Employee Reward

SECOND EDITION

Michael Armstrong graduated from the London School of Economics, and is a Fellow of the Institute of Personnel and Development and a Fellow of the Institute of Management Consultants. He has had over 25 years' experience in personnel management, including 12 as a personnel director. He has also practised as a management consultant for 16 years and is now chief examiner, employee reward, for the IPD. He has written a number of successful management books, including *Management Processes and Functions* (1990); (with Phil Long) *The Reality of Strategic HRM* (1994); *Using the HR Consultant* (1994); and *The Job Evaluation Handbook* (1995) and *Performance Management* (1998), the latter two co-written with Angela Baron. All are published by the IPD.

ID

Other titles in the series:

The Institute of Personnel and Development is the leading
publisher of books and reports for personnel and training
professionals, students, and all those concerned with the
effective management and development of people at work. For
full details of all our titles, please contact the Publishing
Department:

tel. 020 8263 3387
fax 020 8263 3850
e-mail publish@ipd.co.uk

The catalogue of all IPD titles can be viewed on the IPD
website:

www.ipd.co.uk

P

PEOPLE AND ORGANISATIONS

Employee Reward

SECOND EDITION

MICHAEL ARMSTRONG

INSTITUTE OF PERSONNEL AND DEVELOPMENT

Design by Curve

Typeset by Fakenham Photosetting Ltd, Fakenham, Norfolk

Printed in Great Britain by
Short Run Press, Exeter

British Library Cataloguing in Publication Data
A catalogue record of this book is available from the British
Library

ISBN 0-85292-820-3

**INSTITUTE OF PERSONNEL
AND DEVELOPMENT**

IPD House, Camp Road, London SW19 4UX
Tel: 020 8971 9000   Fax: 020 8263 3333
Registered office as above. Registered Charity No. 1038333
A company limited by guarantee. Registered in England No. 2931892

Contents

Editors' foreword

People hold the key to more productive and efficient organisations. The way in which people are managed and developed at work has major effects upon quality, customer service, organisational flexibility and costs. Personnel and development practitioners can play a major role in creating the framework for this to happen, but ultimately they are dependent upon line managers and other employees for its delivery. It is important that personnel and development specialists gain the commitment of others and pursue professional and ethical practices that will bring about competitive success. There is also a need to evaluate the contribution that personnel and development approaches and processes make for organisational success, and to consider ways of making them more effective. Such an approach is relevant for all types of practitioner – personnel and development generalists and specialists, line managers, consultants and academics.

This is one of a series of books under the title *People and Organisations*. The series provides essential guidance and points of references for all those involved with people in organisations. It aims to provide the main body of knowledge and pointers to the required level of skills for personnel and development practitioners operating at a professional level in all types and sizes of organisation. It has been specially written to satisfy new professional standards defined by the Institute of Personnel and Development (IPD) in the United Kingdom and the Republic of Ireland. The series also responds to a special need in the United Kingdom for texts to cover the knowledge aspects of new and revised National and Scottish Vocational Qualifications (N/SVQs) in Personnel and Training Development.

Three 'fields' of standards have to be satisfied in order to gain graduate membership of the IPD: (i) core management (ii) core personnel and development and (iii) any four from a range of more than 20 generalist and specialist electives. The three fields can be tackled in any order, or indeed all at the same time. A range of learning routes is available: full or part-time educational course, flexible learning methods or direct experience. The standards may be assessed by educational and competence-based methods. The books in the series are suitable for supporting all methods of learning.

The series starts by addressing *core personnel and development* and four generalist electives: employee reward, employee resourcing, employee relations and employee development. Together, these cover the personnel and development knowledge requirements for graduateship of the IPD. These also cover the knowledge aspects of training and development and personnel N/SVQs at Level 4.

Core Personnel and Development by Mick Marchington and Adrian Wilkinson addresses the essential knowledge and understanding required of all personnel and development professionals, whether generalists or specialists. Practitioners need to be aware of the wide range of circumstances in which personnel and development processes take place and consequently the degree to which particular approaches and practices may be appropriate in specific circumstances. In addressing these matters, the book covers the core personnel and development standards of the IPD, as well as providing an essential grounding for human resource management options within business and management studies degrees. The authors are both well-known researchers in the field, working at one of the UK's leading management schools. Professor Marchington is also a chief examiner with the IPD. *Employee Reward* by chief examiner Michael Armstrong has been written specially to provide extensive subject coverage for practitioners required by both the IPD's new generalist standards for employee reward and the personnel N/SVQ Level 4 unit covering employee reward. It is the first book on employee reward to be produced specifically for the purposes of aiding practitioners to gain accredited UK qualifications. *Employee Relations*, by chief examiner Professor John Gennard and associate examiner Graham Judge, explores the link between the corporate environment and the interests of buyers and sellers of labour. It also demonstrates how employers (whether or not they recognise unions) can handle the core issues of bargaining, group problem-solving, redundancy, participation, discipline and grievances, and examines how to evaluate the latest management trends. *Employee Development*, by chief examiner Rosemary Harrison, is a major new text which extends the scope of her immensely popular earlier book of the same name to establish the role of human resource development (HRD) and its direction into the next century. After reviewing the historical roots of HRD, she considers its links with business imperatives, its national and international context, the management of the HRD function, and ways of aligning HRD with the organisation's performance management system. Finally, she provides a framework that sets HRD in the context of organisational learning, the key capabilities of an enterprise and the generation of the new knowledge it needs.

These books, like Stephen Taylor's *Employee Resourcing*, are tailored to the new IPD and N/SVQ standards, whereas Malcolm Martin and Tricia Jackson's *Personnel Practice* is focused on the needs of those studying for the Certificate in Personnel Practice. This also gives a thorough grounding in the basics of personnel activities. The authors are experienced practitioners and lead tutors for one of the UK's main providers of IPD flexible learning programmes.

In drawing upon a team of distinguished and experienced writers and practitioners, the People and Organisations series aims to provide a range of up-to-date, practical texts indispensable to those pursuing IPD and N/SVQ qualifications in personnel and development. The books will also prove valuable to those who are taking other human resource management and employment relations courses, or who are simply seeking greater understanding in their work.

Mick Marchington – Mike Oram

Foreword to the second edition

WHAT'S NEW IN THIS EDITION?

This edition has been updated to incorporate the findings of important research projects on performance-related pay and performance management conducted by the Institute of Personnel and Development.

This is a fast-moving area of human resource management. Since the first edition was written in 1996 there have been considerable developments in such areas as broad-banding and job family structures. Much more is known about how competence-related pay and the new concept of contribution-related pay has been introduced. The Halpern committee has reported on executive pay. All these changes have been covered in this new edition, which also includes many more examples of what best-practice companies are doing about employee reward. Reward strategy and conducting pay reviews are given separate and more comprehensive treatment. The concept of the psychological contract and its implications for reward are explored more thoroughly in the light of a series of research projects carried out for the IPD.

This new edition also includes summaries for each chapter.

Plan of the book

The book consists of the following nine parts.

- *Part 1* deals with the conceptual framework: an introductory chapter describes the basic features of employee reward systems, and four chapters cover the reward context and the various economic, psychological and motivation theories that underpin reward policy and practice.

- *Part 2* examines the main reward processes that cover those aspects concerned with philosophy, strategy, policy and the planning and evaluation of reward systems.

- *Part 3* concentrates on job evaluation, the important subject of equal pay, market surveys and job analysis.

- *Part 4* deals with the main types of pay structures, especially graded, broad-banded and job family structures.

- *Part 5* examines the various forms of 'contingent pay' – ie pay that is related to performance, competence, contribution and/or skill. It also deals with the important area of non-financial rewards.

- *Part 6* considers performance management processes, with particular reference to the link between these processes and pay.

- *Part 7* deals with employee benefits and pension schemes.

- *Part 8* reviews reward systems for executives, international pay and rewarding sales staff.

- *Part 9* examines all aspects of managing the reward system.

Part 1

THE CONCEPTUAL FRAMEWORK

1 Employee reward systems

Employee reward is about how people are rewarded in accordance with their value to an organisation. It is concerned with both financial and non-financial rewards and embraces the philosophies, strategies, policies, plans and processes used by organisations to develop and maintain reward systems.

The term 'compensation' is often used as an alternative to 'pay' or 'remuneration', especially in the USA, although it is becoming more common in the UK. The problem with 'compensation' is that it implies that employee reward is only about making amends for the distasteful fact that people have to work for a living. It is in accordance with Robert Elliott's (1991) proposition that: 'For most people work is, in the main, a source of disutility, and they therefore require payment to compensate them for the time they devote to it.' This may well be true in many cases but it provides an unsatisfactory basis for a pay philosophy which can and should adopt the stance that people ought to be valued according to their contribution and competence – which is what this book is about – not just compensated because they have to come to work.

At the end of this chapter the reader will understand:

- the concept of the reward system
- the elements of the reward system: base pay, variable pay, employee benefits and non-financial rewards
- the concepts of reward philosophy, strategy and policy
- the need for integration and to treat employees as stakeholders
- the aims of employee reward from the point of view of the organisation and its employees
- the conventional view of reward management

- the notion of 'the new pay', which is claimed to be a major development in thinking about employee reward, and how it is being developed

- what organisations are paying for

- current trends in reward practice.

On the basis of this understanding, the reader will be able to take an overall view of a reward system and provide advice on reward strategies, policies and practices.

THE EMPLOYEE REWARD SYSTEM

The concept of a reward system

An employee reward system consists of an organisation's integrated policies, processes and practices for rewarding its employees in accordance with their contribution, skill and competence and their market worth. It is developed within the framework of the organisation's reward philosophy, strategies and policies, and contains arrangements in the form of processes, practices, structures and procedures which will provide and maintain appropriate types and levels of pay, benefits and other forms of reward.

The components of a reward system

A reward system consists of financial rewards (fixed and variable pay) and employee benefits, which together comprise total remuneration. The system also incorporates non-financial rewards (recognition, praise, achievement, responsibility and personal growth) and, in many cases, performance management processes. The main components of the system are:

- *processes* for measuring the value of jobs, the contribution of individuals in those jobs, and the range and level of employee benefits to be provided; these processes consist of job evaluation, market rate analyses and performance management

- *practices* for motivating people by the use of financial and non-financial rewards; the financial rewards consist of base and variable pay and employee benefits and allowances, and non-financial rewards are provided generally through effective management and leadership, the work itself, and the opportunities given to employees to develop their skills and careers

- *structures* for relating pay and benefit levels to the value of positions in the organisation and for providing scope for rewarding people according to their performance, competence, skill and/or experience

- *schemes* for providing financial rewards and incentives to people according to individual, group or organisational performance

- *procedures* for maintaining the system and for ensuring that it operates efficiently and flexibly and provides value for money.

Some people object to the use of the term 'reward system' because it seems to refer to a set of mechanisms that can be applied rigidly by employers to guarantee the results they require. Of course this is not the case, and one of the recurring themes of this book is the need for flexibility and a contingency approach to the management of reward – ie an approach that fits the particular needs of the organisation in relation to its business strategies and internal and external environment. Employee reward is chiefly about process – ways of getting things done – rather than about rigid structures and sets of procedures.

However, a 'system' is defined by the *Oxford English Dictionary* as 'a set or assemblage of things connected, associated or interdependent, so as to form a complex whole'. And that is certainly what reward is about. It deals with a number of associated, interdependent and complex areas which have to be developed and managed as a coherent whole. It can also be said that the way people use the reward system is the system.

THE ELEMENTS OF EMPLOYEE REWARD

Base pay

Base (or basic) pay is the level of pay (the fixed salary or wage) that constitutes the rate for the job. It may provide the platform for determining additional payments related to performance, competence or skill. It may also govern pension entitlement and life insurance. The basic levels of pay for jobs reflect both internal and external relativities. The internal relativities may be measured by some form of job evaluation which places jobs in a hierarchy (although the trend now is to play down the notion of hierarchy in the new process-based organisations). External relativities are assessed by tracking market rates. Alternatively, levels of pay may be agreed through negotiation: by collective bargaining with trade unions or by reaching individual agreements. The base rate for a job is sometimes regarded as the rate for a competent or skilled person in that job. Such a rate may be varied in a skill-based or competence-based system according to the individual's skill or competence.

Levels of pay may be based on long-standing structures the origins of which are shrouded in the mists of time and which have been updated in response to movements in market rates and inflation, and through negotiations. In many organisations pay levels evolve – they are not planned or maintained systematically. Rates are fixed by managerial judgement of what is required to recruit and retain people. They may be adjusted in response to individual or collective pressure for increases or upgradings. This evolutionary and *ad hoc* process can result in a chaotic and illogical pay structure which is inequitable, leads to inconsistent and unfair decisions and is difficult to understand, expensive to maintain and the cause of dissatisfaction and demotivation.

Base pay may be expressed as an annual, weekly or hourly rate. This is sometimes referred to as a time rate system of payment. Such systems are simple but they can be made more complex by the addition of various kinds of allowances such as overtime or shift payments. Time rates may be 'spot rates' – ie comprising one rate for the job – or there may be a range of pay for each job grade in which progression takes place according to time in the job, performance, competence and/or skill. The rate may be adjusted to reflect increases in the cost of living or market rates by the organisation unilaterally or by agreement with a trade union. Service-related, performance, skill-based or competence-related pay increases may be added to, or 'consolidated' into, the basic rate, and these form the basis for pension contributions, sick pay, payment for overtime, and bonuses or profit shares when these are awarded as a percentage of base pay.

Contingent pay

Additional financial rewards may be provided that are related to performance, skill, competence and/or experience. These are referred to as 'contingent pay'. If such payments are not consolidated into base pay, they can be described as 'variable pay'. Variable pay is sometimes defined as 'pay at risk', as in the CBI/Wyatt survey (1993). For example, the pay of sales representatives on a 'commission-only' basis is entirely at risk. The main types of contingent pay are:

- individual performance-related pay – in which increases in base pay or cash bonuses are determined by performance assessment and ratings (also known as merit pay)

- bonuses – rewards for successful performance which are paid as cash (lump) sums related to the results obtained by individuals, teams or the organisation

- incentives – payments linked with the achievement of previously-set targets which are designed to motivate people to achieve higher levels of performance; the targets are usually quantified in such terms as output or sales

- commission – a special form of incentive in which sales representatives are paid on the basis of a percentage of the sales value they generate

- service-related pay – which increases by fixed increments on a scale or pay spine depending on service in the job; there may sometimes be scope for varying the rate of progress up the scale according to performance

- competence-related pay – which varies according to the level of competence achieved by the individual

- contribution-related pay – which relates pay to both outputs (performance) and inputs (competence)

- skill-based pay (sometimes called knowledge-based pay) – which varies according to the level of skill the individual achieves

- career development pay – which rewards people for taking on additional responsibilities as their career develops laterally within a broad grade (a broad-banded pay structure).

Allowances

Allowances are elements of pay in the form of a separate sum of money for such aspects of employment as overtime, shift working, call-outs and living in London or other large cities. London or large-city allowances are sometimes consolidated: organisations which are

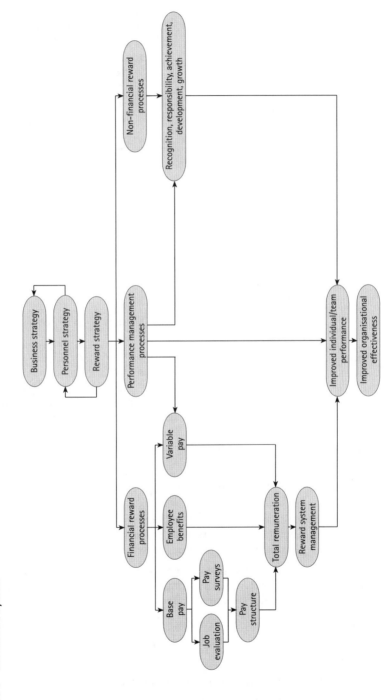

Figure 1 The reward system

ıe total pay system at Bass Brewers

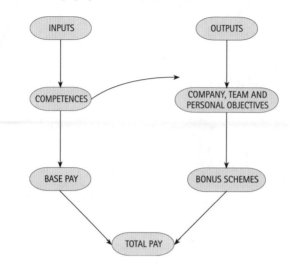

simplifying their pay structure may 'buy out' the allowance and increase base pay accordingly.

Total earnings
Total earnings are usually calculated as the sum of base pay and any additional payments.

Employee benefits
Employee benefits, also known as indirect pay, include pensions, sick pay, insurance cover and company cars. They comprise elements of remuneration additional to the various forms of cash pay and also include provisions for employees that are not strictly remuneration, such as annual holidays.

Total remuneration
Total remuneration is the value of all cash payments (total earnings) and benefits received by employees.

Non-financial rewards
Non-financial rewards include any rewards which focus on the need people perceive to varying degrees for achievement, recognition, responsibility, influence and personal growth.

The elements of a reward system and their interrelationships are illustrated in Figure 1. But they can be combined in many different ways – there is no ideal pattern for a reward system. An example of how Bass Brewers model their system is illustrated in Figure 2.

REWARD PHILOSOPHY, STRATEGY AND POLICY DEFINED

Reward processes and practices are most effective when they are based on thought-through and appropriate reward philosophies, strategies and policies. These terms are often used imprecisely, even interchangeably. But it is possible, and useful, to distinguish between them:

- *Reward philosophy* represents the broad values and beliefs that an organisation holds about rewards. It specifies the assumptions which underpin the reward system and determine its form. It shapes the way strategies and policies are developed and implemented in the form of practices and procedures. Reward philosophy is examined fully in the next section of this chapter.

- *Reward strategy* directs pay programmes to what the organisation wants to achieve. It is a declaration of intent as to how the organisation is going to put its reward philosophy into practice. It provides a broad perspective on how critical reward issues will be addressed. Strategies should be distinguished from plans. A strategy indicates the direction in which the organisation wants to go in developing its reward processes and structures. A plan spells out how it is going to get there. A plan may include, for example, specified programmes or projects to develop new job evaluation processes, new methods of payment, or different types of pay structure. These programmes are designed to achieve the strategic reward objectives. Reward strategy is discussed in Chapter 7.

- *Reward policy* indicates how reward processes should be designed and managed within the context of the reward philosophy. It provides guidelines for line managers and personnel or pay specialists on how particular and recurring reward issues should be dealt with. It enables consistent decisions to be made where appropriate while recognising the need for flexibility and the perils of rigidity. Reward policy is discussed in Chapter 8.

The components of the reward system described earlier in this chapter must be considered as a whole – hence the importance of the concept of total remuneration. This is what employees get, and organisations need to communicate to them the totality of their rewards.

But it is also important to have a coherent philosophy and to achieve the integration of corporate, personnel and reward strategies. This can take the form of vertical integration in which steps are taken to ensure that there is a good fit between business strategy and personnel and reward strategies. The latter flow from the former, but reward strategies can and should support the attainment of organisational and personnel and development strategies.

The integration of reward and other personnel and development processes is equally important. This is sometimes called 'bundling' – the processes of bringing all HR policies and processes together so that they form a coherent and mutually reinforcing whole.

Reward can directly affect:

- resourcing through competitive pay

- employee development through competence-related and skill-based pay that encourage the development of competence and skill (enlarging the skill base) and performance management processes that further continuous development through such means as personal development planning

- career development and planning by establishing a framework for lateral career progress in a broad-banded pay structure or mapping out a career ladder in a job family structure

- employee relations by helping to generate a reward culture based on mutual trust, involvement, transparency and fair dealing

- organisational effectiveness by providing the means to motivate superior performance, to align individual and organisational objectives and to gain commitment.

To facilitate integration it is important to treat reward as part of the total approach to managing and developing people. It should not be regarded as a separate entity. Reward management cannot take place in isolation from people development and other business and personnel management processes. Frequently, new reward structures and systems are developed to fit or support a new organisational structure or following a business process re-engineering exercise. Glaxo Wellcome, for example, operate on the basis that a business case must be made for changing any part of a reward system.

EMPLOYEES AS STAKEHOLDERS

Another recurring theme in this book is the need to treat employees as stakeholders – people who have a legitimate claim to share in the prosperity of the organisation and to be involved in decisions affecting their pay and other terms and conditions of service. This implies the generation of a climate of mutual trust.

The Institute of Personnel and Development's (IPD) statement *People Make the Difference* (1994) makes the point that much has been done in recent years to introduce a sense of reality into employee relations. But, according to the IPD:

> Managers should not kid themselves that acquiescence is the same thing as enthusiastic involvement. The pace of life and changing work patterns in the future will put a strain on the best of relationships between employees and managers.

The IPD suggests that building trust is the only basis on which commitment can be generated and the tensions contained. For these reasons, attaining or sustaining world-class levels of performance will be increasingly unlikely in organisations that do not treat their employees in ways which are consistent with their status as the key business resource. This means that:

- Employees cannot be treated just as a factor of production.

- Organisations must translate their values into specific and practical action. In too many organisations inconsistency between what is said and what is done undermines trust, generates employee cynicism and provides evidence of contradictions in management thinking.

The formulation of reward strategies and policies must take account of the need for trust and the need for integration. Like the process of developing the reward system, this should take place within the conceptual framework described in this Part.

THE AIMS OF EMPLOYEE REWARD

The organisation's requirements

A reward system expresses what the organisation values and is prepared to pay and provide non-financial rewards for. It is governed by the need to reward the right things to convey the right message about what is important. The basic philosophy is that people should be rewarded for the value they create.

As O'Neal (1994) points out: 'Pay is a function of the work system it supports ... Pay systems will need to support the development of intellectual capital, universal use of information technology, strategic alliances, continuous learning, and employee populations that come and go.'

Overall aim

The overall aim of employee reward is to support the attainment of the organisation's strategic and shorter-term objectives by helping to ensure that it has the skilled, competent, committed and well-motivated workforce it needs. This means providing for the continuing improvement of individual, team and therefore organisational performance, and taking steps that contribute to the creation of added value and the achievement of competitive advantage.

As Lawler (1990) has noted:

> The challenge is to develop pay programmes that support and reinforce the business objectives of the organisation and the kind of culture, climate and behaviour that are needed for the organisation to be effective.

He also made the important point that 'Pay practices are only as good as the impact they have on organisational effectiveness.'

It has been emphasised by Schuster and Zingheim (1992) that 'People are the principal variable in organisational success.' Pay programmes should aim to accomplish the following organisational objectives:

- to make excellent performance financially worthwhile

- to communicate to satisfactory performers the importance of acceptable and better performance

- to communicate to less-than-satisfactory performers the need to improve.

Contribution to added value

In accounting language, added value is the difference between the income of the business arising from sales (output) and the amount spent on materials and other purchased goods and services (input). In more general terms, it is the development and use of any resource in such a way as to ensure that it yields a substantial and sustainable higher return on whatever has been invested in it. Added value often means the creation of more out of less, and an increasingly popular index of overall organisational performance is added value per £ of employment costs.

Added value is generated by people. It is people at various levels who create visions, define values and missions, set goals, develop strategic plans, and implement those plans in accordance with the underpinning values. Added value will be enhanced by anything that is done to obtain and develop the right sort of people, to motivate and manage them effectively, to gain their commitment to the organisation's values, and to build and maintain stable relationships with them based on mutual trust.

Employee reward contributes to the creation of added value by helping to ensure that people with the required competences and levels of motivation are available, and by playing a part in creating a culture and environment that stimulate high-quality performance.

Contribution to competitive advantage

Sustainable competitive advantage as formulated by Porter (1985) arises when a firm creates value for its customers, selects markets in which it can excel, and presents a moving target to its competitors by continually improving its position. According to Porter, three of the most important factors are innovation, quality and cost leadership, but he recognises that all these depend on the quality of an organisation's human resources. The ability to gain and retain competitive advantage is crucial to a business's growth and prosperity.

Unique talents among employees, including superior performance, high productivity, flexibility, innovation, and the ability to deliver excellent personal customer service are ways in which people provide a critical ingredient in the development of the competitive position of a business. People are also the key to managing the pivotal interdependencies across functional activities and important external relationships. It can be argued that one of the benefits arising from competitive advantage based on the effective management of people is that such an advantage is hard to imitate. An organisation's personnel strategies, policies and practices are a unique blend of processes, procedures, personalities, styles, capabilities and organisational culture. One of the keys to competitive advantage is the ability to differentiate what the business supplies to its customers from what its competitors offer. Such differentiation can be achieved by having better-quality people. Employee reward practices can make an important contribution to getting and keeping such people and to providing them with the incentives which will motivate them to achieve higher levels of performance.

Management and reward

An organisation's performance depends ultimately on the quality of its management and employees, and the reward system can help to improve that quality. But the improvement of organisational effectiveness cannot be left to the reward system alone: the culture, values and management style of the organisation, together with its performance management and employee development programmes, are equally important. Reward systems, however well conceived and effective, are no substitute for good management.

Reward aims from the organisation's point of view

From the organisation's point of view, the specific aims of employee reward are to:

- help to attract, retain and motivate high-quality people
- play a significant part in the communication of the organisation's values, performance, standards and expectations
- encourage behaviour that will contribute to the achievement of the organisation's objectives and reflect the 'balanced score-card' of the key performance-drivers of customers, finance, processes and people – two of the basic questions to be answered when developing reward systems are 'What sort of behaviour do we want?' and 'How can reward processes promote that behaviour?'
- underpin organisational change programmes concerned with culture, process and structure
- support the realisation of the key values of the organisation in such areas as quality, customer care, teamwork, innovation, flexibility and speed of response
- provide value for money: no reward initiative should be undertaken unless it has been established that it will add value, and no reward practice should be retained if it does not result in added value.

Reward aims from the employees' point of view

From the employees' point of view the reward system should:

- treat them as stakeholders who have the right to be involved in the development of the reward policies that affect them
- meet their expectations that they will be treated equitably, fairly, and consistently
- be transparent – they should know what the reward policies of the organisation are and how they are affected by them.

It is sometimes said that to achieve these aims an organisation's pay practices should be 'internally equitable and externally competitive'. This is all right as far as it goes, but it is not always easy to attain and it represents a somewhat limited point of view. The first problem is that the goals of internal equity and external competitiveness are often hard to reconcile. The pressure of market forces may overcome internal equity considerations when people with scarce talents have to be recruited. On the other hand, a crude wish to be competitive may be inappropriate. As Schuster and Zingheim (1992) point out: 'The strategic view of competitive practices suggests that achieving competitive pay should be contingent upon providing a level of work quality, productivity, or performance which must justify pay levels that reflect expected reasonable goal performance.' Competitive pay should be linked with competitive performance.

Achieving the aims

The employee reward system will achieve its aims if:

- it adopts a strategic approach that is aligned to the business and HR strategies and is congruent with the culture of the organisation
- reward policies and processes are modified in accordance with the changing needs of the business

- employees are valued according to their contribution, skill and competence

- the reward system is transparent and employees are treated as stakeholders who are entitled to make representations on any area of reward that affects their interests and who will be involved in the development of reward processes

- employee relations strategies are designed to build mutual trust and to develop a partnership approach which provides for increases in prosperity to be shared with all employees (not just the favoured few at the top)

- reward policies emphasise the need for equity, fairness and consistency while recognising that the ideal of internal equity may not be sustainable in full because of market pressures

- maximum freedom is devolved to line managers to manage the reward system within their budgets and in accordance with broad policy guidelines

- there is a constant thrust to maximise the performance leverage of any money spent on pay

- reward initiatives are taken only when their interaction with other business and personnel policies has been assessed, and an integrated approach adopted to the development of mutually supportive processes.

TRADITIONAL APPROACHES TO MANAGING PAY

The traditional approach to managing pay in the 1960s and 1970s embraced all the processes described above concerned with financial rewards. But in line with typical personnel management practices of the time it did not recognise the strategic elements and failed to integrate pay with other personnel processes. It also ignored the total approach to reward management which has emerged in the 1990s and which emphasises the significance of performance management rather than conventional appraisal schemes and the need to pay as much attention to non-financial as to financial rewards.

Salary administration, as it used to be called, placed pay in a subordinate role. Salary administrators, if they existed at all, policed the system, ensuring that everyone adhered to rigidly defined procedures for grading jobs and progressing pay. Line managers did what they were told. As their title indicates, salary administrators were concerned only with white-collar staff. The pay of manual workers was left to industrial relations officers, work study engineers and rate-fixers.

However, as Schuster and Zingheim (1992) remark, 'traditional pay practice was not unplanned or poorly directed'. It emphasised the need to 'attract, motivate and retain' employees but the focus was on 'competitive attributes rather than on the more important strategic or tactical issues'.

Traditional pay practices understandably reflected how organisations were structured and managed. They tended to be bureaucratic and geared to extended hierarchies and vertical communication systems – the organisational 'chimneys' largely separate from other organisational chimneys. Progress up the hierarchy was largely by regrading and, frequently, by means of fixed increments within grades or a pay spine. (These still persist in public or ex-public organisations and in the voluntary sector.)

Job evaluation concentrated on measuring job size, so that jobs could be slotted into an appropriate grade in the hierarchy and job-holders could be upgraded if they were promoted to a job with a higher points rating. Job evaluation schemes were often complex, rigid, administratively cumbersome and paper-intensive. The emphasis was on managing internal relativities and on jobs that were defined by means of elaborate and lengthy job descriptions. The focus was on jobs rather than on people. The need for pay to be competitive was, of course, recognised, but market-rate pressures were regarded as unwelcome intrusions, and if the organisation had to bow to such pressures, jobs were 'red-circled' to indicate that they were exceptions to the rule.

Employee benefits – 'fringe benefits', as they were known – tended to proliferate, often so as to avoid income tax. Little attempt was made to get value for money, and the system was administered rigidly. Everyone got what management felt they ought to get. There was no choice.

During the 1980s some elements of this traditional approach were changing in many organisations. Incremental pay structures were largely abandoned in the private sector and performance-related pay (PRP) suddenly became popular. The government of the day discovered PRP like religion and sought to impose it on the public sector in the naive belief that it invariably improves performance and transforms everyone into entrepreneurs overnight. The entrepreneurial 1980s were, of course, the decade of greed, when the ultimate answer to motivation, transformation and success was money through PRP, share options, and so on. It was a decade characterised by Gordon Gekko, in the film *Wall Street*, whose creed was that 'greed was good'. It harked back to Jonas Chuzzlewit, whose education, as described by Dickens (1844), 'had been conducted from the cradle on the strictest principles of the main chance. The very first word he learnt to spell was "gain" and the second (when he got into two syllables), "money".'

There were also movements towards more flexibility in managing pay and benefits, and some organisations began relating shop-floor pay to skill levels. Traditional job evaluation schemes were attacked by Lawler (1990) and others as unsuited to the new flexible and de-layered organisations and inappropriate for the knowledge workers increasingly employed in high-technology industries.

THE ADVENT OF REWARD MANAGEMENT

Traditional approaches to pay therefore began to change in the late 1980s, a change that was signalled by the emergence of the term 'reward management'. Armstrong and Murlis (1988) pointed out that:

> The essentially static techniques of 'salary administration' have developed into the dynamic approach of 'reward management'. The emphasis is first on performance, recognising that the motivation to improve and the rewards for achievement must extend not only to the high-flyers but to the staff at all levels who help to achieve the success of the organization. Secondly, the emphasis is on flexibility. Reward management processes need no longer be confined to the straitjackets of rigid salary structures and elaborate job evaluation schemes.

The concept of reward management was influenced by writers such as Rosabeth Moss Kanter (1987), who commented:

> Status, not contribution, has traditionally been the basis for numbers on employees' pay-checks. Pay has reflected where jobs ranked in the corporate hierarchy – not what comes out of them.

Some commentators have assumed that the reward management concept is solely about performance-related pay. But that is a gross oversimplification. As Armstrong and Murlis (1998) point out, 'Reward management is not just about money. It is also concerned with those non-financial rewards which provide intrinsic or extrinsic motivation.' They concede that 'the impact of PRP as a direct motivator may be arguable' and recognise that:

> PRP need not be regarded as the only motivator. Attention should also be given to the non-financial approaches to motivation and recognition. An integrated approach to performance management can motivate all types of employees (not just the high-flyers) by providing the basis for a mix of financial and non-financial rewards.

They emphasise that 'It is neither possible nor desirable to be prescriptive [about reward management] in the sense of providing easy and superficial answers to subtle and far-reaching problems of motivation and reward.'

The reward management movement was the first challenge to the universalist prescriptions of salary administration. In the post-entrepreneurial 1990s there were further developments in the direction of rewarding for skill and competence, de-emphasising the role of money as a motivator, emphasising the significance of continuous development and of the support reward management can give to that process, and recognising the importance of employee involvement, partnership, mutuality, trust and transparency. In the early 1990s many of these beliefs were encapsulated in the concept of the 'new pay' which emerged as a force to be reckoned with.

THE NEW PAY

Lawler (1990) originated the phrase 'new pay' to reflect the need for an understanding of the organisation's goals, values and culture, and of the challenges of a more competitive global economy when formulating reward policies. He made a significant initial contribution to the new pay concept, especially through his advocacy of people-based as distinct from job-based pay – paying people according to their value in the market and in relation to their knowledge and skills.

Lawler sees new pay as helping to achieve the individual and organisational behaviour that a company needs if its business goals are to be met. Pay systems must flow from the overall strategy, and they can help to emphasise important objectives such as customer retention, customer satisfaction and product or service quality. Lawler's concept of the new pay was further developed by Schuster and Zingheim (1992). They describe the fundamental principles of new pay as that:

- Employees are the primary reason the organisation is able to remain competitive and to compete effectively. New pay is consistent with the organisation's becoming world-class by forming a partnership with its employees.

- Management means leadership rather than hierarchy and bureaucracy.

- Employee communications are crucial to success. Pay is one key element of communication that can be managed so as to convey the right message about the organisation's values, performance expectations and standards.

- Total compensation programmes should be designed to reward results and behaviour consistent with the key goals of the organisation.

- Pay is above all an employee relations issue: 'Employees have the right to determine whether the values, culture and reward systems of the organization match their own.'

- Total compensation should be regarded as an element of the organisation's total management processes. Pay can be a positive force for organisational change.

- Base, variable and indirect pay are elements of a total compensation strategy, not separate and independent.

- New pay starts with the external labour market and does not try to create internal equity across the organisation. Rather, it establishes internal equity within broad job functions and pays the market rate for those functions. (Note, however, that in the USA there is no generally applied 'comparable worth' legislation equivalent to the 'equal pay for work of equal value' requirement in the UK.)

- The major thrust of new pay is in introducing variable pay to employee groups where most organisations pay only base pay. (Variable pay is defined strictly as pay which does not become a permanent part of base pay.)

- The emphasis is on team as well as individual rewards, and on partnership, such that the employee shares financially in the organisation's success.

- The advantages of variable pay are perceived as its ability 'to form partnerships between employees and the organisation, to vary pay costs with performance, to create the need for high levels of teamwork and collaboration, and to support quality and customer value goals'.

- Organisations should determine the total compensation mix and level of benefit costs they can sustain and then manage benefits so as to free money for spending on direct pay, particularly variable pay, where the return on the organisation's investment is greater.

An important development in reward management practice which does not feature in the new pay orthodoxy is the devolution of responsibility for pay decisions to line managers working closely with their teams – collectively or with individual members. This changes the role of personnel or reward specialists from that of police force to that of internal consultants and coaches.

The new pay concept should not be regarded simply as a lever for use in transforming organisations, and it does rely heavily on the leverage supposedly provided by variable pay. Its prescriptions are neither universally acceptable nor generally applicable. Furthermore, it should be regarded as a conceptual approach to payment rather than a set of prescriptions. As Lawler (1995) points out:

> The new pay is not a set of compensation practices at all, but rather a way of thinking about reward systems in a complex organisation ... The new pay does not necessarily mean implementing new reward practices or abandoning traditional ones; it means identifying pay practices that enhance the organisation's strategic effectiveness.

'New pay' is therefore more a philosophy than a set of practices, although organisations developing competence-related pay schemes, broad-banded pay structures and team pay sometimes group them all loosely under a 'new pay' rubric. Those who pursue the development of 'at risk' payment systems – that is, not consolidating performance, skill and/or competence-related pay into base rates – are certainly putting one aspect of the new pay philosophy into practice. And the CBI/Wyatt (1993) survey of variable pay systems found that after some years of relative decline, variable pay systems are increasing in popularity and sophistication.

Too much significance should not be attached to the concept of new pay except as a way of thinking about reward. The concept certainly does not go as far as claiming that pay can lead organisational change, only that it can help to underpin it. The tail does not wag the dog. Organisational change, for example, comes first, possibly through a de-layering or business process re-engineering exercise. The pay strategy follows this change and supports it by the introduction of broad-banding, career development pay and team pay for cross-functional project teams.

It should also be remembered that the philosophy of new pay is based on US practice. Because of the distinction between exempt and non-exempt employees, new pay concentrates on white-collar workers. It does not take much account of gender considerations because general equal-value legislation on the UK pattern has no counterpart in the USA. And it largely ignores the trade unions, whose power has diminished even more in the USA than in the UK.

New pay is 'managerialist' – it looks at what pay can do for the organisation rather than at what pay can do for the people in the organisation. But it does not ignore the need for the involvement of employees, as has been suggested by some UK commentators. In fact the seminal work on the subject by Schuster and Zingheim (1992) devotes a whole chapter to this topic.

> By reference to the above summary of new pay, and the suggested readings listed at the end of this chapter, produce a critique of the concept. How relevant do you think it is to organisations now and in the future? What are its limitations and drawbacks?

WHAT ARE WE PAYING FOR?

When thinking about reward systems and their design and management it is necessary to start by asking the question: 'What are we paying for?' The answer may seem obvious, along the lines of 'We are paying people what they are worth.' But this is plainly inadequate. We have to ask two more detailed questions: 'How do we know what people are worth?' and 'What are the factors we need to take into account when deciding how much people should be paid, whether they are individuals in a role or numbers of employees in a similar job?' A further associated question is 'Are we paying for the job or the person, or both?' It is important to be clear about this. The traditional approach to deciding on how much a job is worth is job evaluation, as described in Chapter 10. The mantra used when considering job evaluation is 'Evaluate the job, not the person.' This follows the principle that jobs are fixed entities with rigidly-defined duties which are performed in identical ways by job-holders. But in today's more flexible organisations more and more people are carrying out roles – they are playing a part in ensuring that a defined purpose is achieved. That part may well vary according to circumstances – and, indeed, may be modified in accordance with the competence or capability of the person in his or her role. There are far more opportunities for people to 'grow their roles' as new demands and opportunities occur. In these circumstances, it is illogical to say that it is the job that determines the value of the person. It is, in fact, quite the opposite: it is the person that determines the value of the job. The first person who emphasised this point was Ed Lawler who in 1986 wrote that job evaluation 'tends to depersonalise people by equating them with a set of duties rather than concentrate on what they are and what they can do'. He advocated a people-based rather than a job-based approach.

As will be discussed in Chapter 3, pay levels are in general influenced by economic factors and in particular by internal and external relativities – that is, internal comparisons between the levels of jobs and external comparisons with the rate at which similar jobs are paid outside the organisation (market rates). But for individuals, the factors to be taken into account in relation to their rate of pay and any increases to their base rate or cash bonuses may be more complex. These factors are modelled in Figure 3 and consist of:

• the *inputs* made by individuals based on the level of skill and/or competence they have attained and can use effectively

- the *outputs* of individuals which comprise the results they have achieved in the form of achieving targets or meeting standards of performance
- the *contribution* of individuals to achieving the purpose of the organisation, their team or their role – this contribution is based on their skill and/or competence and measured by their results
- *internal relativities* – how the individuals' jobs compare with other people's jobs within the organisation in terms of such factors as skill, knowledge, responsibility, complexity and impact on end-results
- *market worth* (external relativities) – what individuals are worth in the marketplace because of what they can do and the level of expertise they have attained
- *potential* – the pay of individuals may be affected by judgements about their potential to make a greater contribution in the future, such that their current pay reflects estimates of their future worth and serves to deliver the message that individuals are valued not only for what they do now but also for what they can deliver in the longer term.

Figure 3 **What we are paying for**

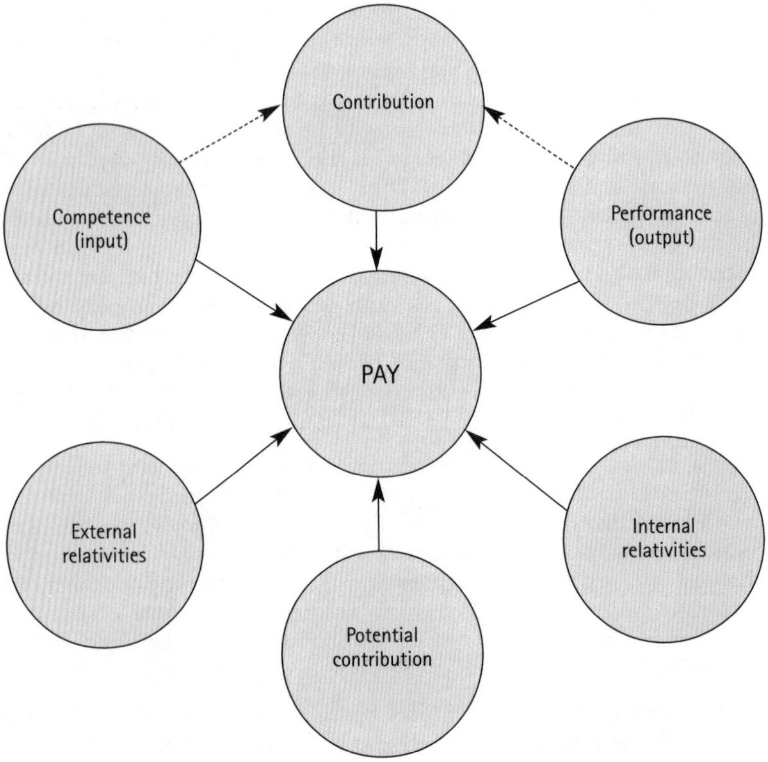

Table 1 Current and projected reward practices

Reward Practice	Using (% of all respondents)	Considering (% of all respondents)
Merit pay	61.5	10.8
Market-based pay	38.2	6.1
Broad-banding	25.5	17.3
Profit-sharing	19.5	7.4
Competence-related pay	13.9	30.3
Skill-based pay	10.0	8.7
Team-based pay	6.1	14.3
Flexible benefits	3.5	29.4
Gain-sharing	3.0	3.5

THE REWARD MANAGEMENT SCENE

The CBI/Hay survey and the IRS survey

A survey of pay systems in 480 UK organisations conducted by the CBI and Hay Management Consultants in 1995 found that 'The most significant factors driving change in pay and benefit policy are the need to strengthen the link to business performance, cost control, support for organisational change and recruitment and retention pressures.' The need for more flexibility in pay and benefits is expected to become more urgent.

The November 1998 survey of reward practices conducted by Industrial Relations Services revealed the current and projected reward practices adopted by the 231 respondents shown in Table 1.

This shows that what IRS calls merit pay (ie performance-related pay) is the leading reward practice. The interest in broad-banding is strong and increasing. Although competence-related pay is not particularly common, it is a major development area together with flexible benefits. Team pay, in spite of all the publicity and interest in teamwork, is relatively rare, although interest is increasing.

THE APPROACH TO REWARDING PEOPLE

According to Pfeffer (1998), the challenge facing organisations is to consider more than simply managing reward. They should devote time and attention not only to pay but to recognition systems, corporate culture and the quality of working life. He has suggested the following six Golden Rules.

1 Include a 'large dose' of collective reward in employees' pay packages.

2 Recognise that pay cannot substitute for a working environment 'high on trust, fun and meaningful work'.

3 Make pay practices open and transparent, thereby sending a positive message about the equity of the system.

4 Use other methods besides pay to signal company values and focus behaviour.

Table 2 **Reward trends**

From	To
Narrowly-defined jobs and job standards	Broader generic roles – emphasis on competence and continuous development
Inflexible job evaluation systems sizing tasks, rewarding non-adaptive behaviour and empire-building and encouraging point-grabbing	Flexible job evaluation processes assessing the value added by people in their roles, often within job families
Hierarchical and rigid pay structures in which the only way to get on is to move up. Focus is on the next promotion	Broad-banded pay structures where the emphasis is on flexibility, career development pay and continuous improvement. Focus is on the next challenge
Emphasis on individual PRP	More focus on team performance through team-based pay
Consolidation of rewards into base pay	More emphasis on 'at risk' pay

5 Realise that pay is 'just one element in a set of management practices which can either build or reduce commitment, teamwork and performance'.

6 Ensure that the messages sent by the pay system reflect what the organisation values, and align pay with other management practices.

THE FUTURE

The main areas in which changes in reward policies and practices are taking place, or are at least being contemplated, are summarised in Table 2.

These movements can be categorised under the headings of competence-related pay, broad-banding and team pay. They are the most forward-looking of current developments in the context of increased devolution of pay decisions to line management and more involvement of employees. All of them will be discussed in later chapters of this book.

SUMMARY

• A reward system consists of an organisation's integrated approaches to valuing and rewarding its employees according to their competence and contribution.

• The system consists of processes, practices, structures, schemes and procedures.

• The elements of reward are base pay, contingent pay, allowances, total earnings, employee benefits, total remuneration and, importantly, non-financial rewards and recognition.

• Reward management is concerned with the development, implementation, communication and evolution of processes which deal with the assessment of relative job values, the design and

Table 3 **The contributions of the gurus**

Rosabeth Moss Kanter	*The Attack on Pay*, 1987	• Move towards reducing the fixed portion of pay and increasing the variable portion.
Ed Lawler	*Strategic Pay*, 1990	• Think more strategically about reward. • Use people-based rather than job-based pay.
Schuster and Zingheim	*The New Pay*, 1992	• Relate pay to results and behaviour consistent with key organisational goals. • Focus on variable pay. • Relate rewards to team and organisational performance.
Flannery, Hofrichter and Platten	*People, Performance and Pay*, 1996	• Align pay with the organisation's culture, values and strategic goals. • Integrate pay with other people processes. • Measure results.

management of pay structures, performance management, paying for performance, competence, skill or contribution (contingent pay), providing employee benefits and pensions, and managing reward procedures.

• The aims of reward management are to support the achievement of the organisation's goals, encourage appropriate behaviour, support the organisation's core values and help to attract and retain high-quality employees.

• The contribution of the 'gurus' to thinking about reward are summarised in Table 3.

FURTHER READING

The basis of reward management is discussed in Armstrong and Murlis (1994: 23–32). M. Beer *et al* provide a thought-provoking view of employee reward in *Managing Human Assets*, New York, Free Press, 1984. Rosabeth Moss Kanter (1987) delivered a number of new pay messages. Lawler (1990) advocates new pay approaches. The definitive exposition of the new pay philosophy is Schuster and Zingheim (1992). Gomez-Mejia and Balkin (1992) discuss the new strategic perspective on pay issues and strategic choices for pay and reward system design issues. The CBI/Hay survey (1996) gives a good summary of UK reward practices. *The Compensation and Benefits Review*, July–August 1995, contains a number of articles summarising the new pay philosophy. Flannery *et al* (1996) provide an insightful and comprehensive review of developments in reward management.

2 The international, national and corporate contexts

Contingency theory in its most extreme form suggests that what organisations want to do should be dependent on their external and internal environments. Reward strategies, policies, plans and processes should thus be developed in the light of the international, national and corporate contexts within which they operate.

However, an extreme, deterministic application of contingency theory would fail to recognise that reward processes can play an important part as drivers of organisational performance and as levers of change. Effective organisations do not simply react to the circumstances in which they find themselves. Instead, they challenge and overcome environmental pressures by making the best use of their distinctive competences – mainly their human resources – and by differentiating themselves from their competitors. It is people who make the difference and people who achieve competitive advantage. Reward systems can help organisations to acquire and develop the capable, committed and motivated people they need.

Reward systems and processes should be designed and developed in the light of an understanding of the organisation's culture. But they can also help to shape that culture by, for example, functioning more flexibly in de-layered organisations where the emphasis is on horizontal processes, teamwork and continuous development, or by focusing on performance, competence and quality expectations.

On completing this chapter the reader will understand the context within which reward strategies and policies are formulated and put into practice.

THE INTERNATIONAL CONTEXT

The international context is global competition, forcing businesses to become more productive and customer-oriented. Severe pressures on manufacturing firms which compete internationally are forcing them into economic restructuring and 'managing away expense'. Hence the pressure for leaner, fitter organisations and the emphasis on de-layering, downsizing, business process re-engineering and developing the capacity to respond flexibly to new opportunities or threats.

The thrust is therefore to achieve world-class performance, which means that what the organisation does and how it does it are as good as, if not better than, the world leaders in the sector in which the organisation operates. Ways of achieving world-class performance include:

- benchmarking to establish world-class standards

- creating an environment dedicated to continuous improvement and high quality

- a strong customer focus

- an unending drive for innovation – product/market and process development, and the introduction of new technology

- determined attacks on costs to achieve cost leadership

- the pursuit of employee resourcing and development goals, and higher levels of motivation and commitment aimed at creating superior levels of individual and team competence and performance.

The global impact on pay systems
The impact of global competition on pay systems has been to focus attention on:

- flexible approaches to pay to help a business react more swiftly to new demands and pressures

- paying for performance and competence to provide competitive edge

- broad-based structures to reflect the 'lean', de-layered organisation and facilitate flexibility in the delivery of pay

- the emergence of globally mobile executives and the challenge as to how they should be rewarded

- how expatriates should be rewarded.

THE NATIONAL CONTEXT

The national context is, of course, strongly influenced by international developments and pressures. The key issues which directly or indirectly affect reward strategies and policies are:

- the introduction of the National Minimum Wage of £3.60 per hour from April 1999 which affects an estimated two million workers

- structural changes in the demand for skills: this started in the 1980s with an emphasis on high levels of attainment and expertise – as a result, the best are now in much greater demand, while the average, sadly, often find themselves out of a job altogether; this may be caused by a number of factors, such as rising competitiveness in commercial life, greater emphasis on knowledge work, higher job mobility, shorter professional careers and, possibly, wider social change in that good people are less prepared than they were to 'carry' mediocre ones

- structural changes in industry: a continuing shift from manufacturing to service industry

- fragmentation in the labour market: this has taken place as the old monolithic manufacturing organisations are breaking up and operational and personnel decisions are being devolved to smaller units closer to their markets and customers

- the lowering of inflation rates – no more double-digit pay awards, and a challenge to the view that everyone is entitled to a base pay increase each year

- skill shortages in some areas which drive the use of pay premiums and the creation of job family or market group structures

- the growth of part-time, temporary and self-employment so that many people are not working full-time: this challenges the reward policy emphasis on full-time employees with long-term employment prospects in large organisations

- a bullish stock market in which executive share option gains has opened up a huge gap between remuneration at the top and remuneration at lower levels in organisations

- a government which persists in believing – against all the evidence – that performance-related pay schemes provide a direct incentive

- decline in the power of trade unions as pay negotiating bodies – with certain exceptions, such as the railway unions, the unions have become a much less powerful force in pay negotiations: this situation has arisen partly because of a reduction in union membership but also because of a trend towards the decentralisation or devolution of pay bargaining (which has contributed to the fragmentation mentioned above)

- social and political trends: social policies adopted by all political parties aim to create new jobs in a low-inflation environment and to improve the skills of the workforce.

The national impact on pay systems
The most important impact on wage systems has been made by the National Minimum Wage Act 1998. Its aim is to provide workers across Britain for the first time with a floor below which their wages will not fall – regardless of where they live or work, or the sector or size of company in which they work. It is *not* a going rate. The Secretary of State for Employment and Industry, as advised by the Low Pay Commission, may prescribe by regulation the minimum wage, which can vary for different cases. The minimum wage was set at a rate of £3.60 an hour in April 1999 for all adult workers with certain exceptions, such as servicemen and -women, voluntary workers, and young people and trainees as indicated below. The Low Pay Commission has advised that this rate should be increased to £3.70 an hour in June 2000. A minimum development rate of £3.00 and hour was set in April 1999 for 18- to 21-year-olds, and for up to six months for those aged 22 or over starting a new job and receiving accredited training, eg towards NVQs. This rate is to be £3.20 an hour in June 2000.

Other national impacts on pay have been to:

- emphasise the need to pay for skill and competence to attract people with the right skills and to develop skill levels

- focus attention on widening differentials and pay inequalities

- encourage pay bargaining, where it exists, at plant level.

THE CORPORATE ENVIRONMENT

The most significant aspects of the corporate environment that affect reward are:

- the overall impact of change and the impact of change on structure

- the impact of corporate environmental change on pay systems

- employer/employee expectations

- organisational or corporate culture

- values

- the 'balanced score-card'.

The overall impact of change

At corporate level, change has affected structures and management processes. The increased focus on the customer as competition becomes more fierce has placed greater emphasis on performance rewards for those at the sharp end of the business. And there has been increased focus on the performance of individuals and teams in the battle to control fixed pay costs so that rewards are targeted on those who are making a greater contribution.

The impact of change on structure

Environmental and technological developments have resulted in fundamental changes to the ways in which firms are structured and managed. We now have:

- the flexible firm – which has to adjust its structure, its product range, its marketing strategies, its manufacturing facilities or its range of services quickly to respond to, and – more important – to anticipate, change: the flexible firm needs flexible people – hence the emphasis on multi-skilling (providing employees with the breadth of experience and training to extend their range of skills) and on ensuring that education, training and development programmes are not overspecialised

- the 'lean' firm – in which 'lean production', as advocated by Womark *et al* (1990), has been introduced with the following characteristics: multi-function teams, flat hierarchy, continuous improvement, flexibility, integrated production change, high-commitment HRM practices, and an emphasis on horizontal processes rather than hierarchical structure

- the information-based firm – in which people are immediately made aware of how they are doing, in which they can therefore direct their own performance through organised and immediate feedback, and in which knowledge is no longer a source of special power because it is shared among all concerned.

The impact of corporate environmental change on pay systems

The impact of the changes at organisational level has been to focus attention on:

- more flexible pay structures – eg broad-banding

- paying for competence, contribution and skill

- team pay

- pay related to organisational performance

- performance management (perhaps using a 'balanced score-card' approach – see page 27)

- single status.

Employer/employee expectations

The conditions of turbulence, even chaos, in which some people exist nowadays means that expectations are obscured and ambiguity is rife, both from the viewpoint of employers, who are often uncertain about what they can reasonably expect their employees to do (although they *should* be uncertain), and from the viewpoint of employees, who mostly know what they expect of life but are not entirely sure what their employers expect from them. Even if the expectations of both parties are quite clear, there may be a mismatch between them, with unfortunate consequences. Agency theory and the concept of the psychological contract, as discussed in the next two chapters, address these issues.

Organisational culture

Organisational or corporate culture is the pattern of shared beliefs, attitudes, assumptions, norms and values in an organisation: they may not have been articulated but, in the absence of direct instructions, they influence the way people act and the way things get done.

This definition emphasises that 'organisational culture' refers to a number of abstractions (beliefs, values, norms, attitudes, etc) which pervade the organisation, although they may not have been defined in specific terms. Nevertheless, they can significantly influence people's behaviour.

Culture is a key component in the achievement of an organisation's mission and strategies, the improvement of organisational effectiveness and the management of change. The significance of culture is that it is rooted in deeply-held beliefs. It reflects what has worked in the past, being composed of responses that have been accepted because they have met with success.

A positive culture can work for an organisation by creating an environment conducive to performance improvement and the management of change. The wrong culture can work against an organisation by erecting barriers which prevent the attainment of corporate strategies. These barriers include resistance to change and lack of commitment. The impact of culture can include:

- conveying a sense of identity and unity of purpose

- facilitating commitment and 'mutuality'

- shaping behaviour by giving guidance on what is expected.

Employee reward philosophies, strategies and policies should be developed by reference to the existing or, if it needs to be changed, the preferred culture. They can reinforce an existing culture or play an important part in changing it. As Vicky Wright, managing director of Hay Management Consultants, has said:

> Work culture analysis helps us to determine whether rewards should, for example, focus on rewarding innovative behaviour rather than orderly, more measured behaviour, and whether the need is for job flexibility or flexibility within a job to service client needs. If we start at this point, it gives us two foundations on which to base change. It focuses on the line management agenda and it sets a direction in which detailed steps can be worked out.

Values

Perhaps the most important aspect of culture which needs to be analysed is that of values. Values are expressed in beliefs about what is best for the organisation and what sort of behaviour is desirable. The 'value set' of an organisation may be recognised only at top level, or it may be shared throughout the firm so that the enterprise can be described as 'value-driven'.

The stronger the values, the more they will affect behaviour and account needs to be taken of them in developing reward policies. This does not depend upon the values' having been articulated. Implicit values that are deeply embedded in the culture of an organisation and are reinforced by the behaviour of management can be highly influential, while espoused values which are idealistic and are not reflected in managerial behaviour may have little or no effect. Areas in which values can be expressed and analysed include:

- care and consideration for people
- care for customers
- employee involvement
- equal opportunity
- equity in the treatment of employees
- innovation
- quality
- social responsibility
- teamwork.

These values may influence policies in such areas as paying for performance, resolving the often competing pressures for internal equity and external competitiveness, the 'transparency' of reward arrangements, and the extent to which employees are involved in the development of reward processes and structures. The values should be taken into account in determining the factors to be considered when using some form of job evaluation to establish the relative worth of jobs or roles.

The balanced score-card

In many organisations the reward system includes some provision for variable pay – that is, pay which is contingent on individual, team or organisational performance, or which is related to the competence or skill levels achieved by employees. Variable pay schemes are effective only if they are based on objective measurements, and they can fulfil their potential only if the measurements are clearly related to the key drivers of organisational performance.

The concept of the balanced score-card as originally developed by Kaplan and Norton (1992) addresses this requirement. They take the view that 'what you measure is what you get', and they emphasise that 'No single measure can provide a clear performance target or focus attention on the critical areas of the business. Managers want a balanced presentation of both financial and operational measures.'

Kaplan and Norton therefore devised what they call the 'balanced score-card' – a set of measures that gives top managers a fast but comprehensive view of the business. Their score-card requires managers to answer four basic questions, which means looking at the business from four related perspectives:

- How do customers see us? (the customer perspective)

- What must we excel at? (the internal perspective)

- Can we continue to improve and create value? (the innovation and learning perspective)

- How do we look to shareholders? (the financial perspective)

Kaplan and Norton emphasise that the balanced score-card approach 'puts strategy and vision, not control, at the center'. They suggest that while it defines goals, it assumes that people will adopt whatever behaviour and take whatever action is required to achieve those goals: 'Senior managers may know what the end result should be, but they cannot tell employees exactly how to achieve that result, if only because the conditions in which employees operate are constantly changing.' They claim that this approach to performance management is consistent with new initiatives under way in many companies in such areas as cross-functional integration, continuous improvement, and team rather than individual accountability.

In the UK the NatWest Bank has adopted the following balanced business score-card:

- business success

- customer service

- quality and people

- business efficiency.

In *The Empty Raincoat* (1994) Charles Handy produced his own version of a balanced score-card:

- the intellectual assets of the company (including its brands, its patents, its skill base)

  - expenditure on the enhancement of those assets, including R&D, training and development

- the introduction of new products or services

- employee morale and productivity

• the customer

- quality of goods and service

- customer satisfaction

• the environment

- investment and expenditure on environmental control and improvement

- expenditure on community work

- investment in the community.

The employees' point of view

Many commentators seem to look at employee reward entirely from the organisation's point of view. Insufficient attention is paid to the needs and wants of employees. As Vicky Wright points out:

> Employees are not naive. They know that the old reward policies need to change not only because their organisations are changing, but also because their expectations and plans are changing. They recognise that there is a new employment deal. For example, where the guarantee of a job until retirement is no longer cast-iron, employees are developing a degree of self-reliance in planning their careers, their lifestyle, and how to manage their rewards.

As mentioned in Chapter 1, employee reward policies should embrace the stakeholder concept. They should take account of the aspirations and needs of all those with a stake in the organisation, especially the owners, managers and employees, but including customers, suppliers and the public at large. Reward policies and practices can affect the outside world as well as the internal environment, as was shown in 1995 by controversies about the salaries and share option schemes of certain executives in privatised companies. Where there are trade unions this clearly means that they have an important part to play in independently representing their members' views to management about pay levels and policies.

Employee involvement is crucial to the development of reward policies and programmes. The wishes of employees need to be ascertained. Their comments on existing practices should be listened to and acted upon. They should be involved in the initiation of new reward processes – for example, job evaluation, performance management and variable pay (performance, competence or skill-related). They should continue to be involved in the development, implementation and evaluation of these processes.

SUMMARY

• The international context has been one of global competition requiring pay policies which emphasise flexibility, paying for performance and broader pay grades.

• The national context is one of considerable structural change in the demand for skills, fragmentation, widening differentials and trade union decline. The impact has been to emphasise paying for competence or skill, the need for competitive pay and the development of plant-level bargaining (where it exists at all).

• The corporate context is one of more flexible and leaner organisations in which the focus is on flexible pay, team pay, paying for organisational success, and performance management.

FURTHER READING

Perhaps the best general text on organisational culture is Ed Schein, *Organisation Culture and Leadership*, New York (Jossey Bass, 1987). The Stationery Office's publications *Social Trends* and *The New Earnings Survey* provide data on earnings and employment. The *Financial Times*'s business and management sections give what is probably the most comprehensive review in a daily newspaper of business trends.

3 Economic theories relating to pay

Reward strategies, policies and plans need to be developed against the background of the economic theories which explain the factors that affect labour markets, pay levels and relations between employees and employers. This chapter summarises the main theoretical concepts in the field of labour economics and draws conclusions on what these theories tell us about reward management. On completing this chapter the reader should understand and be able to explain the factors that affect levels of pay and the key economic theories that influence reward policies and practices.

The main theories of labour economics affecting reward relate to:

• the nature of the external and internal labour market

• economic determinants of pay

• agency theory (also known as principal agent theory)

• the effort bargain.

THE LABOUR MARKET

Like all other markets, the labour market has buyers (employers) and sellers (employees). The efforts of buyers and sellers to arrive at an employment relationship constitute a labour market. An external market may be local, national or international. It may be related to specific occupations, sectors or industries in any of these areas. It is within these markets that pay levels are determined economically.

However, in any sizeable organisation there is also an internal labour market. This is the market that exists in firms that fill their jobs from the ranks of their employees. Pay levels and relativities in the internal market may differ significantly between firms in spite of general external market pressures. Differences arise particularly when long-term relationships are usual, even though these are becoming less common. Pay progression related to length of service and an 'annuity' approach to pay increments (ie pay goes up but does not come down – what economists call 'the sticky wage') may lead to higher internal rates. Pay in the internal market will also be affected by decisions on what individuals should be awarded for their particular contribution or specialist expertise, irrespective of the market rate for their job. But the relationship between internal and external rates will also depend on policy decisions within the firm on its levels of pay generally, or on the rates for specified occupations compared with the 'going rate' – ie the market rate for comparable jobs.

From a pay determination and reward management point of view, the significance of labour market theory is that a firm must be fully aware of the external markets in which it is operating in order to make decisions about pay levels in the light of market intelligence and of its policies on where it wants to be in relation to the market. Internal market theory tells us that there are factors besides market pressures which may affect pay levels, such as the perceived need for equity and the necessity of rewarding individual contributions, and competence, long service and loyalty.

ECONOMIC DETERMINANTS OF PAY

The basic economic determinant of pay is supply and demand, but pay levels and movements are further explained by efficiency wage and human capital theory.

Supply and demand

Classical economic competition theory states that pay levels in labour markets are determined by supply and demand. Other things being equal, if the supply of labour exceeds the demand, pay levels go down; if the demand for labour exceeds the supply, pay goes up. Pay stabilises when demand equals supply at the 'market clearing' or 'market equilibrium' wage. This is sometimes known as the theory of equalising differences. It was first stated over 200 years ago by Adam Smith, who wrote that 'The whole of the advantages and disadvantages of different employments and stock must, in the same neighbourhood, be either perfectly equal or continually tending to equality.'

As Elliott (1991) has noted:

> Competitive theory predicts that the forces of supply in the market as a whole will determine the rates of pay within each firm. The relative pay of any two occupations in a single firm will be the mirror image of the relative pay of the same two occupations in the market as a whole.

Classical theory, however, is based on the premises that 'other things are equal' and that a 'perfect market' for labour exists. In the real world, of course, other things are never equal and there is no such thing as a universally perfect market – that is, one in which everyone knows what the going rate is, there is free movement of labour within the market, and there are no monopolistic or other forces interfering with the normal processes of supply and demand. The existence of internal markets means that individual firms exercise a good deal of discretion about how much they pay and how much attention they give to external market pressures. Human capital theory as discussed in the next section also explains why individual rates of pay may be influenced by forces other than supply and demand. And imperfections in the market exist because of poor information, lack of opportunity and immobility. They also arise when employers or trade unions exert pressure on pay levels or when governments intervene in normal pay determination.

The significance of classical economic theory is that it focuses attention on external pressures and the perceived need for 'competitive pay' – that is, pay which matches or exceeds market rates. Classical theory is used as a justification for concentrating on external competitiveness at the expense of internal equity in the belief that 'a job is worth what the market says it is worth'. Pay determination within firms may therefore be based more on 'market pricing' than on job evaluation. As traditionally defined, the latter is concerned only with measuring the relative worth of jobs within the organisation and does not take account of external relativities.

Efficiency wage theory

Efficiency wage theory proposes that firms will pay more than the market rate because they believe that high levels of pay will raise productivity by motivating superior performance, attracting better candidates, reducing labour turnover and persuading workers that they are being treated fairly. This theory is also known as 'the economy of high wages'.

Organisations are using efficiency wage theory (although they do not call it that) when they formulate pay policies which gauge them as market leaders or at least above the average.

Human capital theory

Human capital theory, as stated by Ehrenberg and Smith (1994),

> conceptualises workers as embodying a set of skills which can be 'rented out' to employers. The knowledge and skills a worker has – which come from education and training, including the training that experience brings – generate a certain stock of productive capital.

For an employee the returns on human capital investment are a higher level of earnings, greater job satisfaction and, at one time, if less so now, the belief that security of employment is assured. For the employer the return on investment in human capital is improved performance, productivity, flexibility and the capacity to innovate resulting from an enlarged skill base and increasing levels of competence.

From a pay point of view, the implication of human capital theory is that investment in people increases their value both to the firm and to other employers. Individuals expect a return on their own investment, and firms recognise that the greater value of their employees should be rewarded. Human capital theory encourages the use of skill-based or competence-related pay as a method of reward. It also underpins the concept of individual market worth, which indicates that individuals have their own value in the marketplace which they acquire and increase through investment by their employer and themselves in extra expertise and competence through training, development and experience. The market worth of individuals may be considerably higher than the market rate for their jobs, and if they are not rewarded accordingly they may take their talents elsewhere.

AGENCY THEORY

Agency theory, or principal agent theory, in its purest form recognises that in most firms there is a separation between the owners (the principals) and the agents (the managers). However, the principals may not have complete control over their agents. The latter may therefore act in ways which are not fully revealed to their principals and which may not be in accordance with the wishes of those principals. This generates what economists call agency costs, arising from the difference between what might have been earned if the principals had been the managers, and the earnings achieved under the stewardship of the managers. To reduce agency costs, the principals have to develop ways of monitoring and controlling the activities of their agents.

Agency theory as outlined above can be extended to the employment contract. The employment relationship may be regarded as a contract between a principal (the employer) and an agent (the employee). The payment aspect of the contract is the means used by the principal to motivate the agent to work to the satisfaction of the principal. But according to this theory, the problem of ensuring that agents do what they are told remains. It is necessary to clear up ambiguities by setting objectives and monitoring performance to ensure that the objectives are achieved.

Agency theory also suggests the desirability of a system of incentives to reward acceptable behaviour. This process of 'incentive alignment' consists of paying for measurable results which are deemed to be in the best interests of the owners. Such incentive systems track outcomes in the shape of quantifiable indices of the firm's performance, such as earnings per share, rather than being concerned with the activities that led up to them. The theory is that if their incentive schemes are designed properly, top managers will out of sheer self-interest closely monitor performance throughout the organisation.

Agency theory has been criticised by Gomez-Mejia and Balkin (1992) as 'managerialist'. In other words, it looks at the employment relationship purely from a manager's point of view and regards employees as objects to be motivated by carrot and stick. It is a dismal theory, which suggests that people cannot be trusted. In this respect it has affinities with McGregor's Theory X. McGregor (1960) described managers' traditional assumptions about people and work as follows:

> The average human being has an inherent dislike of work and will avoid it if he can. Because of this human characteristic of dislike of work, most people must be coerced, controlled, threatened with punishment to get them to put forth adequate effort towards the achievement of organisational objectives.

McGregor, of course, advocated his much more optimistic Theory Y as an alternative approach:

> External control and the threat of punishment are not the only means for bringing about effort toward organisational objectives. Man will exercise self-direction and self-control in the service of objectives to which he is committed ... Commitment to objectives is a function of the rewards associated with their achievement.

McGregor's philosophy underpins many of the tenets held by those who advocate the 'new pay' approach as described in Chapter 1, although agency theory and its associated Theory X still pervade much managerial thinking about rewards and punishments. One of the recurring themes of this book is that effective reward policies depend on trust between management and employees.

However, agency theory does perform the useful function of directing attention to the ambiguities in the employment relationship and to the importance of managing expectations. These aspects of reward are covered by the concept of the psychological contract and by expectancy theory as discussed in the next chapter.

THE EFFORT BARGAIN

The concept of the effort bargain is referred to less frequently nowadays and it is not strictly an economic theory. But it has its uses as a further means of describing the employment relationship because it affects pay. The concept states that one of the tasks of management is to assess what level and type of inducements it has to offer in return for the contribution it requires from its workforce.

The workers' aim is to strike a bargain over the relationship between what they regard as a reasonable contribution and what the employer is prepared to offer to elicit that contribution. This is termed the 'effort bargain'. It is, in effect, an agreement which lays down the amount of work to be done for a rate of pay or wage rate, not just the hours to be worked. Explicitly or implicitly, all employees are in a bargaining situation with regard to pay. A system will not be accepted as effective and workable until it is recognised as fair and equitable by both parties and unless it is applied consistently.

The notion of an effort bargain therefore highlights the fact that pay levels are subject to collective and individual negotiation. It also draws attention to the need for equity, fairness and consistency in reward systems.

FACTORS THAT AFFECT PAY LEVELS WITHIN ORGANISATIONS

Within most organisations there are defined or generally understood pay levels for jobs. They usually take the form of a pay structure which may cover the whole organisation or groups of related occupations (job families). There may be different structures at various levels – for example, senior management, other staff, manual workers. In some organisations, however, the pay system is flexible and relatively unstructured. It may, for example, consist simply of individual rates for the various jobs (spot rates) which bear no apparent logical relationship to one another and are determined by management intuitively. Structures for manual workers may also consist of spot rates which are based on negotiations and custom and practice.

Pay levels and ranges may be determined by job evaluation, which assesses the relative internal worth of jobs (internal relativities), and by market pricing, which assesses external relativities. It is also possible that pay levels may respond to increases in the cost of living (inflationary pressures).

Individual rates may be governed by the pay structure, in the form of a fixed rate for the job or by a scale of fixed increments. (A fixed increment is a predetermined addition to an individual's rate of pay related to service in the job.) The increments may apply within a pay bracket, with fixed minima and maxima in a graded structure, or by progress through defined pay ranges in a pay spine (a series of incremental pay points extending from the lowest to the highest jobs covered by the structure within which pay ranges for the jobs in the hierarchy are established). Alternatively, pay progression within brackets or bands or within job families may vary according to individual performance, competence and/or skill.

Essentially, three factors affect the level of pay of individual employees: the value of the job to the organisation the value of the person to the organisation, and the value of the job or the person in the marketplace. These three factors can be defined in more detail:

- *internal job value* – Organisations generally relate pay to the relative contribution or internal value of the jobs people do. The bigger the job the more they are paid.

- *external job value* – The rate of pay for jobs and people will be influenced by market rates in accordance with the policy of the organisation on how it wants its own rates to relate to market levels and the degree to which market forces affect the salaries required to attract and retain people of the quality the organisation needs.

- *the value of the person* – Individual employees may be paid more because it is perceived that they are making a bigger contribution, are performing better (however that is measured), have achieved a higher level of skill or competence than other employees, or have been in a job longer.

The relations between these factors are illustrated in Figure 4.

Figure 4 **Factors that affect levels of pay**

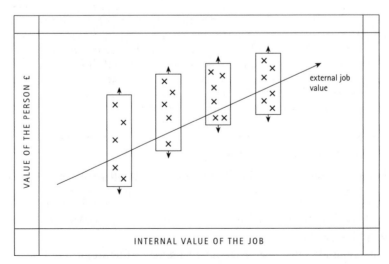

There are, however, other important factors that can affect pay levels generally:

- The employer. Three issues which concern employers may affect levels of pay. The first is affordability – how much is the organisation prepared to pay employees in general or individuals in particular? The second is the policy of the business on whether it is a high payer (prepared to pay above market rates to get and keep good-quality people), a medium payer (willing simply to match market rates, possibly relying on other features of the organisation to attract and retain employees) or a low payer (having to accept, probably for financial reasons, that it must pay less than the market rate). The third is the National Minimum Wage, which will particularly affect employers in low-wage companies.

- Trade unions. Pay levels may be determined through collective bargaining. Trade unions will want their members' pay to keep ahead of inflation, to match market rates and to reflect any increase in the prosperity of the business. The amount of pressure they can exert on pay levels will depend on the bargaining strengths of the employer and the union in pay negotiations.

SUMMARY

- Pay is determined by conditions in both the external and internal labour markets.

- The economic determinants of pay are:

  - *supply and demand* (if labour is scarce, pay is likely to go up, and vice versa)

  - *efficiency wage theory*: paying more raises performance

  - *human capital theory*: investing in people to develop their skill or competence is necessary, and this should influence individual pay.

- Agency theory suggests that incentives should be used to reward acceptable behaviour (incentive alignment).

- The concept of the effort bargain refers to the agreement reached between employers and employees on how the latter should be rewarded according to their effort and contribution.

- The factors affecting levels of pay are:

  - internal relative value of jobs

  - external relative value (market rates)

  - individual value (contribution)

  - what employers can afford

  - management policy on how it wants pay levels to relate to market rates.

FURTHER READING

Labour markets
The general concept of a labour market is defined by Elliott (1991)

and by Ehrenberg and Smith (1994). Labour supply and demand characteristics in labour markets are discussed by Elliott (1991: 7–9). The nature of internal labour markets is dealt with by Ehrenberg and Smith (1992: 27) and Elliott (1991: 357–8).

Economic factors affecting pay levels

Competition theory as a basis for explaining differences in pay is discussed in Elliott (1991: 312–17). Elliot also covers the theory of equalising differences and Adam Smith's theory of net advantage and efficiency wage theory (1991: 346–52). Demand and supply considerations in determining labour market equilibrium and the 'market-clearing' wage are discussed in Ehrenberg and Smith (1994: 43–8). Human capital theory is covered by Elliott (1991: 153–63) and by Ehrenberg and Smith (1994: 279–80).

Agency theory

Agency theory is dealt with by Elliott (1991: 368–70) and by Gomez-Mejia and Balkin (1992: 165–8).

4 The psychological contract

The employment relationship is a fundamental feature of all aspects of people management including those concerned with employee reward. At its most basic level the employment relationship consists of a unique combination of beliefs held by an individual and his or her employer about what they expect of one another. This is the psychological contract, and to manage the employment relationship effectively it is necessary to understand what the psychological contract is, how it is formed, and its significance for those concerned with formulating and implementing reward policy as a key aspect of relationships with employees.

On completing this chapter the reader will:

- have learned about the meaning and significance of the psychological contract

- have found out in broad terms what is happening to the psychological contract in the UK

- appreciate how the concept affects reward policies, and how the latter can be developed in ways that will lead to more positive contracts.

THE PSYCHOLOGICAL CONTRACT DESCRIBED

A psychological contract is a system of beliefs which encompasses the actions employees believe are expected of them and what response they expect in return from their employer.

As described by Guest *et al* (1996), 'It is concerned with assumptions, expectations, promises and mutual obligations.' It creates attitudes and emotions which form and govern behaviour. A psychological contract is implicit. It is also dynamic – it develops over time as experience accumulates, employment conditions change and employees re-evaluate their expectations.

The psychological contract may provide some indication of the answers to the two fundamental employment relationship questions which individuals pose: 'What can I reasonably expect from the organisation?' and 'What should I reasonably be expected to contribute in return?' But it is difficult, often impossible, to ensure that the psychological contract and therefore the employment relationship will be fully understood by either party.

Employees may expect to be treated fairly as human beings, to be provided with work which uses their abilities, to be rewarded equitably in accordance with their contribution, to be able to display competence, to have opportunities for further growth, to know what is expected of them, and to be given feedback (preferably positive) on how they are doing. Employers may expect employees to do their best on behalf of the organisation – 'to put themselves out for the company' – to be fully committed to its values, to be compliant and loyal, and to enhance the image of the organisation with its customers and suppliers. Sometimes these expectations are fulfilled – often they are not. Mutual misunderstandings can cause friction and stress and lead to recriminations and poor performance, or to a termination of the employment relationship.

To summarise in the words of Guest and Conway (1998), the psychological contract lacks many of the characteristics of the formal contract: 'It is not generally written down, it is somewhat blurred at the edges, and it cannot be enforced in a court or tribunal.' They believe that:

> The psychological contract is best seen as a metaphor: a word or phrase borrowed from another context which helps us make sense of our experience. The psychological contract is a way of interpreting the state of the employment relationship and helping to plot significant changes.

An operational model of the psychological contract

An operational model of the psychological contract as formulated by Guest *et al* (1996) suggests that the core of the contract can be measured in terms of fairness of treatment, trust, and the extent to which the explicit deal or contract is perceived to be delivered. The full model is illustrated in Figure 5.

Figure 5 **A model of the psychological contract**

Causes	Content	Consequences
Organisational culture	Fairness	Organisational citizenship
HRM policy and practice	Trust	Organisational commitment
Experience		Motivation
Expectations		
Alternatives	The delivery of the deal	Satisfaction and well-being

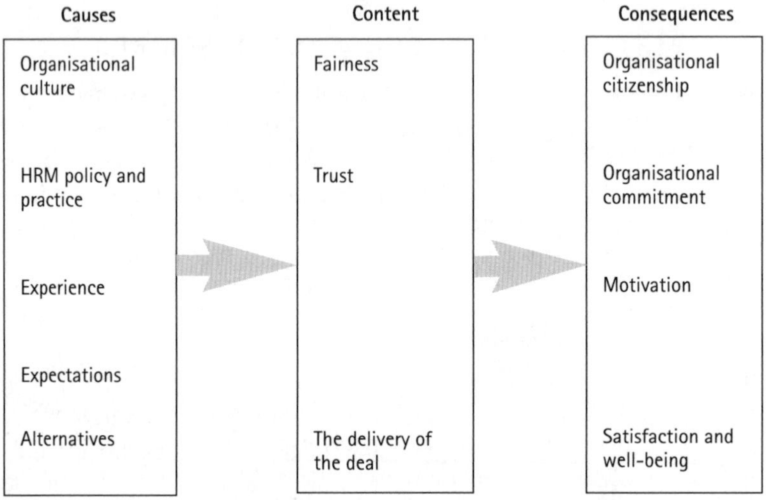

Source: D. Guest, N. Conway, R. Briner and M. Dickman, 'The State of the Psychological Contract in Employment', *Issues in People Management*, Institute of Personnel and Development, 1996.

THE SIGNIFICANCE OF THE PSYCHOLOGICAL CONTRACT

As suggested by Spindler (1994), 'A psychological contract creates emotions and attitudes which form and control behaviour.' The significance of the psychological contract was further explained by Sims (1994):

> A balanced psychological contract is necessary for a continuing, harmonious relationship between the employee and the organisation. However, the violation of the psychological contract can signal to the participants that the parties no longer share (or have never shared) a common set of values or goals.

The concept highlights the fact that employee/employer expectations take the form of unarticulated assumptions. Disappointments on the part of management as well as employees may therefore be inevitable. These disappointments can, however, be alleviated if managements appreciate that one of their key roles is to manage expectations, which means clarifying what they believe employees should achieve, the competencies they should possess and the values they should uphold. And this is a matter not just of articulating and stipulating these requirements but of discussing and agreeing them with individuals and teams.

The psychological contract governs the continuing development of the employment relationship, which is constantly evolving over time. But how the contract is developing and the impact it makes may not be fully understood by any of the parties involved. As Spindler (1994) comments:

> In a psychological contract the rights and obligations of the parties have not been articulated, much less agreed to. The parties do not express their expectations and, in fact, may be quite incapable of doing so.

People who have no clear idea about what they expect may, if such unexpressed expectations have not been fulfilled, have no clear idea why they have been disappointed. But they will be aware that something does not feel right. And a company staffed by 'cheated' individuals who expect more than they get is heading for trouble.

The importance of the psychological contract was emphasised by Schein (1965), who suggested that the extent to which people work effectively and are committed to the organisation depends on:

1 the degree to which their own expectations of what the organisation will provide them with and what they owe the organisation in return matches what the organisation's expectations are of what it will give and get in return

2 the nature of *what is actually to be exchanged* (assuming there is some agreement) – money in exchange for time at work; social need satisfaction and security in exchange for hard work and loyalty; opportunities for self-actualisation and challenging work in exchange for high productivity, high-quality work, and creative effort in the service of organisational goals; or various combinations of these and other things.

And as Guest *et al* (1996) comment:

> While employees may want what they have always wanted – security, a career, fair rewards, interesting work, and so on – employers no longer feel able or obliged to provide these. Instead, they have been demanding more of their employees in terms of greater input and tolerance of uncertainty and change, while providing less in return, in particular less security and more limited career prospects.

Comment on David Guest's views, especially on any implications concerning employee reward practices.

THE CHANGING NATURE OF THE PSYCHOLOGICAL CONTRACT

Many commentators have delivered warnings about changes to the psychological contract which are not all advantageous to employees. And the nature of the psychological contract *is* changing in many organisations in response to changes in their external and internal environments. This is largely because of the impact of global competition and the effect this has had on how businesses operate, including moves into 'lean' forms of operation.

Until recently, the psychological contract has not been an issue because it usually did not change much. This is no longer the case because:

- business organisations are neither stable nor long-lived – uncertainty prevails; job security is no longer on offer by employers who are less anxious to maintain a stable workforce; as Mirvis and Hall (1997) indicate, organisations are making continued employment explicitly contingent on the fit between people's competences and business needs

- flexibility, adaptability and speed of response are all-important and individual roles may be subject to constant change – continuity and predictability are no longer available to employees

- leaner organisations mean that careers may mainly develop laterally – expectations that progress will be made by promotion through the hierarchy are no longer so valid

- meaner organisations may make greater demands on employees and are less likely to tolerate people who no longer precisely fit their requirements.

But, more positively, some organisations are realising that steps have to be taken to increase mutuality and to provide scope for lateral career development and improvement in knowledge and skills through opportunities for learning. They recognise that because they can no longer guarantee long-term employment they have the responsibility to help people to continue to develop their careers if they have to move on. In other words, they take steps to improve employability. Even those which have full embraced the 'core-periphery' concept may recognise that they still need to obtain the commitment of their core

Table 4 The changing psychological contract

From	To
Imposed relationship (compliance, command and control)	Mutual relationship (commitment, participation and involvement)
Permanent employment relationship	Variable employment relationship – people and skills obtained or retained only when required
Focus on promotion	Focus on lateral career development
Finite job duties	Multiple roles
Meeting job requirements	Adding value
Emphasis on job security and loyalty to company	Emphasis on employability and loyalty to own career and skills
Training provided by organisation	Opportunities for self-managed learning

employees and pay attention to their continuous development, although in most organisations the emphasis is likely to be on self-development.

The ways in which psychological contracts are changing have been suggested by Hiltrop (1995) (Table 4).

Hiltrop suggests that a new psychological contract is emerging – one that is more situational and short-term and which assumes that each party is much less dependent on the other for survival and growth. He believes that in its most naked form, the new contract could be defined as follows:

> There is no job security. The employee will be employed as long as he or she adds value to the organisation, and is personally responsible for finding new ways to add value. In return, the employee has the right to demand interesting and important work, has the freedom and resources to perform it well, receives pay that reflects his or her contribution, and gets the experience and training needed to be employable here or elsewhere.

But this could hardly be called a balanced contract. To what extent do employees in general have 'the right to demand interesting and important work'? Employers still call the shots, except when dealing with the special cases of people who are much in demand and in short supply. In the UK, as Mant (1996) points out, 'people often really are regarded as merely "resources" to be acquired or divested according to short-term economic circumstances'. It is the employer who has the power to dictate contractual terms unless they have been fixed by collective bargaining. Individuals, except when they are highly sought-after, have little scope to vary the terms of the contract imposed upon them by employers.

THE STATE OF THE PSYCHOLOGICAL CONTRACT

But the dire warnings which are frequently made about the state of the psychological contract have not been borne out by three recent research projects commissioned by the Institute of Personnel and Development. The research conducted by Guest *et al* (1996) established that the psychological contract (defined in terms of workers' judgements of fairness, trust and organisational delivery of 'the deal') was in better shape than many pundits suggest. A follow-up survey (Guest and Conway, 1997) found that a very high proportion of employees (90 per cent) believe that on balance they are fairly treated by their employers and 79 per cent say they trust 'a lot' or 'somewhat' management to keep its promises. Job security is not a major concern – 86 per cent feel very or fairly secure in their jobs. A majority (62 per cent) believe management and workers are on the same side, and only 18 per cent disagree. However, job satisfaction was only moderate (38 per cent express high satisfaction, but 22 per cent express low satisfaction) although commitment to the organisation was high (49 per cent felt 'a lot' and 36 per cent 'some' loyalty to their organisation).

A further survey (Guest and Conway, 1998) established that:

* there had been no significant changes in attitudes and behaviour since the previous survey

* workers continue to believe that they are fairly treated – 67 per cent report fair treatment by management and 64 per cent say that they get a fair day's pay for a fair day's work

* the number of progressive HRM practices in place is the key determinant of whether workers believe they are fairly treated because they exert a major influence on work attitudes

* people report that home is for relaxation, work is for challenge

* feelings of security remain high – 88 per cent felt 'very' or 'fairly secure' in their jobs

* people still expect a career – 60 per cent believe that their employer has made a career promise, and of these, 65 per cent think that management has largely kept its promise (these feelings are more prevalent amongst younger workers).

The overall conclusion of the researchers in 1998 was that 'the psychological contract is very healthy. On the whole, management is seen as fair, trustworthy and likely to keep its promises. The key influences on a healthy psychological contract are the use of progressive human resource practices, scope for direct participation at work, and working in a smaller organisation.

DEVELOPING AND MAINTAINING A POSITIVE PSYCHOLOGICAL CONTRACT

As Guest *et al* (1996) remark: 'A positive psychological contract is worth taking seriously because it is strongly linked to higher commitment to the organisation, higher employee satisfaction and better employment relations. Again this reinforces the benefits of pursuing a set of progressive HRM practices.' They also emphasise the importance of a high-involvement climate and suggest in particular that HRM practices such as the provision of opportunities for learning, training and development, focus on job security, promotion and careers, minimising status differentials, fair reward systems and comprehensive communication and involvement processes will all contribute to a positive psychological contract.

General approaches to developing a positive psychological contract

The general steps that can be taken to develop a positive psychological contract include:

- defining expectations during recruitment and induction programmes

- communicating and agreeing expectations as part of the continuing dialogue which is implicit in good performance management practices

- adopting a policy of transparency on company policies and procedures and on management's proposals and decisions as they affect people

- generally treating people as stakeholders, relying on consensus and co-operation rather than control and coercion.

The part played by employee reward and performance management processes

Employee reward and performance management processes can help to clarify the psychological contract and make it more positive by:

- providing a basis for the joint agreement and definition of roles

- communicating expectations in the form of targets, standards of performance, behavioural requirements (competencies) and upholding core values

- obtaining agreement on the contribution both parties (the manager and the individual) have to make to getting the results expected

- defining the level of support to be exercised by managers

- providing financial rewards through schemes which deliver messages about what the organisation believes to be important

- providing non-financial rewards which reinforce the messages about expectations

- giving employees opportunities at performance review discussions to clarify points about their work.

> Review reward practices in your own organisation or one familiar to you and identify how well they support the achievement of a productive psychological contract.

SUMMARY

- The psychological contract refers to what employees and employers want and expect from one another. It is concerned with assumptions, expectations, promises and mutual obligations.

- The 'psychological contract creates emotions and attitudes which form and control behaviour' (Spindler, 1994).

- New work contexts mean that the psychological contract is changing.

- Research conducted by Guest *et al* (1996) established that the psychological contract (defined in terms of workers' judgements of fairness, trust and organisational delivery of 'the deal') was in better shape than many pundits suggest.

- 'A positive psychological contract is worth taking seriously because it is strongly linked to higher commitment to the organisation, higher employee satisfaction and better employment relations' (Guest *et al*, 1996).

- To develop a positive psychological contract it is necessary to agree and communicate expectations, adopt policies of transparency and treat people as stakeholders.

- Employee reward practices, especially performance management, can play a significant part in clarifying the psychological contract and making it more positive.

FURTHER READING

The concept of the psychological contract is introduced by Schein in (1965: 22–5, and 98–101: the latter includes an analysis of the relationship between motivation and the psychological contract). Rousseau and Wade-Benzoni (1994: 466–8), describe forms of psychological contracts. Rousseau and Greller (1994) define the concept at pp. 385–6 and consider its significance in 'compensation' at pp. 395–6.

5 Motivation and reward

A number of motivational theories explain how rewards affect the behaviour of individuals and teams. Some people seem to believe that theories are *per se* impractical. But in the field of personnel and development management it can be said that there is nothing so practical as a good theory. A good theory is based on rigorous research into organisational practices and individual and team behaviour. Such research should account for and explain the data it produces, which can be used to help in analysing situations and alternative courses of action and in making predictions about behaviour in different circumstances. The reward philosophies of an organisation can be no better than the motivational theories upon which they are based.

This chapter covers:

- the process of motivation as goal-directed behaviour and the two types of motivation – intrinsic and extrinsic

- the main motivational theories – that is, instrumentality theory, behavioural theory, needs or content theory, Herzberg's two-factor model, and cognitive or process theory (which includes expectancy, goal, reactance, equity, self-efficacy and attribution theory)

- the relationship between money and motivation (pay and performance)

- the factors that affect satisfaction with pay

- the practical implications of motivation theory

- the need for fairness, equity and consistency in reward systems.

On completing this chapter the reader should understand and be able to explain the key motivational theories which influence reward policies and practices.

THE PROCESS OF MOTIVATION

Motivation theory examines the process of motivation. It explains why people at work behave in the way they do in terms of their efforts and the directions they are taking. It also describes what organisations can do to encourage people to apply their efforts and abilities in ways which will help to achieve the organisation's goals as well as satisfying their own needs.

What is motivation? Motivation takes place when people expect that a course of action is likely to lead to the attainment of a goal – a valued reward that satisfies their particular needs. Motivation at work operates in two ways. First, people can motivate themselves by seeking, finding and doing work which leads them to expect that their goals will be achieved. Second, people can be motivated by management through such methods as pay, promotion and praise.

These two types of motivation can be described as:

- intrinsic motivation – the self-generated factors which influence people to behave in a particular way or to move in a particular direction. These factors include responsibility (feeling that the work is important and having control over one's resources), freedom to act, scope to use and develop skills and abilities, interesting and challenging work, and opportunities for advancement and growth.

- extrinsic motivation – what is done to or for people to motivate them. This includes rewards such as increased pay, praise or promotion, and punishments such as disciplinary action, withholding pay, or criticism.

Extrinsic motivators can have an immediate and powerful effect, but it will not necessarily last long. The intrinsic motivators, which are concerned with the 'quality of working life' (a phrase and a movement promoted by proponents of the notion of intrinsic motivation), are likely to have a deeper and longer-term effect because they are inherent in individuals and not imposed from outside.

MOTIVATION THEORIES

The process of motivation in the description above is broadly based on a number of motivation theories which attempt to explain in more detail what it is all about. The theories have proliferated over the years. Some of them, like the crude 'instrumentality' or behaviourist theories have largely been discredited, at least in psychological circles, although they still underpin the views of many managers about motivation and pay systems.

The immensely popular and influential motivation theories of Maslow (1954) and Herzberg *et al* (1957) have been severely criticised, although they are still regarded by many as *the* motivation theories. More convincing 'cognitive' theories have been developed over the years, and in their different ways they help us to appreciate the complexity of the process of motivation and the futility of believing that there are any easy answers to motivating anybody. The main motivation theories are summarised below.

Instrumentality theory

'Instrumentality' is the belief that if we do one thing it will lead to another. In its crudest form, instrumentality theory states that people work only for money. The theory emerged in the second half of the nineteenth century, when the emphasis was on the need to rationalise work and to concentrate on economic outcomes. It assumes that people will be motivated to work if rewards and penalties are tied directly to their performance. Instrumentality theory has its roots in the

scientific management methods of Taylor (1911),
impossible, through any long period of time, to get
much harder than the average men around ther
assured of a large and permanent increase in their

This theory is based on the principle of reinforce
that with experience in taking action to satisfy nee
that certain actions help to achieve their goals v
successful. Success in achieving goals and reward
positive incentive and reinforces the behaviour, which is ...
next time a similar need emerges. Conversely, failure or punishment
provides negative reinforcement, suggesting the need to seek alternative
means of achieving goals. This process has been called the law of
effect.

Motivation using this approach has been and still is widely adopted
and can be successful in some circumstances. But it is based
exclusively on a system of external controls and fails to recognise a
number of other human needs. Nor does it take account of the fact
that the formal control system can be seriously affected by the informal
relations between workers.

Behavioural theory
Behavioural psychologists such as Skinner (1974) emphasise that
behaviour is learned from experience – specific types of behaviour are
strengthened or weakened by the consequences of the behaviour. This
process is called operant conditioning. Behaviourists play down, even
dismiss, the significance of internal psychological factors and instinct.
They are interested only in the external factors that directly influence
behaviour. They believe that learning takes place mainly through the
processes of positive and negative reinforcement.

Needs (content) theory
The basis of this theory is the belief that an unsatisfied need creates
tension and disequilibrium. To restore the balance a goal is identified
which will satisfy the need, and a behaviour pathway is selected which
will lead to the achievement of the goal. All behaviour is therefore
motivated by unsatisfied needs.

Not all needs are equally important to a person at any one time.
Some may constitute a more powerful drive towards a goal than others,
depending on the individual's background and situation. Complexity is
increased because there is no simple relationship between needs and
goals. The same need could be satisfied by a number of different goals.
The stronger the need, and the longer its duration, the broader the
range of possible goals. At the same time, one goal may satisfy a
number of needs. A new car provides transport as well as an
opportunity to impress the neighbours.

Needs theory has been developed by:

• Maslow (1954), who formulated the concept of a hierarchy of needs
  which start from the fundamental physiological needs and lead
  through safety, social and esteem needs to the need for self-fulfilment,
  the highest need of all – He said that 'man is a wanting animal';
  only an unsatisfied need can motivate behaviour, and the dominant

need is the prime motivator of behaviour. This is the best known theory of needs but it has never been verified by empirical research.

- Alderfer (1972), who produced a simpler and more flexible model of three basic needs relating to existence, relatedness and growth (ERG theory)

- McClelland (1975), who identified three needs which motivate managers, and who, while agreeing with Maslow that motives are part of the personality, believed they are triggered by environmental factors – The three needs are achievement, affiliation (friendly relations with others) and power. Different individuals have different levels of these needs. Some have a greater need for achievement, others a stronger need for affiliation, and still others a stronger need for power. Although one need may be dominant, however, it does not mean that the others are non-existent.

Herzberg's two-factor model
Herzberg and his colleagues (1957) developed the two-factor model of motivation following an investigation into the sources of job satisfaction and dissatisfaction among accountants and engineers. It is sometimes called the motivation–hygiene theory. The basic research and various studies which replicated the method led to the conclusion that the factors giving rise to job satisfaction (and motivation) are distinct from the factors that lead to job dissatisfaction. There are two groups of factors. The first consists of the satisfiers or motivators which are intrinsic to the job. These include achievement, recognition, the work itself, responsibility and growth. The second group comprises what Herzberg calls the 'dissatisfaction avoidance' or 'hygiene' factors, which are extrinsic to the job and include pay, company policy and administration, personal relations, status and security. These cannot create satisfaction but, unless preventive action is taken, they can cause dissatisfaction. He also noted that any feeling of satisfaction resulting from pay increases was likely to be short-lived compared with the long-lasting satisfaction from the work itself. One of the key conclusions derived from the research is therefore that pay is not a motivator, except in the short term, although unfair payment systems can lead to demotivation.

Herzberg's two-factor model draws attention to the distinction between intrinsic and extrinsic motivators, and his contention that the satisfaction resulting from pay increases does not persist has some face validity. But his research and the conclusions he reached have been attacked – first because, it is asserted, the original research is flawed and fails to support the contention that pay is not a motivator, and second because no attempt was made to measure the relationship between satisfaction and performance. As David Guest (1992) has said:

> Many managers' knowledge of motivation has not advanced beyond Herzberg and his generation. This is unfortunate. Their theories are now over 30 years old. Extensive research has shown that as general theories of motivation the theories of Herzberg and Maslow are wrong. They have been replaced by more relevant approaches.

Cognitive theory
The more relevant approaches to which Guest refers are the cognitive theories. In cognitive theory, also known as process theory, the

emphasis is on the psychological processes or forces which affect motivation, as well as on basic needs. It is known as cognitive theory because it is concerned with people's perception of their working environment and the ways in which they interpret and understand it. Cognitive theory can be more useful to managers than needs theory because it provides more realistic guidance on motivation techniques. The processes covered by cognitive theory are:

- expectations (expectancy theory)

- goal achievement (goal theory)

- behavioural choice (reactance theory)

- feelings about equity (equity theory)

- self-efficacy theory

- attribution theory.

Expectancy theory

The core cognitive theory is expectancy theory. As Guest (1992) notes, most other approaches adapt or build on it. The concept of expectancy was originally contained in the valency–instrumentality–expectancy (VIE) theory formulated by Vroom (1964). Valency stands for value; instrumentality is the belief that if we do one thing it will lead to another; and expectancy is the probability that action or effort will lead to an outcome.

The strength of expectations may be based on past experience (reinforcement), but individuals are frequently presented with new situations – a change of job, payment system or working conditions imposed by management – where past experience is an inadequate guide to the implications of the change. In these circumstances, motivation may be reduced.

Motivation is likely only when a clearly perceived and usable relationship exists between performance and outcome, and the outcome is seen as a means of satisfying needs. This explains why extrinsic financial motivation – for example, an incentive or bonus scheme – works only if the link between effort and reward is clear and the value of the reward is worth the effort. It also explains why intrinsic motivation arising from the work itself can be more powerful than extrinsic motivation. Intrinsic motivation outcomes are more under the control of individuals, who can judge from past experience the extent to which advantageous results are likely to be obtained by their behaviour.

This theory was developed by Porter and Lawler (1968) into a model which follows Vroom's ideas by suggesting that there are two factors that determine the effort people put into their jobs:

- the value of the reward to individuals in so far as it satisfies their need for security, social esteem, autonomy and self-actualisation

- the probability that reward depends on effort, as perceived by individuals – in other words, their expectations of the relationship between effort and reward.

Thus, the greater the value of a set of rewards, and the higher the probability that receiving each of these rewards depends upon effort, the greater the effort that will be made in a given situation.

But, as Porter and Lawler emphasise, mere effort is not enough. It has to be effective effort if it is to produce the desired performance. The two variables additional to effort which affect task achievement are:

- ability – individual characteristics such as intelligence, manual skills, knowhow

- role perceptions – what the individual wants to do or thinks he or she is required to do: they are good from the viewpoint of the organisation if they correspond with what it thinks the individual ought to be doing; they are poor if the views of the individual and the organisation do not coincide.

Goal theory
Goal theory as developed by Latham and Locke (1979) states that motivation and performance are higher when individuals are set specific goals, when the goals are difficult but accepted, and when there is feedback on performance. Participation in goal-setting is important as a means of securing agreement to the setting of higher goals. Difficult goals must be agreed, and achieving them must be helped by guidance and advice. Finally, feedback is vital in maintaining motivation, particularly towards the achievement of even higher goals.

Reactance theory
Reactance theory as formulated by Brehm (1966) starts from the premise that to the extent that people are aware of their needs and of the behaviour that will satisfy them, and provided they have the necessary freedom, they can choose behaviour so as to maximise need satisfaction. If, however, their freedom to act is threatened, people will react – that is, they will be motivated to avoid any further loss of freedom. As Brehm says:

> In other words, individuals are not passive receivers and responders. Instead, they actively strive to make sense of their environment and to reduce uncertainty by seeking to control factors influencing rewards. Management may have all sorts of wonderful ideas about motivating employees, but they will not necessarily work unless they make sense to the people concerned in terms of their own values and orientations.

Equity theory
Equity theory as described by Adams (1965) states that people will be better motivated if they are treated equitably and demotivated if they are treated inequitably. It is concerned with people's perceptions of how they are being treated in relation to others. To be dealt with equitably is to be treated fairly in comparison with another group of people (a reference group) or a relevant other person. Equity involves feelings and perceptions, and it is always a comparative process. It is not synonymous with equality, which means treating everyone alike. That would be inequitable if they deserved to be treated differently.

Equity theory is linked with the 'felt-fair' principle as defined by Jaques (1961) which states in effect that pay systems will be fair if they are felt to be fair. His assumptions are that:

- there is an unrecognised standard of fair payment for any level of work

- unconscious knowledge of the standard is shared among the population at work

- to be equitable, pay must be felt to match the level of work and the capacity of the individual to do it

- people should not receive less pay than they deserve by comparison with their fellow workers.

This felt-fair principle has passed into the common language of those concerned with employee rewards. It is often used as the final arbiter of how a job should be graded, sometimes overriding the conclusions reached by an analytical job evaluation exercise.

Self-efficacy theory
This theory was developed by Bandura (1982) who defined self-efficacy as 'how well one can execute courses of action required to deal with prospective situations'. It is concerned with an individual's belief that he or she will be able to accomplish certain tasks, achieve certain goals or learn certain things. Locke (1984) has established that self-efficacy is positively related to goal level and goal commitment for self-set goals and performance.

Attribution theory
Attribution theory as defined by Kelley (1967) is concerned with how we explain our performance after we have invested considerable effort and motivation in a particular task. Four types of explanation may be used to account for success or failure – ability, effort, task difficulty and luck. For example, if success or failure is explained in terms of effort, then high motivation may follow. If, on the other hand, failure to achieve is explained in terms of task difficulty or bad luck, the result may be a loss of motivation. Incorrect attributions may be the result of inadequate feedback, and managers can do much to influence attributions and therefore motivation by feedback, communication, appraisal and guidance. This will affect subsequent motivation.

MONEY AND MOTIVATION

People need money and therefore want money. It can motivate but it is not the only motivator. It has been suggested by Wallace and Szilagyi (1982) that money can serve the following reward functions:

- It can act as a goal that people generally strive for, although to different degrees.

- It can act as an instrument which provides valued outcomes.

- It can be a symbol which indicates the recipient's value to the organisation.

- It can act as a general reinforcer because it is associated with valued rewards so often that it takes on reward value itself.

It can be argued that money motivates because it is linked directly or indirectly with the satisfaction of many needs. It satisfies the basic need for survival and security, if income is regular. It can also satisfy the need for self-esteem (it is a visible mark of appreciation) and status – money can set you in a grade apart from your fellows and can buy you things they cannot afford. Money satisfies the less desirable but nevertheless prevalent drives of acquisitiveness and cupidity. So money may in itself have no intrinsic meaning, but it acquires significant motivating power because it comes to symbolise so many intangible goals. It acts as a symbol in different ways for different people, and for the same person at different times. Pay is often a dominant factor in the choice of employer, and pay is an important consideration when people are deciding whether or not to stay with an organisation.

But doubts have been cast on the effectiveness of money as a motivator by Herzberg *et al* (1957). They claimed that while the lack of it may cause dissatisfaction, money does not result in lasting satisfaction. There is something in this, especially for people on fixed salaries or rates of pay who do not benefit directly from an incentive scheme. They may feel good when they get an increase because apart from the extra money it is a highly effective way of making people feel they are valued. But the feeling of euphoria can rapidly die away. However, it must be re-emphasised that different people have different needs, and Herzberg's two-factor theory has not been validated. Some will be much more motivated by money than others. What cannot be assumed is that money motivates everyone in the same way and to the same extent.

But do financial incentives motivate people? The answer, according to Kohn (1998), is absolutely not. He challenges what he calls the behaviourist dogma about money and motivation. And claims that 'no controlled scientific study has ever found a long-term enhancement of the quality of work as a result of any reward system'. Kohn quotes with approval Slater (1980), a sociologist who wrote that 'The idea that everybody wants money is propaganda circulated by wealth addicts to make themselves feel better about their addiction.' When you look at how people are motivated, claims Kohn, 'It becomes disturbingly clear that the more you use rewards to "motivate" people, the more they tend to lose interest in whatever they had to do to get the rewards.' He quotes research that has 'repeatedly shown that the more salient or reinforcing the reward is, the more it erodes intrinsic interest' and points out that 'various devices can be used to get people to do something, but that is a far cry from making people *want* to do something . . .'

Pfeffer (1998) also contends that: 'People do work for money – but they work even more for meaning in their lives. In fact, they work to have fun. Companies that ignore this fact are essentially bribing their employees and will pay the price in lack of loyalty and commitment.' He believes that pay cannot substitute for a working environment 'high on trust, fun, and meaningful work'.

In contrast, Gupta and Shaw (1998) emphasise the instrumental and symbolic meaning of money. The instrumental meaning of money concerns what we get for it – better houses, clothes, cars, etc. The symbolic meaning of money concerns how it is viewed by ourselves and others – money signals our status in and worth to society. They take the basic behaviourist line on money: 'When certain behaviours are followed by money, then they are more likely to be repeated. This means that employees will do the things for which they are rewarded; it also means that they ignore the things for which they are not rewarded.'

The views expressed by Kohn are convincing, except that he seems to think that the only types of rewards to be considered in this debate are financial. He does not seem to recognise that non-financial rewards *can* motivate if handled properly. Pfeffer, however, makes this point when he emphasises the importance of trust and meaningful work. Gupta and Shaw weaken their argument by adopting a crude behaviourist viewpoint. To assume that financial incentives will always motivate people to perform better is as simplistic as to assume, like Kohn, that they *never* motivate people to perform better. Some people will be more motivated by money than others, and, if handled properly, an incentive scheme can encourage them to perform more effectively as long as they can link their effort to the reward and the reward is worth having. But others may be less interested in money and will respond more to intrinsic or non-financial rewards. Yet others will react positively to a judicious mix of both financial and non-financial rewards. What is clear is that simplistic assumptions about the power of money to motivate can lead organisations into developing simplistic performance-related pay schemes or other forms of incentives. For example, the government assumes that the best way to improve examination results is to introduce performance-related pay because, after all, it is well known that teachers are only motivated by money(!).

All we can be certain about is that a multiplicity of interdependent factors are involved in motivating people, and that money is only one of those factors which may work for some people in some circumstances but may not work for other people in other circumstances.

> Consider the arguments presented above about the power of money to motivate. What do you think, and why?

FACTORS THAT AFFECT SATISFACTION WITH PAY

As Lawler (1990) points out, people's feelings about the adequacy of their pay are based upon comparisons they make between their own and others'. External market comparisons are the most critical because they are the ones which strongly influence whether individuals want to stay with the organisation. Many people, however, are unlikely to leave for pay reasons alone unless the increase they expect from a move is substantial – say, 10 per cent.

Lawler also suggests, 'Sometimes it seems that individuals are never satisfied with the pay.' Research in the USA by Porter (1961) and Lawler (1971) has indicated that between 67 per cent and 80 per cent of the managers interviewed expressed dissatisfaction with their remuneration. One of the reasons discovered by Lawler for low pay satisfaction seems to be that individuals seek out unfavourable comparisons. First they look externally: if comparisons there are favourable, they focus on internal comparisons. Only if these are favourable as well are they likely to be satisfied. He comments that:

> A finding that employees are dissatisfied with pay is, in effect, a non-finding. It is to be expected. The key thing that the organisation needs to focus on is whether its employees are more dissatisfied with their pay than are employees in other organisations.

It is possible to argue that some people project their dissatisfaction with other aspects of organisational life – their work and working conditions, opportunities for training, security, etc – on to pay, but there is no hard evidence to support the contention.

Reactions to reward policies and practices will depend largely on the values and needs of individuals and on their employment conditions. It is therefore dangerous to generalise about the causes of satisfaction or dissatisfaction.

However, it seems reasonable to believe that, as mentioned above, feelings about external and internal equity (the 'felt-fair' principle) will strongly influence most people. Research by Porter and Lawler (1968) and others has also shown that higher-paid employees are likely to be more satisfied with their rewards but that the satisfaction resulting from a large pay increase may be short-lived. People tend to want more of the same. In this respect, at least, the views of Maslow and Herzberg have been supported by research.

Other factors which may affect satisfaction or dissatisfaction with pay include the degree to which:

- individuals feel their rate of pay or increase has been determined fairly

- rewards are commensurate with the perceptions of individuals about their ability, contribution and value to the organisation (but this perception is likely to be founded on information or beliefs about what other people, inside and outside the organisation, are paid)

- individuals are satisfied with other aspects of their employment – for example, their status, promotion prospects, opportunity to use and develop skills, and relations with their managers.

THE KEY MESSAGES OF MOTIVATION THEORY

Extrinsic and intrinsic motivating factors
Extrinsic rewards provided by the employer, including pay, will be important in attracting and retaining employees and, for limited periods, increasing effort and minimising dissatisfaction. Intrinsic rewards related to responsibility, achievement and the work itself may have a longer-term and deeper impact on motivation. Reward systems should therefore include a mix of extrinsic and intrinsic rewards.

The significance of needs
People will be better motivated if their work satisfies their social and psychological needs as well as their economic needs.

The influence of goals
Individuals are motivated by having specific goals to work for, and they perform better when they are aiming at difficult goals which they have accepted, and when they receive feedback on performance.

The importance of expectations
The degree to which people are motivated will depend not only upon the perceived value of the outcome of their actions – the goal or reward – but also upon their perceptions of the likelihood of obtaining a worthwhile reward – ie their expectations. They will be highly motivated if they can control the means of attaining their goals. This indicates that contingent pay schemes – that is, those in which pay is related to performance, skill and/or competence – are effective as motivators only if (1) people know what they are going to get in return for certain efforts or achievements, (2) they feel that what they may get is worth having, and (3) they expect to get it.

Behavioural modification
This uses the behavioural principle 'operant conditioning' (ie influencing behaviour by its consequences). Five steps for behavioural modification have been defined by Luthans and Kreitner (1975):

1 Identify the critical behaviour – what people do or do not do which needs to be changed.

2 Measure the frequency – obtain hard evidence that a real problem exists.

3 Carry out a functional analysis – identify the stimuli that precede the behaviour and the consequences in the shape of reward or punishment which influence the behaviour.

4 Develop and implement an intervention strategy – this may involve the use of positive or negative reinforcement to influence behaviour (ie providing or withholding financial or other rewards).

5 Evaluate the effects of the intervention – what improvements, if any, have taken place, and if the intervention was unsuccessful, what needs to be done next?

Self-efficacy
Some people have to be helped and encouraged through guidance, counselling and coaching to believe that they can do more or better.

Attribution theory
This indicates that if people are told they are doing well (positive feedback), if the source is credible and if there is no other information, they will be inclined to believe that they are doing well and therefore to persist in their behaviour. This points the way to performance management processes which motivate by giving feedback and providing the basis for personal development.

Figure 6 **Approaches to motivation (Guest, 1994)**

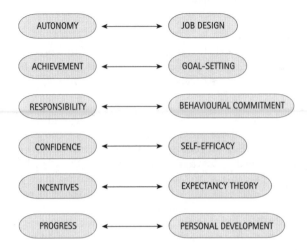

David Guest (1994) has neatly summed up some of the ways in which the process of motivation can further a number of desirable aims in the management of people (Figure 6).

FAIRNESS, EQUITY AND CONSISTENCY

Motivation strategies should incorporate all the elements referred to above. In particular they should influence reward strategies by indicating how the reward system is:

- fair – The reward system should not only be fair, it should be seen to be fair in accordance with the 'felt-fair' principle. It must therefore be transparent – everyone should know how the various parts of the system operate and how they are personally affected by them. Employees and their representatives should be involved in the design of the system and should be given opportunities to comment on how it is working.

- equitable – Equity is achieved when people are rewarded appropriately in relation to others within the organisation and in accordance with their worth and the value of their contribution. An equitable reward system ensures that relative worth is measured as objectively as possible, that the measurement processes are analytical, and that they provide a framework for making defensible judgements about job values and grading.

- consistent – The system should allow consistent decisions to be made about reward levels and individual rates of pay. Policy guidelines should be available to line managers to ensure that they avoid making decisions which deviate irrationally from what would be generally regarded as fair and equitable. But consistency should not be enforced through rigid rules and by insistence on slavishly following precedents. There has to be some flexibility in dealing with reward issues in the light of the current situation and its particular

Table 5 **Summary of motivation theories**

Taylor Skinner	*Instrumentality (behaviourist) theory*	People will be motivated to work if rewards and punishments are directly related to their performance (a popular but largely discredited theory).
Maslow	*Need-hierarchy theory*	A sequence of five needs exists. Needs at a higher level emerge only when a lower-level need has been satisfied.
Herzberg	*Two-factor*	Two groups of factors affect model job satisfaction: (1) those intrinsic to the job (intrinsic motivation or satisfiers) such as achievement, recognition, the work itself, responsibility and growth; (2) those extrinsic – the extrinsic motivators or hygiene factors.
Vroom Lawler and Porter	*Expectancy theory*	Motivation and performance are influenced by: (1) the perceived link between effort and performance; (2) the perceived link between performance and outcomes; and (3) the significance (valence) of the outcome to the person. Effort (motivation) depends on the likelihood that rewards will follow effort and the value of the reward.
Latham and Locke	*Goal theory*	Motivation and performance are higher when individuals have difficult but accepted goals and there is feedback on performance.
Adams	*Equity theory*	People will be better motivated if they are treated equitably, and demotivated if they are treated inequitably.

demands, but such decisions should be consistent with the organisation's reward philosophies, strategies and policies, as discussed in Part 2. The guiding principle should be constancy towards ends but flexibility about means.

SUMMARY

• Motivation is concerned with behaviour instigated by needs and directed towards the goals that can satisfy those needs.

• Motivation theories can be divided into three main categories:

   – *instrumental/behaviourist*, which in effect state that people are only motivated by money

   – *content theory* (eg Maslow and Alderfer) which is concerned with the specific needs of people

   – *process* or *cognitive theory*, which examines the psychological processes involved in motivation (eg expectancy, goal and equity theory).

• The principal theories are summarised in Table 5.

• There are differing views on the extent to which money motivates but its attraction varies between different people and the motivational effect may not persist.

• Satisfaction with pay is largely influenced by feelings about external and internal equity (the 'felt-fair' principle).

FURTHER READING

General reviews of motivation theory are contained in T. M. Ridley, *Motivating and Rewarding Employees*, ACAS, 1992, and M. Armstrong, *A Handbook of Personnel Management Practice*, fifth edition, Kogan Page, 1995 (pp. 149–72). Expectancy theory is expounded by Vroom (1964), pp. 17–18. Vroom also discusses the role of motivation in work performance, pp.191–209. Herzberg summarises his two-factor model in 'One More Time: How do you motivate your employees?' *Harvard Business Review*, pp. 56–8, January–February 1968.

Part 2

EMPLOYEE REWARD PROCESSES

6 Reward philosophy

Reward philosophy provides the guiding principles and sets out the beliefs and values upon which reward strategies, policies and procedures are based. At the end of this chapter the reader will understand the issues with which reward philosophy may be concerned and how it can be developed.

ISSUES

The basic beliefs and values expressed by an organisation's reward philosophy relate to such issues as:

- the role reward plays in achieving performance goals and ensuring continuous improvement
- how reward underpins the organisation's values regarding innovation, teamwork, flexibility and quality
- achieving fairness, equity and consistency
- the extent to which the emphasis should be on achieving internal equity or external competitiveness
- the importance attached to relating pay to individual performance
- the importance attached to team as distinct from individual rewards
- assumptions about the rights of stakeholders in the organisation – owners, management and employees
- the degree to which employees should be regarded as partners, sharing in the success of the organisation
- to what extent employees should be involved in developing reward policies and processes
- to what extent responsibility for pay decisions should be devolved to line management

- how much flexibility, if any, should be allowed in administering the reward system.

Philosophies in these areas may not be articulated – in fact they seldom are, however desirable that may be. Different organisations emphasise some aspects and ignore others. They can become part of the culture of the organisation, which will consist largely of unwritten norms and values, and as such will have been developed over long periods of time and accepted as 'custom and practice'.

THE ROLE OF THE DOMINANT COALITION IN FRAMING PHILOSOPHY

In accordance with the behavioural theory of the firm, as expressed by Cyert and March (1963), an organisation can be viewed as a coalition of individuals who are, in turn, members of sub-coalitions. Various coalitions within the firm are likely to have different ideas about how the reward system should operate. But there will be a dominant coalition (usually the top management team, but sometimes a combination of top managers and powerful senior managers) which will exert considerable influence on reward philosophy and practice. For example, as Gomez-Mejia and Balkin (1992) note on the basis of their research:

- Organisations run by entrepreneurs tend to adopt more flexible and adaptive reward patterns (what Gomez-Mejia and Balkin call 'experiential compensation') than those run by professional management.

- High-technology firms adopt similar approaches based on the value systems of their dominant coalitions – their research engineers and scientists – as do firms in which venture capitalists play an important role.

- Firms in which the dominant coalition at the top consists of risk-avoiders with a high need for order and predictability emphasise the need for predetermined, bureaucratic and tightly-controlled reward processes.

- Family-run companies may adopt a patriarchal system for distributing rewards and often favour company-based rather than individual bonuses.

EXAMPLES OF REWARD PHILOSOPHIES

This variety of dominant coalitions and the almost infinite range of circumstances in which organisations function mean, of course, that there can be no such thing as a model reward philosophy. Here are some examples of how different organisations have expressed their reward philosophy.

- *Birmingham Midshires Building Society*

  - reward will be used as a mechanism to encourage good performance and discourage bad performance

  - upper-quartile salaries will be paid for upper-quartile performance

- variable reward will be used as a means of ensuring value for money

- local incentives should not discourage mobility between business areas

- reward should reflect not just short-term business performance but also growth over the long term

- the total value of reward should be transparent in that people are fully informed of the size of investment made in them by the Society

- reward should, where possible, introduce choice and encourage individuals to take some responsibility for the shape of their overall package.

• *BP Amoco*

The performance of BP Amoco will be dependent on the quality and commitment of its workforce. The board believes that directors and senior executives of the right calibre will be attracted and incentivised to maximise shareholder returns if the BP Amoco group adopts remuneration policies which are comparable to the highest standards of international industry. The aim is to provide a competitive reward for delivering on-target performance while superior rewards can be earned for delivering outstanding results. The remuneration package balances long-term and short-term goals through three elements: base salary, annual bonuses and long-term incentive plans. As the seniority of the executive increases, so the proportion of the base salary declines and the proportion of the two performance-linked 'at risk' elements increases.
(extract from BP Amoco annual report, 1998)

• *Cable & Wireless Communication*

- pay should reflect market need and individual performance

- pay is pitched at the market median for competent performers who achieve objectives

- performance levels are assessed through at least two formal review meetings each year

- the system is owned and driven by managers

- performance is assessed in relation to both 'hard' targets related to business imperatives and 'soft' personal-development ones

- where jobs involve more discretion, the scope for performance-related pay is increased

- the organisation no longer offers any cars on account of 'status'.
(*Source*: IDS, 1998)

• *Civil Aviation Authority*

The philosophy as expressed by the management aims of the reward system is to support corporate objectives, to ensure that CAA can recruit, to train and motivate high-calibre staff, to develop a close relationship between pay and individual performance in order to move towards pay's being mainly determined by line managers, and to provide simple and flexible pay structures.

- *Customs and Excise*

The key pay principles are that pay schemes should directly support the business needs of the organisation; effective communication procedures should be in place; the management of schemes should be delegated as far as possible; paybill modelling and robust control systems should be in place before schemes are introduced; schemes should be fair and open, and should be supported by effective performance agreements and appraisal systems; schemes should provide rewards for the majority of staff, not just the outstanding performers (but poor performers should not receive pay increases); the operation of schemes should be regularly monitored and evaluated.

- *Digital*

Pay provides the competitive edge for skills and is a major contributor to releasing every employee's potential.

- *District Audit*

The organisation's philosophy concerning pay is

- to motivate and reward individual achievement which contributes to business results

- to provide real pay differentiation between those who achieve and those who do not

- to support and enable the development of careers and new skills

- to support the new roles and teamworking

- to retain and attract key staff with relevant skills and experience

- to align pay determination and budget responsibility

- to provide flexibility to respond to changing business circumstances

- to identify for District Audit a clear relationship with 'market rates', recognising that these may differ on a geographical and functional basis

- to be affordable

- to recognise the need at an individual level to be clear, credible and equitable.

(*Source*: IDS Study 650, June 1998)

- *First Direct*

For base pay, salary increases will be based on market movements and the skills required of an individual in a role. It is believed that a clear and well-defined career-development framework is an essential part of the motivation and reward equation.

- *Guy's and St Thomas' Hospital Trust*

The guiding principles are to integrate reward with key strategies for growth and improved performance to underpin the organisation's values, to indicate what behaviour will be rewarded and to provide the competitive edge to attract and retain the level of skills needed.

- *Halifax Bank*

  - the reward you receive will more accurately reflect your contribution to the Halifax

  - there is a need to reflect changing business needs – the new structure is designed to encourage staff to respond better to the needs of customers

  - there is a need to identify yourself by your contribution rather than by grade

  - there is a need to encourage contribution through a performance management process which gives greater responsibility to line managers to develop and reward performance

  - if you fulfil agreed expectations, we will fulfil expectations on reward – if you do not perform, rewards will be less.

- *IBM*

  The emphasis is on contribution pay – 'what you do, counts' – and decisions on pay are primarily owned by line managers.

- *ICL*

  The aim is to strengthen the performance culture by rewarding employees who develop capabilities that clearly relate to the company's business needs.

- *Post Office*

  Pay systems should be integrated, not looked at in isolation, but pay is only one of many tools and must not stand alone. Pay philosophy must support and add value to the organisation as a whole and to the individual units.

- *Rover Group*

  Pay is viewed as a key tool, to be used not only as an incentive to an end result but also to pave the way towards culture change and a focus on achievement. The philosophy is concerned with focusing on individuals, promoting the development of the individual in both a business- and a personally-related way, reinforcing the importance of the individual contribution and reinforcing line management leadership.

- *Shell*

  The philosophy is to provide better rewards for better performance and continue to recognise personal accountability and responsibility within a more flexible salary structure. This will help the company to retain a strong competitive position as an employer.

- *Sun Life*

  The organisation is moving towards a performance-oriented culture;

pay decisions are being devolved to line management; performance management is now a crucial part of the managers' role; we shall reinforce teamworking, focusing attention on excellence of customer service while endeavouring to effect a reduction in labour costs.

• *3M*

Rewards have to be tied directly to successful innovation.

Philosophies in new pay companies
On the basis of their survey of 60 major US corporations, Schuster and Zingheim (1992) differentiated between the philosophies of what they called new pay companies and traditional pay companies as follows:

New pay companies

• focus on key organisational goals and objectives to get a differential advantage

• emphasise excellence.

Traditional pay companies

• focus on fairness, competitiveness and equity

• emphasise 'good pay practice'.

EFFECTIVE REWARD PHILOSOPHIES

An effective reward philosophy is one that:

• reflects and underpins a positive organisational culture – one that recognises the importance of people as a key asset and the need to reward them accordingly

• provides management with guiding principles on how reward strategies and policies should be formulated, bearing in mind that this is an evolutionary process and the fundamental philosophies themselves may need to be adapted when new circumstances arise

• addresses the key issues facing the organisation relating to people and their contribution

• expresses values and beliefs that can be communicated to employees and will be acceptable to them, at least in general terms. (Clearly, what matters to employees is not the philosophies themselves but the pay practices emanating from them.)

DEVELOPING PAY PHILOSOPHIES

Pay philosophies can be developed by taking the following steps:

• Establish what the existing pay philosophy is. All organisations have one, although it may not have been articulated. In that case, ask around. Identify the dominant coalition and, if you can get at them, ask each of its members what he or she thinks the philosophy is. If you can't talk to them, ask other people what they think. You may get a number of different answers but there should be some common thread. It might be best to avoid using the somewhat pretentious phrase 'pay philosophy'; instead, just ask the following questions:

- What contribution do you think our pay policies/practices make to improving organisational performance?

- To what extent do you think pay practices can and do help to promote innovation, teamwork, flexibility (assuming that is what is wanted) and quality?

- How much importance do you attach to equity, fairness and consistency in our pay practices? (The answer will probably be 'A lot', but follow up with questions on how far pay practices are thought to live up to those ideals.)

- What do you think is the more important – internal equity or external competitiveness? Or are they equally important? If so, how can any conflict between the two factors be resolved?

- Should we emphasise rewarding people according to their individual performance? If so, why? Are there any problems in doing so?

- What importance do you attach to rewarding team rather than, or as well as, individual performance?

- Should employees share in the success of the organisation, and if so, how?

- What right do you think employees have to be involved in decisions about reward processes and practices which affect them?

- Do you think more responsibility for decisions should be devolved to line management? If so, how do you believe the implementation of pay policies should be controlled?

- How far is it possible – in fact desirable – to achieve complete consistency in pay decisions across the organisation?

Raise these questions, or something like them, with other people in the organisation besides those in, or close to, the dominant coalition.

• Review existing pay policies and practices to establish the extent to which they are congruent with the espoused philosophy or people's perception of it.

• Form a view on the extent to which the pay philosophy is functional or dysfunctional – and, if the latter, what needs to be done about it. If the philosophy is embedded in the culture of the organisation or is totally owned by the dominant coalition, there is not much that can be done about it in the short term unless you are an influential member of that dominant coalition.

Changing pay philosophies can be a slow process because it involves cultural change. But in the longer term progress can be made by addressing reward strategies and policies as discussed below, with the focus on how they can contribute to improved organisational performance. Evolution in reward philosophy can be achieved by demonstrating the effectiveness of new approaches to reward processes and practice.

> Why is it important to develop and communicate a reward philosophy?

SUMMARY

- Reward philosophy provides the guiding principles and sets out the beliefs and values upon which reward strategies, policies and procedures are based.

- Reward philosophy will be concerned with such issues as the role reward plays in achieving performance goals and ensuring continuous improvement, and in underpinning the organisation's values regarding innovation, teamwork, flexibility and quality.

- There will be a dominant coalition (usually the top management team, but sometimes a combination of top managers and powerful senior managers) which will exert considerable influence on reward philosophy and practice.

- An effective reward philosophy is one that reflects and underpins a positive organisational culture, provides management with guiding principles on how reward strategies and policies should be formulated, addresses the key issues facing the organisation relating to people and their contribution, and expresses values and beliefs that can be communicated to employees and will be acceptable to them.

- Pay philosophies can be developed by establishing what the existing pay philosophy is, reviewing existing pay policies and practices to establish the extent to which they are congruent with the espoused philosophy or people's perception of it, forming a view on the extent to which the pay philosophy is functional or dysfunctional – and, if the latter, what needs to be done about it.

- Changing pay philosophies can be a slow process because it involves cultural change.

- Evolution in reward philosophy can be achieved by demonstrating the effectiveness of new approaches to reward processes and practice.

FURTHER READING

Examples of reward philosophies and policies are contained in *Putting Pay Philosophies into Practice,* Incomes Data Services, 1992.

7 Reward strategy

Reward strategy is concerned with what the organisation wants to do about reward over the next two or three years. It defines the intentions of the organisation on how its reward policies and processes should be developed to meet business needs.

On completing this chapter the reader will understand what strategy is, what it looks like, and how it can be developed.

WHAT IS REWARD STRATEGY?

Reward strategy is a business-focused statement of the intentions of the organisation concerning the development of future reward processes and practices which are aligned to the business and human resource strategies of the organisation, its culture, and the environment in which it operates. As Schuster and Zingheim (1992) indicate: 'Reward strategies provide a road-map from where the organisation is presently to where it wants to be in the future.'

A more comprehensive description is to be found in Gomez-Mejia and Balkin (1992), who define it as:

> The deliberate utilisation of the pay system as an essential integrating mechanism through which the efforts of various sub-units and individuals are directed toward the achievement of an organisation's strategic objectives, subject to internal and external constraints. When properly designed, contingent upon the organisation's strategic objectives and constraints, it can be an important contributor to the firm's performance.

The key words in this complex definition are 'integrating mechanism', 'contingent upon the organisation's strategic objectives' and 'an important contributor to the firm's performance'. The importance of integration and a contingency approach are discussed later in this chapter, which includes an assessment of how reward strategy can contribute to business results.

A strategic orientation to reward means understanding the 'big picture' – what the organisation is there to do, where it is going, and how it is going to get there. It requires the development of a longer-term vision of the future.

REWARD STRATEGY – PERFORMANCE AND BEHAVIOUR

Reward strategy and performance

Reward strategy is concerned with the achievement of higher levels of organisational, team and individual performance as illustrated in Figure 7. This means focusing on resourcing, organising, communicating and rewarding for contribution to value added as well as providing recognition for accomplishment and growth.

Reward strategy and behaviour

Reward strategy will also be concerned with ways in which people's beliefs and expectations about how they will be rewarded can be influenced. As Lawler (1990) explains, 'Expectations are particularly important in influencing behaviour ... the key issue from the organisation's point of view is how it can influence the beliefs that individuals develop.'

WHY HAVE A REWARD STRATEGY?

A reward strategy provides a sense of purpose and direction which will help to establish priorities for developing reward plans which can be aligned to business and HR strategies. The strategy will necessarily be expressed in general terms and it will evolve and be amended as new circumstances arise. But it will express as clearly as possible the intentions of the organisation and form the basis for communicating those intentions to employees.

THE FEATURES OF AN EFFECTIVE REWARD STRATEGY

An effective reward strategy

• is based on corporate values and beliefs

Figure 7 Reward strategy and performance

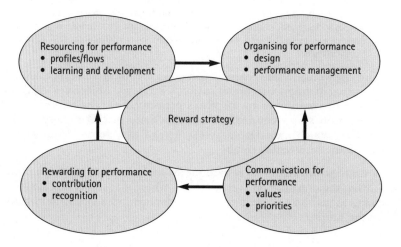

- flows from the business strategy but also contributes to it
- is driven by business needs and 'fits' the business strategy
- aligns organisational and individual competencies
- is integrated with other HR strategies
- is congruent with the culture and internal and external environment of the organisation – the content of the strategy will be contingent on those environments
- rewards results and behaviour that are consistent with key organisational goals, thus, as Armstrong and Murlis (1998) assert, driving and supporting desired behaviour
- is linked with business performance, adopting a competitive strategy perspective
- is practical and implementable
- has been evolved in consultation with key stakeholders.

These features are discussed below.

Linking reward strategy to values and beliefs

Reward strategy provides an opportunity to reinforce the organisation's values and beliefs in such areas as performance, quality, teamwork and innovation. To do this, it should be developed in the light of these values and should state the intention to take account of them in the design of reward processes and in the operation of the reward system. There could, for example, be an indication that teamwork values will be upheld by team rewards and by including effectiveness as a teamworker among the competences assessed in performance management reviews. Or a job evaluation scheme used to measure the relative worth of jobs could incorporate factors or criteria which reflect core values such as innovation, quality and teamwork. Job evaluation factors deliver a message on what is considered important in valuing jobs, roles and people.

Overall, the aim should be to establish a culture in which individuals and teams take responsibility for the continuous improvement of business processes and of their own skills and contributions.

Flowing from but contributing to business strategy

Reward strategy flows from the business strategy. The latter indicates how the business intends to achieve competitive advantage through innovation, quality, performance and cost leadership, and what action it proposes to take to increase shareholder value through growth, diversification, product/market development, performance/productivity improvement, process re-engineering and better cost management. As Lawler (1995) emphasises:

> The business strategy, in particular, serves as a crucial guide in designing organisational systems because it specifies what the company wants to accomplish, how it wants to behave, and the kinds of performance and performance levels it must demonstrate to be effective.

Here are some actual examples of reward strategies flowing directly from the business strategy.

- A large catering firm which, following a business process re-engineering exercise, has concentrated on horizontal processes and project teams. The reward strategy therefore focuses on flexibility, team pay and competence development.

- A venture capital company in biotechnology for which the business strategy is to develop and market highly innovative products. The reward strategy focuses on attracting and retaining the best talents in this particular field. The financial rewards are linked with competence development, team achievement and organisational performance, while non-financial rewards include the opportunity for professional development and 'applause' on successfully completing a project.

- A manufacturing firm in which the business strategy is to differentiate through concentrating on quality rather than on price. Reward strategy therefore focuses on any aspects of design, development, manufacturing and administration where rewards (financial and non-financial) could be related to quality. The strategy includes the intention to conduct research on how best to measure contributions to quality. This has resulted in the introduction of 360-degree feedback, with the emphasis on quality as a product of good teamwork and something on which all team members are expected to comment.

- A large retailer in which a business strategy of differentiation by offering better-quality service in its retail outlets is regarded as the key to increasing shareholder value (the overriding objective of the firm). The reward strategy emanating from this business strategy focuses on relating rewards to increases in levels of competence, customer service being the key competence.

- A mail order firm's strategy for growth is diversification. This depends not only on acquiring the right sort of businesses but also on developing the general management skills required to run them (conspicuously lacking in this highly marketing-oriented company, where an 'easy come, easy go' approach is adopted towards its key marketing executives, the product managers). The implication for the reward strategy is that reward packages are developed which in the short term will attract, retain and motivate entrepreneurs with general management skills (not a widespread combination) but will also encourage high-flying existing product managers to develop the skills and competence required in general management positions.

- A housing association providing sheltered accommodation to people with learning difficulties in which the business strategy was to win more contracts by becoming more competitive though delivering higher levels of care and cutting costs. The issues were that many of the staff delivering the care were not sufficiently competent and a major contributor to the low costs was the pay system which consisted of a pay spine in which, because staff turnover was low, most staff had drifted to the top. The reward strategy to address these business issues was first to develop competence frameworks and performance management and job evaluation processes which were linked to generic and role-specific competences (defined in terms of what people had to be able to do to carry out their work competently). The pay spine was abolished and replaced by a pay spine in which position and progression were determined by the competence levels required and attained.

These are clear cases in which reward strategies flow from business strategies. But what about the other way round? How can they contribute? Reward considerations make an impact if when the business strategy is being formulated there is someone who can point out, for example, how reward initiatives can enable the company to differentiate through diversification or product/market development by getting and keeping the right people or widening the skill base. Negatively, a constraint on business growth may be due to deficiencies in the reward packages for key players which will need to be remedied if the firm is to move forward.

Integrating reward strategies

As Corkerton and Bevan (1998) comment:

> Of all the holy grails that HR professionals seek, the one that aligns reward strategy with business strategy offers the greatest prize. But in many ways it is also the most elusive. By aligning reward and business strategies, elements of the paybill can be targeted at the employees who add most value. And it allows reward to exert leverage over employees' behaviour and performance by sending a clear message about what outputs or skills attract most financial recognition and pay progression. As long as the leverage is on aspects of employee performance that lead directly and unambiguously to improved business performance, everyone (except poor performers) is bound to win.

Integrating reward and business strategies means combining them as a whole so that they contribute effectively to achieving the mission or purpose of the organisation. The processes of linking strategies is the best way of achieving integration, or 'fit', in the sense that business and reward strategies are in harmony. But it is necessary to see that reward goals are aligned with business goals and reward strategies are defined in a way which spells out how they will contribute to the achievement of the strategic objectives contained in the business plan. This process of 'alignment' is perhaps the most important feature of reward strategy. It means aligning what the organisation thinks it should do about reward with:

- what the business wants to do strategically

- the culture of the business as it is now or what it needs to become

- the needs of the people in the business

- the other HR strategies.

The last point is crucial. Vertical integration with the business strategy may be the first aim but it is important to achieve horizontal integration so that reward strategies and those concerned with employee resourcing, development and relations are mutually supportive. Various studies have shown that when organisations 'bundle' related strategies together a much greater impact on organisational performance is achieved. A model of the process of integration is given in Figure 8.

Figure 8 A model of the process of integrating strategy

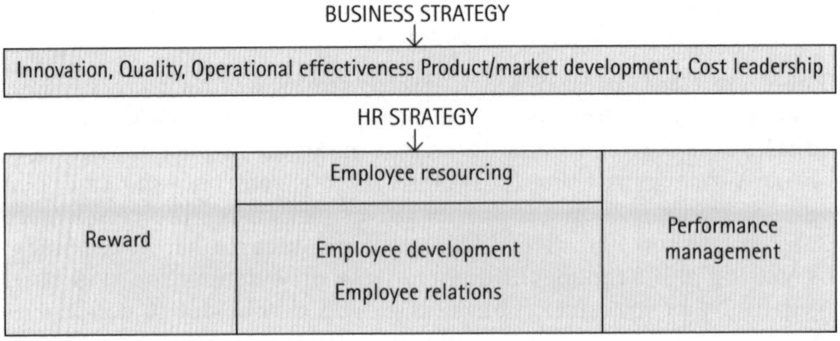

BUSINESS STRATEGY
↓

Innovation, Quality, Operational effectiveness Product/market development, Cost leadership

HR STRATEGY
↓

Reward	Employee resourcing	Performance management
	Employee development	
	Employee relations	

This model illustrates the fact that the HR strategy flows from the various aspects of the business strategy (vertical integration). Reward strategy and performance management strategy are both aligned with the basic resourcing, development and employee relations strategies.

Achieving vertical integration

Vertical integration is achieved by obtaining answers to broad questions derived from business strategy imperatives such as these:

• What sort of people do we need in the future?

• What sort of skills do we need in the future?

• What sort of behaviours do we want in the future?

• What sort of values (for performance, quality, customer service, etc) do we need to operationalise in the future?

• How can our reward policies and practices help us to get and keep the people we need, encourage skill development and appropriate behaviour, and underpin our values?

Examples of how business and reward strategies can be aligned are given in Table 6.

Achieving horizontal integration

Horizontal integration means being aware of the ways in which reward and performance management can support other HR processes. For example, reward processes can impact on recruitment and retention rates, encourage skill development and help to reduce the risk of an unsatisfactory employee relations climate. Performance management can help people to identify and develop the skills and behaviours which the future requires as well as clarify expectations about what each party has to do to 'deliver the deal'.

A CONTINGENT APPROACH TO REWARD STRATEGY

The process of aligning reward strategy means achieving good fit not only with the business and other HR strategies but with the context in which the firm operates – its culture, technology, type of people employed and external environment. The reward strategy will be contingent on all these factors as well as the business strategy.

Table 6 **Achieving vertical integration**

Business strategy	Reward strategy
Achieve added value by improving employee motivation and commitment.	Introduce or improve performance pay plans – individual, team, gain-sharing.
Achieve added value by improving performance/productivity.	Introduce or improve performance pay, plans and performance management processes.
Achieve competitive advantage value by developing and making the best use of distinctive core competences.	Introduce competence-related pay.
Achieve competitive advantage by technological development.	Introduce competence-related or skill-based pay.
Achieve competitive advantage by delivering better value and quality to customers.	Recognise and reward individuals and teams for meeting and exceeding customer service and quality standards/targets.
Achieve competitive advantage by developing the capacity of the business to respond quickly and flexibly to new opportunities.	Provide rewards for multi-skilling and job flexibility. Develop more flexible pay structures (broad-banding).
Achieve competitive advantage by attracting, developing and retaining high-quality employees.	Ensure that rates of pay are competitive. Reward people for developing their competencies and careers in a broad-banded pay structure.

Contingency theory states that to be effective, organisational policies and practices should be appropriate to the firm's unique characteristics. There is no one best way to do things in organisations except to fit what is done to the particular circumstances. As Lawler (1995) points out:

> Particular practices are neither good nor bad in the abstract. Instead, they must make sense within the context of the business strategy and other systems, such as those designed to manage information, human resources, production, finance and, of course, compensation.

It can be argued their there is no such thing as 'best practice' in reward management or, indeed, any other form of management. Benchmarking may and should establish what other organisations believe is good practice in their circumstances, but these are not necessarily right elsewhere. The context is the deciding factor. And this includes not only the business context but the culture of the organisation – its ways of doing things, its values and its norms.

Contingency theory as applied to reward strategy tells us that:

• Diverse organisational strategies and cultures require different reward strategies.

- The usefulness of different reward strategies, policies and practices varies according to the context.

- Business strategies may drive reward strategies but within an organisational context there will be, in the words of Gomez-Mejia and Balkin (1992), 'reciprocal effects because managers and employees will influence emergent (*ad hoc*) strategies at different levels in the organisation'.

- It cannot be assumed that any one reward practice will have an equal effect on all those who experience it. Not everyone is motivated in the same way and people's reaction to a practice such as performance-related pay will be contingent on what motivates them individually.

As Gomez-Mejia and Balkin conclude: 'The notion of general principles in personnel management is essentially bankrupt and, unless legally mandated, is bound to produce sub-optimal results.'

THE CONTENT OF REWARD STRATEGY

A reward strategy should not attempt to do too much. It should focus on no more than one or two critical issues at any one time. Remember that strategy formulation is an evolutionary process. New strategic demands on organisations mean that new strategies will have to be evolved to meet them. Committing too much in advance may increase the problem of flexing strategy in changing circumstances as well as potentially dissipating energy on projects which will add little value in new situations.

Strategy which focuses on critical success factors will enable the organisation to marshal its resources in areas which will maximise added value. It will make life easier for reward strategists, who have to persuade all concerned of the right direction to take – they will be able to concentrate on what really counts.

Reward strategy statements should spell out an *intention* to do something, a *purpose* to achieve something, and a *measure* to determine the extent to which the purpose has been achieved (success criteria). For example, if the business strategy emphasises the need to improve quality, a reward strategy statement could read:

- The intention is to develop new methods of rewarding people for high-quality performance.

- The purpose is to enhance the company's strategy for differentiating through the delivery of high quality to customers.

- The success criteria will be, in general, sales figures and in particular the outcome of customer opinion surveys.

Key strategic issues

The aspects of reward policy and practice which may be regarded as key strategic issues include:

- performance improvement

- increasing levels of competence and enlarging the skill base (support to multi-skilling)

- competitive pay

- achieving a more equitable and definable pay system

- restructuring the pay system to take account of – indeed, to underpin – organisational changes; for example, introducing broad-banding after a de-layering exercise

- culture change

- devolution of pay decisions to line managers

- involvement of employees in reward matters

- developing teamwork.

WHAT A REWARD STRATEGY LOOKS LIKE

Reward strategies come in all shapes and sizes. The following are some examples.

Cadbury Schweppes

The international reward strategy formulated by Cadbury Schweppes stated that it is:

- geared to individual business strategies and practices but recognises the increasingly international nature of our business

- an integral part of an overall human resource strategy geared to those business requirements

- market-driven within each country, thus enabling us to attract, select and retain world-class employees

- designed to motivate and reinforce superior performance

- flexible and increasingly individually-oriented, yet soundly constructed and providing a relevant framework and basis for proper control and reasonable equity

- the subject of regular review as to its continuing relevance and effectiveness in meeting strategic business requirements

- an effective framework for

  - international moves

  - situations where there is multi-business presence in a particular country

  - trans-national arrangements to meet business needs.

The key elements in the Cadbury Schweppes's reward strategy are:

- a basic salary structure which is competitive in the market and in which individual salary is performance-driven via regular reviews geared to the business cycle: performance is assessed against clear and consistent standards relating to the achievement of individual business objectives and competence development

- variable pay in the form of bonuses geared to the success of the business: this needs to reflect the performance of the team at each senior level of the business and to reflect achievement against annual budget

- benefit programmes geared to local market requirements but recognising the multinational nature of the business by the provision of an international share option for senior people.

Glaxo Wellcome

At Glaxo Wellcome the key features of the new reward strategy developed in 1995 were expressed as:

- competitive market rates to attract, develop, motivate and retain quality staff

- levels of reward that vary, depending on the contribution of the individual, team, and operating company to overall business success

- designed to maximise the potential contribution of all employees (a strong emphasis on continuous development)

- cost-effective employee choice in determining component parts of their own benefits package.

The strategic reward processes at Glaxo Wellcome are modelled in Figure 9.

Figure 9 **Reward strategy at Glaxo Wellcome**

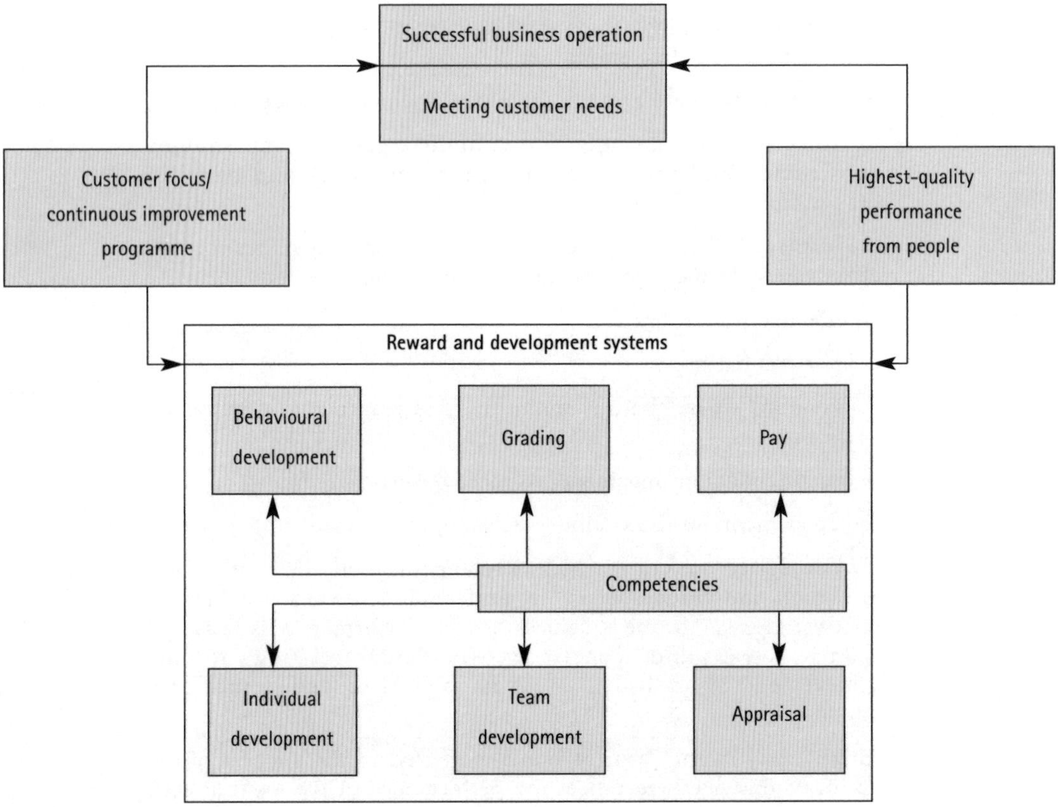

British Airways

As described by Greenham (1998), the reward strategy at British Airways flows from an analysis of business requirements and people needs and the resulting people strategy. The aim is to achieve integration in order to engage people to satisfy business needs. He emphasises that reward strategy is about intrinsic motivation and non-financial rewards as well as pay. There is no holy grail and no such thing as a tramline which takes you along in pre-determined grooves. Strategy has to be a broad church. Its formulation is a living and evolving process. The strategic planning process is illustrated in Figure 10.

Further examples of reward strategies
Benders Paper Disposables

The strategy is to attract and retain the best people by pitching ourselves to be one of the best payers in the area.

BOC Gases (UK)

As described by Corkerton and Bevan (1998), the business strategy was to increase profitability. The reward strategy was to develop a new incentive pay plan based upon the achievement of both individual profit targets and wider business targets.

Customs and Excise

The aims of the pay strategy are to support departmental business needs, to secure the confidence of staff, to provide a clear link between performance and reward, to be consistent with other aspects of personnel policy (eg performance management and equal opportunities), to be affordable, and to lie within the framework set by the government for public sector pay.

Figure 10 Paths to the reward strategy – British Airways

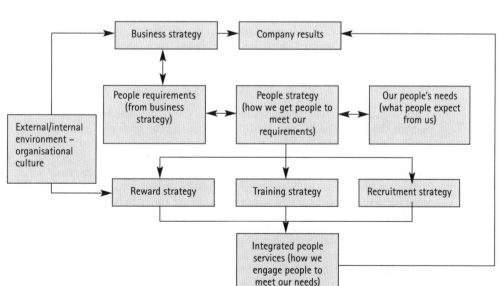

First Direct

The overriding objective in developing the strategy was to ensure that it complemented the overall business objectives and that individuals throughout the organisation were involved in the development of its component parts. Above all, it was seen as crucial that this strategy was seen not as a personnel initiative but rather as something which was owned by the company as a whole.

Guys' and St Thomas' Hospital Trust

The aim is to integrate reward with key strategies for growth and improved performance to underpin the organisation's values, to indicate what behaviour will be rewarded, and to provide the competitive edge to attract and retain the level of skills needed.

Halifax Bank

The strategy is intended to

• change the emphasis from measuring a job and its accountabilities to recognising the person and the contribution he or she makes to the business

• reflect the way the organisation is changing by encouraging staff to be more responsive and flexible to customers' needs

• improve reward for excellent performance by freeing up salary ranges.

Rover Group

The pay strategy takes account of business needs, the views and aspirations of associates, and the collective bargaining environment. The strategy has to balance the following: individualism versus team approach, work groups versus overall performance, control of current processes versus innovation, achievement of goals versus calculated risk-taking, individual contribution versus market-related pay competitiveness.

Royal and Sun Alliance

The aim is to reward the acquisition and application of skills and competence, and to give staff the opportunity to contribute to and share in the company's success.

DEVELOPING A REWARD STRATEGY

A reward strategy 'will be characterised by diversity and conditioned by both the legacy of the past and the realities of the present' (Murlis, 1996). From a business point of view it has to take account of trends such as a concentration on core businesses, the segmentation of key markets, the need to get maximum value from the reward system, flatter organisations, and an emphasis on flexibility and horizontal processes. To meet these needs often requires a sharp break with past practices, away from

• job evaluation and pay systems which focus reward on the size of hierarchies controlled by job-holders and on the nominal job content, such as the job function they are supposed to fulfil, rather than on their real contribution and effect on the business

- implicit belief that reward is about jobs, not people – this is the traditional approach to job evaluation, and it fails to take account of the fact that in the new organisations jobs are shaped to a considerable extent by the way in which individuals do them; what is becoming important is the role that individuals perform, not their specified job

- career development systems designed to assure progress through fixed and extended hierarchies which enable organisations to reproduce themselves, generation after generation.

From the individual's point of view, reward strategy should point the way to the design of reward systems not only that are fair and equitable but also that operate consistently and recognise individual needs.

Reward strategy has to resolve the inevitable differences between these points of view. Hence the importance of communication, involvement and participation.

Basic questions
When formulating reward strategy there are three basic questions to answer:

1 Where are we now?

2 Where do we want to be?

3 What's the business case?

Development steps
The following steps are required to develop reward strategy:

- Identify the key issues in the business strategy and plans which affect the reward policies and practices of the organisation.

- Identify the crucial success factors of the organisation, and consider their implications for human resource and reward strategies.

- Canvass the opinions of the 'dominant coalition', middle managers, team leaders, professional and technical staff, employees generally and their representatives about what they believe to be the key reward issues that need to be addressed in the reward strategy. (Methods of surveying attitudes to reward are dealt with in Chapter 9.)

- Review existing reward practices to identify any areas where change or improvement is required, bearing in mind that reward policies and processes must evolve continuously to adapt to the changing requirements of the organisation.

- Study the human resource plans of the organisation to establish future requirements for different levels and categories of employees, and decide on the implications these plans have for reward strategies and pay levels.

- Consider current and projected changes in the organisation's structure and methods of operating; in particular, establish the significance for reward of such processes as de-layering (reducing the number of levels of management), increases in operational flexibility, multi-skilling and the outcome of business process re-engineering exercises.

- Consult union representatives on their views about how reward practices should develop.

- Analyse external trends and issues which may affect reward strategy – for example, economic trends, government policies, changes in income tax regulations, reports on such issues as top people's pay, and competitive pressures (national and international).

- Benchmark with other organisations on how they have developed reward strategies and with what effect.

- Analyse the existing corporate culture and consider how reward strategy can help to underpin the culture or change it.

- Assess the degree to which the organisation's reward philosophy and proposed reward strategy are consistent with each other, and take steps to resolve any significant inconsistencies.

- Discuss the proposed reward strategy with top management and other interested parties, and amend it in the light of comments and suggestions.

- Set out and communicate the reward strategy and prepare plans for its implementation.

As mentioned earlier, reward strategy need not – in fact, should not – be an elaborate affair. The aim is to keep it simple, focusing on the crucial issues and ensuring that it is realistic and practical. The reward strategy could quite properly concentrate on one key issue only – for example, developing pay-for-performance systems.

CONCLUSION

Even if it is expressed in the broadest terms, reward strategy will point the way. But it must be aligned, relevant and achievable, and it should reflect the belief of the organisation that people should be valued and rewarded accordingly and that reward is a key element in its total management process.

SUMMARY

- Reward strategy is concerned with what the organisation wants to do about reward over the next two or three years. It defines the intentions of the organisation on how its reward policies and processes should be developed to meet business needs.

- The aim of reward strategy is to achieve higher levels of organisational, team and individual performance.

- A reward strategy provides a sense of purpose and direction that will help to establish priorities for developing reward plans which can be aligned to business and HR strategies.

- An effective reward strategy is based on corporate values and beliefs, is driven by business needs, is integrated with business and

HR strategies, rewards results and behaviour that are consistent with key organisational goals, and is practical and implementable.

• The process of aligning reward strategy means achieving good fit not only with the business and other HR strategies but with the context in which the firm operates – its culture, technology, type of people employed and external environment.

• A reward strategy should not attempt to do too much. It should focus on no more than one or two critical issues at any one time.

• The key strategic issues include performance and competence improvement, competitive pay, achieving a more equitable and definable pay system, restructuring the pay system, underpinning culture change.

• When formulating reward strategy there are three basic questions to answer:

1 Where are we now?

2 Where do we want to be?

3 What's the business case?

FURTHER READING

Gomez-Mejia and Balkin (1992: 34–58) examine strategic choices in compensation. Schuster and Zingheim (1992: 29–39) discuss the design of new pay strategies. The concept of strategic HRM is analysed by Armstrong and Long (1994: 38–54).

8 Reward policy

Reward policy sets guidelines for decision-making and action. It may include statements of guiding principles or common purposes. Reward policies may be written or implied, and can be identified by the following features:

- They provide a positive indication of what the organisation and its management may be expected to do and how they will behave in given circumstances.

- They indicate the amount of discretion line managers can exercise, suggesting answers to the question 'How do I deal with this reward issue in the circumstances?'

REWARD POLICY ISSUES

A reward policy addresses such issues as:

- competitive pay – the 'pay policy' or 'pay stance' of the organisation indicates the extent to which it wants to be 'market-led' – ie the relationship it wishes to maintain between its pay levels and market rates

- internal equity – the degree to which internal equity is a prime consideration and the circumstances in which the need to be competitive may override the principle of internal equity

- variable pay – the extent, if any, to which the firm believes that pay should vary according to performance, competence and/or skill

- individual or team reward – the need for rewards to concentrate on individual or team performance

- employee benefits – the types and levels of employee benefits to be provided and the extent to which employees can choose the benefits they want

- the total reward mix – the mix of total rewards as between base pay, variable pay and indirect pay (employee benefits)

- structure – the extent to which the organisation wants a hierarchical and relatively formal (narrow-banded) structure or one that is flexible and broad-banded

- reward priorities – the degree to which the organisation wants to concentrate on 'piling the rewards high' for the relatively small number of key players, or recognises the need to provide rewards which will support the steady improvement of the many. (In other words, who are the people likely to exert the most leverage on overall business performance who should be rewarded accordingly?)

- differentials – the levels of reward at the top of the organisation compared with average and minimum reward levels

- flexibility – the amount of flexibility allowable in operating the reward system; the degree of consistency required in applying policies; the amount of control exercised from the centre

- uniformity – the extent to which pay structures and policies should apply to the whole organisation or be flexible for different levels or categories of employees

- devolution – the amount of authority to be devolved to line managers to make pay decisions

- control – how much control should be exercised from the centre over the implementation of reward policies

- gender neutrality – the approach to be adopted towards eliminating gender bias in reward processes and structures so as to ensure equal pay for work of equal value

- partnership – the extent to which the organisation believes in sharing success with employees

- involvement – how much employees are involved in pay decisions that affect them.

The approaches to dealing with many of these issues should be guided by the reward philosophy of the organisation. In developing a reward policy framework the aim is, in effect, to convert philosophies into guidelines for decision and action which can be communicated to all concerned.

THE CONTENT OF REWARD POLICIES

There is no such thing as an ideal set of reward policies or a list of headings that should be included, although most policy statements refer to at least some of the issues listed above.

DEVELOPING REWARD POLICIES

Reward policies should be developed by:

- referring to the list of policy issues and adding or subtracting items which appear to be most relevant, taking into account the structure, culture, management style and values of the organisation, its reward philosophy and its business, personnel and reward strategies

- deciding under each heading, in consultation with those concerned, what policy approach is likely to be most relevant to the business priorities of the organisation and the needs of its employees

- ensuring that the policies are practical (implementable) and will provide the requisite level of guidance for decision and action

- deciding on the amount of training and guidance which will be required to enable line managers and others to implement policies with an appropriate degree of consistency

- communicating the policies to all affected by them: ideally, they should be expressed in writing and the communication process should include briefing-groups to ensure that employees have the opportunity to seek clarification and make suggestions.

REVIEWING POLICIES

It needs to be re-emphasised that all aspects of reward management are dynamic and evolutionary. They cannot stand still. They must be continually reviewed and modified in line with changes in organisation structures, strategic priorities, core values, processes, technologies and the new demands such changes make on people.

The fundamental beliefs expressed in the reward philosophy should be re-examined from time to time to ensure either that they reflect the current values of the organisation or that they are modified to assist in achieving cultural change. Reward strategies are likely to be in a constant state of flux as new strategic business imperatives emerge. This also applies to reward policies, which must express the realities of the new or anticipated situation.

It is necessary therefore to review current reward policies at regular intervals to answer such questions as:

- Are they still relevant?

- Are they providing the level of guidance required?

- What problems, if any, are being encountered in implementing them?

- Are there any new areas of reward policy which need to be covered?

- Does anyone (top managers, line managers, personnel specialists, employees, union representatives) want them changed, and if so, in what respect?

The review should be carried out by personnel specialists or, possibly, outside consultants, and ideally should include an attitude survey and the use of focus groups (small groups of employees who discuss and comment on various issues) as described in Chapter 9.

The need to monitor reward policies regularly in order to identify the need for changes extends to all reward processes. It is a good idea to include a firm review date – one or two years ahead – following the introduction of any new reward system or structure. And this should not preclude earlier reviews if the necessity arises.

Examples of reward policies
Bass Brewers
The aim is

- to establish an integrated approach to the management and reward of all our staff and to ensure that this is aligned with the needs and objectives of the business

- to ensure that our salaries and benefits remain competitive with the leading companies in our market sector, so that we can retain and attract employees of the highest quality

- to reduce artificial barriers caused by the previous emphasis on grading in favour of much broader categories, in order to encourage personal development through learning opportunities and the development of skills

- to develop a benefits structure which begins to lay greater emphasis on flexibility and employee choice

- to motivate employees sufficiently so that they will ensure that the company remains successful, enabling us to provide market-competitive remuneration and greater reward for superior performers.

Book Club Associates

Staff should be rewarded appropriately in relation to:

- the contribution they are expected to make towards achieving the firm's objectives

- the results they achieve

- the performance of the firm and its economic and commercial environment

- the value placed on comparable jobs within the firm

- the value placed on comparable jobs in other companies.

GE Plastics

The rate of expansion for GE Plastics is accelerating ... To maintain our entrepreneurial thrust as we grow requires a flatter, more responsive organisation, with talented professionals who have a broad business perspective. The new GEP compensation system will encourage professionals to focus on development of their talent and will continue to deliver competitive salary treatment.

Triplex Safety Glass

The principles of the pay and reward structure are that the structure must be consistent with Triplex values, in line with business needs, and must:

- be fair and equitable

- apply to all employees

- be reviewed periodically (eg every two years or in line with business needs)

- encourage and recognise skills development of individuals and teams

- reward effort and performance

- encourage a flexible approach.

Review the reward policies in your own organisation or one familiar to you against the headings listed in this chapter. How well-articulated and effective are they? What changes would you propose?

SUMMARY

- Reward policy sets guidelines for decision-making and action. It may include statements of guiding principles or common purposes.

- Reward policies provide a positive indication of what the organisation and its management may be expected to do and how they will behave in given circumstances, and indicate the amount of discretion line managers can exercise.

- Reward policies are concerned with competitive pay ('pay stance'), internal equity, variable pay, individual or team reward, employee benefits, the total reward mix, structure, reward priorities, differentials, flexibility, uniformity, devolution to line managers, control, partnership and involvement.

9 Reward planning

Approaches to employee reward will be based upon the organisation's reward philosophy, strategies and policies, as discussed in the last three chapters. But the processes and practices within the reward system itself need to be planned so that philosophies are upheld, strategies are implemented and policies applied. In addition, planning is required to ensure that the reward system is integrated with other personnel and development systems. Reward planning as described in this chapter comprises:

* auditing the reward system – analysing current arrangements to identify strengths and weaknesses and to diagnose any changes or improvement required

* setting objectives – what is to be achieved, when it is to be achieved, and the anticipated costs and benefits

* project planning and management – determining the sequence and time-scale of operations and events to achieve results on time and to ensure the optimum use of resources, and deciding how the work should be done; setting terms of reference, establishing and briefing project teams, planning implementation and monitoring progress

* evaluating processes and innovations as a basis for improvement.

Reward planning should not only ensure that the right things get done but also that procedures and systems are set up for monitoring, evaluating and auditing the outcomes of plans.

On completing this chapter the reader should be able to:

* assist in auditing reward processes in order to evaluate their effectiveness and ensure value for money

* take part in the preparation of reward plans.

AUDITING THE REWARD SYSTEM

An audit of the reward system starts with a general review and continues with analyses of the nature of the organisation, the organisation's culture, the point in its life-cycle the organisation has reached, the reward system itself and the attitudes of employees, through surveys and focus groups.

General review

The general review collects factual data on the organisation's mission, business strategies, business performance and results, the state of employee productivity and morale, and the organisation's structure, technology and processes. An analysis of the strengths and weaknesses of the business, and of the opportunities and threats facing it (a SWOT analysis), may be carried out.

Type of organisation

Organisations can be analysed in terms of their stability or instability within the environment using the Miles and Snow (1984) typology of defenders, prospectors or analysers.

Defenders are firms which exist in a historically stable environment. They pursue strategies of maintaining market share, persisting with existing products and services and fostering a 'strong culture' (well-established norms and values). In such organisations, people in professional or administrative jobs tend to be recruited straight from school or university, promotion practices create internal labour markets, long-term and predictable career paths are available, and labour turnover is low. The structure is hierarchical and the administration tends to be bureaucratic. The reward system supports the hierarchy and is also bureaucratic. Tight control is exercised over rewards and emphasis is given to internal equity. Pay may be related to performance but the amounts available for distribution are small and only a small proportion of earnings is variable or at risk.

Prospectors are firms in markets subject to radical and unpredictable change. They compete by continued innovation and adaptation. Their aim is to be 'early to market'. People are recruited at all levels and the emphasis is on present performance, not future potential. There are no obvious career paths, professional staff and managers typically view the organisation as a stepping-stone to opportunities elsewhere, and labour turnover is high. Pay is strongly related to performance, the focus being on rewarding 'individual contributors'. A high proportion of earnings may be variable and at risk. Pay systems tend to be informal and flexible, and managers are given a fair amount of freedom to make pay decisions.

Analysers operate in diversified markets, in some of which the conditions are stable while in others they are unstable. Sub-units may pursue either defender or prospector strategies, depending on the markets they serve. Reward practices therefore tend to be more diverse, with little uniformity between divisions or units.

Culture analysis

Culture analysis covers:

- values of care and consideration for people, enterprise, equity, excellence, growth, innovation, performance, quality, social responsibility, teamwork, etc

- norms (unwritten rules of behaviour) concerning how people relate to one another, the work ethic, the importance of status, loyalty, the use of power and politics, etc

- the organisational climate (how people feel about the organisation and its culture) in terms of being trusted, valued, allowed freedom to act and express opinions, a valuable member of a working team, etc

- management style – the degree to which managers are autocratic or democratic, tough or soft, demanding or easy-going, considerate or unfeeling, etc.

Cultures may be categorised as:

- command-and-control – authoritarian and bureaucratic, where people are expected to do as they are told

- empowering – giving people more scope to exercise control over, and take responsibility for, their work, thus making good use of their ability and enthusiasm

- high-involvement – getting people involved in discussing and agreeing the decisions that affect them

- high-commitment – encouraging everyone to identify with the organisation and to be committed to its purpose and values

- high-performance – emphasising the need for high levels of performance and competence.

The reward system, as noted in earlier chapters, can be used to underpin the culture or as a lever for changing it. Reward plans should take account of what the culture is like under the headings listed above, with particular reference to any values or norms that relate to individual performance and behaviour and that may be influenced by rewards. Account should also be taken of the organisational climate and management style, to assess the extent to which either factor is conducive to the implementation of reward strategies, and if not what, if anything, may be done about it.

Life-cycle analysis
Organisations, like products, have life-cycles. They can proceed from launch (start-up), through growth, maturity and into decline, with the possibility of regeneration if they do not fail or get taken over. It is interesting to assess where an organisation is in its life-cycle and when it is likely to move to the next stage unless something is done about it. The analysis can look at present and future stages in the life-cycle in terms of the typical reward characteristics for each stage as set out below.

Start-up
The start-up is when a new organisation is set up by large or small-scale entrepreneurs or venture capitalists. Decisions on rates of pay, bonuses and employee benefits are made informally and on a highly individual basis by top management. Pay levels are determined almost entirely by market rates. There is no job evaluation scheme or formal pay structure. This is a 'prospector'-type organisation in which a high degree of flexibility and adaptability is essential. The system will probably work perfectly well for the sort of people attracted to work in such an organisation.

Growth
The new organisation has established itself and is growing steadily

through product market development. The culture is still primarily entrepreneurial, innovative and risk-taking and the firm could be classified as a 'prospector'. But decisions on pay are likely to be more considered, while still making reference to market-rate data. The management is probably against or at least indifferent to any formal structure or processes of job evaluation and performance management. However, as growth continues and the organisation becomes more complex, the need for more order becomes apparent. A professional personnel manager may be appointed and briefed to introduce some logic into what is becoming a chaotic pay structure. At the same time, managers and other employees may express the wish for a more transparent performance-related pay system in which rewards are based on achievement in relation to agreed objectives. But a considerable degree of flexibility in administering rewards will be retained.

Maturity

The organisation is now fully established and begins to take on the characteristics of a 'defender'. Formal job evaluation is installed (probably point-factor rating or a proprietary band), a multi-graded structure is designed to match the well-established hierarchy, and performance appraisal and rating systems are introduced by an enthusiastic personnel department as the basis for carefully and centrally controlled performance-related pay decisions.

Decline

Decline takes place when the organisation becomes stultified and concerned only with defending the market share of its existing range of products or services. Administrative and payroll costs are escalating, job evaluation has become bureaucratic and paper-intensive, and people are encouraged to empire-build by being given extra points for the number of staff they manage and the budgets they control. The pay structure simply reproduces the existing hierarchy and pay progression is mainly through upgrading (often achieved by manipulating a corrupted job evaluation scheme). The performance-related pay system has fallen into disrepute because no one understands how their pay is linked to their performance. Performance appraisal is owned entirely by the personnel department, and line managers either pay lip-service to it or ignore it altogether.

Regeneration

Regeneration occurs when an organisation fights out of the corner into which it has backed itself. The emphasis is on values concerned with innovation, quality, performance and teamwork. Unnecessary costs have been managed out of the business by processes of de-layering and downsizing. Business process re-engineering is used to emphasise the importance of streamlining and integrating horizontal processes, and the organisation relies more on project work and self-managed teams than on the management hierarchy. The emphasis is on flexibility and continuous improvement through the development of competences and the scope to use them effectively. The organisation moves from 'traditional pay' to 'new pay', as described in Chapter 1. Competence-related pay and broad-banded structures are developed. Performance management processes emphasise continuous development and do not include ratings for performance-related pay.

They are owned by line managers, to whom pay decisions are largely devolved. Personnel specialists take on an internal consultancy and coaching role. Gain-sharing may be introduced as a means of enabling people to benefit from the organisation's success.

ANALYSING THE REWARD SYSTEM

The existing reward arrangements should be analysed against the background of what has been learned about the organisation in general (mission, strategy, performance, technology, etc), the type of organisation it is (defender, etc), its culture, and the stage it has reached in its life-cycle. The points to be covered in this analysis are:

Reward philosophy, strategy and policy

1 Is there a reward philosophy which reflects a positive organisation culture, provides clear guiding principles, addresses the key issues and can be used to communicate to employees how they are valued?

2 Is there a reward strategy which supports the business and personnel strategies, is fully integrated with them, is directed at driving and supporting desired behaviours, and has been developed in consultation with interested parties?

3 Is there a reward policy which provides clear guidelines on the major issues faced by the organisation in managing reward – eg considerations of equity and competitiveness, the reward mix, reward priorities, differentials, flexibility, devolution, individual and team rewards, equal value, partnership and involvement?

4 Is there evidence that the reward philosophy, strategies and policies are not only relevant to present requirements but also under constant review to ensure that they are adapted to the changing circumstances of the organisation?

Pay determination

5 Is there a formal job evaluation scheme? If so:

– Does it consistently and systematically measure relative values?

– Are the factors representative of the organisation's values?

– Is it measuring the right things (eg competences)?

– Are the results generally accepted by those concerned as fair and equitable?

– Is it being manipulated?

– Is it generating too much paper and/or taking up too much time?

– Does it need to be substantially changed or replaced because it has decayed in some way or is no longer appropriate?

6 If not, are internal relativities illogical or difficult to defend?

7 Are market rates tracked thoroughly by reference to reliable survey data?

8 Are any inconsistencies between the need for internal equity and the need to be externally competitive identified and dealt with satisfactorily?

Pay structure

9 Is the pay structure logical, coherent and relevant to the organisational structure?

10 Is there any need to move from a narrow-banded and rigid structure to a broad-banded and more flexible structure?

11 Is the structure defensible as being fair and equitable?

12 Does it enable the organisation to manage internal and external relativities effectively?

Performance management

13 Is there a performance management system in place which:

  - is owned by line managers?

  - helps in the process of managing expectation?

  - operates on the basis of performance agreements and plans and of regular feedback and reviews?

  - provides valid and acceptable data on performance as the basis of performance-related pay decisions?

Variable pay

14 Is there any performance-related pay or other type of incentive scheme? If so, for any scheme:

  - Are rewards clearly related to performance?

  - Do employees feel that the basis for paying out rewards is fair?

  - Is there any evidence that the scheme does in fact motivate employees?

  - Is variable pay detrimental to quality or teamwork?

  - Is there any evidence of wage drift?

  - Is the operation of the scheme carefully monitored?

15 Is team pay being used where appropriate? If so, do the arrangements meet the criteria set out under 9 above?

16 Is effective use made of company-wide schemes such as profit-sharing and gain-sharing?

Employee benefits

17 Is there a balanced and cost-effective approach to the provision of employee benefits?

18 Are employees given a reasonable amount of choice on the type or scale of benefits they receive?

Reward procedures

19 Are there clearly-defined and properly-operated procedures for conducting pay reviews and deciding on levels of pay? To what extent are they computerised?

20 Has sufficient authority been devolved to line managers to deal with pay issues, without losing control?

Communication and involvement

21 Are reward policies and practices sufficiently 'transparent' – ie communicated clearly to employees?

22 Are employees involved in decisions on key aspects of the reward system?

Overall

23 Is the organisation getting value for money from its reward system?

24 What is the general opinion of managers and employees about the effectiveness of the system? What do they see as its main strengths and weaknesses?

25 What impact is the reward system having on the performance of the organisation?

ATTITUDE SURVEYS

Attitude surveys can be used to gauge the feelings of employees about reward policies and practices. They are a valuable way of involving people by seeking their views on matters which affect them. It is highly desirable, if not essential, to preface any review of the organisation's reward policies and practices with an analysis of the opinions and feelings of employees about them.

A typical survey would ask employees to indicate the extent to which they agree or disagree with certain statements about the reward systems. The views could be expressed on a scale such as:

- agree strongly

- agree a little

- neither agree nor disagree

- disagree a little

- disagree strongly.

Statements like these could be included in a fairly succinct survey:

- I am properly paid for the work I do in relation to other people in the company.

- Rates of pay in the company compare favourably with those paid elsewhere for similar jobs.

- I know what is expected of me.

- If I meet expectations I know that my achievements will be fully and fairly recognised.

- I understand what the pay policy of the company is and how it affects me.

- I get full feedback on how I am doing from my manager/team leader.

- The job evaluation system for grading jobs is fair.

- I understand how decisions are made about my pay.

- Decisions about my pay are made fairly and consistently.

- If I have any queries about my pay, they are answered fully and quickly.

- I feel that this company gives me good opportunities to take on extra responsibilities and thus earn more.

- The performance-related pay/bonus/incentive schemes provide rewards which are clearly and fairly related to my performance.

- The grade structure functions well.

- I think the level of employee benefits (pensions, sick pay, etc) is high.

- I would like more choice over the benefits I receive.

These are fairly general statements and they could comprise the core of a questionnaire which could usefully be reissued every two or three years to check on the extent to which opinions are changing. This is a good way of assessing the overall effectiveness of reward policies.

Specific questions can be added to the core questions to obtain reactions to particular aspects of reward practice or to sound out opinion on possible changes. For example, an organisation that is contemplating the introduction of performance-related pay could assess likely reactions in advance.

It can also be helpful to test reactions retrospectively by surveying attitudes to a new reward process after it has been introduced. A typical survey testing views about a performance management system might ask employees to react to statements such as the following on a five-point scale:

- I like the scheme because it ensures that I am quite clear about the performance standards I am expected to achieve.

- My views were listened to when discussing the performance agreement.

- The objectives and personal development plan agreed at the end of the meeting were fair and attainable.

- I receive regular and fair feedback from my manager on my performance throughout the year.

- At the formal review meeting I was given the opportunity to assess my own performance.

- The performance review meeting was positive – focusing on the future rather than dwelling on the past.

- I was given a good opportunity to express my point of view during the meeting.

- The feedback I got from my manager during the meeting was objective and fair.

- At the end of the review meeting I felt motivated to do even better next year.

Questionnaires could also be issued to managers to find out what they think of the system. (Most managers will, of course, be at the receiving end of reviews as well as conducting them.)

Attitude surveys can be a useful means of testing opinion and gauging reactions. But they will not be effective as methods of involvement unless a comprehensive summary of the results is issued to all employees and, even more important, the organisation is seen to take action on unfavourable views, preferably in consultation with employees.

FOCUS GROUPS

Focus groups can be used as an alternative to an attitude survey or, even better, as a method of obtaining views on particular issues raised by a survey and on what should be done about them. As the name implies, a focus group of employees addresses specified areas of interest or concern. The group should consist of no more than 10 people to facilitate discussion. Its members should be representative of the different activities and occupations in the organisation.

If run well, focus groups can encourage people to express feelings and exchange views more fully and freely than they might in interviews. The person who facilitates a group will gain greater insight into the depth and variety of opinion than is possible from just studying the result of a survey. The facilitator can probe and obtain a feel for the climate and culture of the organisation which an attitude survey cannot provide.

The effectiveness of a focus group depends on having people (internal or external consultants) who are competent facilitators – experts at getting everyone involved, good at ensuring that people listen to each other and capable of achieving consensus without dominating the group when it is desirable. As facilitators they should also ensure that the group focuses on the key issues, and that it makes progress and does not get bogged down. They will start the discussion with a general question such as 'How do you feel about the pay policies of this company?' and then introduce more specific questions. The questions should be limited to half a dozen or so, and the group should meet for not more than two hours. A good facilitator will also intervene from time to time and ask probing questions or encourage people who want to express a different point of view. The aim should be to achieve but not to enforce consensus. If a consensus of opinion is reached on any issue the fact should be recorded. Focus groups should receive feedback on any action taken as a result of their deliberations.

DIAGNOSIS

An employee reward audit is useful only if it leads to a diagnosis which identifies the key issue as a basis for action planning and can be objectively justified by the information obtained. And a diagnosis is worth while only if it provides a basis for relevant, practical and implementable programmes which will address the real issues in line with the strategy. The diagnosis can, of course, contribute to the formulation of strategy. As was pointed out in Chapter 7, strategy is always in a state of evolution and will constantly need to be revised as new situations arise or new information emerges from the audit on what is needed. The development of reward strategies and plans is often an iterative process – each feeding off the other.

The diagnosis should identify the key issues, to indicate where action needs to be taken under the main headings of the reward system:

- reward strategy

- reward policy

- job evaluation

- market-rate surveys

- pay structures

- base levels of pay

- variable pay

- indirect pay (employee benefits)

- total remuneration, including the mix of base, variable and indirect pay

- processes for managing the reward system, including audit and review procedures, computerisation and clarifying the roles of line managers and personnel specialists and the rights of employees as stakeholders.

SETTING OBJECTIVES

Reward plans may cover a complete re-engineering of the system or they may deal with one or more specific aspects of it. In either case the objectives to be achieved by implementing the plan must be defined, first because they will form the basis for defining terms of reference to any individuals, project teams or consultants who may take part in implementation, and second because the objectives will provide criteria for evaluating the reward initiative – measuring the degree to which the plan has been successfully implemented.

No initiative should be planned without making a business case for it. The extent to which it will add value rather than create work should be assessed. A value-added approach means that processes and schemes will not be introduced or updated without assessing the effect they are expected to have on the motivation, commitment and performance of people, on the ability of the organisation to get and to keep the right sort of employees, and, ultimately, on the results achieved by the organisation.

The objectives of a complete re-engineering of the reward system could be expressed like this:

- The aim is to develop a fully integrated and coherent reward system which will help to achieve the organisation's goals as well as meet individual needs for reward and recognition.

- The system design should reflect and underpin the structural and process changes taking place in the organisation and the increased emphasis on values for continuous improvement, quality, innovation and teamwork.

- The system should operate flexibly, and the maximum amount of authority should be delegated to line management.

- The present grade structure should be replaced by a broad-banded structure and the evaluation scheme replaced by a process based on competence levels.

- The performance management and performance-related pay schemes should be reviewed and modified as necessary to ensure that they fit in with the new pay approach.

- Consideration should be given to introducing a flexible benefit system and gain-sharing.

- Line managers, employees and their representatives should be involved in developing the new system.

- It is recognised that this will constitute a major change programme and the objective includes a requirement to phase the programme in accordance with an assessment and agreement of priorities, and then to manage the requisite change effectively.

If the plan is to concentrate on one or two developments, the objectives of a single development could be expressed more succinctly along the following lines:

To introduce a gain-sharing plan which will

- enable employees to share in the success of the company

- establish and communicate clear targets, generally for increasing added value, and specifically for improvements in productivity, quality, customer service, delivery and costs

- increase focus on performance improvements

- provide a framework for involving employees in the improvement of operating processes and methods.

At Glaxo Wellcome the objectives of a complete review of the reward system were:

- emphasis on development and continuous improvement

- less complexity – line ownership

- movement across functional boundaries

- greater differentiation in payment levels

- reinforcement of the future competences required by Glaxo Wellcome.

PROJECT PLANNING AND MANAGEMENT

Project planning means:

- allocating responsibility for the project to a project manager and, preferably, a project team which includes line management and employee representatives

- deciding on the sequence of activities required to complete the project – these are grouped into main stages or phases, and responsibility is allocated for each stage and for the overall control of the project

- deciding on the timetable for completing the project and the timing of each stage (starting and finishing times)

- deciding on the resources required (people and money) – this may mean making a decision on the use of outside help in the form of management consultants.

Project management

Project management means controlling the progress of the project against the plan. It should include progress reports at each 'milestone' (key event) and meetings to review progress by a steering committee. For each item information should be supplied on the planned completion date, the actual achievement and the forecast completion date.

Implementation plan

Project management should continue after the process or system has been developed in order to ensure that it is implemented smoothly. An implementation plan is required, which may include pilot-testing (trialling) and phasing the introduction of the process.

Pilot-testing is highly desirable in order to find out how the system works in practice, to ensure that people understand what they need to do and then do it properly, and to indicate where any changes are required in the system itself or how it is communicated. (Communication is important.) Pilot-testing of, for example, new performance management processes can be carried out in a part of the organisation where people are interested and are likely to be co-operative. If it is successful, their enthusiasm can be conveyed to less interested areas.

Phasing may be necessary. Sometimes new systems – for example, a pay structure – can be introduced only in one step. Other processes or systems, such as performance management, may benefit from being introduced progressively.

The implementation plan should cover how the new process or system is to be communicated and, importantly, how line managers and employees generally should be trained. It should also set up procedures for evaluating effectiveness and monitoring progress against the objectives and the implementation plan. A full audit should be planned after the system has been in operation for a year or two to ensure that it is delivering the results expected of it. If not, corrective action can be taken, either to amend the system and/or to carry out more training in its use.

The whole implementation programme should be the responsibility of the line management concerned, on the grounds that it is their system and they should own it. But personnel specialists can play a vital part in giving guidance and help and in monitoring progress.

Assessing the effectiveness of reward plans

Reward plans are effective if they ensure that reward strategy is implemented and project objectives are achieved. The plans themselves can be assessed according to the degree to which they are specific, relevant, measurable and have a time constraint. They should show clearly how the reward strategy is to be implemented, monitored, evaluated and audited. They should also indicate how the different parts of the system developed by the plans should cohere and how individuals will be affected by it as far as their own pay package is concerned.

PUTTING IT ALL TOGETHER

The aim of the plan should be to achieve integration and coherence in the system as a whole. But it is also necessary to plan the system from the viewpoint of how it affects individuals through their pay and reward packages.

The reward system as a whole

Integration and coherence are achieved by reflecting on the basic reward philosophy, strategy and policies and considering how mutual support can be provided by each part of the system. Performance management, for example, can be an integrating force because it affects so many aspects of reward, especially performance pay and motivation. Competence frameworks can also assist integration because the language of competence is common to such processes as progression within broad-banded or job family structures, performance management and performance pay. Competence frameworks and performance management processes can be powerful aids to the integration of reward and other personnel processes such as selection, training and continuous development.

No reward development project should be planned in isolation. As Armstrong and Baron (1995) conclude from their research, 'Job evaluation is no longer a separate entity – a personnel technique – it has to be developed and managed as an integral part of the people management processes of the organisation.' And the same principle applies to any other aspect of reward management.

What total reward systems look like

All organisations are different and therefore all reward systems are different. There is no such thing as a model system. A good reward system is one that meets the needs of the organisation and its employees.

Planning the total system

The total system should be planned in accordance with the information derived from audits and organisational and system reviews. There will always be a choice as to the approach to be adopted in the reward mix – the types of payment systems that are appropriate to the organisation's culture and which will enable it to achieve its strategic objectives. There will also be a choice regarding the extent to which the organisation wants to provide variable pay (the proportion of total pay at risk) and between the various types of contingent pay that can be used. The possible impact of the different variable of such pay is summarised in Table 7. More detail on the advantages of each type of pay and the approach the organisation can adopt to the main

Table 7 The effect of different types of contingent pay

	TYPE	DEFINITION	IMPACT						
			Motivation	Commitment	Cultural change	Quality	Teamwork	Competence/skill	Flexibility
Individual	Incentive	Payments related to the achievement of targets added to basic pay	••	=	=	-	-	-	-
	Bonus	Rewards for success paid as a lump sum	••	=	=	-	=	=	-
	Commission	Payments for sales people based on a percentage of the sales they generate	••	=	=	=	-	=	-
	Performance-related pay	Payments based on ratings of performance	•	=	•	=	=	=	=
	Competence/skill-related pay	Pay progression linked with the competences or skills people develop and use	•	•	•	••	•	••	••
Team	Group bonus	Shop-floor payments related to output or time taken	•	•	•	•	••	=	••
	Team pay	Payments to staff teams related to achievement of targets	•	•	•	•	••	=	••
Organisational	Profit-sharing	Payments of cash or shares related to company profits	=	••	•	=	=	=	=
	Gain-sharing	Payment of cash bonuses to employees related to added value increases	•	••	••	•	•	=	•
	Profit-related pay	Government-sponsored scheme in which pay is linked to profit with tax advantages	=	•	=	=	=	=	=
	Share option	Allocation of shares with opportunity to sell in future at higher price	•	••	•	=	=	=	=

Scale   •• High   • Moderate   = Neutral   – Negative.

elements of the pay system (job evaluation, pay structures, performance management systems and employee benefits) is given in later chapters of this book.

Individual reward packages

It is necessary to consider how the total reward system can be described in terms of the make-up of an individual's reward package. This is what has to be communicated to people when they join the organisation and when they move into a new role or are promoted. Line managers must be able to explain to their people how their pay has been determined and how improvements in performance, increased levels of competence and more responsibility will be rewarded. They should be equipped to answer queries, although personnel specialists should be available to help when required.

Depending on the reward system, the following aspects of reward need to be clarified:

- how jobs are evaluated and graded

- how base rates are determined and the circumstances in which they may be altered (eg market-rate forces)

- the basis upon which individual performance is measured and rewarded

- the basis upon which individual skill or competence is assessed and measured

- the basis upon which teams are rewarded

- how increases in responsibility are rewarded

- the part played by organisation-wide schemes such as profit-sharing and gain-sharing

- the employee benefit provisions, including the extent of any choice

- the total mix of base pay, variable pay and indirect pay

- the amounts which employees can expect to earn in their job if they achieve an acceptable level of performance and if they exceed expectations – this means explaining the proportion of total pay which may vary according to performance, skill or competence

- any other allowances employees may receive for shift work, unsocial hours, etc

- how employees can appeal against job evaluation or any other pay decisions.

DEVELOPING THE SYSTEM

Lawler (1994) suggested that the following questions should be answered when thinking about reward innovations:

- What are the policy goals?

- Why are we doing this?

- How does it support business objectives?

- What are the design mechanics? For example: is merit pay right for us? What about team bonuses?

- What is the reality of the operation? How well will we implement changes?

The points to bear in mind when developing a reward system, as suggested by Steve Kear (1999), remuneration manager with Bass Brewers, are:

- Make it simple and easy to use.

- Ensure that it is relevant and helpful in doing the job, not something extra that managers have to do.

- The debate about money and motivation will never be settled.

- It is a good idea for people to know what is expected of them and to get feedback.

- In the final analysis, communication is the most important thing of all. The cleverest schemes will fail if they are not communicated properly and repeatedly.

Developing reward systems: a 12-point plan

1 Always be aware of business needs and how reward systems can help to meet them.

2 Focus on the whole, not the parts (an integrated approach).

3 Allow flexibility but develop basic frameworks – structures, processes and guidelines.

4 Accept that there are always options, but that they may be limited.

5 Benchmark, but remember that 'best fit' (to culture, structure and technology) is more important than 'best practice'.

6 Set objectives (in terms of meeting business needs) and evaluate outcomes.

7 Set up projects and manage them effectively.

8 Remember the need for fairness, equity, consistency and transparency.

9 Get managers and employees to own the processes.

10 Devolve as much responsibility to managers as possible.

11 Ensure affordability (cost-effectiveness).

12 *Involve, communicate and train.*

EVALUATION

One of the more remarkable findings of the IPD research into performance management and performance-related pay conducted in 1997–8 was how few organisations made any formal attempt to evaluate the effectiveness of their reward practices. They either accepted them as an act of faith or gave up before they started on the grounds that it would be too difficult. But evaluation through attitude surveys, focus groups and discussions with individuals can and should be done. It is even better, although it may be more difficult, to attempt an assessment of the impact of the reward initiative on value added, performance, productivity, quality or customer service. This could be based on the simple ratio of value added per employee.

SUMMARY

- Reward planning is concerned with auditing the reward system, setting objectives, project planning, and management and evaluation.

- An audit of the reward system starts with a general review and continues with analyses of the nature of the organisation, the organisation's culture, the point in its life-cycle the organisation has reached, the reward system itself, and the attitudes of employees, through surveys and focus groups.

- An employee reward audit is useful only if it leads to a diagnosis which identifies the key issues as a basis for action-planning and can be objectively justified by the information obtained.

- Planning reward projects means allocating responsibility for the project to a project team, deciding on the sequence of activities required to complete the project and its timetable, and establishing the resources required (people and money).

- Project management involves reviewing progress against the plan and taking swift corrective action if required. It should continue after the process or system has been developed to ensure that it is implemented smoothly.

- Reward plans are effective if they ensure that reward strategy is implemented and project objectives are achieved. The plans themselves can be assessed according to the degree to which they are specific, relevant, measurable, and have a time constraint.

- The total system should be planned in accordance with the information derived from audits and organisational and system reviews. There will always be a choice as to the approach to be adopted.

- Reward innovations and systems should be evaluated through attitude surveys, focus groups and discussions with individuals.

FURTHER READING

Case-studies of employee reward systems in action are often given in the Incomes Data Services publications *The IRS Employment Review* and *People Management*. A detailed exposition of the evolution of reward processes is given in M. Armstrong and H. Murlis, *Reward Management*, fourth edition, Kogan Page 1994, pp. 15–19. An extended checklist for evaluating reward processes is also given in that edition at pp. 58–67. A compete description of reward auditing is given in Michael Armstrong *The Rewards and Benefits Audit*, Cambridge Strategy Publications, 1999. A questionnaire on the development of total compensation strategy is given in J. R. Schuster and P. K.

Zingheim, *The New Pay*, Lexington Books, 1992, at pp. 317–23. An example of an attitude survey on reward policy is given in the fourth edition of *Reward Management* at pp. 591–6.

Part 3

EVALUATING, PRICING AND ANALYSING JOBS AND ROLES

10 The approach to job evaluation

The aim of this chapter is to provide a conceptual framework for the process of job evaluation covering the following areas:

- definition

- purpose

- key features of job evaluation

- basic methodology and types of schemes

- job-ranking schemes

- job-classification schemes

- internal benchmarking

- point-factor schemes

- market pricing

- competence-based job evaluation

- the case for and against job evaluation.

The choice of approach and methods of introducing and maintaining job evaluation will be dealt with in Chapter 11; Chapter 12 examines equal value considerations.

On completing this chapter the reader will understand the objectives and limitations of job evaluation and be familiar with the various methods available.

JOB EVALUATION DEFINED

Job evaluation can be defined strictly as a systematic process for establishing the relative worth of jobs within an organisation. This definition implies that job evaluation is concerned solely with internal equity. Conventional job evaluation philosophy says that it is about getting internal relativities right so that jobs are equitably placed at appropriate points in the organisation's job hierarchy. The process of 'pricing' the jobs or attaching pay scales to job grades is completely separate. In order to produce a pay structure or to decide on 'the rate for the job', the procedure is first to evaluate the jobs to define internal relativities, then to establish external relativities through surveys of market rates.

However, decisions on the internal relative value of jobs are made only in order to express them ultimately in terms of rates or levels of pay and benefits. The decisions normally take account of market comparisons, to ensure that the pay levels of the organisation are externally competitive even when the first consideration is internal equity or comparable worth. In fact many organisations rely entirely on 'market pricing' to determine both rates of pay and internal relativities.

THE PURPOSE OF JOB EVALUATION

The purpose of job evaluation is to:

* provide a rational basis for the design and maintenance of an equitable and defensible pay structure

* help in the management of the relativities existing between jobs within the organisation

* enable consistent decisions to be made on grading and rates of pay

* establish the extent to which there is comparable worth between jobs so that equal pay can be provided for work of equal value.

Job evaluation enables a framework to be designed which underpins pay decisions. It can help with internal comparisons and, to a degree, external comparisons by providing a common language for use in discussing the relative worth of jobs and people.

Research conducted by Armstrong and Baron (1995) confirmed that the primary reason for organisations to introduce job evaluation is to ensure a more equitable pay structure. Belief in job evaluation is based, in Quaid's (1993) words, on 'the greater power and validity of the "quantitative" (over the qualitative) of the "formal" (over the informal) and of the "objective" (over the subjective)'. Organisations commonly introduce job evaluation because they want to replace chaos with order, inconsistency with consistency, and political judgement with rational judgement.

However, some people think, naively, that job evaluation is a scientific and objective 'system' which, when it has been 'installed', will at a stroke remove all the problems they have experienced in managing internal relativities, fixing rates of pay and controlling the pay structure. This, of course, is asking far too much. Job evaluation, as Pritchard and Murlis (1992) suggest, should be regarded as a process rather than a system. It can certainly be argued that it is a process which, while it can be systematic and can reduce subjectivity, will always be more art than science, and, because it relies on human judgements, will never be fully objective.

KEY FEATURES OF JOB EVALUATION

Job evaluation can be regarded as:

- a comparative process – it deals with relationships, not absolutes

- a judgemental process – it requires the exercise of judgement in interpreting data on jobs and roles (job and role definitions or completed job analysis questionnaires), comparing one job with another, comparing jobs against factor level definitions and scales, and developing a grade structure from a rank order of jobs produced by job evaluation

- an analytical process – job evaluation may be judgemental but it is based on informed judgements which in an analytical scheme are founded on a process of gathering facts about jobs, sorting the facts out systematically in order to break them down into various elements, and re-assembling them into whatever standard format is being used

- a structured process – job evaluation is structured in the sense that a framework is provided which aims to help evaluators make consistent, reasoned judgements: this framework consists of language and criteria which are used by all evaluators, although, because the criteria are always subject to interpretation, they do not guarantee that judgements will be either consistent or rational.

Jobs and roles

Is job evaluation concerned with jobs or roles, or both? The terms 'job' and 'role' are often used interchangeably, but there is an important difference:

- A job consists of a group of finite tasks to be performed (pieces of work) and duties to be fulfilled in order to achieve an end result.

- A role describes the part played by people in meeting their objectives by working competently and flexibly within the context of the organisation's objectives, structure and processes.

When describing a job, the traditional approach has been to concentrate on why it exists (its overall purpose) and the activities to be carried out. The implication is that the latter are fixed and are performed by job-holders as prescribed. On the face of it, there is no room for flexibility or interpretation of how best to do the work. Jobs are the same – in fact, should be the same – whoever carries them out.

The concept of a role is much wider because it is people and behaviour-oriented – it is concerned with what people do and how they do it rather than concentrating narrowly on job content. When faced with any situation – eg doing a job – individuals have to enact a role in order to perform effectively in that situation. In a sense, people at work are often acting a part; they are not simply reciting the lines but interpreting them in terms of their own perception of how they should behave in the work context. Role definitions cover the behavioural aspects of work – the competences required to achieve acceptable levels of performance and contribution – as well as the tasks to be carried out or the results to be achieved. They stress the need for flexibility and multi-skilling, and for adapting to the different demands that are made on people in project- and team-based organisations where the emphasis is on process rather than hierarchical structure.

Jobs and people

By focusing on jobs, rather than roles, traditional job evaluation deliberately avoids considering the value of people. Human beings seem to be treated as an unnecessary intrusion in the pure world of job hierarchies with which job evaluation is concerned. Of course, the reason for the dogma that 'job evaluation measures the value of jobs, not of people' is to avoid contaminating the process of evaluation with considerations of the performance of individual job-holders. And indeed it would be undesirable for job evaluators to get involved in performance assessment – a separate matter.

But the traditional view still implies that people have nothing to do with the value of the job they perform, and that is clearly ludicrous. It is equally misguided to accept the universal assumption that people adapt to the fixed specification of their jobs rather than that jobs should be adapted to the characteristics of the people in them. In the new flexible organisation jobs are created and evolve according to the strengths and limitations of the people who design and fill them. To sum up, it is people who create value, not jobs.

BASIC METHODOLOGY

The process of job evaluation begins by identifying which jobs are to be examined and the total number to be evaluated. A decision also has to be made on whether there should be one scheme for all employees or separate schemes for different levels or categories of people. The next step is to choose one of the methods described later in this chapter. The final stages are to

- select the representative 'benchmark' jobs which will be used as the basis of comparisons

- decide on the factors to be used in evaluating the jobs

- analyse the jobs and roles

- establish the relative value of jobs by applying a process of evaluation

- develop a pay structure: this usually means designing a grade structure and then deciding on the rates or ranges of pay in the structure through internal comparisons and 'market pricing'.

Benchmark jobs

Benchmark jobs are those identified as representative of the range of jobs to be considered. They serve initially as the basis for the design or modification of a job evaluation scheme, and then function as reference points for the internal assessment of job relativities in order to help in the understanding and evaluation of less obvious jobs. They are also used in the external process of matching jobs with those in other organisations in order to make market-rate comparisons.

Job evaluation factors

Job evaluation is essentially about comparing the different characteristics or elements of jobs in order to establish relativities. When jobs are evaluated, even if there is no formal evaluation scheme, those concerned always have some criterion in mind, even if it is only a general concept of the level of responsibility compared with other jobs, or a comparative assessment of the impact of the job on end results, or its critical dimensions (eg turnover, output, resources controlled). In analytical schemes, as described below, these characteristics are termed factors (in the US the term 'compensable factor' is used). Even in non-analytical schemes where 'whole jobs' are compared with one another – ie they are not broken down into their separate elements or factors – there may be explicit or implicit assumptions about the factors to be taken into account when making comparisons for ranking them or slotting them into a grade structure.

Factors are the main characteristics or elements which are common to the range of jobs being evaluated but are present in differing degrees in different jobs. They are used as a basis for assessing relative values. If, in common parlance, one job is held to be more 'responsible' than another, responsibility is being used as a factor, however loosely responsibility is defined.

Job and role analysis

This provides the factual data about the jobs and roles people carry out upon which the evaluation will be based. The information is collected systematically and presented in a structured form which covers the factors to be used in the evaluation. Normally it is set out in a job description or role definition, but it can be recorded as answers to a structured questionnaire which directly provides the information for job evaluation.

The job evaluation process

This covers the methods used to decide on the rank order of a job, its position in a job grade or its comparative worth. In point-factor schemes it indicates how jobs will be scored. The process describes how comparisons will be made, in either of the following ways:

- job-to-job, in which a job is compared with another job to decide whether it should be valued more, less, or the same (ranking, factor comparison and 'internal benchmarking' processes)

- job-to-scale, in which judgements are made by comparing a whole job with a defined hierarchy of job grades (job classification) or comparing the different factors or elements of a job with a graduated scale of points for each of these factors (point-factor rating).

Developing a pay structure
Grading

Most job evaluation systems are linked with job grades. The job evaluation process may simply enable jobs to be slotted into a predetermined hierarchical structure. Alternatively, a job evaluation exercise may lead to the design of a new grade structure or the revision of an existing one.

Market pricing

Market pricing is the final stage in the process of valuing jobs and developing pay structures. It establishes market rates and external relativities as the basis for attaching pay scales to job grades or fixing individual rates.

JOB EVALUATION SCHEMES

Job evaluation schemes can be divided broadly into the following types: non-analytical, analytical, single-factor, skill- or competence-related, market pricing, and the management consultants' schemes, the so-called proprietary brands.

Non-analytical schemes compare whole jobs with one another and make no attempt to distinguish between the factors within the jobs which may differentiate them. Job ranking, paired comparison and job classification are usually regarded as the three main non-analytical schemes, although paired comparison is simply a statistical method of establishing rank order. Other non-analytical approaches, which are not generally dignified with being called schemes, are internal benchmarking and market pricing. They may not be recognised as a proper form of job evaluation but they are, nevertheless, practised by a lot of organisations, even if they do not call them by that name. And once they have carried out their initial analytical job evaluation exercise, many organisations do in effect slot in jobs by internal benchmarking whenever they perceive a close affinity between the job in question and a benchmark job.

The analytical schemes are point-factor rating, as it is universally known in the USA (in the UK it is often called simply points rating or a points scheme), and factor comparison. Because of its complexity and a number of other fundamental flaws, the latter is little used in its traditional form and is therefore not dealt with in this chapter. (A full description is given in Armstrong and Baron, 1995.) A modified form of what may be called graduated factor comparison is, however, sometimes adopted by the job evaluation 'experts' commissioned by industrial tribunals to report on equal value cases.

Market pricing is used in conjunction with other internally-oriented evaluation schemes to price jobs by reference to market rates.

Competence-based schemes value people rather than jobs in terms of their attributes and competences.

A number of management consultants such as Hay Management Consultants, KPMG Management Consulting, PA Consulting, PE Consulting, Price Waterhouse, Saville & Holdsworth, Towers Perrin and Watson Wyatt offer their own 'proprietary brands' of management consultants' schemes. These are usually analytical and generally rely on some form of point-scoring. Details of these and other consultants' schemes are provided in Neathey (1994).

The principal features of the job ranking, job classification, internal benchmarking, point-factor and market pricing approaches are summarised below.

JOB RANKING

Ranking is the simplest method of job evaluation. It is what everyone does, perhaps intuitively, when deciding on the relative position of a job in a hierarchy and the rate of pay which should be attached to it. This happens when the pay has not been determined by the price needed to attract or retain someone, or where there is no negotiated or generally accepted rate for the job.

The process of job ranking

Ranking is carried out by comparing jobs with one another and arranging them in order of importance, or difficulty, or their value to the organisation. In one sense, all evaluation schemes are ranking exercises because they place jobs in a hierarchy. The difference between ranking and analytical methods such as point-factor rating is that job ranking does not attempt to quantify judgements. Instead, whole jobs are compared – they are not broken down into factors or elements, although, explicitly or implicitly, the comparison may be based on some general concept such as the level of responsibility. Ranking may be carried out by identifying and placing in order a number of clearly differentiated and well-defined benchmark jobs at various levels. The other jobs can be ranked by comparing them with the benchmarks and slotting them in at an appropriate point.

Ranking may simply involve identifying the jobs which are perceived to be the ones with the highest and lowest value, then selecting a job midway between the two, and finally choosing others at lower or higher intermediate points. The remainder of the jobs under review are then grouped around the key jobs, and the ranking carried out within each sub-group. This achieves a complete ranking, which should be subjected to careful scrutiny to identify any jobs which appear to be 'out of line' – wrongly placed in the rank order.

The statistical technique of paired comparison can be used to ease the process of making judgements about the rank order of jobs. The technique requires each job to be compared separately with every other job. If a job is considered to be of higher value than the one with which it is being compared, it receives two points; if it is thought to be equally important, it receives one point; if it is regarded as less important, no points are awarded. The scores are added for each job and a rank order is obtained. The advantage of paired comparison is that it is easier to compare one job with another than to make multi-comparisons. The procedure is fairly complex, and a detailed explanation of how it is carried out is to be found in Armstrong and Murlis (1994). The final stage is to divide the ranked jobs into grades as described in Chapter 16.

Subsequent gradings or regradings are usually carried out by internal benchmarking – comparing the descriptions of the jobs to be graded with any benchmark jobs that appear to be broadly similar in relation to their level of responsibility, then slotting them into the appropriate grade. It may sometimes be necessary to carry out a special ranking exercise for a selection of jobs to establish where a new or a changed job should be slotted into the hierarchy.

The advantages and disadvantages of job ranking

The advantages of job ranking are that:

- It is in accord with how people instinctively value jobs.

- It is simple and easily understood.

- It is quick and cheap to implement, as long as agreement can be reached on the rank order of the jobs without too much argument.

- It is a way of checking the results of more sophisticated methods to indicate the extent to which the hierarchies produced are 'felt fair'. But this may simply reproduce the existing hierarchy and fail to eliminate gender bias. The question is, 'Felt to be fair by whom?'

The disadvantages are that:

- There are no defined standards for judging relative worth. There is therefore no rationale to defend the rank order – it is simply a matter of opinion (although it can be argued that even analytical schemes do no more than channel opinions in certain directions).

- Ranking is not acceptable as a method of determining comparable worth in equal value cases.

- Evaluators need an overall knowledge of every job to be evaluated, and ranking may be more difficult when a large number of jobs are under consideration.

- It may be difficult if not impossible to produce a felt-fair ranking for jobs in widely different functions where the demands upon them vary significantly.

- It may be hard to justify slotting new jobs into the structure or to decide whether or not there is a case for moving a job up the rank order – ie regrading.

- The division of the rank order into grades is likely to be somewhat arbitrary.

The use of job ranking
Because of the disadvantages listed above, job ranking is little used in large or sophisticated organisations except as a check on the results of an analytical evaluation exercise or as guidance on weighting in a point-factor scheme. Job ranking in its crudest form is more often used in the relatively informal environment of small or uncomplicated businesses where everyone has a clear notion of relativities.

JOB CLASSIFICATION

Job classification or job grading is a non-analytical method which slots jobs into grades by comparing the whole job with a scale in the form of a hierarchy of grade definitions.

The process of job classification
Job classification is based on an initial definition of the number and characteristics of the grades into which jobs will be placed. The grade definitions refer to such factors as the key tasks carried out, skill, competence, experience, initiative and responsibility. The number of grades is usually limited to between four and eight, and there should be clear differences in the demands made on jobs in all the grades. Each grade therefore represents a threshold which must be crossed

before regrading occurs. Classification systems with more than eight grades become unmanageable because of the difficulty of defining clear differences between successive grades. If there are fewer than four grades it may be just as hard to produce a sensible definition that distinguishes one grade clearly from another, although this may not be a problem in a broad-banded structure (see Chapter 17).

The advantages and disadvantages of job classification

The advantages of job classification are that:

- Standards for making grading decisions are provided in the form of the grade definitions.

- Explicit account can be taken of the training, experience, level of responsibility and specific demands of a job in comparison with other jobs.

- Jobs can quickly be slotted into the structure.

- It is easy and cheap to develop, implement and maintain.

- Its simplicity means that it is easily understood.

The disadvantages of job classification are that:

- It cannot cope with complex jobs which do not fit neatly into one grade.

- The grade definitions tend to be so generalised that they may not be much help in evaluating borderline cases, especially at more senior levels.

- It often fails to deal with the problem of evaluating and grading jobs in dissimilar occupational or job families where the demands made on job-holders are widely different – eg technical and administrative job families.

- Grade definitions tend to be inflexible and unresponsive to technological and organisational changes affecting roles and job content.

- The grading system can perpetuate inappropriate hierarchies.

- Because it is not an analytical system, it is not effective as a means of establishing comparable worth and is unacceptable in equal value cases.

The use of job classification

Because of its simplicity, job classification is sometimes used by organisations that want to introduce job evaluation and a grading system easily and cheaply. Some organisations with broad-band structures in effect use a form of job classification. A definition is produced of the responsibilities attached to the typical roles in the band which may be amplified by reference to generic competence profiles. The problem of producing meaningful and properly differentiated grade definitions covering the whole population in an organisation has led some businesses to develop special job classification systems for different job families. Others have abandoned the idea of job classification altogether and, if they do not want to use an analytical method, adopt the relatively informal approach of internal benchmarking.

INTERNAL BENCHMARKING

Internal benchmarking is what people often do intuitively when they are deciding on the value of jobs, although it has never been dignified in the job evaluation texts as a formal method of job evaluation.

The process of internal benchmarking

Evaluation by internal benchmarking simply means comparing the job under review with any internal benchmark job which is believed to be properly graded and paid, and slotting the job under consideration into the same grade as the benchmark job. The comparison is usually based on the 'whole job' without analysing the jobs factor by factor. However, internal benchmarking is likely to be much more accurate and acceptable if it is founded on the comparison of role definitions which indicate key result areas and the knowledge, skills and competence levels required to achieve the specified results.

The advantages and disadvantages of internal benchmarking

The advantages of internal benchmarking are that:

• It is simple and quick.

• It is realistic – it is a natural way of valuing jobs.

• It can produce reasonable results as long as it is based on the comparison of accurate job or role descriptions.

The disadvantages of internal benchmarking are that:

• It relies on judgement which may be entirely subjective and could be hard to justify.

• It is dependent on the identification of suitable benchmarks which are properly graded and paid, and such comparisons may only perpetuate existing inequities.

• It would not be acceptable in equal value cases.

The uses of internal benchmarking

Internal benchmarking is perhaps the most common method of informal or semi-formal job evaluation. It can be used after an initial analytical job evaluation exercise as a means of slotting jobs into an established grade structure without going to the trouble of carrying out a separate analytical evaluation (although if there is an agreement with employees or representatives that all jobs should be properly evaluated, this would not be feasible).

POINT-FACTOR SCHEMES

Method of operation

Point-factor schemes operate as follows:

• A number of factors are selected and defined – eg skill, responsibility and effort.

- The levels or degrees at which the factor can be present in the organisation's jobs are defined.

- Each factor may be assigned a percentage weighting to indicate its relative significance and hence its value in the job. This weighting is translated into the maximum points score that can be given for any factor, and the sum of the scores for each factor indicates the maximum score that can be allotted to any job. However, some schemes deliberately avoid weighting on the grounds that it is always arbitrary and subjective as well as potentially discriminatory. The designers of such schemes aim to create a factor plan in which all the factors are equally important.

- The maximum points for each factor are divided between the levels or degrees for that factor. Thus each level has a points score or range of points assigned to it.

- Benchmark jobs are selected and analysed in terms of the factors.

- The level at which each of the factors is present in the benchmark jobs is determined by reference to the factor plan (see below).

- Scores are allotted for each factor in accordance with the factor plan and added together to produce a total score for the benchmark jobs and a ranking of jobs in accordance with those values.

- A grade structure is designed which divides the rank order into a number of grades which are defined in terms of points brackets.

- The remaining non-benchmark jobs are then evaluated and slotted into the grade structure.

- The job grades are priced by reference to market rates and/or existing rates of pay and relativities.

The factor plan

The factor plan consists of:

- the factors themselves

- the factor level definitions

- the total scores allotted to each factor in accordance with the factor weighting (assuming the factors are weighted)

- the factor scale – the scores available for each factor, divided between the various levels.

An example of a typical weighted factor plan is shown in Figure 11.

Figure 11 **A factor plan**

	FACTORS	LEVELS					
		1	2	3	4	5	6
1	Knowledge and skills	50	100	150	200	250	300
2	Responsibility	50	100	150	200	250	300
3	Decision-making	40	80	120	140	180	220
4	Complexity	25	50	75	100	125	150
5	Contacts	25	50	75	100	125	150

Selecting factors

The choice of factors is crucial because

- It expresses the values of the organisation on how the contribution people make should be recognised and rewarded.

- It can influence the extent to which the scheme constitutes a fair basis for assessing relative values.

- It can affect the degree to which the scheme may be held to be discriminatory in equal value cases.

In selecting factors, organisations are explicitly declaring what values they believe to be important when assessing job worth. And the fact that this declaration has to be made is one of the virtues of job evaluation, which can be used either to underpin existing values or to change values if they are no longer functional. The process of selecting factors must also take account of equal value considerations as discussed in Chapter 12.

There is plenty of choice. Armstrong and Baron revealed that the 15 point-factor schemes they studied had between them 50 different factors, although many undoubtedly overlapped. The types and numbers of factors are discussed below. Methods of designing factor plans are described in Chapter 11.

Types of factors

Job evaluation factors break down the components of jobs which, collectively, represent each of the most important elements of those jobs. In devising a factor plan, it is necessary to remember that job evaluation is essentially about valuing work and the contribution made by the people who do the work. The criteria or factors chosen for the purpose should therefore represent the reality of what work is all about. If the main aspects of work are not covered in the factor plan it will be inadequate as an instrument for comparing relative worth. The plan must cover all the key characteristics of the jobs to be evaluated and it must not discriminate on grounds of sex. To ensure that the factor plan is comprehensive it is helpful to base it on the input–process–output model for describing work, which is illustrated in Figure 12.

Work is done to fulfil a purpose which is defined in terms of the contribution expected from job-holders and the effect they have on end results – their output. The output is initiated by the job-holders' input – what they bring to the job in the form of skills, knowledge and expertise. All work is essentially about transforming inputs into outputs, and this is the process aspect of a job in which job-holders use skills and knowledge and bring to bear competences in such areas as decision-making, problem-solving, innovation, interacting with people or carrying out a complex or diverse range of tasks. The process

Figure 12 The input–process–output model

Table 8 Numbers of factors in factor plans

No. factors	No. schemes
4	2
5	6
6	2
7	1
8	2
10	2

aspect involves the application of behavioural competences. In addition, jobs can make mental and physical demands on people and may involve unpleasant or demanding working conditions.

Numbers of factors
The number of main factors included in the schemes analysed by Armstrong and Baron (1995) are shown in Table 8.

Advantages and disadvantages of point-factor schemes
The advantages of point-factor schemes are that:

• Evaluators are forced to consider a range of factors which, as long as they are present in all the jobs and affect them in different ways, will reduce the danger of the oversimplified judgements which can be made when using non-analytical schemes.

• Points schemes provide evaluators with defined yardsticks that should help them to achieve a degree of objectivity and consistency in making their judgements.

• They at least appear to be objective (even if they are not), and this quality makes people feel that they are fair.

• They provide a rationale which helps in the design of graded pay structures (see Chapter 16).

• They can assist in matching jobs when making external comparisons for market pricing purposes.

• They can be acceptable in equal value cases as long as the factor plan is not discriminatory.

• They adapt well to computerisation (see Chapter 37).

Points schemes have these disadvantages:

• They are complex to develop, install and maintain.

• They give a somewhat spurious impression of scientific accuracy. It is still necessary to use judgement in selecting factors, defining levels within factors, deciding on weightings, and interpreting information about the jobs in relation to the definitions of factors and factor levels.

• They assume that it is possible to quantify different aspects of jobs on the same scale of values and then add them together. But the attributes and job characteristics cannot necessarily be added together in this way.

Apart from the complexity issue, however, the list of disadvantages simply confirms what is already known about any form of job evaluation. It cannot guarantee total objectivity or absolute accuracy in sizing jobs. It can do no more than indicate broadly where jobs should be placed in a pay structure in relation to other jobs. But the analytical nature of point-factor rating does at least give a more accurate indication than non-analytical methods. If the use of this method is carefully managed, the results are more likely to be acceptable (to be felt-fair), and a sound basis for dealing with equal value issues will have been established.

Conclusions

Point-factor rating is the most popular approach because people generally feel that it works. And so it does, in the sense that if carried out properly it is seen to be analytical, thorough and fair as a means of determining internal relative values.

But it is a big leap from the ranking produced by the evaluation to devising a grade structure. This can be mainly a trial-and-error process. And the jobs still have to be priced, which is largely judgemental. Furthermore, people can be well satisfied with the progress of a job evaluation exercise until they find out how it will affect their pay. Whatever the protestations of management to the contrary, employees usually feel that job evaluation equals more pay. This stage of the process can cause a lot of grief and has to be very carefully handled.

It is still possible to feel uncomfortable about the impression of accuracy conveyed by scoring jobs. The quantification of subjective judgements does not make them any more objective and gives an entirely spurious aura of scientific accuracy. Emerson (1991) believes that 'The actual distinctions between jobs in organisations are neither measured nor empirically accounted for in point-factor schemes.'

MARKET PRICING

Market pricing is the process of assessing rates of pay by reference to market rates – what similar organisations pay for comparable jobs. Market pricing takes two forms:

• It establishes external relativities.

• It can act as a form of job evaluation in itself by using the relativities or differentials between the market rates for comparable jobs as the logic for defining internal relativities or differentials.

Market pricing is often used in association with internal benchmarking. The market rates for a number of benchmark jobs are first established and a grade structure is produced. The remaining jobs are then slotted into the grades. Market-rate surveys also provide information on movements in the 'going rates' so that adjustments can be made to the organisation's pay structure or job rates to ensure that they remain competitive.

Market pricing is based on the assumption that it is always easy to get hold of comprehensive and accurate information on market rates. The assumption is ill-founded, as will be discussed in Chapter 10. Market pricing therefore has to rely on a number of general assessments of external relativities which, although they broadly indicate the going rate for a job, cannot be relied upon for definitive guidance. There is also the problem that for some highly specialist jobs there may be no reliable market data. Such cases have to be slotted into the pay structure, and a more conventional evaluation scheme can help to show where they should be placed in relation to already evaluated benchmark jobs.

Market pricing evaluation can be conducted in the following six stages:

- The jobs to be evaluated are identified.

- The jobs are analysed and described in terms of job content and characteristics. In a large organisation only a representative sample of jobs will be analysed at this stage. They will be jobs for which external comparisons can be made and will be designated the benchmark jobs.

- A pay structure is developed that incorporates pay ranges or scales to cover all the jobs. The limits of the structure will be related to the highest and lowest market rates for those jobs. The number of grades between these limits will depend on the size and complexity of the organisation, the policy on the width of the bands (the amount of pay progression allowed within one job) and the overlap between bands. It may be necessary to have more than one structure to cover different market groups where jobs in some functions are subject to special market pressures. They could then be grouped together in such a way that movements in pay for one job within the group are likely to be associated with movements for other jobs in the group, but not for those in other groups.

- The benchmark jobs are slotted into the structure by reference to the information obtained on market rates for each of the jobs and graded according to the band into which that figure falls.

- A final choice is made on the grading of the benchmark jobs by checking to ensure that the provisional allocation has not upset any well-established and appropriate internal relativities.

- The remaining jobs are slotted into the grades by comparison with the benchmark jobs. The greater the number and range of occupations or functions covered by the benchmarks the better.

The advantages and disadvantages of market pricing
This approach has the merit of being practical, straightforward and quick, and many firms use it for those reasons. If jobs are analysed thoroughly, if the pay survey is comprehensive, and if good judgement is exercised in allocating jobs to grades, the results can be quite satisfactory. However, these are big 'ifs'. The drawback is that it relies on the accuracy of the market rate information, and this may not be easy to obtain, especially in companies in specialised fields that tend to grow their own staff. And judgement may be fallible in situations where no yardsticks are available and where it has not been possible

to subject the jobs to comparisons based on detailed analysis of defined criteria.

Another drawback of market pricing is that it can perpetuate discrimination against women. If market rates for jobs generally held by women are depressed because of long-standing gender bias, the fact will be reflected in the pay structure. This may result in tensions between the principle of internal equity and comparable worth and the perceived need to be competitive. Pay structures often do incorporate a compromise between the competing imperatives of internal equity and external competitiveness but the compromises may discriminate against women. A market pricing system of job evaluation is not analytical and as such may be discriminatory.

If, however, an organisation is satisfied that this approach is non-discriminatory, it could adopt it as the simplest and most realistic method of valuing jobs in financial terms, although it would always have to remember that it might be building its pay structure on the shifting sands of a number of doubtful assumptions about what are the true market rates.

COMPETENCE-BASED JOB EVALUATION

Competence-based job evaluation is an analytical approach which aims to value the work people do in terms of the competences required to perform effectively in different roles and at different levels in the organisation. It measures both the value of roles and the contribution of people against the same criteria.

Approaches

Competence-based job evaluation concentrates on people in their roles, not jobs. There are three varieties, as described below, two of which resemble traditional methods (point-factor and job classification schemes), except that the emphasis is on competences rather than the traditional factors or criteria used in such schemes. The third type is far more radical, in that there is no 'scheme', only an approach which evaluates people in their roles on an individual basis.

1 – Point-factor competence-based evaluation

This is the most common method. The headings in the factor plan consist entirely or mainly of core or generic competences included in a competence framework. The levels at which the generic competences can be applied in roles are defined and scores are allocated to each level. The competence-based factors may not be weighted. Individual role competence profiles are defined and these are compared with the generic competence-level definitions and scored in exactly the same way as in a conventional point-factor scheme. A broad-banded structure may be adopted with the bands defined in points terms and roles allocated to bands accordingly. Within the bands pay is related to market rates, and progression depends on individual levels of competence and contribution.

A typical set of factors, as used by Thomas Cook, comprises:

• knowledge and skills

- human relations skills required in such areas as: influencing other people, leadership, selling or negotiating, contact with others, training, communicating

- thinking and reasoning

- numerical, logic and information technology skills

- personal qualities – responsibility, flexibility, freedom of action, etc

- physical skills.

The factors incorporated in the Triplex Safety Glass scheme are:

- knowledge/experience

- functional skills

- organisational skills

- communication (interpersonal) skills

- initiative/problem-solving.

2 – Role classification competence-based job evaluation
In this approach the grades in a broad-banded structure are defined generally as in a job classification scheme. However, the grade definitions are expressed in terms of the organisation's core or generic competences. Roles are slotted into bands on the basis of comparisons between individual competence profiles and the band definition. Alternatively, a job family structure is adopted in which the levels in the job family are defined in competence terms. Pay progression within the job family is along curves related to individual competence and contribution.

3 – Individually-based competence-related role evaluation
This approach is based on a broad-banded or job family structure. The bands may be designated very broadly by reference to generic roles but no attempt is made to define them in competence terms. Progression within and between bands is related to individual competence and contribution as demonstrated by the capacity to take on additional responsibilities and new roles.

The advantages and disadvantages of competence-based job evaluation
Competence-based job evaluation can

- direct attention to the things that really matter in delivering performance

- focus on roles

- provide for jobs and people to be measured against the same criteria

- clarify 'aiming' points – the requirements which must be met to advance or broaden a career

- provide a framework for continuous development and self-managed learning

- help to extend the skill-base of the organisation.

But competence-based job evaluation

- depends on the definition of competences and competence levels which are too often developed without sufficiently rigorous analysis so that factor or level definitions are vague, obscure or irrelevant

- can be just as bureaucratic and difficult to introduce and manage as any other form of job evaluation

- requires competence frameworks to be constantly updated, and this is time-consuming and easily neglected

- could lead to problems with equal value – gender bias can just as easily creep into a competence-based pay system as into any other system, and there could be real difficulties in assessing comparative worth unless a more conventional factor comparison scheme is used to supplement it (and why should the process of job evaluation be further complicated in this way?); it is also possible that generic role definitions could be discriminatory

- depends on a clear understanding of the slippery and often confusing language of competencies

- can contain jargon and complexities which too easily become part of an 'over-engineered' system that will be unacceptable to line managers (leaving it as the property of the HR department)

- lead to over-emphasis on inputs rather than outputs; knowledge, skills and behaviour rather than results.

The uses of competence-based job evaluation

Competence-based job evaluation can work in any type of business but it is particularly appropriate in organisations with numbers of knowledge workers where the emphasis is on people in flexible and developing roles rather than on rigid job hierarchies. It could be relevant in project and process-based organisations where this type of role flexibility is important and where the contribution of people can be significantly and measurably enhanced if they acquire additional skills and competences *and* are able to use them to good effect. It can work well in job families. A good reason for adopting this approach is the opportunity it gives to integrate organisational core competences and individual competences.

> Compare competence-based job evaluation with the more conventional methods described earlier. What does it offer, if anything, that those methods do not?

JOB EVALUATION: THE PROS AND CONS

The case for job evaluation

A case for job evaluation does not really have to be made. Organisations have no choice. It is impossible to avoid making decisions on rates of pay, and, if they are not negotiated, pay decisions will be based on beliefs or assumptions about where the job fits into the organisation, the contribution job-holders make and the market rate for the job or the market worth of the individual in the job.

However, the use of formal methods of job evaluation needs to be justified.

The arguments in favour of a formal approach are powerful – most people believe that they are indisputable. They can be summarised as follows:

- An equitable and defensible pay structure cannot be achieved unless a systematic process is used to assess job values and relativities.

- It provides a logical framework and a common language for making consistent decisions on the relative value of jobs.

- It reduces the risk of pay discrimination by defining when work is of equal value, as long as an analytical process is used.

- A formal process of job evaluation is more likely to be accepted as 'felt-fair' than informal or *ad hoc* approaches – and the degree of acceptability will be considerably enhanced if the whole process is transparent.

But many practitioners and commentators are dubious about the usefulness of traditional formal approaches to job evaluation in flexible organisations where people are likely to have flexible roles. A formidable list of objections has been drawn up.

The case against job evaluation
A number of attacks on traditional methods of job evaluation have come from academics, two of the most spirited having been mounted by Ed Lawler and Maeve Quaid.

Ed Lawler
Ed Lawler's (1986) major contentions about point-factor job evaluation are that:

- Because it was originally developed to support traditional bureaucratic management, the point-factor approach discourages organisations from changing – 'the kind of work it takes to create job descriptions and job evaluations generates a high investment in the status quo.'

- Job evaluation can create unnecessary and undesirable pecking orders and power relationships.

- The point-factor approach emphasises doing the job as described rather than doing the right thing.

- Virtually every point-factor system creates an internal wage structure in which promotion is the main way to increase compensation.

- Point-factor schemes reward people for creating overheads and higher cost to get more points and thus more pay.

- People tend to go in for point-grabbing – they realise that creatively-written job descriptions can lead to pay increases.

- Job evaluation schemes are expensive to administer.

He concluded his attack by stating that:

These criticisms of the point-factor approach highlight that it is more than just a pay system. It reinforces a particular value system and a particular orientation to management. The decision to adopt it should therefore not be taken lightly.

Maeve Quaid

Maeve Quaid (1993) bases her comments on job evaluation on her two years' experience as a job evaluation specialist helping to install the Hay system in a Canadian province. She subsequently researched the subject in Oxford, then went back to conduct research into how the Hay system had been applied in the same province and how well it was working. She suggests that job evaluation functions as a 'rationalized, institutional myth' and believes that it

> provides organisations with a set of language, rituals and rhetoric that has transported an otherwise impossible and indeterminable process to the realm of the possible and determinable. In this way, what job evaluation seems to do is to code and recode existing biases and value systems to re-present them as objectifiable data.

Summary of main criticisms

Research conducted by Towers Perrin in 1994 (unpublished) indicated that the major criticisms of job evaluation in large UK organisations revolve around

- inflexibility in reacting to business and work changes

- inefficiency in terms of time-consuming and expensive operation.

The criticisms of job evaluation by other commentators are summarised below.

- It relies on human judgement. Job evaluation guidelines are subject to different interpretations and varying standards among evaluators. Madigan and Hills (1988) say that criteria for establishing job worth often vary and that 'objective' or non-biased measurement of that worth is therefore impossible.

- It is inflexible. As Grayson (1987) points out, 'Job evaluation systems have usually been designed on the basis of traditional systems of work: the result is job evaluation schemes which are seen to be too slow, inflexible, unhelpful in implementing change, and more geared to preserving the status quo.' Emerson (1991) commented that job evaluation fosters rigidity 'by paying people to remain in positions that require and reward non-adaptive behaviour'. Incomes Data Services (1992) asserted that 'The whole panoply of job descriptions, the scoring of jobs, grading appeals, evaluation teams and so on convey a message which is at odds with flexibility.' An aspect of flexibility which traditional job evaluation also fails to recognise is the increased emphasis on teamwork and the need for people to be multi-skilled.

- It unrealistically ignores market forces. As Supel (1990) argues, 'From both rhetorical and empirical perspectives ... the point-factor system is redundant vis-à-vis a market pricing system, and the case is extremely strong for firms to allocate resources so that market pricing is given a larger role in their pricing procedures.'

- It focuses on jobs rather than people. As Fowler (1992) noted, some organisations 'criticise job evaluation for its assumption that employees adapt to a fixed specification of the job, rather than jobs being adapted to fit the characteristics of employees'.

- It cannot prevent *a priori* judgements. There is a tendency for managements to judge the validity of a job evaluation exercise by the extent to which it corresponds with their preconceptions about relative worth. As Armstrong (1993) suggests, 'Despite emphasis on objective and balanced decisions based on job analysis assisted by a paraphernalia of points and level definitions, evaluators tend instinctively to pre-judge the level of a job by reference to their own conception of its value. The information presented to them about the job is filtered through these preconceptions and the scheme is used to justify them.'

In addition, Edwards *et al* (1995) have suggested that traditional job-based evaluation leads to

- inappropriate focus on promotion – People are led to believe that a job is more important than the individual in the job. This implies that the only way to get on is by being promoted rather than by maximising contribution and competence in the present role.

- inability to reward knowledge workers – Traditional job-based pay systems which reward position in the job hierarchy and the number of people supervised generally do not work well for knowledge workers, whose performance is based on specialist applied learning rather than general skills.

- inability to keep pace with high-speed organisational changes – In the new flexible fast-moving organisations, where the emphasis is on process and on self-directed teams that carry out variable project assignments, employee roles often do not fit traditional job evaluation methodologies.

Conclusions

The case for formal job evaluation may be incontrovertible because it

- makes the value criteria used to judge relative job values explicit

- structures the judgement process

- helps to ensure that equal pay is provided for work of equal value.

But there are powerful counter-arguments, as described above. Admittedly, most of them are related to traditional point-factor schemes, but it is, after all, by far the most popular form of job evaluation. Job evaluation has indeed been heavily criticised because it creates or perpetuates hierarchical pecking orders but, as Hillage (1994) comments, 'The counter-argument is that this is a criticism of how job evaluation is conducted and not an inevitable consequence of the process.'

The point has been made by Armstrong and Murlis (1994) that:

> Job evaluation methodologies which emphasise place in hierarchy, numbers of people supervised or resources controlled, without taking

into account technical expertise or complex decision-making, have little to contribute. Indeed, in more flexible environments, it is frequently *not the scheme itself which is at fault but the way it is applied.* [Italics added]

As suggested by Pritchard and Murlis (1992), job evaluation should be regarded as a process rather than a system – a process which consists of a series of steps each of which 'can be designed and when necessary modified, simply and practically, to meet specific needs and the changing of these needs'.

Job evaluation processes in fluid and adaptive organisations must therefore be designed and operated flexibly. Job evaluation schemes continue to be used, and there are strong arguments for using them, because they are perceived to be logical, systematic, fair and a good basis for handling 'equal pay for work of equal value' issues. A review by Pickard and Fowler (1999) concluded that 'Job evaluation will continue to have an important role in establishing pay relativities – not least in the hands of those who wish to challenge society's traditional pecking order.'

But job evaluation should

- not be applied too rigidly to support or create inappropriate hierarchies

- reflect the degree of flexible working now taking place in most organisations, which increasingly have to cater for individuals in dynamic roles, not static jobs, who are expected to behave adaptively and to extend their capacity to use their skills and competences to deal with new work requirements and challenges

- recognise that it is concerned with the contribution of people, not just the demands of a job

- take account of the increased emphasis on teamworking

- not rely on elaborate, constricting and misleading job descriptions

- not involve the organisation in expensive and time-consuming routines

- be reasonably simple to operate so as to facilitate the devolution of job evaluation decisions

- provide a framework for making consistent judgements on comparable worth

- be amended or replaced if it has decayed or is no longer appropriate

- be transparent – everyone concerned should know how it works and how it affects them

- be acceptable as equitable and fair: this is more likely if employees and their representatives have been involved in the development and implementation of the scheme.

Job evaluation does no more than provide a framework within which judgement can be exercised. It does not remove the necessity for judgement. And it should be accepted that, while job evaluation is concerned with the inputs provided by people in the shape of their knowledge, skills and competence, it should also focus strongly on outputs – the contribution people make in their roles. Ultimately, people are rewarded for what they do and what they achieve – their delivered performance – not just for their attributes.

The choice of approach and methods of introducing a point-factor scheme and maintaining job evaluation are considered in the next chapter.

What sort of job evaluation would be most appropriate in the following types of organisations, and why?

• a research and development organisation

• a local authority

• a large retail store

• an insurance company

• an engineering company.

SUMMARY

• Job evaluation is a systematic process for establishing the relative worth of jobs in an organisation. It provides a basis for designing pay structures, managing relativities, making decisions on grading, and ensuring that equal pay is provided for work of equal value.

• Job evaluation is a comparative, judgemental, analytical and structured process.

• The two main types of scheme are non-analytical (eg job ranking, job classification, internal benchmarking and market pricing) and analytical (eg point-factor, competence-based).

• The case for job evaluation is that it provides a rational and, it is hoped, a defensible basis for 'felt-fair' pay decisions.

• The case against job evaluation is that it relies on human judgement, is inflexible and inefficient, ignores market forces, focuses on jobs rather than people and imposes a hierarchy which may be inappropriate.

• Job evaluation in some form is necessary but it should be regarded as a process for valuing jobs rather than an infallible system.

FURTHER READING

Armstrong and Baron (1995) provide a comprehensive guide to job evaluation practice on the basis of their 1995 research. Pritchard and Murlis (1992) take a broad view of job evaluation processes, drawing to a large extent on their considerable experience at Hay Management Consultants. The most comprehensive analysis of consultants' schemes is given by Neathey (1994). Hillage (1994) contains an analysis of the research carried out by the then IMS (now the Institute of

Employment Studies) and draws conclusions about the changing role of job evaluation. Grayson (1987) provides an interesting review of the impact on job evaluation of changes in technology. Quaid (1993) delivers a spirited attack on point-factor job evaluation. McHale (1990) describes approaches to competency-based job evaluation.

11 Job evaluation in action

This chapter describes the application of job evaluation – the extent to which it is used, selecting the right approach, designing and introducing a point-factor scheme and maintaining job evaluation. On completing the chapter the reader will be able to advise management on the choice of a scheme, including whether it should be a home-grown (tailor-made) one or a consultant's proprietary brand. The reader will also be able to plan and implement the introduction of job evaluation and to ensure that it is working effectively.

THE INCIDENCE OF JOB EVALUATION

All organisations practise some form of evaluation, although it is often highly informal. The research conducted by the Institute of Personnel and Development (Armstrong and Baron, 1995) established that 55 per cent of the 316 organisations taking part in the survey used formal evaluation processes. Other figures from previous surveys reveal varying proportions of organisations with job evaluation schemes. For example:

- ACAS (1988) – 40 per cent of manufacturing establishments and 35 per cent of service sector establishments have some form of evaluation for at least some of their employees.

- Wyatt and IPM (1989) – 61 per cent of a sample of 376 had a formal evaluation scheme in operation and 11 per cent were about to introduce a scheme.

- Workplace Industrial Relations Survey (Millward *et al* 1992) – about 26 per cent of workplaces had job evaluation schemes.

- IRS (1993) – 75 per cent of the 164 organisations participating in their survey used job evaluation.

- CBI/Hay (1996) – around 50 per cent of the participating organisations used job evaluation.

The variation among these figures could be attributed to differences in the samples.

Both the ACAS and the Wyatt/IPM surveys showed that the use of job evaluation was increasing, especially in the public sector. The Wyatt/IPM survey and the IPD survey revealed that job evaluation was more common in larger organisations. Formal job evaluation methods are less likely to be used in manufacturing organisations, especially where wage rates are negotiated.

SELECTING THE APPROACH

The questions to be answered when selecting an approach to job evaluation are dealt with below.

Is job evaluation necessary?

There is no choice about job evaluation. All organisations must make decisions on rates of pay and those decisions are based on judgements about relative job values within the organisation or on market rate imperatives or perceptions. The choice is therefore concerned not with the need to evaluate jobs but with whether or not a formal evaluation scheme is required. Many organisations seem to be quite happy to do without formal job evaluation. Their organisational structure and methods of working may, in their view, clearly indicate the relative values of roles without the need for a bureaucratic and, they may feel, inflexible process of job evaluation. In some cases negotiations or custom and practice determine pay relativities and organisations see no point in superimposing job evaluation. If asked about the danger of an equal-value claim they may reply that they are quite satisfied that their pay structure is not discriminatory and that they are certainly not going to become obsessed by equal-value considerations. They may feel that a formal process would be at odds with their culture as manifested in their flexible and non-bureaucratic approach to managing their affairs.

Other organisations, including the majority of those contacted by Armstrong and Baron (1995), believe that an orderly approach is essential in order to develop and maintain a logical and fair structure which enables them to manage relativities and minimise the risk of a successful equal-value claim. The arguments in favour of a formal approach to job evaluation were set out in the previous chapter. In essence they are that formal evaluation schemes provide the best basis for making fair, consistent and defensible decisions about the relative and comparable worth of jobs. Moreover, a formal approach can and should be transparent.

The arguments that people sometimes use against formality are that job evaluation is:

- unnecessary – management already knows what rates to pay without such a system

- inflexible

- bureaucratic

- costly, in time as well as money.

Everyone is quite happy with the system as it is, so why bother?

The choice will be dependent on the organisation's culture, management style and methods of organising and conducting business. But even if the decision is against formality in the shape of a set-piece job evaluation scheme, it is difficult to deny that a systematic approach to assessing job values is desirable. The arguments in favour of some degree of formality are very powerful, and it is perfectly possible to develop and use flexible methods of job evaluation which fit flexible firms and do not impose a costly and time-wasting system on the them.

At this stage an initial decision can be made on which jobs or occupations should be covered and how many schemes may be required. But no final decisions should be made without a further analysis of requirements and discussions with employees.

Is it necessary to change the existing arrangements?

Job evaluation schemes can decay. They can be corrupted and subject to manipulation and they can either create or fail to control grade drift (upgradings unjustified by an increase in the value of the job). They may become out-of-date, no longer relevant in a rapidly changing organisation. Changes can take place in organisational structures and processes, the composition of the workforce or the values held by management and employees generally about what is important when assessing relative worth. These values may be quite different from those existing when the scheme was originally introduced. The scheme may be perceived by those who run it and/or by those who are affected by it as inflexible, inappropriate, bureaucratic and time-wasting.

The questions to be answered when reviewing the operation of an existing job evaluation scheme are:

- Do management, employees and trade union representatives feel that it operates fairly?

- To what extent are inequities perceived in the ways in which jobs have been graded or paid?

- Is there any gender bias built into the scheme's factor plan or evidenced in the way it functions – the outcome of evaluations?

- Will the scheme provide an adequate defence against equal-value claims?

- Is the scheme being manipulated?

- Does grade drift take place?

- Are the values expressed by the factors contained in the scheme appropriate and acceptable to all concerned?

- Can it respond adequately to the new role requirements emerging in the organisation – for example, increased flexibility, more project/teamwork, multi-skilling?

- Is it appropriate to all the new occupations/jobs being created in the organisation?

- Is it relevant to the new structure of the organisation (eg de-layered, an emphasis on horizontal processes rather than vertical hierarchies)?

- Is the factor plan unsuitable? For example, are there too many or too few factors, duplications, omissions, imprecise definitions of factors or factor levels, inappropriate weightings?

• Is the scheme over-complex and/or inflexible?

• Is it time-consuming and bureaucratic?

This audit could be carried out by the personnel function or, preferably, by an internal working party, which should not necessarily consist of members of existing evaluation panels. External help may be desirable, if only in the form of someone who can facilitate the working party's investigations.

It is unlikely that any job evaluation scheme which has been in operation for more than five years or so will stand up to this sort of audit in its entirety. There will always be room for improvement by total replacement, rejigging the factor plan or altering the various analytical, evaluation and grading processes. If it is believed that a radical revision is required, the decisions required are discussed below. If, however, it is decided that only relatively minor changes should be made to the factor plan or to methods of operating the scheme, they could be decided internally in discussion with managers and employee representatives.

Should employees and their representatives be involved?
Some employers see the whole process of valuing jobs as a management prerogative. They do not involve employees at all, either in developing or in operating the scheme. Organisations which adopt this policy probably save time and money, and they may produce a result which is perfectly satisfactory from management's point of view. But what about the workers? It affects them too. Not involving them at all can convey the clear message that the organisation does not recognise their interest in something which affects them deeply – ie how they are rewarded. Transparency is important.

Employees and their representatives together with line managers should participate as members of a project team or job evaluation panel in the process of designing or modifying a tailor-made scheme, customising a consultant's proprietary brand (so far as this is possible), conducting job analyses, preparing job descriptions or role definitions, and evaluating jobs. They may take part in discussions of the grade structure but are much less frequently involved in grading decisions, and never in decisions on rates of pay for individuals, although rates of pay for jobs and pay scales may be negotiated with unions if they are present and have negotiating rights. Importantly, panel members can take part in communicating information about the scheme to their fellow employees. They can also be represented on the steering group which oversees the whole exercise. A further advantage of using panels is that they provide a forum for discussing any organisational issues that emerge from the job analyses.

Who should be covered by job evaluation?
Having decided who should or should not be involved, the next decision is which jobs, occupational groups or levels in the organisation should be subject to job evaluation. Ideally everyone, except possibly

board members and senior managers on individual contracts and terms and conditions of employment, should be included.

How many schemes?

Decisions on who should be covered lead naturally to the consideration of how many schemes are necessary. Preferably, one scheme should be used for all occupations and levels, but this ideal may not be practicable in situations where there is a considerable range of occupational groups. There are circumstances in which an organisation may contain a number of job families – clearly differentiated groups of occupations where people work within a distinct function, using a common range of knowledge, skills and competences at different levels. These job families may also comprise 'market groups' in which market-rate levels are generally different from those in other occupational groups. Each job family can have its own sequence of defined levels or bands, and progression through the bands may be determined by assessments of competence rather than a conventional job evaluation scheme. But job evaluation may be used for 'read-across' purposes – ie to assess comparable worth between job families.

What are the objectives?

It is essential at this stage to be clear about the objectives of the exercise before defining criteria for choice and deciding what type of scheme to use. These objectives can form the basis for communicating to employees and for briefing consultants in order to develop terms of reference for an assignment. Objectives could be defined along the following lines:

• to develop and implement a systematic and analytical process for evaluating jobs which will enable fair and consistent decisions to be made on their relative worth – This is intended to provide a basis for the design and operation of a logical and equitable grade and pay structure, and for managing relativities within that structure.

What criteria should be used for the scheme?

This question needs answering as a basis for preparing a system specification which can be used when assessing the relative merits of different approaches. The criteria could be set out under the following headings:

• integrated with other HR processes

• structured

• analytical

• systematic

• people-oriented

• free of gender bias

• transparent

• accepted as fair and equitable

• defensible

• developed and operated with the involvement of all concerned

- flexible

- inexpensive to introduce and operate

- easily administered and maintained

- computerised, but user-friendly.

Tailor-made scheme or consultants' package?

The process/system specification will form the background against which the next decision can be made: whether to develop a tailor-made scheme or whether to purchase a consultant's package.

In a tailor-made scheme the factor plan is aligned to the culture of the organisation and to the particular occupations and roles within it. The plan will deliver an important message to employees to the effect that 'These are our values and these are the factors we believe to be important when deciding on the relative worth of jobs and people.'

A reason for developing a tailor-made scheme in-house was provided by Alan Fowler (1992) who wrote, 'A major test of any scheme is its credibility within the workforce, and this may be enhanced by the knowledge that it has been designed by and for the organisation.' However, the design and development of a tailor-made scheme can be a major exercise, not to be embarked upon without thinking very carefully about the amount of expertise required and the time and effort involved. These considerations may make it advisable to enlist outside help from management consultants in developing a bespoke scheme.

A decision to use a proprietary brand may be made because well-established schemes are thought to be

- credible – they are well tested and tried in a wide variety of organisations

- offered by consultants who are experienced, good at facilitating working parties, expert at dealing with problems, and who are convincing

- relatively easy to install – the consultants will have developed well-honed methods of introducing their scheme, including job analysis, questionnaires, the format of job descriptions, methods of evaluation and methods of converting evaluation scores to gradings; if they wish, personnel specialists can take a back seat and let the consultants drive the installation programme

- proof against equal-value claims – the consultants' schemes are usually analytical and, so far, none has been found to be discriminatory (although it is said that some unions are only waiting for the right opportunity to challenge one or other of them)

- convincing to employees when presented with the help of consultants who are expert in communicating the virtues of their scheme

- computerised to save installation and administration costs and time – either as part of the package or as an add-on

- frequently linked to a database of market rate comparisons – this can be a particularly powerful incentive to adopt a scheme which obtains data from organisations that use the same analytical evaluation method, thus, it is claimed, ensuring that like is compared with like.

The arguments sometimes advanced for not using a proprietary brand are that:

- The factors included in the scheme and the factor weighting (if any) may not be appropriate to the types of job to be evaluated or to the organisation's values regarding what should be rewarded. Factors which, as in some consultants' schemes, emphasise the number of people supervised and the size of budgets controlled, may be irrelevant in research, development and creative jobs, and the contribution of people doing such work could be undervalued. There is also the possibility that they may encourage empire-building, totally inappropriate in today's leaner and flatter organisations.

- The schemes may be inflexible and bureaucratic.

- In spite of what the consultants say, the schemes can be manipulated by people determined to inflate job levels.

- No consultants' scheme has yet been developed which wholly eliminates subjective and possibly prejudiced judgements about job values.

Management consultants may assert in reply to these criticisms that:

- They are prepared to modify their factor plans and guide charts (ie to 'customise' the scheme) to suit a particular organisation and its values.

- There is no need for the schemes to be run bureaucratically (except, presumably, in a bureaucratic organisation).

- Manipulation of job descriptions and evaluations can be controlled through well-trained and experienced job evaluation panels, the members of which are familiar with the jobs and are encouraged to probe wherever a job description appears to be inflated. In any case, manipulation is possible in any job evaluation scheme, whether or not it is a consultants' proprietary brand.

- No job evaluation scheme has ever been devised which totally eliminates subjective judgements, but at least a well tried and tested consultant's scheme is more likely to do so than one developed from scratch.

A decision can be made only by weighing the pros and cons in the light of the circumstances. The key questions to answer are:

- Is a scheme wanted which will fit the particular requirements of the organisation?

- Is a proprietary scheme preferable because of its reputation, the expertise of the consultants, the market-rate data available, or, importantly, the perceived ease with which the scheme can be introduced?

Cost will also be a consideration. Consultants can be expensive. A fairly typical assignment in a medium-sized firm of 250 to 1,000 employees could easily cost between £20,000 and £30,000.

Depending on the decision, the next questions to be answered are either 'Which method should be used in a bespoke plan?' or 'Which consultant's scheme should be selected?'

What type of tailor-made scheme?

The advantages and disadvantages of each of the main types of job evaluation schemes were outlined in Chapter 10. The method selected depends, of course, on the particular needs of the organisation as summarised in the objectives and criteria developed for the project. The following needs may be taken into account:

- If the first requirement is to achieve internal equity and equal pay for work of equal value, an analytical point-factor scheme may be appropriate.

- If the need is to have a scheme which is easy to operate and takes account of market forces, and if equal value is not an important consideration, a combination of internal benchmarking and market pricing might be used.

- If flexibility is a prime consideration and the scheme has to cover knowledge workers, a competence-related approach as described in Chapter 10 may be desirable. This could be incorporated in a broad-banded structure as discussed in Chapter 17.

- If the aim is to reduce administration to the minimum, an analytical evaluation scheme could be computerised, as described in Chapter 37.

Which consultant's scheme?

Summaries of the better-known consultants' 'proprietary brands' are given in the IRS publication *Job Evaluation in the 1990s* (Neathey, 1994). Points to be considered when making a choice are:

- the reputation of the scheme and of the consultants who offer it

- the experience of the consultants in installing the scheme in similar organisations

- the degree to which the factors included in the scheme appear to fit the requirements and values of the organisation

- the extent to which the consultants can customise their scheme to suit the requirements of the organisation

- gender neutrality (an absolute requirement)

- the availability of reliable market-rate data linked with the scheme

- the likely acceptability of the scheme to employees and their representatives

- the ease with which the scheme can be installed and operated

- the quality of the questionnaires, the checklists and the briefing and supporting material provided by the consultants

- the availability of computerised systems to help in job analysis, job evaluation and scheme maintenance

- the ability of the consultants to train job analysts and evaluators

- the capacity of the consultants to provide advice and help with related reward and HR issues, including the design of pay structures, pay modelling, performance management, competence analysis and profiling, and organisational development

- the time it would take to introduce the scheme

- the costs involved (always a consideration but not necessarily the first consideration).

The selection and use of consultants is discussed further in Chapter 35.

DEVELOPING AND IMPLEMENTING A POINT-FACTOR JOB EVALUATION SCHEME

The job evaluation programme for a point-factor scheme (the most common method) can be conducted in the stages shown in Figure 13 following decisions on the method of approach.

Project planning

The first step should be to clarify who has overall responsibility for the project and who is going to be involved in each stage, either carrying out the work or facilitating a working party or evaluation panel. A common approach is to have a steering committee (composed of directors and senior managers) to oversee the whole project and a working party or job evaluation panel to carry out the detailed work.

Although overall control of the project may be assigned to a steering committee, a project director should be appointed from within the organisation to direct it in detail: monitoring progress, providing for quality assurance, co-ordinating the activities of job evaluation panels, carrying out consistency checks, ensuring that the cost budget is not exceeded, dealing with problems as they arise, and ensuring that the consultants, if they are used, deliver. This is an important, demanding and time-consuming role. It is often performed by the head of personnel or the head of a pay and benefits (remuneration) function, if one exists. But there is no reason why it should not be a line manager.

If consultants are involved in a large-scale exercise, they will appoint a project manager, but she or he should be accountable to the organisation's project director for deliverables, quality, keeping to the timetable and not exceeding the cost budget.

The project plan should set out:

- the stages of the project

- the deliverables at each stage

- the completion date for each stage

- the milestones at which the progress of the project will be reviewed formally

Figure 13 **Job evaluation programme**

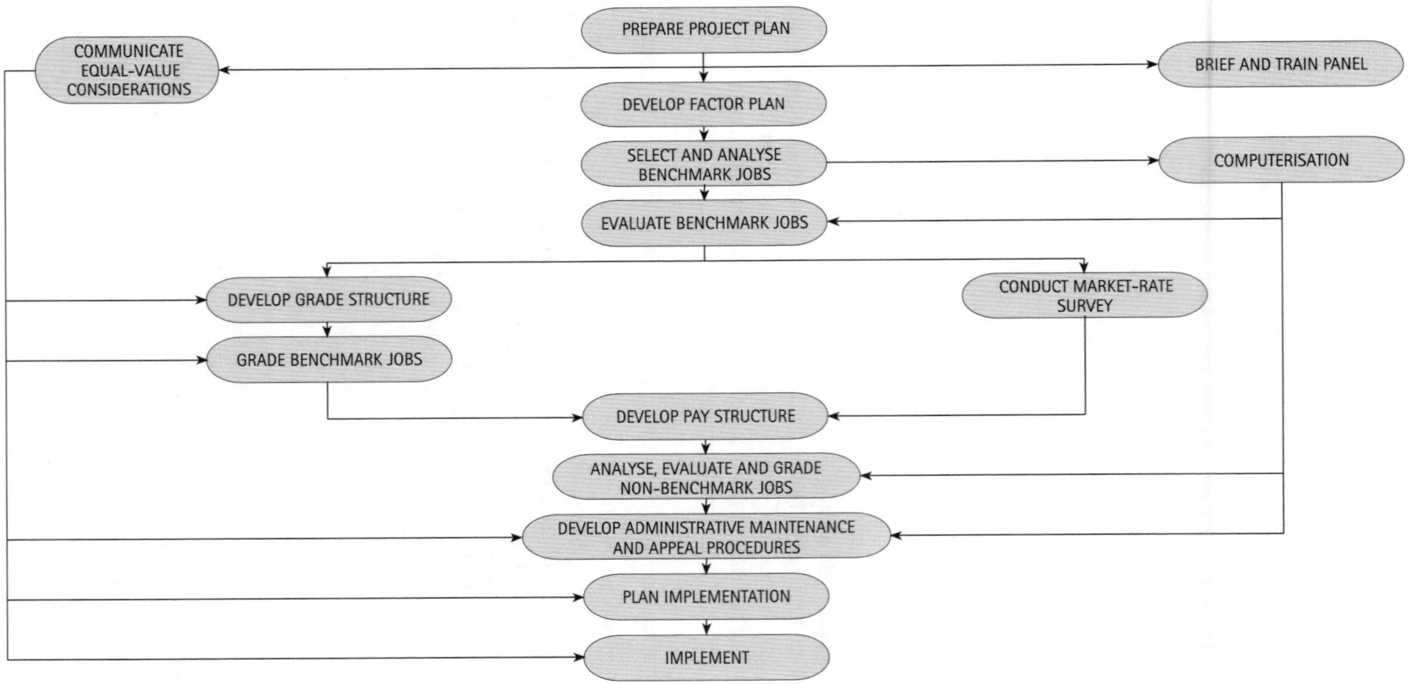

- who is responsible, individually or jointly, for each stage and the overall management of the project. This will cover the roles of the steering committee, the project director, the job evaluation panel and its chairperson, and the role of facilitator, if one is used (either an internal or external consultant).

The timetable should be based on realistic estimates not only of the time that is likely to be spent on each activity but also of the elapsed time, taking into account the intervals required between meetings and the time it takes to conduct job analyses and evaluations. The rules of thumb which can be used to estimate times are:

- *Job analysis* – It will take between half a day and a whole day to carry out a job analysis and prepare a job description, allowing for some iteration in gaining agreement to the description. (This time can be considerably shortened by the use of computers to record and summarise answers to questionnaires.)

- *Job evaluation* – A job evaluation panel may take between 30 minutes and an hour initially to evaluate a benchmark job but will speed up as they become familiar with the factor plan and more used to interpreting the level descriptions and relating information about the job to them. It is probably advisable to plan for about five to six jobs to be evaluated during the first day's meeting, which can later be increased to seven to eight. Job evaluation panels can run out of steam if they try to do too much at one sitting. The result may be that the evaluations are superficial and consensus is too readily reached. Ideally, the panel should meet for only half a day or at most a short day (eg 10.00 am to 4.00 pm). This time can also be reduced if the evaluation is carried out with the help of a computer, possibly without the use of a panel at all, involving only the job-holder, the manager, a specialist job evaluator and perhaps a trade union representative.

- *Market rate surveys* – If a special survey is being conducted, it may be necessary to allow about four weeks between inviting organisations to take part and getting their replies. It can take longer.

Communicate to employees
The evaluation process should be as transparent as possible. Employees should be informed at this stage that the evaluation exercise is going to take place, and why. They can be given broad details of how the programme will be conducted and told that the steering group and job evaluation panel have been set up to develop and implement the scheme. These bodies' terms of reference might be summarised and information given on any outside help that may be enlisted to carry out the exercise.

It should be emphasised that the project is concentrating on internal relativities in order to develop a more rational and equitable grade structure. As far as possible, people should be disabused of any expectations that it will result in pay increases all round – or any pay increases at all. If this point is not made clear now, there will be trouble in store. Few organisations conducting a job evaluation exercise have ever been able completely to suppress expectations of pay increases but they can at least be damped down at the start of the exercise. At the same time, it should be pointed out that no one's pay will be reduced as a result of the project.

Brief and train the panel

The panel members should be briefed carefully on the objectives of the exercise and their terms of reference. Their role in developing the factor plan, selecting benchmark jobs, analysing and evaluating jobs and advising on the grade structure should be explained. They will need to be trained in job analysis and evaluation techniques.

Develop a factor plan

The main decisions required when developing a factor plan are the choice and definition of factors, the weighting, if any, of the factors, the number of levels required for each factor and the points scale that should be attached to the levels.

The number of factors

The number of factors required is a matter of judgement. If there are too few – say, less than four – the individual factors may cover too many aspects of the job and the level definitions may be confusing. If there are two criteria in the definition of a level – say, numbers managed and size of budget – it may be difficult to decide between them.

If there are too many factors – say more than 12 or 13 – there is a risk of overlap and duplication, and the evaluation process may become complicated. The risk may, however, be reduced if sub-factors are clustered together under main factor headings.

There is no rule which says that one factor or set of factors is always better than another. However, it can be argued that a larger number of factors will facilitate more accurate comparisons, especially in equal-value (comparable worth) situations, where it is essential to compare specifically each facet of the jobs under consideration.

It cannot be emphasised too often that the factor plan should represent the values of the organisation as regards what it believes to be the key criteria in establishing the worth of jobs. For example, the focus could be on competences, especially those concerned with working flexibly in complex situations, interpersonal relationships, teamworking and quality. The impact of the job on organisational performance would also be covered and, possibly, the mental and physical effort involved, and the working conditions.

Ultimately, decisions on the types and numbers of factors will be a matter of judgement, although it will be influenced by equal-value requirements. Every organisation must make this judgement in accordance with its needs, whether it is designing its own scheme (with or without the help of consultants) or selecting a proprietary one.

To summarise, a factor plan should ensure that:

- all the characteristics of the jobs (male and female) are covered

- the factors are not duplicated – it is necessary to avoid the risk of double-counting

Table 9 **A factor matrix**

| | | INTERPERSONAL SKILLS | | | |
		A	B	C	D
	a	10	20	30	40
	b	20	30	40	50
TYPICAL CONTACTS	c	30	40	50	60
	d	40	50	60	70

- as far as possible, only one criterion is included in each factor although two related factors can be incorporated if a matrix format is used as illustrated in Table 9. In this example, a rating of B for the interpersonal skills required and C for the frequency and level of typical contacts with others (within and outside the organisation) would produce a score of 40 points.

Defining factors

The guidelines for defining factors are:

- Include as few criteria and dimensions as possible; aim for one criterion per factor.

- Ensure that a key criterion is only included once in a set of factors; do not include a very similar criterion in another factor.

- Be as precise as possible about what the factor is intended to cover.

- Wherever possible refer to specific measures, observable conditions and types of behaviour or competences that can easily be linked with the demands made on actual job-holders, the requirements they must meet to satisfy those demands, and the results they are expected to achieve by meeting these requirements.

- Make the definitions as succinct as possible – too many words confuse.

- Remember that the aim is, so far as possible, to ensure that the factor has the same meaning for all those who carry out evaluations.

Factor levels

The number of levels required depends on the range between the highest and lowest incidence of the factor in any of the jobs and the degree to which it is possible to differentiate between the levels in that range.

Factors need not all have the same number of levels. The scope or range of the different factors may vary considerably. The minimum number of levels is usually three and the use of more than six or seven levels is rare. It is undesirable to impose too many levels, which could result in problems of differentiation between them.

Defining levels is perhaps the most critical and it is certainly the most difficult task when designing a traditional point-factor scheme. It is the level definitions that will be referred to most frequently when comparing the job analysis with the factor plan. The guidelines for defining levels are:

- Aim to capture all the differences in the nature, type and extent of the work done relevant to each factor.

- Define only the levels required to differentiate clearly between the degrees to which the factor may apply.

- Define the levels so that there are obvious differences between them. It is helpful if they are seen as a series of steps, each representing a progressively greater amount or incidence of the relevant job criterion.

- Do not duplicate the description of a criterion in another degree.

- Concentrate on what the work actually entails at that level, or the specific outputs expected. Avoid relying solely on a series of comparative adjectives or adverbs (eg 'small', 'medium', 'large') without qualifying them with a description of what 'small' means, where possible expressed in quantified terms (frequency of contact, numbers supervised, size of budget, length of time required to become fully competent, weight of objects to be lifted, etc).

- Define the levels in a way that will facilitate the development of a structured questionnaire for job analysis purposes.

- Use language that conveys succinctly, directly and unequivocally what is involved at that particular level and facilitates comparisons between the job analysis and the level definition.

These requirements are not easy to satisfy. The problem with defining levels is that it can become an exercise in semantics. It is easy to fall into the trap of simply producing a series of comparatives and superlatives which have no meaning in themselves and lend themselves to varied interpretations.

Weighting
If the significance of the factors in determining relative values is believed to differ, weighting may be carried out by assigning to each factor a proportional value: a percentage of the total size of the job expressed as 100 per cent. For example, in the example of a factor plan given in chapter 10, the factors were weighted as shown in Table 10. There is nothing magical about the weightings in this example – every factor plan can and should have its own weighting pattern. What matters is that the weighting

- properly reflects the values of those affected by job evaluation – ie employees and their representatives as well as management

Table 10 Factor plan weighting

Factor	Maximum	%
1 Knowledge and skills	300	27
2 Responsibility	300	27
3 Decision-making	220	20
4 Complexity	140	13
5 Contacts	150	13
Total	1,100	100

Table 11   Factor score divided evenly

Level	Points
6	300
5	250
4	200
3	150
2	100
1	50

Table 12   Progressively widening scores

Level	Points
6	300
5	230
4	170
3	120
2	80
1	50

- does not discriminate against women or men (equal-value considerations in designing factor plans are discussed fully in Chapter 12).

Weightings are based on judgemental assumptions about the relative significance of the factors. These assumptions can be tested and adjusted by trial and error or by the statistical technique of multiple regression (see Armstrong and Baron, 1995) to find out whether, when applied to actual evaluations during a pilot run of the scheme, they produce a 'felt-fair' rank order of jobs. As mentioned below, when developing a new factor plan it is often better to defer weighting until the factor plan has been tested on the basis of assigning levels only – ie not scoring the jobs.

Factor rating scales
These consist of the points assigned to each level. There may be just one point value for each level; or the level may be defined as a range; or scope may be given for a three-point scale at each level (eg standard, standard-plus and standard-minus). Allocating a range to each level suggests a degree of accuracy in rating which is unachievable. Even allowing for three points in the level scale may be asking too much for the discriminatory powers of evaluators – although when they are deciding on levels they will often want to award a plus or a minus. People tend to dislike being constrained, and the feeling can be respected by allowing some variation upwards and downwards.

The simplest approach is to divide the total factor score equally between the levels, giving an arithmetic progression like that in Table 11. Some organisations prefer the differences between the value of levels to widen progressively upwards, as in Table 12. This is based on the assumption that differences in the degree of responsibility and accountability, etc, are likely to be greater at higher levels. But this could be just as arbitrary as valuing the levels as if they were equidistant.

To summarise, the key points to be remembered when designing a factor plan are that:

- The plan should reflect the values of the organisation in respect of what it believes are the most important considerations determining the relative worth of jobs.

- The factors should be appropriate to the jobs being covered, taking account of the range of work carried out in the organisation generally and, in particular, the characteristics of women's work (which have often been treated as invisible in traditional factor plans).

- There should be no duplications or omissions in the factors and no double-counting (ie more than one factor measuring the same characteristics).

- The factors should be defined as clearly as possible – broadly enough to cover all the work but not so vaguely as to leave too much room for interpretation.

- Factor levels should be defined in a way which captures significant differences in the nature of the work carried out, clarifies those differences step by step, and focuses on what the work actually entails at each level.

- The weighting process should be based on reasonable and tested assumptions about the relative significance of the factors, and it should not discriminate against women or men. It may be decided that arbitrary weighting decisions should be avoided by selecting factors which are assumed to be of equal value, although, in a sense, that would also be an arbitrary decision.

The panel should be given as much freedom as possible to identify the factors they believe to be important, in line with the parameters listed above and on the understanding that too many factors make the scheme unwieldy and may lead to duplication. At this stage it is preferable not to decide on the weighting of the factors. This should be done after an initial selection of benchmark jobs have been evaluated. The panel will by then have gained a clearer understanding of the scheme and will be in a better position to determine whether weighting is necessary, and if so, what it should be.

Select benchmark jobs
Benchmark jobs provide the reference points for evaluation, bearing in mind that job evaluation is essentially a comparative process. They are the representative jobs which enable standards to be developed and refined for making judgements about comparative worth and form the datum points which are the basis of the framework within which other jobs are evaluated. Benchmarks consist of the key jobs at different levels and in different functions of the organisation and need to be selected whenever the total number of jobs is too large for them all to be compared with one another. (As a rule of thumb, such may be the case when there are 40 jobs or more, although the number could be smaller if there are wide variations between a smaller number of jobs.) Normally between 15 per cent and 30 per cent of the total number of jobs may be selected, depending on the complexity of the

organisation, although some jobs may be done by a number of people and the percentage is therefore likely to be less than the total number employed.

The criteria for selecting benchmarks are that they should

- represent the entire range of jobs according to level and function, and the extent to which job-holders are predominantly male or female

- be well recognised jobs with which the members of the job evaluation panel between them are familiar

- be reasonably stable – ie unlikely to change much in content (although this presents difficulties in a rapidly changing organisation)

- be precisely defined with regard to skills, responsibilities and work requirements

- stand out clearly from other jobs so that they can be easily identified

- include at least some jobs which can form the basis of external comparisons.

Analyse benchmark jobs
The analysis of benchmark jobs can be carried out by means of interviews and/or questionnaires (see Chapter 14) or the process can be entirely computerised as described in Chapter 37.

Evaluate benchmark jobs
Initially the panel should evaluate a selection of four or five benchmark jobs. This exercise can be treated as a pilot-scheme to familiarise panel members with the evaluation process and to indicate where changes are necessary to the factor plan. It will also provide the information required to decide on factor weighting.

Ground rules for evaluating jobs can be given to panel members as follows:

- Evaluate the requirements and demands of the job/role on those who perform it but do not be influenced by the performance of the person(s) in the job.

- Recognise that some roles will have been built round the particular skills and competences of the people who perform them, but concentrate on what these people actually do and the attributes they need rather than on their personalities.

- Consider what the job-holder is normally responsible for doing; do not allow what may occur very occasionally to over-influence the evaluation. At the same time, recognise that many roles now require a considerable degree of flexibility, and this should be taken into account as a 'normal' demand on people in the role.

- Consider the job/role requirements and demands in terms of what a fully competent individual will be expected to do. Avoid focusing on what outstanding performers do on the one hand or on what people manage to do when they have not yet completed an orientation and induction period.

- Assess each factor independently of the others. Remember that this is an analytical process, which means that each element of the job – ie the factors – must be considered separately prior to making an overall judgement.

• Do not allow any preconceived notions of the value of the job or the work carried out to sway judgement on the level of each factor. Forget the present grade or rate of pay both when evaluating each factor separately and when you look at the overall profile of the job as expressed in the factor levels assigned to it.

• Ensure that every aspect of the role is covered. Do not attach undue significance to any one characteristic.

• Be aware of the danger of gender bias. Do not allow judgement to be affected by unsupported assumptions about the relative value of women's and men's work.

• Use judgement in selecting the factor level which is closest to describing the incidence of that factor in the role. The fit may not be exact, because factor level definitions can never be written with enough precision to guarantee it. But remember that the definitions will become more useful as the panel increases its understanding of the meaning of the words by interpreting how they apply to the benchmark jobs at different levels.

• Consider the relative value or comparable worth of the job within the organisation; do not take any account of the current or anticipated market value of the role.

When carrying out evaluations, the role of the panel facilitator is to assist in the process of making judgements and to ensure that as far as possible thorough and objective discussions take place. The facilitator should not take the responsibility for making decisions from the panel.

The steps usually taken by a panel to evaluate a job are:

• Panel members independently read the job/role definition and analysis, taking up with the analyst (who should be present if he or she is not a member of the panel) any queries on matters of fact. They can also be discussed between members of the panel. If the panel members feel that the analysis and description are inadequate, they can request a further analysis to fill in gaps or to answer specific questions. Alternatively, they may co-opt someone who has direct knowledge of the job to attend a panel meeting and answer queries.

• The panel members independently evaluate the job by reference to the factor and level definitions in the factor plan. Because the weighting (if any) and the factor scales should not yet have been determined, panel members should indicate only the level for each factor. They should not be encouraged to give a plus or minus to their ratings because such fine distinctions cannot be made with any validity by reference to the necessarily general factor definitions (although many people like to make such fine distinctions and it may be difficult to dissuade them). The facilitator should not commit himself or herself to an evaluation at this stage.

- The panel members record their judgements, with any explanatory comments they may wish to make.

- The facilitator reproduces all the individual ratings on a flipchart. Starting with the more significant deviations, the panel members are asked to explain their reasoning. It is essential that facilitators manage this part of the process with great care. No panel member should be forced on to the defensive or feel threatened by critical comments. Facilitators should ask other panel members for their views but the focus should always be on matters of fact, not opinion. Any views must be substantiated by reference to the evidence, and the facilitator may have to step in to ask probing questions about the factual basis of the views expressed, but only as a last resort. Where necessary, facilitators can suggest that the panel should re-examine the factor or level definition very carefully to make sure it is fully understood or to note any ambiguities which have served to cloud their judgement. Such ambiguities should be noted for future reference when amending the draft factor plan. As the panel gains experience its members, possibly helped by the facilitator, will be able to refer to previous evaluations which will clarify the definitions.

- The process described above continues for the four or five jobs which are being used to pilot-test the scheme. When the evaluation has been completed the panel can pause and consider any changes that it would like to make in the factor plan. If the proposed changes are significant, it may be necessary to re-evaluate the pilot-scheme jobs. To be absolutely certain that a substantially revised factor plan is appropriate and usable, it may be necessary to test it again before producing a final version for the rest of the evaluations. Even this version may benefit from fine-tuning. No factor plan should be regarded as sacrosanct during the benchmark job evaluations. But it should not be amended once the evaluations have been completed.

- The panel considers what factor weighting, if any, is required. If it decides that the factors should be weighted, it carries on along the lines described in Chapter 10.

- The panel decides on the points scales for each of the factors. This is a crucial but essentially judgemental and iterative process which continues until the panel feels that the scales are satisfactory. The pilot-scheme jobs are then scored, using the agreed factor scales, and the panel forms a judgement as to whether or not they rank the jobs properly and reflect the differences between them. If the panel is not satisfied with the result, it has to test other configurations (scales and weightings) until a satisfactory result is obtained. This is the last opportunity to check the plan before embarking on the full benchmark job evaluation.

- The remaining benchmark jobs are evaluated by the panel in the same way, using the full factor plan.

- The job evaluation panel scrutinises the completed evaluations of all the benchmark jobs. Even if the process has not been fully computerised the results can usefully be loaded into a computer to form the database for analysis and future evaluations.

- The panel assesses the factor level gradings across all the benchmarks to identify any inconsistencies or what appear to be out-of-the-ordinary judgements. (This process is sometimes called 'sore-thumbing'.)

- The jobs can then be listed in rank order according to their scores, and the panel members have to assess whether this order and the points differentials between jobs are reasonable – ie 'felt-fair'.

- As necessary, the panel re-evaluates any jobs where the evaluation is believed to be inconsistent or the relativities are not felt fair. A final revision of the factor plan could also be undertaken at this stage in the light of the analysis in the previous two stages of the results of the benchmark evaluation.

It is in these final stages that a point-factor job evaluation exercise is in danger of simply reproducing the existing hierarchy, and that is what many equal-value commentators accuse it of doing. The only way of avoiding this trap is to ensure that as far as possible the panel concentrates on the facts – the evidence produced by the analysis and evaluation processes which it has been considering. If panel members do this, their 'felt-fair' judgements would at least be based on the factual analysis rather than on preconceived notions of the 'correct' rank order. If there is still any reasonable doubt about comparable worth, then the jobs in question should be re-evaluated before the decisions on benchmark job scores and the factor weighting plan are confirmed. The rest of the exercise can then go ahead as described below.

Develop a grade structure
Methods of developing a grade structure following an evaluation are described in Chapter 16. It is, however, worth reiterating that this is a highly judgemental process.

Grade benchmark jobs
If a point-factor scheme is used, each grade in the structure is defined in terms of points such that any benchmark job with a points score within the grade bracket will be allocated to that grade. All jobs within that grade will be paid within the same pay range attached to the grade. At this stage, therefore, the job evaluation score is no longer significant in a graded structure except as an indication of the grade into which the job is to be placed. In other words 'points do not equal pounds', and that has to be made clear to all concerned.

Survey market rates
Market-rate surveys are usually conducted by the personnel function, possibly with outside help but not involving a job evaluation panel. However, trade union representatives taking part in pay negotiations may challenge the data if they have not taken part in obtaining it. Methods of conducting surveys are described in Chapter 13.

Design the pay structure
Methods of designing a graded pay structure are described in Chapter 16. It will be particularly important at this stage to cost the implications of the alternative structures that might be developed. After a job evaluation exercise individual rates of pay may go up but they

seldom if ever come down. In other words, the rate of pay of employees who have been upgraded will be brought up to the new pay point or range for their new grade, possibly in stages, while the pay of employees who are now overgraded will not be reduced. It will 'mark time'. Computer pay modelling software can be used to develop iterations on the costs of alternative structures before a final decision is made (see Chapter 37).

Evaluate non-benchmark jobs

Non-benchmark jobs are sometimes allocated to grades by a process of internal benchmarking. This can lead to inequitable decisions if it is not based on the results of thorough job analysis. From an equal-value point of view, it is preferable to deal with non-benchmark jobs in exactly the same way as the benchmark jobs. And individuals may be aggrieved if they realise that they have simply been slotted into the structure without any consideration of the characteristics of their particular jobs or role.

Develop procedures

There may be circumstances in which the administration of job evaluation is handled entirely by the personnel function. But there is everything to be said for involving other people – line managers and employee representatives. Job evaluation will be much more acceptable and therefore effective if it is regarded as their scheme.

If a job evaluation panel developed the scheme, the panel could become the body that maintains it. The panel could then act as the guardian of the scheme's integrity. It could carry out that role by ensuring that job analyses and evaluations are conducted thoroughly, that no one is allowed to manipulate the wording of role definitions or the process of evaluation in order to enable unjustified upgradings to take place, and that evaluations are consistent across occupational and functional boundaries. The panel should ensure that equal-value considerations are given constant attention so that gender bias is eliminated and jobs of comparable worth are paid equally. It would be responsible for evaluating new jobs and re-evaluating jobs in which the responsibilities have changed. The panel should not, however, hear appeals, because it would be considering appeals against its own decisions.

The role of the personnel function should be to service the panel, providing information, conducting analyses, facilitating meetings and auditing evaluations to ensure that they are consistent. It could also be responsible for training new panel members and providing refresher training for existing members.

Administration

The procedures to be administered by the panel or the personnel function, if a panel is not used, are:

- the general processes and methods used to analyse and evaluate jobs

- the arrangements for evaluating and grading new jobs, including how the analysis should be conducted and what supporting information will be required to explain the context in which the new role will be carried out

- the arrangements for re-evaluating existing jobs: the arrangements should spell out how the case for re-evaluation should be put together (ie what information is required and who prepares it), how the job or role analysis will take place, and who will make the final decisions on the evaluation and regrading

- the arrangements for hearing appeals.

Plan implementation

The implementation plan should cover:

- the general communication to all employees of the outcome of the job evaluation exercise

- decisions on how employees who are over- or undergraded as a result of evaluation should be dealt with (see below)

- how individual employees should be informed of the effect of the evaluation on their grading and pay, if it affects them at all.

The decisions on over- or undergraded employees are crucial. If this part of the exercise is mishandled, the result could be serious demotivation and disaffection. The usual practice is to 'red-circle' those employees who are now overgraded – ie maintain their pay at its present level until it falls within the new pay bracket or scale for the grade after any general increases in pay scales.

Employees who are undergraded should be placed in the pay bracket or scale for their new grade. The cost of doing this should have been estimated when earlier decisions were made on gradings and the pay structure, and adjustments may have been made to the gradings and scales to minimise the costs. But if it is felt that the additional payroll costs cannot be sustained all at once, it may be decided to phase increases over two or at most three years. Employees are said to have been 'green-circled' when this happens. However, phasing pay-rises can cause dissatisfaction, and the organisation should avoid doing so unless it truly cannot afford a once-and-for-all increase. Ideally, the costs should have been anticipated and budgeted for. But there may be more readjustments than were anticipated, even if care was taken to minimise them when devising the pay structure and grading jobs.

DEVELOPING A COMPETENCE-BASED FACTOR PLAN

The most typical approach is to develop a competence-based factor plan using one of the three methods summarised below.

1 – Adapting an existing scheme to an existing competence framework

The first step is to analyse the scheme's factors to identify those which appear to fit the framework (possibly with some modification) and those which do not fit at all. It is then necessary to review those factors which do fit within the competency framework and decide whether any additional factors are required.

2 – Adapting an existing competence framework to create a factor plan

This method starts by taking an existing competence framework as a basis for a factor plan which, apart from the inclusion of competence headings, would resemble a conventional point-factor scheme. Not all the competence headings would necessarily be used and additional 'output'-type headings might have to be added. Such schemes could best be described as competence-related rather than competence-based.

3 – Developing a completely new competence-framework and competence-related job evaluation plan

This is the most radical approach. It requires the initial definition of generic competences, followed by the development of a method of evaluation, which is often computerised. The development process could start with an analysis of the organisation's core competences and then create generic role competence profiles which support the development and effective use of those competences.

The analysis is not confined to generic behavioural competences. It also focuses on the *work* required to deliver results – the occupational-related competences which determine the extent to which what is done achieves the outputs required. The outcome of this analysis could be a point-factor competence-related scheme, a role classification scheme or a job family structure as described below.

Developing a competence-related point-factor job evaluation scheme

The process of developing a competence-related point-factor evaluation scheme is much the same as that described for a conventional points scheme. A factor plan has to be produced, and this requires the selection of factors, the definition of factor levels and the development of factor scales following a decision on how the factors should be weighted. The difference is that competence-related job evaluation is based on a competence framework which provides the starting-point for selecting factors and defining levels. These factors should

- spell out the underlying skills and competences required to meet the demands placed on people in their roles at different levels in the organisation or within a job family – this implies that it will be possible to define levels at which any particular competence or cluster of competences will be required

- cover all the areas of behaviour and performance which need to be valued in order to establish the worth of a job

- contribute specifically to the creation of added value by people in their roles, taking into account the goals and critical success factors of the organisation

- reflect and reinforce the core competences and values of the organisation

- be able to cope with rapidly changing and flexible roles.

MAINTENANCE

Job evaluation schemes decay. This seems to be almost inevitable, perhaps because no one involved in job evaluation can be infallible or completely objective all the time. And there will always be pressure for upgrading from individuals and their managers which may be supported by enhanced job descriptions and tendentious arguments, often phrased in the language of the factor plan to indicate that the job is operating at, say, level four rather than level three.

Preventive maintenance

Preventive maintenance is required to minimise the risk of rapid decay. It is carried out by periodic audits of evaluations and gradings and, on a sample basis, the re-evaluation of jobs to check on the validity of the original evaluation or to establish whether changes mean that the evaluation ought to be amended.

Consistency checks

Consistency checks should be made periodically by means of cross-evaluations and by analysing the outcome of any new evaluations compared with the benchmarks. Too much reliance should not be placed on the benchmarks as the anchors of the job evaluation and grading process. Benchmark jobs can change, just like any other job, and therefore ought to be re-evaluated or even replaced by new benchmarks. A re-evaluation or replacement of a benchmark for this reason should not be allowed to have a knock-on effect on the evaluation of non-benchmark jobs which have remained unchanged. Any evaluation, once completed, should stand on its own merits, irrespective of what happens to the benchmark job with which it was originally compared.

SUMMARY

- There is no choice about job evaluation. Some form is essential.

- Job evaluation schemes can decay and may need to be rejuvenated. This should be carried out following an audit and employees should be involved. Clear objectives and criteria for effectiveness should be set.

- The development of a typical point-factor scheme involves:
  - project planning
  - communicating to employees
  - setting up and training a panel
  - developing a factor plan
  - selecting, analysing and evaluating benchmark jobs
  - developing a grade structure
  - developing procedures

- Much of the work of introducing and operating job evaluation can be reduced by using a computerised system.

- The importance of job evaluation is less evident in broad-based pay structures.

FURTHER READING

The best practical guides to installing a job evaluation scheme are Armstrong and Baron (1995), ACAS (1988) and Fowler (1992).

12 Equal pay for work of equal value

This chapter covers the background to discrimination and deals with the legislation concerning equal pay for work of equal value and what organisations can do to achieve gender neutrality in their payment systems. It also refers to the need to avoid discrimination because of race or any other reasons.

On completing the chapter the reader should be able to analyse and audit a pay structure to assess whether it implicates sex or other discrimination and to suggest ways of designing job evaluation schemes and pay structures free of bias. The reader should also understand the reasons for pay discrimination and the basic principles of the Equal Pay legislation and case law.

WHY DISCRIMINATION TAKES PLACE

As Robert Elliott (1991) has stated: 'Discrimination arises when equals are treated unequally.' Historically, it has been generally accepted by men in a man's world that women's place was in the home, unless they were needed to carry out menial and therefore underpaid jobs. Women's work has been undervalued because of the low rates of pay. Prior to the Equal Pay Act 1970, collective agreements tended to have only one rate of pay for women workers, with no differentiation between grades of work or levels of skill.

The entry of women into the professions in the nineteenth century and pressures for women's rights in the twentieth heralded a very gradual change in this climate of discrimination. But it needed the Treaty of Rome (1957), Article 119 of which enshrined the principle of equal pay for equal work, to stimulate anti-discriminatory law in the UK. The first British legislation was the Equal Pay Act 1970, amended by the Equal Pay Amendment Regulations 1983.

Discrimination in the determination of the relative rates of pay for men and women may not be so blatant now as it was before 1975, when the 1970 Equal Pay Act came into force, but it still exists. The 1998 New Earnings Survey showed that women's average gross hourly earnings (excluding overtime) were 80.1 per cent of men's. This was indeed better than in 1970, when women's earnings were 62.1 per cent of men's. But there is still a 20 per cent differential.

It seems that historical attitudes about the fundamental value of women compared with men continue to exert a powerful influence on relative rates of pay. This means that women tend to be concentrated in lower-paying jobs, a problem aggravated by the relative lack of training opportunities for women. Undoubtedly this is because the value of work undertaken by women has been insufficiently recognised. The demands their work makes in terms of knowledge and skill have consistently been undervalued compared with the work undertaken by men. Such undervaluation occurs right across the pay market but has also arisen because of inherent gender bias in the design of job evaluation, grading and performance appraisal schemes or in the application of such schemes.

In a comprehensive analysis of the economics of equal value Jill Rubery (1992) suggested that the undervaluing of women's employment is caused by three interrelated factors:

- gender discrimination in the ways in which jobs are graded and paid

- widespread occupational segregation by gender

- differences in the labour supply and labour market conditions which allow the differences to be perpetuated.

She indicated that job segregation was the mechanism by which jobs performed by women may be undervalued relative to jobs performed by men, and that the four main theories which explain the causes of segregation are:

- *Human capital theory* – Segregation arises not from the undervaluation of women's jobs but from the lower levels of skill possessed by many women because they have had less opportunity to gain training and qualifications. This leads to women's becoming segregated in low-paying occupations. Women's lack of 'human capital' can arise from institutional and societal discrimination – for example, within the education system, or from women's decision to invest less in 'human capital' because they expect lower returns on such investment than men, given their expectations of leaving the labour market to have children.

- *Crowding theory* – Women are constrained or 'crowded' into one part of the labour market by custom, prejudice and hostile working arrangements. There is therefore oversupply of women to the female part of the labour market, and firms operate labour-intensive techniques and work on a low-productivity basis. Women are constrained to work in low-productivity jobs not because of their low potential but because such jobs are all that is available to them.

- *Patriarchal and 'family wage' theory* – Low pay arises from women's subordinate social and familial positions or from their traditional position as secondary-income earners. These perceived historical differences in the economic role of men and women have become embedded in payment structures. According to this theory, women are low-paid because of their gender, and the jobs that they do are low-paid regardless of their actual value or contribution to the firm.

- *Labour market segmentation theory* – Women are employed in low-paid jobs because labour market discrimination has resulted in their being available at lower wage levels than men.

To summarise, inequalities in pay exist because of prejudice, segregation and inequalities of opportunity in selection, training, development and promotion. The overall differential in rates of pay is partly a result of the fact that because of the inequalities there are fewer women than men doing the more demanding and better-remunerated jobs.

Discrimination in employment is also legislated against. The Sex Discrimination Act 1975 makes it unlawful for employers to discriminate on grounds of sex or marriage against their methods of access to non-contractual benefits, or by denying such access. The Act additionally outlaws discrimination by employers against job applicants in the terms on which they are offered employment. Discrimination also takes place on the grounds of race, and it too is caused by job segregation, unequal opportunities for training and promotion and, to an even greater extent, prejudice. The Race Relations Act 1976 prohibits discrimination on racial grounds and between racial groups, and states that discrimination arises when a person is treated less favourably than other persons on racial grounds. The Act specifies that it is unlawful to discriminate on grounds of race against employees in the terms of employment given to them and in the way in which they are afforded facilities for promotion, transfer, training or access to any other benefits.

EQUAL PAY FOR WORK OF EQUAL VALUE: THE LEGAL FRAMEWORK

The equal pay for work of equal value legal framework is based on the provisions of Article 119 of the Treaty of Rome, 1957, the Equal Pay Act 1970 as amended by the Equal Pay (Amendment) Regulations 1983, plus the case law. The Act and its amendment are implemented through employment tribunals, which may call for reports from 'independent experts' to undertake a job evaluation study.

Article 119

Article 119 of the Treaty of Rome prohibits any discrimination with regard to pay between men and women, whatever the system which gave rise to such discrimination. This was supplemented by the Equal Pay Directive 1975, which is designed to facilitate the practical application of the principle of equal pay. It has been invoked in some key cases, for example, *Barber* v *Guardian Royal Exchange Assurance Group* in which the European Court of Justice held that occupational pensions under a contracted-out pensions scheme constitute 'pay' under Article 119 and so must be offered to men and women on equal terms.

The Equal Pay Act 1970

Under the Act, which came into force in 1975, an employee in the UK is entitled to claim pay equal to that of an employee of the opposite sex in the same employing organisation in only two situations:

• where they are doing the same or broadly similar work, 'like work'

- where the work they do is rated equivalent under a job evaluation scheme.

The basis of the Act is that every contract of employment is deemed to contain an equality clause which is triggered in either situation. The equality clause modifies any terms in a woman's contract which are less favourable than those of a male comparator. Thus, if a woman is contractually paid less than a man doing the same work, she is nonetheless entitled to the same rate of pay.

The three important points to note about the original Act are that:

- Because it was confined to like work and work rated as equivalent, the scope of comparison was fairly narrow.

- It did not make job evaluation compulsory, but did establish the important point (or made the important assumption) that where job evaluation did exist and valued two jobs equally there was a *prima facie* entitlement to equal pay.

- The Act recognised that a job evaluation scheme could be discriminatory if it set 'different values for men and women on the same demand under any heading'. It gave effort, skill and decision-making as examples of headings.

However, the European Commission's Equal Pay Directive 1975 stated that the principle of equal pay should be applied to work of equal value. The Commission successfully argued before the European Court of Justice in 1982 that the UK had failed to implement the directive because the Equal Pay Act enabled individuals to obtain equal pay for work of equal value only where their employer had implemented job evaluation. As a result the UK government had to introduce the 1983 Equal Pay (Amendment) Regulations of the Act, which came into force in 1984. These are often referred to as the equal-value regulations.

The Equal Pay (Amendment) Regulations 1983
Under this equal-value amendment women are entitled to the same pay as men (and vice versa) where the work is of equal value 'in terms of the demands made on a worker under various headings, for instance, effort, skill, decision'.

This removed the barrier built into the Act which had prevented women from claiming equal pay where they were employed in women's jobs and no men were employed in the same work. Now any woman can claim equal pay with any man and vice versa, subject to the rules about being in the same employment. Equal-value claims can now be brought even if there have been no job evaluation arrangements, although the existence of a non-discriminatory job evaluation which has been applied properly to indicate that the jobs in question are not of equal value can be a defence in an equal-value case.

The amendment also provided for the assignment of 'independent experts' by employment tribunals to assess equality of value between claimant and comparator under such headings as effort, skill and decision-making without regard to the cost or the industrial relations consequences of a successful claim.

Equal-value claims can be made across sites and across employers within an umbrella organisation, with potentially far-reaching consequences, provided applicant and comparator are deemed to be 'in the same employment'. This happens when they have common terms and conditions of employment. In *Leverton* v *Clwyd County Council* (1989) the House of Lords held that it was sufficient for applicants to be covered by the same 'Purple Book' agreement, despite differences in their individual terms and conditions.

The material factor defence

If the employer can show that the difference in pay is due to a material factor, the claim may be rejected even when the jobs have been shown to be of equal value. The term 'material' means significant and relevant. The purpose of the material factor defence is to limit the right to equal pay to situations where the difference in pay is due to discrimination which cannot be justified by the employer.

The following factors have been held in case law to justify a difference in pay, but in each case it is a question of fact for the tribunal as to whether the factor is 'material' and whether the difference in pay is due to that factor.

- market forces – In *Enderby* v *Frenchay Health Authority* (1993) the European Court of Justice ruled that 'the state of the employment market, which may lead an employer to increase the pay of a particular job in order to attract candidates, may constitute an objectively justified ground' for a difference in pay. But tribunals will want clear evidence that a market-forces material factor defence is based on 'objectively justified grounds', bearing in mind that the labour market generally discriminates against women. They may view with suspicion evidence gleaned only from published surveys which they may hold to be inherently discriminatory because they simply represent the status quo.

- red-circling (cf *Snoxell* v *Vauxhall Motors Ltd* 1977) – This occurs when an employee's job is downgraded but the employee's pay is not reduced. The protection may not last indefinitely. A tribunal might expect that the pay of the red-circled employee would be frozen until the pay of other employees in the same grade catches up (cf *Outlook Supplies Ltd* v *Parry* 1978).

Employers cannot defend equal-value cases on the grounds of the cost of implementation or the effect a decision could have on industrial relations, and part-time working *per se* cannot provide a defence to a claim. Employers will find it difficult to defend a case unless they use an analytical evaluation scheme. In *Bromley* v *Quick* (1988) the Court of Appeal ruled that a job evaluation system can provide a defence only if it is analytical in nature. The employer must demonstrate the absence of sex bias in the job evaluation scheme, and jobs will be held to be covered by a job evaluation scheme only if they have been fully evaluated using the scheme's factors. Slotting whole jobs against benchmarks is insufficient.

OTHER EQUAL-VALUE ISSUES

Other equal-value issues which have been dealt with by case law include the following.

Transparency

In what is usually referred to under an abbreviated form as the 'Danfoss' case, the European Court of Justice in 1989 ruled that:

> The Equal Pay Directive must be interpreted as meaning that when an undertaking applies a pay system which is characterised by a total lack of transparency, the burden of proof is on the employer to show that his [sic] pay practice is not discriminating where a female worker has established, by comparison with a relatively large number of employees, that the average pay of female workers is lower than that of male workers.

The number of comparators

In the case of *Pickstone* v *Freemans* (1988) the House of Lords ruled that females were not precluded from claiming equal pay for work of equal value with higher-paid men performing different work just because there were a small number of men doing the same work as themselves.

The basis of comparison

The case of *Hayward* v *Cammell Laird* (1988) concerned Julie Hayward, who was a cook in her employer's canteen and who claimed equal pay with a joiner, a painter and an insulation engineer. Following an independent expert's report the tribunal ruled that her work was of value equal to that of the comparators' and should be paid at the same rate. Some of Julie Hayward's terms and conditions of employment other than pay were more favourable than those of the comparators and the company argued that they should be taken into account to offset the difference in pay levels. However, the House of Lords ruled that the Act required a comparison of each term of the contract considered in isolation. Julie Hayward was therefore entitled to the same rates of basic and overtime pay as the men, even though the other terms of her contract were more favourable.

Separate bargaining units

In *Enderby* v *Frenchay Health Authority* (1993) the European Court of Justice made another important ruling in this case relating to separate bargaining units, stating that:

> The fact that the rates of pay at issue are decided by collective bargaining processes conducted separately for the professional groups concerned without any discriminating effect within each group, does not preclude a finding of *prima facie* discrimination where the results of these processes show that two groups with the same employer and the same trade union are treated differently.

Otherwise, it would be easy for employers to 'circumvent the principle of equal pay by using separate bargaining processes'.

Employment tribunal procedures in equal-value cases

Unless it is satisfied that there are no reasonable grounds for determining that the work in question is of equal value, an employment tribunal must require an independent expert to prepare a report. This requirement stipulates that the expert must

- evaluate the jobs concerned analytically – that is 'in terms of the demands made on that person employed in the work, for instance, under such headings as effort, skill and decision'

- take account of all information supplied and representations which have a bearing on the question

- before reporting, send the parties a written summary of the information and invite representations

- include the representations in the report, together with the conclusion reached on the case and the reason for that conclusion

- take no account of the difference in sex, and at all times act fairly.

The independent expert's task differs in a number of ways from that of someone carrying out a full-blown job evaluation mainly because a conventional job evaluation will aim to establish the relative values of a number of jobs, whereas an independent expert will be concerned with comparative value – comparing the value of a fairly narrow range of jobs. In the case of *Hayes and Quinn* v *Mancunion Community Health Trust and South Manchester Health Authority* 1996, the tribunal was strongly critical of the expert evidence provided by the employer which was based on a proprietary system of job evaluation. It questioned whether the generalised nature of that scheme was appropriate and expressed the view that it was 'preferable to identify factors which arise directly from the job functions being assessed' (which is what independent experts generally attempt to do).

JOB EVALUATION AND EQUAL VALUE

The original legislation and subsequent case law clearly state that the existence of an analytical and non-discriminatory job evaluation scheme which is applied to all the parties, between whom comparisons can be made, provides a good defence against equal-value claims. But job evaluation is often attacked because it does no more than reproduce existing hierarchies and, therefore, inequalities.

Job evaluation as a perpetuator of existing hierarchies

Michael Rubinstein (1992) has pointed out that from the management standpoint there is one overriding criterion of whether a particular job evaluation scheme is successful, and that is acceptability. The results of the scheme must be acceptable to those covered by it and those responsible for its administration. It is hardly surprising, then, he argued, that what is seen by the majority as acceptable or fair will usually be that which has the effect of establishing a rank order which is very similar to the existing pay structure.

It is certainly the case that any whole-job-ranking exercise based on 'felt-fair' judgements is likely to do no more than reproduce the existing hierarchy. Indeed, from the point of view of equal pay the felt-fair principle will tend to re-endorse management's preconceptions if it is they who make the judgement on whether or not a rank order or grading is fair. And it is worth remembering that decisions on grade structures are often made by management alone after a joint management/employee panel has completed the job evaluation exercise.

Another factor which may lead to the perpetuation of the existing hierarchy is the selection of benchmark jobs. Traditional job evaluation practice requires that benchmark jobs should represent the various levels in the pay structure. In other words, as McNally and Shimmin (1988) suggest:

> The original rank order of the jobs is reproduced by the reaffirmation of the status of these key posts. The remaining jobs are then grouped around the benchmark jobs and, with the exception of a small number which are regraded, the 'new' job hierarchy takes on an appearance which, to all intents and purposes, is identical to the old.

Perhaps this traditional approach is less common nowadays, but if it is followed trade unionists may suspect that once selected as benchmarks, the jobs concerned will not be regraded as a result of the job evaluation exercise. This could be because employers would not want a 'knock-on' effect to disturb the grading and therefore the pay levels of non-benchmark jobs. Thus, it is argued, benchmarks will help to perpetuate the existing hierarchy and differentials.

Is gender bias in job evaluation inevitable?

Sue Hastings (1989) believes that 'there is no such thing as a non-discriminatory job evaluation scheme' but then goes on to say that it is possible to identify the obvious sources of discrimination and the associated risks. Arvey (1986) comments that 'Because many of the procedures involved in job evaluation are inherently subjective, these practices have been suspect for being biased and discriminatory against jobs held predominately by females.'

Gender bias can exist in the components of the scheme (the choice of factors and their weighting), and this is the discriminatory aspect of job evaluation which has been given most attention by the Equal Opportunities Commission and trade unionists, possibly because some employers are introducing job evaluation schemes solely as a means of avoiding equal-value problems. As Sue Hastings (1989) remarks: 'The present state of equal pay legislation is such that an employer introducing a job evaluation scheme covering all potential "equal value" applicants and comparators is effectively protecting itself against "equal value" claims.' However, it should be remembered that it is not only the scheme itself which can discriminate but also the way in which the scheme is applied. In other words, the process of job evaluation can be discriminatory as well as the system used.

Gender bias does exist in society and therefore it is reasonable to suppose that it can be present within the organisations in that society. It can be argued that because people are subjective the technique must also be subjective. And subjective judgements in a climate where gender bias exists may well be discriminatory.

Achieving gender neutrality

The issues raised above suggest that if an organisation is determined to achieve gender neutrality and end discrimination it should not be obsessive about equal-value law. It should instead concentrate on the evaluation scheme it is developing and the processes used to implement it. These processes go beyond merely establishing internal relativities – they extend to the key decisions made on grade structures and the relationship between internal rates of pay and market rates. The rest of this chapter examines the issues concerning discrimination in job evaluation and what organisations can do to achieve gender neutrality.

DISCRIMINATION IN JOB EVALUATION

Discrimination in job evaluation starts with the design of the scheme, and as the Trade Union Research Unit (Hastings, 1991) noted:

> It is the Unit's view that most discrimination, and the most serious forms of discrimination because they are the most difficult to identify and the least easy to do anything about, occur in the design of the scheme. The reason for this is simple. A job evaluation scheme will achieve the aims, broadly speaking, of those who design it. If those aims are directly discriminatory (to make sure that women's jobs remain at the bottom of the structure) or indirectly discriminatory (to replicate the existing hierarchy), then they will have been achieved through the scheme's structure.

Clearly, the first thing to do when attempting to eliminate discrimination is to look at the scheme itself. But as noted earlier, the way in which the scheme is implemented can discriminate, especially when organisations simply install off-the-shelf schemes which appear to be non-discriminatory, and then proceed to allow grading and pay decisions to be made which continue to be gender-biased. Both these issues need to be considered.

How job evaluation schemes themselves can discriminate against women

The ways in which job evaluation schemes can discriminate against women as described by Sue Hastings (1991, 1992) are considered below.

Type of scheme
If the scheme is non-analytical (a whole-job ranking or classification scheme) it may simply replicate existing views on job demands which may be biased against women.

Appropriateness
A scheme will be non-discriminatory only if it takes account of the significant features of all the jobs it covers. A scheme designed for a different type of organisation or area of work may fail to do so.

Choice of factors
Examples of discriminatory and non-discriminatory job factors provided by the Equal Opportunities Commission (1985) are given in Tables 13 and 14.

Number of factors
Conventional wisdom has dictated that the number of factors must be kept to a minimum to avoid duplication and complexity. It was, and still is, argued that the same results can be obtained with a smaller as with a larger set of factors.

The impact of equal value means that more factors may be needed than in a traditional scheme in order to cover all the significant features of both men's and women's jobs. The number of factors required will depend on the number of jobs to be covered. A scheme for jobs of a similar structure or type will need a smaller number of factors than one

Table 13 Examples of discriminatory job factors

Factors	Maintenance fitter	Company nurse
Skill		
experience in job	10	1
training	5	7
Responsibility		
for money	0	0
for equipment and machinery	8	3
for safety	3	6
for work done by others	3	0
Effort		
lifting requirement	4	2
strength required	7	2
sustained physical effort	5	1
Conditions		
physical environment	6	0
working position	6	0
hazards	7	0
Total	64	22

Note: Each factor is scored on a scale from 1 to 10. For the sake of simplicity no weights have been applied.

Table 14 Examples of non–discriminary job factors

Factors	Maintenance fitter	Company nurse
Basic knowledge	6	8
Complexity of task	6	7
Training	5	7
Responsibility		
for people	3	8
for materials and equipment	8	5
Mental effort	5	6
Visual attention	6	6
Physical activity	8	5
Working conditions	6	1
Total	53	53

Note: Each factor is scored on a scale from 1 to 10. For the sake of simplicity no weights have been applied.

covering a whole organisation. Sue Hastings suggests that six to 12 factors may be sufficient if a limited range of jobs have to be covered, while up to 20 may be necessary in a large organisation where a wide range of jobs, functions and services need to be catered for. Attempting to cover all the jobs in an organisation with a multiplicity of factors can, however, be difficult and confusing. There is a real danger of duplication, and the time taken to analyse and evaluate jobs will increase considerably.

Factor measurement
Particular care needs to be exercised with the definition of levels for skills, knowledge and experience factors. Discrimination can be introduced if some sorts of qualifications are assumed to be of a higher level than others. This could produce an arbitrary hierarchy

where, for example, the questionable assumption may be built in that a formal qualification leading to a certain level of applied knowledge and skill is inherently better than the same level of knowledge and skills acquired through some combination of education, training and experience.

The scoring system may also result in discrimination if the size of the steps simply reinforces the existing hierarchy, making it more difficult for women's jobs to be upgraded or to be found equal at the end of the exercise.

Factor weighting
Factor weighting is likely to be discriminatory if it favours factors predominantly related to male jobs (eg physical effort) or to women's jobs (eg manual dexterity). Some form of balance must be achieved between any factors which may favour either men or women. Weighting based on regression techniques linked to 'felt-fair' rankings may reinforce existing differentials and could therefore perpetuate discrimination.

Weighting can be either explicit (the variations between the maximum scores attached to different factors) or implicit (when some factors have more sub-factors than others or where there are different numbers of levels for each factor but each level carries the same number of points).

How the introduction and application of job evaluation can discriminate against women
The introduction and application of job evaluation can discriminate against women in the ways described below.

Job evaluation processes
These may be discriminatory if the job evaluation panels are not fully representative of both men and women. A prejudiced evaluation could result if the sex of the job-holder is identified.

Job analysis and job descriptions
Job analysis may not take account of all the features of both men's and women's jobs. Gender bias can exist in the job analysis phase of job evaluation in the following ways:

* Job analysts may perceive and recall differential information, depending on whether the job involves 'women's work' or whether the work is carried out predominantly by men.

* Job analysts may neglect information more likely to be related to women's work – for example, asking about working conditions that involve considerable physical exertion but neglecting aspects of work such as sitting still for long periods of time, visual strain, etc.

* Job analysis information may be 'pre-selected' by questionnaires or job inventories which are in themselves biased.

These sort of risks can best be reduced by extensive training of job analysts in the system and in awareness of how gender bias occurs.

Computer-assisted job evaluation
Computer-assisted job evaluation systems could be held to be

discriminatory if they are based on biased questionnaires or 'rules' in terms of factors, weightings and the conversion of questionnaire responses to evaluation scores. These points should be checked for gender bias before the system is implemented (it may be more difficult to change it later). There is also the question of transparency – how much is revealed or can be revealed about what goes on inside the black box? Such systems have not yet been tested in an equal-value case.

Reducing the danger of discrimination in a job evaluation scheme

To eliminate or at least reduce the risk of discrimination it is necessary to ensure that:

- The scheme is appropriate to the jobs it covers.

- A comprehensive and non-discriminatory factor plan is developed – attention has to be paid to the choice and definition of factors and factor weighting, and the factors should not omit any important job demands.

- The factor and level definitions are precise and unambiguous.

- There is a rationale for the weightings which reflect the importance of the job demands to the organisation as a whole and do not perpetuate the existing hierarchy.

- Weightings of factors do not discriminate against men or women.

- Job descriptions are specific and reliable (generic job descriptions are not relied upon) and the job-holder is involved in writing them.

- Job titles are not gender-based and the sex of the job-holder is not revealed.

- Comprehensive and unbiased questionnaires are used.

- Job analysts are given proper training in conducting job analyses and producing fair job descriptions, which should include bias-awareness training.

- A proper proportion of female as well as male employees are involved in the development of the scheme, as are also trade union representatives if the organisation is unionised. (Involvement should extend to the choice of the scheme, the design of the factor plan, job analysis, the actual process of evaluation and the design of grade structures.)

- A proper proportion of female as well as male employees (and trade union representatives) are involved in the operation of the scheme through job evaluation panels or by some other joint process of evaluation in which employees and their representatives take part.

- Appeal processes are created, using bodies with both management and employee representatives.

- The aims, methods of working and impact of job evaluation is explained to all employees (not just the members of the working party or panel).

- Care is taken over the selection and use of benchmark jobs so that they are fully representative of both men's and women's jobs and the process does not simply reproduce the existing hierarchy.

DISCRIMINATORY PAY STRUCTURES

Pay structures can be discriminatory in the following ways:

- The grade boundary lines in a multi-graded structure are based purely on judgements which may simply reinforce existing inequalities.

- Generic job descriptions take insufficient account of significant differences between male and female roles.

- An analytical job evaluation scheme is not used to define grades or allocate jobs to grades – whole jobs are slotted into a graded, broad-banded or job family structure by a process of internal benchmarking which could simply perpetuate existing discrimination.

- Benchmark jobs do not fairly represent the distribution of male and female jobs.

- Market-related pay levels and differentials reproduce marketplace gender discrimination and do not take account of internal relativities.

Drawing grade lines

As mentioned above, the process of drawing grade lines between jobs in a graded pay structure is largely judgemental and can give rise to discrimination. The Equal Opportunities Commission suggests that boundary lines should be drawn when a point-factor evaluation scheme is used wherever there is a significant gap in the distribution of scores between job clusters. This sounds like good advice and follows the precepts of most standard texts on job evaluation. What the EOC fails to appreciate, however, is that scattergrams of points scores do not always arrange themselves with convenient gaps. It may be impossible to avoid boundary lines which dissect clusters of jobs, and there will inevitably be problems of deciding which jobs should fall on either side. This problem may be alleviated in a broad-banded system because there will not be so many boundaries. In such systems it may therefore be easier to draw the lines where there are convenient gaps, although broad-banded structures may create other problems, as suggested below.

Broad-banded structures

Broad-banded structures can facilitate flexibility and reduce the problem of grade drift so often encountered with more narrowly-banded structures. But they may discriminate indirectly if they rely entirely on 'anchoring' zones by reference to market rates and if they slot jobs into bands by means of whole-job comparisons. The former approach could be attacked from an equal-value point of view unless 'objectively justified' grounds can be produced, and that may not be easy. It would probably be insufficient to rely on published pay surveys or advertised rates. The latter approach can form the basis of an equal-value claim on the grounds that an analytical job evaluation scheme has not been used to grade all the jobs. Simply defining the grade boundaries in points terms and then slotting jobs into the bands may not be enough.

Competence-related structures

If these are designed by reference to an analytical competence-related job evaluation scheme (ie one in which competence headings are used as factors), they will not be discriminatory *per se*. Discrimination will arise only if there is gender bias in the choice of the competence-related factors. A job family structure which uses competence levels to define the bands or levels within job families could, however, be regarded as discriminatory, as discussed below.

Job family structures

Whether or not job family structures are competence-related, there are three ways in which they may be found discriminatory:

- if the levels are defined as in a job classification scheme – ie evaluation is non-analytical, being conducted by slotting whole jobs into the job family levels

- if there is no 'read-across' by means of an analytical evaluation process between job families

- if they are in effect 'market groups' containing jobs which it is believed because of market forces need to be paid higher than is indicated by the internal evaluation process – market-rate differentials of this nature may need to be 'objectively justified'.

Job families have not yet been tested as such in an equal-value case but the decision of the European Court of Justice in *Enderby* v *Frenchay Health Authority* (1993) indicates that any differences in average earnings between job families of different predominant gender would have to be objectively justified by the employer.

Generic role definitions

The use of generic role definitions could be discriminatory if insufficient account is taken of the particular characteristics of individual roles.

Implementation of the pay structure

Following the creation of a new grade and pay structure by means of job evaluation and market pricing, employees may have to be regraded or placed in a radically redesigned grade structure.

It is generally regarded as good and fair practice not to reduce the pay of anyone whose job is overgraded following evaluation. In this situation, employees are normally 'personally protected' or 'red-circled' – in other words, their rate of pay is frozen until it falls within the proper grade, following general increases in the pay brackets for grades. But in order to cut the costs of implementing the new structure, organisations may phase the increases required to bring undergraded employees up to the level of pay appropriate to their new grade. This 'green-circling' procedure could be held to be discriminatory if the preponderance of red-circled employees were men and most if not all the employees whose pay increases were being phased were women. The practice of simply transferring employees into their new grade on their existing level of pay, even where the job evaluation has indicated that their jobs are worth more, may be regarded as discriminatory if it mainly affects women and they are still underpaid in comparison with men whose jobs have been evaluated at the same level.

DESIGNING NON-DISCRIMINATORY PAY STRUCTURES

To design a non-discriminatory pay structure, it is necessary to ensure that:

- 'Read-across' mechanisms are provided between different job families and occupational groups if they are not all covered by the same plan.

- Great care is taken over grade boundary decisions – the aim should be to avoid placing them between jobs which have been evaluated as virtually indistinguishable, bearing in mind that the problem will be most acute if grade boundaries are placed between traditionally male and female jobs (in any situation where such boundary problems exist it is good practice to re-evaluate the jobs, possibly using a direct 'comparable worth' or equal-value approach which concentrates on the particular jobs).

- Market-rate comparisons are treated with caution to ensure that differentials arising from market forces can be objectively justified.

- Care is taken over the implementation of the pay structure to ensure that female employees (indeed, any employees) are not disadvantaged by the methods used to adjust their pay following regrading.

- A non-discriminatory analytical job evaluation system is used to define grade boundaries and grade jobs.

- Discriminatory job descriptions are not used as a basis for designing and managing the structure.

- Men's jobs or women's jobs do not cluster respectively at the higher and lower levels of the hierarchy.

- Any variation between pay levels for men and women in similarly evaluated jobs (for example, for market-rate reasons) can be objectively justified.

- Red-circling is free of sex bias.

- There are objectively justifiable reasons for any inconsistency in the relation of the grading of jobs in the structure to job evaluation results.

THE EQUAL OPPORTUNITIES COMMISSION CODE OF PRACTICE ON EQUAL PAY

In its 1997 Code of Practice, the Equal Opportunities Commission (EOC) states that: 'Sex discrimination in pay occurs primarily because women and men tend to do different jobs or to have different work patterns. As a result it is easy to undervalue the demands of work performed by one sex compared with the demands associated with jobs typically done by the other.'

The EOC recommends that a pay system review should be conducted in the following stages:

1 Analyse the pay system to produce a breakdown of all employees, covering for example sex, job, whether full- or part-time, rates of pay, benefits and allowances, and performance ratings.

2 Examine each element of the pay system against the data produced at stage 1.

3 Identify any elements which may be discriminatory.

4 Change discriminatory practices in consultation with employees, trade unions and staff representatives as appropriate.

5 Analyse the likely impact of proposed changes.

6 Give equal pay to current employees.

7 Set up a system for regularly monitoring pay practice.

8 Draw up and publish an equal-pay policy which should set out clear objectives which enable priorities for action to be identified and an effective programme to achieve them to be implemented.

MINIMISING OTHER TYPES OF DISCRIMINATION

Eliminating unequal pay because of racial discrimination is more a matter of developing and implementing an equal opportunity policy and operating the evaluation scheme without bias than of the design of the scheme itself. Clearly, segregation and prejudice are the most likely causes of discrimination, and they can be removed only if there is a policy for ensuring equal opportunities in employment, promotion and training and if the policy is underpinned by a continuous programme of education and training.

AUDITING EQUAL PAY

Equal pay audits should be carried out regularly in order to ensure that:

- The job evaluation scheme remains free of bias and properly reflects the type and levels of work.

- New jobs are properly evaluated and graded without bias.

- Evaluations are made purely on job content without reference to the sex of job-holders or historical position in the pecking order.

- Evaluations are updated to reflect changes in jobs.

- Sex bias has not crept into evaluations and gradings.

- The allocation of jobs to grades or bands does not indicate bias.

- Jobs which appear to be paid unequally for work of equal value are identified and action taken to remove unjustified inequalities.

SUMMARY

- Discrimination arises because women tend to be concentrated in different and/or lower-paid jobs, women have fewer training opportunities, women are more likely to be employed in low-paid part-time jobs, inherent gender bias exists, and the value of women's work has been under-recognised.

• The Equal Pay Act 1970 provides that employees can claim equal pay to that of employees of the opposite sex where:

   – they are doing like work: ie the same or broadly similar work

   – they are doing work which is rated as equivalent under a job evaluation scheme.

• The Equal Pay (Amendment) Regulations 1983 (the equal-value amendment) provided that women are entitled to the same pay as men where the work is of equal value in terms of the demands made on the worker.

• The essential features of the equal-value amendment are that:

   – it enables *any* women to claim equal pay with *any* man, and vice versa, if they are in the same employment. In contrast, the Equal Pay Act prevented women from claiming equal pay if they were employed in women's work and no men were employed in the same work

   – it enables equal-value claims to be made even if there are no job evaluation arrangements

   – in an equal-value case held before an employment tribunal the existence of a non-discriminatory analytical evaluation scheme can be used as evidence that equal pay for work of equal value does exist (cf *Bromley* v *Quick*, 1988)

   – the 'material factor' defence means that an equal-value claim can be rejected if the employer can show that the difference in pay is due to a material (ie significant and relevant) factor, even when the jobs have been shown to be of equal value (the leading cases referring to the material factor defence so far have been *Enderby* v *Frenchay Health Authority,* 1993 and *Snoxell* v *Vauxhall Motors,* 1977) – the case of *Hayward* v *Cammell Laird* (1988) defined the basis of comparison.

• The amendment also provided for the assignment of 'independent experts' by employment tribunals to assess equality of value between claimant and comparator under such headings as effort, skill and decision-making.

• Discrimination in job evaluation can take place because of the type of scheme, an inappropriate scheme, the use of discriminatory factors or discriminatory weightings, biased definitions of factors and levels, and the way in which it is introduced and managed.

• To reduce the risk of discrimination it is necessary to ensure that: the scheme is appropriate to the jobs it covers, a comprehensive and non-discriminatory factor plan is developed with precise factor definitions, weightings do not discriminate, job descriptions are reliable, and care is taken over the selection and use of benchmark jobs so that they are fully representative of both men's and women's jobs and the process does not simply reproduce the existing hierarchy. And there is no discrimination in the involvement of women or men in the scheme.

• Pay structures can be discriminatory when: the grade boundary lines in a multi-graded structure are based purely on judgements which may simply reinforce existing inequalities, generic job descriptions take insufficient account of significant differences between male and female roles, an analytical job evaluation scheme is not used to define grades or allocate jobs to grades, benchmark jobs do not fairly represent the distribution of male and female jobs, market-related pay levels and differentials reproduce marketplace gender discrimination and do not take account of internal relativities.

• To design a non-discriminatory pay structure it is necessary to ensure that: great care is taken over grade boundary decisions, market-rate comparisons are treated with caution to ensure that differentials arising from market forces can be objectively justified, care is taken to ensure that female employees (indeed, any employees) are not disadvantaged by the methods used to adjust their pay following re-grading, a non-discriminatory analytical job evaluation system is used to define grade boundaries and grade jobs, discriminatory job descriptions are not used, men's jobs or women's jobs do not cluster higher up or lower down the hierarchy, and there are objectively justifiable reasons for any inconsistency in the relation of the grading of jobs in the structure to job evaluation results.

• Equal-pay audits should be carried out regularly in order to ensure that bias does not exist in the operation of job evaluation or the pay structure.

FURTHER READING

Jill Rubery's pamphlet for the Equal Opportunities Commission (1992) provides the best analysis of the background to discrimination. The *Equal Opportunities Review* provides useful updates on the legislation and case law. The publications of the Equal Opportunities Commission and the Trade Union Research Unit provide the best guidance on how to avoid discrimination.

13 Conducting pay and benefit surveys

Pay and benefit surveys collect information on pay (market rates) and employee benefit provisions in other organisations to provide guidance on levels of pay and benefits within the organisation in line with its policies on reward comparabilities.

On completing the chapter the reader should be able to contribute to the conduct of a local or national pay and benefit survey on the basis of an understanding of the concept of a market rate in local and national labour markets and of methods of obtaining, interpreting and using market-rate data as a basis for market pricing decisions.

THE OBJECTIVES OF PAY AND BENEFIT SURVEYS

The objectives of pay and benefit surveys are to provide information which will enable the organisation to:

- maintain a competitive pay and benefit position in relation to the marketplace, thus enabling it to attract and retain people of the quality it needs

- determine levels of pay for individual jobs and pay brackets or scales for pay structure grades

- provide guidance on internal differentials by reference to the differentials in the external labour market

- provide information on any adjustment required to general or individual pay levels by means of pay reviews.

The information is collected from the markets in which the organisation is recruiting new staff or to which existing employees may be tempted to move for more pay. This may mean surveying either the national and regional markets or the local markets or all three. The national and regional labour markets will most likely be for managerial, professional and technical staff while other employees such as clerical and sales staff and manual workers will probably be drawn from the local market, although highly-skilled workers may be recruited nationally or regionally.

Many organisations go in for 'market pricing' – that is, determining internal pay levels by reference to market rates. And in 'broad-banded' structures, as described in Chapter 17, rates of pay are usually 'anchored' by reference to market rates. In these circumstances, and in any organisation that has a policy of competitive pay (which means most organisations), market-rate tracking is a major activity. But, as discussed below, accurate market-rate information may be difficult to obtain.

To achieve these objectives it is necessary to understand:

- the concept of a market rate

- the type of data that can be collected on pay and benefits

- the sources of market-rate data

- methods of presenting and analysing data

- methods of conducting pay and benefit surveys

- how to set up a 'pay club'

- how to use survey data.

THE CONCEPT OF A MARKET RATE

People commonly talk about the market rate for a job as if there were such a thing as the market rate. The concept of a market rate is elusive. As Gomez-Mejia and Balkin (1992) state:

> While the myth persists that the market wage can be accurately and scientifically determined as a single rate, in fact there is a wide range of market pay rates available for each occupation, and the determination of the going rate for a job is a combination of art and science. Thus, the combination of decisions that determine the market wage for a firm leaves room for a great deal of subjectivity due to the many judgements that must enter into these decisions.

No pay survey will ever produce a result which states, unequivocally, the correct rate of pay for a job. In external labour markets there is always a choice of rates. This is because:

- different firms have different policies as to what they need to pay

- individuals in effect have their own market rate, depending on their expertise and ability and the degree to which their talents are unique

- this individual 'market worth' will vary widely and will often be as much a matter of perception as of fact

- larger firms tend to pay more, and rates of pay are higher in some local labour markets than in others.

There are two other factors which compound these problems:

- *Job-matching* – The accuracy of market-rate data depends on the extent to which 'like is compared with like'. Job-matching aims to achieve this but it can be difficult. Simply comparing jobs that have similar titles will be totally misleading. A sales manager in one company will almost always have a different range of responsibilities from one in an adjacent firm. Job-matching can be improved, but without going to a great deal of trouble and expense it is very hard to achieve an accurate and therefore meaningful comparison. (Methods of job-matching are discussed later in this chapter.)

- *Timing* – The information in published surveys, upon which many people rely, is often out of date. Pay levels may have changed and people may have moved in or out since the date of the survey. Estimates can be made of likely movements since the survey took place and these will be more accurate in times of low inflation. But they are still mainly guesswork.

The range between the highest and lowest levels of pay for a job as established by an individual survey can be as much as 50 per cent or more. To overcome this problem a measure of 'central' tendency such as the average or the median will be incorporated in the survey findings and the distribution of rates will be defined in such terms as the 'interquartile range' – the middle 50 per cent of a 100 per cent distribution. (This and other statistical terms used in pay surveys are defined on pages 182–3.)

Considerable differences are to be found between the market-rate figures given by the various published surveys and any other surveys conducted for jobs with similar titles. This difference can be as much as 25 per cent between the average or median rates. It will be greater in surveys of the national labour market. It is often easier to obtain fairly consistent data for the local labour market.

The result is that there will be a range of rates to choose from, especially for managerial, professional and technical jobs in the national labour market. It is therefore necessary to estimate what may be called a 'derived market rate' for such jobs. The source of this estimate is the various data available, and what is in effect a weighted average is calculated to arrive at a judgement on the rate to be used. The weighting is based on assessments of the relative accuracy and relevance of the various sources of market-rate information. This means committing the statistical sin of averaging averages, but there is no alternative.

However, the judgements will be more accurate if they are based on the systematic analysis of valid and reliable data. This can be achieved by understanding what types of data can be collected, the possible sources of the data, and the methods of presenting and analysing them. These requirements are discussed in the next four sections of this chapter.

TYPES OF DATA

Data on pay and benefits can be obtained and analysed under the following headings:

- *base or basic pay* before deducting National Insurance, income tax and pension contributions – it includes any incremental or performance payments or special allowances which have been consolidated into the base salary but it excludes additional incentive or bonus earnings, the value of employee benefits, overtime and shift or other unconsolidated allowances; location allowances (eg a London allowance) may or may not be consolidated and it is necessary to establish which is the case

- *variable pay* in the form of payments under incentive or bonus schemes which are not part of basic pay, but excluding special allowances

- *total earnings* – the sum of the basic pay and variable incentive or bonus payments over the previous 12 months: the value of employee benefits and special allowances is excluded

- *employee benefits* – entitlement to benefits such as pensions, company cars, petrol for private use, mortgage assistance, loans, permanent health insurance, medical insurance, health screening, relocation packages, holidays and other forms of leave, sick pay, etc

- *other allowances* – cash payments made in special circumstances such as shift or night work, call-outs, car mileage allowances and location allowances (if they are not consolidated)

- *total remuneration* – the total value of all cash payments and benefits received by employees: this figure is seldom collected in surveys because the valuation of benefits depends on a number of assumptions which are difficult to apply consistently in different organisations

- *pay scales* – the pay scales for specified jobs, as distinct from the actual base pay or earnings of job-holders: this information is of interest in making general comparisons but it does not indicate actual market rates

- *pay movements* – percentage increases in levels of pay since the last survey: this figure may be misleading if it is based on overall averages, because the population in the survey companies will have changed; surveys more rarely measure the difference between the pay levels of people who remain with the organisation to give an indication of average increases which may arise because of merit payments or promotion (the figure is not particularly useful if these factors are not separated)

- *pay increases* – details of across-the-board cost-of-living or market-rate increases, or average merit or performance-related pay increases.

SOURCES OF DATA

The main sources of data on pay and benefits are described below. The criteria governing choice are considered at the end of the section.

General national and regional published surveys

General published surveys contain data on a variety of occupations (often restricted to managerial and professional jobs), usually for the whole of the UK, and often analysed by regions. The data include details of base salary and total earnings levels at a given date, with some information on the provision of employee benefits. Pay movements may also be included.

The data are presented by job title and function. There is usually some indication of the level of the job and sometimes a brief description of typical responsibilities. The data may be analysed in terms of organisation size (sales turnover or number of employees), location and industry sector.

General surveys give an overall picture of pay levels in the national and regional labour markets but their value is diminished by the problems of job-matching. It is difficult to be certain that either the surveys or the analyst are comparing like with like. This difficulty, and differences in sampling, explain why data on seemingly similar jobs may vary widely between the surveys. Variations are also caused because the surveys may have been conducted on different dates and some time ago.

General survey information may not be wholly reliable, although it at least gives a general picture of pay levels. But if a comprehensive national or regional survey is being carried out it is best to consult more than one source.

General national and regional surveys include those published by Reward, Monks Publications and PE International.

General local published surveys

Some organisations such as locally-based management consultants conduct and publish surveys of the local labour market, covering office and manual occupations as well as managerial and professional jobs.

Such surveys can usefully provide relevant information for the market in which an organisation is doing most of its recruiting. It is necessary, however, to ensure that the survey includes data from a reasonable number of organisations (no fewer than 20 or so), and that it has been conducted professionally, with some care to ensure an acceptable level of job-matching.

Management consultants' databases

The larger management consultancy firms, especially those specialising in pay, maintain their own database of pay levels which can be accessed by clients or, at a cost, by non-clients. Hay Management Consultants, for example, also provide the clients who use the Hay job evaluation system with market-rate data where job-matching is achieved through the use of a common evaluation process by survey contributors.

Sector surveys

Sector surveys can produce useful information on a sector where pay levels and occupations may be distinct from those in other sectors. For example, in the voluntary sector special surveys are conducted by Charity Recruitment and Reward.

Industrial surveys

Industrial surveys can be conducted by employers and trade associations on jobs specific to their industry for which other data may not be available. They are a useful source of industry job-specific data, and job-matching is often quite precise. But they may be conducted only occasionally, and the results are often made available only to participating companies.

Consultants may also publish industrial surveys. For example, Towers Perrin survey executive pay in the electronics industry and Watson Wyatt produce data on the insurance industry and investment staff.

Occupational surveys

Occupational surveys obtain information on the pay of members of professional institutions such as chartered accountants and specific categories of people such as computer specialists, sales or office staff. The data from professional institutions are often confined to pay in relation to age, qualifications and membership status rather than to jobs. But they give useful information on general levels of salary for professional people.

Occupational surveys may be conducted by consultants or professional firms. William M. Mercer, for example, publishes data on company secretaries and legal staff and facility management.

A survey conducted by the organisation

The organisation can conduct its own survey or arrange for a firm of management consultants to conduct one on its behalf. This may be a national, regional or sector survey, or it may be confined to the local labour market. It could cover a range of occupations or focus on particular jobs.

Such surveys can be as sophisticated as those conducted by the organisations which publish general surveys, or they can be relatively simple. They have the advantage of being able to concentrate on the jobs in which the organisations are particularly interested. They can also seek information from competitor organisations in the national or local labour market who may be quite willing to co-operate as long as they think the benefit of the extra information with which they are provided on a reciprocal basis justifies the time and effort in replying to a survey questionnaire. Methods of conducting special surveys are described later in this chapter.

Pay club surveys

Pay clubs are groups of organisations which exchange information about levels of pay and benefits on a regular basis. They often operate within a particular industry or sector, or locally, and, if properly run, they can provide well-matched and therefore reliable data. Methods of setting up and running pay clubs are discussed later in this chapter.

Published data in journals

Up-to-date company and national pay data can be obtained from:

- Incomes Data Services and IRS *Employment Review* (Pay and Benefits Section) which monitor pay settlements and publish details of agreements: details of pay structures and trends in individual companies are also supplied

- the government's Labour Force Survey and New Earnings Survey for information on trends

- the Business News sections of the *Financial Times* and other top newspapers.

Job advertisements

A lot of people, especially line managers, rely on job advertisements in the national and local press or in specialist journals such as *Marketing Week* (for product managers), *Accountancy UK* and *People Management*.

Advertisements provide some indication of levels of pay but they should be treated with caution, especially in the case of managerial and professional jobs advertised nationally. Differences in the levels of responsibility and scope of jobs with the same job title can be considerable, and levels of pay vary accordingly. The brief descriptions of the jobs are often full of hyperbole and may be misleading. This problem is not so acute for the clerical, sales and manual workers who are advertised for in local papers.

Nevertheless, even for managerial and professional jobs, advertisements provide an additional source of information which cannot be ignored. Remember that employees will also be looking at them and will be drawing their own conclusions about what they are worth in the marketplace.

Recruitment consultants and agencies
Recruitment consultants and agencies should have a good 'feel' for levels of pay in the posts they are helping to fill. They obtain data from employers and from applications. Executive search consultants are particularly knowledgeable about rates of pay in the senior management job market.

Analysis of recruitment data
It is sometimes possible to get ancillary data about levels of pay by analysing information obtained from recruitment campaigns. Data provided in CVs, if any, may be suspect, but some indication of what is the going rate can be obtained by establishing how much money is required to attract a particular type and level of applicant.

Other market intelligence
Data on market rates can be obtained from informal contacts or networks. Information can usefully be exchanged on rates of pay for specific jobs, increases in pay levels, performance or merit pay increases, and data obtained from separate market rate surveys. Building up and maintaining an informal or semi-formal network can be very helpful, especially if it consists of employers or personnel managers who are interested in the local labour market.

Criteria
A check on the rate for a job in local labour markets can be carried out simply by ringing round or writing to a few local organisations, studying advertisements in the local paper and checking with an agency or two. A more comprehensive local labour market study may mean conducting a much wider-ranging postal survey and, possibly, joining or forming a pay club.

To obtain information on national, regional, sector or occupational rates of pay and benefits means considering the use of the published general surveys and any other specialist surveys. It is always advisable to obtain data from more than one published source and to supplement them by information from other sources – journals, market intelligence and even advertisements, as long as the latter are treated with caution.

Information on what published surveys are available is published every other year by Incomes Data Services in its *Directory of Salary*

Surveys. This summarises what the surveys provide in the shape of jobs covered, sample data, cost and availability, as well as comments on the quality and reliability of the data.

When selecting a published survey the criteria are:

- Does it cover relevant jobs in similar organisations?

- Does it provide the information on pay and benefits required?

- Are there enough participants to provide acceptable comparisons?

- So far as can be judged, is the survey conducted properly in terms of its sampling techniques and the quality of job-matching?

- Is the survey reasonably up to date?

- Are the results well presented?

- Does it provide value for money?

If reliable published information is available which can easily be supplemented from other sources, you may decide to be content with the data thus provided. If more specific data are required, it may be necessary to conduct a special survey. This can be time-consuming and may be costly, especially if outside consultants are brought in to help. A judgement has to be made on whether or not the additional or specific information is worth the effort and expense.

Pay clubs can be a very good source of focused data and it is well worth joining one if it is appropriate and has room for an additional member (entry may be restricted). Consideration can be given to setting up a club if a good network already exists – a special survey could provide the nucleus of the club's membership.

FACTORS THAT AFFECT THE QUALITY OF SURVEY DATA

The main factors that affect the quality of survey data are job-matching, timing, and the importance of matched samples in comparing increases from one survey to the next.

Job-matching

Job-matching aims to ensure that as far as possible like is compared with like. Matching methods in order of increasing reliability are:

- Matching by job title can be completely misleading. Titles convey little of what the job actually entails.

- A brief description of duties and levels of responsibility which is used for matching jobs in many national surveys provides better guidance, but there is still plenty of scope for interpretation and inaccuracy in the matching process.

- Capsule job descriptions which sum up the key characteristics of the jobs to be compared are often used in special surveys and can help to produce a more accurate match. But the descriptions are necessarily general, and fully accurate comparisons are still somewhat elusive (an example is given on p. 187).

- Complete job descriptions should in theory allow for a better fit, but they require time and effort to prepare in a form suitable for pay comparison purposes. Moreover, the organisations with which comparisons are being made (the comparators) may not have equivalent descriptions and will certainly be unwilling to prepare special ones for the survey.

- If a common system of job evaluation is used properly, it can provide the most accurate form of comparison. In the UK surveys are run on this basis by both Hay and Watson Wyatt management consultants. This method can be much more difficult to organise unless a common system of job evaluation is already in use (generally a consultants' scheme, the so-called 'proprietary brands').

Timing of surveys
The data provided by published surveys can soon become out-of-date, although this problem is not so acute in times of low inflation. Some survey firms update their information annually, and one firm (Monks Partnership) has changed from a yearly collection of data to rolling collection – participants provide data at the time of year that is most convenient to them.

It is possible to make some assumptions about movements since the survey date on the basis of trend data available in such publications as the IRS *Employment Review*, but they do not produce a reliable result.

Pay increases over time
Information on trends in pay increases are provided in some published surveys. But they are largely invalid unless they are based on a matched sample – that is, the data are based on comparisons between an identical set of organisations in successive years. Even then the comparisons may be dubious unless they refer to exactly the same job-holders who have remained in the same job. This information does not, however, distinguish between general and individual increases. It is often best to settle for the trend figures provided by journals such as the IRS *Employment Review*.

PRESENTING THE DATA

The pay data from surveys are received in the form of an actual rate if there is only one person in a job or an average figure if there is more than one. The average can be represented as an arithmetic mean or a median as defined below. What has to be done then is to convert the data from each respondent in each job (the data set) into what statisticians call an array. This sets out the data in order of increasing size, thus producing a distribution of the items in the data set from the lowest to the highest average rates for the job. The data are made meaningful for analysis purposes by measuring the position of the average value or the middle of the data set (measures of central tendency – the arithmetic mean or median) or the value which occurs with the greatest frequency in the data set (the mode). These are called measures of location.

It is also helpful to know how the data are spread around the average or middle value. This is discovered through measures of dispersion such as the range, quartiles and deciles.

Measures of location

The *arithmetic mean* or *average* is calculated by adding together all the individual items in the data set (ie the total of all the items of pay-rate information produced by the survey) and dividing by the number of items in the data set (ie the number of rates of pay collected). The problem with the arithmetic mean is that the calculation can be distorted if there are some extremely high or low values in the distribution of data.

The *median* is the value falling in the middle of a distribution or array of data items. Fifty per cent of the reported rates of pay will be equal to or above the median and 50 per cent of the rates will be equal to or below the median. If there is an odd number of values, the median is the middle one. If there is an even number of values the median is obtained by calculating the average of the middle two items. This measure is less influenced by extreme values or by the data's being bunched up at one end or the other (ie skewed). The median is therefore the most frequently-used measure of central tendency in pay surveys, although it is not appropriate when there are fewer than five items.

The *mode* is the value that occurs with the greatest frequency in a set of data. It may not always be in the centre. In pay and benefit surveys the mode is often used to describe benefit provisions where there are not many alternative items. For example, a survey of benefits for sales managers might show that five out of 12 had a 2,000-cc car, three a 2,500-cc car and four a 1,800-cc car. The mode would therefore be 2,000 cc.

Measures of dispersion

Because of the wide range of rates of pay usually contained in a distribution, a measure of central tendency does not convey sufficient information about market rates to use in formulating pay level policies. It is necessary to calculate the amount of dispersion or spread between the pay figures collected in the survey. The measures used are described below.

The *range* extends from the lowest to the highest figures in a distribution – for example £14,000 to £20,000. It may be expressed by the arithmetic difference between those figures – £6,000. The range is a useful measure when the difference is fairly small or when there is a limited number of items (say, fewer than 10). But it is misleading if there are one or two extreme figures at either end of the distribution, which is why upper and lower quartiles are more frequently used when there are sufficient items to justify them (10 or more).

The *upper quartile* is the value in a distribution which a quarter of the values exceed or three-quarters of the values are lower than. In setting their pay policies or 'pay stance' organisations that want to be competitive often express their pay level policy as 'We aim to pay at the upper quartile' or 'Our policy is to pay between the median and the upper quartile.' The term 'upper quartile' also refers to the top 25 per cent of the distribution, and some organisations express their policy as being to pay *in* rather than *at* the upper quartile. Intentions of paying at or in the upper quartile are not always achieved – which is just as well. If everyone set their pay levels at or in the upper quartile, rates of pay would be in a state of perpetual inflation. But if an organisation establishes that its rates of pay are broadly equivalent to the upper quartile market rates, then at least it knows that its levels of pay are competitive for the time being, as long as the figures are reliable.

The *lower quartile* is the value in a distribution which three-quarters of the values exceed and a quarter of the values fall below. Organisations seldom set their sights at the lower quartile when formulating their pay policies but a survey may indicate that they are paying that much below the median rate and they must do something about it if they are to remain competitive, assuming that is what they want and the figures are trustworthy.

The *interquartile range* is a measure of spread between the upper and lower quartiles. It covers the middle 50 per cent of values and is therefore a useful way of expressing dispersion which eliminates extreme figures at each end.

The *upper decile* is the value in a distribution which 10 per cent of the values exceed and 90 per cent fall below.

The *lower decile* is the value which is exceeded by 90 per cent of the distribution, 10 per cent of the values being lower.

Statistical presentation
The findings from pay surveys are usually presented statistically in the format shown in Table 15. The average figure (the arithmetic mean) may also be given and, if the size of the sample is fairly small, the lower and upper deciles may be omitted.

Table 15 Format of pay survey findings (£)

	Lower decile	Lower quartile	Median	Upper quartile	Upper decile
Basic salary	17,800	19,250	22,000	23,050	24,600

Benefits may be shown by an indication of the distribution of benefits amongst the comparator organisations; for example, the employee's contribution to a pension scheme may be set out as in Table 16.

Table 16 Example of the distribution of employee contributions to a pension scheme

Contribution	%
Non-contributory	11
Up to 3%	12
3% to under 5%	16
5% to under 6%	42
6% and over	19

Figure 14 Marketing management: range of market rates

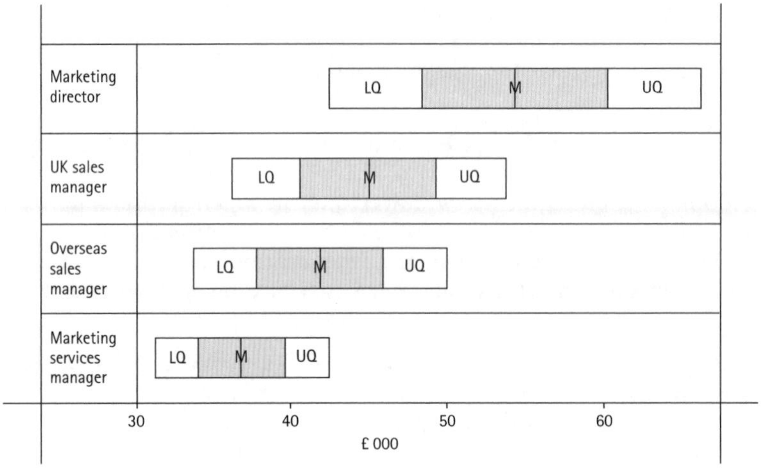

The data may be analysed under the following categories:

- size of organisation in terms of sales turnover or income, and number of employees (levels of pay are usually directly related to size)

- occupations or levels of management

- type of industry or sector

- location (a regional analysis).

Graphical presentation
It can be helpful to illustrate the statistical data with a graphical presentation as illustrated in Figure 14.

CONDUCTING A PAY SURVEY

Pay surveys are carried out by an organisation when it wishes to collect specific information about pay and benefits provided by comparable companies for similar jobs. They may be conducted in the local or national labour markets. The organisation originating the survey can invite other organisations to take part on a reciprocal basis. Information is exchanged confidentially, and if a number of organisations are involved, the originator of the survey sends out a summary of the results to all the participants. In its simplest form a local labour market survey can be conducted by getting on the telephone to the firm down the road and persuading them to exchange information. The more elaborate approach described below is to contact a number of local or national firms by telephone or by letter in order to build up a large sample. Members of the sample are then provided with full details of the jobs and a standard format for their replies, which are returned for analysis to the originator.

The steps in conducting a pay survey are as follows:

• Draw up a list of suitable organisations.

• Invite the organisations to participate.

• Prepare job data and distribute them to the participating organisations.

• Analyse and prepare and distribute a summary of replies.

The list of participating organisations

The organisations invited to take part should be chosen on the basis of their compatibility with regard to industry, size and the sort of jobs they have. Selection will also be governed by estimates of the likelihood of the organisations' agreeing to participate. It is obviously best to start with companies and individuals known to the originator of the survey who can be contacted informally by telephone. Preferably, the organisations selected should be ones in which there are personnel or pay specialists who will be able to obtain and present the information required. It is generally easier to conduct a local market survey because good networks are more likely to exist.

The number of organisations invited will depend on the time available and on whether the survey is to be by post or by personal visit. Personal visits are ideal, but they are time-consuming and the participating organisations may prefer to deal quickly with a return rather than having to entertain a visitor. Clearly, the more sources of information there are, the better. The aim should be to attract at least 20 participants, although in a specialised area it may be necessary to be content with a smaller number. Experience has shown that unless the originating company is fortunate, at least a third of the companies invited to take part will decline on the grounds that they do not reveal pay data, or that they will get nothing out of it, or that they have contributed to enough surveys already. The proportion of refusals can be minimised by adopting an impressively professional approach, but some refusals are inevitable and should be allowed for when drawing up the list of organisations.

Approaching organisations

Known contacts are best but a direct approach often has to be made out of the blue. It can be done by telephone or by letter or both. If time is available, a letter is to be preferred because it can be drafted carefully to be read at leisure and the recipients are not so likely to feel that they are being bounced into taking part. Letters can be ignored and sometimes are, but the risk is minimised if they are worded properly.

In a letter of invitation to a company you do not know, the message to be got across is that:

• a responsible individual is conducting the survey

• the survey will be carried out competently

• the company will obtain relevant and useful information

• the company will not be put to too much trouble

Such a letter might read like this:

Pay Survey

I am writing to ask if you would be prepared to take part in a survey designed to obtain information on the salary levels appropriate for the following appointments in my company:

- marketing director

- UK sales manager

- marketing services manager

- international sales manager.

We are proposing to conduct the survey by exchanging information on the salary ranges and actual salaries paid for positions broadly comparable to those mentioned above with you and with some 20 other companies which we hope will accept our invitation to take part. It is appreciated that exact comparisons will be impossible, but we intend to supply enough detail about the jobs in my company to enable participants to identify any jobs in their companies which will provide valid comparisons.

The details will cover such matters as level of responsibility, number of people controlled, sales turnover, and budgets.

When the replies have been received from all the companies taking part, we will prepare and circulate a summary of the data on salary levels which we believe you would find of considerable interest. It will include details of the remuneration of the job-holders in my company but it would not, of course, be possible to identify from the summary the names of your company or of any of the other companies taking part. Apart from this anonymous summary, the individual details of salary levels would be treated in complete confidence by me.

If you agree to take part, I will send brief descriptions of the jobs and a short questionnaire which you should be able to complete quite quickly. Alternatively, if it is more convenient, you could let me have the answers by telephone, or I could visit you to discuss them.

I should be grateful if you would let me know whether you would like to take part in this survey. I hope that you will feel able to do so on the confidential basis I have described above and on the understanding that you will receive in return a full summary of the results.

Preparing job data and survey forms

The data for distribution to comparator organisations should consist of a capsule job description which identifies the main responsibilities and gives some data indicating the extent of those responsibilities and the place of the job in the organisation. What might be called the critical dimensions of the job could include such items as the number of people controlled, the annual sales turnover or value of output, the value of the assets controlled, and/or the actual volume of output for which the job-holder is responsible. It is best to avoid quoting current salaries at this stage because that will inevitably bias the replies from the survey companies who, when making comparisons, will look for jobs paid the same salary rather than jobs with similar responsibilities. An example of a capsule job description is given below.

Job title: Marketing director

Reports to: Managing director

Direct reports

UK sales manager

Marketing services manager

International sales manager

Dimensions

Annual turnover: £78 million

Staff: 46

Overseas sales agencies: 9

Responsibilities: Develops short- and long-term marketing and sales plans. Directs and controls UK and overseas marketing operations. Identifies new markets and product development opportunities. Contributes as an executive director to the formulation of the strategic objectives and plans of the company.

The forms upon which the comparator organisations are asked to record their replies should be as simple as possible in order to minimise the time and trouble taken in completing them, and to facilitate the analysis and summary of the survey data. An example of a pay survey form is illustrated in Figure 15.

FORMING A PAY CLUB

Pay clubs consist of members who periodically exchange information amongst themselves on the pay and benefits provided for a selected range of jobs. Their advantage is that more accurate job-matching can be achieved and the information is obtained in a standardised form on a regular basis.

Pay clubs should consist of a sufficient number of members, 10 or more, to ensure that a good spread of information is obtained. They can be set up by an existing network, the members of which already exchange information informally and who want to obtain comparative data more systematically. If such a network does not exist already, a company may take it upon itself to form a club. In that case other companies with which the originating organisation has no contacts may have to be invited to join. Such invitations are best made in a letter which sets out how the club will operate – by exchanging information on the remuneration of a sample of jobs – and the benefits that will result from matching jobs more accurately with the help of agreed capsule job descriptions.

It is useful to invite interested parties to a meeting at which agreement

Figure 15 Salary survey form

SALARY SURVEY

SHEET _____

NAME OF ORGANISATION _____

Ref no.	Job Title	Scope + = –	No. job-holders	Actual basic salary			Salary scale			Location allowance £ pa	Bonus £ pa	Date of last review	Car (make or cost)	Pension (emp contrib.)	Holidays pa
				Min.	Median	Max.	Min.	Max.	No. increments						

can be reached on the jobs to be covered, the data to be collected for those jobs, the method of analysis and presentation, and how the club may be run. The originating company may undertake to administer the drawing up of capsule job descriptions and the initial survey. However, the aim would be to get club members interested enough to take turns in administering the survey. They may even agree to contribute to retaining a management consultant to conduct the survey. (Pay clubs involve quite a lot of work and, ideally, it is best to get outside help with the administration.) The methods used to produce and

> Market pricing is a process for determining internal rates and relativities by reference to external levels of pay. What problems might an organisation meet if it adopted this approach, and what would you do about them?

analyse the data and the format of the capsule descriptions can be the same as for individual surveys.

SUMMARY

- Pay and benefit surveys collect information on pay (market rates) and employee benefit provisions in other organisations to provide guidance on levels of pay and benefits within the organisation in line with its policies on reward comparabilities.

- The objectives of pay and benefit surveys are to provide information which will enable the organisation to maintain competitive rates of pay, determine levels of pay for individual jobs and pay ranges, provide guidance on internal differentials, and provide information for pay reviews.

- No pay survey will ever produce a result which states, unequivocally, the correct rate of pay for a job.

- The main sources of data are general national and regional published surveys, general local published surveys, management consultants' databases, sector surveys, industrial surveys, occupational surveys, surveys conducted by the organisation, pay club surveys, published data in journals, advertisements (treat with care) and recruitment consultants and agencies.

- The main factors that affect the quality of survey data are job-matching, timing, and the importance of matched samples in comparing increases from one survey to the next.

- To obtain information on national, regional, sector or occupational rates of pay and benefits, consider the use of the published general surveys and any other specialist surveys.

- It is always advisable to obtain data from more than one published source and to supplement it with information from other sources – journals, market intelligence and even advertisements, as long as the latter are treated with caution.

14 Job and competency analysis

The reliability and validity of many employee-reward processes, including job evaluation, job-matching when conducting in-depth market-rate surveys, and pay structure design, depend largely on the quality of the analysis of jobs, roles and competences which provides the information upon which the evaluation, comparison and design are based. The analysis also provides the data for a number of key personnel processes, including organisation design, human resource planning, recruitment, performance management and training and development. It is therefore an important aid to the creation of integrated personnel plans and practices.

This chapter first defines job, role and competence analysis and the concept of generic roles. It then deals with the techniques of job, role and competence analysis and the preparation of job descriptions and role definitions for job evaluation and job-matching purposes. On completing the chapter the reader will understand how to carry out job and competence analyses and produce job descriptions and role definitions.

DEFINITIONS

Job analysis

Job analysis is the process of collecting, analysing and setting out information about the content of jobs in order to provide the basis for a job description and data for recruitment, training, job evaluation and performance management. Job analysis concentrates on what job-holders are expected to do. The term 'job analysis' is sometimes used generally to cover skills and competence analysis and the analysis of the elements or factors which will be used when evaluating or comparing jobs.

Competence analysis

Competence analysis is concerned with functional analysis to determine work-based competences and behavioural analysis to establish the behavioural dimensions that affect job performance. Work-based or occupational competences refer to expectations of workplace performance and the standards and outputs that people carrying out specified roles are expected to attain. Behavioural or personal competences are the personal characteristics that individuals bring to their work roles.

Job description

A job description sets out the overall objectives of a job, where it fits in the organisational structure, and the key result areas or principal accountabilities of job-holders, or the main tasks they have to carry out. It may include a description of the context within which the job is carried out and an analysis of the job in terms of the criteria used in a job evaluation factor plan.

Role definition

A role definition describes the part to be played by individuals in fulfilling their job requirements. It concentrates on the purpose of the role in the form of outputs (accountabilities), and expands on the information contained in a job description by setting out the competencies required to perform the role satisfactorily.

Generic role definitions

Generic role definitions contain descriptions of typical roles performed by a number of job-holders which are essentially similar, with only minor differences. They specify overall role requirements in terms of the common characteristics of individual roles without spelling out the details of any particular job. A generic role definition therefore fits the role of, say, all team leaders, but the accountabilities of individual job-holders may be defined as outputs – the objectives and standards of performance to be achieved. Generic role definitions may also be used to indicate where any particular role should be placed in a broad-banded or job family pay structure.

Job families

A job family is a group of jobs in which the essential nature and purpose of the work are similar but the work is carried out at different levels.

JOB ANALYSIS TECHNIQUES

Job analysis aims to get the facts about a job from the people in the job, their manager or team leader and their colleagues or fellow team members. It is not a matter of obtaining opinions or making judgements. What goes into a job description definition should be what actually happens and why, not what people would like to think happens.

Job analysis is not easy. The 'facts' about jobs may have to be interpreted because responsibilities are ill-defined or even because there is a difference of opinion between the job-holder and his or her manager about exactly what the job entails. Some people find it difficult to explain what they are doing succinctly, and job analysts can be overwhelmed with detail. This is why some people advocate the use of structured questionnaires or computerised approaches rather than an interview, however structured it may attempt to be.

Job analysis can be conducted by means of interviews or questionnaires or through a computer-assisted job analysis program.

Interviews

The aim of the interview should be to obtain the basic facts about the job:

• the job title

- organisational details – reporting relationships, team membership

- a brief description (one or two sentences) of the overall purpose of the job

- a list of what people in the role are expected to achieve: it may be described as key result areas, principal accountabilities, key tasks, or main responsibilities.

The interview can be structured around questions designed to elicit information about the characteristics of the job and the role played by the job-holder. Where appropriate, these questions should be linked explicitly with the factors included in the evaluation scheme. The questions could cover such aspects of the job as:

Overall purpose
What is the job for?

Main activities and tasks
What does the job holder do?

Objectives
What is the job holder expected to achieve, overall and in respect of each of the key result areas?

Inputs (knowledge and skills)
What does the job-holder need to know and be able to do in such aspects as:

- carrying out specified tasks or administrative routines

- processing data

- planning and organising activities

- leading teams, working as a team member, relating to internal and external customers and clients, networking, persuading people to take a course of action, communicating, taking care of people, handling people problems, and assessing, training and developing employees

- analysing and interpreting data and arranging and presenting complex information in a clear and logical manner which facilitates understanding and decision-making

- using equipment and machines, covering what individuals have to know and being able to do to operate them effectively

- exercising any manual skills, including dexterity and the skills required to carry out particular tasks

- understanding and making use of information technology and computer applications such as integrated or computer-controlled systems (manufacturing, design, financial, administrative, etc), including data-processing, electronic communication systems, managing databases and working in networked data-processing systems and automated offices

- handling numerical and financial data

- understanding company policies, organisation, procedures, technical processes, systems, products, services, customers or clients and sources of supplies

- understanding the business, economic, social and political environment in which the organisation functions?

Process

How is the job-holder expected to behave in achieving his or her objectives and carrying out the various activities required? This may cover such aspects as:

- relating to and co-operating with other people

- teamworking

- exercising leadership qualities

- working flexibly

- achieving high-quality standards (continuous improvement)

- focusing on internal and external customer needs

- responding quickly and efficiently to new challenges

- innovating

- communicating clearly, orally or on paper

- commitment to the organisation and the task.

Outputs

What is the job-holder expected to achieve? This relates specifically to:

- the contribution to achieving the objectives of the team, department or organisation

- the impact on results

- the degree to which influence is exerted over activities and decisions and the effect of that influence

- the specific (quantifiable) targets for profit, sales, output, added value and cost reduction

- deliverables in terms of innovations, implementation of new processes, systems, etc, and satisfactory completion of projects.

Job demands

What does the job require of the job-holder?

- accountability for results

- responsibilities – accountability for managing resources (people, money and plant and equipment) and/or handling confidential information

- the degree to which the work is routine or repetitive

- the extent to which the role involves making independent decisions requiring the exercise of judgement

- the amount of supervision received and the degree of discretion allowed in making decisions (freedom to act)

- the typical problems to be solved and the amount of guidance available when solving the problems

- the complexity of the job in terms of the diversity of tasks to be carried out, the responsibilities to be fulfilled, skills to be used, problems to be solved or people to deal with

- the relative difficulty of the tasks to be performed

- the physical effort which has to be exerted by job-holders in terms of lifting, carrying, manoeuvring heavy weights, or other physical exertions and activities such as digging, bending, stretching, etc

- the stamina required – working for long periods at physically demanding tasks, standing or working in confined conditions or in situations where movement is restricted

- the mental, visual and allied effort associated with work involving continuous visual examination, concentration, precision or the co-ordination of hand and eye

- the amount of stress involved in working at speed or with small or delicate items, the stress/pressures of frequent changes or discontinuities, the need to reschedule work and the requirement to work to deadlines, schedules or exacting standards, or to achieve ever-increasing targets

- the extent to which the work is carried out under disagreeable conditions

- any hazards associated with the work

- any special requirements in such aspects of the job as unsocial hours, lengthy shifts or travelling.

Conducting a job analysis interview
Job analysis interviews should be conducted as follows:

- Work to a logical sequence of questions which help interviewees to order their thoughts about the job.

- Probe as necessary to establish what people really do. Answers to questions are often vague, and information may be given by means of untypical instances.

- Ensure that people do not give imprecise or inflated descriptions of their work.

- Sort out the wheat from the chaff. Answers to questions may produce a lot of irrelevant data which must be sifted before preparing the role definition.

- Obtain as clear a statement from people as possible about their authority to make decisions and the amount of guidance they receive from their manager or team leader. This is not easy. If asked what decisions they are authorised to make, many people look blank because they think about their role in terms of duties and tasks rather than abstract decisions.

- Avoid asking leading questions which make the expected answer obvious.

- Allow the individual ample opportunity to talk by creating an atmosphere of trust.

It is helpful to use a checklist derived from questions such as those listed above when conducting the interview. Elaborate checklists are not necessary. They only confuse people. The essence of job analysis is to 'keep it simple'. The questions should be structured specifically to obtain the information required for evaluation and comparison purposes. They should therefore cover each of the main factors or criteria which will be referred to when evaluating the job. The points to be discussed will vary according to the occupation and level of the individual and the job evaluation factors.

It is always advisable to check the information provided by individuals with their managers or team leaders. Different views can be held about the job, and if they are, they should be reconciled. Job analysis often reveals such differences as well as various organisational problems. This information can provide a useful spin-off from the analysis process.

The advantage of this method of analysing jobs is that interviews can be carried out flexibly. Properly handled, they provide a picture of what the job is really like, including its more subtle aspects (eg interpersonal relationships). But interviewing can be time-consuming and the results are not always easy to analyse. Much depends on the skill of the analyst in getting the facts and appreciating the significance not only of the facts but of the behavioural requirements of the role. And job analysts can consciously or unconsciously be prejudiced. That is why, in large evaluation exercises, general or structured questionnaires are often used, thus speeding up the interviewing process and minimising prejudice (as long as the questionnaire itself is not prejudiced). Questionnaires can even replace the interview altogether, although it may mean failing to capture the true 'flavour' of the job.

When carrying out job analysis for job evaluation purposes it is necessary always to bear in mind what the analysis is going to be used for, namely to provide the basis of a job description which will in turn be used by a job evaluator or a job evaluation panel to give guidance on the ranking, classification or rating of the job. The problem is to convey this information in a way which will facilitate objective judgements, and the written word is not always adequate in achieving that purpose.

General questionnaires
Questionnaires covering points such as those included in the checklist above can be completed by individuals and approved by their manager or team leader. They are helpful when a large number of roles are to be examined. They can also save interviewing time by recording purely factual information and by enabling the analyst to structure questions in advance to cover areas which need to be explored in greater depth. Questionnaires can produce information quickly and cheaply on a large

number of jobs and can be phrased in non-discriminatory ways. But a substantial sample is needed, and the construction of a questionnaire is a skilled job which should be done only on the basis of preliminary fieldwork. It is highly advisable to pilot-test questionnaires before launching into a full-scale exercise. The accuracy of the results also depends on the willingness and ability of individuals to complete questionnaires. Many people find it difficult to express themselves in writing about their work, however well they know and do it.

There are two problems with general questionnaires:

- analysing the facts – Even when the interview or questionnaire is carefully structured, the information is unlikely to come out neatly and succinctly in a way which can readily be translated into a job description. It is often necessary to sort out, rearrange and sometimes rewrite it.

- using the information for evaluation purposes – Too many questionnaires provide only general data, even if they follow the points listed above. Evaluators therefore have difficulty in aligning their answers with level or grade definitions.

Structured questionnaires

Structured questionnaires aim to overcome the problems mentioned above by asking detailed questions about all the key aspects of a job. The aim is in effect to pin people down by getting them to cover every point as specifically as possible and to facilitate the subsequent evaluation of the job. Structured questionnaires are often used in computer-assisted job evaluation systems – the answers are loaded into the computer and the software generates a score.

Such questionnaires can eliminate the need for job descriptions as the basis of job evaluation and therefore reduce the often tedious time it usually takes to prepare such descriptions. One day per job is a typical amount of time if allowance is made for checking and iteration.

It is possible to reduce the amount of work involved even further if the individual and his or her manager input the data about the job direct into the computer, for which a program has been devised that asks the questions and processes the answers to deliver a score. This eliminates the need for written questionnaires and job description. The Gauge job evaluation system developed by the Burnley Health Care Trust as mentioned in Chapter 37 comes into this category.

Structured questionnaires are often offered by consultants as part of their computerised job evaluation package, and they save much time and effort. The design of such questionnaires is not easy, and they should always be pilot-tested to ensure that job-holders have no problems in completing them and that the information can readily be translated into a job evaluation score.

ANALYSING ROLES

Role analysis concentrates on the behavioural aspects of the job. It therefore uses competence analysis techniques, as described below. Role analysis may start with individual roles and then distil the information to produce generic role definitions. Alternatively, it may start by carrying out an overall analysis of a generic role such as team leader, primarily in competence terms, and then developing individual profiles. The latter method can produce perfectly valid results but there is much to be said for the distillation process which helps to capture the key common characteristics of the role. A generalised approach could mean that something important is omitted.

COMPETENCE ANALYSIS

Competence analysis is used to produce competence profiles and frameworks for human resource planning, recruitment, performance management and training and development activities. But it can also provide the information required for competence-related pay processes, as described in Chapter 21, and the results of the analysis may be incorporated in a role definition or contribute to the definition of the layers in a job family.

The most common methods of competence analysis are expert opinion, workshops, structured interviews and functional analysis, as described below. The critical-incident technique or repertory grid analysis are sometimes used to produce behaviourally-oriented lists of competence dimensions but the techniques are probably too elaborate for most competence-based pay applications.

Expert opinion

The simplest method is for 'experts' (members of the personnel department and representatives of line management) to get together and draw up a list from their own understanding of 'what counts', possibly by reference to other published lists. This will certainly save time and trouble, but it may not be particularly analytical, and reliance on other people's ideas could result in a list being drawn up which is irrelevant to the real needs and requirements of the business. When defining generic, or individual, role competences it is essential to ensure that they flow directly from the core competences of the business so that people competences are fully integrated with and support business competences.

Workshops

A more structured approach through a workshop is likely to produce better results, particularly if the workshop is mainly comprised of people who are actually doing the job. The competence definitions will then be expressed in the language of the job-holders and are likely to be much more acceptable as well as realistic. The experience of the Derby City General Hospital NHS Trust was that very considerable benefits in the shape of 'ownership' emerged when this approach, involving the nurses and midwives concerned, was used.

Such a workshop usually begins by defining the job-related competence areas – the key functions in terms of the outputs required for the roles under consideration. Using the competence areas as a framework, the members of the group develop examples of effective and less effective behaviour which may be recorded on flipcharts. Such questions can be put to the group as: 'What sort of things do the really effective people in this job do?' 'What sort of things do people who are ineffective in this job do?'

The workshop facilitator's roles are to help the group to analyse its findings, to prompt, to provide examples and to assist generally in the production of a set of competence dimensions which can be illustrated by behaviour-based examples. The facilitator may have some ideas about the sort of headings that may emerge from this process but should not try to influence the group to come to a conclusion which it has not worked out for itself, albeit with some guidance.

The structured interview

This method starts from a list of competences drawn up by 'experts' or a workshop and proceeds by subjecting a number of individuals to a structured interview. It begins by identifying the key activities or result areas of the role and goes on to analyse the behavioural characteristics which distinguish performers at different levels of competence.

The basic question is: 'What are the positive or negative indicators of behaviour which are conducive or non-conducive to achieving high levels of performance?' The answers may be analysed under such headings as:

- personal drive (achievement motivation)

- impact on results

- analytical power

- strategic thinking

- creative thinking (ability to innovate)

- decisiveness

- commercial judgement

- team management and leadership

- interpersonal relations

- ability to communicate

- ability to adapt and cope with change and pressure

- ability to plan and control projects.

One of the problems with this approach is that it relies too much on the ability of the interviewer to draw information out of people. It is also undesirable to use a deductive approach which pre-empts the analysis with a prepared list of competence headings. It is better to adopt an inductive approach which starts from specific types of behaviour and groups them under competence headings. This can be done in a workshop.

Functional analysis

Functional analysis is the method used to produce competence-related standards for NVQ frameworks, but it can equally well be applied to the definition of work-based or occupational competences within an organisation. Functional analysis starts by describing the overall purpose of the job or occupation and then identifies the key functions undertaken.

In NVQ language, a distinction is drawn between tasks, the activities undertaken at work, and functions, the purposes of those activities. The distinction is important because the analysis must focus on the outcomes of activities in order to establish expectations of workplace performance. This is the information required to define standards of competence at the various levels in job families or for individual roles.

When the units and elements of competence have been established, the next question is 'What are the qualities of the outcomes?' in terms of the performance criteria at each level which can be used to judge whether or not an individual's performance meets the required standards. The response can feed information into performance management reviews.

Functional analysis can also lead to definitions of the behavioural dimensions of competence, especially when generic role definitions are required for a whole occupational area – for example, managers or team leaders.

JOB DESCRIPTIONS

Structured questionnaires can sometimes replace job descriptions for job evaluation purposes but job descriptions still remain the most common means by which information about jobs is communicated to evaluators. It is therefore necessary to give some consideration as to how they should be laid out. The format of job descriptions will depend upon the requirements of the organisation. There are many varieties, but one which is commonly used consists of the following sections:

Purpose
This is a short statement of why the job exists. It should be expressed in a single sentence. When defining the purpose of a job it is helpful to consider questions like:

• What part of the organisation's or team's total purpose is accomplished by people in this job?

• What is the unique contribution of this job that distinguishes it from other jobs?

• How would you summarise the overall responsibility of individuals in this job?

Organisation
This section explains where the job fits into the organisation. It sets out the job title of the person to whom the individual is responsible and the job titles of the people who are directly responsible to the job-holder.

Key result areas
Key result areas (also known as key tasks, main responsibilities or principal accountabilities) are statements of the end-results or outputs required of the job. They answer the question 'What are the main areas in which people in this job must get results to achieve its purpose?'

For most jobs, up to eight or 10 headings are sufficient to cover the major result areas. Fewer than four or five headings probably mean something is missing; more than 10 may mean that the job description is going into too much detail.

The complete key result area schedule should be expressed on the proverbial one side of one sheet of paper. The emphasis should be on contribution and outcomes.

Key result area statements should have the following characteristics:

- Taken together, they represent all the major outputs expected of the job.

- They focus on what is required (results and outputs), not on how the job is done (detailed tasks and duties).

- Each key result area is distinct from the others and describes an important aspect of the job in which results are to be achieved.

- They suggest (but need not state explicitly) measures or tests which could determine the extent to which results are being achieved.

A key result area statement is written in the form: 'Do something in order to achieve a stated result or standard.' Where possible, it should point to performance measures. Each statement is made in one sentence beginning with an active verb such as 'prepare', 'produce', 'plan', 'schedule', 'test', 'maintain', 'develop', 'monitor', 'ensure'. For example:

- Prepare marketing plans which support the achievement of corporate targets for profit and sales revenue.

- Control manufacturing operations to achieve output targets, quality specifications and delivery to time requirements within cost budgets.

- Maintain a stock control system which optimises inventory levels.

- Deal promptly and accurately with queries from customers on products and prices.

- Provide an accurate, speedy and helpful word-processing service to internal customers (fellow team members).

Critical dimensions
The critical dimensions of a job include any quantitative data that indicate its size and the range of responsibilities involved. For example: output, number of items processed, sales turnover, budgets, costs controlled, number supervised, number of cases dealt with over a period.

Factor analysis
If a point-factor job evaluation scheme is used, an additional section may be added to the job description which describes the demands made by the job under such headings as skills, responsibilities, complexity, interpersonal relations and mental and physical demands. An example of a job description might be as follows.

Job title: personnel officer

Responsible to: personnel manager

Responsible to job-holder: personal assistant (half-time)

Overall purpose: to provide personnel services (recruitment, job evaluation, induction training, and counselling) for headquarters office staff.

Key result areas

- Provide advice and efficient services which enable the company to recruit staff of the quality it requires.

- Organise induction training programmes which ensure that new staff understand the organisation and the policies and procedures that affect them, easily settle down in their jobs, and gain a favourable impression of the company.

- Analyse jobs and prepare job descriptions which provide the information required by the job evaluation panel.

- Give advice on implementing discipline and grievance procedures, equal opportunity issues and maternity leave entitlement which helps managers to deal with departmental employment matters effectively.

- Counsel junior staff in order to help them to solve their work-related problems.

- Provide efficient administrative support in conducting the annual salary review.

- Input personnel data promptly and accurately to the company's computerised personnel information system.

Critical dimensions: 400 office staff; 60 to 70 jobs to fill a year.

ROLE DEFINITIONS

Role definitions cover what people do and how they are expected to behave in such aspects of work as interaction with other people, the amount of flexibility required, the sort of problems that regularly have to be solved, the decisions they have to make, and the skills, knowledge and behavioural competences required. A role definition may be expressed as a structured narrative covering:

- the impact made by the person in the role on end-results – the contribution made to achieving the objectives of the organisation, department or team

- the amount of influence the individual is expected to exert on policy-making, planning and the decisions or actions of other people

- how the role fits in with other key aspects of the work of the organisation or team

- decision-making authority

- how work is assigned, reviewed and approved

- the particular knowledge, skills and experience required

- the complexity of the job – the degree of flexibility needed to undertake different tasks or use different skills

- the particular demands on the job in such areas as communication skills, customer relations, interpersonal skills, quality management, team leadership, teamworking, planning, project management, etc

- the major problems individuals are likely to meet in doing their work

- pressure – to meet deadlines, achieve exacting targets and quality standards, cope with constantly changing priorities, deal with potentially difficult interpersonal situations, etc.

An example of a role definition follows:

Job title: client services administrator

Reports to: client services manager

Overall purpose: to administer life and pension policies, ensuring that customers' expectations of quality service are fully achieved.

Key result areas

– Provide a quality customer service in accordance with industry regulations which ensures that customers' needs are satisfied by:

   identifying and responding to service opportunities

   making reasoned decisions by assessing the customer's individual circumstances when applying policy rules

   resolving complex cases by carrying out required investigations, ensuring that the customer is aware of progress at all times

   actioning all enquiries accurately and quickly.

– Understand the company's life and pensions products, and administer them correctly within the specified guidelines.

– Use systems relating to products accurately, from inputting new application details through to processing claims.

– Action high volumes of work correctly within predetermined time-scales, while meeting the standards of quality required.

– Interpret and respond promptly to correspondence relating to new and existing policies, ensuring that all aspects are answered in detail, in line with the customers' expectations.

– Monitor accounts where claims are pending, ensuring that all follow-up procedures are actioned as quickly as possible.

– Complete paperwork in a comprehensive and accurate manner, including statistics as and when required.

Expected behaviours and skills

– organised, self-disciplined and timely in handling administration and paperwork associated with the job

– listens to customers to identify needs, and checks that their needs have been met

– takes responsibility for own actions

- aware of the impact of own behaviour on others and responds appropriately to achieve results

- actively participates as a team member in achieving team goals

- responds positively to new situations and challenges

- works flexibly – capable of effectively using a full range of the skills required within the team

- conveys information and ideas concisely and accurately, orally and in writing

- sets high standards of performance for self

- pro-active and committed to developing own knowledge and skills.

GENERIC ROLE DEFINITIONS

Generic role definitions covering groups of roles that are essentially similar are prepared by means of normal role and competence analysis techniques as described earlier in this chapter. Such techniques aim to identify the common characteristics of the roles and distil them into a general definition. An example follows:

Generic role: team leader

Overall purpose of role: to lead teams in order to attain team goals and help achieve the organisation's objectives

Key result areas

- Agree with team members targets and standards which help achieve the organisation's objectives.

- With team members, plan work schedules and resource requirements which will ensure that team targets will be reached – indeed, exceeded.

- Agree performance measures and quality assurance processes with team members.

- Agree with team members the allocation of tasks, rotating responsibilities as appropriate to achieve flexibility and the best use of the skills and abilities of team members.

- Co-ordinate the work of the team to ensure that team goals are achieved.

- Ensure that the team members collectively monitor the team's performance in terms of achieving output, speed of response and quality targets and standards.

- Agree with team members any corrective action required to ensure that team goals are achieved.

- Conduct team reviews of performance to agree improvement plans.

- Conduct individual reviews of performance to agree areas for improvement and personal development plans.

- Recommend appropriate team performance rewards and

individual rewards related to the acquisition and effective use of skills and abilities.

Abilities

- builds effective team relationships, ensuring that team members are committed to the common purpose

- encourages self-direction amongst team members but provides guidance and clear direction as required

- shares information with team members

- trusts team members to get on with things; not continually checking

- treats team members fairly and consistently

- supports and guides team members to make the best use of their abilities

- encourages self-development by example

- actively offers constructive feedback to team members and positively seeks and is open to constructive feedback from them

- contributes to the development of team members, encouraging the acquisition of additional skills and providing opportunities for them to be used effectively.

JOB FAMILY DEFINITIONS

Job family definitions aim to define the different levels of competence or capacity within a job family as a basis for grading and rewarding people in the occupational category covered by that family. When competences are used to define job family levels they should focus on actions and outcomes as well as personal attributes and behaviour. Role and competence analysis techniques are used to identify the different levels within a family. The number of levels is usually restricted to three or four and the aim is to ensure that the definitions establish a clear gradation from the lowest to the highest, although progress within the job family may be a matter of continuous development rather than of distinct steps.

Some job families are more diverse than others and may be divided into homogeneous groups. For example, a professional engineer job family could be divided into design, development and project engineers. As Pritchard and Murlis (1992) suggest, this broad family approach is more appropriate when career development is not simply up a series of parallel ladders but includes diagonal moves as people gain experience in a variety of roles: 'What is wanted is a wide staircase or scrambling net which can accommodate a diversity of roles and career paths.' An approach along these lines may alleviate what is perhaps the biggest potential drawback of job families – that they confine people to separate categories and therefore inhibit flexibility in developing their capacity to take on different or wider responsibilities in other functions or occupations.

Table 17   Extract from level descriptions for research group job family

Job family	Level 1	Level 2	Level 3
Leadership	Leads a number of teams of professional scientists and technicians	Leads a project team of professional scientists and technicians	Conducts scientific experiments as a member of a multi-disciplinary team
Planning	Defines aims, programmes and priorities for research	Plans project programmes and priorities	Determines day-to-day priorities within overall project programme
Project management	Co-ordinates and controls a number of research projects	Controls research project to achieve objectives and deadlines	Monitors own performance as a team member against project objectives and deadlines
Performance delivery	Delivers and communicates results as agreed in overall development programme	Delivers and communicates results as agreed for project programme	Delivers expected results as a team member
Relationships	Maintains close links with (a) customer group managers and (b) relevant external research institutions to ensure that (a) their needs are being met and (b) up-to-date information is obtained on latest developments and best research practice	Liaises with customer group team leaders to ensure that the project is meeting their needs	Contributes to building and maintaining good relations inside the team and with colleagues in other units
Professional competence	A recognised expert in this field inside and outside the organisation	A fully seasoned professional with substantial understanding at a high level of the scientific methodology required to carry out original research in this field	Proficiency in the application of scientific knowledge and techniques to projects involving applied research
Budgetary control	Exercises budgetary control for units	Exercises budgetary control of project	Keeps within budgeted limits of expenditure for work on project

An example of level definitions in a job family expressed under a set of competence headings is illustrated in Table 17.

SUMMARY

- Job analysis is the process of collecting, analysing and setting out information about the content of jobs in order to provide the basis for a job description and data for recruitment, training, job evaluation and performance management.

- Competence analysis is concerned with functional analysis to determine work-based competences and behavioural analysis to establish the behavioural dimensions that affect job performance.

- A job description sets out the overall objectives of a job, where it fits into the organisational structure and the key result areas or principal accountabilities of job-holders, or the main tasks they have to carry out.

- A role definition describes the part to be played by individuals in fulfilling their job requirements. It concentrates on purpose in the form of outputs (accountabilities) and expands on the information contained in a job description by setting out the competencies required to perform the role satisfactorily.

- Job analyis aims to get the facts about a job from the people in the job, their manager or team leader and their colleagues or fellow team members.

- Job analysis can be conducted by means of interviews or questionnaires or through a computer-assisted job analysis program.

- Role analysis concentrates on the behavioural aspects of the job.

- Competence analysis is used to produce competence profiles and frameworks for human resource planning, recruitment, performance management and training and development activities. But it can also provide the information required for competence-related pay processes, and the results of the analysis may be incorporated in a role definition or contribute to the definition of the layers in a job family.

- The most common methods of competence analysis are expert opinion, workshops, structured interviews and functional analysis.

Part 4

PAY STRUCTURES

15 Pay structures: purpose, criteria and types

This chapter starts with an overall definition of a pay structure and its purpose, then summarises the characteristics of the main types of structure, namely graded, broad-banded, job family, pay curve, pay spine, spot rate, individual pay range, manual workers', integrated and rate for age. Graded structures – the most common form – are dealt with in detail in chapter 16. The more recent developments in the form of broad-banded and job family structures are covered in chapters 17 and 18 respectively. In many ways these can be more appropriate in de-layered and flexible organisations than the traditional approaches.

On completing this chapter the reader will understand the need for pay structures and the main features of the different types of pay structures.

DEFINITION OF A PAY STRUCTURE

A pay structure

- defines the different levels of pay for jobs or groups of jobs by reference to their relative internal value as established by job evaluation, to external relativities as established by market rate surveys, and, where appropriate, to negotiated rates for the job

- except in the case of 'spot rates', provides scope for pay progression in accordance with performance, skill, competence or service

- contains an organisation's pay ranges for jobs grouped into grades, individual jobs or job families; or

- pay scales for jobs slotted into a pay spine; or

- pay or progression curves; or

- the spot rates for individual jobs where there is no scope for progression.

There may be a single, integrated pay structure covering the whole organisation or, more commonly, there may be one structure for managerial, professional, technical, sales and administrative staff and another for manual workers. Executive directors may be treated separately.

Organisations sometimes have separate parallel structures for different occupations. For example, there may be 'technical ladders' for scientists or research and development engineers, which recognise that progression can sometimes depend more on professional competence than the assumption of managerial responsibility for people and other resources. This principle may be extended to setting up separate structures for different job families as described in Chapter 18. Some companies create separate 'market group' structures to cater for categories of employees such as accountants, computer specialists and marketing executives, whose levels of pay are heavily influenced by market pressures and who may therefore have to be treated differently from other groups of people. This may be inconsistent with the principle of internal equity but, as perceived by companies which adopt this policy, it is an inevitable requirement if high-quality staff are to be recruited and retained in a competitive labour market.

Pay structures are needed to provide a logically-designed framework within which equitable, fair and consistent reward policies can be implemented. They enable the organisation to determine levels of pay for jobs and people and are the basis upon which the effective management of relativities and of the processes of monitoring and controlling the implementation of pay practices can take place. The pay structure is also a medium through which the organisation can communicate the pay opportunities available to employees.

CRITERIA FOR PAY STRUCTURES

Pay structures should

- be appropriate to the characteristics and needs of the organisation and its employees

- facilitate the management of relativities and the achievement of equity, fairness and consistency in managing employee reward

- be capable of adapting to pressures arising from market-rate changes and skill shortages

- facilitate operational flexibility and continuous development

- provide scope as required for rewarding performance and increases in skill and competence

- clarify reward and career opportunities

- be constructed logically and clearly so that the basis upon which they operate can readily be communicated to employees

- enable the organisation to exercise control over the implementation of pay policies and budgets.

Analyse the pay structure of your own organisation or one familiar to you against these criteria and assess its strengths and weaknesses.

TYPES OF PAY STRUCTURE

Graded pay structures

A conventional graded pay structure consists of a sequence of job grades into which jobs of broadly equivalent value are slotted. A pay range is attached to each grade. The maximum of each range is typically a rate between 20 per cent and 50 per cent above the minimum. For example, a '40 per cent' range could span from £20,000 to £28,000.

The pay range or band provides scope for pay progression. There may be anything from around six to 15 grades in a structure. Grades may be defined by job evaluation in points terms, by grade definitions or simply by the jobs that have been slotted into the grades. Differentials between pay ranges are typically around 20 per cent, and there is usually an overlap between ranges, often of about 50 per cent.

Graded structures as illustrated in Figure 16 are the most common form of structure in the private sector because they provide an orderly basis for managing pay relativities, especially if they have been designed and are maintained through systematic job evaluation and market-rate comparison processes. However, broad-banded structures, as described below, are interesting many organisations that want to adopt a less hierarchical approach to managing relativities and pay progression and feel the need to provide more flexibility. Graded pay structures are described in detail in Chapter 16.

Figure 16 **A typical graded pay structure**

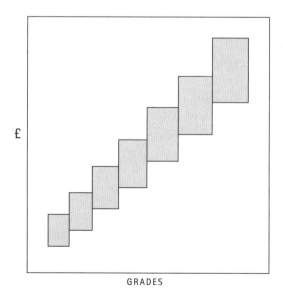

£

GRADES

Figure 17 **A broad-banded structure**

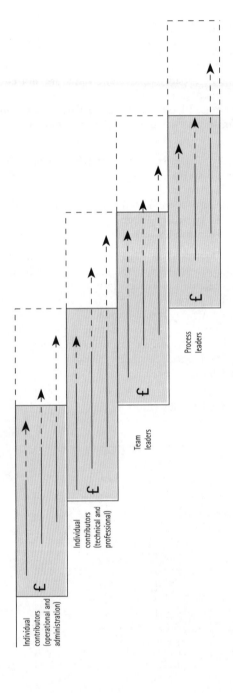

Individual contributors (operational and administration)

£

Individual contributors (technical and professional)

£

Team leaders

£

Process leaders

£

—————— Pay zone for role   – – – ▶ Scope for further progression

Broad-banded pay structures

In a broad-banded structure, as illustrated in Figure 17, the range of pay in a band is significantly higher than in a conventional graded structure. The band width may be as much as 100 per cent or even more, and there may be only four or five bands in the structure. The band boundaries are often, but not always, defined by job evaluation. Jobs may be placed in the bands purely by reference to market rates or by a combination of job evaluation and market-rate analysis. Bands are often described in terms of generic roles relating to the band. They are not defined hierarchically.

Although 'zones' may be defined which indicate normal progression, there is much more scope in a broad-banded structure for additional 'career development pay' by moving horizontally through the band and indeed beyond the notional band limits on the basis of increases in the scope of activities, contribution and competence. Pay progression and career development are not simply a matter of getting promotion to a higher grade. The aims are to fit the pay structure to a de-layered organisation, to reflect an emphasis on horizontal processes in such organisations, and to support flexibility and teamworking.

Broad-banded structures are more likely to be introduced in flexible organisations which do not believe in extended hierarchies, are concerned about continuous development, and employ a high proportion of knowledge workers. Such organisations have often been through a business process re-engineering exercise which looks at the fundamental processes of the business from a cross-functional perspective and aims to break away from the constraints of conventional organisational boundaries. Broad-banded structures are fully described in Chapter 17.

Individual job range structures

Individual job range structures, as illustrated in Figure 18, simply define a separate pay range for each job. The relativities between jobs are usually determined by point-factor job evaluation, which may in effect convert points to pounds by the application of a formula. The range is often defined as the plus or minus percentage of its midpoint. For example, a range of £16,000 to £24,000 could be described as

Figure 18 Individual job ranges

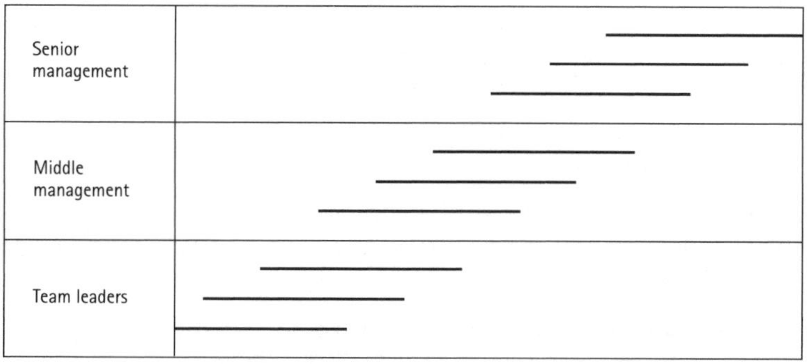

Figure 19   A competence- and performance-related pay curve

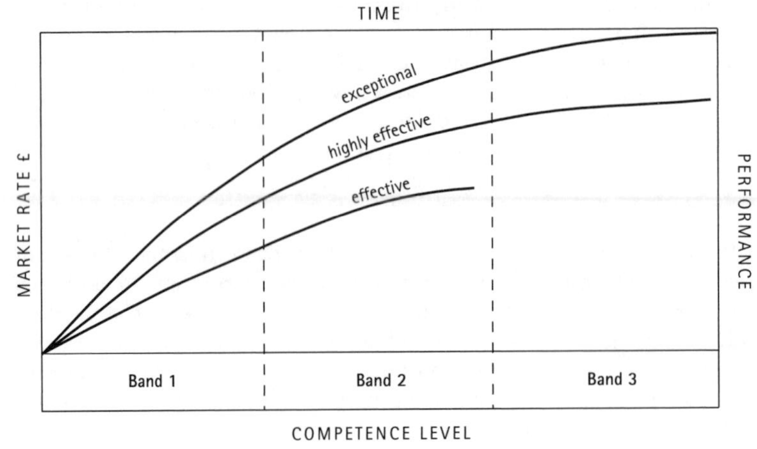

plus or minus 20 per cent of the midpoint of £20,000 (ie plus or minus £4,000). The midpoint would be aligned with market rates in accordance with the organisation's pay stance. Where reliable market data are available this can be done job by job, which means that individual ranges can more readily be changed in response to market-rate movements.

Job family structures
A job family structure consists of separate pay structures for jobs which are related through the activities carried out and the basic skills used, but are differentiated by the level of responsibility, skill or competence required.

Pay curves
Pay curves (sometimes referred to as maturity or progression curves), as illustrated in Figure 19, provide different pay progression tracks along which people in a family of jobs can move according to their levels of competence and performance. A number of competence 'bands' are defined, each of which constitutes a definable level of skill, competence and responsibility. Pay curves can be incorporated in a job family structure for each family.

Individuals move through these bands at a rate which is related to their performance and their capacity to develop. They do not move into a new band until they have demonstrated that they have attained the level of competence required. It is assumed that:

• Competence develops progressively through various levels or bands rather than between a number of fixed points.

• Individuals develop at different rates and will therefore achieve different levels of performance, which should be rewarded accordingly.

• Market-rate considerations should be taken into account when determining levels of pay at each point on the curve.

Pay curves may be introduced primarily because they provide a flexible means of rewarding staff who are increasing their competence and their performance through a process of continuous development. They are therefore often used for knowledge workers. However, they do not suit all organisations, especially when there are clearly-defined job hierarchies and where it would be in conflict with the culture to distinguish between employees in separate job families.

Spot rate structures

A spot or individual job rate structure allocates a specific rate for a job. There is no scope for the basic rate for the job to progress through a defined pay range, although individual rates of pay for job-holders whose rates have not been negotiated with a trade union may change, possibly at the whim of management. Job-holders may be eligible for performance pay or an incentive or bonus scheme. Spot rates can be fixed entirely by reference to market rates in a market-driven structure. Alternatively, job evaluation may be used to assess relative job worth. The rates may be negotiated with trade unions.

Spot rate structures are typical for manual workers but they are adopted for other types of staff by some organisations that want the maximum scope to pay what they like.

Spot rate structures can be modified so that levels of pay may vary other than by means of incentives. Such modifications can produce something akin to an individual job grade structure. There will be provision for paying less than the spot rate to those on a learning curve where they are not fully qualified to do the job, or for paying more for specified skills, job responsibilities or conditions of work.

Figure 20 **A pay spine**

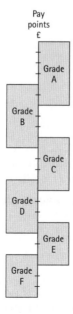

Pay spines

Pay spines as illustrated in Figure 20 consist of a series of incremental points extending from the lowest- to the highest-paid jobs covered by the structure. A pay spine increment may be standardised at, say, 3 per cent from the top to the bottom of the spine, or the increments may be wider at higher levels. Pay scales or ranges for different job grades may then be superimposed on the pay scales. If performance-related pay is introduced, individuals can be given accelerated increments.

Pay spines are most often found in the public sector or in agencies and voluntary organisations which have adopted a public sector approach to reward management.

Pay structures for manual workers

A pay structure for manual workers consists of the rates paid to employees who work on the shop floor, in distribution, transport, public services or anywhere else where the work primarily involves manual skills and tasks. The structure will be similar to any other pay structure in that it will incorporate pay differentials between jobs. These will reflect real and assumed differences in skill and responsibility, but they are also influenced by pressures from the local labour market, by custom and practice and by settlements reached between management and trade unions.

The pay structure may include a number of 'spot rates' – that is, fixed base-rates for each job which do not vary according to skill or merit. Alternatively, there may be a formal structure in which there are defined job grades into which jobs are slotted according to their level of skill or responsibility. There may be a fixed rate for each job in the grade, or there may be a pay bracket to allow individual skill or merit payments to be made above the minimum time rate. In the latter case the pay structure closely resembles a graded structure. Some structures are based entirely on levels of skill, as when there is a skill-based pay scheme (see Chapter 23).

Pay levels in the structure are determined in a number of ways. They may be agreed following national, local or plant negotiations, or they may be fixed by management in relation to the rates paid for similar jobs in the local labour market.

Incentive payments may be made in addition to the base or day rate through some form of payment-by-results (PBR) scheme, such as piecework or a work-measured system. However, many manufacturing companies have abandoned PBR and replaced it with 'high day rates' (a higher level of base pay), sometimes accompanied by a skill-based pay scheme and gain-sharing, or both.

Many structures incorporate various 'plus rates' for particular skills, shift work, 'unsocial working hours', overtime and difficult or unpleasant working conditions.

Integrated pay structures

Integrated pay structures cover all or most employees, including manual workers, but sometimes leaving out senior management and sales representatives. They may be based on the same system of job evaluation for all jobs covered by the structure and will provide for the harmonisation to some extent of employee benefits and conditions of employment such as holidays, hours of work, sick pay and pensions, although the scale of such benefits may still be related to position in the grade hierarchy.

Integrated pay structures have become more common recently for the following reasons.

• Differences between manual and non-manual employment have become blurred, partly through the introduction of new technology but also as a result of a change in the social climate. The belief that someone operating, say, a word processor should be accorded higher status than someone operating, say, a computer-numerically-controlled machine tool is no longer tenable.

• The introduction of new manufacturing technology and processes and the widespread use of information technology have entailed greater flexibility and changes in skill requirements. Some office jobs have, in effect, been de-skilled while the skill requirements of many shopfloor jobs have been considerably enhanced. Knowledge workers now function on the shop floor as well as in the office.

• Many US and Japanese companies with subsidiaries in the UK have a company philosophy of offering single-status employment conditions.

• There has been a move towards single-table bargaining with trade unions (all negotiations on one site involving all unions, including those traditionally concerned with white-collar as well as manual workers). The introduction of this form of bargaining as a means of reaching joint agreements has encouraged the integration of the pay structure.

• It is felt that a unified structure is required to meet equal pay for work of equal value requirements.

Integrated pay structures are usually formed round grades, although it is possible to adopt a job family approach. The grades are usually established by job evaluation, generally a points-factor scheme, although ranking has been used.

The introduction of integrated pay has frequently been accompanied by the abolition of old payment-by-result schemes and their replacement by one consolidated rate of pay. Some schemes, however, have introduced performance-related pay for all categories of staff, including manual workers who were previously receiving incentive pay. Skill-related or competence-related pay processes may be introduced. A gain-sharing plan is also sometimes introduced as part of the integrated pay structure.

An integrated structure will not necessarily lead to the abolition of all plus payments. Allowances may be paid for shift or unsocial hours, and separate overtime payments up to a certain level in the structure may be made.

Rate-for-age scales
Rate-for-age scales provide for a specific rate of pay or a pay bracket

to be linked with age for staff in certain jobs. They are relatively uncommon nowadays because of changing patterns of work. The rationale of rate-for-age scales used to be the learning curve, but that can be catered for in a graded pay structure. They are, however, still used by some organisations for employees below the age of 21 on formal training schemes extending over two or three years.

CHOICE OF STRUCTURE

The choice of structure depends on the type of organisation and the type of people it employs. Larger enterprises and institutions with formal, hierarchical organisation structures tend to prefer conventional graded structures which permit orderly administration and ease in managing internal relativities. High-technology organisations that want to achieve rather more flexibility but within a defined framework may opt for a broad-banded structure.

Individual job ranges may be favoured by organisations that want a degree of formality, for example in progressing people through a range, but do not wish to put 'one-off' jobs into what they may perceive as the straitjacket of a graded structure.

Organisations that are particularly concerned with maintaining competitive pay levels and that have a number of different market groups amongst their employees may prefer a job family structure. They may also introduce such a structure if there are a number of distinctive job families. If they employ a large proportion of knowledge workers who are continually developing in their jobs, especially in their formative years, they may go further and introduce a pay curve system for certain categories of staff.

A spot rate structure may be preferred by smaller organisations, those whose environment induces a more flexible, less formal approach to administration, companies which are market-rate driven, and fast-moving entrepreneurial companies which demand high performance.

> Under what circumstances might an organisation prefer to have a spot rate structure?

> What are the potential advantages and disadvantages of a pay spine structure in a typical public-sector organisation?

EXAMPLES OF STRUCTURES

Every structure is different. Here are some examples:

- *Automobile Association* – five 'tiers' to cover all management jobs

- *BP* – the 10 grades for the international cadre reduced to two bands

- *British Rail Research* – a five-grade matrix which groups generic families of jobs

- *British Waterways* – six wage grades for its 1,000 canal staff: workers move up through the grades subject to achieving and delivering the level of competence defined for each grade

- *Cancer Research Campaign* – nine grades for all staff (previously 27 grades)

- *Thomas Cook* – separate broad-band salary scales for general staff, field operations and technical staff; in the general structure there are five role levels which overlap

- *First Direct* – 10 'development levels' with roles clustered into job families

- *Glaxo Wellcome* – six broad bands overlaid with a competence framework

- *Prestige Group* – four straight day rates for production operators, operators/adjusters, setters and skilled toolroom operators (replacing 12 levels of pay)

- *Rover Group* – in 1994 replaced five hourly grades and six salaried grades with a single-status structure of three levels

- *Toshiba* – seven grades to cover all operational staff.

SUMMARY

- A pay structure defines the different levels of pay for jobs or groups of jobs by reference to their relative internal value as established by job evaluation, to external relativities as established by market-rate surveys and, where appropriate, to negotiated rates for the job.

- There may be a single, integrated pay structure covering the whole organisation or, more commonly, there may be one structure for managerial, professional, technical, sales and administrative staff and another for manual workers. Executive directors may be treated separately.

- Pay structures are needed to provide a logically-designed framework within which equitable, fair and consistent reward policies can be implemented.

- Pay structures should be appropriate to the characteristics and needs of the organisation and its employees, facilitate the management of relativities and the achievement of equity, fairness and consistency in managing employee reward, facilitate operational flexibility and continuous development, and be constructed logically and clearly so that the basis upon which they operate can readily be communicated to employees.

- The main types of pay structures are graded, broad-banded, job family, individual job grade, pay curve, spot rate and pay spine.

- The choice of structure depends on the type of organisation and the type of people it employs.

16 Graded pay structures

A conventional graded pay structure consists of a sequence of job grades into which jobs of broadly equivalent value are slotted. A pay range is attached to each grade. The main features of graded structures (the most common type) are described below under the following headings:

- job grades

- pay ranges

- pay progression

- the advantages and disadvantages of graded structures

- designing a graded structure

- adjusting the structure.

On completing this chapter the reader will understand the main features of graded pay structures and how they are designed.

JOB GRADES

Jobs are allocated to grades on the basis of an assessment of their relative internal value. Grades may be defined in terms of a points bracket if a point-factor job evaluation scheme is used. Alternatively, they may be defined verbally if a job classification system is used or by reference to the benchmark jobs slotted into the grade. In the latter case, the allocation of jobs may be helped by the existence of generic role profiles. All jobs in a grade are treated the same for pay purposes. In other words, they are assumed to be of broadly comparable value and are rewarded within the same pay range.

PAY RANGES

A pay range is attached to each grade. It indicates the minimum and maximum rates payable for any job in the grade and the scope for the pay of job-holders to progress while they are in that grade. (This may be governed by performance, skill or competence criteria as described under the heading of pay progression later in this chapter.)

Defining a pay range
A pay range may be defined in terms of the percentage increase between the lowest and highest points in the range. For example, a

range where the minimum and maximum are £20,000 and £28,000 respectively could be described as a 40 per cent range. Ranges can also be defined as a percentage of the midpoint. For example, a range in which the midpoint is £25,000 and the minimum and maximum rates are £20,000 and £30,000 could be described as an 80 per cent to 120 per cent range. The latter method can be used to indicate where the pay of an employee is placed in the range. Thus an employee paid £22,500 in a £20,000 to £30,000 range could be described as being paid at 90 per cent of the midpoint of £25,000. This is sometimes called a 'compa-ratio' (short for 'comparative ratio'), a figure often used as a method of describing the relationship of the actual pay of employees in a grade to the midpoint.

Range width

The width or span of a range provides scope for performance-related pay and for dealing with incremental increases in responsibility that are insufficient to justify upgrading but need to be recognised by additional pay. Spans can vary widely. In a narrow- or fine-banded structure the span may be about 20 per cent above the minimum for each range. In a conventionally-banded structure the span of the ranges may be around 30–50 per cent above the minimum. Broad-banded structures as described in the next chapter can have spans of 100 per cent or more.

The span or width of a range may be influenced by the extent to which the performance and responsibilities of people holding jobs in the grade vary. Range spans are often increased at higher levels in recognition of the fact that there is more scope for differences in performance – for example, 30 per cent ranges for junior jobs, 40 per cent for middle managers and 50 per cent for senior managers.

Assigning pay ranges to job grades

The process of assigning pay ranges to job grades is influenced by three considerations:

- the pay differentials that are believed to be appropriate between the adjacent grades – these are often defined by reference to the midpoint of the pay range

- the policy on the width or span of the grades (the difference between the minimum and maximum levels of pay in a grade)

- the market rates for jobs in the grade.

The midpoint of a grade is often regarded as the 'target' rate for a fully competent job-holder in the grade, although this reference-point could be anywhere in the range – some companies may place it at, say, 90 per cent of the midpoint rate to allow more scope for progression. In principle the aim may be to align the midpoint or reference-point with market rates in accordance with policy on market-rate relativities. Such policy, sometimes called the pay stance or pay posture, may indicate that the organisation aims to be a high payer in order to get and to keep good-quality staff. The policy could be expressed as 'We aim to pay in the upper quartile,' in other words, within the top 25 per cent of the distribution of market rates for the jobs in the grade. Alternatively, it could be stated as an intention broadly to match market rates – ie pay at the average market-rate levels of jobs in the grade. However, this may be difficult to put into practice, for two reasons. First, it is seldom, if ever, possible to obtain precise information on market rates, as was explained in Chapter 13. Second, even if it were possible, the market rates for the various jobs in a grade may differ.

One method of aligning pay ranges with market rates is to equate the minimum with the lower-quartile figure of the job in the grade with the lowest market value, and to equate the range maximum with the upper-decile figure for the job with the highest market value. But it may be difficult to obtain comprehensive market rate information which is reliable enough for this procedure to be adopted with confidence. It may be necessary to make assumptions about the market rates of the various jobs in the grade, and the assumptions are often judgemental. Range limits and range midpoints can only broadly indicate market-rate relativities. The final decision is therefore often made on the basis that 'On balance, this seems to be about right.' This may mean that the market rates for some jobs in a grade are outside the pay range for that grade.

The number of pay ranges
The number of pay ranges will be influenced by:

- the organisation structure – flatter organisations need fewer grades

- the corporate culture – the degree to which it is hierarchical

- the amount of flexibility required

- the total range of pay to be covered by the structure

- the span or width of the pay ranges which, as mentioned above, can vary considerably

- the differentials between ranges – which may be between 15 per cent and 20 per cent – to recognise differences between the value of jobs in adjacent grades

- the overlap between pay ranges – ie the proportion of a range which is covered by the next lower range. Overlaps can be as much as 50 per cent and increase flexibility by allowing highly experienced people in one grade to be paid more than inexperienced people in the grade above.

A conventional graded structure in a typical hierarchical organisation may be designed with differentials increasing from 15 per cent in the lower grades to 20 per cent at the top, while the width of the ranges or bands may increase from 30 per cent to 40 per cent. This could result in an eight-graded structure if salaries from £10,000 to about £44,000 had to be covered, as illustrated in Table 18. An arrangement along these lines, which could be termed a medium-banded structure, is fairly typical. But there are many variations of this pattern. Plenty of choice is available – there are no rules stating that one type of structure is 'best': it all depends on what the organisation wants and needs.

Table 18 **A graded structure**

Grade	Range (£)	Span (%)	Differential (%)	Overlap (%)
1	10,000–13,000	30	–	–
2	11,500–14,950	30	15	43
3	13,225–17,192	30	15	43
4	15,208–19,771	30	15	43
5	18,250–25,550	40	20	20
6	21,900–30,660	40	20	42
7	26,280–36,792	40	20	42
8	31,536–44,150	40	20	42

PAY PROGRESSION

Graded pay structures are based on the belief that individuals should progress through ranges by reference to their performance, skill, competence or time in the job. It is also usual to recognise that people may be paid above the minimum for the range when they are appointed or promoted to a job in a grade. This can take place when it is necessary to offer people a competitive rate of pay if they are recruited from outside the organisation, or to provide them with an appropriate increase on promotion. Policies and procedures are required to govern when this happens and the amount above the minimum that can be offered (see Chapter 36). Progression can be variable in accordance with performance-related, competence-related or skill-based schemes as described, respectively, in Chapters 20, 21, and 23.

Alternatively, progression can be through fixed increments. This means that individuals move through a scale for the grade by predetermined steps related to service, although some basically fixed incremental schemes do allow variations for performance, eg double increments. Fixed incremental scales are little used now except in some parts of the public and voluntary sectors. The reason is that most organisations do not approve of paying people more simply for being there. However, it is sometimes argued that this system at least avoids the bias that can result from relying on managerial judgement to determine the size of increases. The main methods of varying progression are described below.

Variable progression without guidelines
In this approach, performance-related (merit) increases are awarded on an *ad hoc* basis and the rate of progression is not controlled. No limits are defined and individuals who remain in the same job may drift up to the top of their range, perhaps at different rates. Ultimately they may all be paid the same, irrespective of their performance. This approach is not uncommon but, clearly, it can lead to overpayment and inequities. Without guidelines the distribution of awards may be arbitrary and inconsistent.

Variable progression with guidelines
This method uses guidelines on the level of performance-related increases which can be given according to performance ratings. (Rating methods are discussed in Chapter 29.) Managers will be given a

Figure 21 Performance-related variable progression

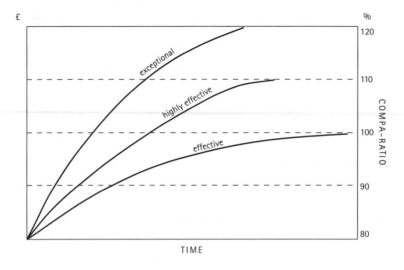

budget for increases of, for example, 5 per cent and may be instructed to make awards to people according to their performance of not more than, say, 10 per cent and not less than 3 per cent (on the assumption that any increase of less than that amount is not worth giving). No specific guidelines are issued on rates or limits of progression. This approach is quite common. It provides a better basis for monitoring proposed increases to ensure a degree of consistency. But individuals can still drift to the top of the range.

Performance-zoned variable progression
Performance-zoned variable progression systems spell out the basis upon which individuals can move further and faster through the range for various performance levels. This approach represents the 'performance-track' concept in which individuals can follow a track of pay opportunity based on assessed performance. The full range at the fastest rate of progression is reserved only for those who sustain high levels of performance, while smaller parts of the range at slower rates of progression are available for those who are not achieving top levels. This approach is modelled in Figure 21.

A performance-zoned system divides the range into zones. If compara-ratios are used, these zones would be defined as a percentage of the midpoint, as in the example of an 80 per cent to 120 per cent range shown in Table 19. There are many variations on this structure. For example, at Thomas Cook 'salary scale range points' are determined for each role level. There are six points covering the following percentages of the range from the minimum to the notional maximum: 0–16, 16–33, 33–50, 50–66, 66–83 and 83–100. A salary bracket is fixed for each of these zones.

Table 19 Defining the range in zones by reference to performance

Zone	Compa-ratio (%)	Pay range (%)
1	80–90	10,000–11,250
2	91–100	11,251–12,500
3	101–110	12,501–13,750
4	111–120	13,751–15,000

Limits to progression may be determined by reference to performance ratings. For example, the type of scale shown in Table 19 could be used in an 80–120 per cent (£10,000 to £15,000) range. Guidelines on the percentage of job-holders who may be expected to reach each level of competence are sometimes given, as in Table 20. But they will always be arbitrary and should be used flexibly. For assessment purposes, each level of competence would have to be defined as specifically as possible, and this definition would emphasise that assessments should be based on the effective use of competences, not simply their acquisition.

Table 20 Limits of pay progression by reference to performance

Assessment	Compa-ratio (%)	Maximum pay (£)	Guideline (%)
Developing competence	90	11,250	20
Achieved required level of competence	100	12,500	60
Exceeded required level of competence	110	13,750	15
Achieved exceptional level of competence	120	15,000	5

Even more specific guidance on progression within a range can be provided by the use of a performance-related pay matrix as explained in Chapter 36. The matrix relates percentage increase to performance rating and position in the range (compa-ratio).

Variable progression related to the learning curve
Pay progression is often planned to follow the pattern of the learning curve, as illustrated in Figure 22. This means that increases are related

Figure 22 Variable progression related to the learning curve

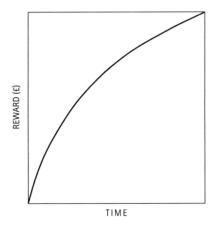

to the rate at which people are likely to learn the job and thus become fully competent. Learning is assumed to decelerate – in other words, people learn most quickly when they start the job, and the pace of learning decreases as the necessary skills and competences are acquired.

Pay progression to the fully competent rate

Pay ranges in graded structures can contain a target rate or reference-point which is the rate for a fully competent person in any job in the grade. (This is often, although not necessarily, the midpoint.) Progression from the minimum to the target rate can be planned in a series of increments which correspond to specified increases in competence or successive skill blocks, as long as the individual has demonstrated that he or she has used them to good effect. For example, there might be four increments each of 5 per cent of the midpoint in an 80 per cent to 120 per cent range to take someone who started at the minimum level of competence required to enter the grade to the fully competent 100 per cent level. Full increments are given only if the competence criteria at each level are completely satisfied, although some flexibility might be allowed to give more or less than, say, 5 per cent if progress had been higher or lower than expected. Above the midpoint or reference-point further pay progression would be entirely related to performance, which would have to be at a higher level than the norm for a fully competent individual. This method is modelled in Figure 23.

An alternative to permanent increases in pay above the reference-point is to award only cash sums. This avoids the annuity aspect of

Figure 23 **Pay progression to the fully competent rate and beyond**

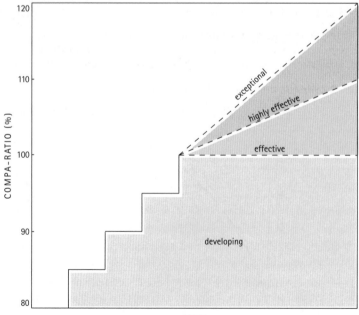

any system which provides permanent increases in base pay (pay may go up but it seldom if ever comes down) and answers the question 'Why should we go on paying someone more for last year's performance which he or she is clearly not sustaining this year?' A policy along these lines would restrict the span of the range. The principle of cash lump-sum bonuses (ie variable pay) can be adopted in any system, whether or not the initial progress is governed by increases in competence.

THE ADVANTAGES AND DISADVANTAGES OF GRADED STRUCTURES

The advantages of graded structures are that they

- clearly indicate pay relativities

- provide a framework for managing relativities and for ensuring that jobs of equal value are paid equally

- allow better control over the fixing of rates of pay and pay progression

- are easy to explain to employees.

The disadvantages are that:

- Defining grade boundaries is a matter of judgement which may not always be easy to defend.

- If there are too many grades, there will be constant pressure for upgrading, leading to grade drift.

- Pay ranges create the expectation that everyone is entitled to reach the top of the scale.

- Graded structures can create or maintain hierarchical rigidity which is at odds with the requirement of flexibility in new team- and process-based organisations.

DESIGNING A GRADED STRUCTURE

How the need may arise
The need to design or redesign a graded structure can be prompted by a major change in the organisational structure of the business or because a diagnostic review has established deficiencies in the present arrangements such as:

- an over-extended hierarchy

- inflexibility

- anomalies and inequities arising either from the lack of a job evaluation system or from the decay of an existing scheme

- inadequate control of gradings and regradings leading to grade drift (unjustified upgradings)

- unsatisfactory provision for pay progression, leaving insufficient scope for differentiating between levels of performance and competence

- over-engineered or bureaucratic pay systems which give rise to unnecessary work and expense and do not add value.

Before embarking on a design or redesign exercise it is worth assessing the amount of work involved and the cost. Redesigns can be expensive if they result in pay rises for numbers of employees (and they never seem to result in reductions).

The basis of graded pay structure design

The first aim of the design is to group together jobs which are of a similar value and separate those which are significantly different. So far as possible, the range of pay for the grade should accommodate the range of market rates for the jobs in the grade, although this is an ideal arrangement which may be very difficult to put into practice, not least because of the often imprecise and incomplete nature of market-rate data.

Account must be taken of the perceptions of people in the organisation about different job levels. If jobs which up till now have been generally considered to be of the same value are placed in different grades, the structure will not be acceptable unless convincing reasons for the change are produced. This is one of the many reasons why employees should be involved in the job evaluation exercise and why the rationale underpinning a new structure should be explained carefully to them. The positioning of grade boundaries needs to be handled with particular care. Failure to do so can result in considerable pressure for regrading.

Policy considerations

It will be necessary during the exercise to formulate policy on the following graded structure variables which were considered earlier in this chapter:

- the number of grades which may be required

- how pay ranges should be assigned to grades – this will include the policy on the relationship between internal pay levels and market rates

- the width or span of pay ranges

- the differentials between ranges

- the degree of overlap between ranges

- the arrangements for progressing pay through ranges.

These points should be given some initial consideration, especially policy on market-rate relativities. But firm decisions on structure will probably develop only during the course of the exercise.

Ways of designing a graded pay structure

There are four methods of designing a graded pay structure:

- on the basis of assumptions about the number of grades required and the jobs that should be allocated to those grades – the empirical approach

- by reference to market-rate data – the market pricing approach

- following a job-ranking exercise – the job-rank approach

- following a point-factor job evaluation exercise – the analytical approach.

The empirical approach
This almost entirely judgmental method starts by looking at what are felt to be the different levels of jobs in the hierarchy and then proceeds more or less arbitrarily to allocate jobs to those grades by a process of internal benchmarking. Pay ranges are attached to grades by reference to existing rates of pay and market rates.

The market pricing approach
This approach relies mainly on market-rate data to decide which jobs can be grouped together in pay ranges. The number of grades and the boundaries between grades are decided empirically to answer the question 'Does this look and feel right?' Reliance on market rates is based on the dubious assumption that precise market-rate data can be obtained. There could also be equal-value problems such that it would be difficult to explain the logic of the resulting structure.

The job-ranking approach
Following a job-ranking exercise an initial estimate is made of the number of grades likely to be required on the basis of an assessment of the range of jobs to be covered and any natural boundary-lines in that range, coupled with an analysis of the present or proposed structure of the organisation – the number of levels in the hierarchy or any natural ladders of promotion. Grade boundaries may be drawn between groups of jobs with common features, the aim being to separate the groups to achieve a real distinction between the content and levels of jobs in adjacent grades. This is easier said than done, and drawing the boundary-lines is always a matter of judgement which may involve reconsidering the initial estimate of the number of grades required. To achieve a 'felt-fair' result it may be necessary to experiment with a number of alternatives.

Pay ranges have then to be allocated to the grades by reference to existing scales and market-rate information. Arriving at an acceptable sequence of pay ranges may involve further iteration and adjustment of scales and the allocation of jobs to grades. This is by no means a scientific procedure.

One of the advantages claimed for point-factor rating is that it provides the basis for an analytical approach to the design of graded structures in the three stages described below, namely: designing the grade structure, pricing the grade structure and developing the total graded pay structure.

The analytical method of designing grade structures
The analytical method is based on a point-factor job evaluation exercise. The first step is to evaluate the benchmark jobs and rank them according to their scores. The next step is to draw grade boundary-lines at appropriate places in this rank order. The points scores will indicate the difference between jobs in quantified terms. In theory this makes it easier first to establish the extent to which similar jobs are clustered together, and second to identify gaps between

clusters where grade boundary-lines can be drawn which distinguish clearly between adjacent grades.

The criteria for judging whether correct grade boundaries have been drawn are:

- the existence of clusters of jobs with natural breaks between them so that when there is a distinct difference between the levels of the clusters the jobs are allocated to separate grades

- the degree to which jobs of a similar size and with common features as indicated by the job evaluation factors are grouped together

- the extent to which the structure reduces the risk of boundary problems by not placing jobs which are nearly the same size on either side of a grade boundary. There should ideally be a distinct gap between the highest-rated jobs in one grade and the lowest-rated jobs in the grade above.

These criteria are quite exacting and often difficult to satisfy, especially when the grades are fairly narrow. Wide grades do not eliminate boundary problems, but there are likely to be fewer of them and they may be easier to manage.

The initial attempt at producing a grade structure is therefore often unacceptable and other configurations will have to be considered. This process is made easier by the use of computer software to model different alternatives as described in Chapter 37. At a later stage the same programs can be used to cost the various options so that the most affordable alternative is selected – affordability is a very important consideration.

At this stage any pretence that defining job grades is a scientific process has to be abandoned. Even with computerised assistance, it now becomes a matter of judgement, often based on trial and error. Grade structure design usually involves iteration, trying something out, testing against various criteria and, if necessary, trying something else, until it feels right. And the operative word is *feels*. There is no objective test of the rightness or otherwise of a grade structure.

One approach is to try a number of different configurations based on alternative grade widths, as illustrated in Figure 24. This example assumes that all grades should be of equal width in percentage terms. But there is no rule that says this should be the case. Range widths and scales can vary according to the types of job which may be allocated to the grades.

Each alternative can be evaluated against the criteria for grade boundaries listed earlier until one emerges which feels about right. And, ultimately, the 'felt-fair' principle is the only one that can be used to judge whether or not a sensible grade structure has been developed.

The analytical method of pricing grade structures

Following the design of a grade structure as described above, decisions have to be made on pricing the structure – ie attaching pay ranges or scales to the grades. Prices are decided by reference to both internal and external considerations.

Figure 24 **Alternative grade structures**

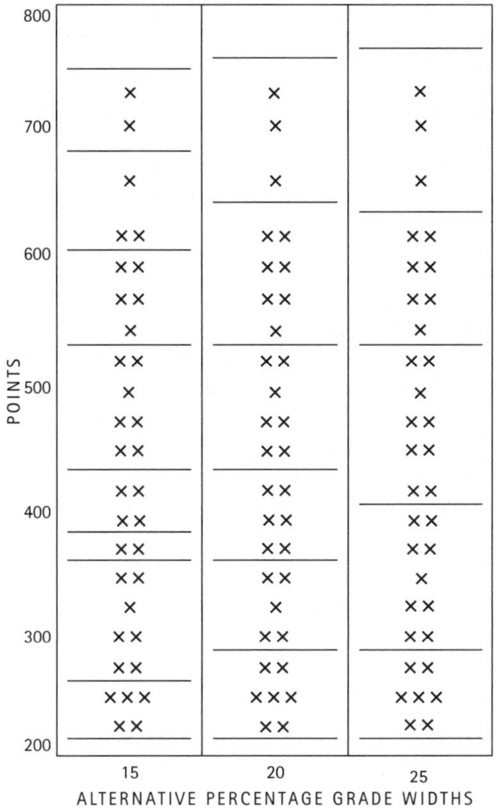

Internal considerations come first. These will refer to internal relativities, the differentials between grades, and the scope for pay progression within grades – the size of the pay range or scale. Differentials need to be high enough to reflect increases in job sizes between adjacent grades. The size of the differential will vary according to the number of grades in the structure and the level of the grade. It will probably be not less than 10 per cent in the lower grades and it could be 15 per cent to 20 per cent at higher levels.

The size or span of the range will depend on policy as to the amount of pay progression which should be allowed in a grade through some form of performance-related or competence-related pay. The greater the scope for improving performance, developing competence levels and working flexibly in a role, the greater the width of the range. But this, like many other aspects of pay structure design, is a matter of judgement.

External relativities also have to be considered. These will involve the relation between market rates and the rates for jobs in the organisation. Market-rate pressures will vary but there will generally be some jobs for which competitive rates must be paid if key people are to be attracted and retained. In these circumstances market rates cannot be ignored and it will be necessary to reconcile the competing claims of internal equity and external competitiveness. However, there is still the problem, as mentioned earlier, that the concept of a market rate is less precise than it seems.

The analytical method of designing a complete graded pay structure

These steps are required to design or redesign a graded pay structure following a point-factor evaluation exercise:

Establish internal relativities

Plot the scores resulting from the rating exercise against existing rates of pay for the benchmark jobs. This is illustrated in Figure 25. A trend line of actual pay is drawn to show the relationship between points and pay. This will give a preliminary indication of the pay ranges which will be needed to accommodate the jobs which are fairly close to the trend line. The trend line also highlights any apparent anomalies – jobs for which the rate of pay is some distance above or below the line. These will need to be investigated to establish the extent to which they are a result of one or more of the following causes:

• individuals' being overpaid in relation to the work they do

• market-rate forces

• incorrect job evaluation outcomes.

Establish external relativities

Plot market rate data for benchmark jobs on the scattergram and draw a market-rate trend line as shown in Figure 26. This is usually confined to median rates.

The relationship between internal rates and market rates is a policy matter – a policy, for example, that they should broadly be matched or that the organisation wants its pay levels to be above the median market rate, say in the upper quartile or even the upper decile.

Figure 25 Scattergram of actual pay data

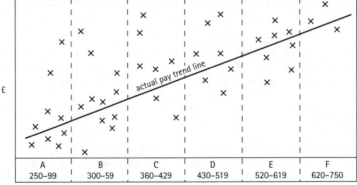

GRADES AND POINTS RANGES

Figure 26 Scattergram of market–rate data

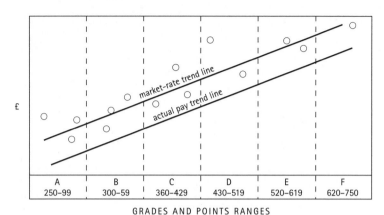

GRADES AND POINTS RANGES

The implications for the pay structure can then be considered and decisions made on where the range limits should be placed, taking into account policy on the width of the ranges and the desirability of having ranges which, as far as possible, accommodate the market rates for all the jobs in the grade. Clearly, the wider the range the greater the likelihood of fitting in all the jobs. But there may well be some jobs for which market rates are much higher than the pay range for the grade to which they have been allocated on the basis of internal comparisons. In such cases, market-rate premiums may have to be added to the rates for those jobs. It is undesirable for jobs to be placed in a grade higher than that indicated by internal equity simply because of market-rate pressures.

If there are a number of jobs in a job family for which market rates are significantly higher, it may be appropriate to set up a separate market group structure. In the event of market rates being significantly lower than the scale, internal relativity considerations should prevail.

Design the proposed structure

The information collected, presented and analysed as above is now put together to produce a design for the structure, as illustrated in Figure 27. In this example the midpoints of each grade broadly correspond with the median market trend line. The graph also shows where the rates of pay of existing employees are placed in relation to the proposed pay ranges.

If the first design results in an undue proportion of anomalies (individuals paid above or below the range limits) it may be necessary to reconsider the grade structure and pay ranges. Computer modelling techniques as described in Chapter 37 can greatly facilitate this process. They can be used on a 'what if?' basis to establish the extent to which different grade configurations reduce or increase the anomalies and therefore reduce the problems and costs of implementing the new or revised structure. Iteration may be necessary to obtain an optimum solution. Unless the grades are very broad, it is

Figure 27 **Grade structure**

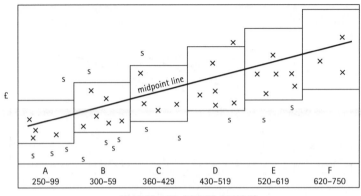

GRADES AND POINTS RANGES

unusual to redesign a structure without giving rise to some anomalies, although the need to avoid them should be constantly borne in mind when producing the initial proposal.

Assess the new structure and its cost implications and iterate as necessary

This assessment takes place when the iterative procedure described above has produced what is believed to be the optimum design. The questions which should be answered before accepting the new structure are:

- Does it meet the objectives set for the exercise?

- Does it generally look reasonable – ie is it 'felt-fair'?

- Is it likely to be acceptable to all concerned? If not, can it at least be justified?

- More specifically, do jobs appear to be correctly grouped together in the grades?

- Are there any anomalies? If so, why?

- Are boundary problems likely to arise because jobs of nearly equal value have been placed on opposite sides of a grade boundary?

- Does it ensure that jobs of equal value are paid equally?

- Can higher rates of pay because of perceived market pressures be objectively justified?

- Will it be manageable?

- Will the costs of implementation be acceptable?

The costs will depend first on the extent to which the optimisation process still leaves people who are paid below the minimum of the new range for their job, and second on policy for dealing with such cases and the pay of those whose current rate is above the new maxima. Employees who are paid less than the new minimum rate of pay for their grade should be brought up to that minimum. If, however, the gap is considerable, the increase may be given in two or three stages. It may be necessary to accept that some people will have to be paid above the range maxima for their job. In the circumstances they can be treated as a special case – 'red-circled' – and their pay could be frozen. But this is obviously demotivating, and special achievements or sustained levels of high performance could be rewarded by lump-sum bonuses. Their pay might also be protected against inflation.

If people paid below the new range limits receive a pay increase, immediately or staged, while the pay of those paid above the limits is protected, there are clearly going to be some extra costs. Typically, such costs amount to 3 per cent or more of the paybill. Cost levels can be calculated with the help of a computer program. If they are unacceptable, in spite of the earlier design iterations, it may be necessary to reconsider the structure yet again, using the computer to model alternative costs.

If the earlier work was thorough and, importantly, if key issues were raised in advance with those concerned (management and employees), it should be possible to answer the above questions satisfactorily. If not, then it is a case of 'back to the drawing-board'.

Plan implementation
Finally, plans are made for implementation. They include communicating generally to employees the details of the new structure and its implications, and discussing with any individual special cases how they will be affected. It is best not to leave individuals too long in doubt about the impact the new structure will have on them. Arrangements have also to be made for employees to appeal against their gradings or to raise through a grievance procedure any complaints about how they have been treated.

Because a new structure will convey some telling messages about the reward philosophies and policies of the organisation, great care should be taken in communicating what it means to employees. It is equally important to consult line managers and employees before embarking on the exercise and to get them to participate as much as possible in the various activities involved.

Conclusions
The judgements, iterations and compromises that are inevitable in any pay structure design or redesign exercise using the approaches described above (including the analytical approach) indicate that it is not a scientific process, and it is usually difficult to please all the people all the time. The design of pay structures is a demanding exercise involving hard choices and, possibly, heavy costs. It should not be embarked upon lightly.

ADJUSTING THE STRUCTURE IN RESPONSE TO GENERAL INCREASES IN PAY LEVELS

A decision to increase pay levels generally to ensure that the pay structure remains competitive, or following pay negotiations, can be implemented by proportionate increases in the midpoint of each range. If the span of the existing ranges is to be retained, their maxima and minima are similarly increased. It may be decided, however, that it would be appropriate to alter the size of the ranges by increasing the maxima or the minima less or more than proportionately.

SUMMARY

- A conventional graded pay structure consists of a sequence of job grades into which jobs of broadly equivalent value are slotted. A pay range is attached to each grade.

- Jobs are allocated to grades on the basis of an assessment of their relative internal value. Grades may be defined in terms of a points bracket if a point-factor job evaluation scheme is used. Alternatively they may be defined verbally if a job classification system is used or by reference to the benchmark jobs slotted into the grade.

- A pay range is attached to each grade. It indicates the minimum and maximum rates payable for any job in the grade and the scope for the pay of job-holders to progress while they are in that grade.

- Graded pay structures are based on the belief that individuals should progress through ranges by reference to their performance, skill, competence or time in the job.

- The advantages of graded structures are that they: clearly indicate pay relativities, provide a framework for managing relativities and for ensuring that jobs of equal value are paid equally, allow better control over the fixing of rates of pay and pay progression, and are easy to explain to employees.

- The disadvantages are that: defining grade boundaries is a matter of judgement which may not always be easy to defend, If there are too many grades, there will be constant pressure for upgrading, leading to grade drift. Pay ranges create the expectation that everyone is entitled to reach the top of the scale. They can also create or maintain hierarchical rigidity which is at odds with the requirement of flexibility in new team- and process-based organisations.

- The design process groups together jobs which are of a similar value and separates those which are significantly different. The range of pay for the grade should accommodate the range of market rates for the jobs in the grade.

- The four methods of designing a graded pay structure are (1) empirical – making assumptions about the number of grades and where jobs should be slotted in; (2) by reference to market-rate data – the market pricing approach; (3) following a job ranking exercise; and (4) following a point-factor job evaluation exercise – the analytical approach.

FURTHER READING

The most comprehensive description of graded pay structures and their design is given in *Reward Management* by Michael Armstrong and Helen Murlis (Chapters 14 and 17), fourth edition (1998).

17 Broad-banded pay structures

An increasing number of fast-changing businesses are facing the problem of what to do with a traditional pay system which is ill-suited to their needs in the 1990s and beyond. They have to ask the question 'Do we want to continue with what has worked well in the past, or do we experiment with a new and untested approach?' Broad-banding offers a solution to this dilemma. Essentially, it involves reducing the number of grades into a relatively small number of much wider 'bands' in which pay is managed more flexibly than in a conventional graded structure, and increased attention is paid to market relativities. Broad-banding started in the USA: a William Mercer study in 1997 of 3,000 US organisations found that close to 45 per cent had either installed broad-banding or were considering it. Broad-banding got off to a slow start in the UK but research conducted by Watson Wyatt in 1996 showed that 20 per cent of the 346 firms surveyed had introduced the system. Of the remainder, more than half planned to introduce it. Since then, there has been a considerable increase in the number of organisations with broad bands. The IRS 1998 survey revealed that 38 per cent of the respondents had introduced a form of broad-banding and 19 per cent were intending to do so.

This chapter starts with a definition of broad-banding and then discusses its aims, its main features, the reasons for its introduction, its advantages and disadvantages, and the factors that influence the degree to which it is appropriate. The chapter ends with a description of methods of introducing broad-banding. On completing the chapter, the reader will understand the rationale of broad-banding, the problems it may create and the circumstances in which it might be introduced.

BROAD-BANDING DEFINED

Broad-banding is the compression of a hierarchy of pay grades or salary ranges into a small number (typically four or five) of wide bands. Each of the bands will therefore span the pay opportunities previously covered by several separate pay ranges, as illustrated in Figure 28.

THE AIMS OF BROAD-BANDING

The aims of this process of collapsing job clusters or tiers of positions into a few wide bands are to

Figure 28 Converting from traditional ranges to broad bands

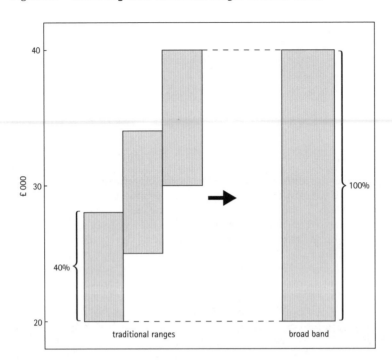

- provide pay structures which fit de-layered (flatter) organisation structures

- enable processes originally created to sustain hierarchy and vertical movement to be replaced

- support operational and role flexibility and teamworking

- reflect the new emphasis on horizontal processes which is frequently a product of a business process re-engineering exercise

- produce a better framework for communicating what the organisation values and is prepared to pay for

- develop alternative methods of payment that reflect a broader spectrum of employee development and contribution, including increased levels of competence, skill acquisition, career development, continuous learning, adaptability and flexibility

- facilitate lateral career moves and internal mobility in flatter organisations by providing rewards for such moves (career development pay), thus conveying the message that advancement can take place by horizontal as well as vertical movement within the organisation

- help to simplify the administrative processes involved in the delivery of pay by, for example, reducing dependence on elaborate job evaluation systems.

FEATURES OF BROAD-BANDING

There is a wide range of terms and approaches taken by companies in implementing broad bands. There is no such thing as a model broad-banded structure – but there are some features which are generally present in a fully-realised broad-banded structure. These shared characteristics are:

- A much smaller number of pay grades exist.

- There is a considerably wider spread between the minimum and maximum pay limits of bands (the pay range or span).

- There may be considerable overlap in pay terms between bands.

- Bands may be described in terms of the roles allocated to them and defined by reference to job evaluation points or to generic definitions.

- The 'band architecture' may be relatively unstructured to foster maximum flexibility, but some structure may be incorporated by designating 'anchor rates' for roles or clusters of roles, and defining zones within which progression in the same role can be rewarded.

- Pay levels in bands are strongly influenced by market rates – most broad-banded structures could be said to be 'market driven' – market relativities may therefore be the most important factor in positioning roles in bands, but the relative size of roles is usually also taken into account.

- Formal analytical job evaluation schemes may not be used at all, or if they do exist, they have a mainly supporting role once the band structure has been designed.

- Roles are slotted into bands by reference to band definitions – the positioning of roles in the band will be determined by referring to both external and internal relativities.

- There is provision for lateral progression through the band rather than vertical progression (promotion or upgrading) through an extended hierarchy of grades.

- Progression is often based on competence and contribution, never on service, and infrequently on performance alone (high levels of achievement in a role are most probably rewarded by a cash bonus).

- Progression along the band does not depend on taking on new roles – people can move beyond the rate for their role if it has expanded or if they are making a contribution above the level expected of them.

- Progression in a band may be related to career development.

- There is an emphasis on flexibility in delivering pay and rewarding people in roles: the focus is on paying the person rather than paying for the job.

- More responsibility for managing pay in bands is usually devolved to line managers within their budgets and in accordance with general guidelines about pay and career management.

- Effective budgeting and control processes are particularly important to avoid escalating costs in broad-banded structures.

- Broad-banding provides a framework for managing and developing people and for career planning: it is not just about delivering pay.

The number of bands

Broad-banded structures typically have four or five bands to cover all salaried employees. Some organisations which exclude directors from the system have only three bands. A structure with more than six or seven bands could be better described as a 'fat-graded' structure. According to Gilbert and Abosch (1996), the number of bands depends on how many 'value-adding tiers' exist in an organisation. A value-added tier is defined by them as a cluster of roles that have common responsibilities and accountabilities – in other words, the distinguishable levels of management, supervision, professional and technical staff and operatives, administrators or support workers. Watson Wyatt found that the median number of bands in the companies covered by their 1995 survey was five.

The following are examples of the number of bands in different organisations:

- *Bass Brewers* – five (all staff: group resource, senior management, management, professional/technical, and support)

- *British Aerospace Holdings Inc.* – seven bands (senior management 1 and 2, professional 1 to 3, senior specialist, specialist)

- *Citibank* – six (all staff except senior managers)

- *Glaxo Wellcome* – six (all staff)

- *IBM* – nine (all staff)

- *Inland Revenue* – five (all staff except senior management)

- *Midland Bank* – three (all managerial staff)

- *RAC Motoring Services* – five (all managers)

- *Reckitt & Colman* – six (global senior executives).

Width of bands

A typical 'salary spread' for a band is about 100 per cent – ie at least twice as wide as a traditional salary range. The width may, however, vary from level to level. The following are examples of broad-band pay spans adopted by organisations covered by the recent IPD research (*IPD Guide on Broad-banding* 1997):

- *Bass Brewers* – 78 to 100 per cent

- *BP* – no defined widths

- *Glaxo Wellcome* – 100 per cent plus

- *Inland Revenue* – 74 to 101 per cent

- *Midland Bank* – band minima only

- *RAC Motoring Services* – no defined widths

- *Reckitt & Colman* – 50 per cent.

Organisations such as the RAC with no defined widths are in effect operating on the assumption that the width of bands has to be flexible in accordance with the spread of market rates for jobs placed in the band.

Overlap between bands

There is usually a large overlap between bands, of 50 per cent or more. This provides room for more flexibility in pay provision by recognising that people in roles in one band may deliver more added value than some in the next higher band. For example, a high-level individual contributor such as a very specialised research scientist working at the leading edge could be more valuable to the organisation than his or her team leader. It also enables individuals in a band to continue receiving 'career development' pay increases as they expand their roles without having to be upgraded to a higher band.

Band structure

The structure of bands ('band architecture' as it is termed in the USA) is much more flexible than it is in a graded structure. Because of their spread, broad bands do not have midpoints. There is no reference- or control-point for all jobs in the band which represents the market-related norm and is used as a basis for the traditional control systems of compa-ratios and midpoint management.

However, within the band, 'target' rates of pay may be assigned to individual roles or clusters of related roles which are usually determined by reference to market values, although when setting up the structure roles may be 'sized' within the band through job evaluation. There may be no definition of the range of pay around this target rate which can be earned by individual employees. It would depend entirely on an assessment of their contribution and competence, and pay progression may be primarily related to career development without any defined limits within the band.

Alternatively, pay zones may be established for jobs within the band which are 'anchored' by market rates. These define the target rate for a competent individual in the role and indicate that when someone is paid below market value, pay should be brought up to that rate as long as the individual achieves the required level of competence. People can be paid above the target rate within the zone if their delivered performance is above that normally expected of their role. There is scope to move beyond the zone as far as the upper limits of the band, but only if people develop their competences and their range and level of expertise and thus extend or enlarge their existing role to make a larger contribution and deliver added value. As Hofrichter (1993) emphasises: 'These payment zones are not merely salary ranges within a band, since individuals are not paid above market value merely for doing a job well or establishing seniority or tenure.' The purpose of zones is to provide managers with guidance in making pay decisions, and, unlike traditional salary ranges, it is possible for employees to be paid outside the zone without the need for special approval or job evaluation. Pay zones are not defined in job evaluation point terms so that a move to a higher zone is a matter of taking on greater responsibility in a new or expanded role which requires higher levels of competence. It is not about acquiring more points.

Figure 29 Zones with target rates and scope for individual progression in band

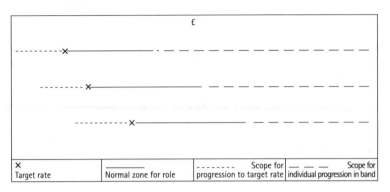

The use of pay zones in a broad band is illustrated in Figure 29.

Although it is always emphasised that pay zones within a broad band are not the same as orthodox pay ranges, they can look remarkably similar. IDS (1995) give an example of their use at Sun Life where, in one particularly wide range, five overlapping sub-ranges defined by 'trigger-points' and 'pay ceilings' have been created. The IDS comment on this approach was that 'The use of such pay zones casts doubt on the view that broad-banding represents a radical new departure from traditional organisations. From the employee's perspective, there may be little difference between grades and pay zones.' And this comment is justified if pay zones impose strict limits on pay progression in a job – even more so if pay progression in a band depends on moving to successive pay zones. (In the latter case the system would just be a traditional grade structure under a more fashionable name.)

Describing bands
Bands can be described simply in terms of the broad characteristics of jobs that may be allocated to them. To underline the message that a broad-banded structure is not the same as traditional graded structure hierarchies, most companies which introduce broad-banding do not designate bands by numbers or letters. Instead, they use general descriptive labels such as senior management, management, team leaders, individual contributors (professional and technical) and individual contributors (administrative and support).

Defining bands
Bands are sometimes defined by means of job evaluation points – as at Bass Brewers and Glaxo Wellcome – so that all jobs with a score of between, say, 750 and 1,000 points are placed in one band. Bands may, however, be defined simply in terms of the generic roles allocated to them – so, for example, a band for managers may be described by a general description of the characteristics of the managerial roles in the band. This is a form of job classification and this process could therefore be described as the use of a non-analytical job evaluation method. Another approach is to describe bands by reference to the different levels of competence required. This method is used at BP

Exploration where the headings of the company's competence framework provide the basis for defining the levels of competence in each band.

Determining the pay range of bands

An indication of the pay range of a band is provided by the market rates of the roles assigned to it. In a zoned band, the bottom of the range is determined by the starting-point of the zone for the role with the lowest market rate, while the top of the range is the upper limit of the zone for the role with the highest market rate. This means that the width of the band may be adjusted whenever there is a significant increase in market rates at the upper end. Such adjustments could be frequent, in contrast to the rigid nature of a conventional grade. This is an illustration of the flexible approach to managing pay in a broad band. If reliable market rates are not available at the upper or lower end of the band, an assumption is made on what scope there should be for pay progression by reference to other benchmark roles in the same or adjacent bands.

Allocating and positioning roles

One of the avowed aims of some companies which introduce broad-banding is to reduce the administrative burden of running a traditional grade structure. This is achieved by abandoning elaborate point-factor evaluation schemes and relying on market pricing to determine both the total range of pay in the band and the target rates for individual jobs. Because there are relatively few bands, each of which clearly covers a readily identifiable group of jobs, some organisations simply slot jobs into bands by a process akin to internal benchmarking or by reference to band definitions (job classification). As Braddick *et al* (1992) of Hewitt Associates comment:

> In most cases [*of broad-banding*] the need for detailed job evaluation diminishes. It is far easier to determine what the correct band is when there are only five to choose from than it is to determine the correct salary grade when the evaluation process involves 25 grades.

Organisations with broad bands do, however, often underpin the structure with some form of job evaluation. It may be used simply to define band boundaries, as mentioned above, target rates within bands being established by market pricing. Alternatively, job evaluation can establish the relative size of all the roles in a band when it is established and then be used to place new roles in the band or to compare roles from an equal pay for work of equal value viewpoint. However, decisions on placing roles in bands may be mainly influenced by external relativities.

Many organisations in the USA have simplified their approach to job evaluation. In 1993 David Hofrichter, vice-president and managing director of the Hay Group, noted that:

> Rather than evaluating specific jobs, the company considers each individual's 'primary focus of output'. It then assigns each output a market value that reflects the incumbent's job understanding, mastery and performance. Next the company establishes 'payment zones' in which movement beyond market value is linked to an increase in the

incumbent's competences – those skills and behaviours associated with peak performance in his or her specific job and within the company's overall culture.

As Braddick *et al* (1992) remark:

> Market pricing is more important with broad bands than with traditional salary structures. About half of Hewitt's survey respondents expect their use of external salary data to increase. This need is driven in part by the use of market data to determine pay targets within bands.

Harbig Garabedian, manager of organisation and human resources development at GE Plastics, says that 'We've increased our participation in job-matching surveys, which allow us good insight into market worth. We've made that information available to our managers, who use it as a reference-point in setting individual salaries.'

A survey of five major US companies with broad-banding by the Corporate Leadership Council (1994) found that their methods of managing broad bands 'typically involve utilising market surveys for general band ranges and relying upon strictly-defined development plans, competency levels and skill assessments for deciding compensation within bands'.

The position of roles within bands (selecting anchor rates) may be primarily determined by market relativities, but when designing the structure the relative size of the role as determined by job evaluation may indicate where roles should be placed. Additionally, positioning on an internal equity basis may have to be modified to respond to market conditions. In common with all approaches to pay structure design, job evaluation may be used when valid and reliable market-rate comparisons cannot be made. In these circumstances, the relative 'size' of the role can be used to position it in relation to roles for which market comparisons are available.

Pay progression according to competence and contribution

In traditional graded structures it is usual to have rigid or prescribed methods of progressing pay through the relatively narrow grades. A much more flexible approach can be adopted in wider and less structured broad bands. Progression is based on managerial judgements about the individual's contribution, competence and ability to continue developing. It is recognised in today's flexible organisations that people are not restricted to the set of prescribed duties in a stable job. Instead, they carry out dynamic roles in which their level of competence is likely to be a major factor in determining what they do as well as how they do it. This particularly applies to the increasing proportion of knowledge workers, who generally have greater scope to influence the content of their work because of the skills they can bring to bear on it. People not only grow in their roles, they can also grow their roles. In a broad-banded structure, progression is people- rather than job-oriented. The emphasis is on growth and continuous development for which people will receive both financial and non-financial rewards – the opportunity to develop and achieve more recognition as well as more pay.

Broad-banding is thus focused on competency-development, but competencies are much more than a set of skills that may or may not be used. As Hofrichter (1993) points out, they consist of 'skills, knowledge, abilities, characteristics and other attributes, that in the right combination and under the right set of circumstances, predicate superior performance'. Progression within a band is based not on the existence of knowledge and skills but on their application in a series of career moves in which people are faced with new opportunities and challenges.

Relating pay progression to career progression

One of the most important reasons for broad-banding is to recognise and reward continuous development. Bergel (1994) remarks that:

> In a banded pay structure, career development pay is viewed as a strategic pay delivery system for rewarding employees for improving their flexibility, experience and knowledge by making lateral moves to other parts of the organisation. Such moves can be made in role (eg from manager to individual contributor), function (eg from sales to marketing), business line (eg from product A in division C to product B in division D), and so on.

Broad-banding facilitates lateral career moves which broaden experience and develop competences. Holbeche (1998) suggests that career planning in the flatter organisation is best catered for by creating broad career bands through which lateral development can take place. Broad-banding encourages people to use their abilities to achieve results in roles which they might have been unwilling to move into as seeming no more (or even less) important than their present one.

For example, a manager in one department might take a job as assistant manager in another with a greater need of his or her talents and brighter opportunities for career development and extra rewards. The move would be made without loss of pay. There could even be an increase if the new challenge were sufficiently demanding. The manager of a large established branch might be moved to a smaller new one with an increase in pay. The rise would be a recognition that special skills and abilities are required to develop the new outlet and that the successful application of these skills will benefit both the company in terms of profitable growth and the individual in terms of increased career potential. A marketing manager may be more willing to move into sales if he or she perceives it as a career opportunity which will be suitably rewarded. A senior accountant might take a new career path in a lower-level job as a financial analyst without sacrificing any pay.

Career development pay can be combined with performance management processes which include performance improvement and personal development plans. Pay progression can be related to success in hitting agreed targets for improvement and development which meet expectations on levels of performance, behaviour and the knowledge and skills to be acquired.

Managing broad bands

One of the reasons often advanced for broad-banding is that it reduces the burden of pay administration. But in practice it can be more difficult to manage and control than a conventional grade structure system. This is because broad-banding operates more flexibly. By definition, there is more scope for the pay of employees to progress within a broad band than in the relatively small pay limits imposed by a typical grade structure. Greater responsibility for managing pay is usually, and rightly, devolved to line managers. Their freedom to make decisions is not inhibited by a fixed incremental system or constrained by rigid guidelines.

Perhaps the most important question that needs to be answered about broad-banding is therefore 'How, in the absence of clearly defined and fairly narrow limits for pay progression, accompanied by strict guidelines, are we going to (1) control pay costs and (2) achieve a proper degree of equity and consistency in making decisions on rates of pay for jobs and people?' This question can be answered in one of the following ways.

Total payroll budgeting

Payroll budgets are determined for the organisation and each of its departments. Managers have to work generally within these budgets during the period, although the budgets may be flexed to reflect increases or decreases in activity levels and the need to create new roles or reduce the number of employees. If there is a formal pay review a fixed budget of, say, 5 per cent is allocated to managers which they must not exceed but which they can distribute amongst their staff in the form of career development pay related to increases in contribution and competence. This approach controls costs and grants managers the maximum freedom and flexibility within their budgets. But it relies on their capacity to distribute rewards appropriately and without discrimination. It is desirable, therefore, to adopt one or more of the other methods described below to achieve a proper degree of equity, fairness and consistency.

Briefing, education and training

No broad-banding system will work unless line managers and their staff are briefed on how it will be applied. Line managers need to be educated in the principles governing the system and trained in how to operate it in their departments. The education and training should emphasise the need for fairness and consistency and provide guidance on how the need can be met through performance and career management and salary planning. The points to be covered by the training are discussed in Chapter 28.

Guidelines

These can take the form of information on target rates for jobs in line with market values (the minimum that should be supplied). More guidance can be provided by the definition of payment zones indicating typical ranges on either side of the target rates within which pay may be progressed – up to the target rate as individuals acquire the levels of competence they need to carry out the role effectively; above the target rate to recognise further growth. This is a fairly common method of providing guidance, and it can be appropriate as long as the flexibility inherent to broad-banding is preserved by giving managers the authority to go beyond the zone limits to reward growth through career development pay.

Specific performance-related pay guidelines can be provided on the increases recommended for different performance ratings. But the excessive use of comprehensive and mandatory guidelines can compromise the key features of broad-banding – flexibility and freedom for managers to manage their most important resource on the basis of what they believe to be in the interests of their department and the people who work in it.

Monitoring

Personnel or pay specialists can monitor proposals by line managers for pay increases. They can study the distribution of pay within bands and question any instances when unusual decisions appear to have been made.

The extent to which monitoring is necessary will clearly depend on the capacity of line managers to exercise their powers responsibly and the perceived need to take special care to avoid gender or any other form of bias. Judgement is necessary on how much monitoring takes place and on what happens if line and personnel managers disagree.

Flexibility

Broad-banding enables pay to be managed much more flexibly than in a conventional graded structure. Flexibility extends to both placing roles in bands and progressing pay within and between bands. Pay decisions are not governed by rigid job evaluation procedures and they are not usually subject to the confines of a pay matrix or the forced distribution of ratings and increases. More scope is often available for managers to vary pay in relation to contribution and continuous development within pay budgets and in accordance with broad guidelines. There is, of course, a penalty to be paid for this. Many people, managers as well as employees, feel uncomfortable without structure. The basis for decisions may not be so clear, managers may not like to be accountable to their own staff as well as their superiors for their proposals, and staff may suspect that decisions will be inconsistent and unfair. These problems have to be addressed when setting up the structure and deciding how it should be managed and controlled.

Devolution to line managers

The extent to which the management of pay is devolved to line managers is often greater in broad-banded structures. This could be because broad-banding is a relatively recent innovation and the trend has generally been towards giving managers more responsibility for pay. But it is also because the philosophy of broad-banding is to empower managers to be more involved simply because they are in the best position, within limits, to make decisions about how people should be rewarded in constantly changing situations.

Placing more onus on managers does mean, however, that they need to be briefed and trained in their responsibilities and given guidance and help as required. And their decisions will have to be monitored to ensure that they are in accord with policy guidelines.

Broad-banding is not just about pay

The question to be answered in developing a broad-banded structure is: 'How will this support the needs of the business?' not: 'How will this deliver pay better?' Broad-banding should not just be regarded simply as an alternative pay structure. It should instead be treated as a framework for managing people and their personal and career development.

REASONS FOR INTRODUCING BROAD-BANDING

Research conducted by Hewitt Associates in 1992 covering 27 major US companies established that the top five reasons for broad-banding were:

- to facilitate internal transfers/job mobility (65 per cent)

- to de-emphasise promotion (54 per cent)

- to support a new organisation culture/climate (46 per cent)

- to foster a flatter organisation (38 per cent)

- to simplify/reduce administrative effort (35 per cent).

A survey by *Employee Relations and Human Resources Bulletin* (1992) identified the following reasons for broad-banding in a selection of US companies:

- GE Plastics introduced broad-banding to complement and accentuate changes in its corporate value system and to move away from a rigid hierarchy. Twenty-one pay grades were reduced to five career bands.

- PSI Energy was seeking to create a simpler organisation and believed broad-banding was one of the needed steps. It also wanted to encourage teamwork, to get employees more involved in information flow, and to break down barriers. It was felt that banding would help to eliminate some of the old emphasis on grades and titles.

- At Consumers Power Association the decision to introduce broad-banding arose because of the company's compressed structure and the need for a new type of evaluation system for jobs that would support that structure.

As reported in the IDS *Management Pay Review* (1995), flexible roles, flexible working and flexible pay are the key themes of recent developments in the USA. In the UK they are the major reasons for the move to broad-banding by such organisations as National Freight Corporation and Sun Life.

At BP, broad-banding was introduced for the following reasons:

- better 'fit' with the de-layered organisation

- to correspond to the changing nature of the work

- to emphasise development, not grade progression

- greater management involvement in pay.

At British Rail Research, broad-banding – as described in 1994 by Kate Johnson, personnel director at a Hay Management Consultants conference – has:

- led to fewer job descriptions and has relaxed perceptions of traditional job boundaries

- engendered generic and professional families, with the potential for building teams and valuing more highly the contribution made by support staff

- reduced layers, thus providing fewer barriers to change

- lessened the bureaucracy of job evaluation

- provided a platform for a better remuneration policy

- been a powerful tool for achieving cultural change.

British Aerospace Holdings Inc. stated in a 1997 communication to staff:

> BAe has introduced broad-banding to increase the flexibility of our organisation and to simplify our compensation system. Simply put, our old system of grade levels was unnecessarily bureaucratic and cumbersome. It might have been right for us years ago, but times have changed. We wanted to become more flexible, and broad-banding will do that.

Armstrong and Baron (1995) found that companies such as Bass Taverns introduced broad-banding to support strategies for organisational and cultural change with the emphasis on horizontal processes and lateral development. At Glaxo Wellcome broad-banding was installed to promote flexibility and, again, continuous development.

Bergel (1994) indicates that organisations are introducing broad-banding to improve teamwork and eliminate barriers to communication and development. They are achieving this by:

- requiring fewer grade levels and titles

- providing alternative career tracks for individual contributors

- rewarding lateral career development moves within wider salary ranges.

The best-known example of broad-banding is provided by General Electric in the USA. It was pioneered in the late 1980s to support the vision of GE's chief executive officer Jack Welch, who wanted the company in the 1990s to become a 'boundaryless' organisation in which the barriers and distinctions that separated employees from each other on the inside and from key constituencies on the outside would be eliminated. As explained by Dan Gilbert, staff consultant (compensation) at GE:

> Career bands support that vision by enabling employees to evaluate new positions based on job content and impact rather than the role's position level, and to see jobs for what they can become as opposed to what they are. (Abosch et al, 1994)

In 1994, GE had four 'career bands' for all non-executive salaried employees, as shown in Table 21. They replaced a 14-grade structure in which there was automatic progression to the midpoint and merit-

Table 21   Broad-banding at GE

Band title	Width (%)	Minimum ($)	Maximum ($)
Senior professional	115	48,000	102,000
Lead professional	124	33,000	76,000
Professional	160	20,000	52,000
Associate professional	188	16,000	35,000

increase grids related to quartiles. This structure, according to Gilbert, sent the message that 'success is measured quartile by quartile, position level by position level'. It gave employees 'the sense that their world within the firm is a high-definition world, unlike the world outside the business'. He believes that 'With their lack of definition, bands help people experience an internal culture that more closely mirrors the external competitive environment, and as a result makes it easier for employees to re-orientate themselves to the marketplace.' Above all, it is claimed by GE that 'broad-bands facilitate the internal mobility of employees from job to job, help employees focus on a new position's high-impact characteristics rather than the salary grade, and present less complexity than traditional structures.'

THE ADVANTAGES AND DISADVANTAGES OF BROAD-BANDING

The main advantages of broad-banding are that it

- enhances organisational flexibility by reducing the number of vertical break-points

- reduces the time spent analysing and evaluating jobs because there are fewer levels between which distinctions need to be drawn

- speaks more directly to each employee's personal growth by paying for skills and competences

- supports teamworking by encouraging the development of multi-focus roles and a 'boundaryless' organisation

- can, as indicated by Bergel (1994), help organisations to reward 'lateral career development, continuous learning, team flexibility and outstanding performance ... the end-result is a rewards system that motivates employees to develop new skills, to experiment with their careers within the organisation, and to focus on the organisation's performance goals'

- enhances the ability of the organisation to reward people for what they 'bring to the party' beyond their job descriptions

- directs employee attention towards career growth, indicating through the wider spread of pay opportunities that only significantly larger job responsibilities merit moving to a higher pay band

- provides greater flexibility along with a wider array of career-building opportunities

- offers pay increase opportunities for mastering new competences within the band

- allows more responsibility and accountability to be given to managers to make pay decisions: they can no longer blame the personnel department if things go wrong.

The advantages of broad-banding may seem considerable but there are some important disadvantages. Broad-banding

- appears to restrict the number of promotional opportunities: lateral career development pay may alleviate the problem but employees may still look elsewhere to further their career (although it could be said that this problem is a function of de-layering rather than of the broad-banding which often mirrors a flattened organisation)

- may mean that employees formerly in higher grades feel that it has devalued their jobs by placing them in the same band as employees previously in a lower grade – team leaders could find themselves in the same band as their staff

- may create concern amongst employees at the apparent lack of structure and precision – they could find it difficult to understand how pay decisions affecting them are made and why they are placed at certain points in the bands

- may create management problems for HR – the lack of structure and rules may mean that the department has to spend more time in monitoring pay decisions and coaching or helping line managers

- can ask much more from line managers than a conventional structure in which all the decisions were often made for them – they may or may not be able or willing to respond to this challenge

- requires a significant commitment of training and communication resources if it is to be successful

- can build up employee expectations of significant pay opportunities which are doomed in many cases if proper control of the system is maintained – this danger underlines the need for very thorough communications about how the system will operate which, while indicating that there will be room to reward career development, emphasises that rewards will have to be earned

- may lead to escalating payroll costs unless careful control is exercised over the operation of the system – but there is a delicate balance to be achieved between allowing sufficient flexibility and simultaneously maintaining the right amount of control.

Perhaps the greatest difficulty with broad-banding in the UK arises if it means that an analytical job evaluation process is no longer used for every job. This approach could lead to lack of control over gender bias and problems in defending an equal-value case. It should be remembered that the USA, where the concept of broad-banding originated, does not enjoy the same sort of universal equal-value legislation that exists in the UK. Equal-value considerations have therefore been relatively much less important in the USA.

WHEN IS IT APPROPRIATE TO INTRODUCE BROAD-BANDING?

Broad-banding is being introduced by a growing number of organisations which are in the midst of transformation seeking a new pay structure to fit a new organisational structure. It can be appropriate in organisations where promotional opportunities have disappeared as the organisations have become leaner and flatter but where there is still a need to develop a more broadly-skilled and flexible workforce that can take on new challenges, tasks and projects and adapt rapidly to change.

Braddick *et al* (1992) showed that companies which are the strongest candidates for a successful broad-band system have the following characteristics:

- They are looking to support a new culture and are most likely to have just experienced a precipitous event.
- Top management strategy supports the change.
- Communication channels within the organisation are effective.
- Line managers are skilled at setting and managing employee pay.

Organisations that are least likely to benefit from broad-banding may have some or all of the following characteristics:

- They may already be very successful with their pay programme.
- They may have a strong culture that values a traditional organisational hierarchy.
- They may have an effective career management system.
- Their job structure already supports their business strategy.
- They may be looking to broad-banding to solve salary administration problems such as the 'topping out' of employees at the peak of their salary range.

INTRODUCING BROAD-BANDING

The first thing to remember is that there are many different approaches to broad-banding, none of which is intrinsically better than another. It all depends on what the organisation needs and wants, and many organisations can do without it altogether. The following steps are required.

General considerations
Consider the advantages and disadvantages of broad-banding, the extent to which it would be appropriate (by reference to the points listed above), and the benefits it might bring.

Assess whether the organisation is ready for broad-banding. Hofrichter (1993) suggests that the following questions need to be answered:

- Have we a clear idea of what our compensation programme should compensate?
- Do we know what types of performance we want the separate elements of our pay structure to reinforce?

- Are our employees and managers ready to accept a new pay structure? (They may be concerned about what they perceive as a lack of structure or precision.)

- Have we the necessary support mechanisms, such as good survey data, a clear understanding of the roles in the organisation, and computerised pay information systems?

- Will broad-banding make a 'value-added' difference to the organisation? (It should not be introduced simply to solve existing compensation problems.)

- Have we a clear vision of how to link pay with our organisational competences? (Any change in compensation must be tied to larger business objectives.)

Steps required to develop and introduce broad-banding

1 Decide in principle that broad-banding is desirable.

2 Make an empirical and provisional judgement on how many bands will be required by reference to an analysis of the organisation structure and the various roles carried out at each level.

3 Decide on the band architecture – the width of bands, the degree of overlap, the anchor points and zones.

4 Carry out a job evaluation exercise using benchmark (generic) roles to establish band boundaries and provide data on relative size. Revise the band structure as appropriate on the basis of this data.

5 Conduct a pay survey to establish market rates.

6 Position roles in bands (singly or in clusters) on the basis of relative size as established by job evaluation and by reference to market rates. As always, this will be a judgemental process to establish the relative weight to be given to internal and external relativities – the decision will depend on the extent to which it is policy to provide for market relativities to drive pay decisions.

7 Decide on the basis for progressing pay within zones and for adjusting pay levels following a change in role (an expansion of the existing role, or movement to an entirely new role).

8 Decide on the role of job evaluation in defining band boundaries, guiding band positioning decisions and dealing with new roles or equal-value queries.

9 Examine the existing rates of pay for individual employees, identify any increases that may be required (immediately or phased), and establish any cases where red-circling is necessary.

10 Draw up procedures for managing the structure, including the allocation of roles to bands, the use of job evaluation, the conduct of pay reviews, fixing salaries for recruiting purposes or following a change in role, maintaining data on market rates and the use of performance management processes to assist in making pay review decisions.

11 Brief and train managers on the new structure and their roles in managing pay.

12 Communicate details of the new structure and how it affects them to staff.

SUMMARY

- Broad-banding is the compression of a hierarchy of pay grades or salary ranges into a small number (typically four or five) of wide bands. Each of the bands will therefore span the pay opportunities previously covered by several separate pay ranges.

- The aims of broad-banding are to provide pay structures which fit de-layered organisation structures, support operational and role flexibility and teamworking, reflect the new emphasis on horizontal processes, and reward people for lateral development in the organisation.

- The main features of a broad-banded structure are:

  - a much smaller number of pay grades

  - there is a considerably wider spread between the minimum and maximum pay limits of bands

  - there may be considerable overlap in pay terms between bands

  - bands may be described in terms of the roles allocated to them and defined by reference to job evaluation points or to generic definitions

  - the 'band architecture' may be relatively unstructured to foster maximum flexibility, but some structure may be incorporated by designating 'anchor rates' for roles or clusters of roles, and defining zones within which progression in the same role can be rewarded

  - pay levels in bands are strongly influenced by market rates

  - formal analytical job evaluation schemes may not be used at all, or if they do exist, they have a mainly supporting role

  - roles are slotted into bands by reference to band definitions – the positioning of roles in the band is determined by referring to both external and internal relativities

  - there is provision for lateral progression through the band rather than vertical progression (promotion or upgrading) through an extended hierarchy of grades

  - more responsibility for managing pay in bands is usually devolved to line managers.

- Typical reasons for introducing broad-banding are the introduction of de-layered organisation structure, need for increased flexibility in managing pay, and to emphasise lateral development, not grade progression.

- The advantages of broad-banding are that it enhances organisational flexibility by reducing the number of vertical breakpoints, speaks more directly to each employee's personal growth by paying for skills and competences, and helps organisations to reward lateral career development, continuous learning, flexibility, competence and contribution.

- The disadvantages of broad-banding are that it appears to restrict the number of promotional opportunities, may create concern amongst employees at the apparent lack of structure and precision, and may create management problems for HR – the lack of structure and rules may mean that the department has to spend more time monitoring pay decisions and coaching or helping line managers.

FURTHER READING

Broad-banding is a fairly recent and mainly US phenomenon. With one exception (the IPD's 1997 *Guide on Broad-banding*), references sources are all from US publications. They give a good picture of the US scene but experience there is not necessarily transferred readily across the Atlantic (for example, differences in the approach to equal value).

18 Job family pay structures

Job family pay structures are being introduced in some organisations in response to the need to pay particular attention to how related occupational groups are managed in both pay and career development terms. A job family may be treated for pay purposes as a separate market group although attention will be paid to internal relativities between job families. From a career viewpoint, progression both in career and pay terms may be vertical within a family, lateral into related roles, or diagonal through promotion to another job family. Job families are often incorporated in broad-banded pay structures.

On completing this chapter the reader should understand:

• the concept of a job family and a job family pay structure

• how job family pay structures can be developed and managed.

THE JOB FAMILY

A job family is a group of jobs in which the essential nature and purpose of the work is similar but the work is carried out at different levels. Job families may be functional in that they cover specific work groups within an area, such as marketing, finance or personnel. Or they may be generic in that they cover similar types of work across functional boundaries – for example, professional staff, administrators, managers or team leaders.

The jobs within a family may be linked in any of the following ways:

• the nature of the work undertaken – eg administration, data-processing, customer relations

• the technical or professional discipline – eg scientists, engineers, designers, creative workers, accountants, personnel specialists

• a common function – eg production or sales management

• a hierarchy in a regionalised organisation – eg regional, area and branch managers

• the same job operating at different levels – eg secretaries

• branch managers – eg in building societies with different sizes of branches to reflect local conditions.

Within each type of job family there will be a number of common factors, but there will also be differentiating factors which can be used to distinguish the various levels of work.

Job family structure

A job family structure consists of separate pay structures for job families which may be graded in terms of levels of skill or competence. Each level may have its own finite pay range as in a conventional graded pay structure. Alternatively, progression may be managed more flexibly in a pay curve system as described in Chapter 15 which is predicated on a policy of continuous development.

Some organisations have conventional graded structures for the majority of their jobs but introduce job families where it is felt that an occupation needs to be dealt with separately, especially one in which job-holders are mainly professional staff or knowledge workers. Separate job families may only cover some roles in the organisation. The others may be catered for as single jobs in a common graded pay structure.

Job family structures may also be set up for 'market groups' where the occupations concerned are subject to particular market pressures. The market rates for such jobs are higher than those for other occupations which would be placed in the same grade on the basis of internal relativities alone. However, the creation of market groups means that there is increased risk of gender discrimination.

The overall job family structure consists of a number of separate job family graded pay structures which have been identified for this purpose. Each of these structures is aligned to market rates and

Figure 30 **A job family structure**

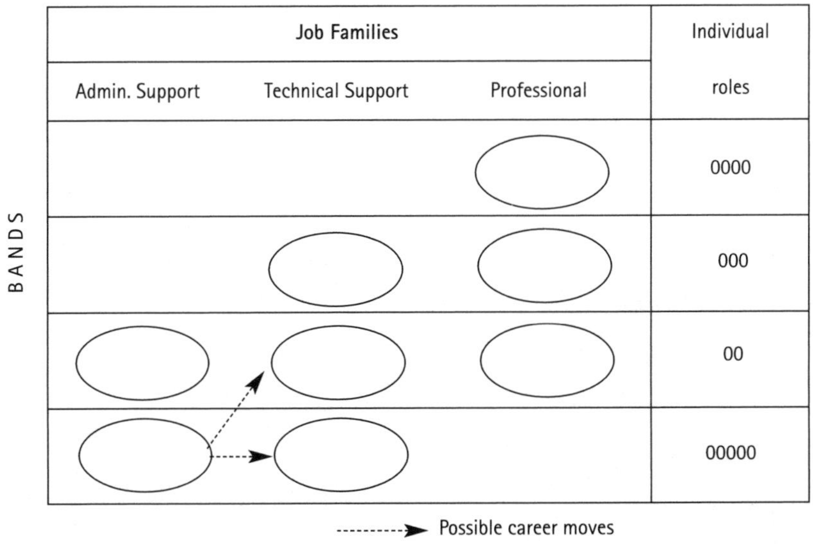

Job Families			Individual
Admin. Support	Technical Support	Professional	roles
		⬭	0000
	⬭	⬭	000
⬭	⬭	⬭	00
⬭	⬭		00000

`--------▸` Possible career moves

Source: Armstrong, M. and Murlis, H. *Reward Management,* 4th edition, Kogan Page, 1998.

contains a number of pay ranges which reflect the levels of work within the job family as defined by job evaluation. Any occupations not included in a job family are catered for by a common graded pay structure. This is easier to do within a broad-banded structure which provides a framework for both the job families and the individual roles and is likely to be defined in competence-level terms and use competence and contribution as the criteria for progression. The job evaluation process should preferably use a plan which is constructed on the basis of competence factors. A job family structure within a broad-banded structure is illustrated in Figure 30.

A broad-banded structure at IBM which incorporates job families is illustrated in Figure 31.

JOB FAMILY MODELLING

Job family modelling, as conducted by Hay Management Consultants, is the process of

- identifying groups of roles in which the type of work is similar but where the actual work is carried out at different levels

- analysing the essential nature of each of these groups or job families

- establishing the levels of work carried out within each family

- defining the differentiating factors between each level in the family in terms of role size

- producing functional or generic role specifications

- defining the pay ranges for bands or levels in the job family hierarchy by reference to market-rate data but taking into account internal relativities.

Figure 31   Broad-banding and job families at IBM

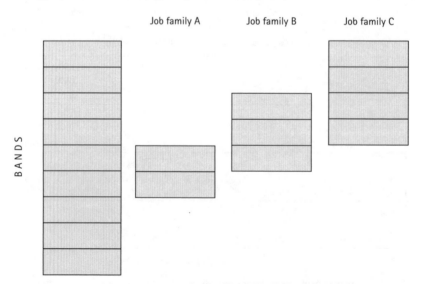

Source: The *IPD Guide on Broad-banding*, 1997.

Job family modelling analyses individual job families vertically and defines differences in role size at each level. It is complementary to level-of-work analysis, which is a horizontal process that establishes the relative similarities in role size across functions. Job family modelling and levels-of-work analysis are therefore related concepts which are applied side by side in a job family modelling exercise. A critical element of job family modelling, as carried out by Hay, is establishing the size of roles at different levels. Levels-of-work analysis allows work to be measured using reputable job measurement methodology. To meet equal-value requirements it is important to underpin job family modelling with analytical job evaluation.

Each job family describes a career path and clarifies the criteria for advancing from one level of the family to the next. Additional career paths are identified through grouping similar job families together. These represent the most likely career routes (after advancement through a family) because of the similarities in behavioural competencies and skills. Career paths between unrelated families can also be mapped.

Why have job family structures?
Job family structures are used because it is felt that some occupations need distinct treatment from both the reward and the career development points of view. One of their perceived advantages is that career progression on the basis of increases in skill or competence can be planned and individuals can be made aware of the development opportunities available to them in their job family. Such an approach should be designed to underpin organisational flexibility, fostering and encouraging lateral and diagonal career moves and supporting the concept of employability.

DISADVANTAGES

Although it can be argued that some occupations are best treated separately because they are different or because of their special market-rate position, job family structures can be divisive. They can further career development within a family but at the same time inhibit career flexibility (moving between different job families). Equity is more difficult to achieve, especially where job families provide rewards that are strongly oriented towards market rates and individual competencies.

WHEN JOB FAMILIES ARE APPROPRIATE

Job families are most likely to be appropriate when there are groups for whom it is thought special treatment is necessary, in terms either of career and pay planning or of particular market-rate pressures. They are often used for professional and other knowledge workers for whom career opportunities can readily be defined within the organisation.

Do you think job family structures are likely to be adopted more widely? If so, why?

SUMMARY

- A job family is a group of jobs in which the work is similar but it is carried out at different levels.

- A job family structure consists of separate structures for job families, often within a broad-banded framework. Some individual jobs may be left outside the job family structure.

- Job family structures can be designed by the Hay Management Consultants' process of job family modelling which involves identifying job families, analysing and defining levels of work in each family, establishing levels of work between job families by job evaluation and defining pay ranges.

- Job family structures enable distinct treatment to be given to related occupations for pay and career planning purposes. Job families can be treated as separate market groups and the structure as a whole can facilitate career planning. But job families can be divisive and equal pay could be a problem.

- Job family structures are most common in organisations which employ professional and knowledge workers.

FURTHER READING

The only detailed description of job family pay structures and job family modelling is to be found in Michael Armstrong and Helen Murlis, *Reward Management,* fourth edition, 1998, Kogan Page, Chapter 16.

Part 5

REWARDING INDIVIDUAL AND TEAM CONTRIBUTIONS AND ORGANISATIONAL PERFORMANCE

19 Contingent pay – general considerations and criteria

Pay systems are usually constructed around a base rate which constitutes the rate for the job or role and is determined by reference to internal relativities (job evaluation) and external relativities (market rates). The base rate can be regarded as the rate for a person who is fully capable of carrying out the role. In a spot rate structure, that is the fixed level of reward. But additions can be made to this rate which are contingent on factors other than the rate for the job. These factors may refer to the individual's length of service in the job, performance, competence, contribution or skill, team performance, or organisational performance.

Contingent pay may be consolidated in base pay, in which case it forms the basis for allowances such as sick pay and for pension arrangements. Alternatively it may be awarded in the form of a cash lump sum. The latter arrangement is called 'variable pay'. This is sometimes referred to as 'pay at risk' which has to be re-earned, as distinct from consolidated pay which is usually regarded as continuing as long as the person remains in the job and performs it satisfactorily.

The consolidated rate of pay can be raised generally (an 'across-the-board' payment) to recognise increases in the cost of living or market rates or following a negotiated settlement. Pay levels may be generally reduced in times of financial stringency.

The expression 'contingent pay' is a useful blanket term which covers the various methods of providing additional rewards for individuals or teams. On completing this chapter the reader will understand:

- the difference between the concept of a reward and that of an incentive
- the various forms of contingent pay
- variable pay
- the arguments for and against contingent pay
- the criteria for contingent pay
- the strategies available for introducing contingent pay.

The various types of contingent pay are considered in the next seven chapters (19 to 26). The last chapter in this part (Chapter 27) examines approaches to providing non-financial rewards and recognition.

THE DISTINCTION BETWEEN INCENTIVES AND REWARDS

When developing contingent pay policies and processes it is necessary to be clear about the extent to which a scheme is designed to provide an incentive or a reward. Incentives are forward-looking while rewards are retrospective.

- *Financial incentives* aim to motivate people to achieve their objectives, improve their performance or enhance their competence or skills by focussing on specific targets and priorities.

- *Financial rewards* provide financial recognition to people for their achievements in the shape of attaining or exceeding their performance targets or reaching certain levels of competence or skill.

Financial incentives are designed to provide direct motivation – 'Do this and you will get that.' A shopfloor payment-by-result scheme and a sales representative's commission system are examples of financial incentives. An achievement bonus or a team-based-pay lump-sum payment are examples of financial rewards. Financial rewards provide a tangible form of recognition and can therefore serve as indirect motivators, as long as people expect that further achievements will produce worthwhile rewards.

This distinction is important because it highlights the fact that reward schemes designed to 'incentivise' and therefore motivate people may fail to do this directly, although they could be a useful means of recognising contribution.

TYPES OF CONTINGENT PAY

Service-related pay
Service-related pay provides fixed increments which are usually paid annually to people on the basis of continued service either in a job or a grade in a pay spine structure. Increments may be withheld for unacceptable performance (although this is rare) and some structures have a 'merit bar' which limits increments unless a defined level of 'merit' has been achieved. This is the traditional form of contingent

pay and is still common in the public and voluntary sectors and in education and the health service although it has largely been abandoned in the private sector.

Service-related pay is supported by some unions because they perceive it as being fair – everyone is treated equally. It is felt that linking pay to time in the job rather than performance or competence avoids the partial and ill-informed judgements about people which managers are prone to make. Some people add that the principle of rewarding people for loyalty through continued service is a good one.

The arguments against service-related pay are that:

* It is inequitable in the sense that an equal allocation of rewards according to service does not recognise the fact that some people will be contributing more than others and should be paid accordingly.

* It does not encourage good performance – indeed, it rewards poor performance equally.

* It is based on the assumption that performance improves with experience, but this is not automatically the case – it has been said that a person with five years' experience may in practice only have had one year's experience repeated five times.

* It can be expensive – everyone may drift to the top of the scale, especially in times of low staff turnover, but the cost of their pay is not justified by the added value they provide.

The arguments against service-related pay have convinced most managements, although some are concerned about managing any other form of contingent-pay schemes (incremental pay scales do not need to be managed at all). They may also have to face strong resistance from their unions and can be unsure of what exit strategy they should adopt if they want to change. They may therefore stick with the status quo.

Other types of contingent pay for individuals
Organisations may decide, for good reasons or bad, to stick to service-related pay. But many already have some form of contingent pay or are moving towards it.

It is sometimes believed that the only alternative methods are either performance-related pay (see Chapter 20), which links pay to an assessment of performance, usually the results achieved against objectives, or payment-by-result schemes for shopfloor workers and sales staff (see Chapters 24 and 34 respectively). But there are other approaches, namely:

* *competence-related pay* – which links pay to an assessment of the level of competence achieved (see Chapter 21)

* *contribution-related pay* – which links pay both to performance as measured by results and competence (see Chapter 22)

* *skill-based pay* – which provides additional payments that reflect the level of skill attained (see Chapter 23).

Contingent pay for teams

Another alternative to individual performance-related pay is to link pay to the performance of teams, as described in Chapter 25. This is sometimes the sole method of contingent pay but it may be accompanied by some form of payment for competence or skill and/or pay related to organisational performance.

Contingent pay based on organisational performance

The third group of contingent pay arrangements relate rewards to organisational performance as measured by profits, added value or some other criteria linked to the achievement of targets or standards. These can be the only form of contingent pay but they can operate in conjunction with individual schemes. The main types of organisational schemes are:

- *profit-sharing* – which provides a cash payment related to the level of profits (see Chapter 26)

- *profit-related pay* – which provides for a proportion of pay to go up or down in line with profits (these schemes originally offered considerable tax advantages but these will have been withdrawn by 2000 (see Chapter 26)

- *gain-sharing* – which shares gains in terms of added value or some other measure between the company and its employees, and includes various forms of involvement (see Chapter 26).

GENERAL ARGUMENTS FOR AND AGAINST CONTINGENT PAY

Individual contingent pay

Arguments for

- It is right, proper and equitable that those who perform better, successfully apply higher levels of competence or skill, and contribute more, should receive higher financial rewards than those who do not – as stated by ACAS (1997): 'There is a strong and widely-shared belief that those who perform well should gain greater benefits, and that allocating rewards this way is the fairest principle to follow.'

- Contingent pay can motivate people to achieve higher levels of performance, competence, contribution or skill and thus improve organisational performance.

- It can communicate organisational performance requirements, priorities and values.

Arguments against

- It depends on the existence of accurate and reliable methods of measuring performance, competence, contribution or skill, which might not exist.

- It relies on the judgement of managers which, in the absence of reliable criteria, could be partial, prejudiced, inconsistent or ill-informed.

- It assumes that performance is completely under the control of the individual when in fact it is affected by the system in which individuals work.

- Because of the above problem, management's attention may be diverted away from system defects which need to be given urgent attention.

- There is no proof that these schemes motivate people to improve their performance: indeed, they can serve to de-motivate them if badly managed, which they often are.

- Contingent pay, especially individual performance-related pay schemes, can militate against quality and teamwork.

- Contingent pay schemes imply that the only way to reward people is financially, but non-financial rewards can make a deeper and longer-lasting impact on motivation and therefore performance.

Conclusions

The arguments against contingent pay appear to be formidable. But they generally focus more on the *process* of contingent pay for individuals rather than on the principle. If it is believed that better performers or people with higher levels of competence or skill should be rewarded more, then the question has to be asked: 'What's the alternative?' Should organisations pay everyone in a job the same irrespective of what they deliver? Or should organisations adopt or maintain service-related incremental scales? And if either of these alternatives is adopted, should greater attention be paid to using non-financial rewards?

But it can be argued strongly that most people do believe that their pay should be related to performance. And this contention was supported by the research conducted by Guest and Conway (1998) for the IPD. The alternative of service-related increments may provide an easy way out but it conflicts with the belief that people generally want their pay to reflect their contribution and competence.

As mentioned above, it is not the principle of contingent pay for individuals that is wrong but the way it is operated. The criteria for effectiveness in terms of providing an incentive or a motivating reward as set out in the next section are very demanding. If these cannot be met, then consideration has to be given to some form of payment related to team or organisational performance and/or more focus on non-financial methods of reward or recognition schemes.

Team pay

Arguments for

- It reinforces teamwork and team identity.

- It focuses the team's attention on key performance expectations.

- It enhances flexible working and encourages multi-skilling.

Arguments against

- It only works if the team is well-defined, has clear and measurable objectives and contains interdependent members; but it may be difficult to meet these conditions.

- It may be difficult to isolate the impact of the team.
- Counter-productive team rivalry can be created.

Rewards related to organisational performance
Arguments for
- They communicate organisational priorities.
- They enable the organisation to share success with its employees.
- They can increase identification and commitment.

Arguments against
- They can be complex.
- They are not effective motivators because of the difficulty of tracing any connection between individual contribution and reward.
- They tend to focus on financial targets so that other 'balanced score-card' measures of organisational effectiveness – ie customers, processes and staff – are neglected.

VARIABLE PAY

Variable pay in the sense of payments in cash rather than consolidated increases is growing in popularity. It means that rewards can be made immediately after the achievement. A cash sum which can be spent now is to many people more meaningful than the small increase in their base pay which is normally available in times of low inflation and cost pressures. Consolidated pay is in effect a fixed cost, and as Abosch (1998) has pointed out: 'Variable pay allows the organisation to shift increased compensation from the fixed-cost to the variable-cost category, paying out only when the money is there to allow a layout.' Some organisations are now adopting a policy of providing scope for base pay to increase as competence increases to a target rate for a fully competent person – ie competence-related pay. Thereafter, unless the role expands, people are rewarded by one-off achievement bonuses, although a 'sustained-performance' bonus can be given when a conspicuously high level of contribution is maintained.

CRITERIA FOR CONTINGENT PAY AS A MOTIVATOR

The 'line of sight' criterion
The 'line of sight' criterion, as originated by Ed Lawler (1990), sums up the key requirement of any contingent pay scheme, especially one related to performance. This is that individuals and teams should have a clear line of sight between what they do and what they will get for doing it. A line of sight model adapted from Lawler (1996) is shown in Figure 32.

The line of sight concept expresses the essence of expectancy theory: that motivation takes place only when people expect that they will get worthwhile rewards for their effort and contribution.

Figure 32 Line of sight model

Specific criteria

For a performance-, competence- or skill-related pay scheme to provide an incentive or motivating reward, it should ideally meet the following criteria.

1 Individuals or teams know the targets and standards they are required to meet.

2 The reward is clearly and closely linked to accomplishment or effort.

3 People know what they will get if they achieve targets or standards, and can track their performance against them.

4 Fair and consistent means are available for measuring or assessing performance, competence or skill.

5 People must be able to influence their performance by changing their behaviour, and/or they should be able to develop their competences and skills.

6 The rewards should be meaningful.

7 The reward should follow as closely as possible the accomplishment that generated it.

These are ideal requirements and few schemes meet them in full. That is why contingent pay arrangements can often promise more than they deliver.

> Assess any PRP or other types of performance pay scheme you know against these criteria.

Figure 33 Contingent pay strategy

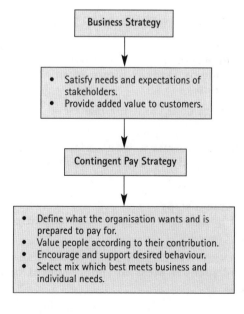

Table 22 Impact of different contingent pay schemes

Method	Impact: on motivation as an incentive	on motivation as a reward	on commitment
Performance-related pay	low	medium	low to medium
Competence-related pay	medium	medium	medium
Contribution-related pay	medium	high	medium
Skill-based pay	high	high	medium
Payment-by-result	high	medium	low
Team pay	medium	high	medium
Profit-sharing	low	low	medium to high
Gain-sharing	medium	medium	high

CONTINGENT PAY STRATEGY

Basic considerations
The basic considerations affecting the basis and content of a contingent pay strategy are summed up in Figure 33.

Choice of approach
The choice of approach will be influenced by the following factors:

• the culture and business strategies/needs of the organisation

• the degree to which the approach is likely to meet these needs

• the type of people employed

• the existence of appropriate measures

• the capacity of the organisation and its managers to administer the system efficiently and fairly

• the views and likely reactions of employees and their representatives.

In the light of an analysis of these factors, the choice can be made by reference to Table 7 (page 102) and Table 22 above.

DEVELOPING CONTINGENT PAY SCHEMES

Main considerations
The following important points about developing contingent pay schemes were made by Duncan Brown in an address to the 1998 Compensation Forum:

• 'If you are going to do it, do it and manage it properly or don't do it all.'

• 'Tailor and tie pay schemes to what performance actually means in your organisation and also to the culture in which you manage.'

• 'Improve; don't remove.'

Twelve development steps
1 Be aware of business needs and how contingent pay can help to meet them.

2 Analyse present arrangements and circumstances (including culture) and identify areas for improvement or change. Set objectives.

3 Survey employee opinion and consult staff and, if appropriate, trade union.

4 Consider the choice or mix of schemes – for example, individual, team or corporate; paying for performance, competence contribution or skill. Identify alternatives and in consultation with employees evaluate the alternatives against the objectives and criteria for contingent pay.

5 Review methods of defining targets or standards of performance and aligning corporate and individual objectives.

6 Decide how performance should be measured and who measures it.

7 Consider how performance management processes will be used as a means of assessing performance, competence and contribution.

8 Design the scheme in consultation with employees, ensuring that it produces differential rewards for individuals or teams in a fair, equitable and consistent way.

9 Decide how pay reviews will be conducted.

10 Communicate the proposed scheme to employees.

11 Train managers and staff in operating the new scheme.

12 Evaluate the effectiveness of the scheme in operation against the objectives, and improve as necessary.

SUMMARY

- Contingent pay consists of those additional rewards which are related to (contingent on) length of service, performance, competence, contribution or skill.

- Contingent pay may be awarded to individuals or teams or it may be based on organisational performance.

- A distinction should be made between forward-looking incentives and backward-looking rewards.

- Variable pay (cash rather than consolidated) is becoming more popular.

- For contingent pay to be effective there should be a 'line of sight' between what people do and what they will get for doing it.

- There is a choice of approach which will depend on the organisation's culture, people, the existence of appropriate measures, the capacity of the organisation to administer it fairly, and the views of staff.

20 Performance-related pay

Performance-related pay (PRP) provides individuals with financial rewards in the form of increases to basic pay or cash bonuses which are linked to an assessment of performance, usually in relation to agreed objectives. PRP emerged in the entrepreneurial 1980s as *the* answer to motivating people and developing performance-oriented cultures. It was seen as a major lever for change, and the government of the day adopted it with much enthusiasm but little understanding as a means of transforming public sector bodies into businesses.

Most schemes are for managers and other salaried staff. Relatively few organisations have introduced PRP for manual workers although Kinnie and Lowe (1990) give some examples. PRP schemes may be restricted to certain categories of employees, such as senior managers.

But in the post-entrepreneurial 1990s there was a backlash against PRP. First-generation schemes installed in the 1980s were not delivering the expected results. A number of research studies failed to demonstrate that there was any causal link between PRP and performance or productivity. Some organisations are introducing second-generation schemes which aim to avoid earlier mistakes. Others are questioning the validity of PRP in its original form and are trying competence-related or contribution-related pay, often in a broad-banded structure.

At the end of this chapter, the reader should be able to:

- analyse the case for and against the introduction of performance-related pay
- advise on the introduction and implementation of an appropriate performance-related pay scheme
- audit and evaluate the effectiveness of the performance-related pay scheme.

In addition, the reader should know and understand:

- how performance-related pay schemes function
- the criteria for an effective performance-related pay scheme
- the conditions required in an organisation for performance-related pay to operate well.

METHOD OF OPERATION

Methods of operating PRP vary considerably but its typical main features are as follows.

Pay structure

If pay progression is provided for within a graded structure, this is designed to provide scope for increases within pay brackets attached to job grades. In a broad-banded structure, provision may be made for pay progression perhaps through zones but the scope for progression will not be defined so rigidly as in a conventional graded structure.

In a pay spine, the structure will incorporate a series of pay points which represent standard increments. But if PRP exists, additional increments can be given for highly-rated performance and increments can be withheld for poor performance.

Methods of paying increases

Performance-related pay increases may be added cumulatively to basic pay (ie consolidated) until either the maximum rate of pay for the grade or a limit within the grade defined in terms of a level of performance is reached.

Alternatively they may be paid as cash bonuses (variable pay) for special achievements or sustained levels of high performance. Individuals could be eligible for such bonuses when they reach the top of the pay bracket for their grade, or when they are assessed as being fully competent, having completely progressed along their learning curve. The rate of pay for someone who reaches the required level of competence can be aligned to market rates according to the organisation's pay policy.

The principle of paying cash bonuses avoids the annuity approach which takes place in any system where PRP or merit increases are perpetuated as part of the basic pay. This could be described as a gift which goes on giving, and it raises questions such as 'Why should this person still be rewarded now for an isolated achievement which took place many years ago?' The consolidation of PRP increases means that pay costs will escalate without any guarantee that such extra costs are financed by increases in performance and productivity. The principle of variable pay is that bonuses have to be re-earned and will only be paid if it is believed that they will be financed by performance improvements.

Bonus payments may be made when there is a spot rate structure in which individuals who are qualified and competent are paid a single rate for the job – there is no pay range. But they could be eligible for cash bonuses as a substitute for increases to their basic rate.

Consolidated pay progression

When pay increases are consolidated, the rate and limits of progression through the pay brackets are usually determined by performance ratings which are often made at the time of the performance management review but may be made separately in a special pay review which can determine a PRP increase, as discussed below.

Pay progression in a graded structure is typically planned to decelerate through the grade for two reasons. First, it is argued in line with learning curve theory that pay increases should be higher during the earlier period in a job when learning is at its highest rate. Second, It may be assumed that the central or reference-point in a grade represents the market value of fully competent people. According to the pay policy of the organisation this may be at or higher than the median. Especially in the latter case, it may be believed that employees should progress quite quickly to that level, but beyond it they are already being paid well and their pay need not progress so rapidly.

A common method of deciding PRP increases is to use a pay matrix. This indicates the percentage increase payable for different ratings according to the position of the individual's pay in the pay range. This is sometimes referred to as an individual's 'compa ratio' (short for comparison ratio) and expresses pay as a percentage of the midpoint in a range. Thus if the compa ratio were 100 per cent, the individual's salary would be at the midpoint. An example is illustrated in Chapter 36.

Pay progression within a broad-banded structure can take place in an entirely unstructured band or one which is semi-structured by the use of zones. Such structures are designed to support a continuous development policy by rewarding people for acquiring and using necessary skills and competences and through career development pay (methods of progressing pay in broad-banded structures are described in more detail in Chapter 17).

Variable pay
Bonus decisions when a variable pay system is used may also be based on ratings but are quite commonly made by a process of managerial judgement.

Measuring performance
The essence of performance-related pay is that it requires performance to be measured and these measurements serve as the basis for an assessment, most often expressed as a rating. Clearly, you cannot pay for performance unless you can measure performance. This presents a stumbling-block for many people contemplating PRP: how, they ask, can you measure performance which cannot be quantified in terms of sales or output without being subjective and, therefore, potentially unfair or prejudiced?

A common answer to this question is that 'anything which can be managed can be measured'. But how can it be, if to measure is defined as 'to find the extent or quantity of a thing by comparison with a fixed unit or an object of known size'? What is the 'fixed object' in the seemingly subjective world of performance appraisal? The usual reply to these questions is that the 'fixed unit or an object of a known size' takes the form of a performance objective which is as clearly defined as possible in quantified or output terms and against which the results achieved can be compared and therefore measured.

But it is often impossible to quantify every aspect of a job, and this can create the problem of focusing attention on a few quantifiable objectives while neglecting other important aspects of the role – eg quality and teamworking. Some role requirements can only be expressed in qualitative terms, and in some jobs it may be difficult to identify quantifiable measures.

However, more precision can be achieved in defining qualitative requirements by agreeing objectives in the form of performance standards which state that 'a certain aspect of the role will be well done if a certain thing happens'. And this provides a basis for comparison. Approaches to establishing and agreeing objectives in the form of targets and standards are discussed in Chapter 28.

But the main problem with PRP is not so much measuring performance as translating measurements into ratings when these determine PRP awards.

Rating performance

Most PRP schemes depend on performance ratings to indicate the size of an increase or whether there is to be an increase at all. Ratings as part of a performance management process (see Chapter 28) are usually on a four- or five-point scale. Similar scales may be used in separate pay reviews, or the pay decisions may be based on a broad assessment of whether the increase in pay should be in line with a predetermined norm or above or below that norm. Approaches to rating and methods of conducting pay reviews when a performance-related pay scheme is in use are described more fully in Chapters 28 and 36 respectively.

The difficulty of rating consistently and fairly is probably the weakest aspect of the concept of performance-related pay. The problem can only be overcome by very carefully and thoroughly guiding and training managers on how to rate, and by monitoring the actual ratings to identify inconsistencies or potential areas of unfairness. This can be done by the personnel function, but there is a danger, if they carry out this role too enthusiastically, of their becoming the 'PRP police'. Such a development would undermine the highly desirable process of getting managers to handle their own personnel decisions. Some organisations such as IBM avoid this by bringing a peer group of managers together to review and, as necessary, adjust each other's assessments on the basis of their common knowledge of the individuals who have been rated.

Other organisations avoid rating altogether. Of those covered by the IPD 1997 survey with PRP, 24 per cent did not incorporate rating in the process.

Table 23 Distribution of PRP awards as established by the 1998 IPD survey

PRP awards as a percentage of base pay	Percentage of respondents
0	3
1–3	32
4–6	26
7–10	16
11–20	14
More than 21	9
	100

Size of increases

In times of low inflation, the size of increases tend to be small. An IRS study of merit awards in the 1997/1998 pay round established that at the median, increases amounted to 1.5 per cent of the paybill. This was in addition to an average across-the-board increase of 3.5 per cent. One of the problems facing PRP schemes is that the motivational impact of such small increases when they are consolidated is likely to be small. It has been suggested by Lawler that a pay change of 10 per cent to 15 per cent is probably required to increase motivation significantly. Small increases may provide a form of recognition expressed in financial terms but even a pay increase of 3 per cent to 5 per cent, while noticeable, may not be sufficient to make an impact on performance. Some companies are relying more on variable pay on the grounds that a lump sum will be more welcome and make more impact than a similar percentage increase to base rate. The effect of a cash bonus may be even greater if it is given soon after an achievement.

The IPD 1997 survey of 357 organisations found that the distribution of pay awards was as shown in Table 23.

> Many organisations, especially in the public and voluntary sectors, retain fixed incremental systems in which pay progresses more or less automatically in line with length of service. What are the arguments for and against such systems?

THE APPLICATION OF PERFORMANCE-RELATED PAY

Organisations with PRP do not necessarily extend it to all employees. There are those which want to maximise what is often called 'leverage' by restricting it to people who are considered to be the 'drivers' of performance – eg senior management. Manual workers and sales staff are usually excluded because they have their own incentive or commission schemes or because it is felt that PRP would be inappropriate. There may be different schemes for different levels of staff. Some organisations introduce PRP at or near the top and cascade it down through successive layers in their hierarchy.

THE INCIDENCE OF PERFORMANCE-RELATED PAY

The 1997 IPD research into performance management practices established that 43 per cent of respondents with performance management had PRP. A survey conducted in 1998 by IRS revealed that 61 per cent of respondents had what they call merit pay. The IPD 1998 research on PRP found that 40 per cent of 1,158 respondents had adopted performance-related pay. As the IPD commented; 'Contrary to the popular belief that organisations are becoming disillusioned with performance-related pay, the results strongly suggest that the use of all forms of PRP is growing.' Fifty-nine per cent of the respondents had introduced it during the five years prior to 1998, whereas 23 per cent of respondents who currently do not have performance pay processes had discontinued them between 1990 and 1998. This represents an annual cessation rate of 3 per cent a year – smaller than the growth experienced over the last five years. As Brown and Armstrong (1999) point out, this indicates that newer practices such as competence-related pay or team pay are growing *alongside* rather than instead of individual PRP.

The incidence of PRP varies between sectors. A 1997 IDS study of 400 UK organisations found that the proportion of all-merit pay awards had continued to expand slowly up to 1996 but there had been a marked shift in this pay method to the service sector, especially financial services, where the proportion had more than doubled since 1990. A 1998 *Personnel Today* study showed that a majority of organisations used performance pay but that the incidence by sector varied from 41 per cent in the public sector to 72 per cent in financial services.

THE IMPACT OF PERFORMANCE-RELATED PAY

The use of performance-related pay can be justified on the general grounds that superior performers should be paid more than inferior performers. But the thrust for PRP has mainly been based on the belief that it will produce improvements in individual and organisational performance. Is this the case? Surveys and research have generated both positive and negative findings.

Positive findings
There have been a number of studies which showed that survey respondents believed that PRP was making an impact on performance.

The 1998 IPD survey established that 74 per cent of respondents believed that PRP improves performance. This is a strong vote of confidence in the system. The only reservation that can be made about this information is that it represents the opinion of the respondents, who were mainly personnel specialists and might be expected to be bullish about PRP. The opinion of employees in receipt of PRP was not sought.

The survey found that respondents largely believed PRP delivered a clear message about organisational performance (67 per cent) and rewarded people in a way they think is fair (57 per cent), although 14 per cent felt that PRP had worsened perception about fairness.

In the opinion of the survey respondents, PRP schemes made their most positive impact on the behaviour of the high performers (21 per cent, compared with 4 per cent for average performers and 4 per cent of poor performers). The writers of the IPD's executive summary commented that: 'These high performers may be precisely the type of employee that many employers wish to nurture and develop.' This may be so – except that it could be argued that these high performers may well be motivated by a number of other factors (eg achievement) rather than money. The survey does reveal that 41 per cent of respondents thought there was no real change in average performance as a result of PRP, and 52 per cent believed there was no real change in poor performers. But these are the very people whose performance should be addressed by PRP. Other methods of motivation provided by performance management have to be deployed as well as money.

An IRS study in 1994 revealed that 76 per cent of respondents believed that PRP had a positive effect on individual performance and 54 per cent thought that it improved organisational performance. The findings of another survey on the impact of PRP have been published by *Personnel Today* (1995) which indicated that 36 per cent of respondents reported predominately positive gains while 24 per cent indicated that the impact had been negative.

As cited by Brown and Armstrong (1999), Marc Thompson conducted a study of 400 companies in the aerospace sector (reported in 1998). This used a fairly sophisticated measure of added value per employee in each company which was then correlated with the application of various HR practices. The high-value-added and low-value-added companies were clearly differentiated in terms of their pay practices, virtually double the number of high-value-added companies applying performance-related pay to more than two-thirds of their staff.

Negative findings
However, other studies have failed to prove that a clear link exists between PRP and performance. The 1991 IPM research project found no link between improved company performance and PRP. In contrast to his later research quoted above, Marc Thompson in 1992 stated that he had not been able to find any relationship between corporate performance and the use of PRP. In 1998 he resumed the attack on PRP by asserting that:

> The new forms of pay can have a damaging impact on trust and work relations. The trouble is, it is a predominately negative one ... Managing reward is thus a job for damage limitation and perhaps not the 'strategic lever for organisational transformation' that appears so seductive in the writing of American commentators.

A well known and much quoted study by Marsden and Richardson (1994) into the effects of 'merit pay' in the Inland Revenue concluded that: 'Although the principle of relating pay to performance was widely accepted among Revenue staff, our results strongly suggest that the system as it operated had, at most, only a small positive motivational effect on staff.' The lack of impact was primarily attributed to staff perceptions that the system operated unfairly, believing that however well they performed, their box marking (rating) was not appropriate because of a quota system and favouritism. A follow-up study by the same researchers in 1997 found that in spite of the changes made to the system by the Inland Revenue management, staff still tended not to trust it. 'Around half of line managers operate with management' compared with one-fifth five years before. Furthermore, in lateral trust relationships between staff it was found that staff were much more inclined to agree that merit pay had 'caused jealousies' and 'discouraged teamworking'. And, as Thompson (1998) comments: 'Most interesting of all, the operation of performance pay appears to have increased employees' instrumental and transactional view of work with less than a third agreeing that "personal satisfaction of my work is enough incentive" compared to nearly two-thirds five years previously.'

On the basis of their study of seven organisations, Kessler and Purcell (1992) came to the conclusion that 'the link between pay and performance remains as obscure as ever'.

The IPM/NEDO 1992 research showed that most managers were not convinced that they could pinpoint the effect of PRP on individual or overall performance. As one personnel manager said: 'The fundamental problem we have is that you can't compare what we have done with how it would have been had we not done it.'

Establishing causality – the impact of PRP on performance – will always be difficult because of the multiplicity of factors which affect results. And the companies involved in the research conducted by Kessler and Purcell resisted a suggestion that an attempt be made to measure the effect of PRP and performance because, they said, a direct link between PRP and company performance was never envisaged.

Commentary
Brown and Armstrong (1999) comment that:

> We have researched the academic literature and research in some depth, going back as far as the 1920s, and the main conclusions we have drawn from this are twofold:
>
> • it is an extremely difficult area in which to carry out research, given the difficulty of isolating variables and identifying and attributing causation, and due to the broader political and social philosophies and debates which inevitably interfere with objective research
>
> • there are at least as many research studies suggesting that performance-related pay can reinforce and support high organisational and individual performance as there are suggesting that it doesn't.

A particular problem in assessing the outcome of PRP is that huge claims were made for its effectiveness in the 1980s which could never be lived up to. They were based on naive assumptions about the instrumental value of money as a motivator without taking any account of the lessons from expectancy theory, the problems of administering PRP fairly, and the fact that it might work better in some organisations than others and would certainly make different impacts on individuals which could neither be presumed nor predicted.

Another problem is that too often organisations have not specified what they wanted to achieve except in such vague terms as 'to develop a performance-oriented culture'. Moreover, as Cannell and Wood (1992) established by their research, little attempt is made by organisations to subject PRP to rigorous evaluation against clearly-defined criteria. It is hardly surprising, therefore, that the impact of PRP has been difficult to measure and prove.

REASONS FOR INTRODUCING PERFORMANCE-RELATED PAY

Research conducted by Kessler and Purcell (1993) found that there were two main reasons the organisations contacted introduced PRP:

• to attract the 'right' type of applicant and to send strong messages to those employees the organisation wanted to lose as well as those they wanted to retain

- to achieve organisational transformation by promoting values suggesting that the company was performance-driven, cost-conscious, and flexible, and by encouraging employee commitment – 'locking' individuals in through objectives cascading from the company's business plan.

The research conducted by Thompson in 1991 indicated that the two most important factors that influence the decision to introduce PRP were the desire to link pay and productivity more closely and the need to motivate employees.

The IPM/NEDO research conducted by Cannell and Wood in 1992 found that rewarding the better performers at the expense of the poorer ones was central to many of the recently-introduced PRP schemes. The key consideration was the relativities – 'not to reduce everyone to the lowest common denominator' as one interviewee put it. The general impression was that although motivation was certainly a factor in the introduction of schemes, it was less significant than rewarding good performance. Another important reason for introducing PRP was to achieve cultural change by increasing accountability and by encouraging people to concentrate on key objectives. One private sector manager stressed to the researchers that when his firm introduced PRP for its senior executives, 'The purpose was not to provide more money for senior executives but to get them to focus on things which mattered to the business. It was a way of crystallising managers' minds on what are seen by the managing director to be the key targets.'

At NatWest, their Performance-Related Reward plan was introduced 'to improve the business performance of the Bank. The scheme was intended to encourage greater concentration on corporate and personal objectives by clarifying at each level what the key objectives were, relating them to specific circumstances and rewarding managers according to how well they achieve them.' This is a good example of an approach which links PRP clearly to performance management processes where the emphasis is on assessing performance against agreed objectives and integrating individual objectives with those of the organisation.

The reward manager (Amanda Stainton) at Yorkshire Water Services is quoted by Brown and Armstrong (1999) as saying: 'Money is not the most important motivator in life, but is a lever for change – a symbol, a way to change behaviour.' Without the pay linkage, she feels that the new performance management system would not have had the power and the priority to really impact on management and behaviour in the organisation: 'The history was that of managers' backing off from tough decisions.'

THE BENEFITS OF PERFORMANCE-RELATED PAY

Those who advocate performance-related pay and those that introduce it believe that it provides the following benefits:

- It motivates people and therefore improves individual and organisational performance.

- It acts as a lever for change.

- It delivers a message that performance generally or in specified areas is important.

- It links reward to the achievement of specified results which support the achievement of organisational goals.

- It helps the organisation to attract and retain people by offering them financial rewards and helping to make pay competitive.

- It meets a basic human need – to be rewarded for achievement.

RESERVATIONS ABOUT PERFORMANCE-RELATED PAY

A number of research studies, some of which have been referred to above, have been carried out in recent years on the impact of PRP, and there has been a considerable amount of debate amongst academics, practitioners and consultants on its effectiveness. The main reservations expressed about PRP by the researchers and the other people who have joined in the debate are:

- It is not the only motivator, or even an effective motivator – it can positively demotivate.

- It simply does not work.

- There are problems in measuring and therefore paying for performance.

- It relies on the skill and judgement of managers who may not be capable of exercising it.

- It focuses on quantity rather than quality.

- It can inhibit teamwork.

- It could be discriminatory.

- It may not deliver value for money.

- It may not be appropriate.

- It is too often taken on trust.

- PRP may be right in principle but it is very hard to make it work in practice.

Pay is not the only motivator, or even an effective motivator
As Michael Beer (1984) has commented:

> Tying pay and other extrinsic rewards to performance may actually *reduce* the intrinsic motivation that comes when individuals are spontaneously involved in work because they are given freedom to manage and control their jobs. By making pay contingent upon performance (as judged by management), management is signalling that it is they – not the individual – who are in control, thus lowering the individual's feeling of competence and self-determination.

Kohn (1988) has remarked that:

> Extrinsic rewards can erode intrinsic interest. ... Higher-quality work, particularly on jobs requiring creative thinking, is more likely to occur when a person focuses on the challenge of the task itself, rather than on some extrinsic motivator, and feels a sense of self-determination, as opposed to feeling controlled by praise or reward.

In 1993 Kohn delivered an even more scathing attack. He contended that:

> Research suggests that, by and large, rewards succeed at securing one thing only: temporary compliance. When it comes to producing lasting changes in attitudes and behaviour, however, rewards, like punishment, are strikingly ineffective.... There is no firm basis for the assumption that paying people more will encourage people to better work or even, in the long run, more work.

The personnel managers interviewed during the IPM/NEDO research project (Cannell and Wood, 1992) were uncertain about the precise role of money as a motivator. Most respondents felt that money was only one of several factors, and several interviewees felt that once monetary reward was at a satisfactory level, recognition became the major factor. As one put it: 'If there is good basic pay, then recognition is the greatest motivator – especially feedback on performance from the manager.'

The IPD survey into the psychological contract (Guest and Conway, 1988) found that in response to a question about pay, 51 per cent claimed that it did motivate them to perform better on a day-to-day basis while 49 per cent felt that it did not. Opinions about pay as a motivator are therefore equally divided although they well may be affected by the perceived fairness of the scheme and the amount of money available.

Can PRP demotivate?
The research conducted for the Institute of Manpower Studies on *Pay and Performance: The employee experience* (Thompson, 1992) led to the conclusion that: 'PRP does not serve to motivate [even those with high performance ratings] and may do more to demotivate employees.'

Marsden and Richardson's (1994) study of Inland Revenue staff established that 55 per cent of those surveyed felt that PRP had helped to undermine staff morale and 62 per cent believed that it caused jealousies between staff. The survey conducted by the Society of British Telecom Engineers in 1993 found that 63.2 per cent of respondents believed that PRP was applied unfairly in practice. However, the IPD's research into the psychological contract (Guest and Conway, 1998) established that no one believed that performance-related pay demotivated them.

Does PRP work?
The Kessler and Purcell (1992) research distinguished the following problems when assessment is linked to pay:

- *tunnel vision* – where employees concentrated on those aspects of the job linked to pay to the neglect of other aspects of their job

- *cost of living* – the strong tradition of cost-of-living increases can still lead employees to refer to inflation in their evaluation of any pay increase, so diluting the performance linkage

- *mismatch between appraisal and pay* – the small amount of money sometimes devoted to PRP could cause positive appraisal ratings to result in only small pay out-turns

- *diversion of merit money* – in cases where grading anomalies or labour market pressures existed, line managers might use the pay pot to address these problems rather than to directly reward performance

- *the wrong message may be sent* – 'If it is a system which depends on sending messages to employees, the organisational consequences of sending the wrong messages could be severe.'

A diatribe against 'merit pay' was delivered by Helen Hague in 1996. Quoting extensively from the usual academic studies and one practitioner, she concluded that 'performance-related pay, far from rewarding performance, is demotivating staff'.

It can be argued, as does Caulkin (1999), following the total-quality guru, William Deming (1986), that: 'Performance-related pay diverts management from doing its proper job: improving the system.' Caulkin also asserts that managers in private industry have discovered to their cost that performance-related pay is 'either too crude to be useful or too complicated to be workable'.

You can't reward what you can't measure
As Lawler (1988) says, the key to any successful performance-related reward system is effective performance measurement. Indeed, he asserts, the most common reason that individual pay-for-performance plans fail is their lack of a good appraisal system. Riley (1992) has stated in an ACAS report that: 'There is something wrong with the proposition that you can measure in reliable terms the output and effort of people in a wide variety of jobs.'

Kessler and Purcell (1993) noted the following difficulties at the objective-setting stage:

- *inconsistency* – variation between managers in the same organisation in the definition of objectives and the substantive character of those selected

- *viability* – difficulties in setting meaningful objectives, particularly on a continuing basis, for certain occupational groups – eg R&D scientists and administrative and clerical workers.

Reliance on managers
PRP puts much greater pressure on line managers to possess and exercise skills in agreeing objectives, providing feedback, conducting performance reviews and rating or assessing performance. If these task are carried out badly, PRP is likely to demotivate employees because they will perceive it as being operated unfairly and inconsistently by incompetent people.

An important element in the ideal PRP model is that the responsibility and 'ownership' of the payment system should be devolved to line managers. Yet, as Thompson (1992) noted, the IMS research found that it was this issue which led to some of the most difficult problems in practice. In several of the organisations covered by the research line managers perceived PRP as being 'yet another bureaucratic system imposed by corporate personnel'. Employers reported that line manager commitment to the system and its objectives tended to be very patchy, particularly in the first year of operation.

The following problems were found by the Kessler and Purcell research at the performance assessment stage:

- *easy options* – a centring tendency such that managers were reluctant to mark people too high or too low

- *labels* – the attachment of descriptive labels or rankings which might send demoralising messages to staff

- *subjectivity* – where managers might use their own criteria to assess employees or apply established criteria to different employees in an inconsistent way.

Prejudicial to teamwork

A survey conducted in a large pharmaceutical company as quoted by Robinson (1992) found that 82 per cent of the staff believed that PRP did not encourage teamwork. Several of the organisations surveyed in the IPM/NEDO study acknowledged that PRP can have a negative effect on teamwork by over-emphasising incentives for the individual.

Focus on quantity, not quality

PRP often focuses on the results obtained as measured in quantitative terms. It may ignore the need to deliver high-quality results. People may therefore go for output targets at the expense of quality.

Sex discrimination

At the 1991 Trades Union Congress the Association of First Division Civil Servants alleged that 52 per cent of male civil servants in grades 5 to 7 qualified for extra performance-related payments, while only 38 per cent of women did so. In 1990 the Local Authorities Conditions of Service Advisory Board wrote on PRP (*Report No. 4*):

> So far as the coverage of PRP schemes is concerned, they are at present mainly applied to senior employees, who are primarily male, and even where PRP has been extended down the organisation more generous payments tend to be available to those at the top of the hierarchy. In many cases, therefore, it is probable that the introduction of PRP will widen internal pay relativities and will also widen the salary gap between male and female local government officers.

Thompson (1992) noted that only two of the 20 organisations visited during the study were concerned with the equal opportunities aspects of their schemes' operation. And only two were aware of the 1989 *Danfors* ruling under the EC Equal Pay Directive which states that:

> The quality of work carried out by a worker may not be used as a criterion for pay increments where its application shows itself to be systematically unfavourable to women.

There is a possibility that assessments made by managers (the majority of whom are still male) of their female staff could be biased.

Value for money

In theory, PRP should be self-financing, but there is little or no convincing evidence that this is the case. The organisations surveyed in the Thompson 1992 study which had measured costs (only two out of 20) found that PRP had led to an increase in the salary bill of 2 per cent in one case and, after three years, 14 per cent in another. If, as normally happens, PRP awards are consolidated into basic pay and are not subsequently reduced if performance falls, then as the CBI/Wyatt report (1994) points out, PRP can ratchet up fixed costs.

There are other costs associated with PRP, including the use of consultants, training, communications to employees and the direct and indirect expense of running the scheme. A full PRP scheme backed up by performance management can make considerable demands on the time of line managers. The fact that they might resent diverting their attention to an area of lower priority, as they perceive it, is a very good reason for taking steps to convince them of the value of PRP.

PRP is not necessarily appropriate

Many people in public and voluntary organisations and, frequently, their trade unions, have expressed disquiet at the spread of PRP on the grounds that it conflicts with the ideal of public or community service or individual care. In education it raises suspicion that it will damage the collegiate basis on which educational establishments can operate. An organisation with a strong culture which incorporates the notion of rewarding people for loyalty and length of service and where there is an emphasis on values for fairness and equity may run into difficulties if it tries to install PRP too brusquely.

Too often, schemes are introduced as packages irrespective of the organisational context and culture. As Flannery et al (1996) observe, perhaps the key design failure has been the uniform, management-driven merit pay model in such a wide variety of situations.

PRP is often introduced as a lever to achieve cultural change – for example, to make the organisation more businesslike with a focus on accountability for the achievement of objectives. But a too-rapid shift away from the prevailing culture may lead to failure.

There is also the question of affordability. PRP, as noted earlier, can be costly. If an organisation cannot afford to pay out performance-related increases which provide worthwhile incentives or rewards, then it has to ask itself if there is any point in going to the trouble of introducing and maintaining PRP.

PRP taken on trust

Research has shown that managements have tended to take PRP on trust. It seems to be an act of faith on their part that it will improve performance, help to change the culture, or deliver messages to employees about key performance, quality and customer service values.

PRP is difficult to manage well

Many research studies such as those conducted by Bowey and Thorpe (1982), Thompson (1992) and Kessler and Purcell (1992) have revealed that performance pay problems are rooted in implementation and operating processes. And Vicky Wright, managing director of Hay Management Consultants (1991), has emphasised that: 'Even the most ardent supporters of performance-related pay recognise that it is extraordinarily difficult to manage well.'

The demands made on management by PRP are that it is necessary to

- communicate its purpose and processes to staff clearly and persuasively

- ensure that 'SMART' objectives are defined and agreed

- ensure that performance is measured fairly and consistently by managers, and that they properly differentiate between good and poor performers

- convince staff that pay decisions have been fair and unprejudiced (it is commonly held that favouritism determines the size and distribution of rewards)

- ensure that limited performance pay budgets are distributed appropriately in accordance with performance

- distribute relatively small sums in a way which will avoid demotivating staff

- avoid prejudicing the effectiveness of the developmental aspects of performance management because review meetings focus on ratings and their pay implications.

These are all considerable demands and it is hardly surprising that PRP schemes fail because they have not been met.

DEALING WITH THE RESERVATIONS

According to Brown and Armstrong (1999) clarity and communication of scheme objectives generally linked to business strategy and goals has been found to be the key differentiator between successful and unsuccessful performance pay schemes.

These reservations can be addressed along the following lines:

1 *PRP not the only motivator* – Do not use PRP as the sole motivator. Rely as much, if not more, on the intrinsic and non-financial motivators including the use of a performance management system for this purpose.

2 *PRP expectations* – Do not expect too much from PRP. There are other ways of improving performance. But it can still deliver messages about performance values – as long as these are the right messages – and help to implement cultural change.

3 *PRP as a demotivator* – PRP will demotivate if it is felt to be unfair. Take steps to ensure that performance is measured as objectively as possible, and that ratings, if they are used, truly reflect the individual's contribution. Ensure that the scheme is fully transparent, and involve employees and trade unions in developing the plan so that fears about unfairness can be resolved.

4 *Reliance on line managers* – Train managers thoroughly in providing feedback and rating performance. Ensure that they understand what the performance rating levels mean and how to translate these into recommendations on pay increases by reference to the organisation's guidelines. By all means devolve as much accountability to managers for making performance pay decisions as possible, but provide reasonably close help and guidance when PRP is introduced and to newly-appointed managers. Involve managers in developing PRP to ensure ownership.

5 *Teamworking* – Include competence as a teamworker as one of the factors to be considered when assessing and rewarding performance. Emphasise to managers that they should not define individual performance requirements in a way which is so internally competitive that it is detrimental to teamwork. But get them to bear in mind that situations in which poor individual performance can be hidden within the team should be avoided. Consider the use of team pay (see Chapter 25).

6 *Focus on output not quality* – Introduce quality criteria as performance standards, and measure and assess performance against them.

7 *Sex discrimination* – Monitor PRP awards to ensure that they are not discriminatory.

8 *Value for money* – Evaluate PRP to ensure that it is delivering what it is meant to deliver at a reasonable cost. Consider paying performance-based awards as lump-sum unconsolidated bonuses rather than consolidating them into basic pay.

9 *Inappropriate* – Introduce or maintain PRP only if it fits the existing culture or management is confident that it will successfully help to change the culture.

10 *Taken on trust* – Be clear about the objectives of PRP and what it can realistically attain, bearing in mind the critical success factors of the organisation. Evaluate the impact of PRP against these objectives.

11 *Making it work*

- Define the objectives of the scheme.

- Ensure that the method of operation will, so far as this can be judged, achieve those objectives; account should be taken of the lessons provided by expectancy theory.

- Communicate the purpose of the scheme and how it works – transparency is essential.

- Involve as many people as possible in developing the scheme.

- Develop a comprehensive performance management process, again involving staff.

- Train *everyone* (staff as well as managers) in the skills and processes necessary to make performance management effective – this should include practice and training in objective-setting.

- If the scheme includes ratings, define each of the levels as carefully as possible and issue guidelines on their application.

- Train managers in rating performance to ensure that they understand what is involved and gain familiarity with what the different levels mean by reference to real examples.

- Issue guidelines on how judgements on PRP increases should be made, whether or not ratings are used.

- Provide one-to-one tuition for managers on rating and pay-decision procedures.

- Monitor ratings and pay decisions against the guidelines and provide advice on dealing with inconsistencies or doubtful judgements.

> To what extent do you believe that these approaches are realistic and will really address the inherent problems of PRP? As far as possible answer this question by reference to the circumstances in an actual organisation.

CONCLUSIONS ON WHAT PRP CAN OFFER

Even if these measures do not overcome the reservations completely it can be argued that they are not so much concerned with the concept of PRP as with how PRP is managed. The process of PRP can be said to be more important than the pay itself. In spite of all the criticisms, the most convincing argument for PRP is that people should be rewarded according to their contribution – the value they create.

But it is still necessary not to be starry-eyed or to believe that it is an easy option. PRP is most likely to fail if it is introduced complacently, without sufficient thought, on the basis of simplistic views about what it can do. Brown and Armstrong (1999) make the following points about how PRP can be made to work and its strengths and limitations.

PRP is not a universal solution
PRP cannot be endorsed universally, out-of-hand – it appears to work in some situations but not in others. It is more likely to work in high-involvement cultures and in entrepreneurial cultures in which performance can be measured readily. Situational variables (culture, management style, type of people involved, technology, etc) rather than the scheme's design are important determinants of success or failure. Success is far more dependent on communications and support systems as mentioned above.

PRP is not universally successful or successful
All PRP schemes have their strengths and weaknesses, and the key issue for practising managers is not only to pick out the most appropriate pay scheme for their situation but also to try and maximise the potential advantages and minimise the disadvantages.

Simplistic views about the power of money to motivate are unhelpful
It is a bad mistake to believe that money by itself will result in sustained motivation. It can assist in the motivation process but, as

Kohn correctly points out, rarely in a crude, behaviourist, Pavlov's-dog type of way. People react in widely different ways to any form of motivation. The assumption that money in the form of PRP will motivate all people equally is untenable. And it is this belief that has led governments, as well as managements, in the direction of making the naive and unjustified assumption that PRP by itself can act as a lever for change and can make a major impact on performance.

The significance of goal-setting

The objective-setting and review processes associated with performance management can make at least as much impact on performance as PRP. Goal theory (see Chapter 5) indicates that objective-setting is a powerful motivator in its own right. As Brown and Armstrong comment: 'Who is to say whether a pay scheme influences behaviour because of the money on offer, or because of the objectives and target achievements which have to be satisfied?'

Conclusions

The limited power of PRP to provide an incentive through financial means alone should be recognised, but that does not mean that it should be rejected out of hand. It *does* work as a reward process in some circumstances, and it does satisfy the basic principle that it is equitable to reward people who do well more than those who do badly. Rewards can be provided by non-financial means, but tangible recognition can be a valuable part of a total reward system as long as it is appropriate in the situation and is well-conceived and managed. The rest of this chapter is devoted to providing an answer to how PRP can be successful in the right circumstances by examining the conditions favourable and unfavourable to PRP, approaches to introducing PRP, and methods of evaluation.

> List the advantages and disadvantages of PRP. To what extent do you think the advantages outweigh the disadvantages or vice versa?

CONDITIONS FAVOURABLE OR UNFAVOURABLE TO PRP

Favourable conditions

Success in introducing and operating PRP is most likely if

- the culture is entrepreneurial with an emphasis on growth, competitiveness and the achievement of financial objectives

- top management is convinced that PRP can bring about cultural changes leading to significant performance improvements

- performance management processes are in place that include the agreement of objectives integrated with the overall objectives of the organisation, that involve feedback and review, and that provide a sound basis for making fair and consistent pay decisions

- line managers 'own' the scheme and believe that it will help them to achieve their objectives

- line managers are skilled in the processes of objective-setting and giving feedback and assessing performance

- the expectation of what employees need to do to achieve a reward are clarified

- the scheme is transparent so that everyone knows how it works – as Lawler (1998) says: 'If you are doing something good, flaunt it! If you feel you have to hide it, maybe you shouldn't be doing it'

- there is a tradition of involving employees in decisions on matters that affect them

- the organisation can afford to award worthwhile PRP increases

- PRP processes are integrated with other personnel and development practices.

Unfavourable conditions

Obviously, the absence of any of the characteristics listed above will reduce, if not eliminate, the possibility of success for PRP. The prospects will be even more unfavourable if

- the organisation is not prepared to spend time and money in training managers and communicating with employees about PRP

- there is lack of trust between management and employees

- there is a powerful trade union which is strongly against PRP

- PRP does not fit the culture – for example, when there is a strongly embedded fixed incremental pay system or when there is an emphasis on teamwork rather than individualism, on quality rather than quantity

- promises made about the benefits of PRP to managers and employees alike are not fulfilled

- in spite of all management's efforts, employees feel that performance pay decisions are unfair

- the core of employees on whom the organisation depends is neglected by PRP

- the scheme itself is unlikely to act as a motivator because it does not satisfy the criteria set out in Chapter 17.

> To what extent do you think the circumstances in your own organisation (or any organisation you know) are favourable or unfavourable to PRP in each of the respects listed above (or any others you can think of)?

INTRODUCING PRP

General considerations

The process of introducing PRP often is – indeed, should be – an iterative one in which alternative ideas are considered and a fresh start made if they are modified or rejected. It involves choice from a wide and expanding menu, and it is necessary to be flexible in fitting the choice to the requirements of the organisation.

Basically, a contingency approach should be adopted – ie one in which the plan meets the particular requirements and circumstances of the organisation. But those concerned with developing PRP should not be too constrained by the existing situation. They need to assess where changes to the culture, values and management processes of the company are required to meet future challenges.

The development programme

The development programme should involve people who are close to the business. These include top management, line managers, team leaders and employees generally, the latter through joint consultation, focus groups and surveys. It should not be left to the personnel function, although personnel specialists have an important role in discussing requirements, benchmarking (finding out what works well elsewhere), producing and testing ideas, and facilitating the whole process.

It should be remembered throughout the development programme that it will not be a one-off exercise. The results will have to stand the test of time and the plan should be capable of being modified if new circumstances arise.

The programme should consist of the following stages:

1 *Define the objectives* under such headings as

 – impact on performance

 – delivering messages on performance priorities and values

 – helping to achieve cultural change

 – rewarding people according to their contribution

 – who should be covered by the plan and why.

2 *Analyse the existing situation* in terms of

 – the organisation's culture

 – its objectives and critical success factors

 – the work carried out and the type of people employed

 – who has the most leverage on key results

 – the reward system: its strengths and weaknesses in relation to the objectives defined for the development programme

 – the extent to which it will be possible to set realistic objectives and measure performance

 – the approach to assessing performance (if any) and its effectiveness

 – related personnel processes concerned with resourcing and employee development

 – the capacity of line managers to operate PRP

 – the employee relations climate, including an assessment of likely attitudes to PRP and the extent to which employees should be involved in the development programme (or will insist on being involved)

– how much the organisation can afford to spend on PRP.

3 *Decide on the involvement processes* – line managers, team leaders, employees and trade unions. A decision is required at this stage on who should be involved, how they should be involved, and when they should be involved. Ownership and acceptance is much more likely if the maximum degree of involvement of all concerned is built into each stage of the programme.

4 *Consider alternative designs,* including

– methods of measuring performance

– methods of assessing performance, including an evaluation of the use of ratings

– methods of converting performance assessments or ratings into performance pay increases – eg PRP matrix

– the value of the PRP increases related to different levels of performance

– whether PRP increases should be consolidated with base pay or awarded in the form of cash bonuses generally or in certain circumstances.

5 *Consider the process elements of the plan*

– performance management procedures including the use of rating (if at all)

– the arguments for and against separating the performance review from the pay review: many organisations believe that they should be separated because the forward and developmental aspects of the performance review meeting may be submerged by concerns about pay decisions (this is discussed more fully in Chapter 35)

– the extent to which responsibility will be devolved to line managers

– budgeting for PRP increases

– the type of guidelines provided for line managers and the training with which they should be provided

– monitoring ratings and pay recommendations to ensure that an appropriate degree of objectivity and consistency is achieved and that there is no gender bias

– controlling PRP expenditure against budget.

(Arrangements for conducting pay reviews are considered in Chapter 36.)

6 *Produce the overall design* covering each element of the plan and the processes used in operating it. This design should be based on

discussions and consultations held with interested parties at stages 5 and 6 before finalising the details.

7 *Prepare implementation programme* covering

– communications to employees

– training of line managers *and* employees on how the plan should be operated and the role each of the parties involved should play

– any phasing of the introduction of the plan thought appropriate.

8 *Implement communication and training programmes.*

9 *Implement the plan.*

10 *Evaluate the impact of the plan.*

EVALUATING PRP

Almost every research project into PRP has commented adversely on the failure of organisations to evaluate PRP. The problem of evaluating its impact on individual and organisational performance is, of course, causality – how can you distinguish the effect of PRP from the other possible causes of performance improvement. In the case of individuals, this could arise from training and the objective-setting, feedback and personal development aspects of performance management rather than from PRP awards linked to performance ratings. In the case of the organisation, improvements or declines in levels of performance can arise from a multiplicity of causes – external events, competition, the introduction of new technology, restructuring, a successful business process re-engineering exercise, the vision and drive of a chief executive supported by an effective top management team, etc. Studies of performance figures following the introduction of PRP reveal nothing of any significance about its effectiveness. But neither do they indicate what might have happened if PRP had not been introduced.

The evaluation should attempt to assess improvements in performance if data is available. But it may have to concentrate on process rather than output issues – how PRP is functioning, what people feel about it in terms of its influence on their performance, and the degree to which it is perceived as being fair and equitable. The best way to do

---

OPINION SURVEY

The PRP scheme:

• has made a significant impact on my performance

• has not led to any significant change in my behaviour at work

• operates fairly

• is not being implemented consistently across the organisation

• ensures that I get good feedback on my performance

• is based correctly on the principle that rewards should be related to performance.

Table 24 The advantages and disadvantages of PRP

Advantages	Disadvantages
Motivates	Is not the only motivator
Is a lever for change	Is not an effective motivator
Links reward to results	Can demotivate
Delivers message that performance is important	May deliver the wrong message
Helps to attract and retain staff	Problems of measuring performance
Meets basic human need – to be rewarded for achievement	Relies on managerial judgement which may be partial
	Emphasises quantity at the expense of quality
	Is prejudicial to teamwork
	May be discriminatory
	May not deliver value for money
	May not be appropriate
	Is too often taken on trust
	May be right in principle but is hard to make work in practice.

this is to survey opinion – of top management, line managers, team leaders, employees, members of the personnel function and the trade unions. This need not be a full-blown attitude survey. It could be restricted to a simple set of statements and a request for respondents to indicate the extent to which they agree or disagree with them, as in the example on page 289.

Clearly, there is no point in carrying out this type of survey unless the organisation is prepared to take action on the basis of the results. If opinions are somewhat negative about the process aspects of the scheme, this may mean that better communication and training programmes need to be developed, or the quality of the guidelines for line managers should be improved. It will not necessarily mean that the basic features of the plan will have to be changed, although that could be necessary.

CONCLUSIONS

It is difficult to argue with the basic principle underpinning PRP – that it is equitable to reward people according to their contribution. But it is not easy to ensure that PRP works well, and much more rigorous approaches are necessary to its introduction and management than were adopted in the heady days of the 1980s.

PRP is not for all organisations and there are alternatives to consolidating rewards into basic pay. Achievement and sustained-performance bonus can make more impact and can be used not only for outstanding employees but as a special means of recognising the contribution of the core of employees upon which the organisation depends.

Other alternatives should be considered – team pay for organisations in which teamwork is vital; competence-related and skill-based pay for organisations where the emphasis is on improving competence and skill, as long as they deliver better performance; contribution-related pay schemes embracing both input and output measures; and organisation-wide reward schemes such as gain-sharing, profit-sharing and profit-related pay to promote commitment and ensure that everyone, especially core employees, shares in the organisation's success.

For organisations which meet the conditions set out earlier in this chapter PRP could well be the right answer, but it has to be planned and operated with great care and the organisation has to be prepared to be flexible – amending the scheme in the light of changed circumstances and feedback from managers and employees.

SUMMARY

- Performance-related pay (PRP) provides individuals with financial rewards in the form of increases to basic pay or cash bonuses which are linked to an assessment of performance, usually in relation to agreed objectives.

- PRP functions within a graded or broad-banded pay structure or a pay spine in which provision is made for pay progression related to performance.

- PRP is usually consolidated in base pay but it can be awarded as a cash bonus (variable pay).

- Awards may be based on rating but not always.

- The most common award is between 1 per cent and 3 per cent of base pay.

- A number of studies have suggested that PRP does make a positive impact on performance but others have failed to make a connection. The case is not proven, mainly because of the extreme difficulty in proving it.

- The reasons given for introducing PRP include motivation, improving performance, linking pay to performance, delivering a message about the importance of high performance, and maintaining competitive pay levels.

- The advantages and disadvantages of PRP are summarised in Table 24.

- The disadvantages appear to considerably outweigh the advantages, but the problem with PRP is not so much that it is wrong in principle but that it is difficult to operate well in practice.

- The limited power of PRP to provide an incentive through financial means alone should be recognised, but that does not mean that it should be rejected out of hand. It *does* work as a reward process in some circumstances, and it does satisfy the basic principle that it is equitable to reward people who do well more than those who do badly.

- PRP is more likely to succeed in organisations with an entrepreneurial culture in which effective performance management processes are in place and line managers are skilled in the processes of objective-setting and giving feedback and assessing performance – the organisation should be able to award worthwhile PRP increases.

- PRP is less likely to work if the above conditions are unfulfilled, there is lack of trust between management and employees, a powerful trade union is strongly against PRP, or it does not fit the culture – eg where there is a strongly embedded fixed incremental pay.

- It is essential to evaluate PRP.

PRP is not for all organisations and there are alternatives – eg competence-related, contribution-related or skill-based pay, team pay, and organisation-wide reward schemes such as gain-sharing and profit-sharing.

FURTHER READING

Vicky Wright's chapter in *The Performance Management Handbook* (first edition) is a good piece of prescriptive writing. Ed Lawler's article on 'Pay for Performance' also provides good practical advice. The most comprehensive examination of this whole area is provided by Duncan Brown and Michael Armstrong in *Paying for Contribution*, 1999.

21 Competence-related pay

The focus in today's organisations is on flexibility, multi-skilling and continuous development. The thrust is to extend and increase levels of competence to meet new challenges in a highly competitive environment. Competence-related pay is people-oriented and is seen by some as a valid alternative to performance-related pay.

On completing this chapter, the reader will understand:

- what competence-related pay is

- what concept of competence can be used in competence-related pay processes

- how it works

- its advantages and disadvantages

- when it is appropriate, and how it can be implemented.

COMPETENCE-RELATED PAY DEFINED

Competence-related pay can be defined as a method of rewarding people wholly or partly by reference to the level of competence they demonstrate in carrying out their roles. It is a method of paying people for the ability to perform.

This definition makes three important points:

- Pay is *related* to competence. The link between competence and pay may not be direct enough to imply that pay is *based* on competence. Levels of competence may be difficult to measure with any precision. This contrasts with payment for skills rather than competences. It is appropriate to refer to skill-based pay because the acquisition and use of skills can be measured with a fair degree of accuracy through accreditation or validation processes (eg NVQ levels).

- People may be rewarded wholly *or* partly by reference to their level of competence. Competence-related pay is not an all-or-nothing affair. Competence assessment may be a factor, but is not the only factor, in determining pay levels or increases. Performance may also be a factor to a greater, equal or lesser extent. Increases in pay may be made in response to market pressures – increases in the individual's 'market worth'. And the rate of pay of individuals will be related to that of their peers. The fact that in practice competence is often not the only consideration is another good reason for referring to competence-related rather than competence-based pay.

- Competence pay is related to the level of competence people *demonstrate* in carrying out their roles. Competence is about performance. It is concerned with behaviours which deliver performance, not the behaviours themselves. Competence-related pay does not confine itself to the acquisition of competence. It is about the effective use of competence to generate added value. Competence levels cannot properly be measured simply by observing how people behave. They can only be assessed by considering the impact people's behaviour has on their performance at work.

THE INCIDENCE OF COMPETENCE-RELATED PAY

The use of any of the many versions of competence-related pay is not yet widespread. The 1998 IRS survey revealed that 13.9 per cent of respondents had competence-related pay (compared with 61.5 per cent with performance-related or merit pay). However, interest is growing; 30.3 per cent of respondents indicated that they were thinking about introducing it.

Research conducted by the IPD, IDS and NHS Personnel has revealed a great diversity of practice in organisations which claimed to have competence-related pay. As is the case with the other recent reward innovations (or fads, as some people would say), broad-banding and team-based pay, there is no generally accepted definition of what competence-related pay is, perhaps in this case because there are so many definitions of what competence is.

THE CONCEPT OF COMPETENCE AND PAY

One of the problems surrounding the concept of competence-related pay is defining what 'competence' means. This is a jargon-ridden area haunted by academics indulging in semantic obfuscation.

The most familiar definition of competence was produced by Boyatzis (1982). He defined a 'competency' as 'an underlying characteristic of an individual which is causally related to effective or superior performance'.

The implication of this and other definitions of competence or competency is that it refers to the capacity of people to meet the requirements of both their present and their future roles. Competence does not, therefore, just relate to present performance; it also predicts future performance because it is deemed to be a continuing characteristic which is normally irreversible. This contention is arguable, but it underpins one of the common assumptions of competence-related pay, that competence-related increases should be consolidated into base pay.

One of the problems surrounding the concept of competence or competency is that the term is used to refer to the ability to perform a job or task competently and also to how people ought to behave in order to carry out a role with competence. Many academic commentators are concerned that a distinction should be made between competence (hence competences) and competency (hence competencies). Dire consequences, we are told, result for anyone who mixes these two things up. Following Boyatzis, it is suggested by Woodruffe (1991) that these two concepts should be kept quite separate:

- *competence* should be used to refer to areas of work in which the person is competent

- *competency* should be used to refer to the dimensions of behaviour lying behind competent performance.

Another way of making this distinction is to distinguish between work-based 'hard' competences and behavioural or 'soft' competences.

- *Work-based or hard competences* refer to expectations of work performance and the standards and outputs that people carrying out specified roles are expected to attain. They are concerned more with effect rather than effort; with impact rather than input. This is broadly in line with the NVQ definition of an element of competence as 'a description of something which a person who works in a given occupational area should be able to do. It reflects action, behaviour or outcomes which have real meaning in the occupational sector to which it relates.'

- *Behavioural or soft competences* refer to the behavioural or personal characteristics which people bring to their work roles in such aspects as teamworking, achievement-orientation, leadership and strategic perspective.

This may not be the sort of jargon that appeals to line managers but at least it clarifies the difference between approaches tied to the ability to perform a role and those which refer to behavioural traits.

One way out of this semantic jungle is to remember that competence-related pay must depend on some method of measuring competence. To do this, it is useful to distinguish between the input, process and output aspects of performance and how competence can be measured under each heading.

As an *input*, competence can be measured by the capacity within people to do their work well. Capacity refers to what people bring to their work in the form of knowledge, skills and personal attributes.

As a *process*, competence can be measured in terms of the behaviour required of people in order effectively to convert inputs into outputs.

As an *output*, competence is measured by the outcomes of the behaviour of people in making the best use of their knowledge, skills and attributes.

In a sense, these are three models of competence, and organisations have to choose which model or combination of models to use in relating pay to competence.

Here are some definitions of competence used by organisations with competence-related pay:

Bass Brewers

- Displayed behaviours or attitudes which have been identified as key to the success of a business and are shared by everyone at every level. They are a reflection of knowledge, skill and personal qualities.

Blue Circle Cement

- Attributes necessary to be successful at the job.

Thomas Cook

- The knowledge, experience and skills required to meet the demands of a role and the aptitudes required to perform a role to the required standard.

Colonial

- Descriptions of core knowledge, skills, attitudes and abilities which result in effective performance at different job levels. They provide a structured way of describing effective performance in terms of observable behaviour.

Glaxo Wellcome

- What you know, what you do and how you do it, which when applied by an individual or a team, leads to positive outcomes for the company.

Unisys

- The ability to perform a job-related task to a predetermined standard.

Volkswagen UK

- The key attributes, skills and knowledge required for a job.

Woolwich Building Society

- The characteristics needed to achieve successful performance.

Many of these definitions refer in one way or another to the 'input' aspect of competency – ie knowledge, skills, attitudes, attributes and abilities. Most of them also refer to outputs in the shape of effective performance. The 'process' aspect of competency (behaviour, *how* the work is done) is mentioned by four of the companies. At the Bank of Scotland, a distinction is made between *technical competences* (the actual things and relative value of what people do in their work) and *personal competences* (the attributes and behaviours that determine how employees carry out their work).

Competence in these organisations is therefore often treated as a mix of 'hard' and 'soft' competence or by reference to each of the input, process, output aspects of competence. Some companies such as Glaxo Wellcome are now trying to get out of the semantic morass into which organisations have been plunged by the competence industry. They are anxious to produce definitions of competence which, mercifully, are free from management jargon. Others such as ICL and HSBC have abandoned the word *competence* altogether and use 'capability' instead.

Competence frameworks

A considerable number of organisations have developed competence frameworks of various degrees of elaboration: it has been estimated by Brown (1998) that the proportion is as high as 70 per cent. This may be an exaggeration but it is certainly an aspect of personnel management which has become very prominent over the last decade.

Most organisations develop their own frameworks, although there is quite a lot of common ground – perhaps because there are only so many headings that can be used and, of course, a lot of benchmarking goes on in this area.

Competency magazine in 1996 reported that the 10 most common competence headings used by the 126 organisations they surveyed were:

- communication
- achievement-/results-orientation
- customer focus
- teamwork
- leadership
- planning and organising
- commercial/business awareness
- flexibility/adaptability
- developing others
- problem-solving.

Most frameworks contain a number of items from this list.

HOW DOES COMPETENCE-RELATED PAY WORK?

Competence-related pay works through the processes of:

- competence analysis to develop competency frameworks – a number of methods may be used, such as workshops, expert opinion, critical incident or repertory grid
- agreeing competence requirements in a particular role – this may be based on a standard competence profile for generic (similar) roles or it may be determined specifically for a role: in either case performance management agreements as described in Chapter 29 may refer to competence requirements as a basis for development plans and for the assessment of the levels achieved
- assessing levels of competence for individuals against the profile and the performance agreement
- relating the pay of individuals to these assessments.

For competence-related pay purposes, after the framework and profiles have been agreed the key actions are to assess competence and relate pay to that assessment.

ASSESSING COMPETENCE LEVELS

To relate individual rates of pay and pay progression to competence

Figure 34   Assessment of competence levels against a target role profile

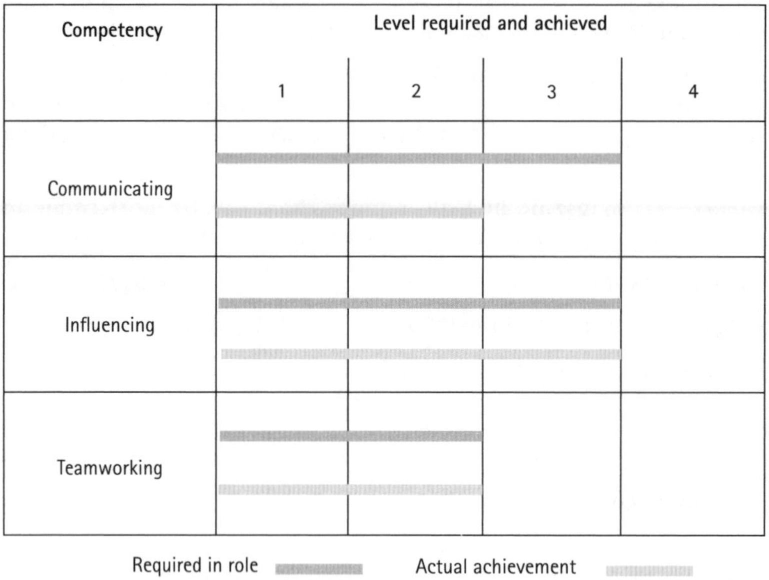

Competency	Level required and achieved			
	1	2	3	4
Communicating				
Influencing				
Teamworking				

Required in role ▒▒▒▒▒▒▒▒   Actual achievement ▒▒▒▒▒▒▒▒

Adapted from: M. Armstrong and D. Brown, *Compensation and Benefits Review*, May/June 1998, p.35

means that there has to be a method of measuring competence. This may be carried out by reference to defined competence levels. At Glaxo Wellcome these are called 'competency dimensions' and describe the level at which the competency needs to be performed by reference to the demands of the role in terms of complexity and impact rather than of the individual's effectiveness in the role. For example, for the competency 'establishing a plan' within the 'planning to achieve' competency area, the dimensions as described to GWUK staff are:

• At the lowest level you might only be planning your own daily or weekly work; the impact is therefore just on yourself.

• At the next level you may be involved in team plans; your impact is therefore on the whole team plan.

• At the next level you may be involved in planning for a department or therapy area.

• At the next level you may be involved in company-wide plans which would effect everyone.

Not all competencies in the framework have dimensions – some are required to be performed at the same level regardless of the role.

The assessment process
As described by Armstrong and Brown (1998) the aim is specifically to assess people in each competency area. A target role profile as illustrated in Figure 34 can be used in which each competency is

defined in general terms and then separate definitions are produced for each level of the profile against which the individual's level of competence can be measured.

These guidelines do not eliminate subjectively. However, they at least provide a framework within which more objective judgements can be made, especially when these cover the contribution and impact which can be measured by reference not only to behaviour but also to the results of that behaviour.

Measurement problems
Although it is perfectly possible to define competence dimensions, as at Glaxo Wellcome, difficulties may arise when it comes to measuring them. Even if people feel that they know competence when they see it (ie by observing behaviour), they cannot really measure it in quantitative terms. To minimise subjectivity, assessments need to be based on evidence of both what the individuals have achieved and also how they have achieved it. Increased objectivity can be obtained if agreements in advance are made between the parties on what competences will be assessed, what evidence will indicate the level of competence achieved, and how that evidence will be collected and analysed. There is much to be said for using competence (what people are capable of doing) as the basis for pay rather than competency (how people behave). This is because the former can be easier to measure if competence profiles have been produced which define what people must to do to perform well, and if the assessment process compares evidence of what people have shown themselves to be able to do against those profiles.

Some organisations get their managers to rate people's competence against a scale for each heading and add up the ratings to produce a total score. But as can be said for point-factor job evaluation, quantifying subjective judgements does not make them any more objective.

The alternative to rating individual competence is to produce an overall rating (often numerical or alphabetical) of competence levels. This is what happens in performance-related schemes, and criticisms of the subjectivity of these PRP ratings could equally well be levelled at overall competence ratings.

The most subjective approach of all is a holistic one which leaves managers or team leaders scope to agree with individuals how they are getting on in competence terms, and which feeds this judgement into a decision on pay that will be strongly influenced by external (market-rate) and internal relativity considerations. This method is used in some of the more advanced broad-banded structures.

An analysis of 15 competence-related pay schemes showed that eight used ratings for each heading, four had overall ratings, and three avoided ratings altogether. It is interesting to note that the most popular approach is to rate individual competence headings, typically on a five-point scale. Clearly these organisations believe that the advantage of having a scale to guide judgements (and to monitor assessments) outweighs any inherent weaknesses of such scales (they do not eliminate subjectivity and by themselves they cannot guarantee consistent judgements).

The companies that use overall assessments without ratings all have broad-banded systems and have devolved considerable responsibility for managing pay to line managers. As quoted by IDS (1996), ICL say that formal standards of measurement are not needed because the market plays a vital role, and therefore only broad indications of competence are needed. Bass Brewers similarly believes that competency measurement need not be rigorous because it is only one of the factors that determine pay. At Glaxo Wellcome, although competence-related pay decisions are not linked to a formal overall rating, they are influenced by assessments of how the competency profiles of individuals fit the competency profile for their role in a broad band.

Assessment problems

A number of competence pay issues have been raised by Sparrow (1996). These include the performance criteria on which competences are based, the complex nature of what is being measured, the relevance of the results to the organisation, and the problem of measurement. He concluded that 'we should avoid over-egging our ability to test, measure and reward competencies'. But this conclusion was based on the assumption that only 'behavioural competencies' are being linked to pay. This is not the case. A number of organisations such as the Bank of Scotland, Bass Brewers, ICL, Guinness Brewers and Portsmouth Housing Trust use job-related competences: competence definitions which focus on outputs, or 'technical competences' (the key things people should be able to do if they are fully competent). Sparrow believes that competence pay schemes usually 'hang on the back of an existing performance-related pay system'. In fact, many organisations such as Bass Taverns, Glaxo Wellcome and Volkswagen have competence pay schemes which are not linked in any way to a conventional performance-related pay system. He also states that 'managers have a limited ability to handle complex assessment decisions across multiple competencies or dimensions', and asserts that 'The law of "cognitive limits" tells us that managers can differentiate seven ideas, plus or minus two, so we should not expect to pay reliably for many competencies.' Whether or not the suspiciously exact figure of seven plus or minus two is correct, it is certainly true that any process of assessing competence must be kept simple. Six or seven competence headings are the maximum that should be incorporated in a scheme.

> To what extent do you think Sparrow has a point?

Another criticism of competence pay was provided by Lawler (1996). He expresses concern about schemes that pay for an individual's personality traits and emphasises that such plans work best 'when they are tied to the ability of an individual to perform a particular task and when there are valid measures available to show how well an individual can perform a task'. He also points out that 'generic competencies are not only hard to measure, they are not necessarily related to successful task performance in a particular work assignment or work role'. And Hofrichter and Spencer (1996) assert that 'competency-based systems that pay for generic personality traits not clearly related to task performance are at best trivial, and at worst damaging'.

An answer to these points was provided by Brown and Armstrong (1997) who emphasised that in competence-related pay people are paid for what their role demands, directly related to their performance. Businesses are developing well-researched competence frameworks and defining the standards of competence required. They are using performance management processes which generate specific evidence about what people have done and the results they have achieved as the basis for assessments. Brown and Armstrong assert that competence-related pay is not just a case of fashion: 'Increasingly, organisations are finding that success depends on a competent workforce. Paying for competence means that an organisation is looking forward, not back.'

Other reservations

ICL was one of the competence-related pay pioneers but, as described by Adams (1998), has rethought its approach. The focus has shifted from paying for competence in job families (called job communities by ICL) which led people to be more concerned about pay progression in their communities than career development, especially lateral career development, which had been the main purpose in setting them up. ICL then decided to reinforce the link between competencies and career development and play down the pay element. The employment relationship was changed to make it more performance-focused, more market-oriented. There is now no direct link between competence and pay. Although competencies are still being used in conjunction with other factors to support pay decisions, reward is now tied more closely to market norms.

The trade unions have expressed some doubts about competence-related pay. As quoted by Adams (1998), The Institute of Professionals, Managers and Specialists (IPMS) has stated that:

> It may be that competency-based schemes which focus on rewarding skills, experience and capability are preferable to the other performance pay measures, particularly in the light of moves towards broader pay bands and de-layering. However, in broad-banded systems, competencies can be used to create bars to pay progression, and there are usually other restrictions built in.

In fact, as described in Chapter 17, the opposite happens in a well-conceived broad-banded structure – pay can progress as people's careers progress when they increase their level of competence and contribute more.

Unison believes that competence-related pay may be used by organisations to generate individualised pay packets that leave unions out in the cold. But individualised pay packets are not unique to competence-related pay – they are a feature of any scheme in which pay is related to performance or contribution. And there should be no question of leaving unions out if a competence-related or indeed any other pay scheme is being developed. At Portsmouth Housing Trust, for example, Unison was involved from the beginning in developing a competence-related pay scheme.

The Banking and Finance Union (BIFU) is doubtful about the use of behavioural competencies because their assessment will be subjective. It prefers the use of competences firmly rooted in skills.

RELATING COMPETENCE ASSESSMENTS TO PAY

The relationship between competence assessment and pay may be formal or informal to varying degrees. In this aspect of competence-related pay, as in all the others, there is much diversity in practice.

A completely formal relationship can take the form of a pay matrix. This functions in exactly the same way as a performance-related pay matrix by relating increases to competence assessments and the individual's position in the salary range (his or her compa-ratio). This approach is used by Derby General Hospital NHT Trust and Scottish Equitable.

Another equally formal arrangement is that practised by Volkswagen United Kingdom by which each job family has its own salary range with between 30 and 40 increments. Progression through these ranges is entirely based on competence development.

A less formal relationship, as practised at Bass Brewers and Glaxo Wellcome, treats competence as just one of the factors that line managers are expected to take into account, the others being market rates, relativities between the rate of pay of individuals and others in similar roles or the same job family and, in some cases, potential (career development pay). At ICL the emphasis is actually put on the new salary paid rather than the salary increase. This is partly due to a desire to keep its salaries commensurate with the market, but is also intended to give the message that capability development does not necessarily lead to a salary increase. In a fast-changing business, existing capabilities may become irrelevant.

The mixed model
A number of companies conduct pay reviews by reference to both competence and performance assessments. The Performance Review and Development scheme at Severn and Trent Water, for example, assesses individuals against both work inputs (competences) and work outputs (performance objectives). At Mobil Oil (UK) staff are appraised against both objectives and competences. At the Woolwich Building Society pay increases are related to both the demonstration of competence and performance outcomes. The competences are organisation-wide and cover the following areas:

- team management/membership
- priority-setting/personal organisation
- networking
- customer service orientation

- staff and personal development

- change orientation

- performance management

- communicating information.

Other companies with hybrid performance-/competence-related pay schemes include Colonial, National Power and the Royal Bank of Scotland. It could be argued that these schemes and others like them should be given another name, such as contribution-related pay – and this concept is discussed in Chapter 22.

Method of payment
Competence-related pay processes essentially determine overall pay by reference to the level of competence someone has reached. Because the market worth of people is based on their level of competence compared with those in similar roles, competence pay will be influenced by market rates (external comparabilities). This means that the pay for someone who is fully competent may be aligned to the market rate for fully competent persons in a similar role. If they are less than fully competent they will be paid less; if they are more than fully competent they will be paid more.

It is therefore possible to argue that increases in competence are not rewarded by increments to a base rate of pay but by deciding on a new level of pay which is related to the competence level attained. It is, in fact, usual for competence pay increases to be consolidated rather than treated as variable, 'at risk' pay. The rationale for this approach is that competence implies that an individual's contribution will at least be maintained at the same level. In other words, competence predicts future performance.

COMPETENCE PAY CRITERIA

When developing a competence pay scheme the fundamental question to be answered is: 'To what extent do we want to pay for *what* people do, or *how* people do it, or a combination of the *what* and the *how*?' When people are paid for what they do, this is directly related to their performance and they are being paid for competence. Each competence heading has to provide an answer to the question: 'What does a person in this role have to do and achieve to be regarded as fully competent in this area?' An important subsidiary question has also to be asked: 'What evidence will be available to measure what has been done and achieved, and how will we get it?' These were precisely the questions used when Portsmouth Housing Trust developed their competence assessment process.

If, alternatively, behavioural dimensions are used, then competencies are the criteria. They may be core or generic competencies under general headings like those at Colonial: providing leadership and direction, ensuring the achievement of goals, and maximising others' contribution. Or they may be expressed in terms of core values such as achievement, leadership, customer focus, teamworking, innovation and creativity. Behavioural competencies are frequently used as the criteria for competence-related pay – for example, by Abbey Life, Bass Brewers, Colonial, Derby City General Hospital NHS Trust, and Scottish Equitable. The use of competencies accords with the view expressed in the Jimmy Lunceford number 'It ain't what you do but the way that you do it; that's what gets results.'

A competence approach is concerned more with effect than behaviour, more with impact than input. It is saying that competence is about performance and that increases in competence are rewarded only when they lead to higher levels of contribution. However, a focus on the effective use of competences rather than their acquisition – on delivered performance – means that competence-related pay begins to look suspiciously like performance-related pay.

A behaviour-oriented competencies approach does appear to flow naturally from the construction of competency frameworks for recruitment, promotion and developmental purposes. Competency analysis therefore becomes an integrating process. But there is a danger that assessment will be referred to personality traits so that competency-based appraisal schemes may begin to look like the discredited merit-rating systems of the 1950s and 1960s. And concentrating on behaviour gives the impression that people will be rewarded for behaving nicely, irrespective of the degree to which that behaviour impacts on results.

WHY COMPETENCE-RELATED PAY?

Competence-related pay is appropriate when:

- well-researched competency frameworks have already been established for developmental and recruitment purposes

- criteria are available for the measurement/assessment of competencies

- the organisation is concerned with the development of competence levels

- it is necessary to develop the competences required to take on new or enlarged responsibilities in flatter or process-based organisations.

THE ADVANTAGES AND DISADVANTAGES OF COMPETENCE-RELATED PAY

Advantages
Competence-related pay can

- focus attention on the need for higher levels of competence

- encourage competence development

- fit de-layered organisations by facilitating lateral career moves

- encourage staff to take ownership of their own development

- help to integrate role and generic competences with organisational core competences.

Disadvantages
The disadvantages are these:

- Unless very careful control is exercised, costs may escalate if employees are paid for competences they rarely, if ever, use.

- Assessment and documentation of competence levels can be time-consuming and expensive.

- Its effectiveness depends on the fair and consistent measurement of competence levels, and this may be difficult.

- The link to pay may be arbitrary.

- It requires considerable resources in terms of training and support.

- There is the possibility of gender bias.

- The process makes considerable demands on the commitment and skills of line managers.

It is noticeable that the disadvantages are mainly concerned with the way in which competence-related pay is administered. It is quite certain that it can be time-consuming and can make considerable demands on management and administrative resources. Managers may not want to or be able to cope with the new demands made on them.

But the disadvantages can be contained if

- rewards are related to the effective use of competences rather than merely to their acquisition

- competence levels are described in terms of specific work-related behaviours

- thought is given to the evidence that can be made available to indicate competence levels and how it can be obtained, analysed and assessed

- it is recognised in advance that competence-related pay will require the mobilisation of extensive management resources and will take time to implement and manage

- steps are taken to plan the use of these resources and the implementation and management programmes and procedures on the assumption that all the effort will be worthwhile

- the implementation of competence pay decisions is monitored from an equal value point of view with analytical job evaluation support as necessary

- clear guidelines and training are provided on the identification and assessment of competence levels

- it is recognised that although a key aim of competence pay is to support continuous development, there will be limits to how far anyone can progress and, indeed, to the scope for progression, and the existence of these limits will have to be made clear to employees

- managers are involved in developing the process and trained in its use – the emphasis from the top must be that handling this area of their responsibilities is regarded as a key managerial competence requirement

- continuous support and guidance is available to line managers from HR or specially nominated and trained colleagues.

The advantages are mainly to do with the developmental aspects of competence-related pay in flatter organisations and its use in integrating corporate, HR and reward strategies. These advantages are compelling for those organisations that want to adopt an integrated approach to reward and development. But even if the advantages are believed to outweigh the disadvantages and the latter can be managed, the organisation should consider the extent to which it is ready for competence-related pay before taking any steps to introduce it.

READINESS FOR COMPETENCE-RELATED PAY

An organisation is more likely to be ready for competence-related pay when

- generic competence frameworks have been developed which have been aligned to core competences

- the need for continuous development and improvement is recognised at all levels

- a corporate transformation programme backed up, possibly, by a business process re-engineering exercise, has led to increased emphasis on competence development within a flatter and process-based organisation structure

- it is recognised that in flatter organisations careers are likely to develop laterally and the reward processes should support the development of the competences required

- effective performance management processes are in place

- a broad-banded pay structure has been developed or is being planned

- the organisation is prepared to consult with employees and involve them in the development programme.

Cira and Benjamin (1998) have suggested that: 'Competency-based compensation is not appropriate for every organisation, even an organisation that is already using competencies to manage performance, staffing or development. It is a difficult and often disruptive system to implement and only a company that is committed to significant change should consider it.' They believe that it is only appropriate to make the move when

- it is implemented as part of a broader competency-based human resource programme

- it follows the successful implementation of competency-based performance management

- it is considered that the changes intended from the introduction of an overall competency-based system of HRM need the additional emphasis that should come from linking the system to pay.

They do believe, however, that 'properly implemented and enforced it should lead to superior results for the organisation'.

INTRODUCING COMPETENCE-RELATED PAY

If these conditions are satisfied, the steps required to introduce competence-related pay are:

1 Evaluate need and readiness.

2 Obtain the views of the line managers, team leaders and employees about competence-related pay, having communicated in broad terms how it will work and the benefits to both the organisation and themselves.

3 Set up a cross-functional and fully representational project team to develop the process.

4 Define the broad approach to competence pay and what work has to be done to develop it – the work may include competence analysis programmes, the development of new or revised job evaluation or performance management schemes, the introduction of new broad-banded structures, procedures for linking competence assessments to pay, ways of integrating competence pay and employee development processes, and of controlling how the scheme will be maintained and what resources will be required. The costs of implementation should also be calculated at this stage.

5 Proceed with a development programme. Consultation and communication should continue.

6 Develop the whole process on the basis of the work carried out in the last stage. Communicate the proposals to everyone and involve senior management, managers, team leaders and staff in discussing the implications for the organisation and themselves. As necessary, assess the proposal in the light of the implications for the organisation and themselves.

7 Plan a phased introduction and training programme.

8 Monitor each stage of the implementation and training programme.

9 Evaluate results.

10 Amend or improve as necessary.

CONCLUSIONS

As Brown (1998) points out: 'Competence-related pay is particularly appropriate in organisations where it is recognised that employee skills and behaviours are the key to competitive success ... [especially] for knowledge workers and professional staff.' But he also emphasises that:

> Competence-related pay is in the main not replacing pay approaches but fusing with them, and such a combination can help to address both the measurement concerns of academics and trade unionists and the results-focused orientation of line managers.

This need for a fused approach can be met by developing the relatively new concept of contribution-related pay as described in the next chapter.

It has been suggested that competence-related pay schemes are just merit-rating schemes with a new name. To what extent do you think they are different and better?

SUMMARY

- Competence-related pay is a method of rewarding people wholly or partly by reference to the level of competence they demonstrate in carrying out their roles.

- Competenc(i)es can be defined as *work-based* or *hard competences* which refer to expectations of work performance and the standards and outputs that people carrying out specified roles are expected to attain, or *behavioural* or *soft competencies* which refer to the behavioural characteristics of people which they bring to their work.

- Competence-related pay works through processes of competency analysis, agreeing competency requirements in a particular role, assessing levels of competence for individuals against the requirements, and relating the pay of individuals to these assessments.

- Competence-related pay is appropriate when

  - well-researched competency frameworks exist

  - criteria are available for the measurement/assessment of competencies

  - the organisation is concerned with the development of competence levels

  - managers and staff are properly briefed and trained on the assessment of competence.

- The advantages and disadvantages of competence-related pay are summarised in Table 25.

- An organisation is more likely to be ready for competence-related pay when generic competence frameworks have been developed, the

Table 25 **The advantages and disadvantages of competence–related pay**

Advantages	Disadvantages
Encourages competence development	Relies on appropriate, relevant and agreed competence profiles
Fits de-layered organisations by facilitating lateral career moves	Assessment of competence levels may be difficult
Helps to integrate role and organisational core competences	Might pay for irrelevant competencies
Forms part of an integrated, competence-based approach to people management	Link to pay may be arbitrary
Delivers message that competence is important	Costs may escalate if inappropriate or unused competencies are rewarded.

need for continuous development and improvement is recognised at all levels, there is an increased emphasis on competence development within a flatter and process-based organisation structure, it is appreciated that reward processes should support the development of the competences required and effective performance management processes are in place associated with a broad-banded structure.

FURTHER READING

BROWN, D. (1998) *A Practical Guide to Competency-Related Pay.* London, Financial Times.

MCHALE, P. (1990) 'Putting competencies to work: competency-based job evaluation'. *Competency.* Summer. pp. 39–40.

TIJOU, F. (1991) 'Just rewards: implementing competency related pay'. *Human Resources.* Autumn. pp. 147–150.

22 Contribution-related pay

This is what a compensation and benefits manager in a finance sector organisation said about reward policy:

> Performance in our setting is much more complex than a decision relating to five SMART objectives. Often the most measurable is not the most meaningful ... Contribution talks to a broader series of outcomes, is easier to relate to corporate values, encompasses enthusiasm, future capability and teamwork ... It relates to discretionary effort, rather than the sort of narrow-minded, individual, short-term results focus which stifles innovation in many organisations.

This is the view held by an increasing number of pay specialists who have recognised the limitations of performance-related pay, are not convinced that competence should be the sole factor in influencing reward decisions, and want to take a much broader view of the basis for deciding levels of pay.

The belief that a new approach is required is reinforced by the fact that while it is possible to make a number of distinctions between performance-related and competence-related pay, these can become distinctions without differences – more apparent than real. This happens when competence levels are defined and competence is assessed against those levels not just by observing behaviour but by analysing the impact of that behaviour in achieving results and meeting required standards of performance.

The distinction between them becomes even less real if the evidence of competence is based on *what* people have done as well as *how* they have done it. But if performance can be defined as being both what people achieve (outcomes) as well as how they achieve it (competences), then a mixed model becomes appropriate. This could be described as 'contribution-related pay'.

On completing this chapter the reader will understand the concept of contribution pay, how it works, and the circumstances in which it may be appropriate.

CONTRIBUTION DEFINED

Contribution is what people do to bring about a result. Individuals and teams contribute to the achievement of the purpose of their role. In financial terms, contribution is the difference between the sales revenue for a product and its directly attributable marginal or variable costs. It thus indicates what income a product generates towards achieving profit and covering fixed costs. In the context of pay and performance management, however, contribution is a more general concept which embraces both the results people achieve and the skills and competences they deploy in delivering those results.

CONTRIBUTION-RELATED PAY DEFINED

In accordance with the definition given above, contribution-related pay is based on both output (results) and input (competence) criteria. Contribution-related pay recognises that performance embraces both these factors. It is concerned with *how* results are achieved as well as the results themselves. It is about paying for the skills and behaviours which underpin the future success of the individual and the organisation. Contribution pay is therefore not so narrowly focused on one aspect of performance (outputs or inputs) as are both PRP and competence-related pay. It takes a more rounded view of what constitutes good performance and, therefore, of how it should be rewarded.

The questions to be answered when considering what should be paid for contribution are:

• What impact has the person in this role made on team, departmental or organisational performance?

• What level of competence has been brought to bear in handling the demands made by the role?

• How has the contribution made to end-results been affected by the level of competence displayed and applied?

• What are the indications that the individual's level of competence is increasing so that contribution performance is likely to improve even more in the future?

Contribution-related pay can therefore be defined as a process for making pay decisions which are based on assessments of both the outcomes of the work carried out by individuals and the levels of skill and competence which have influenced these outcomes. It is a holistic process, taking into account all aspects of a person's performance in accordance with the definition produced by Brumbrach (1988):

> Performance means both behaviours and results. Behaviours emanate from the performer and transform performance from abstraction to action. Not just the instruments for results, behaviours are also outcomes in their own right – the product of mental and physical effort applied to tasks – and can be judged apart from results.

THE BASIS OF CONTRIBUTION-RELATED PAY

Contribution pay is a process which encapsulates the developments since the 1980s in approaches to rewarding people for what they do and achieve, as summarised in Table 26 (adapted from Brown and Armstrong, 1999).

Table 26 1980s pay for performance approaches compared with pay for contribution

	Pay for performance	Pay for contribution
Organising philosophy	Formulae, systems	Processes
HR approach	Instrumentalist, people as costs	Commitment, people as assets
Measurement	Pay for results (the 'whats'), achieving individual objectives	Multi-dimensional, pay for results *and* how they are achieved
Measures	Financial goals; cost efficiency	Broad variety of strategic goals; balanced score-card; added value
Focus of measurement	Individual	Multi-level: business, team, individual
Design	Uniform merit pay throughout organisation	Diverse approaches, wide variety of reward methods to meet different needs
Time-scales	Immediate past	Past performance and contribution to achieving future strategic goals
Performance management	Past review and ratings focus; top-down; quantitative	Mix of past review and future development; 360-degree feedback; quantitative *and* qualitative
Pay linkage	Fixed formula; matrix	Looser, more flexible linkage; 'holistic' approach to pay review; pay 'pots'
Administration	Controlled by HR	Owned/operated by line managers
Communication and involvement	Top-down; written	Face-to-face; open; high-involvement
Evaluation of effectiveness	Act of faith	Regular monitoring against clearly-defined success criteria
Changes over time	All or nothing	Continuous improvement

HOW CONTRIBUTION-RELATED PAY WORKS

Contribution-related pay can work effectively within a broad-banded pay structure in which movement across the bands depends on both competence and performance. It also fits well with a belief that the delivery of pay should be based on performance, competence *and* career progression considerations.

Paying for contribution, as suggested by Brown and Armstrong (1999), means paying for results plus competence and for past performance and future success, as illustrated in Figure 35.

Figure 35 **Paying for contribution model**

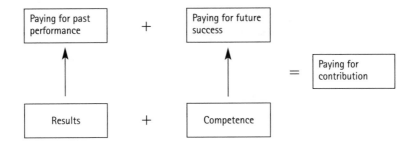

Contribution-related pay therefore works by applying the mixed model of performance management – assessing inputs and outputs and coming to a conclusion on the level of pay that is appropriate for individuals in their roles, looking both at past performance and, importantly, at the future.

There are two approaches. The first is to take a holistic view of what people have contributed on the basis of information about their competence and what they have delivered. This can be based on a competence framework so that behaviour can be considered analytically, although ultimately an overall view will be formed. Similarly, an overview of performance in achieving objectives or meeting standards can be evolved. The information from the sources is then combined and the level of contribution compared with others in similar roles in order to reach a pay review decision.

The second approach involves rating both results and competence and taking both these ratings into account in deciding on pay increases. This could be done somewhat mechanistically with the help of a pay matrix as illustrated in Chapter 36.

Paying for contribution in practice
At Nuclear Electric, as stated in the joint management and trade union communication to employees, paying for contribution involves 'replacing tenure-related increments with progression based on acquiring and using competencies, together with increases based on contribution to the business plan'.

At Bass Brewers pay decisions are based on an overall performance (contribution) rating which is based 50 per cent on competency ratings and 50 per cent on achievement of their five personal objectives.

At Coutts & Co. (bankers) both output and competence are taken into account when reviewing pay. As described by Mead and Pollard (1999), the requirement was to find a balance between rewarding for output and rewarding for behaviour. The decision was made to use output as the only factor which governs cash bonuses but to include it only as a subsidiary when considering base salary. In contrast, competence is used as the major component in determining salary, as illustrated in Figure 36.

Figure 36 **Contribution pay at Coutts & Co.**

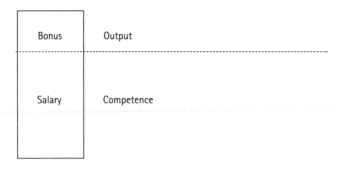

The salary scale at Coutts & Co. has three ranges, as shown in Figure 37.

Figure 37 **Salary range structure at Coutts & Co.**

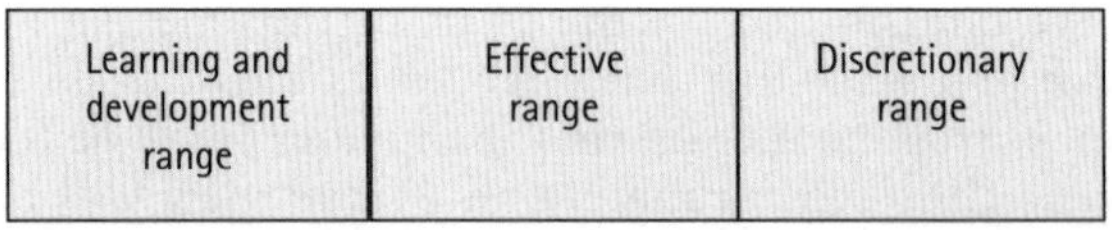

Learning and development range	Effective range	Discretionary range

Movement from the learning and development range depends entirely on 'accreditation' – ie meeting the defined competence requirements for the role. Movement into and within the discretionary range depends on 'continued superior performance'. The market midpoint is within the effective range. Its precise position depends on the company's performance. The ranges are determined by market data and drawn as wide as possible – the maximum can be as much as two and a half times the minimum – ie broad-banding.

WHEN CONTRIBUTION-RELATED PAY IS APPROPRIATE

Paying for contribution is appropriate when it is believed that a well-rounded approach covering both outputs and inputs is required to make pay decisions which are related to the criticality of the role now and in the future. It is used when it is deemed important to get the balance of factors affecting pay right in the light of organisational requirements. But it will work only if there are competence frameworks in place, if outputs can be measured, and if there are fair and consistent methods of assessing competence and measuring output.

> What are the advantages and disadvantages of contribution-related pay?

SUMMARY

- Contribution-related pay is based on both output (results) and input (competence) criteria. It is concerned with *how* results are achieved as well as the results themselves.

- Paying for contribution means paying for results plus competence and for past performance and future success.

- Contribution-related pay works by applying the mixed model of performance management – assessing inputs and outputs and coming to a conclusion on the level of pay that is appropriate for individuals in their roles, looking both at past performance and, importantly, the future.

FURTHER READING

A full description of contribution-related pay is provided by Brown and Armstrong in *Paying for Contribution*, Kogan Page, 1999.

23 Skill-based pay

The notion of linking pay with the acquisition of skills became popular in the USA during the 1980s. Interest in skill-based pay was aroused in the UK during the later 1980s, and the IRS 1998 found that 10 per cent of the respondents had skill-based pay and 8.7 per cent were considering its introduction.

The purpose of this chapter is to define skill-based pay and what it sets out to do, describe the various ways in which skill-based pay functions, assess the problems associated with skill-based pay, and outline methods of introducing it. On completing the chapter the reader will understand how skill-based pay works, its advantages and disadvantages, the circumstances in which it can play a useful role in the reward system, and the principles which should govern its design and use.

DEFINITION, APPLICATION AND AIMS

Definition
Skill-based pay provides employees with a direct link between their pay progression and the skills they have acquired and can use effectively. It focuses on what skills the business wants to pay for and what employees must do to demonstrate them. It is therefore a people-based rather than a job-based approach to pay. Rewards are related to the employee's ability to apply a wider range or a higher level of skills to different jobs or tasks. It is not linked simply with the scope of a defined job or a prescribed set of tasks.

A skill may be defined broadly as a learned ability which improves with practice in time. For skill-based pay purposes the skills must be relevant to the work. Skill-based pay is also known as knowledge-based pay, but the terms are used interchangeably, knowledge being regarded loosely as the understanding of how to do a job or certain tasks.

Application
Skill-based pay was originally applied mainly to operatives in manufacturing firms. But it has been extended to technicians and workers in retailing, distribution, catering and other service industries. The broad equivalent of skill-based pay for managerial, professional and administrative staff and knowledge workers is competence-related pay, which refers to expected behaviour as well as, often, to knowledge and skill requirements. There is clearly a strong family resemblance

between skill- and competence-related pay – both are concerned with rewarding the person as well as the job. But they can be distinguished by the way in which they are applied, as described below and in the next chapter, and by the criteria used.

Aim

The overriding aim of skill-based pay is to improve performance and competitiveness by increasing employee effectiveness and by enhancing the efficiency of working arrangements. The specific aims are:

- *to raise the skills base* by extending the range and depth of the skill possessed and used by employees – Multi-skilling is required where workers are grouped together in manufacturing cells and customer-focused teams or when just-in-time systems are used. They will be expected to be capable of exercising a wider range of skills and to be interchangeable with other team members.

- *flexibility* – A multi-skilled workforce is a flexible workforce. Employees can be transferred between different parts of the operation, thus increasing the ability of the company to vary production or the services it provides in response to changes in customer demand or business peaks and troughs. Multi-skilled workers may be able to carry out their own routine maintenance and minor repairs, thus avoiding downtime spent having to wait for a specialist maintenance worker.

- *operating with a leaner workforce* – A survey by Incomes Data Services (1992) found that all the companies they contacted were able to function with a leaner, more efficient workforce than would have been possible under more traditional, job-based systems with strict demarcations.

Other reasons identified by the IRS (1995) survey were:

- to improve quality

- to raise employee motivation

- to aid efficient labour use

- to increase pay competitiveness.

HOW SKILL-BASED PAY WORKS

Basically, skill-based pay works as follows:

- Skill blocks or modules are defined. These incorporate individual skills or clusters of skills which workers need to use and which will be rewarded by extra pay when they have been acquired and the employee has demonstrated the ability to use them effectively.

- The skill blocks are arranged in a hierarchy with natural break points between clearly definable different levels of skills.

- The additional pay to be awarded for the successful acquisition of the skills contained in each skills block is determined. This defines how the pay of individuals can progress as they gain extra skills.

Table 27 Skill/performance pay matrix

Skill level	Performance rating		
	Not yet competent	Competent	Highly competent
1	–	£a	£b
2	–	£c	£d
3	–	£e	£f

- Methods of verifying that employees have acquired and can use the skills at defined levels are established.

- Arrangements for 'cross-training' are made. These will include learning modules and training programmes for each skill block.

SKILLS AND PAY PROGRESSION

Pay progression beyond general increases is usually linked directly with the acquisition of skills, although some organisations also include an element of performance-rating. The completed acquisition of a skill module or skill block will result in an increment in pay. The value of the increment usually depends on the grade, lower-grade increments being worth less than higher-grade increments. Payment may be linked with the successful completion of training for a 'skill block' defined as a training input. A skill level may be equivalent to a pay grade or equal to an NVQ (National Vocational Qualification) level. Within each skill level there may be a number of skill blocks, each of which can be developed through training.

Some companies combine skill-based pay with performance-related pay to ensure that payment is related to the effective use of skills, not just their acquisition. A skill–performance pay matrix may be used, as illustrated in Table 27. This provides for additional payments above the basic rate. Research conducted by IDS (1992) indicated that the amount paid for a module ranged from about £200 to £700, and that around £300 was the average.

EXAMPLES

At Motorola Easter Inch, a skill-based pay scheme has been introduced to 'define a structured career path for all manufacturing associates'. The aims of the scheme are to improve performance, flexibility and output. The scheme consists of an advancement programme of six steps which links performance, service, skills attainment and the completion of key training goals.

Examples quoted by IDS include Amersham International, which has four craft grades with between five and 11 pay points in each grade that relate to individual skill modules. Promotion from one grade to another is automatic, except for progression to the top grade, which depends on the company's operational needs. British Sugar has three administrative grades with three skill functions per skill block, and on completion of all blocks in a grade employees can gain automatic progression to the next grade. Pirelli Cables (Aberdare) has just two grades, for standard and specialist non-managerial employees, involving seven pay points, each representing one skill module.

IRS (1992) quotes British Home Stores, which gives further pay awards (on top of the annual pay deal) to employees who attain National Training Council (NRTC) qualifications. At West Cumbria Health Authority health-care assistants are placed in a grading structure with job descriptions based on the competences linked with the levels defined in the relevant National Vocational Qualifications. At the London Borough of Southwark's housing department a hybrid arrangement with both performance-related pay and skill-based pay elements has been introduced for neighbourhood housing officers and assistants. The latter can progress from scale 4 to scale 5. To do so they have to demonstrate 'sustained competence' over the assessment period of six months in a range of performance criteria and skills (79 in all) covering nine core task areas such as dealing with housing applications and providing housing management support. In each of these areas a specific target may be set to indicate (for example) the time-scale in which the employee needs to deal with the task or to be able to exercise the skill. Any specific training required is noted down by the individual's manager on the six-monthly assessment form, after ticking the 79 key skills and tasks to indicate the extent to which specific targets have been reached.

At Bayer Diagnostics, as reported by IRS (1996), there is a three-level skills-based structure: (1) start rate, (2) journeyman and (3) multi-skilled. Each area of manufacturing is organised into a number of self-directed teams. There are well-instructed trainers in each team who are expected to work 'on line' as well as carry out their training duties. They base their instruction on task breakdowns. Once taught to perform a particular task, employees are assessed and passed as competent operators by the trainer. The recommendation is checked by the manager, who triggers the pay increase. The skill-based pay grids are designed so that people will develop a set of skills with the objective of eventually becoming multi-skilled across a range of tasks in their area.

TRAINING IMPLICATIONS

Skill-based pay requires a more systematic approach to training. Unless sufficient investment in training resources or attention to the organisation of training is provided, the system may founder. 'Cross-training' to develop multi-skilling is usually part of the training and development process.

It is essential to ensure that training provision and the acquisition and use of new skills are synchronised. If training is inadequate but employees progress through the skill levels anyway, then the main point of the system will be lost. On the other hand, if the criteria for skill acquisition are demanding but no training support is given, so that few people progress, the incentive value of the system may be prejudiced.

The usual approach is for training to be module-based, and employees are expected to achieve a specified level of proficiency in each skill block module. The modules may include a range of related skills at a specified level.

ACCREDITATION

Skill-based pay requires a process for accrediting or validating the acquisition of skills and for assessing the proficiency with which employees use them. Some companies set their own standards and run their own accreditation system. Others use external certifiers such as the National Council for Vocational Qualifications, City and Guilds, or the Engineering Training Authority.

As Cross (1992) noted, the assessment systems used in the companies he studied tended only to recognise competence or no-competence. They did not attempt to establish different levels of competence – for example, the ability to perform the task under supervision, the ability to perform the task without assistance, the ability to support colleagues in the learning of the task. Cross commented that 'the thoroughness of the initial assessment system is important to establish the link between the current capability and the potential of individuals and their future roles'. But only one of his case-study companies had developed a comprehensive assessment process which sought to establish the ability of individuals and to plan their training needs.

PROBLEMS WITH SKILL–BASED PAY

Skill-based pay systems are expensive to introduce and maintain. They require a considerable investment in skill analysis, training and testing. Although in theory a skill-based scheme will pay only for necessary skills, in practice individuals will not be using them all at the same time and some may be used infrequently, if at all. Inevitably, therefore, payroll costs will rise. If this increase is added to the cost of training and certification, the total additional costs may be considerable. The advocates of skill-based pay claim that their schemes are self-financing because of the resulting increases in productivity and operational efficiency. But there is little evidence that such is the case, and there is some indication from the research carried out by Cross (1992) that companies which have introduced skill-based pay schemes have underestimated the costs involved and are finding it difficult to quantify the benefits.

A further problem is that of 'topping out' – employees' moving to the top of the skills hierarchy and then being unable to progress further. If, as is typical, there is no performance pay element, this process of going so far and no further may result in frustration and demotivation. Some US companies as reported by Ziskin (1986) have addressed this issue by introducing gain-sharing plans to supplement skill-based pay.

INTRODUCING SKILL–BASED PAY

Before introducing skill-based pay it is essential to establish that it is right for the organisation and that the organisation is ready for it. Skill-based pay is most appropriate in organisations where

• the level and range of skills needed is high

- flexible working arrangements are required

- the technology is appropriate – skill-based pay is likely to work best in continuous-process technologies or cellular manufacturing systems, although they have been introduced successfully in customer service operations where employees need a wide range of skills if they are to serve people properly

- the organisation is capital equipment-intensive rather than labour-intensive and direct labour therefore accounts for a fairly low proportion of product costs – in this situation, priority has to be given to efficient resource utilisation

- there is a high-involvement management culture which encourages the participation of all concerned in the design and operation of the system – without such involvement success is much less likely

- the trade unions (if any) are likely to be co-operative.

It is also essential at this stage to be quite clear about the objectives of introducing skill-based pay. An attempt must be made to evaluate both the costs and the benefits.

Finally, it is necessary to carry out an initial analysis of skill requirements, training resources and the availability of accreditation and certification processes.

If this analysis indicates that the conditions are favourable to the introduction of skill-based pay, the following steps should be carried out:

- Identify the jobs to be covered by the scheme.

- Define job families. Group individual jobs into job families where the basic skill requirements are similar.

- Analyse skills within job families.

- Define skill bases by reference to the skills analysis – there should be a distinct step in skill levels between each band.

- Devise skill training modules.

- Design 'cross-training' programmes for each module to extend skills.

- Decide on methods of testing and assessment.

- Establish base rates for job families.

- Define the range of payments for each skill.

- Establish procedures for progressing through the bands. These set out the testing and training arrangements and indicate that extra skill payments will be made only if they can be used operationally when required (but they do not need to be used all the time).

SUMMARY

- Skill-based pay provides employees with a direct link between their pay progression and the skills they have acquired and can use effectively.

- The overall aim of skill-based pay is to improve performance and competitiveness by increasing employee effectiveness and by enhancing the efficiency of working arrangements.

- The specific aims are to raise the skills base, enhance multi-skilling and flexibility, and operate with a leaner workforce.

- Skill-based pay works by defining skill blocks or modules which incorporate individual skills or clusters of skills which workers need to use and which will be rewarded by extra pay when they have been acquired and the employee has demonstrated the ability to use them effectively. The skill blocks are arranged in a hierarchy with natural break points between clearly definable different levels of skills. Additional pay is awarded for the verified successful acquisition of the skills contained in each skills block. Arrangements for 'cross-training' are made. These will include learning modules and training programmes for each skill block.

- Skill-based pay is most appropriate in organisations where the level and range of skills needed is high, flexible working arrangements are required, the technology is appropriate (eg continuous-process or cellular manufacturing systems), the organisation is capital equipment-intensive rather than labour-intensive, and there is a high-involvement management culture which encourages the participation of all concerned in the design and operation of the system.

FURTHER READING

Good examples of skill-based pay schemes are given in Cross (1992), IDS (1992) and IRS (1992) (see above). Other readings, all from the USA, are:

BUNNING, R. L. (1992) 'Models for skill-based pay plans'. *HR Magazine*, February, 62–4.

DEWEY, B. J. (1994) 'Changing to skill-based pay: disarming the transition landmines'. *Compensation and Benefits Review*, January–February, 38–47.

LEDFORD, G. E. (1991) 'Three case studies on skill-based pay: an overview'. *Compensation and Benefits Review*, March–April, 11–23.

24 Shopfloor incentive schemes

Shopfloor incentive schemes are based on the principle of payment-by-results (PBR). Modern developments in PBR are closely linked with the ideas of F. W. Taylor (1911), who argued that every manufacturing operation could be broken down by work study in the interests of efficiency. He stated that the object of shopfloor incentive schemes was to reward the input of labour within closely-defined tasks and, by so doing, to stimulate people to work at a faster pace and increase their output. This is in accordance with the instrumentalist view of motivation which is closely associated with 'Taylorism'. The view that employees will only work harder if they get more money still dominates thinking about shopfloor incentive schemes, although the advent of high technology in the shape of computer-integrated manufacture has meant that what were formerly skilled craft workers have now become technicians. The old type of payment-by-results scheme is no longer appropriate for them and they are more likely to be paid a salary. They may also be eligible for individual performance-related pay, but many organisations prefer team pay, especially when the manufacturing operation is conducted on a cellular basis. There is also a trend towards the use of gain-sharing schemes.

The proportion of shopfloor workers taking part in incentive schemes is declining rapidly. The New Earnings Survey for 1983 reported that 47 per cent of all male manual workers and 35 per cent of all female workers received incentive payments. In 1994 the figures were 29 per cent for men and 23 per cent for women. The IPM/IDS research (Cannell and Wood, 1992) found that only 3 per cent of the responding organisations had brought in new schemes during the previous five years, and during the same period 25 per cent of PBR schemes introduced before the mid-1980s had been withdrawn. This is partly because managements, especially in the manufacturing sector, have become increasingly disenchanted with incentive schemes, for reasons discussed later in this chapter. The decline has accelerated for four other reasons associated with changes over the last decade:

- the introduction of new technology – when manufacturing is largely computer-controlled or automated, output is predictable and depends much less on the efforts of the operative

- new methods of working – for example just-in-time (JIT) and cellular and group technology manufacturing systems, where results are achieved through collective effort and it would be inappropriate to reward team members by means of individual incentive schemes

- the need for flexibility and multi-skilling in new manufacturing environments – individual incentive schemes can encourage workers to concentrate on a limited range of tasks and to develop only the skills required for those tasks

- the increased emphasis on quality – PBR schemes encourage speed, which can be at the expense of quality if workers complete tasks to the minimum acceptable standard and ignore defects.

But there are enough schemes still in use to make it necessary for anyone who works in manufacturing to understand the principles affecting the design and operation of incentive schemes for manual workers so that he or she is in a position to advise on whether or not incentive schemes are appropriate, and if so, how they may be developed and used. That is the aim of this chapter, which starts with an analysis of the general considerations that affect the design, operation and maintenance of such schemes, and then describes each of the main types of scheme in turn – namely, piecework, work-measured schemes, multi-factor schemes, measured day work and performance-related pay. It concludes with a brief discussion of group incentive schemes.

GENERAL CONSIDERATIONS

The general considerations to be taken into account in developing and maintaining incentive schemes are the criteria of effectiveness, and the advantages and disadvantages.

The criteria of effectiveness

Incentive schemes aim to motivate employees to exert greater effort. They will do so effectively only if

- the link between effort and reward is clear and easily understood

- the value of the reward is worthwhile in relation to the effort

- individuals are able to influence their level of effort or behaviour in order to earn a reward

- rewards closely follow the effort

- the integrity of the scheme is preserved – it is not allowed to degenerate and cannot be manipulated so that individuals are over-rewarded.

The rationale behind incentive schemes

The basic rationale behind incentive schemes is the simple proposition that people are motivated by money. It is believed that they will work harder if rewards are tied directly to the results they achieve. Certainly the experience of most people, including the writer, who have installed a PBR scheme in a workplace where it did not previously exist is that productivity increases substantially when the scheme is new, although the level of increase is not always maintained. Studies in the USA by Lawler (1971), Guzzo *et al* (1985), Nalbantian (1987) and Binder (1990) have shown productivity increases of between 15 per cent and 35 per cent when incentive schemes have been put into place.

PBR schemes are used in the belief that they yield increased output, lower the cost of production and provide higher earnings for the workers concerned. It is also commonly believed that less supervision is needed to keep output up. Indeed, when direct supervision is difficult, PBR is often advocated as the only practicable form of payment.

The disadvantages of incentive schemes

The argument that people work harder only when they are paid more is regarded by some people as overwhelming. They do not accept the proposition that intrinsic and non-financial motivators can have an equally, if not more, powerful and longer-lasting impact. They may agree that this could be the case with knowledge workers and those who do not directly influence output or sales by their own efforts. But they argue that it certainly does not apply to those who are in a position to make an immediate impact on quantifiable results by their efforts. However, even if this assertion is accepted, there are still a number of compelling arguments against payment-by-result schemes. As long ago as 1960 Douglas McGregor said that:

> The practical logic of incentives is that people want money, and they will work harder to get more of it. Incentive plans do not, however, take account of several other well demonstrated characteristics of behaviour in the organisational setting: (1) that most people want the approval of their fellow workers and if necessary they will forego increased pay to obtain this approval; (2) that no managerial assurances can persuade workers that incentive rates will remain inviolate regardless of how much they produce; (3) that the ingenuity of the average worker is sufficient to outwit any system of control devised by management.

In 1962 Wilfred Brown launched a strong and influential attack on PBR systems as counter-productive and the cause of considerable shopfloor conflict and wage drift (pay increasing without any commensurate increase in productivity). The Office of Manpower Economics (1973) accepted the conclusion of the National Board on Prices and Incomes that: 'Our evidence has shown that some degree of wage drift will accompany any conventional payment-by-results system, no matter how good the managerial or joint controls.'

Currently the main objections to shopfloor PBR schemes are that they lead to:

• unfairness – earnings may fluctuate through no fault of the individual because of lack of work, shortage of materials, design modifications or the need to learn new skills; it may also be felt that the method of altering rates is unfair

• ineffectiveness – workers may have their own ideas about how much they want to earn or how hard they want to work, and regulate their output accordingly

• penalising skill – the more skilled workers may be given the more difficult and often less remunerative jobs

• wage drift – the difficulty of conforming to such criteria as clearly relate pay to effort and the lax approach of some organisations to the management of incentive schemes contribute to increases in earnings at a higher rate than productivity: degeneration and wage drift are a particular problem with work-measured schemes, as discussed later in this chapter

- management's escaping its responsibilities – team leaders and supervisors may rely on the incentive scheme to control output: instead of taking poor performers to one side and informing them that their work is not up to standard, they are tempted to take the soft option and simply point to the figures

- costly maintenance – extra work study engineers, rate-fixers and inspectors are often needed to maintain the scheme and exercise quality control

- strife in the workplace – arguments about rates and accusations of unjustified rate-cutting are common in workshops where incentive schemes are used

- poor quality – concentration on output can lead to neglect of quality

- poor teamwork – individual incentive schemes by definition encourage individual rather than team effort

- accidents and health hazards – workers may be tempted to cut corners and ignore safety precautions to achieve output targets; repetitive strain injury (RSI) may result if they work too hard on tasks requiring repeated small movements.

In spite of these arguments shopfloor incentive schemes persist. The main varieties as described below are piecework, work-measured schemes, multi-factor schemes, measured day work and performance-related pay.

PIECEWORK

Piecework is the oldest and simplest form of shopfloor incentive scheme. Operators are paid at a specific rate according to their output or the number of 'pieces' they produce. Pay is directly proportional to output, although most piecework schemes provide a fall-back rate which indicates a minimum earnings level. The proportion of the minimum rate to average earnings varies. It is typically set at 70 per cent or 80 per cent, although it can be as low as 30 per cent.

Advantages and disadvantages for employers
The advantage of piecework to employers is that it is easy to operate and explain to employees. The variable labour costs of production can be calculated and forecast readily and, in theory at least, it provides a strong incentive as long as a fair rate is set. Piecework systems appear to meet all the criteria for incentive schemes listed earlier in this chapter.

But there are a number of disadvantages. Piecework can function well as an incentive but only if the rates are fair, and that may be difficult to achieve. If the rates are too 'tight', workers will be under pressure to work too hard and will become dissatisfied and less productive or co-operative. If the rates are too 'loose', earnings may be too high in relation to effort and the scheme becomes costly. It may be more difficult to control output when workers are left with a considerable degree of freedom to determine their own rate of production, and quality may suffer.

Advantages and disadvantages for employees

Piecework systems are easy to understand and employees can easily control their earnings by regulating their pace of work. Assuming there is a steady flow of work, they can therefore forecast what their earnings will be in the short term. However, in the longer term, earnings may fluctuate from week to week, thus making it difficult to budget for regular items of expenditure.

When piecework may be appropriate or inappropriate

Piecework may be appropriate in operations where the work is relatively repetitive and unskilled, where workers can control the rate of production and their output by their own efforts, and where speeding up work will not significantly affect quality standards. It may not be appropriate in situations where the work is skilled, where operators have little scope to control the rate of production, where the work involves part of an operation or a series of operations rather than dealing with single units, or where quality considerations are high.

WORK-MEASURED SCHEMES

Work-measured schemes are the most popular form of incentive plan for manual workers. They use work measurement techniques to determine standard output levels over a period or standard times for tasks. The incentive pay is then linked with the output achieved relative to the standard or to the time saved in performing each task.

Calculating standard times using time study techniques

Traditionally, 'rate-fixers' used to set values based on their knowledge and experience, but more sophisticated work measurement techniques are now generally applied. The basic form of work measurement is time study. Jobs are broken down into their constituent parts or tasks, and the time taken by workers to complete each part is measured with a stopwatch by a work study, or industrial, engineer. A number of measurements are made of the time taken by different workers on the same task or the same worker carrying out the task at different times of the day and night.

Time study is based on objective measurements, but account has to be taken of the fact that there will probably be significant differences between the rate at which operators work – the effort they put into the job. Work study engineers have therefore to assess what that rate is – a process known as effort-rating.

Individual effort is rated in terms of 'standard performance'. This is the performance which a qualified and motivated worker should be able to achieve without over-exertion. The effort needed to achieve standard performance is sometimes represented as equivalent to walking at 4 miles an hour (ie quite briskly). All the operators studied are given an effort-rating relative to this standard. The raw times observed by the work study are then adjusted by the work study engineer to produce a basic time which represents at a rating of 75 or 100 (depending on which system is used) the performance of an average operator working conscientiously without financial motivation. This involves a large element of subjectivity, although experienced and well-trained engineers should be capable of making reasonably accurate and consistent assessments.

The basic time is further adjusted to incorporate allowances for relaxation, personal needs, fatigue and any time regularly taken up by other aspects of the work such as cleaning or resetting machines. The result is the standard time for the task, usually expressed as 'standard minutes'.

Incentive payments under work-measured schemes are based on performance-ratings. British Standard Institution (BSI) formulas are generally used. These are expressed as either 100/133 or 75/100, in which 100 or 75 is average performance without an incentive and 133 or 100 is the performance of a fully-motivated operator. Performance-ratings are calculated by the formula:

$$\frac{\text{number of units produced per day} \times \text{standard minutes per unit}}{\text{actual time taken, in minutes per day}} \times 100$$

Thus in a working day of 8 hours (ie 480 minutes of actual time) an operator may produce a total of 120 units. If the standard time to produce each unit was 4 standard minutes, the rating would be calculated as follows:

$$\frac{\text{(day's units) } 120 \times \text{(standard minutes) } 4}{\text{(actual minutes) } 480} \times 100 = \frac{480}{480} \times 100 = 100$$

If the employee produced 132 units in the day the rating would be:

$$\frac{\text{(day's units) } 132 \times \text{(standard minutes) } 4}{\text{(actual minutes) } 480} \times 100 = \frac{528}{480} \times 100 = 110$$

The problem with time study is that although it is based on objective measurements, the standard time that is ultimately obtained is the product of a number of additional subjective judgements. Employees who are being timed may deliberately restrain their performance in order to achieve low standard times and therefore higher bonuses with less effort. It is up to the work study engineer's skill and judgement to detect such restraint, and this can lead to arguments and even strife. In organisations with trade unions it is common practice to train some representatives in work measurement techniques to promote the achievement of acceptable judgements on standard times.

Predetermined motion-time systems

An alternative to time study is to use predetermined motion-time systems (PMTS). These use the times previously obtained from time studies to build up a 'synthetic' standard time. A common form of PMTS is methods-time measurement (MTM), which is based on a library of standard times for each basic physical movement. Work study engineers identify the movements required to complete a task and aggregate the MTM synthetic time for each movement to produce a standard time. MTM synthetic times can be developed within the organisation or obtained from management consultants. MTM eliminates expensive time studies and minimises their subjectivity, thus avoiding dissent as long as the synthetic times upon which the standards are based are acceptable.

Relating reward to performance

There are three basic methods of relating reward to performance.

Proportional payments

Proportional incentive payments increase in direct proportion to performance. On the BSI scale, for example, the bonus could be 1 per cent of basic pay per week per point above BSI. If the employee works at BSI 110, the incentive payment is 10 per cent. If performance is 130, the incentive payment is 30 per cent. An upper limit on bonus earnings of, say, 40 per cent may be imposed. This is the most common approach, and it is straightforward and easy to understand.

Progressive payments

These are payments in which incentive pay increases proportionately more quickly than output, as indicated by performance ratings. A performance of BSI 110 could give an incentive payment of 15 per cent of basic pay, and one of BSI 120 could result in an incentive payment of 30 per cent. Again, an upper limit may be imposed. This method offers employees high rewards and therefore more incentive – but wage costs are higher.

Regressive payments

These are payments in which incentive pay increases proportionately less quickly than output. For example, a performance of BSI 110 could produce a payment of 5 per cent of basic pay, while at BSI 120 the payment would be 10 per cent. This method means that wage costs are decreased but the incentive is reduced, and although from the employer's point of view it may be reasonable for employees to share more of the cost savings from higher productivity with their employer, the rationale of this approach may be difficult to explain.

The three basic methods of payment are illustrated in Figure 38.

Degeneration

The problem with work-measured schemes is that they tend to degenerate unless they are controlled tightly. Control is often difficult in the rough and tumble of a typical shop floor. The result is the phenomenon known as wage drift – incentive earnings increasing at a higher rate than productivity. Degeneration is caused by:

• special allowances – shop average earnings are paid for unmeasured work or waiting time; weak supervisors or rate-fixers too easily give in to demands for average earnings

Figure 38 Incentive scheme models

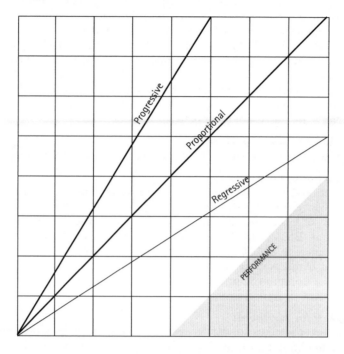

- erosion of standards – the type of work or the work mix can change over time: it may be difficult to point to a change in method sufficient to justify a retiming of the job under the rules of the scheme

- loose rates – however carefully the work study engineers have measured the original timings, some rates will be slack (ie more time will be allowed than is justified) and the natural tendency of employees and their representatives is to encourage and perpetuate loose rates

- cross-booking – workers may cross-book from difficult tasks on which it is hard to earn a good bonus to easier ones: the ability of operators to find ways of manipulating a scheme to their advantage should never be underestimated.

When work-measured schemes may be appropriate
A work-measured incentive scheme is likely to be more appropriate when

- short-cycle repetitive work predominates

- changes in the work mix, tasks or methods are infrequent

- shopfloor hold-ups and downtime are rare and not prolonged

- management and supervision, with the help of work study engineers, are capable of managing the scheme and preventing degeneration

- productivity is so low that the stimulus of an incentive scheme, even when it may cause problems later, is still worthwhile.

Advantages and disadvantages for employers

Work-measured schemes offer a more 'scientific' method of relating reward to performance and therefore providing financial motivation. But schemes can all too easily degenerate and, for reasons mentioned at the beginning of this chapter, employers are becoming increasingly hostile to any form of incentive pay, even if it is based on work measurement.

Advantages and disadvantages for employees

Work-measured schemes appear to offer a more objective method of relating pay to performance. But ratings are still prone to subjective judgement and earnings can fluctuate badly through no fault of the worker.

MULTI-FACTOR SCHEMES

With multi-factor schemes two or more indices of performance – such as quantity and quality of output – are combined to calculate the bonus. The advantage is that they can take into account other considerations than the sheer volume of output, quality being the most important one. But they can be complex and are little used.

MEASURED DAY WORK

Measured day work schemes became popular in large-batch or mass-production factories in the 1950s and 1960s, when it became evident that despite all efforts it was impossible to control wage drift. They are, however, much less common now. Manufacturing firms often prefer to pay a 'high day rate' (a rate of pay which is significantly above the base rate used in an incentive scheme and which is usually related to market-rate pay levels for similar jobs. Firms that adopt this approach may consider a factory-wide bonus scheme such as gain-sharing.

When they exist, measured day work schemes provide for the pay of employees to be fixed on the understanding that they will maintain a specified level of performance, but in the short term pay does not fluctuate with their performance. The arrangement depends on work measurement to define the required level of performance and to monitor the actual level. The fundamental principles of measured day work are that there is an incentive level of performance and that the incentive payment is guaranteed in advance, putting employees under the obligation to perform at the effort level required. In contrast, a conventional work-measured incentive scheme allows employees discretion as to their effort level but relates their pay directly to the results they achieve. Between these two extremes there are a variety of alternatives, including banded incentives, stepped schemes and various forms of high day rate.

Measured day work seeks to produce an effort–reward bargain in which enhanced and stable earnings derive from an incentive level of performance. Its disadvantage is that the set performance target can become an easily attainable norm and may be difficult to change, even after extensive renegotiation.

The essentials for success in operating measured day work are:

- total commitment of management, employees and trade unions, which can be achieved only by careful planning, joint consultation and the staged introduction of the scheme

- effective work measurement, and efficient production planning and control and inventory control systems

- the establishment of a logical pay structure with appropriate differentials from the beginning of the scheme's operation: the structure should be developed by job evaluation and in consultation with employees

- good control systems, so that swift action can be taken to correct any shortfalls on targets.

These are exacting requirements, which is why measured day work is relatively rare and has been abandoned by a number of organisations in favour of a high day rate system, possibly topped up with team or factory-wide bonuses.

PERFORMANCE-RELATED PAY

Performance-related pay systems such as those described in chapter 20 can be used for manual workers. Employees receive a high base rate and an additional performance-related payment which is either a lump-sum bonus or consolidated into basic pay. The award is governed by assessments of skill and performance-ratings under such headings as quality, flexibility, contribution to teamworking and ability to hit targets. The percentage award is usually small – up to 5 per cent.

Performance-related pay is sometimes introduced for manual workers as part of a programme for harmonising their conditions of employment with those of salaried staff. It can be appropriate in circumstances where work measurement is difficult or impossible to use, in high-technology manufacturing where operations are computer-controlled or automated and teamwork and multi-skilling are important, in organisations where the emphasis is on quality, and in those where just-in-time (JIT) systems are used.

However, performance-related pay for manual workers suffers from all the problems referred to in Chapter 15. It is not particularly effective as a motivator and it will be resented by workers who have been earning high incentive payments.

ALTERNATIVES TO INCENTIVE PAY

The main alternatives to incentive pay are:

- high day rates plus skill-based pay (see Chapter 23)

- high day rates accompanied by a factory-wide bonus or gain-sharing system (see Chapter 27)

- high day rates plus some form of performance-related pay (on the assumption that PRP does not act as an incentive).

If it is believed that some form of incentive is still required in a teamwork environment, or if JIT is in operation, some form of team reward as described in Chapter 25 could be considered.

CHANGING A PAY SYSTEM FOR MANUAL WORKERS

There are three main directions in which change can take place:

- introducing an incentive scheme

- changing an existing scheme

- abandoning incentive schemes altogether, possibly replacing them with a high day rate or introducing an integrated pay structure in which no distinction is drawn between the pay arrangements of staff and manual workers. (In the latter situation PRP or skill-based pay might be used.)

In each of these cases the steps to be taken are as follows:

- Analyse existing working methods and plans for future change. Account should be taken of such developments as computer-integrated manufacturing, cellular working and just-in-time systems.

- Analyse existing pay arrangements to assess their strengths and weaknesses.

- Assess the critical success factors of the company.

- Consider in the light of the analyses and assessments in the first three stages what changes may be desirable to reflect current or future working methods to overcome weaknesses in the present pay arrangements (eg wage drift, focus on quantity rather than quality), and to take account of the critical success factors (eg quality, customer service, speed of response, time to market, flexibility, teamwork).

- Before making any decisions, consult trade unions and employees on what they would like to do about pay arrangements. Assess the degree to which they might accept change or some sort of quid pro quo (eg increased security, a higher level of guaranteed pay, staff conditions of employment) to persuade them to agree to changes in the payment system and working arrangements, eg more flexibility.

- Involve trade unions and employees in developing the new arrangements.

- If a new incentive scheme is to be introduced, negotiate an agreement with the trade union(s), if any, which spells out how it works, the limits on payment levels, the circumstances in which rates can be changed, the pay arrangements for waiting time, continued work, etc, and, if at all possible, an understanding that the operation of the scheme will be limited to one or two years and will then be subject to revision in the light of experience.

- If a work-measured scheme is to be introduced, ensure that experienced and capable work study engineers are available to run it and that managers and team leaders are trained in their responsibilities.

- Document the arrangements and communicate them to employees, explaining how the scheme functions, the part they will play, and how they will benefit from it.

- Introduce the scheme, possibly in stages or on a piloted basis.

- Monitor and evaluate the impact of the scheme on productivity and the costs of operating it.

- Revise the scheme as necessary in the light of the evaluation.

SUMMARY

- Payment-by-results (PBR) schemes for shopfloor workers are used in the belief that they yield increased output, lower the cost of production and provide higher earnings for the workers concerned. It is also commonly believed that less supervision is needed to keep output up. Indeed, when direct supervision is difficult, PBR is often advocated as the only practicable form of payment.

- The main types of shopfloor incentive schemes are piecework, work-measured schemes, multi-factor schemes, measured day work and performance-related pay.

- Piecework involves operators' being paid at a specific rate according to their output or the number of 'pieces' they produce.

- Work-measured schemes use work-measurement techniques to determine standard output levels over a period of standard times for tasks. The incentive pay is then linked with the output achieved relative to the standard or to the time saved in performing each task.

- Measured day work provides for the pay of employees to be fixed on the understanding that they will maintain a specified level of performance, but in the short term pay does not fluctuate with their performance.

- In performance-related pay systems shopfloor employees receive a high base rate and an additional performance-related payment which is either a lump-sum bonus or consolidated into basic pay.

- In multi-factor schemes two or more indices of performance, such as quantity and quality of output, are combined to calculate the bonus.

FURTHER READING

The basic principles of incentive schemes with examples are summed up well in the ACAS publication, *Introduction to Payment Systems*, 1994. A more comprehensive but denser summary is given in the ILO publication, *Payment by Results*, Geneva, 1984. *IDS Study 488*, August 1991, provides an excellent summary of the whole subject. Cannell and Wood (1992) provides further insight into how incentive pay is operating, with good case-studies. Nick Kinnie and David Lowe review the operation of PRP for manual workers on the basis of their research in 'Performance-related pay on the shop floor', *Personnel Management*, November 1990, 45–9. There are some good case-studies.

25 Team rewards

Teamwork matters in the newly de-layered organisation. It was suggested by Industrial Relations Services (1995) that following this stripping-out process, 'The organisation that is left can only function effectively if teamworking is formalised and made an important part of the business operation.' Katzenbach and Smith (1993) have commented that 'The primary purpose of top management is to focus on performance and the teams that will deliver it.'

The significance of good teamwork as a key factor in organisational success has directed attention to how employee reward systems can contribute to improving team effectiveness. The focus is shifting from individual performance-related pay (which has conspicuously failed to deliver the results expected of it in many organisations) to team pay and other methods of rewarding teams.

This chapter reviews the basic considerations affecting team rewards, then examines the use of non-financial as well as financial team reward systems and processes. By the end of the chapter the reader should be able to identify the scope for team rewards and understand how they can be introduced.

TEAM REWARDS – AN OVERVIEW

Team-based rewards are payments to members of a formally established team or the provision of other forms of non-financial reward which are linked to the performance of that team. The rewards are shared among the members of the team in accordance with a published formula or on an *ad hoc* basis in the case of exceptional achievements. Rewards for individuals may also be influenced by assessments of their contribution to team results.

The purpose of team rewards is to reinforce the sort of behaviour that leads to and sustains effective team performance by:

- providing incentives and other means of recognising team achievements

- clarifying what teams are expected to achieve by relating rewards to the attainment of predetermined and agreed targets and standards of performance or to the satisfactory completion of a project or a stage of a project

- conveying the message that one of the organisation's core values is effective teamwork.

Research conducted by the Institute of Personnel and Development (IPD, 1996) established that the main reason organisations gave for developing team reward processes was the perceived need to encourage group endeavour and co-operation rather than to concentrate only on individual performance. It is argued that 'pay for individual performance' systems prejudice team performance in two ways. First, they encourage individuals to focus on their own interests rather than on those of the team. Second, they result in managers and team leaders treating their team members only as individuals rather than relating to them in terms of what the team is there to do and what they can do for the team. These are powerful arguments, but the take-up of team pay has been fairly small in the UK. The IRS (1998) survey established that only 6.1 per cent of participants had team pay, although 14.3 per cent were thinking about introducing it. That the number of schemes is small may be because organisations find it difficult to meet the quite exacting conditions for team pay set out later in this chapter. Others may believe that they have to focus their incentive schemes on individual rather than group effort.

To develop and manage team rewards as part of a total reward system it is necessary to understand what a team is, how teams function and the way in which the types of teams that operate within organisations differ.

The nature of a team

A team has been defined by Katzenbach and Smith (1993) as:

> a small number of people with complementary skills who are committed to a common purpose, performance goals and approach for which they hold themselves mutually accountable.

The essential characteristics of an effective team are that:

- It exists to attain a defined purpose and is successful in doing so.

- Members of the team are committed collectively and individually to achieving that purpose.

- Team members reinforce each other's intentions to pursue their common purpose irrespective of individual agendas.

Teams are concerned with task completion (results) and the building of relationships (process). Team rewards therefore need to recognise not only what the team has achieved (its outputs) but also how the results have been obtained (inputs).

Types of teams

The choice of team rewards will be influenced by the type of team. There are four categories.

Organisational teams

Organisational teams consist of individuals who are linked together organisationally as members of, for example, the 'top management team', departmental heads in an operational or research division, section heads or team leaders in a department, or even people carrying out distinct and often separate functions, as long as they are all contributing to the achievement of the objectives of their department or section. Members of organisational teams can be related to one another by the requirement to achieve an overall objective, but this may be loosely defined and the degree to which they act in concert will vary considerably. In a sense, organisations are entirely constructed of such 'teams', but team reward processes may be inappropriate unless their members are strongly united by a common purpose and are clearly interdependent. If such is not the case, some form of profit-sharing or gain-sharing system could be adopted to provide people with a share in the success of their function and the organisation.

Work teams

Work teams are self-contained and permanent teams whose members work closely together to achieve results in terms of output, the development of products or processes, or the delivery of services to customers. This type of team is clearly focused on a common purpose and its members are interdependent – results are a function of the degree to which they can work well together. Team rewards may be appropriate as long as team targets can be established and team performance can be measured accurately and fairly. Rewards can then be linked clearly with the achievement of the targets.

Project teams

Project teams consist of people brought together from different functions to complete a task lasting several months to several years. When the project is completed, the team disbands. Examples include product development teams or a team formed to open a new plant. Project teams may be rewarded with cash bonuses payable on satisfactory completion of the project to specification, on time and within the cost budget. Interim 'milestone' payments may be made as predetermined stages of the project are completed satisfactorily.

Ad hoc teams

These are functional or cross-functional teams set up to deal with an immediate problem. They are usually short-lived and operate as a taskforce. It is unusual to pay bonuses to such teams unless they deliver exceptional results.

THE BASIS OF TEAM REWARDS

In a sense, all of us do what we get rewarded for doing, whether acting as individuals or as members of a team. When considering the introduction of team-based rewards there are two fundamental questions to be answered:

- Should teams be rewarded by financial means, by non-financial means, or by a combination of the two?

- To what extent can we rely on extrinsic (external) rewards, whether financial or non-financial, as distinct from intrinsic (internal) rewards?

Teams, just like individuals, respond to both extrinsic and intrinsic rewards. Examples of extrinsic rewards include pay, bonuses, praise, public recognition and various forms of gifts. Examples of intrinsic rewards include satisfaction from accomplishing the team goals and a sense of well-being derived from strong work relationships, creative challenges, increased responsibility and learning opportunities.

The emphasis in team reward systems is usually on team pay rather than on other forms of non-financial rewards. Pay is of course important, as a tangible recognition, reward and, in certain circumstances and within limits, as a motivator. This chapter therefore devotes a large portion of its contents to team pay. However, the ultimate reward for teams, especially project teams, is often the successful completion of a task, as long as the achievement is recognised. And cash is not the only means of recognition. The choice is not between financial and non-financial rewards but between financial team rewards enhanced by non-financial rewards and non-financial rewards alone.

Team rewards in context

It is individuals who receive team rewards. The total team reward system is built upon the foundation of the main element of reward – basic pay. It is necessary to get this right before considering any form of team pay. As reported by the IDS (1993), some organisations such as Ind Coope and Baxi Heating see little need for team incentives. At both companies, team members are paid simple spot rate basic salaries. Ind Coope believes that if all team members are on the same rate, there are fewer arguments about who does what. Other companies such as the Body Shop recognise that flexible working, by which team members share management responsibilities, implies greater pay equality.

The IDS also noted that teamworking is generating divergent pay strategies. On the one hand there are those who are devising a range of incentive arrangements, team bonuses being coupled with individual performance-related pay. On the other hand, companies are flattening pay differentials and placing little or no emphasis on incentive arrangements. According to IDS, 'It is the very novelty of trying to combine co-operative behaviour, group performance and a separate emphasis on individual contribution that has produced these conflicting approaches.'

TEAM PAY IN ACTION

The basic approach

The IPD research and other recent research projects conducted by Industrial Relations Services (1995) and the Institute of Employment Studies (Thompson, 1995) showed that the most common method of providing team pay for managerial, professional, technical and office staff was to distribute a cash sum related to team performance amongst team members. Various formulas are used for calculating the bonus pool, and there are a number of different ways in which bonus pools are divided between team members. There is no such thing as a typical team pay scheme for people in these categories. That is to be expected. The design of such schemes is contingent on the requirements and circumstances of the organisation, and these will always differ.

In contrast, shopfloor group incentive schemes tend to follow a similar pattern, bonuses being linked either with the physical output of the team or, in work-measured schemes, to the time saved on team tasks – the difference between allowed time and actual time. Because of the relatively straightforward nature of such schemes, this chapter concentrates on describing team pay methods for other categories of staff covering the formula, methods of distribution and catering for individual as well as team performance.

Bonus formulae

Bonus formulae relate the amount individual team members receive to one or more measures of team performance or to the achievement of specifically agreed team objectives.

There are many ways of calculating team bonuses, but the IPD research identified three basic approaches:

- *Performance related to defined criteria* – as at Lloyds Bank and Norwich Union, where the criteria are sales and a measure of customer satisfaction. At Pearl Assurance bonuses are related to three performance criteria: speed of processing, accuracy, and customer service and satisfaction. At Sun Life the bonus is based on a customer service index expressed as a percentage of the customer cases dealt with over a period. Note that in each of these financial service companies customer service is used as a criterion.

- *Bonus related to an overall criterion* – as at the Benefits Agency, where team bonuses are paid if there has been 'a valuable contribution to performance as determined by local unit managers'. At Portsmouth Hospitals NHS Trust the bonus for directors and senior managers is based on the trust's outturn figures.

- *Bonus related to the achievement of predetermined team objectives* – as at Rank Xerox.

Methods of distributing bonuses

Bonuses can be distributed to team members in either of two forms:

- the same sum for each member, usually based on a scale of payments, as at Lloyds Bank and Norwich Union

- a percentage of base salary, as at the Benefits Agency, Pearl Assurance, Portsmouth Hospitals NHS Trust and Sun Life.

Payment of bonus as a percentage of base salary is the most popular method. The assumption behind it is that base salary reflects the value of the individual's contribution to the team. The correctness of this assumption clearly depends on the extent to which base salary truly indicates the level of performance of individuals as team members.

Team pay and individual pay

Some organisations, such as Lloyds Bank, Portsmouth Hospitals NHS Trust and Sun Life, pay team bonuses only. Others, such as the Benefits Agency, Norwich Union and Pearl Assurance, pay both team and individual bonuses.

REQUIREMENTS FOR TEAM PAY

Team-based pay schemes aim to provide:

- financial incentives to motivate team members to work effectively together and thus improve their team's performance

- financial rewards that recognise team achievements and usually take the form of cash bonuses which are distributed amongst team members.

The distinction between incentive and reward is important because it highlights the fact that schemes designed to motivate through financial incentives may fail to do so directly unless they meet the stringent conditions for a contingent pay scheme as set out in Chapter 19. But bonuses paid as a reward can be a useful means of recognising the team's contribution, and recognition of achievement can be a powerful motivator. Awarding a bonus is a way of demonstrating that the business values the team and its efforts and appreciates success.

Team pay works best if teams

- stand alone as performing units for which clear targets and standards can be agreed

- have a considerable degree of autonomy – team pay is likely to be most effective in self-managed teams

- are composed of people whose work is interdependent – it is acknowledged by members that the team will deliver the results expected of it only if they work well together and share the responsibility for success

- are stable – members are used to working with one another, know what is expected of them by fellow team members, and know where they stand in the regard of those members

- are mature, well-established, used to working flexibly to meet targets and deadlines, and capable of making good use of the complementary skills of their members

- are composed of individuals who are flexible, multi-skilled and good team players while still being able to express a different point of view and carrying the point if it is for the good of the team.

These are desirable requirements but they are not all essential. For example, mature teams may respond best to team pay, but there may be good reasons for providing team rewards during the start-up phase (although not necessarily financial rewards).

If the requirements above can be met, there may be a good case for team pay. But, as Vicky Wright (1993) has pointed out, 'The philosophy of pay for teams cannot ignore that it is individuals who receive rewards. Although team dynamics can affect individual perceptions, perceived individual fairness is a key to success.' Individuals may be motivated best and perform most effectively in a team setting, but the reward system has to meet their particular needs, as well as the needs of the team.

DEVELOPING TEAM PAY

Initial analysis
An initial analysis should be made of the following factors.

Situation and requirements

The success of team pay depends upon the rigour with which the initial analyses are conducted of the scope for introducing it and of the requirements of the organisation and its members. The analyses should cover:

- the identification of teams for which team pay may be appropriate

- an assessment of the team behaviour the organisation wants to reinforce

- how the performance of teams can be measured in relation to their objectives

- the opinions of employees about team pay.

Types of teams

Analyse:

- the types of teams in the organisation, divided into the four main categories defined earlier in this chapter – ie organisational teams, work teams, project teams and *ad hoc* teams

- the extent to which any of the teams are recognisable as clearly-defined units which are required to deliver specified results

- the degree to which members of the teams are interdependent and are required to be flexible and multi-skilled in achieving their team's purpose

- the amount of autonomy given to the teams. (Can any be described as 'self-managed'?)

Team behaviour

The analysis should assess the type of team and team member behaviour the organisation wants to encourage through team reward processes. This aspect could include such facets of team behaviour as:

- team direction – whether through an appointed team leader or by a process of self-management

- team commitment – the identification of individual team members with the team and the achievement of its purpose

- team orientation to performance objectives such as the achievement of goals, innovation, quality, customer service and cost management

- co-operation – the willingness of team members to work with each other and to subordinate their own objectives and needs to those of the team

- flexibility – the willingness of team members to work flexibly in the interests of achieving team targets

- skill/competence acquisition – the need for team members to acquire the necessary skills and competences to work well in a team environment (including the need for multi-skilling).

Team objectives

The analysis should establish what types of objective – in the form of targets, standards, deadlines and budgets – can be set for teams.

Team performance measures

How the performance of the teams can be measured in relation to their objectives must also be analysed. Wherever possible, the aim should be to identify quantifiable measures of output, income, quality, customer service, etc.

Employee opinion

The analysis should sound out and take note of the opinions of line managers, team leaders, existing team members and employees who may be included in teams on whether team performance needs to be rewarded specifically, and if so, how. Employee opinions can be ascertained through an attitude survey, individual interviews or focus groups. The latter approach has much to commend it, especially if it covers a representative sample of employees and existing teams. The questions which could be put to focus groups are:

- How important do you think good teamwork is in this organisation?

- Why do you think it is important?

- Do you believe that team members should be rewarded specifically for the achievements of their teams?

- If so, what sort of rewards do you think should be provided?

- What do you think would be the best basis for deciding on the scale of awards for teams?

- What do you think would be the fairest way of distributing a team bonus among the team's members?

- Do you believe it is right for individuals to be rewarded for their performance, irrespective of that of their team?

Setting objectives for team pay

The initial analysis should provide the basis for deciding on whether or not to go ahead with team pay, and if so, for whom and in what form. It should also provide the background against which specific objectives for team pay can be set. These objectives will form guidelines in the design and implementation of the system and, importantly, on how its impact should be monitored and evaluated. The objectives can be defined in such areas as:

- achieving cultural change – moving from an individualistic to a co-operative culture

- reflecting and reinforcing organisational changes in structure and process arising from de-layering and/or increased emphasis on lateral processes involving teamworking and project groups

- focusing the attention of teams on the organisation's critical success factors

- improving the effectiveness of teams

- achieving measurable improvements in organisational performance through increased profit, productivity and quality, better customer service, innovation or cost control

- the basis upon which team pay should be financed: the aim should be to make it self-financing through productivity improvements and/or cost savings.

Involving employees

The philosophy driving the development programme should be that 'people support what they help to create'. Team pay schemes must be 'felt fair' by those whom they affect – otherwise, like many of the original PRP schemes, they can act more as demotivators than motivators.

Employees who will be affected by team pay should therefore be involved as members of taskforces in the design of the scheme, with particular reference to the sort of objectives that will be set, the extent to which team members will take part in setting and agreeing the objectives, how performance should be measured, and the basis upon which team rewards should be distributed to team members.

Designing the scheme

Scheme design requires decisions to be made on the following elements of a team pay system.

Team eligibility

Which teams will be eligible for team pay and why? (Specific team pay objectives may have to be set for different teams according to their type and purpose.)

The quantitative measures

These are the criteria to be used in judging performance. They will vary according to the type of team. The criterion for a top management team may be improvements in any of the following: net profit, profitability, outturn (however measured) or earnings per share. For a work team, depending on the type of activity it engages in, the criteria could include such measures as output or sales figures, productivity, speed and accuracy of order-processing, quality levels achieved or customer satisfaction indices. The criterion for a project team could be completing the task to specification, on time and within the cost budget.

The qualitative criteria

What are the qualitative measures that may be used to assess team performance? For instance, how well do team members work together? How does the team fit in with other teams in the organisation?

The size of team bonuses

This is a matter of judgement. As reported by Caudron (1994), Stephen Gross, US vice-president and managing director of the Hay Group, has suggested in connection with team pay that 'Conventional wisdom, which is always suspect, says that variable compensation, to be meaningful, needs to be about a month's pay... At minimum, it needs to be in the range of 5 per cent to 10 per cent of the base salary.' In the UK the amounts paid out by organisations in team pay vary considerably. No limits are laid down in the Benefits Agency scheme but the bonus has to be self-financing. The highest target payment at Rank Xerox is around £4,000 a year, although the average payment has recently been about £1,500 a year. The Lloyds Bank scheme pays out a maximum of £400 a quarter. The maximum team pay bonus for Norwich Union Financial Planning Consultants is £3,000 a year.

The amount available depends on the following factors:

- a 'feel' for what a worthwhile payment is in the particular organisation: this will represent the view of management on the size of bonus required to provide an adequate incentive or reward and therefore to motivate team members

- the importance generally attached to financial rewards by the organisation and its members

- policy on the proportion of total remuneration which it is believed should be at risk

- what the organisation believes it can afford to pay: this will be related to the extent to which the scheme is expected to be self-financing in terms of increased productivity or cost savings.

The team pay formula

This establishes the relationship between team performance, as measured or assessed in quantitative or qualitative terms, and the reward. It also fixes the size of the bonus pool or fund earned by the team to be distributed among its members, or the scale of payments made to team members in relation to team performance with regard to certain criteria. There are many methods of doing this.

A bonus fund or pool may be appropriate when some flexibility is required in setting the level of payment to a team in relation to its performance and in distributing the sum among team members. The size of the fund allocated to a team may be based, as at Sun Life, on the cost savings generated by the team through increased productivity.

Other approaches include basing team bonus payments on:

- performance related to defined criteria

- an overall performance criterion

- the achievement of team objectives.

Dealing with high and low individual performance in a team

It is sometimes assumed by advocates of team pay that all members of a team contribute equally and should therefore be rewarded equally. In practice the contribution of individual team members will vary, and if this is the case, for example, in shopfloor groups, team pressure may oblige everyone to work at the same rate so as to avoid 'rate-busting'. (This is an example of how a highly cohesive team can work against the interests of the organisation.)

When designing a team pay scheme decisions have to be made on the likelihood that some people will perform better or worse than others. It may be decided that even if this happens, it would be invidious and detrimental to single anyone out for different treatment. It could, however, be considered that 'special achievement' or 'sustained high performance' bonuses should be payable to individuals who make an exceptional contribution, while poor performers should receive a lower bonus or no bonus at all.

Project team bonuses

The design considerations described above apply to permanent work teams. Different arrangements are required for project teams specially set up to achieve a task and, usually, disbanded after the task has been completed. Project team bonuses should, wherever possible, be self-financing – they should be related to increases in income or productivity or cost savings arising from the project. Project teams can be set targets and their bonus can be linked with achieving or surpassing targeted results. Alternatively, a fixed bonus can be promised if the project is on time, meets the specification and does not exceed the cost budget. The bonus could be increased for early completion or to reflect cost savings. For lengthy projects, interim payments may be made at defined 'milestones'.

Ad hoc bonuses

Where there are no predetermined arrangements for paying bonuses to project teams a retrospective bonus can be paid to a project or *ad hoc* team in recognition of exceptional achievement.

INTRODUCING TEAM PAY

Team pay may be an unfamiliar device and it should therefore be introduced with care, especially if it is replacing an existing system of individual PRP. The process will be easier if employees have been involved in developing the scheme, but it is still essential to communicate in detail to all employees the reasons for introducing team pay, how it will work, and how it will affect them.

It is easier to introduce team pay into mature teams whose members are used to working together, trust one another and can recognise that team pay will work to their mutual advantage. Although it may seem an attractive proposition to use team pay as a means of welding new work teams together, there are dangers in forcing people who are already having to adapt to a different situation to accept a radical change in their method of remuneration. It should be remembered that it may not be easy to get people in work teams to think of their performance in terms of how it impacts on others. It can take time for employees to adapt to a system in which a proportion of their pay is based on team achievement.

Clearly, this problem does not arise when teams are set up to tackle a special project. All the members of project or *ad hoc* teams know, or should know, that the project or task will be completed successfully only if they work well together.

When it comes to launching team pay it may be advisable to pilot it initially in one or two well-established teams. Experience gained from the pilot scheme can then be used to modify the scheme before it is extended elsewhere. If the pilot-scheme teams think it has been a success, other teams may be more willing to convert to team pay.

MONITORING AND EVALUATING TEAM PAY

Even when team pay has been planned and introduced carefully its success is not assured. It will be a new concept to most if not all the people affected by it – team leaders as well as team members. Team pay should be closely monitored in its early stages and evaluated regularly to establish the extent to which it is achieving its aims and providing value for money.

Monitoring and evaluation processes should aim to find out

- the extent to which team pay is achieving its objectives

- the opinions of line managers, team leaders and team members about team pay

- what improvements in performance have resulted from team pay

- what problems have been met

- how those concerned believe the problems can be overcome.

A team pay audit should look at performance figures before and after the introduction of team pay and obtain the views of those involved through attitude surveys, individual interviews and focus groups.

THE ADVANTAGES AND DISADVANTAGES OF TEAM PAY

Team pay can

- encourage teamworking and co-operative behaviour

- clarify team goals and priorities and provide for the integration of organisational and team objectives

- reinforce organisational change in the direction of increased emphasis on teams in flatter and process-based organisations

- act as a lever for cultural change in the direction of, for example, quality and customer focus

- enhance flexible working within teams and encourage multi-skilling

- provide an incentive for the group collectively to improve performance and team process

- encourage less effective performers to improve in order to meet team standards

- serve as a means of developing self-managed or self-directed teams.

The disadvantages of team pay are that:

- The effectiveness of team pay depends on the existence of well-defined and mature teams – but they may be difficult to identify, and even if they can be, do they need to be motivated by a purely financial reward?

- Team pay may seem illogical to individuals, whose feelings of self-worth could be diminished. It is not always easy to get people to think of their performance in terms of how it affects other people.

- Distinguishing what individual team members contribute could be a problem. It may not be regarded as a disadvantage by a fervent believer in teams, but it might demotivate individual contributors, who may still have much to offer, inside as well as outside a team setting.

- Peer pressure which compels individuals to conform to group norms could be undesirable. Insistence on conformity can be oppressive. Should the organisation provide financial rewards for such behaviour?

- Pressure to conform, which is accentuated by team pay, could result in the team's maintaining its output at lowest-common-denominator levels – sufficient to gain what is thought collectively to be a reasonable reward, but no more.

- It can be difficult to develop performance measures and methods of rating team performance that are seen to be fair. Team pay formulae may well be based on arbitrary assumptions about the correct relationship between effort and reward.

- Problems of unco-operative behaviour may be shifted from individuals in teams to the relationship between teams.

- Organisational flexibility may be prejudiced. People in cohesive, high-performing and well-rewarded teams could be unwilling to move, and it might be difficult to reassign work between teams or to break teams up altogether in response to product-market or process developments or to competitive pressures.

The arguments for team pay look good in theory but there are some formidable disadvantages and it has not yet been proved that team pay for white-collar workers will inevitably be cost-effective. (This is in contrast to work-measured group incentive schemes, which can produce significant increases in productivity.) Perhaps this is why, in the UK, team pay has been more talked up than put into practice, as the IPD and other research projects have shown.

This does not mean that team-based pay should be dismissed as yet another flavour of the month. The IPD research identified a number of organisations that truly believed it works well for them, even if they could not always quantify the benefits.

OTHER APPROACHES TO REWARDING TEAMS

Financial rewards can motivate teams as long as the teams are composed of people who are strongly motivated by money and whose expectations that they will receive a worthwhile financial reward as a result of the efforts of the team are high. But the motivational impact of money may not persist, and it may be diminished for individual team members because they find it hard to establish a link between their behaviour and the reward. Some people may feel that their pay should be related to their own efforts rather than being dependent on the performance of other people. For these reasons it may be undesirable to rely upon team pay alone, and consideration should be given to the other forms of non-financial extrinsic and intrinsic rewards which can be used specifically to supplement or even replace financial rewards.

Extrinsic non-financial rewards
The extrinsic non-financial rewards for teams include positive feedback, which can be given formally at team review meetings by team leaders who itemise precisely what the team has achieved in each of its key

performance areas. Praise from management or a team leader for work well done or a notable achievement can be part of a formal feedback process, but it can also be used less formally and more spontaneously during the everyday work of the team. As long as the praise is sincere and deserved it can have an immediate motivational effect.

Positive feedback and praise are both methods of recognition, but they can be even more effective if they are put in writing, preferably by higher management. Greater impact will be made if the team's performance is recognised publicly in house magazines, on noticeboards or at special events.

A tangible form of recognition which, while it costs the company money, is not strictly a financial reward, is to provide a special occasion for the team, such as a dinner, a trip to the theatre, or even a visit abroad to one of the company's overseas establishments. The team can also be called upon to represent the company or its business unit at outside or corporate events.

Intrinsic rewards

Intrinsic rewards are the self-generated factors which induce people to behave in a particular way or to move in a particular direction. The intrinsic motivators can work equally well in teams which feel that they are accomplishing something worthwhile and have a degree of autonomy to manage their own affairs and to make operational decisions. Individual motivation will increase if team members believe that they can exert more influence as part of a high-performance and self-directed team. Moreover, they may see more opportunities for personal growth in a team where the emphasis may be on flexibility and multi-skilling.

Providing non-financial rewards

Extrinsic rewards can be given by the organisation (eg public recognition) but will mainly be forthcoming from team leaders. Intrinsic motivation can be provided by increasing the degree to which teams are allowed to act autonomously.

World-wide research conducted by Coil and Frohman at Motorola (unpublished) showed that the following team reward and recognition approaches could be used at each stage of a team's development.

Definition

Reward and recognition help team members to become familiar with their assignment and goals and the challenge they have been given. So do any actions that help them to get better acquainted with one another and grasp the different skill-set requirements to support team performance.

Support

Reward and recognition help a team fully to understand and deal with its assignment, agree to procedures for itself and members' expectations of each other. The rewards should encourage team members to support one another and develop into a team with its own identity.

Reinforcement

Recognition acknowledges the progress (or lack of it) of the team and its members as it pursues its assignment. Informal and formal rewards that provide feedback and encouragement are most effective.

Celebration

Reward and recognition acknowledge achievement by the team as a whole and its members (eg performance evaluation). There is a clear message that the team effort is appreciated and its results will count. The acknowledgement of poor performance, if that is the case, is also important. However, the appropriate reward and recognition in previous stages should reduce the likelihood of poor performance.

CONCLUSIONS

The UK organisations which have introduced team pay are convinced that it works for them, and no doubt there are many other organisations for which the culture and the importance of good team work make team pay an attractive proposition. Team pay as a means of improving team performance does appear to promise much. But relatively few organisations seem to believe that it is relevant for them or that it will achieve its promise, if the number of examples of formal team pay systems identified by the IPD and others is anything to go by. A number of organisations that have expressed interest in developing team pay have gone no further. Indeed, this is hardly surprising if the onerous conditions for success and the disadvantages of team pay, as set out earlier in this chapter, are taken into account.

Perhaps one of the limits on the wider spread of team pay is that every scheme is unique – it is not possible to take one down from the shelf. And they are not always easy to design or manage. Many organisations will not venture into team pay because they are perfectly satisfied with their individual PRP scheme. It is these businesses which might consider the deliberate deployment of non-financial team rewards if they do want to improve teamwork. And they can assist the process if they include teamwork as a competence to be assessed and rewarded in their performance management system.

SUMMARY

- Team-based rewards are payments to members of a formally established team or the provision of other forms of non-financial reward which are linked to the performance of that team. The rewards are shared among the members of the team in accordance with a published formula.

- The purpose of team rewards is to reinforce the sort of behaviour that leads to and sustains effective team performance.

- The most common method of providing team pay for managerial, professional, technical and office staff is to distribute a cash sum related to team performance amongst team members.

- Bonus formulae relate the amount individual team members receive to one or more measures of team performance or to the achievement of specifically agreed team objectives.

- Bonuses can be distributed to team members either as the same sum for each member or as a percentage of base salary.

- Team pay works best if teams

  - stand alone as performing units for which clear targets and standards can be agreed

  - have a considerable degree of autonomy

  - are composed of people whose work is interdependent

  - are stable – members are used to working with one another, know what is expected of them by fellow team members and know where they stand in the regard of those members

  - are mature, well established, used to working flexibly to meet targets and deadlines, and capable of making good use of the complementary skills of their members

  - are composed of individuals who are flexible, multi-skilled and good team players.

- Team pay can

  - encourage teamworking and co-operative behaviour

  - clarify team goals

  - enhance flexible working within teams and encourage multi-skilling

  - provide an incentive for the group collectively to improve performance and team process

  - encourage less effective performers to improve in order to meet team standards

  - serve as a means of developing self-managed or self-directed teams.

- The disadvantages of team pay are that:

  - the effectiveness of team pay depends on the existence of well-defined and mature teams – but they may be difficult to identify

  - individuals may prefer to be paid for their own contribution

  - people in well-rewarded teams could be unwilling to move and there can be pressure from individuals to 'migrate' to better teams.

- Teams can be rewarded effectively by non-financial means, such as the various forms of recognition described in Chapter 27.

FURTHER READING

ARKIN, A. (1994) 'Team-based pay – an incentive to work together'. *Personnel Management Plus*, November, 22–3.

MACHIN, D. H. (1994) 'Evaluating and rewarding team performance'. *Compensation and Benefits Review*, March–April, 67–76.

THE PAY FORUM (1995) *Team-based Reward*. Winchester.

ZIGAN, J. (1994) 'Measuring the performance of work teams'. *ACA Journal*, Autumn, 18–32.

26 Profit-sharing and profit-related pay

Rewards can be related to organisational performance by means of profit-sharing, gain-sharing, profit-related pay and share ownership schemes. Of these, profit-sharing is the most popular (19.5 per cent of companies in the IRS 1998 survey had such schemes). Gain-sharing is still relatively rare – only 3 per cent of the companies surveyed by IRS used it.

On completing this chapter the reader will understand the nature and use of each of these main approaches to linking pay with how well the organisation does.

AIMS

The aims of relating rewards to organisational performance are to

- enable employees to share in the success of the organisation

- increase the identification of employees with the organisation

- focus employees' attention on what they can contribute to organisational success

- obtain tax advantages for employees through approved profit-sharing or share schemes – such 'tax-efficient' schemes enable the business to get better value for money from its expenditure on employee remuneration.

Schemes relating rewards to organisational performance – sometimes known as company-wide or factory-wide schemes – can be used to bring areas for improvement to the attention of employees. But they are not effective as individual motivators because the links between effort and reward are too remote.

PROFIT-SHARING

There are two forms of profit-sharing: non-approved schemes and approved schemes.

Non-approved profit-sharing schemes

Non-approved profit-sharing schemes are the traditional schemes which usually provide eligible employees with cash from a 'pool' on the basis of a formula that may or may not be published.

As reported by IDS (1995), in almost a third of the schemes covered by their survey the size of the pool is decided at the discretion of the directors or the executive council. At General Accident the directors are bound by one proviso: the size of the pool is subject to a minimum of 2–3 per cent of aggregate basic salaries.

In some companies the payout is triggered by the attainment of a set profit level. Others use a defined formula. At British Gas a set percentage of 3 per cent of group profits is paid to employees. Greene King contributes 10 per cent of the amount by which pre-tax profit for the year exceeds 80 per cent of the average profit for the three previous years, after allowing for the effects of inflation. A maximum and/or a minimum percentage of profit may determine the size of the pool. For example, the Bank of Scotland contributes a minimum of 2 per cent of pre-tax profits and a maximum of 6 per cent.

In most non-approved schemes the profit-share is distributed to employees as a percentage of their pay. In some schemes, as at Norwich Union and Thomas Cook, employees with low performance ratings get no payment. The level of payouts varies between 2 or 3 per cent of salary and 10 per cent or more. Employees have to pay income tax and National Insurance contributions on the sums they receive from a non-approved scheme.

Approved profit-sharing schemes

All-employee approved profit-sharing schemes were originally introduced by the 1978 Finance Act. Such schemes, which must be company-wide, allow bonuses to be paid in free shares rather than in cash. Although they are known as profit-sharing schemes, there is no statutory requirement for share allocations to be directly related to company profits.

In an approved profit-sharing scheme shares are set aside or appropriated for employees. The shares are then held for a minimum of two years by a trust specially set up for the purpose. After this period, employees may dispose of their shares. They will, however, be liable for income tax on the original value of the shares when they were issued unless the shares remain in trust for a further year, at which time they may be disposed of free of income tax charges. The share bonus does not attract National Insurance contributions but capital gains tax is payable at 25 per cent or 40 per cent when the shares are sold if the gains in any one year exceed the individual's threshold, which in 1995 was £6,000.

Under an approved scheme an employer may set shares aside for an employee up to an annual maximum value of £3,000 or, if greater, 10 per cent of the employee's salary, subject to a ceiling of £8,000 in any one tax year.

If it is to gain approval, all employees with five years' service must be able to participate in the scheme. Employers are free to allow employees with less than five years' service to join.

GAIN-SHARING SCHEMES

Gain-sharing is a formula-based company- or factory-wide bonus plan which provides for employees to share in the financial gains made by a company as a result of its improved performance. The formula determines the share by reference to a performance indicator such as added value or another measure of productivity. In some schemes the formula also incorporates performance measures relating to quality, customer service, delivery or cost reduction. The most popular formula is value added, as described below, but there are various kinds of special formulae such as the Rucker Plan, also described later.

Gain-sharing differs from profit-sharing in that the latter is based on more than improved productivity. A number of factors outside the individual employee's control contribute to profit, such as depreciation procedures, bad-debt expenses, taxation and economic changes. Gain-sharing aims to relate its payouts more specifically to productivity and performance improvements within the control of employees.

Aims

Fundamentally, the aim of gain-sharing is to improve organisational performance by creating a motivated and committed workforce who want to be part of a successful company. More specifically, as described by Armstrong and Murlis (1998), the aims of gain-sharing are to

- establish and communicate clear performance and productivity targets

- encourage more objective and effective means of measuring organisational performance

- increase focus on performance improvement in the areas of productivity, quality, customer service, delivery and cost

- encourage employees to participate with management in the improvement of operating methods

- share a significant proportion of performance gains with the employees who have collectively contributed to improvements.

At BP Exploration (BPX), as reported by IRS (1996), gain-sharing involves paying employees a bonus for 'stretching performance beyond the business plan'. These plans focus on the key performance measures of production, cost and safety, with an additional element tied to the performance of the company as a whole. According to BPX, the scheme has

- helped to align employees with performance targets

- increased staff participation and commitment

- enabled the company to reinforce its teamworking arrangements by providing a direct link between business performance and team reward.

At Rank Xerox as reported by IRS (1997) the added-value gain-sharing plan was defined as 'a scheme designed to encourage all employees across the site to participate and contribute in order to improve our competitive advantage and share the benefits'.

The key characteristics of gain-sharing

The most important aspects of gain-sharing are:

- ownership by employees of the plan – they should be involved in its development and operation

- the opportunity provided for increasing identification and commitment

- the scope it provides for employees to be involved in performance improvements to the benefit of themselves as well as the company

- the basis it provides for improving the quality of communications so that employees understand the key issues facing the company, its critical success factors and the part they can play.

The value-added formula

Many versions of gain-sharing are based on value added as the key performance measure. Value added is calculated by deducting expenditure on materials and other purchased services from the income derived from sales of the product. It is, in effect, the wealth created by the people in the business. A manufacturing business 'adds value' by the process of production as carried out by the combined contribution of management and employees.

In a value-added gain-sharing plan, increases in value added are shared between employees and the company. Typically, the employees' share is between 40 per cent and 50 per cent. Payments are triggered off if added value rises above a threshold or norm. If this happens, the surplus is shared between employees and the company on the grounds that normal payroll and other costs have been covered and the profit target has been met. If added value does not reach the standard, there are no payments.

Other formulae

The Scanlon Plan

The Scanlon formula measures labour costs as a proportion of total sales. A standard ratio – say, 50 per cent – is determined, and if labour costs fall below that proportion the savings are distributed between employees and the company on the basis of a pre-established formula.

The Rucker Plan

The Rucker Plan is also based on labour costs, but they are calculated as a proportion of sales less the costs of materials and supplies (ie value added). Allen Rucker contended that the pay proportion of value added remains a near-constant share unless the organisation suffers from severe mismanagement or a drastic change of policy. On the strength of this assumption the Rucker Plan determines a constant share of whatever added value is created by the joint efforts of management and employees.

Improshare

Improshare is a proprietary plan based on an established standard which defines the expected hours required to produce an acceptable level of output. The standard is derived from work measurement. Any savings resulting from an increase in output in fewer than the expected hours are shared between the organisation and employees by means of a pre-established formula.

Other factors
Some gain-sharing schemes introduce other factors besides added value into the formula such as quality and customer service.

Non-financial aspects of gain-sharing
Although the financial element is obviously a key feature of gain-sharing, its strength as a means of improving performance lies equally in its other important features – ownership, involvement and communication. The success of a gain-sharing plan depends on creating a feeling of ownership that first applies to the plan and then extends to the operation. When implementing gain-sharing, companies enlist the support of employees in order to increase their commitment to the plan.

The involvement aspect of gain-sharing means that information generated on the company's results is used as a basis for giving employees the opportunity to make suggestions on ways of improving performance, and for giving them scope to make decisions concerning their implementation.

Gain-sharing plans are always based on key performance measures such as added value. Companies therefore need to ensure that everyone involved knows exactly what is happening in these performance areas, why it is happening, and what can be done about it. The communication process is two-way: management communicates performance information to employees, who in turn communicate their proposals for improvement back to management. The financial basis of gain-sharing provides extra focus for the processes of communication and involvement.

Advantages and disadvantages
The great advantage of gain-sharing over any other form of organisation-wide scheme is that there is a stronger line of sight between what employees do and what they get. They know the formula and how they can contribute to increasing value added. Moreover, gain-sharing is essentially a participative process – it provides a platform for communications and involvement in key aspects of a company's performance, and this is a valuable means of developing identification and commitment in the light of a better understanding of how both managers and employees contribute and can share in the gains they jointly produce. The only restriction, which partly explains the low take-up of gain-sharing, is that it is most appropriate in manufacturing environments.

The disadvantages are, first, that gain-sharing takes time to plan and operate if it is to work well. Second, management must be committed to it and employees should be prepared to play their part in the involvement process. Neither of these requirements is easy to achieve or maintain. Managements and/or employees can become bored or indifferent, and the scheme will be no more than a method of handing out money without a measurable return, as is the case with profit-sharing.

Introducing gain-sharing
The steps required to introduce gain-sharing are:

- Define the reasons for introducing gain-sharing and justify the decision to develop a plan on the basis of benefits resulting from increased productivity, identification and commitment.

- Determine the specific objectives of the scheme.

- Draw up preliminary proposals on the design of a scheme.

- Obtain opinions from managers, employees and trade unions on these broad proposals.

- Involve employees in discussions on the design of a scheme.

- Evaluate alternative formulae, carry out a cost/benefits analysis, and select the one that is most likely to meet the objectives in a cost-effective way.

- If added value is going to be the basis for the scheme, determine how it will be calculated (there are different methods of doing this).

- Decide, in consultation with employees, on the threshold when payments will be made and the basis on which added value above this figure will be shared.

- Communicate to employees the purpose of the scheme, how it will work, the contribution they will be expected to make, and the benefits they may receive.

- Establish the administrative arrangements for the scheme (calculating added value and the value of the share, providing supporting data on performance and productivity for dissemination to and discussion with employees).

- Set up arrangements for communicating performance data, and for involving employees in discussing results and actions which can be taken to improve them.

- Monitor the scheme and evaluate its impact against objectives. (It may be advisable to agree that the scheme should run for a trial period of one year after which it could be revised on the basis of the evaluation, which should be carried out in consultation with employees and trade unions.)

At Rank Xerox the main lessons learned from introducing gain-sharing were that:

- Good communication is vital.

- Employees must feel motivated, committed and involved in the scheme's operation.

- Performance objectives must be clearly identified.

- There must be a direct line of sight for employees between their pay and their performance.

PROFIT-RELATED PAY

When profit-related pay schemes were introduced, they had the following features:

- A portion of pay moved up and down with profit.

- Profit-related pay could be introduced or increased in place of a conventional increase in pay, and this could be coupled with the conversion of some existing pay to profit-related pay. The latter is known as a salary-sacrifice scheme, and in such schemes employees have to accept that their pay may increase or decrease as profits rise or fall.

- Profit-sharing pay was free of income tax when it was the lower of 20 per cent of pay or £4,000 a year.

- All employees except controlling directors were eligible for tax relief under approved schemes.

Profit-related pay schemes became very popular because they provided substantial tax advantages. Some companies introduced profit-related pay in place of a pay rise, particularly when costs had to be tightly contained, there was no opportunity to increase prices and the pressure to meet profit targets was considerable.

But all this is now changing. In 1996 the government announced that the tax relief would be phased out by 2000. Companies with profit-related pay have therefore had to devise exit strategies.

Strategies to exit from profit-related pay
The main exit strategies are:

- to return to the position before profit-related pay was introduced – this is the most popular approach, but it means that the earnings of employees may be reduced because they no longer get tax relief; some companies, but by no means all, are providing compensation for this loss by, for example, increasing employees' gross salary to maintain take-home pay

- to develop new performance-related pay or company-wide profit-sharing schemes

- to replace profit-related pay with a share-based incentive scheme

- to enhance benefit provisions and/or introduce flexible benefits

- to retain PRP as a company-wide scheme or on an individual basis – relatively few companies are adopting either of these approaches.

SHARE OWNERSHIP

Share ownership can be provided through approved profit-sharing schemes but also by means of an SAYE share option scheme or an employee share option plan (ESOP).

SAYE share option schemes
'Save-As-You-Earn' share option schemes give employees the option to buy shares in their company on a specified future date at the share price prevailing at the beginning of the contract or with an allowed discount off that price.

The shares can be bought only from the proceeds of a Save-As-You-Earn (SAYE) contract. Such contracts are valid for a period of three, five or seven years, at which time employees may either use the proceeds to buy shares or withdraw their savings plus a bonus. Employees must decide at the outset whether to take a three-year, five-year or seven-year share option.

If share prices rise over the contract period, the option price will be below the market price and a profit will be made. Whether employees opt for shares or cash, there is no income tax to pay.

Employee share option schemes (ESOPs)

The classic ESOP involves setting up an employee benefit trust which borrows money and uses the funds to buy shares from the company to distribute to employees (including directors). The trust holds the shares on behalf of the employees to whom they have been distributed. The employees receive dividends on the shares, which are taxed in the normal way. If the employees leave their shares in the employee benefit trust for at least five years, they pay no tax on them (unless the rise in the value of the shares pushes an individual's gain over the capital gains tax threshold).

ESOP shares can be issued free, although some schemes require a contribution from employees, who can therefore be given a stake in the company and can, on leaving or on selling the shares at some other time, receive a substantial lump sum. The company also has a new source of capital – the money it receives from the employee benefit trust in return for new shares.

SUMMARY

- The aims of relating rewards to organisational performance are to enable employees to share in the success of the organisation, to increase the identification of employees with the organisation, and to focus employees' attention on what they can contribute to organisational success.

- Approved profit-sharing schemes enable bonuses to be paid in free shares rather than in cash.

- Non-approved profit-sharing schemes are the traditional schemes which usually provide eligible employees with cash from a 'pool' on the basis of a formula that may or may not be published.

- Gain-sharing is a formula-based company- or factory-wide bonus plan which provides for employees to share in the financial gains made by a company as a result of its improved performance. The formula determines the share by reference to a performance indicator such as added value or another measure of productivity. In some schemes the formula also incorporates performance measures relating to quality, customer service, delivery or cost reduction.

- Share ownership can be provided through approved profit-sharing schemes but also by means of SAYE share option schemes or an employee share option plan (ESOP).

FURTHER READING

ARMSTRONG, M. AND MURLIS, H. (1998) *Reward Management*, (4th Edition). Kogan Page – Chapter 29 covers gain-sharing in more detail, and Chapter 31 examines profit-related pay exit strategies in depth.

BELL, D. W. AND HANSON, C. G. (1987) *Profit Sharing and Profitability*. London, Institute of Personnel Management.

GRAHAM-MOORE, B. AND ROSS, T. L. (1990) *Gainsharing*. Washington DC, Bureau of National Affairs.

KRUSE, D. L. (1993) *Profit Sharing: Does it make a difference?* Kalamazoo, MI, W. E. Upjohn Institute.

MASTERNAK, R. AND ROSS, T. (1992) 'Gainsharing bonus plan or employee involvement?' *Compensation and Benefits Review*, January–February, 46–54.

27 Non-financial rewards and recognition schemes

The purpose of a reward system is to support the achievement of corporate objectives by motivating people to join the organisation, stay with it, and deliver sustained high levels of performance. Money can help to attract and retain people – but will it motivate them? Well, Latham and Locke (1979) noted that 'Money is obviously the primary incentive, since without it few, if any, employees would come to work.' But they go on to say that 'money alone is not always enough to motivate high performance'. Kohn (1998) goes even further in denying that money can motivate.

It can be said that money may motivate some of the people all the time and all of the people some of the time, although even the latter point can be disputed. But to rely on it as the sole motivator is misguided. Money has to be reinforced by non-financial motivators and recognition schemes. In fact, when motivation is achieved by non-financial means, it can have a more powerful and longer-lasting effect on people, and financial and non-financial motivators can be mutually reinforcing.

Reward systems should therefore be designed and managed in such a way as to provide the best mix of all types of motivators according to the needs of the organisation and its members. This chapter concentrates on alternatives to pay in the form of non-financial rewards and recognition schemes. By the end of the chapter the reader should be able to identify areas for furthering the use of non-financial motivators and the introduction of recognition processes as part of a total reward system.

AREAS FOR NON-FINANCIAL MOTIVATION

Non-financial motivators centre on the human need for achievement, recognition, responsibility, influence and personal growth. In each of these areas the approach should be influenced by the implications of the key motivational theories summarised in Chapter 5, especially those concerned with expectations and self-efficacy.

Achievement
Motivation can occur when people are given the opportunity to achieve. This can involve empowerment: providing more scope for people to make decisions and use their skills. The need to achieve applies in varying degrees to all people in all jobs, although the level

at which it operates will depend on the orientation of the individual and the scope provided by the work to fulfil the need for achievement. Individuals in managerial, sales, marketing, and research and development jobs may be strongly motivated to achieve but the aim is by no means restricted to people in those occupations or roles.

High achievement motivation results in such behaviour as taking control of situations or relationships, directing the course of events, creating and seizing opportunities, enjoying challenges, reacting swiftly and positively to new circumstances and relationships, and generally 'making things happen'. People who are driven by the need to achieve are likely to be proactive, to seek opportunities and to insist on recognition. Those whose orientations are not as strongly defined can be helped to satisfy achievement needs by being given the scope and encouragement to develop and use their abilities productively.

Achievement motivation can be increased by organisations through processes and systems such as job design, performance management, and skill-based or competence-based pay schemes.

Recognition
Recognition is one of the most powerful motivators. People need to know not only how well they have achieved their objectives or done their work but also that their achievements are appreciated. Recognition needs are linked with the esteem needs in Maslow's (1954) hierarchy of needs. These are defined by Maslow as the need to have a stable, firmly-based, high evaluation of oneself (self-esteem) and to have the respect of others (prestige). These needs are classified into two subsidiary sets: first, 'the desire for achievement, for adequacy, for confidence in the face of the world, and for independence and freedom', and second 'the desire for reputation or status defined as respect or esteem from other people, and manifested by recognition, attention, importance or appreciation'.

Recognition can be provided by positive and immediate feedback. However, praise should be given judiciously – it must be related to real achievements. And it is not the only form of recognition. Financial rewards, especially achievement bonuses awarded immediately after the event, are clearly symbols of recognition to which are attached tangible benefits. They are an important way in which a mutually reinforcing system of financial and non-financial rewards can operate. And there are other forms of recognition, such as public 'applause', status symbols of one kind or another, sabbaticals, treats, trips abroad and long service awards, all of which can be part of the reward system.

Recognition is also provided by managers who listen to and act upon the suggestions of their team members and, importantly, acknowledge their contribution. Other action which accords recognition includes promotion, allocation to a high-profile project, enlargement of the job to encompass more interesting and rewarding work, and various forms of status or esteem symbols. However, caution has to be exercised in the use of status symbols, because they can be divisive. Virtually all informal rewards form a zero-sum game: one person's recognition also implies an element of non-recognition to others, and the consequences of having winners and losers, while almost inevitable, need to be carefully managed.

This problem is present in all aspects of the reward system. High-flyers get the best rewards – but what about everyone else? The latter's rewards may be limited because they have reached the top of their pay scale and there are few prospects of promotion. But the high-flyers depend on the foundation provided by these core employees. The latter should be eligible for special achievement (ie recognition) bonuses when these are deserved. However, the scope for awarding them may be limited, and non-financial rewards, especially those related to the recognition of consistent and steady achievement, become more important. As described in the last section of this chapter, more interest is currently being expressed in recognition schemes. The recognition system of an organisation should be integrated with the financial reward system through performance management processes.

Responsibility

People can be motivated by being given more responsibility for their own work. This is in line with the concept of intrinsic motivation, which is related to the content of the job or 'the work itself'. It is also related to the fundamental concept that individuals are motivated when they are provided with the means to achieve their goals.

Three characteristics have been distinguished by Lawler (1969) as being required in jobs if they are to be intrinsically motivating:

- *feedback* – individuals must receive meaningful feedback about their performance, preferably evaluating their own performance and defining the feedback they require: this implies that they should ideally work on a complete product, or on a significant part of it which can be seen as a whole

- *use of abilities* – the job must be perceived by individuals as requiring them to use abilities they value in order to perform the job effectively

- *self-control* – individuals must feel that they have a high degree of self-control over setting their own goals and over defining the paths to these goals.

In jobs the internal structure of each task consists of three elements: planning (deciding on the course of action, its timing and the resources required), executing (carrying out the plan), and controlling (monitoring performance and progress, and taking corrective action when required). A completely integrated job includes all these elements for each of the tasks carried out by the job-holder. Individuals or teams, having been given objectives in terms of output, quality and cost targets, decide on how the work is to be done, assemble the resources, do the work and monitor output, quality and cost standards. Responsibility in a job is measured by the amount of authority someone has to do all these things.

Providing motivation through increased responsibility is a matter of job design and the use of performance management processes. The philosophy behind motivating through responsibility was expressed in McGregor's (1960) Theory Y: 'The average human being learns, under proper conditions, not only to accept but also to seek responsibility.'

Influence

People can be motivated by the drive to exert influence or to exercise power. Power-seekers are almost by definition self-motivators, but more ordinary – and possibly more normal – mortals can be motivated if they feel they are given scope to use their abilities to influence decisions. This is partly a matter of the working relationships between individuals and their managers, and it is linked closely with the other motivation factors inherent in such relationships concerning achievement, recognition and responsibility. But the organisation, through its policies for involvement, can provide motivation by putting people into situations where their views can be expressed, listened to and acted upon.

Personal growth

The importance of growth needs as one of the three key elements is stressed by Alderfer (1972) in his ERG theory (the others being existence and relatedness needs). He believes that growth needs impel people to make creative or productive efforts for themselves: 'Satisfaction of growth needs depends on a person finding the opportunities to be what he [or she] is most fully and to become what he [or she] can.'

Ambitious and determined people will seek and find these opportunities for themselves, although the organisation should clarify the scope for growth and development that it can provide. (If it does not, they will go away and grow elsewhere.)

Increasingly, however, individuals at all levels of organisations, whether or not they are eaten up by ambition, recognise the importance of continually upgrading their skills and of progressively developing their careers. Many people now regard access to training as a key element in the overall reward package. The availability of learning opportunities, the selection of individuals for high-prestige training courses and programmes, and the emphasis placed by the organisation on the acquisition of new skills as well as the enhancement of existing ones, can all act as powerful motivators. This is particularly important in de-layered organisations in which upward growth through promotion is restricted but people can still develop laterally.

Researchers can be motivated by the opportunity to advance the frontiers of science and their own reputation. And if they can acquire a PhD at the same time, so much the better. They will also be more motivated if they are given the tools (ie laboratory equipment) to do the job. Managers can be motivated by being given the opportunity to acquire a professional or academic qualification, such as an MBA, and information on how this will help with their career development. In offices and on the shop floor people can be motivated by providing opportunities to enlarge and extend their skills. If all this is linked with the financial incentives provided by a skill-based pay system the motivational impact can be considerably increased.

RECOGNITION SCHEMES

Recognition schemes aim to publicly acknowledge and reward success. They are a means of generating 'applause' for achievement. The recognition can be simply by nominating and publicising someone as 'employee of the month' or a team as 'team of the month'. Particular achievements can be recognised in the company magazine or on notice-boards.

More tangible means of recognition can be provided by gifts, vouchers, holidays or meals out. Companies often make a point of providing gifts which will also be welcomed by the employee's partner.

At Pearl Assurance, as reported by Rose (1998), a recognition scheme was introduced as part of a culture change programme. The philosophy behind the programme was to 'catch people doing something right'. Pearl wanted something informal that could be delegated down to junior managers and would provide immediate reward such that when a team or individual does a particularly good job – for example, in terms of customer service – the manager can provide a suitable gift such as flowers, or dinner up to the value of £50 a person.

Although available to individuals, the emphasis has been on team performance. Paying for the team to have dinner together can thus be a team-building experience as well as a reward.

Armstrong World Industries have both formal and informal recognition programmes. The formal programmes are based on clear criteria and allow any employee to nominate an employee or a team. There are three main awards: the manager's award for a unique contribution to achieving departmental objectives, the general manager's award for a unique contribution to company objectives, and the president's award for extraordinary achievement involving a unique contribution to parent company objectives. The informal systems allow recognition through parties, meals and outings. Finally, there is a culture of simple day-to-day recognition through oral thank-yous and hand-written notes.

CONCLUSIONS

Non-financial motivators and recognition schemes are powerful in themselves but can work even more effectively if integrated with financial rewards in a total reward system. However, it is important to remember that the needs of individuals vary considerably, depending upon their psychological make-up, background, experience, occupation and position in the organisation. It is therefore dangerous to generalise about which mix of motivators is likely to be most effective in individual cases. And that is why it is not possible to rely on nostrums such as performance-related pay, skill-based pay, job enrichment or performance management to work equally well for every person or in every organisation. These processes need to be 'customised' to meet the needs of the organisation and the people who work in it. But this customisation will take place more effectively if judicious use is made of achievement bonuses and pay increases related to the acquisition of specific skills and the development of competence and performance management processes which concentrate on identifying individual needs and gaining the joint commitment of employees and their managers to satisfying them.

SUMMARY

- Reward systems should be designed and managed in such a way as to provide the best mix of all types of motivators according to the needs of the organisation and its members.

- Non-financial motivators centre on the human need for achievement, recognition, responsibility, influence and personal growth.

- Motivation can occur when people are given the opportunity to achieve. This can involve empowerment: providing more scope for people to make decisions and use their skills.

- Recognition is one of the most powerful motivators. People need to know not only how well they have achieved their objectives or done their work but also that their achievements are appreciated.

- People can be motivated by being given more responsibility for their own work. This is in line with the concept of intrinsic motivation, which is related to the content of the job or 'the work itself'.

- People can be motivated by the drive to exert influence or to exercise power.

- The opportunity to 'grow' skills, acquire more expertise and to develop competences can be a strong motivator.

- Recognition schemes aim to publicly acknowledge and reward success. They can simply provide 'applause', or they can utilise more tangible forms of remuneration.

FURTHER READING

ALDERFER, C. (1972) *Existence, Relatedness and Growth*. New York, Free Press.

LATHAM, G. AND LOCKE, E. A. (1979) 'Goal setting – a motivational technique that works'. *Organizational Dynamics*, Autumn, 68–80.

LAWLER, E. E. (1969) 'Job design and employee motivation'. *Personnel Psychology*, Vol. 22, 426–35.

McGREGOR, D. (1960) *The Human Side of Enterprise*. New York, McGraw-Hill.

MASLOW, A. (1954) *Motivation and Personality*. New York, Harper & Row.

ROSE, M. (1998) 'Rewarding with recognition'. *Human Resource Management Yearbook*, London.

Part 6

PERFORMANCE MANAGEMENT

28 The essence of performance management

Performance management is a means of getting better results from the organisation, teams and individuals. It is about the agreement of objectives, knowledge, skill and competence requirements, and work and personal development plans. It involves the joint and continuing review of performance against these objectives, requirements and plans, and the agreement and implementation of improvement and further development plans. The focus is on improvement, learning, development and motivation. However, performance management processes can also be used to produce ratings which govern the distribution of financial rewards in a performance-related pay (PRP) scheme. It is often argued that introducing this pay-related element contaminates the essence of performance management. But if an organisation believes in PRP it should do its best to ensure that performance is measured as objectively and fairly as possible, and that is what performance management aims to do.

This chapter concentrates on performance management as a means of indicating how individuals should be rewarded in relation to their performance and the level of competence they achieve. It covers both the financial reward element and, importantly, the motivation through non-financial rewards that can result from well-conceived and implemented performance management processes.

The chapter starts with a brief analysis of the nature and philosophy of performance management. This is followed by a general description of performance management as a process, not a mechanical 'system'. The performance-rating and motivational aspects of performance management are then examined. By the end of the chapter the reader should understand the nature and philosophy of performance management. Applications of performance management are considered in the next chapter.

THE NATURE OF PERFORMANCE MANAGEMENT

Performance management incorporates that part of management which by objectives philosophy emphasises the importance of goal-setting and feedback – reviewing performance in relation to agreed objectives. It also includes many of the approaches included in traditional appraisal schemes to do with the setting of objectives, as in results-oriented schemes, the use of behaviourally-anchored factors for assessment purposes in the form of competences, and the approaches to be used in conducting formal review meetings.

There are a number of significant differences between performance management and traditional appraisal schemes. Performance management in its most developed form

- involves all members of the organisation as partners in the process – it is not something handed down by bosses to subordinates

- is concerned with performance in its broadest sense, embracing not only outputs (results) but also inputs (levels of competence and how competences are used)

- is based upon agreements on people's roles covering accountabilities, expectations (objectives and competence requirements), and development plans, again seen as part of the normal interactive processes which exist between managers and individuals or teams

- is concerned with team performance as well as individual performance

- is a continuous process, not relying on a once-a-year formal review

- treats the performance review as a joint affair which is primarily concerned with looking constructively towards the future

- focuses on improving performance, developing competence, realising potential and providing non-financial rewards in the form of feedback, recognition and opportunities to develop skills, competences and careers

- concentrates on 'self-managed learning', giving people the encouragement they need to develop themselves with whatever support and guidance they need from their managers and the organisation

- may provide a basis for performance-related pay decisions where such schemes exist, but care is taken over the development of rating systems and the achievement of consistency in ratings

- may not include ratings at all, especially if the process is used primarily for development and performance improvement purposes

- does not rely on elaborate forms or procedures – the records of agreements and reviews may be retained by managers and individuals and are sometimes not held by the personnel department

- recognises the need for thorough training in the skills required to agree objectives, provide feedback, review performance, and coach and counsel employees

- overall, attaches more importance to the 'processes' of forming agreements, managing performance throughout the year and monitoring and reviewing results than to the content of what is often referred to as a 'performance management system' – by implication, a set of mechanisms to get people to do certain things in certain ways.

THE PHILOSOPHY OF PERFORMANCE MANAGEMENT

The philosophy of performance management is based on specific beliefs about how performance should be managed.

Inputs, process and outputs

Performance management emphasises the importance of inputs, process and outputs. Inputs are what employees bring to the job in the shape of knowledge, skills, expertise and competence. Process is how they behave in carrying out their work. Outputs are the results they obtain in terms of achieving objectives and the influence or impact they have on the efforts of their team, their department and the organisation as a whole.

Performance management analyses outputs and diagnoses the reasons for differential performance by reference to the inputs and behaviour of individuals and the circumstances affecting their work. Performance reviews and feedback cover the extent to which results are influenced by the individuals' motivation, ability, knowledge, skill or attitudes, the way in which they are managed, the resources they are given, and external factors beyond their control.

The analysis and diagnosis will be closely linked with specifications of behavioural requirements. These will be focused on the competencies required to achieve the objectives associated with the individual's role, but they will also deal with wider organisational values such as quality, customer service, teamworking and flexibility.

Performance management as a process of management

The philosophy of performance management is strongly influenced by the belief that it is a natural and core process of management. Its emphasis on analysis, measurement, monitoring performance and planning and coaching for performance improvements means that it is concerned with basic aspects of good people management practice.

Managing expectations by agreement

Performance management is based on agreed definitions of the contribution employees are expected to make in achieving the purpose of their team, department or function, and of the organisation as a whole. This leads to the clarification of the individual's role or the team's purpose. It also means spelling out for individuals the knowledge, skills and competences required to perform the role effectively. In the case of teams, this means reaching agreement on how team members should behave in order to achieve effective teamwork and produce the expected standards of performance and results. Expectations about required performance, skill and competence levels are therefore defined, and a basis is provided for managing those expectations so that they are fulfilled. The management of expectations is a joint affair requiring managers, teams and individuals to act in partnership.

Performance management as an integrating process

Performance management is concerned with the interrelated processes of work, management, development and reward. It can become a powerful integrating force, ensuring that these processes are linked together properly as a fundamental part of the human resource management approach which should be practised by every manager in the organisation.

THE PERFORMANCE MANAGEMENT PROCESS

Conceptual framework

Although every organisation that wants to introduce performance management should create its own version to suit its needs, it is useful to have a conceptual framework within which appropriate processes can be developed and operated. This framework will help in deciding the approach to be adopted, and when the decision has been made it will provide guidance to managers and the individuals and the teams they manage on what performance management activities they will be expected to carry out.

The performance management cycle

Performance management processes operate as a continuous management cycle which is in line with what all managers do, or should do. This is what is meant when 'performance management' is described as a natural process of management rather than a separate performance appraisal 'event' orchestrated by the personnel department.

The cycle is illustrated in Figure 39.

Figure 39 The performance management cycle

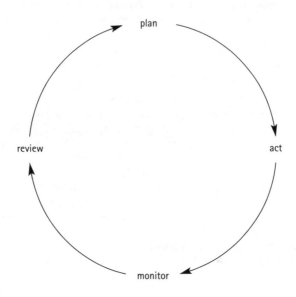

Figure 40 **The performance management sequence**

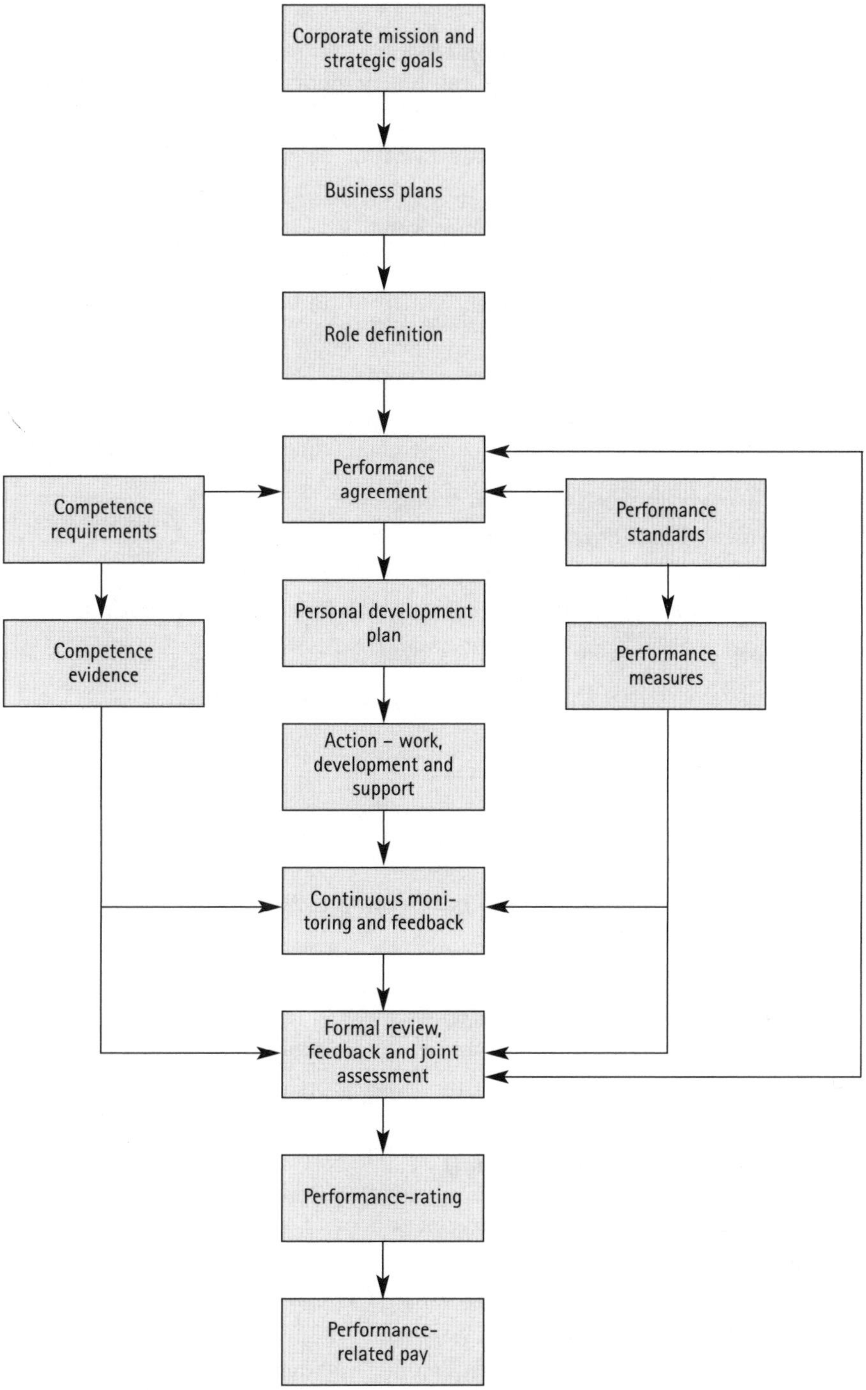

The performance management sequence

The performance management sequence is illustrated in Figure 40. It consists of the following activities.

Corporate strategies and objectives

- preparation of mission and value statements linked with business strategy

- definition of corporate and functional or departmental objectives.

Business plans

- plans to achieve corporate objectives.

Role definition

- the role of the individual in contributing to the achievement of business plans

- accountabilities and competency profile.

Performance agreement

- update of objectives and of competence requirements

- identification and agreement of performance measures.

Personal development plan

- identify and agree development and training needs

- agree action to be taken by individual (self-managed learning)

- agree support to be provided by manager

- agree any special training or development programmes.

Action

- work towards achieving objectives

- carry out personal development and other training activities

- provide management support.

Continuous management of performance throughout the year

- regular feedback

- interim progress reviews.

Formal performance review(s)

- preparation by the manager and the individual for the formal review

- the annual performance review, which leads to a new performance agreement.

Performance-rating (optional)

- rating or ranking performance – although common, this is not an inevitable performance management activity.

Performance-related pay

- as described in Chapter 20, PRP is not always associated with performance management.

These activities are broadly sequential, but they can overlap. There is scope for feedback during the year and from the formal performance review, which can lead to a revised or new performance agreement.

Documentation
The trend is to reduce the complexity of the documentation associated with performance management. Some organisations just ask people to record their conclusions and plans on a blank sheet of paper. But there is much to be said for having an agreed format, although it should be as simple as possible. The review form could just include spaces for recording agreed objectives and achievements and the personal development plan or any other agreed areas for improvement. Ratings, if any, would also be recorded. The form should be completed jointly by the manager and the individual, and copies should be kept by them for reference purposes throughout the year and at the next formal review. It is not the property of the personnel department.

RATING PERFORMANCE FOR PRP PURPOSES

As described in Chapter 20, PRP rewards are frequently but not always determined by ratings. These can be agreed separately from the performance management review on the grounds that the developmental nature of the review will not then be prejudiced because both parties are more concerned about the pay outcomes than identifying performance improvement and training needs. But the results must be read across. The performance assessed for pay purposes is not different from that assessed for development purposes. Separating them in time may take the heat out of the pay elements of the review but does not alter the fact that PRP decisions are being taken as a result of some form of performance assessment. The arguments for and against rating, the various approaches available and methods of achieving consistency are considered below.

Arguments for and against rating
The arguments for rating are that:

• You cannot have performance-related pay without some form of rating (assuming you want or need PRP).

• It is a means of summing up who are the exceptional performers or under-performers, and who are the reliable core performers, so that action can be taken (to develop or to introduce some form of non-financial reward).

• It can provide a basis for predicting potential on the assumption that people who perform well in the present are likely to go on doing so in the future. However, past performance is a predictor of future performance only when there is a connecting link – ie there are elements of the present job which are also important in a higher-level job.

The arguments against rating are that:

• It is largely subjective, and it can be difficult to achieve consistency between different raters.

• To sum up a person's total performance in a single rating is a gross oversimplification of what may be a complex set of factors which influence that performance.

- To make judgements about potential on the basis of an overall rating which masks dissimilarities between these elements is dangerous.

- To place people in boxes and label them as, for example, 'below average', or whatever equivalent terms are used, is both demeaning and demotivating.

Some organisations which do not have performance-related pay reject ratings altogether because of the objections listed above.

If overall ratings are to be included in a performance review procedure, it is necessary to consider how performance levels should be defined, the number of such levels required and the steps necessary to achieve a reasonable degree of accuracy and consistency.

Performance-level definitions

The rating-scale format can either be behavioural, with examples of good, acceptable and unacceptable performance, or graphic, simply presenting a number of scale points along a continuum. The scale points or anchors in the latter may be defined alphabetically (a, b, c, etc), numerically (1, 2, 3, etc) or by means of initials ('ex' for excellent, etc) which purport to disguise the hierarchical nature of the scale. The scale points may be described adjectivally (eg very effective, effective, developing).

Many organisations have taken great care in the wording of their definitions of each level of the scale in the hope that it will ensure greater accuracy and consistency in ratings. Detailed descriptions may be helpful, but only to a certain extent – however carefully such descriptions are worded there will always be room for subjective judgements. Hence the importance of taking further steps to promote understanding of how to apply the scale definitions, as described later in this section. Definitions can be either positive and negative or simply positive.

Positive–negative definitions

Traditionally, definitions have regressed downwards from a highly positive, eg 'exceptional', description to a negative, eg 'unsatisfactory', definition, as in the following typical example:

A Outstanding performance in all respects

B Superior performance, significantly above normal job requirements

C Good all-round performance which meets the normal requirements of the job

D Performance not fully up to requirements: clear weaknesses requiring improvement have been identified

E Unacceptable; constant guidance is required and performance of many aspects of the job is well below a reasonable standard.

Positive definitions

An increasingly popular alternative is a rating scale which as far as possible provides positive reinforcement. It avoids entirely negative feedback although it will indicate where improvements are required, as in the following example.

Very effective Consistently exceeds targets and required standards, and continually performs in a thoroughly proficient manner beyond normal expectations.

Effective Fully achieves required objectives and standards of performance and meets the normal expectations of the job.

Developing A contribution which is stronger in some aspects of the job than others. Most objectives are met but performance improvements should still take place.

Improvable A contribution which leaves much room for improvement in several definable areas.

Definitions like these aim to avoid the use of such terminology for middle-ranking but entirely acceptable performers as 'satisfactory' or 'competent' which seem to be damning with faint praise. Some organisations use the terms 'learner/achiever' or 'unproven/too soon to tell' as categories for new entrants to a grade of whom it is too early to give a realistic assessment.

This scale deliberately avoids including an 'unacceptable' rating or its equivalent on the grounds that if someone's performance is totally unacceptable and unimprovable it should have been identified during the continuous process of performance management and corrective action initiated at the time. This is not action that can be delayed for several months until the next review when a negative formal rating is given which may be too demotivating or too late. If action taken at the time fails to remedy the problem, the employee may be dealt with under a capability or disciplinary procedure and the normal performance review suspended until the problem is overcome. However, the disciplinary procedure should still provide for performance reviews to assess the extent to which the requirements set out in the informal or formal warnings have been met.

Note also that in order to dispel any unfortunate associations with other systems, such as school reports, this 'positive' scale does not include alphabetical or numerical ratings.

The number of rating levels
There has been much debate on what constitutes the 'best' number of rating levels. The choice lies between:

- three level scales on the assumption that people are not capable of making any finer distinctions between performance levels: they know good and not-so-good performers when they see them and have no difficulty in placing the rest where they believe they belong – ie in the middle category. A typical three-level scale would refer to threshold, on target, and exceptional performance.

- four, five, or even six level scales – those who advocate more levels think that more perceptive ratings will be achieved if raters are given a wider range of choice; to avoid the alleged tendency of raters to gravitate to the middle level in a five-point scale, some people advocate four- or six-point scales.

Those who want a larger number of points on the scale also claim that it assists in drawing the finer distinctions required in a performance-related pay system. But this argument is sustainable only if it is believed that managers are capable of making such fine distinctions.

Achieving consistency

Ratings can be inconsistent because managers interpret rating scales in different ways. If rating is used, an attempt must be made to achieve consistency by training, monitoring, moderating and guidance, as explained in Chapter 35.

Doing without ratings

Research conducted by Towers Perrin in the USA as described at the ACA Annual conference (Boston, 1999, unpublished) revealed that a number of US companies, including Amoco Corporation, Cadillac, Dow Chemical, Westinghouse and Xerox, have abandoned 'bottom-line' ratings. The objectives of these and other companies were to facilitate employee development, make the process more future-focused rather than backward-looking, and encourage joint accountability for performance management. The positive outcomes reported by these organisations were that:

- the cultural environment became more open and fair; in particular, discussions about performance were more honest and frequent

- there was a forward focus on development and improvement instead of a backward focus on past performance and missed results

- mutual accountability between managers and employees to make performance management 'work' was increased

- a better link was achieved between performance management and other programmes and business results.

Where a rating-less system is used, the performance review may include a narrative summary of performance – 'John has performed well against the following targets/standards ... There is some room for improvement in the area of ... and these actions were agreed to achieve that improvement ...' Alternatively, the meeting is used simply as the basis for a forward-looking personal development/ performance improvement plan in which the summary does not dwell on past performance. Approaches to handling performance-related pay decisions in the absence of overall ratings are considered in Chapter 36.

NON-FINANCIAL REWARDS THROUGH PERFORMANCE MANAGEMENT

Performance management processes can effectively motivate people through the non-financial rewards associated with feedback, reinforcement and the provision of opportunities for growth.

Feedback

The philosophy of performance management emphasises the importance of feedback on performance. The feedback will be positive when things have gone well but it will also inform employees whose performance is not up to standard so that they are aware of the need for corrective action. As much feedback as possible is self-generated. People are given the opportunity to plan how they are going to achieve their objectives and encouraged to monitor their own performance by obtaining feedback data for themselves.

Reinforcement

Positive reinforcement is provided by the feedback process when behaviour which leads to improved performance is identified. The object is to recognise specific performance improvements as soon as possible after the event. That is why performance management should be regarded as a continuing process. Recognition and therefore reinforcement take place whenever appropriate throughout the year. They are not deferred to an annual performance review session.

Similarly, if someone makes a mistake or fails to reach the agreed standard of performance, the matter is discussed immediately and constructively, so that learning can take place and improvement plans can be agreed.

Growth opportunities

In focusing on continuous development, performance management can motivate people by providing opportunities for growth. Individuals are encouraged to draw up personal development plans which may be expressed in the form of a learning contract. This spells out what employees should do to develop themselves and defines the support that will be given by their managers and the organisation through learning and development programmes.

SUMMARY

- Performance management is a means of getting better results from the organisation, teams and individuals.

- It is about the agreement of objectives, knowledge, skill and competence requirements and work and personal development plans.

- Performance management involves the joint and continuing review of performance against these objectives, requirements and plans and the agreement and implementation of improvement and further development plans.

- The focus of performance management is on improvement, learning, development and motivation.

- Performance management processes can also be used to produce ratings which govern the distribution of financial rewards in a performance-related pay (PRP) scheme.

- Performance management is concerned with performance in its broadest sense, embracing not only outputs (results) but also inputs (levels of competence and how competences are used).

- It is based upon agreements on people's roles, definitions of mutual expectations (a performance agreement) and the preparation of personal development plans.

- It is a continuous process, not relying solely on a once-a-year formal review.

- A formal review is necessary from time to time to discuss progress and agree future plans.

- Performance management may provide a basis for performance-related pay decisions where such schemes exist, but care should be taken over the development of rating systems in order to achieve consistency in ratings.

- Performance management processes can effectively motivate people through the non-financial rewards associated with feedback, reinforcement and the provision of opportunities for growth.

FURTHER READING

Full descriptions of performance management with examples of schemes are given in Armstrong and Baron (1998) *Performance Management: The New Realities*, IPD.

29 Performance management in action

In this chapter, the various ways are explained in which the principles of performance management described in Chapter 28 are put into practice. The basis for much of this information is the comprehensive survey into performance management practices that was conducted by the IPD in 1997–1998 (Armstrong and Baron, 1998). On completing the chapter the reader will be familiar with:

- the fundamental questions to be answered when embarking on the development of performance management processes and when considering the link, if any, to pay

- the information on current practices obtained from the IPD survey

- the use of 360-degree feedback

- the use of the balanced score-card.

FUNDAMENTAL QUESTIONS ABOUT PERFORMANCE MANAGEMENT

When considering the introduction of performance management and, possibly, linking it to pay, the following questions have to be answered:

- Can good or poor performance be identified?

- Can the causes of good or poor performance be established?

- How should good performance be rewarded?

- Can all this be done fairly and consistently?

The answers to these questions will depend on the circumstances, culture and management style of the organisation, and will largely determine the way forward. The rest of this chapter provides data on how other organisations deal with these and related issues, including the use of 360-degree feedback as a basis for measuring performance and the choice of performance measures (balanced score-card).

THE PRACTICE OF PERFORMANCE MANAGEMENT

The use of performance management

Out of the total of 562 organisations that responded to the survey, 388 (69 per cent) said that they operate formal processes to manage performance. Of the 31 per cent who do not operate formal processes, 48 per cent have definite plans to do so within the next two years and

Figure 41 Features of performance management

Feature	Percentage
Objective-setting and review	85%
Annual appraisal	83%
Personal development plans	68%
Self-appraisal	45%
Performance-related pay	43%
Coaching/mentoring	39%
Career management	32%
Competence assessment	31%
Twice-yearly appraisal	24%
Subordinate (180-degree) feedback	20%
Continuous assessment	17%
Rolling appraisal	12%
360-degree feedback	11%
Peer appraisal	9%
Balanced score-card	5%
	0%

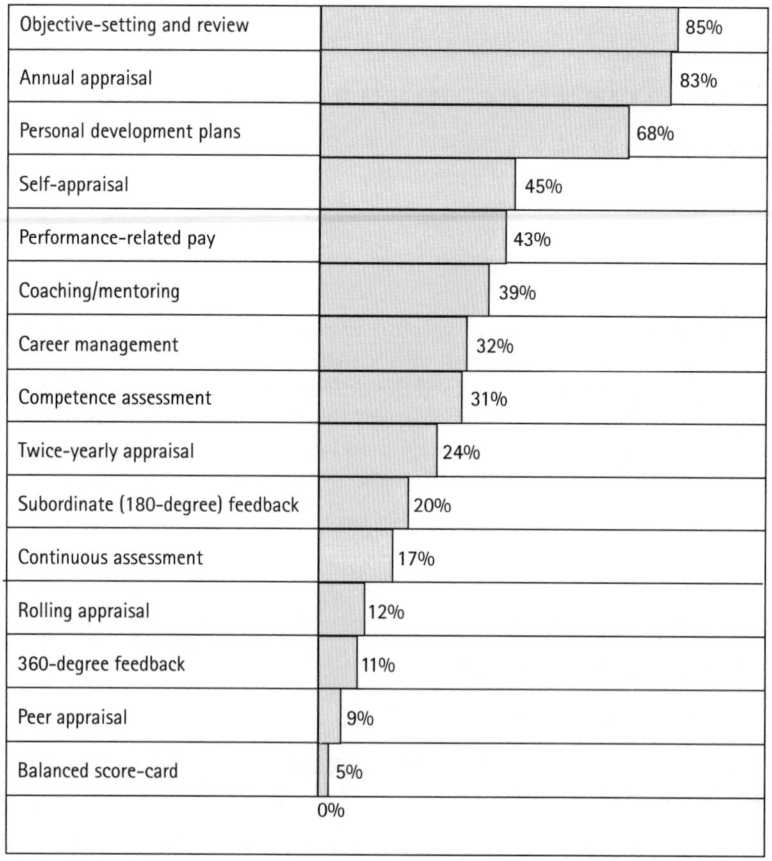

a further 25 per cent are undecided. Only 11 per cent have no plans to implement formal performance management processes.

Features of performance management
The features of the performance management processes operated by the respondents to the survey are summed up in Figure 41.

As might be expected, the most common features are objective-setting and review, and annual appraisal. The high proportion of organisations that use personal development plans is significant – this emphasis is much greater than in the IPD survey conducted in 1991. Less than half the organisations have performance-related pay. This is fewer than might have been expected and contrasts with the 74 per cent of organisations that operated performance-related pay in 1991 (but these are not matched samples).

The effectiveness of key features
Respondents were asked to assess the effectiveness of each of the key features. Their replies are set out in Table 28.

Table 28 The effectiveness of key features of performance management

	Very effective %	Mostly effective %	Partly effective %	Not effective %	No comment %
Objective-setting and review	27	48	18	2	5
Annual appraisal	7	59	28	2	2
Selfappraisal	22	43	30	2	3
Performance-related pay	6	36	37	14	7
Personal development plans	19	40	31	3	7

Objective-setting and review, annual appraisal, personal development plans and self-appraisal are all strongly endorsed. Performance-related pay did not receive such support; less than half of the respondents thought it was very or mostly effective, and there were a substantial number of people (14 per cent) who thought PRP was not effective.

Feelings about performance management
The majority of respondents either strongly agreed or slightly agreed with the following descriptions of performance management:

- is an integrated part of the employee/line manager relationship (85 per cent)

- integrates individual and organisational goals (83 per cent)

- sets stretching goals (79 per cent)

- is owned by line managers (78 per cent)

- motivates individuals (75 per cent)

- is developmental (72 per cent)

- is integrated into other people management processes (72 per cent)

- has aims that are well understood (66 per cent)

- is measured in quantitative terms (62 per cent).

The majority of respondents either slightly or strongly disagreed with the following statements:

- Performance-related pay is an essential part of performance management (59 per cent).

- Performance management is bureaucratic and time-consuming (60 per cent).

Respondents were particularly positive about the integrating, motivating and developmental aspects of performance management, but the majority disliked performance-related pay. Although most respondents did not feel that performance management is bureaucratic and time-consuming, a substantial minority (36 per cent) thought it was.

Rating
The proportion of respondents in whose organisation an overall rating was given for performance was 54 per cent. This compares with the 64 per cent of organisations which had ratings in 1991. Of the respondents who had PRP, 24 per cent did not have ratings.

Figure 42 **Developments in performance management since 1991**

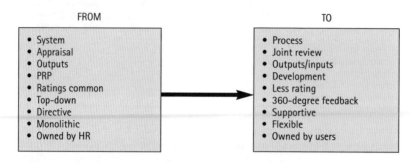

CHANGES IN PERFORMANCE MANAGEMENT PRACTICES

The major changes between the IPD surveys in 1991 and 1998 are summed up in Figure 42.

These developments can be summarised as follows:

From system to process
In 1991 performance management was regarded as a 'system', a sort of mechanistic set of techniques which could be applied rigidly to any organisation with the guarantee that it would deliver results in the form of improved performance. It is now more generally seen as an integrated set of processes which are concerned with ways in which managing performance can be carried out. The emphasis is much more on *how* the management of performance is carried out – what the people involved do and how they do it – than on a set of prescribed procedures and practices which have to be followed rigidly by all concerned.

From appraisal to joint review
Performance management in the early 1990s still carried the baggage of the traditional performance appraisal scheme in which the appraisal meeting was an annual event that involved top-down and unilateral judgements by 'superiors' of their 'subordinates'. Since then, it has increasingly been perceived as a continuous process, involving reviews which focus on the future rather than the past and for which the key words are 'dialogue', 'shared understanding', 'agreement' and 'mutual commitment'.

From outputs to inputs
In 1991, the emphasis was still on objective-setting and the appraisal of results against goals – ie outputs. This was more baggage – a hangover from the discredited management-by-objectives system. What is now happening is the realisation that a fully rounded view of performance must embrace *how* people get things done as well as *what* gets done – ie inputs as well as outputs. This means using the so-called mixed model, considering skills and competence as well as results, inputs as well as outputs.

From performance-related pay to development

In the early days of performance management it was associated closely with performance-related pay, which to many people epitomised the 'system'. Lip service may have been paid to the use of performance appraisal as a means of identifying training needs (to be met by sending people on courses) but the developmental aspects of the process were strangely neglected. It does not seem to have been appreciated that the greatest added value which could be derived from performance management was the role it could play in continuous development and self-development. Personal development plans had not been heard of in 1991. Yet in 1997–1998 they have become a major feature of performance management processes. This does not mean that they always work as well as they are expected to, but the philosophy of planning personal development as part of the overall process has now become firmly embedded in the policies and practices of a large proportion of the organisations covered by our research.

Less prominence given to ratings

At one time, performance appraisal was synonymous with performance rating – another hangover from the old days, in this case merit-rating. The use of rating is often justified by the need to have a basis for performance-related pay decisions. Yet about a quarter of the organisations with PRP which responded to the IPD survey did *not* have ratings. Focus group research revealed the considerable hostility to ratings shared by people at all levels in the organisations concerned. Increasingly, people are realising that ratings, as one HR director put it to us, 'denigrate the performance management process'.

From top down appraisal to 360-degree feedback

The use of 360-degree feedback is still fairly small (11 per cent of the respondents to the IPD questionnaire). But interest is growing as the value of obtaining feedback from a number of different sources is becoming recognised.

From a directive to a supportive approach

'Best-practice' organisations recognise that performance management is not just another means of obtaining compliance to the achievement of objectives which have been cascaded down from some remote height. They treat it as a joint process which requires managers and team leaders in discussion with individual team members or their teams as a whole to identify what support they need to do their work well. This support may be provided in a number of ways, such as by exercising more effective leadership skills, coaching, counselling, guidance, training, redesigning roles or redefining team responsibilities, providing better resources in the form of equipment and facilities and generally demonstrating that people are valued for what they contribute. A supportive approach is in line with the belief that individuals and teams are, in effect, the internal customers of their managers.

From monolithic to flexible

Traditionally, performance appraisal has been a monolithic and bureaucratic system which has been imposed on line managers by the personnel department. Everyone has had to conform to the same procedure and the most important output has been a set of ticks on an elaborate form which once made were soon forgotten. Today there is much less bureaucracy in many organisations – forms are no longer the be-all and end-all of performance management. It has also been recognised by many people that performance management is a tool for managers to use in association with the members of their teams and that they will use it most effectively if they apply it in their own particular way in accordance with their own particular circumstances. It is still desirable to define and communicate certain principles of the approach to performance management that are likely to produce the best results. And it is often desirable to provide structure and guidance which can be built round some fairly simple forms and procedures. Helping everyone to learn about how they can gain the most benefit from performance management is also important. But this is no longer regarded by many of the organisations we contacted as a set of prescriptions that everyone must follow to the letter.

From ownership by HR to ownership by the participants

The best-practice organisations we visited all stressed that they were concerned with the management of performance as the responsibility of line managers in conjunction with their teams. The idea that the personnel function was the sole guardian of performance standards through the performance appraisal schemes it administered has been rejected for the nonsense that it is.

PERFORMANCE MANAGEMENT IN PRACTICE

Aims

The specific aims of performance management mentioned by the survey organisations included:

- the achievement and integration of objectives – a packaging company

- to underpin the statement on management's values and beliefs – a food manufacturer

- to develop a performance-driven organisation – a government agency

- to improve performance and results – a number of companies

- to increase the capacity of managers to manage performance – a software company

- to foster better management – an NHS trust

- to define/clarify expectations – a number of organisations

- to replace a discredited performance appraisal scheme – a shipping line

- to place more focus on development – a shipping line

- to move to individual accountability for development – a manufacturing company

- culture change – a bank

- to overcome problems surrounding the link to pay which inhibited an open and honest discussion – a security company.

PERFORMANCE MANAGEMENT PROCESSES

The following summaries of performance management processes again illustrate the wide variety of approaches, often clearly influenced by the context in which they were introduced, including the culture of the organisation. Some of the more interesting features are:

- cascading objectives – a health authority

- focus on objectives/targets – various organisations

- the importance attached to the measurability of performance targets – a manufacturing company

- emphasis on looking forward – an NHS trust

- focus on development and career progression through the use of competency models – a number of companies

- emphasis on the interaction between managers and individuals – a packaging company

- focus on dialogue in the performance review process – an educational establishment

- the use of an integrated approach – a food manufacturer

- personal development planning – a county council

- team objective-setting and review – a packaging company.

Rating

Rating was a controversial topic, as it generally is. Here is a comment from an HR director:

> A rating system is a tag which is, by its nature, inevitably totally simplistic. How can you take everything that somebody has done and all the strengths and weaknesses they may be exhibiting and boil it down to a single letter on a piece of paper? Clearly, in itself it doesn't mean very much, except where you need a rating for a secondary purpose. But then if you really begin to look at how valid that is, you begin to doubt it. In organisations like ours the scope for individual contributions is ... well, it's still there, but the implications of teams and achievement at team level is much more obvious.

Link to pay

A high proportion of the 35 organisations visited during the research (82 per cent) had performance- and/or competence-related pay. This was much bigger than the proportion of those with PRP that responded to the questionnaire (43 per cent). The discrepancy may be partly attributable to sampling differences. Most of these organisations used one form or another of performance-related pay.

As one personnel manager commented, linking the performance review with pay was out of the question because of scepticism and negative feeling about the old appraisal process, which had a choice of ratings – good, very good, excellent, etc. When it was used, pay became the sole focus of the appraisal meeting:

> Basically people wanted to know what they'd got, and when they knew they'd not got it, there was then an argument trying to justify why they

should have got it. If they knew they had got it, then there was no interest in anything else. We found people covered up and didn't want to admit to any weaknesses, any need for improvement, any need for training, because it might suggest that they shouldn't get the performance reward ... It was normally an exercise in diplomacy on the part of the manager.

360-DEGREE FEEDBACK

Although not many organisations in the IPD survey used 360-degree feedback, interest is growing, and the section below discusses what it is, how it works, and its relationship to pay.

360-degree feedback defined

360-degree feedback is the process of systematically collecting and analysing information about someone's performance from the person's manager, direct reports, colleagues and, sometimes, customers and suppliers. The data is usually fed back in the form of ratings against various performance dimensions.

The use of 360-degree feedback

360-degree feedback is mainly used to support learning and development but a minority of companies use it to inform pay decisions.

The IPD 1998 survey found that the 51 organisations covered by the research with 360-degree feedback predominantly (92 per cent) used it to help in assessing development needs, while 80 per cent used it to help in overall performance coaching and only 20 per cent used it to determine a performance grade or pay award.

Its use for pay

360-degree feedback can be extended to inform performance-related pay decisions. Ratings are influenced by the feedback and in turn govern, or at least guide, proposals on pay increases.

Organisations which reject this link do so because they believe that participants would be so concerned about how their feedback might affect decisions about pay that the development opportunities would be lost. The evidence that the IPD collected from organisations and focus groups highlighted the damage to the developmental nature of performance management that can be caused by incorporating ratings and explicit links to pay. Armstrong and Baron (1998) assert that 'If, as we believe should be the case, performance management is primarily a developmental process, then we contend that, when 360-degree feedback is incorporated into performance management, it should not form the basis for performance ratings and should be entirely divorced from pay. Performance management is *not* simply about judgmental ratings and money.'

The rationale for 360-degree feedback

The rationale for 360-degree feedback is that it can overcome biased appraisals because the organisation is not relying on one person's view and the inherent prejudices he or she may have. It recognises the value of a multi-dimensional view of performance and gives people a more rounded view of performance than they had previously – subordinates and colleagues may have experiences of a manager's behaviour which are unknown to the manager's manager. Finally, a broader perspective of how they are perceived by others can increase self-awareness and, because a number of stakeholders are involved, provide a powerful impetus to self-improvement.

But there may be problems. These include:

- a person's not giving frank or honest feedback
- a person's being put under stress in receiving or giving feedback
- lack of action following feedback
- over-reliance on technology
- too much bureaucracy.

These can all be minimised, if not avoided completely, by careful design, communication, training and follow-up. But most people who have introduced 360-degree feedback have grave doubts about linking it to pay. It is essentially a developmental tool.

THE USE OF A BALANCED SCORE-CARD

The concept of the balanced score-card as described in Chapter 1 requires managers to look at the business from four related perspectives: the customer, internal processes, improvement and learning, and financial (shareholders). This approach was originally conceived by Kaplan and Norton (1996) as a means of measuring organisational performance. But the need to align individual and corporate objectives has led some organisations to adopt an integrated approach to performance measurement and review, using the organisational balanced score-card headings and criteria as the framework for individual performance management.

The NatWest Bank uses the four headings of business success, customer service, quality and people, and business efficiency as the criteria for both corporate and individual reviews. At Bass Brewers a balanced score-card approach is used at corporate level, and each individual has a 'commitment schedule' which details their five objectives and how they link to the balanced score-card. The balanced score-card measures impact directly on the company bonus, and the aim is to encourage employees to take an interest in what they can do in each area to contribute to improvements in results. The Halifax Bank links performance appraisal and pay to a range of activities determined by a balanced score-card. The four perspectives are financial, business, customer and internal. This means that to fulfil expectations managers have to do more than meet their targets. They have additionally to show that they have coached and developed their staff, achieved the required ratings in customer satisfaction surveys and maintained good standards of administration.

INTRODUCING PERFORMANCE MANAGEMENT

Basic questions
There are six basic questions that should be answered before introducing performance management.

Figure 43 The performance management framework

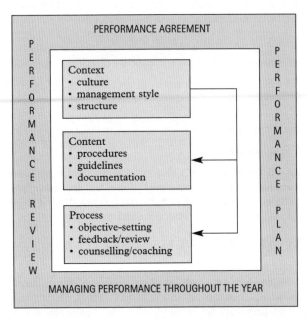

Source: Michael Armstrong and Angela Baron, *Performance Management: The New Realities*, IPD, 1998

1 What is the business case for performance management?

2 What is the performance culture in our organisation?

3 Can we identify good or poor performance?

4 Can we establish the causes of good performance?

5 How can we motivate people to perform well?

6 Can we do all this fairly and consistently?

The framework
The framework for performance management is provided by the arrangements for agreeing performance requirements or expectations, preparing performance plans, managing performance throughout the year and reviewing performance. The factors to be taken into account, as illustrated in Figure 43, are the organisational context, the content in the shape of procedures, guidelines and documentation, and the processes of objective setting, feedback and reviews, and counselling/coaching.

Approaches to introducing performance management
The following are examples of approaches to introducing performance management identified during the IPD research.

An engineering company
The personnel director of this company believes that performance

management should be introduced by an educative process – 'encouraging, supporting and setting a sense of direction'.

A car manufacturer

The importance of context was emphasised by the HR manager, who explained that: 'I had to design something that could be easily understood by everyone that related to this office and to the work in this office.'

A food manufacturer

The implementation of performance management was achieved by pulling together a number of component parts. It was concerned more with making explicit links between the business plan, people plans and individual objectives than it was about making a fundamental change. HR people from all the regions were brought in for training, and given resources and presentation packs to take back to their business units.

A financial services company

A series of focus groups was held with managers to obtain their views about how performance management could best work for them. A set of principles was distilled from the outcome of the discussions and fed back to managers for their approval. After some amendments, these principles were laid down as guidelines for practising performance management which were 'owned' by the managers.

The vital things to do in introducing performance management are to *involve, communicate, train* and *evaluate*. These and other requirements may be spelt out as follows:

- To ensure involvement, managers *and* staff should participate in initial discussions about the aims of the process.

- The objectives of performance management should be agreed following this consultation and used as the basis for developing the process.

- Managers and staff should be further involved in developing the details of how performance management is to operate.

- Pilot tests should be carried out.

- A large-scale communications exercise should be conducted to explain the purpose of performance management and how people will benefit from it.

- A comprehensive training programme should be planned and implemented.

- Following its introduction, the process should be evaluated against its stated objectives by means of attitude surveys and focus groups.

- Action should then be taken to deal with any problems identified by the evaluation – performance management should be treated as an area for continuous improvement.

SUMMARY

- The most common features of current approaches to performance management are objective-setting and review, annual appraisal and personal development plans.

- Fewer than half the organisations surveyed by the IPD have performance-related pay.

- The surveyed organisations believed on the whole that objective-setting and review, appraisal, and personal development planning worked well. They were less confident that PRP was effective.

- 360-degree feedback is a process of systematically collecting and analysing information about someone's performance from the person's manager, direct reports, colleagues and, sometimes, customers and suppliers.

- 360-degree feedback is mainly used to support learning and development, but a minority of companies use it to inform pay decisions.

- The rationale for 360-degree feedback is that it can overcome biased appraisals because the organisation is not relying on one person's view and the inherent prejudices he or she may have.

- The concept of the balanced score-card requires managers to look at the business from four related perspectives: the customer, internal processes, improvement and learning, and financial (shareholders).

- Some organisations adopt an integrated approach to performance measurement and review, using the organisational balanced score-card headings and criteria as the framework for individual performance management.

- The vital things to do in introducing performance management are to involve, communicate, train and evaluate.

FURTHER READING

Further case-study material is given in IDS (1997) *Performance Management: Study No 626*. Incomes Data Services.

Part 7

EMPLOYEE BENEFITS, ALLOWANCES AND PENSION SCHEMES

30 Employee benefits and allowances

Employee benefits are those parts of the total reward package provided in addition to cash pay. There are three types of employee benefits:

- deferred or contingent, such as a pension scheme (dealt with in Chapter 31), sick pay, medical insurance

- immediate, such as a company car or a loan

- benefits which are not strictly remuneration, such as holidays.

Employee benefits are sometimes referred to, somewhat pejoratively, as 'fringe benefits' or 'perks'. These terms should be reserved for those benefits which do not fundamentally care for personal security and needs.

This chapter covers:

- the aims of employee benefit strategies and policies

- the content and development of benefit strategies and policies

- types of benefit

- harmonisation and single status

- administering and auditing benefits and controlling costs

- flexible benefit policies and systems

- tax considerations affecting benefit provision.

At the end of the chapter the reader should be able to

- advise on the development and implementation of benefit policies and packages

- evaluate the case for introducing flexible benefits

- monitor the application of benefit policies to ensure that value for money is obtained.

In addition, the reader should know and understand the basis upon which the various aspects of an employee benefits system works, including flexible benefit, or 'cafeteria', schemes.

AIMS

The principal aims of employee benefits policies and practices are:

• to contribute to the provision of a competitive total reward package

• to provide for the needs of employees in terms of their security and, sometimes, their requirements for special financial help, thus demonstrating to them that they are members of a caring organisation

• to increase the commitment of employees to the organisation (but not their motivation unless a benefit such as a better company car is linked directly with individual achievement)

• to provide a tax-efficient method of remuneration.

EMPLOYEE BENEFIT STRATEGY AND POLICY

Benefit strategy

The employee benefit strategy of an organisation should be directed at achieving the aims set out above. It should form part of the total reward strategy and therefore should contribute to the achievement of the objectives of the business by helping to ensure that it has the high-quality, committed people it needs.

The strategy will aim to meet the real needs of employees rather than what the organisation assumes to be their needs. It will also be concerned with getting value for money from its expenditure on employee benefits. The strategy will cover the range of benefits to be provided in general terms and, broadly, how much the organisation is prepared to spend on providing benefits as a proportion of its total remuneration costs.

To meet real employee needs, the strategy will indicate the extent to which the organisation wants to provide flexibility in its benefit provision – a measure of individual choice for employees. Issues concerning the extent to which benefits should be harmonised may also be covered by the strategy.

Employee benefit policies

Employee benefit policies deal with:

• the types of benefit to be provided

• the allocation of benefits, including levels of benefit for different categories of staff and issues about harmonisation and single status

• the scale of benefits to be provided, taking into account their cost and their actual and perceived value to employees, and bearing in mind that the perceived value of a benefit such as a car or pension may be greater than the cost to the business (especially, in the case of pensions, for older employees)

- the proportion of benefits to total remuneration: if pensions are included, benefit costs can easily exceed 20 per cent of the paybill

- flexibility and choice – one way of providing for choice is to move towards 'clean cash', which diverts expenditure on benefits to the actual pay of employees, for them to spend as they wish; another is to adopt a flexible benefit policy or introduce a 'cafeteria' system as described later in this chapter

- market considerations – the extent to which the company believes it must adopt a competitive benefit level policy: this often applies particularly to company cars and special pension arrangements for senior executives

- fiscal considerations – new and changed tax regulations will affect the relative tax efficiency of benefits.

Trade unions are increasingly concerned with negotiating employee benefit levels, although many organisations resist, especially with regard to occupational pensions.

Developing employee benefit strategy and policy

Employee benefit strategy and policy can be developed by taking the following six steps.

Step 1

Decide objectives. It is first necessary to be clear about what the organisation wants to achieve through its benefit strategy and policy. Consideration should also be given at this stage to how much can be spent. The forces that are likely to shape future benefit design and financing should also be analysed. A survey conducted by Towers Perrin (1994) of 376 UK companies established that in order of importance the key issues were:

- total remuneration (achieving the right mix of benefits in the reward package)

- matching benefit philosophy to corporate objectives

- flexibility and choice of benefits

- regular assessment of employee attitudes toward benefits

- level of benefits

- method of reducing employer risk

- age (providing benefits for older employees)

- job level – who gets what benefits at each level

- benefits for seasonal and part-time workers

- controlling benefit costs through employee cost-sharing

- meeting child-care needs.

Note that harmonisation does not appear in this list, although many organisations have harmonised benefits or are moving in that direction.

Step 2

Obtain the views of employees. The opinions of employees on what

Table 29 Benefits ranked in order of importance

Benefit	%
Sick pay	89
Good salary	81
Training and development	80
Transferable pension	74
Company car	73
Profit-sharing scheme	68
Bonus scheme	68
Non-contributory pension	66

Source: MacMillan (1988)

benefits they would prefer should be obtained by such means as attitude surveys, focus groups and individual interviews. In a survey conducted by Henley Management College (MacMillan, 1988) the rewards and benefits regarded by more than 50 per cent of the sample as extremely or very important were ranked as shown in Table 29. It is interesting to note that training and development rank high as a benefit. This suggests that in formulating benefit policies organisations should broaden their thinking to encompass non-financial rewards as benefits (see Chapter 27).

There is no reason why employees should not be asked to rank the importance of a list of existing or possible benefits to them. It is highly probable that any organisation that carried out such a survey would find that the priorities of its employees would be unique. It is certainly most unlikely that they would replicate the results of the Henley survey. Hence the importance of establishing needs and wants. They will differ in accordance with the organisation's culture, its traditional approach and the type of people it employs. Standard or universally applicable benefit packages do not exist.

Step 3
Analyse the competitive position. Benefit provision in other organisations should be surveyed to establish the organisation's competitive position in each benefit area and decide where it wants to position itself. This can be achieved, as described in Chapter 13, by studying published pay and benefit surveys or by exchanging information with other organisations. Because of the complexity of benefit provision and the wide variety of policies that organisations adopt, a benchmarking exercise may well be appropriate. This would identify a number of other 'best-practice' or 'world-class' organisations from which, on a reciprocal basis, to obtain full information on their benefit policies and practices. The information could include details of the components of their benefit package, the costs involved, the rationale of the package and, importantly, the impact it makes on employee commitment and the extent to which it helps to attract and retain good-quality staff.

Step 4
Design the benefit package. The next step is to consider or reconsider the mix and scale of the benefit package, the allocation of benefits (including the need for harmonisation or single status), the scope for

flexibility and a move to 'clean cash', the cost of benefit provision, and what the organisation is likely to gain from its benefit policies. It is at this stage that the advice of benefit consultants and tax specialists should be obtained. Advice from tax specialists is particularly important as a means of maximising tax efficiency. Benefit consultants can advise on the development of flexible benefit or cafeteria systems, and it is usually desirable to seek such help. Discussions should also take place with providers of benefits – for example, health care services and leasing firms for company cars.

When considering the benefit package it is initially necessary to decide what core benefits the organisation should provide. They usually include an occupational pension scheme, sick pay and life insurance. The scale of benefits in each core area has to be determined, and if benefits are not harmonised, the extent to which core benefit provision may vary for different levels of staff or occupations. Directors and executives may have special pension and life assurance arrangements, and extra insurance should be taken out for employees who travel abroad.

Decisions can then be made on any additional or fringe benefits which the organisation may want to provide. These frequently include medical or permanent health insurance, company cars (status cars) and free petrol above a certain level. Financial benefits such as season tickets, low-interest loans and mortgage assistance may also be provided, although the latter are more common in financial service companies. Such benefits are often made available to all employees, although entitlement may be governed by length of service.

The final area for consideration is holiday entitlement (often increased at higher levels) and personal needs such as maternity and paternity leave and pay, compassionate leave and child care.

When decisions on benefit provision have been made, it is necessary to set out very clearly who is entitled to what and the circumstances in which benefits can be provided. This schedule provides the basis for informing employees of their entitlement, communicating to them what they gain from the employee benefit package (this is essential), and monitoring and costing the operation of the employee benefit system (also essential).

Step 5
Consult employees. Before finalising the benefit package it is highly desirable for employees to be consulted on the proposals and, where possible and desirable, for changes to be made to the arrangements in the light of their comments.

Step 6
Plan the introduction. The introduction of any new benefits or changes in the existing system should be planned at this stage. It is essential to communicate to everyone concerned what is happening, why it is happening, and how it will affect them. A comprehensive and well-planned communication programme is required, involving all types of media and face-to-face discussions with individuals.

TYPES OF BENEFIT

Perhaps the most significant benefit is an occupational pension scheme, as discussed in Chapter 31. The other main benefits, as described below, are concerned with personal security, financial assistance, personal needs and company cars.

Personal security

Personal security benefits include:

- health care services – the provision through medical insurance of private health care to cover the cost of private hospital treatment (permanent health insurance) and making periodic health screening available

- dental insurance

- critical illness insurance

- insurance cover for death in service (if not already provided in a pension scheme), for personal accident and for business travel

- sick pay, providing full pay for a given period of sickness and a proportion of pay (typically half-pay) for a further period – sick pay entitlement is usually service-related: sick pay can be costly unless attendance management and control practices are introduced

- redundancy pay – additions can be made to the statutory redundancy pay, including extra notice compensation, extra service-related payments (eg one month per year of service) and *ex gratia* payments to directors and executives in compensation for loss of office (sometimes called 'golden handshakes')

- career counselling (outplacement advice), which can be provided by specialist consultants to employees who have been made redundant.

Financial assistance

Financial assistance can take the following forms:

- company loans – interest-free modest loans, or more substantial loans with low interest, which are usually earmarked for specific purposes such as home improvements

- season ticket loans – interest-free loans for annual season tickets

- mortgage assistance, which provides for subsidised interest payments on mortgages up to a given price threshold: this benefit is most likely to be provided by financial services companies

- relocation packages for recruits and employees who are being obtained from or transferred to other parts of the country: these may cover the costs of removal, legal and agents' fees, and buying new carpets and curtains

- company discounts on the products or services provided by the organisation

- retail vouchers

- fees to professional bodies such as the Institute of Chartered Accountants and the Institute of Personnel and Development.

Personal needs

The employee benefit package will provide for holidays – usually at least four weeks a year and often five weeks or, much less frequently, six weeks. Holiday entitlement may be service-related, although it is usually a standard part of an executive's package.

The other personal needs that can be provided for include:

- maternity leave and pay above the statutory minimum

- paternity leave and pay – a growing area of benefit provision

- compassionate leave when close relatives are ill or die

- child care – workplace nurseries or crèches or vouchers

- pre-retirement counselling – advice to employees who are about to retire on financial planning, using increased leisure time, health, and local sources of information and advice

- personal financial counselling, which is usually restricted to senior executives and covers investments, tax planning, etc

- restaurant facilities and luncheon vouchers – subsidised restaurant facilities or, when they are not available, luncheon vouchers

- sports and social facilities, as sometimes provided by larger organisations although this form of paternalism is becoming less common.

Company cars

In many ways company cars are the most visible and troublesome of all employee benefits. But in spite of the much higher personal tax liability, the so-called 'status' car is still one of the most highly-valued benefits from the viewpoint of employees. And, although developing and administering company car policies is time-consuming and can cause many headaches, most businesses find that they must provide cars or cash in lieu of cars if they want their total reward package to remain competitive.

In spite of the tougher tax regime for company cars (see the last section of this chapter) it is still more expensive for a private person to own a vehicle than to use a company vehicle. Individuals do not have as much buying power, spend more on running and maintaining the vehicle, and cannot reclaim VAT on maintenance costs.

Recent research conducted by AT&T Capital, as quoted by the Institute of Directors (CBI/Towers Perrin, 1994) showed that a typical car costing a company £435 a month would cost an extra £135, or 31 per cent, for the individual to provide. A further perceived benefit for many individuals is that a company car relieves them of worries about paying for maintenance, repairs, insurance and replacements. Psychologically, to many people, extra pay or cash instead of a car, even if it fully covers the costs, is not the same as getting their employer to carry all the expense and risk.

Because a status company car is still seen by most people as a major benefit, the gap between those who have one and those who have not can become very significant. Company cars can therefore distort the reward structure, demotivate those who are not eligible, and create undue pressure for upgrading from those on the wrong side of the dividing line. Even when employees are entitled to a company car they can be upset about the model they get, the extras they are allowed and the replacement policy. It is therefore essential to have a clearly-defined car policy covering:

- allocation – who gets what

- model entitlement – the choice may be restricted to vehicles on which the business can get the best deal from a supplier (sports cars are usually excluded): it is quite common for some choice to be allowed within benchmark prices or lease costs – some companies allow employees to pay for extras within a ceiling of, say, 10 per cent of the purchase price or lease cost; others require employees to stick rigidly within the cost limit, which may allow a few common extras such as metallic paint

- replacement – cars are usually replaced every two to four years or after about 60,000 miles

- eligibility to drive – it is usual to allow spouses or partners to drive status cars and some companies (insurers permitting) extend this to immediate family, and other named drivers.

Whatever rules are adopted about allocation, model entitlement, replacement and eligibility, it is essential to stick to them rigidly. Making exceptions creates precedents, and the pressure for bigger and better cars and quicker replacements (and, indeed, to become eligible for a car) can become unbearable.

In addition to company cars, a further benefit in the shape of free fuel for private mileage (usually in the UK only) can be provided. But this is taxable and if annual mileage is low, the tax could exceed the cost of the fuel.

HARMONISATION

Harmonisation is the process of introducing the same conditions of employment for all employees. It means the reduction of differences in the pay structure and other employment conditions between categories of employees, usually manual and staff employees. The pressure for harmonisation has arisen for the following reasons:

- new technology – status differentials can obstruct efficient labour utilisation, and concessions on harmonisation are invariably given in exchange for an agreement on flexibility; moreover, technology, by de-skilling many white-collar jobs and enhancing the skills of former blue-collar workers, has made differential treatment harder to defend

- legislation – equal pay, the banning of sex and racial discrimination and employment protection legislation have extended rights to manual workers previously the preserve of staff: the concept of equal value has been a major challenge to differentiation between staff and manual workers

- improved productivity by the more flexible use of labour

- simplified personnel administration, t
- changes in employee attitudes, impro and morale.

ACAS (1982) has suggested that befo harmonisation, organisations should se questions:

- What differences in the treatment of rational result of differences in the wo
- Is it possible to estimate the direct cost
- What differences in status are explicit 'reward package' for different groups in
- What would be the repercussive effects of harmonisation?
- How do the existing differences affect industrial relations in the organisation?

MANAGING EMPLOYEE BENEFITS

The methods used to manage employee benefits should measure accurately how much is spent on each type of benefit and how much the benefit is being used. For example, data should be collected and monitored on the cost to the business of granting season ticket loans and how many loans are being made.

There should be a budget for employee benefit costs and expenditure should be monitored against it so that corrective action can be taken if costs exceed the budgeted figure. Alternatively, if the extra costs are necessary and unavoidable, the budget can be amended.

Regular surveys should be undertaken of the attitude of employees to the benefits package. They may indicate scope for redirecting benefit expenditure to areas where it would be more appreciated. They may also suggest that there is a need to adopt a flexible benefit policy, as described below.

It is also necessary to keep abreast of changes in the tax system, which may well result in some benefits becoming less tax-efficient. Outside help can usefully be obtained from benefit and tax specialists to audit the system and advise on where it could be improved in the light of tax legislation or new developments in benefit provision.

FLEXIBLE BENEFITS

Flexible benefits allow employees to decide, within certain limits, on the make-up of their benefits package. They are allocated an individual allowance to spend on benefits. This allowance can be used to switch between benefits, to choose new ones or to alter the rate of cover within existing benefits. Some core benefits such as sick pay may lie outside the scheme and cannot be 'flexed'. Employees can shift the balance of their total reward package between pay and benefits, either adding to their benefits allowance by sacrificing salary or taking any unspent benefit allowance as cash.

rticularly executives with a wider range of benefits, can
e level of benefits on one item, such as a company car,
s free money to be paid as additional salary or to be
ibuted between other benefits. For example, an allowance of
0 a month for the contract hire of a car could be reduced to £400
month, freeing £200 to be allocated to other benefits or added to
pay. Flexible benefit systems mean that individuals can tailor their
benefits to suit their personal needs and particular obligations and
aspirations. The need to pay a mortgage and support school-age
children may be a priority for someone with a family, but a colleague
with no such commitments may prefer a bigger and better car. The
young and fit may place a low value on free health insurance whereas
the older employee may rate it more highly.

From the employer's point of view a flexible benefit policy can save
money on benefits which are neither needed nor wanted.

Flexible benefit systems

Flexible benefit systems (sometimes called cafeteria systems) can
allow for a choice within benefits and/or a choice between benefits.
Choice within benefits is the typical approach and was adopted by 41
per cent of the companies surveyed by CBI/Towers Perrin in 1994.
The most common areas of choice within the provision of individual
benefits are company cars and pension schemes. Cars can be provided
through a leasing supplier and a choice of models allowed within a set
annual leasing cost. Other options may include choosing a less
expensive car and taking the balance in cash, paying extra to have a
larger car or taking a lump sum instead of a company car. Pension
schemes could provide a choice in the level of individual employee
contributions (say between 3 per cent and 6 per cent) linked with a
similar range of employer contributions, and some trade-off between
normal pension benefits and linked benefits such as widow's/widower's
pensions or death benefits. Some schemes allow employees to trade
holidays for cash or vice versa although a minimum 'core' holiday
period may be laid down.

Choice between benefits is less common (22 per cent of the companies
covered by the 1994 CBI/Towers Perrin survey). It may be a straight
choice between specified benefits such as life and medical insurance.
Alternatively, it may involve selection from a menu of costed items
within an overall budget. In its most developed form the latter is
often called a cafeteria system.

A multi-choice flexible benefit plan is frequently based on a core of
non-negotiable cash and benefits (the latter may include, for example,
pensions, sick pay and holidays), although choice is allowed in some
schemes. A range of benefits which can be varied within a total
annual value is then determined. This is variously termed the benefits
allowance, flex fund, benefits credit or benefits 'pot'. For example,
three types of benefit could be varied – say, life assurance, medical
insurance and a car. Within each benefit there would be a range of
costed options and an annual budget which could not be exceeded. If
the total cost of the selected options is less than the budget the balance
is made available to the employee as a monthly salary credit.

Table 30 Benefit flexibility

Benefit	%
Choosing between a car and cash	65
Taking a higher-value car and contributing cash	63
Taking a lower-value car plus cash	41
Flexible pension benefits	24
Private medical insurance	62

Source: CBI/Towers Perrin (1994)

Options

The options typically presented to employees are:

• to make no change to their existing benefits package

• to increase some benefits while decreasing others with or without sacrificing pay

• to use pay to buy new benefits while retaining existing ones

• to decrease benefits and take the cash released as extra pay.

Flexible benefits in practice

The IRS 1998 survey established that only 3.5 per cent of employers had flexible benefits, but interest is growing fast – 29.4 per cent were considering introducing them. The CBI/Towers Perrin 1994 survey showed the extent to which the companies provided benefit flexibility, as outlined in Table 30. Few companies covered by the survey allowed employees either to buy or sell holidays in exchange for cash or benefits, possibly because it is recognised that allowing employees to sell holidays is a cash cost to the company which may not be made up by increased productivity. However, 57 per cent of respondents did allow employees to carry forward unused holiday into the following year, and 37 per cent allowed employees to take unpaid time off to extend their holiday.

The IDS 1998 survey established that the most common flexible benefits were holidays, private medical insurance and dental insurance. Fairly common flexed benefits included company cars (trading up/down, opting out – ie not having a car), permanent health insurance, health screening and child-care vouchers. The less common flexible benefits included pensions, personal accident insurance, financial counselling and concessionary rail travel.

As reported in the IDS 1998 study, Birmingham Midshires Building Society introduced flexible benefits in 1996 with the following benefits on the menu: holidays, private medical insurance, dental insurance, critical illness insurance, retail vouchers, health screening, life assurance and personal lease car.

At Cable & Wireless as reported by IRS (1998) the 'flex' scheme introduced in what was then Mercury Communications in 1996 allowed employees to choose a standard employment package or to enhance one or more benefits from a set list of six: pensions, life cover, health care, dental insurance, annual leave and child-care vouchers.

Reasons for introduction

The reasons given by the Birmingham Midshires Building Society for introducing flexible benefits, as reported by IDS (1998), were:

- as a response to employees' requests for some flexibility expressed in an attitude survey

- to allow employees more choice over how they were rewarded, allowing them to shape their benefits package so that it more closely matched their personal circumstances

- to help recruit and retain the best staff by making the company more attractive to work for

- to provide a means of improving employee satisfaction which would flow through to improvements in customer satisfaction

- to provide certain benefits for staff in the most cost-effective manner.

At Mercury Communications (now Cable & Wireless) as reported by IRS (1998) 'flex' was introduced in 1996 for two main reasons: first because although the remuneration package focused on the individual, the benefits part was not individualised; and second, management was concerned that the growth in benefits provision could not be sustained and believed that it would be better to offer benefits tailored to individual needs.

The advantages and disadvantages of flexible benefits

The advantages of a flexible approach are that:

- Greater individual freedom of choice in the make-up of the remuneration package can assist in the recruitment and retention of employees.

- It makes economic sense to spend money on things which individuals perceive to be most valuable.

- The needs of different sections of the workforce can be more easily addressed – for example, younger and older and married and unmarried employees will have different priorities.

- Employers are in a better position to manage the costs of providing benefits: as IDS (1998) points out, 'There is always pressure on employers to improve the range and coverage of the benefits they provide. By introducing the element of choice, the package available to staff can be enhanced, while enabling new benefits to be offered at little or no extra cost to the company.'

- Some savings can accrue in the employer's National Insurance contributions which can help to pay for the costs of operating flexible benefits.

- Employees can gain a better appreciation of the value of the benefit package provided for them.

- The fact that employees' priorities change over a period of time can be catered for.

The disadvantages are that:

- Each benefit must be accurately costed for inclusion in the menu.

- Freedom of choice for employees can cause administrative problems for employers – the greater the opportunity to make choices, the greater the potential complexity and the administrative burden (although there is software available to assist in the administration of flexible benefits).

- Giving individuals a range of options may mean that they make the wrong choices unless they are given specialist advice which enables them to choose in their own best interests.

- There is a risk that the cost to employers of insurance premiums for benefits may increase when employees are given more say in whether the benefit is provided and at what level.

- Flexible benefits can be tax-disadvantageous to employees.

Introducing flexible benefits

Professional advice is essential when setting up a flexible benefit scheme, even a fairly simple one. This is a highly technical area of remuneration, and the tax implications need to be examined rigorously by experts. Benefit consultants can provide invaluable assistance in designing the scheme and installing the administrative systems necessary to maintain it. Their advice is helpful at the earliest stage of contemplating the possibility of flexible benefits. If, after due consideration, it is thought that the advantages outweigh the disadvantages, the professional advisers can work with management to

- develop the scheme, identifying the core benefits and any additional benefits which can be flexed

- decide who is to be given the opportunity to take part in the scheme: many companies restrict choice to senior executives, but this can be divisive and some organisations are extending the facility to other levels of staff

- consult employees about the arrangements – it is highly desirable to enlist their support and listen to their views at an early stage

- cost each of the benefits to be included in the flexible package – this can be a complex process and is another area in which professional advice is useful if not essential

- explore the tax implications from both the employers' and the employees' points of view

- set up the administrative arrangements for making choices, recording decisions, adjusting the total remuneration packages of individual employees and collecting cost data

- brief employees on how the scheme works, how they can benefit and what advice they will be able to obtain from qualified and registered pensions and benefits advisers – under the Financial Services Act 1985 any advice on pensions should be given only by approved bodies, companies or individuals.

ALLOWANCES AND OTHER PAYMENTS TO EMPLOYEES

The main areas in which allowances and other special payments may be made to employees are:

- location allowances – London and other large city allowances may be paid because of housing and other cost-of-living differentials. Allowances are paid as an addition to basic pay, although many employers in effect consolidate them by paying the local market rates, taking into account explicit or implicit location allowances and costs.

- subsistence allowances – The value of subsistence allowances for accommodation and meals varies greatly between organisations. Some have set rates, depending on location or the grade of employee. Others allow 'reasonable' rates without any set scale but usually, and desirably, with guidelines on acceptable hotel and meal costs.

- overtime payments – Most manual workers are eligible for paid overtime as well as many staff employees up to management level. Higher-paid staff may receive time off in lieu if they work longer hours. Typically, organisations which make overtime payments give time-and-a-half as an overtime premium from Monday to Saturday, with double-time paid on Sundays and statutory holidays. Some firms also pay double-time from around noon on Saturday. Work on major statutory holidays such as Christmas Day and Good Friday often attracts higher overtime premia.

- shift payments – These are made at rates which usually vary according to the shift arrangement. A premium of, say, one-third of basic pay may be given to people working nights while those on an early or late day shift may receive less – say, one-fifth of basic pay.

- stand-by and call-out allowances – These may be made to those who have to be available to come in to work when required. The allowance may be made as a standard payment added to basic pay. Alternatively, special payments may be made for unforeseen call-outs.

TAX CONSIDERATIONS

General principles

Emoluments from employment are subject to income tax under Schedule E. Emoluments are defined by legislation as 'all salaries, fees, wages, perquisites, or profits whatsoever'. In the courts, emoluments have been defined as rewards for 'services rendered, past, present and future' or, more broadly, payments made 'in return for acting as, or being, an employee'.

In general, much of the taxation on benefits applies only to directors and employees earning over £8,500 a year – in most organisations this is likely to be just about all full-time workers. Such employees are sometimes known as P11D employees, P11D being the form on which employers have to report the benefits received by employees to the Inland Revenue. A non-cash benefit such as a gift is taxable on the price it would command if sold. A benefit which cannot be turned into cash by the recipient is taxable on the annual cost incurred by the employer. For employees earning less than £8,500 a year, such 'non-convertible' benefits are not taxed. Regulations on the taxation of benefits are summarised below as they applied in 1996. They are frequently changed and it is advisable to keep up to date through such publications as the IDS annual guide to taxation for personnel managers.

Taxable benefits

The taxable benefits include:

- company cars – The tax charged on company cars is based on the 'full cost' of a car for a year. 'Full cost' includes running costs and major fixed costs such as depreciation and financial costs. For income tax purposes, full cost is 35 per cent of the list price of the car. The taxable value of the benefit can, however, be reduced to take business use into account. This amounts to a one-third reduction if between 2,500 and 17,999 business miles are driven a year and two-thirds for 18,000 or more business miles a year. Employers have to pay National Insurance contributions on company cars.

- free fuel – This is taxed on the basis of fixed-scale charges for company cars which are available for private use. The scale charge in 1998/99 for a car with an engine capacity over 2,000cc is £1,890, and for a 1,401 to 2,000cc car it is £1,280. The government's intention is to increase scale charges considerably. The scale charge is applied however much private mileage is driven, so that free benefit can be a burden if mileage falls below a certain level.

- car mileage allowances – Under the fixed-profit car scheme (FPCS) a scale lays down the size of allowance that is tax-free according to cylinder capacity and mileage. For example, in 1996/97 the tax-free allowance for a car over 2,000cc for up to 4,000 miles a year was 63p.

- cheap or interest-free loans – Tax is payable on the taxable benefit of a loan. This is calculated as the difference between the interest, if any, paid by the employee and the interest on the loan, calculated at the 'official rate' of interest set by the Inland Revenue.

- living accommodation – All employees and directors are liable for tax on the benefit of employer-provided free or cheap housing, unless they are in certain exempt categories such as those required to live on the premises.

- private medical benefits – Private medical insurance and treatment are taxable on the basis of the cost to the employer.

- gifts and vouchers – These are taxed on the full realisable value of the gift, or their full cost if a voucher or credit token is used to obtain them.

- use of assets – Where assets such as furniture and electrical goods (but not cars or accommodation) are provided as a benefit to employees, they are taxed at 20 per cent of the market value of the asset at the time it was first used by the employee.

- prizes and incentive awards – Cash awards are taxed in the normal way. Awards in the form of goods, vouchers or services, such as holidays, are taxed on the value of the award. Employers can arrange with the Inland Revenue to pay the tax due on non-cash incentive awards on behalf of their employees so that the awards are 'tax-free'.

- mobile telephones provided for private use – These are taxed at the rate of £200 unless the employee makes good the full cost of any private use.

Benefits not usually subject to tax

Benefits not usually subject to tax include:

- meals provided for employees, as long as the free or subsidised meals are on 'a reasonable scale' and all employees can take advantage of them

- child care in workplace nurseries or play schemes

- car parking space if this is at or near the place of work

- subscriptions to approved professional institutions and learned societies

- luncheon vouchers of up to 15p a day

- Christmas parties and other functions – employees are not liable to tax on the value of a Christmas party or other social function provided by the employer as long as it is open to employees generally and the cost is no more than £50 per head

- small gifts and entertainment by third parties – gifts are tax-free up to the value of £100, as is goodwill entertainment provided by a third party (ie not the employer)

- relocation expenses – tax relief is available on relocation packages to a ceiling of £8,000, but this excludes payments by employers to compensate employees for any loss on the sale of their old home

- long service awards – awards given to mark service of over 20 years are tax-free as long as they are 'tangible articles of reasonable cost' or shares in the employing company: reasonable cost is defined as no more than £20 per year of service – the employee must not have received a similar award within the previous 10 years

- suggestion schemes – awards made to employees under suggestion schemes are tax-free up to a maximum of £5,000 as long as the suggestion is outside the scope of the employee's normal duties and is implemented: awards must not exceed either half the net financial benefit expected during the first year of implementation, or 10 per cent of the expected benefit over a period of up to five years – 'encouragement' awards, given where the suggestion shows merit but is not implemented, are tax-free up to a limit of £25

- education and training – employees are not liable to tax on further education or training paid for by their employers as long as it leads to the acquisition of knowledge and skills that are either necessary for the job or will increase an employee's effectiveness at work; if the course is of general education, employees must be aged under 21 when it starts

- outplacement counselling

- workplace nurseries – tax relief is available to employees whose children have a place in an employer-provided workplace nursery

- redundancy payments – the first £30,000 of a redundancy payment is tax-free as long as it is a full and final settlement and there is no question of any part of the money being paid to the individual for services rendered – the Inland Revenue has recently been taking a firm line on the latter provision.

SUMMARY

- Employee benefits are those parts of the total reward package provided in addition to cash pay. There are three types of employee benefits: deferred or contingent, such as a pension scheme, sick pay, medical insurance; immediate, such as a company car or a loan; and benefits which are not strictly remuneration, such as holidays.

- The aims of employee benefits policies and practices are to contribute to the provision of a competitive total reward package, to provide for the needs of employees in terms of their security and, sometimes, their requirements for special financial help, thus demonstrating to them that they are members of a caring organisation, to increase the commitment of employees to the organisation and to provide a tax-efficient method of remuneration.

- Employee benefit policies deal with the types of benefit to be provided, the allocation and scale of benefits and the extent to which choice will be provided (flexible benefits).

- The main types of benefits provided are for personal security, financial assistance and personal needs.

- Flexible benefits allow employees to decide, within certain limits, on the make-up of their benefits package. They are allocated an individual allowance to spend on benefits. This allowance can be used to switch between benefits, to choose new ones or to alter the rate of cover within existing benefits. Some core benefits such as sick pay may lie outside the scheme and cannot be 'flexed'.

FURTHER READING

COOPERS & LYBRAND (1993) *Flexible Benefits*. London, CCH Editions.
INSTITUTE OF DIRECTORS (1994) *Employee Benefits*. London, Institute of Directors.
IDS (annual) *The Personnel Manager's Guide to Taxation*. London, Incomes Data Services.

31 Pension schemes

Pensions are provided by the state and employers. Schemes made available by employers are designed to provide employees with security by currently building up rights which will give a guaranteed income to them or their dependants on retirement or death. Pensions are essentially deferred pay, and they are financed by contributions from the employer and in most, but not all cases, the employee.

Pension arrangements are probably the most complex of all the areas of employee reward with which personnel and development professionals may be concerned. Setting up and administering pension schemes is a highly technical process, the province of actuaries and other specialist insurance, investment, tax and financial advisers.

But it is necessary for personnel specialists to have at least a general understanding of pensions so that they can play their part in administering this important benefit and in communicating to employees how the company's scheme affects them. Readers who complete this chapter will know and understand:

- why organisations have pension schemes

- what a pension scheme is

- the different types of pension scheme, including those provided both by employers and by the state

- the main features of a typical occupational pension scheme

- the factors affecting the choice of pension arrangements

- the basis upon which pension schemes are administered

- the legal framework within which pension schemes operate

- the headings under which the government has made proposals in 1998 on the future of pensions.

On the basis of this understanding, readers should be able to:

- contribute to policy discussions on the development of pension schemes within their organisation

- contribute to the administration of the scheme within their organisation

- provide employees with information on how the pension schemes operate
- forward requests for advice on pension arrangements to qualified advisers.

This chapter concentrates on occupational pension schemes, covering in turn:

- the reasons for providing a pension scheme
- a general description of occupational pension schemes
- the different types of scheme
- the main benefits provided by schemes
- pension scheme administration
- occupational pension schemes in action
- the factors affecting choice.

The chapter concludes with descriptions of the other types of pension arrangements – ie personal pension schemes, the state pension scheme, and a discussion of the legal restrictions on providing advice about pensions.

WHY PROVIDE A PENSION SCHEME?

The usual reasons advanced for having a worthwhile pension scheme are that:

- it demonstrates that the organisation is a good employer
- it attracts and retains high-quality people by helping to maintain competitive levels of total remuneration
- it indicates that the organisation is concerned about the long-term interests of its employees.

A survey by the CBI and the pension consultants William M. Mercer (1994) of what motivated companies to set up pension schemes revealed that the most important reason (advanced by 33 per cent of the senior executives contacted) was that a good pension scheme 'ensures that the company is competitive in the labour market'. The next most important reason, selected by 28 per cent of the respondents, was that 'It is part of the company's paternalistic approach to benefit provision and contributes to our image as a good employer'. Twenty-one per cent believed that their scheme 'acts as an aid to employee motivation'. The motivational impact of pensions may be questionable but the first two reasons are probably those which would be subscribed to by most organisations with pension schemes.

OCCUPATIONAL PENSION SCHEMES – GENERAL DESCRIPTION

Definition
An occupational pension scheme is an arrangement under which an employer provides pensions for employees when they retire, income for

the families of members who die, and deferred benefits to members who leave. A 'group scheme' is the typical scheme which provides for a number of employees.

Operation

Occupational pension schemes are administered by trusts which are supposed to be outside the employer's control. The trustees are responsible for the fund from which pension benefits are paid.

The pension fund is fed by contributions from employers and usually (but not always) employees. The size of the fund and its capacity to meet future commitments depends not only on the size of contributions but also on the income the trustees can generate. They invest fund money with the help of advisers in stocks, shares and other securities, or through an insurance company. In the latter case, insurance companies offer either a managed fund – a pool of money managed by the insurance company for a number of clients – or a segregated fund which is managed for a single client.

Contributions

Pensions may be contributory or, more rarely, non-contributory. In a contributory scheme employees as well as employers make contributions to the pension fund.

The level of contributions varies considerably, although in a typical contributory scheme employees would be likely to contribute about 5 per cent of their earnings and employers would contribute approximately twice that amount. In a non-contributory scheme the employer totally funds the pension.

An approved scheme

Members of an occupational scheme which has been approved by the Inland Revenue (an 'approved' scheme) obtain full tax relief on their contributions. The company also recovers tax on its contributions and the income tax deductible from gains realised on UK investments. This makes a pension fund the most tax-efficient form of saving available in the UK.

Employers can establish unapproved pension schemes which provide benefits in excess of approved schemes but at the expense of the generous tax allowances for the latter type of scheme.

For a scheme to be approved by the Pension Schemes Office (PSO), a special department of the Inland Revenue,

- The pension may not exceed a sum greater than two-thirds of final pay after 40 years' service.

- There is a limit to how much pension can be paid (£82,220 in 1996).

- Three-eighteenths of final earnings for each year of service may be paid as a lump sum free of tax instead of pension – this is termed cash commutation.

- Dependants' pensions may not in total exceed members' pensions, and widows' and widowers' pensions may not exceed the members' pensions.

- Lump-sum death benefits may not exceed four times salary plus a return of the members' contributions when members die in service, or £1,000 when members die in retirement.

- Contributions by employers must not exceed 14 per cent of pay in a final salary scheme. In a personal pension plan higher contributions can be made on a scale starting at 17.5 per cent.

- Contributions by employees must not exceed 15 per cent of their earnings.

- Various complex rules apply to how retained benefits (ie deferred pensions from previous employers) are treated.

Occupational pensions can be described as 'deferred pay' because they are financed by contributions made during an employee's working life.

Retiring age and sex discrimination

Traditionally, the retiring age was 65 for men and 60 for women. However, under the Sex Discrimination Act 1986 it is unlawful for employers to require female employees to retire at an earlier age than male employees. In its judgement on the *Barber* v *Guardian Royal Exchange* case on 17 May 1990 the European Court ruled that pension was 'pay' under Article 119 of the Treaty of Rome (which provided for equal pay), and that it was unlawful to discriminate between men and women with regard to pension rights. It has since been agreed that pensions will not count as pay prior to 17 May 1990.

Benefit statements

Every member of an occupational scheme is entitled to an annual statement setting out his or her prospective benefits.

Contracting out

It is possible for a pension scheme to be contracted out of the State Earnings Related Scheme (SERPS) as long as it meets certain conditions (see p. 419).

TYPES OF OCCUPATIONAL PENSION SCHEME

Defined benefit scheme

A defined benefit or final salary group pension scheme offers a guaranteed pension, part of which may be surrendered for a tax-free cash sum. In its final pay or salary form, the pension is a fraction of final pensionable earnings for each year of service (typically one-sixtieth). To achieve the maximum two-thirds pension in a one-sixtieth scheme would therefore take 40 years' service.

Defined benefit schemes provide employees with a predictable level of pension. But for employers they can be costly and unpredictable because the employer has to contribute whatever is necessary to buy the promised benefits.

Defined contribution scheme

In a defined contribution or money purchase scheme employers fix the contributions they want to pay for employees by undertaking to pay a defined percentage of earnings irrespective of the benefits available on retirement. The retirement pension is therefore whatever annual payment can be purchased with the money accumulated in the fund for a member.

A defined contribution scheme offers the employee unpredictable benefits because they depend on the total value of the contributions invested, the investment returns achieved and the rate at which the accumulated fund can be converted into a pension on retirement. For the employer, however, it offers certainty of costs.

Hybrid schemes

Hybrid schemes combine final salary and money purchase arrangements in various ways. For example, the money purchase may 'underpin' a final salary benefit by paying a pension based on the money purchase formula if this would be higher than that received under the final salary arrangement.

Executive pension plans

Executive pension plans (sometimes known as 'top hat schemes') are arrangements for 'topping-up' pensions for directors or senior executives. Directors or executives may, for example, be members of a group pension scheme with a normal retirement age of 65 and also be members of an executive pension plan arranged specially for them with a retirement age of, say, 60. The maximum benefits payable to members of executive pension plans will take into account their pensions from the group scheme.

If a director's pension is to be topped up by means of a separate executive pension plan and the employer is unwilling to bear the additional cost, the employer's contribution can be made by a practice known as salary sacrifice – the director giving up a part of his or her salary voluntarily.

Group personal pension schemes

In a group personal pension scheme (GPPS) employees have their own personal pension contracts, and the scheme is, in effect, a bundle of individual personal pensions. The employer may simply carry out a payroll function by deducting members' contributions from net pay and remitting them to the pension-provider together with the employees' contributions.

Final salary	Money purchase
Benefits defined as a fraction of final pensionable pay	Benefits purchased by an accumulation of contributions invested
Benefits do not depend on investment returns or annuity rates	Benefits dependent on investment returns, contributions, and cost of annuities at retirement
Employer contributes necessary costs in access of employee contributions	Employer contributions are fixed
Employer takes financial risk	Member takes financial risk
Early leavers often suffer a loss as benefits are broadly linked to prices rather than earnings	Early leavers do not take a loss because their account remains invested within the scheme
Benefits designed for long-serving employees with progressive increases in pensionable pay	Benefits designed for short-serving employees or those whose pensionable pay fluctuates

A GPSS is not subject to the rules of an occupational pension scheme and benefits are unlimited, although contributions are restricted to a prescribed scale which increases with age. It is in effect a defined contribution scheme, because it makes no promise of a specific level of pension benefit on retirement.

Comparison of final salary and money purchase scheme

The most common forms of pension schemes are final salary and money purchase. The main differences between them as described in a *Key Fact* sheet on pensions (Institute of Personnel and Development, April 1999) are summarised on page 412.

BENEFITS FROM OCCUPATIONAL PENSION SCHEMES

The benefits from a pension scheme will clearly depend on a number of factors, especially the type of scheme and the level of contributions. As described below, benefits fall under three headings: benefits on retirement, benefits on death, and benefits on leaving service.

Benefits on retirement

Most members are in occupational defined benefit (final salary) schemes which provide a pension based on pensionable earnings at or near retirement. A typical basis of calculation is to take average earnings over the best three consecutive years in the last 10 years of service.

Size of the pension – final salary scheme

The size of the pension within the two-thirds Inland Revenue limit will depend on the member's service and the accrual rate – the fraction of each year of service which forms the basis of pension entitlement. For example, a member in a scheme with an accrual rate of one-sixtieth would receive the full two-thirds of final salary pension after 40 years' service. The benefits in respect of service up to a specific date calculated in relation to current earnings or projected final earnings are known as accrued benefits or accrued rights.

Size of the pension – money purchase scheme

In a money purchase scheme the final pension will depend entirely on the value of the contributions paid during the member's service and the returns made on investing those contributions.

Commutation

Most occupational pension schemes allow members to take part of their pension in the form of cash. This is known as commutation. No more than a quarter of the pension can be taken in cash, which is tax-free. The amount of pension which has to be given up in exchange for cash will vary from scheme to scheme. Typically, a man aged 65 may have to give up £100 a year pension to obtain £900 cash.

Enhanced benefits

Pension schemes can provide for the payment of enhanced benefits so that it is possible to obtain a two-thirds pension after only 20 years' service (10 years for those who were members of schemes before 1987).

Additional voluntary contributions

Additional voluntary contributions (AVCs) can be made by pension scheme members in order to increase their scale benefits. The contributions made by an employee cannot exceed 15 per cent of total remuneration. Thus an employee who already contributes 5 per cent to a scheme could not make an AVC contribution of more than 10 per cent.

AVCs provided by the employer enable the whole of the members' contribution to be deducted from their pay before tax, which gives relief from income tax at the highest rate. Alternatively, employees can take out a free-standing AVC which is completely separate from their employer's sponsored scheme. In that case, individuals obtain basic tax relief at source and claim any higher tax relief through their tax assessment.

Added years
Public sector schemes may allow 'added years of service' to be purchased. For example, a voluntary contribution of 5 per cent of salary might secure three or four years' additional pensionable service for a young member.

Working beyond normal retirement age
Employees who remain in employment after their normal retirement date can earn additional benefits as long as the benefits are not above the maximum approved pension limit.

Post-retirement pension increase
A substantial majority of pension schemes guarantee some increases in pension following retirement to allow for increases in the cost of living. The Social Security Act 1990 requires all final pay schemes to guarantee post-retirement pension increases in line with increases to the retail price index subject to a maximum of 5 per cent per annum.

Benefits on death
Widows' and widowers' pensions
Widows' and widowers' pensions are normally related to the member's anticipated pension, based on pay at death, counting service to normal retirement date. The most common fraction is half.

Other dependants
Occupational schemes frequently provide pensions for children, and in special circumstances the trustees can decide to choose as beneficiary a person other than the widow.

Lump sum
Occupational pension schemes almost always provide a lump-sum payment if the death takes place in service. It can be from two to four years' pay; two years' is typical. When death takes place after retirement the Pension Schemes Office allows a payment of up to £1,000 provided the deceased member was a member of the pension scheme prior to 1 October 1991.

Benefits on leaving an employer
Individuals who leave an employer can elect to take one of the following options:

• a deferred pension from the occupational scheme they are leaving

- the transfer of the pension entitlement from the present employer to the new employer (but this is not always possible or desirable)

- refund of this contribution, but only if they have completed less than two years' membership of the pension scheme.

PENSION SCHEME ADMINISTRATION

Pension scheme rules

Pension scheme rules are set out in a Trust Deed and cover:

- eligibility – who is eligible to join the scheme, when, and at what age

- contributions – the basis for determining contributions and the rate of contribution

- normal retiring date, which after 17 May 1990 must be the same for men and women

- pensionable service – how this is determined

- pension provisions – the types of scheme, the formula for determining pensions in a defined benefit scheme (the accrual rate), the various benefits provided on retirement, death or leaving.

Trustees

To obtain tax-exempt status an occupational pension scheme must be set up as a trust, with the assets held quite independently of the sponsoring company or organisation. The trustees are entirely accountable for the operation of the trust, and their responsibilities have become even more onerous under the provisions of the Pensions Act 1995.

Trustees have a duty to the trust generally and may not pursue a sectional interest. The primary responsibility of trustees is to supervise the investment of monies which are not immediately required to pay benefits. Their role is to obtain the maximum return consistent with the prudence expected when the future benefits of members and their dependants are at stake. As stated in the High Court ruling in the case of *National Coal Board* v *National Union of Mineworkers and others* (1986): 'Trustees must exercise their powers in the best interests of all present and future beneficiaries. Best interests would usually mean best financial interests.'

Trustees have the following additional duties under the Pensions Act 1995:

- to appoint the investment manager, auditor and actuary

- to compile an investment principles statement

- to refuse a surplus refund if it is not in the members' interest

- to set up internal dispute resolution machinery

- to apply the principle of equal treatment between the sexes.

With limited exceptions, the members of an occupational pension scheme will have the right to select at least one-third of its trustees.

There will be a minimum of two such trustees if the scheme has 100 members or more and a minimum of one if there are fewer than 100 members. The employer can propose an alternative arrangement, which, however, cannot be adopted if more than 10 per cent or a minimum of 1,000 members object.

Under the 1995 Act, member-nominated trustees and other employee trustees have a statutory right to be paid when undertaking their duties or undergoing training. It is particularly important to ensure that trustees are properly trained because of their considerable responsibilities and the complexity of their role.

Funding group pension schemes

Most group schemes promise benefits relating to final earnings, so that, as earnings increase, so do prospective pensions. It is therefore difficult to quantify in advance the exact pension benefit and the cost of providing it. The employer's contribution as a percentage of the total pensionable pay of employees is known as the funding rate. It will be calculated by the actuaries to the fund on the basis of assumptions about the rate at which pay will increase, the prospective yield on the fund, mortality rates, the pay/age profile and ratio of males and females.

At least every three years the actuaries will check the performance of the fund against the assumptions. If the assumptions were incorrect, adjustment of the funding rate may be required.

Funds may run into deficit if pay has increased substantially without corresponding increases in the fund's yield. In that case the deficit may have to be made good by the injection of a lump sum. Funds can also generate surpluses, and often do when the rate of growth has exceeded the growth in earnings and when they make a profit out of early leavers.

Under the Pensions Act 1995 defined benefit schemes (including final salary) will have to meet a new minimum funding requirement, and the trustees of all schemes will have to ensure that contributions are received from the employer regularly according to an agreed schedule.

Security measures

The Pensions Act 1995 introduces new security measures effective from April 1997 to parry predatory raids on an occupational pension fund. The measures will be overseen by a new Occupational Pensions Regulatory Authority (OPRA). The role of OPRA is to take decisive action on being told of irregularities and it will therefore rely to a great extent on scheme trustees and their professional advisers to be its local watchdog.

Equal treatment

All occupational schemes are required by the Pensions Act 1995 to ensure equal treatment for men and women regarding access, contributions and benefits for any period of pensionable service after 17 May 1990. There are certain exceptions to the principle of equality permitted by judgements of the European Court of Justice.

OCCUPATIONAL PENSION SCHEMES IN ACTION

The National Association of Pensions Funds' (NAPF) survey (1994) found that 83 per cent of employees decide to join their employer's pension scheme when they become eligible. The other main findings of the NAPF survey are that:

- Seventy-seven per cent of schemes require employees to contribute.

- The average employer's contribution is 6.4 per cent when employees also contribute and 11.1 per cent in non-contributory pension schemes.

- The average member contribution is 4.6 per cent in contributory schemes.

- Seventy-four per cent of schemes have an accrual rate (pension fraction) of one-sixtieth of final pensionable salary per year of membership; 19 per cent had a more generous fraction (for example one-fiftieth) and 7 per cent a less generous rate (for example one-eightieth).

- Ninety-eight per cent of schemes provide a lump-sum death-in-service benefit.

- Ninety-seven per cent of schemes provide a dependant's pension.

- Sixty-three per cent of schemes provide an additional children's pension.

- Seventy-one per cent of schemes guarantee some increase to pensions currently being paid.

- Sixty-nine per cent of schemes have member trustees.

- Fifty-nine per cent of schemes allow all part-time employees to join, but 12 per cent do not allow any part-timers to join.

- Seventy-nine per cent of schemes allow new employees to join from day one, and in 96 per cent of schemes the qualifying period for membership is one year or less.

The 1994 CBI/Wyatt survey established that the proportions of respondents with different types of scheme were:

- defined benefit schemes   53%
- defined contribution schemes   21%
- group personal pensions   10%
- individual personal pensions   10%
- hybrid schemes   6%

CHOICE OF SCHEME

Considerations to be taken into account when choosing a pension scheme are:

- the organisation's philosophy about the level of pension benefits it wants to provide, which will be dependent on the extent to which it believes it has a moral obligation to offer good benefits and/or the extent to which it believes the level of pension provision will be an important factor in attracting and retaining employees

- costs – level and predictability

- the amount of administration involved.

Cost and predictability considerations are increasing the attractiveness of defined contribution (money purchase) or at least hybrid schemes. According to Self (1995), few defined benefit (final salary) schemes are still being set up. Those that are tend to be confined to situations where the structure of existing pension benefits has to be mirrored in a new scheme for transferring employees.

Where pension benefits are being offered for the first time, a large number of employees are now choosing a money purchase approach. There is also increasing interest in group personal pension arrangements. Some large organisations such as the National Grid and the BBC are using personal pension arrangements as described in the next section to cater for the needs of staff who are on fixed-term contracts.

OTHER ARRANGEMENTS

Personal pension schemes
Under the Social Security Act 1986 employers cannot compel their employees to join their scheme. As an alternative, employees can take out their own personal pension plan. A personal pension plan is a scheme which an employee buys individually from an approved provider, either as an alternative to an occupational scheme provided by the employer or because there is no occupational scheme available. Approved providers can be an insurance company, a bank, a building society or a unit trust company.

Personal pension schemes can be contracted out of the state pension scheme and may take contributions from an employer. They are defined contribution (ie money purchase) schemes, which means that the pension is based on what has been paid into the scheme and not on final salary.

The state pension scheme
State pension arrangements are subject to change, and this section is based on the situation in March 1999. The state pension scheme has two parts, as described below.

The State Flat-Rate Benefit (SFRB)
The SFRB is paid at a standard rate which may be increased each year as long as the required number of National Insurance contributions have been paid. Since 1940 the retirement age has been 65 for men and 60 for women, but it is due to be equalised at 65 by 2020.

The State Earnings-Related Pension Scheme (SERPS)
SERPS pays a pension on earnings for which Class 1 National Insurance contributions have been paid over the years which fall between the lower and the upper earnings limit. The lower earnings limit corresponds roughly with the flat-rate pension (SFRB) for a single person while the upper limit is currently about eight times the lower earning limit. Both limits are adjusted from time to time.

Contracting out

Employers and individuals with a personal pension plan can contract out of SERPS. From November 1986 to 6 April 1997 the scheme had to provide a guaranteed minimum pension (GMP) roughly equivalent to what the individual would have obtained through SERPS.

The arrangements from 6 April 1997 under the Pensions Act 1995 are that no new GMPs will be built up although all existing GMP rights will be preserved. Occupational pension schemes will be able to contract out if they meet an overall quality test. When a scheme is contracted out, both the employer and the employee pay National Insurance contributions at a lower rate. Contracting out is supervised by the Pensions Occupational Board.

ADVISING EMPLOYEES ON PENSIONS

Personnel specialists should be aware of the restrictions placed by the Financial Services Act 1986 on the giving of financial advice. Only those who are directly authorised by one of the regulatory organisations or professional bodies are permitted to give detailed financial advice on investments. There is no problem in giving the following advice to employees:

- They can be informed about the company's occupational pension scheme, since it is not classed as an investment.

- They can be told about the general principles to be borne in mind when comparing an occupational pension scheme with a personal pension. These could include spelling out the benefits of the company's scheme, thus leaving employees in a better position to compare the benefits with whatever an authorised adviser may indicate are the benefits from a personal plan. What should not be done is to tell people categorically that they will be better off with the company's scheme or to advise them to look elsewhere.

- They can be informed of the general advantages of making additional voluntary contributions.

Personnel specialists should therefore avoid giving specific advice on the merits or otherwise of a particular personal pension plan – personal pensions are classed as investments by the Financial Services Act. Any person not authorised to do so who does give specific advice could be guilty of a criminal act, even if he or she had no financial interest in making or preventing the sale.

The problem of what advice, if any, to give may arise if an early leaver approaches a member of the personnel department and asks what he or she should do: preserve their rights in the company's scheme, transfer those rights to the employee's new company, take out a policy with an insurance company, or take out a pension with a personal pensions provider. These can be highly technical questions and personnel specialists should always err on the side of caution in dealing with them. It is best to refer the questioner to the company's own pension specialist or adviser or, if none is available, suggest that the employee should talk to an authorised adviser – for example, the individual's own insurance company or bank. Departing employees can be given information on what their rights will be if they preserve their pension and advised to find out from their prospective employer whether existing rights can be transferred to their scheme, and if so, what the outcome will be in terms of pension rights at the new company. Personnel specialists may also have to be prepared to answer such questions from people they are recruiting or at least refer them to someone who can answer them. But they should always restrict themselves simply to giving information. They should never suggest what people should do.

THE FUTURE OF PENSIONS

The government announced in 1998 that it proposed to retain the basic state pension but discontinue the state earnings-related scheme which will be replaced by a Second State Pension. It will also introduce the 'stakeholder pension' which will be on a defined contribution basis, low-cost and flexible.

SUMMARY

- Pensions are provided by the state and by employers. Schemes made available by employers are designed to provide employees with security by currently building up rights which will give a guaranteed income to them or their dependants on retirement or death.

- The reasons for providing a pension are, first, that it demonstrates that the organisation is concerned about the long-term interests of its employees, and second, that it helps to attract and retain high-quality people.

- An occupational pension scheme is an arrangement under which an employer provides pensions for employees when they retire, income for the families of members who die, and deferred benefits to members who leave. A 'group scheme' is the typical scheme which provides for a number of employees.

- In a contributory scheme employees as well as employers make contributions to the pension fund.

- The main types of pension schemes are *defined benefit* commonly known as a final salary scheme, *defined contribution,* commonly known as a money purchase scheme, *executive (top hat) pensions, group pension schemes* and *hybrid schemes.*

- A defined benefit or final salary scheme offers a guaranteed pension which is calculated as a fraction of final pensionable earnings for each year of service (typically one-sixtieth).

- In a defined contribution or money purchase scheme employers fix the contributions they want to pay for employees by undertaking to invest a defined percentage of earnings irrespective of the benefits available on retirement.

- Executive pension plans are arrangements for 'topping-up' pensions for directors or senior executives.

- In a group personal pension scheme employees have their own personal pension contracts, and the scheme is, in effect, a bundle of individual personal pensions.

- Hybrid schemes combine final salary and money purchase arrangements in various ways.

- As at March 1999 the state pension scheme has two parts: the State Flat-Rate Benefit (SFRB) and the State Earnings-Related Pension Scheme (SERPS). The government is proposing a number of fundamental changes to these arrangements.

- Under the Financial Services Act 1986, only those who are directly authorised by one of the regulatory organisations or professional bodies are permitted to give detailed financial advice on investments. Personnel specialists must avoid giving specific advice on the choice of pension schemes.

FURTHER READING

REARDON, A. M. (1993) *Pensions Handbook*. London, Longman.
OLDFIELD, M. (1994) *Understanding Occupational Pensions*. Croydon, Tolley.

Part 8

MANAGING THE REWARD SYSTEM FOR SPECIAL GROUPS

32 Directors and senior executives

Probably no aspect of remuneration has attracted as much attention in recent years as that of the pay of directors and senior executives. The outcry over top executive reward levels led to the creation of the Greenbury Study Group and the review of the remuneration of directors and chief executives of privatised utilities by the House of Commons Employment Committee, both of which published their findings in 1995. These reports followed that of the Cadbury Committee in 1993 on the financial aspects of corporate governance, which made a number of important recommendations on the remuneration of directors. More recently, the London Stock Exchange in 1997 produced its listing requirements relating to remuneration, and in 1998 the Halpern Committee produced its combined code on corporate governance following its 1997 report.

This chapter starts with an analysis of the pay scene for directors and senior executives and continues with a summary of the findings of the bodies referred to above, all of which significantly affect approaches and attitudes to pay at the top. The chapter concludes with a description of the various types of executive bonus and share schemes – namely, short-term and longer-term bonus schemes, share options, and other forms of long-term incentive.

By the end of the chapter the reader should understand the main provisions made by various bodies on top pay, the role of the remuneration committee and the factors affecting decisions on the remuneration of directors and senior executives. The reader should also be in a position to contribute to discussions on how reward packages can be constructed at this level.

THE REWARD SCENE AT THE TOP

The National Institute of Economic and Social Research (1994) has shown that, in the firms covered by their survey, directors' pay rose in real terms (ie discounting inflation) by 77 per cent between 1985 and 1990, while over the same period average earnings in those firms rose by only 17 per cent. Between 1980 and 1994, IDS (1995) reports that the earnings of chief executives increased by around 250 per cent while those of manual employees increased by about 150 per cent. How has this happened, and what impact has it had on performance?

Until the late 1970s differentials between executives and the rest of the workforce were relatively low, largely as a result of national incomes policies which depressed pay generally and that of executives most of all. Those were the days when the demand from the boardroom and the Institute of Directors was for 'more headroom' – ie wider differentials. This *cri de cœur* was answered in the 1980s when the enterprise culture made greed respectable. Basic executive pay levels increased much more rapidly than pay generally, and this was the decade when executives' share options and uncapped bonus schemes (ie schemes with no upper limit) came into their own.

Another powerful argument used then (and now) was that top executives had to benefit from the high demand for their services and the need to secure their loyalty against the attractions of a competitor. This market argument has been invoked whenever high levels of executive pay have been criticised. It is protested loudly and at length that 'Unless we keep up with what other organisations are paying, our key executive will be headhunted away.'

But to what extent is this market-rate argument valid? The market for top executives in large companies is very small. It can hardly be called a market at all in the real sense of the word. And IDS (1995) has commented that:

> For many top executives, the market has become a modern mantra, invoked every time they face criticism over excessive pay rises.... The market for top executives is not defined in the usual way, by the trading of commodities (executives themselves), but by comparability with similar employees in other organisations, as defined by salary surveys. When top executives talk about the market, what they actually mean is comparability. Real markets play no role at all.

And in their guidelines for remuneration committees the Institute of Directors (not notorious for advocating limits on the pay of directors) states that 'It is important that Remuneration Committees and Boards should avoid setting remuneration packages which are generous in relation to market levels and beware of pressure always to be in the "upper quartile".' The IOD also pointed out the limitations on the extent to which market comparisons, especially international comparisons, are relevant.

Comparability studies could be biased because they select inappropriate comparators or even firms which are known to be high payers. The practice of basing comparisons on high-paying concerns is one that only a disreputable management consultant retained by a remuneration committee would indulge in.

There is also the question of the extent to which high levels of remuneration for directors and executives improve the performance of the firm. The NIESR (1994) found a clear relationship between board-level pay and sales growth, although this finding does not reveal whether higher pay resulted in higher sales or higher sales resulted in higher pay. However, the survey did show that there was only a weak link between board pay and returns to investors. In the USA a study by Berlet and Cravens (1991) of the pay-for-performance of 163 US companies from 1987 to 1989 revealed that the relationship between executive pay and company financial performance was virtually random.

It is possible that a few well-publicised examples of what many people regard as excessive pay-outs to chief executives and directors have misrepresented reality. The Monks Partnership 1995 survey of the earnings of directors in companies worth an equivalent of £50 million in 14 countries showed that British directors were bottom of the international league, with directors' pay averaging £52,000. Directors in Switzerland receive most – about £140,000.

Whether justified or not, fury about the 'gravy train' for top executives resulted in the reports, guides and regulations summarised below.

The Cadbury report

The report of the Cadbury Committee in 1993 on the Financial Aspects of Corporate Governance made the following recommendations concerning the remuneration of directors.

- Directors' service contracts should not exceed three years without shareholder approval.

- There should be full and clear disclosure of directors' total emoluments and those of the chairman and the highest-paid UK director, including pension contributions and stock options.

- Separate figures should be given for salary and performance-related elements, and the basis upon which performance is measured should be explained.

- Executive directors' pay should be subject to the recommendations of a remuneration committee made up of non-executive directors.

- The chief executive role should be separated from that of the board chairman (as a counter to remuneration policies dominated by the chief executive).

The Cadbury Committee's report increased the amount of disclosure and led to a large number of remuneration committees being set up. But this remedy did not work. More information on pay resulted in a greater outcry, and remuneration committees consisting of non-executive directors were criticised on the assumption (not necessarily true) that such committees would be filled by 'old pals' who were also executive directors in other companies and would support higher pay because it was in their own interest.

The House of Commons Employment Select Committee's report

This 1995 report recorded the agreement of the Committee that there should be no direct legal control of executive pay and that the main responsibility for overseeing boardroom rewards rests with shareholders. The majority view of the committee was that in principle service contracts should be for no longer than 12 months. This was in response to huge severance payments for directors on a typical three-year contract. It was also recommended that shareholders should be given the right to approve any new incentive schemes for directors of listed companies.

The Greenbury report

The 1995 Greenbury report expressed the belief that 'UK companies mostly deal with directors' remuneration in a sensible and responsible way'. However, the report did add:

> We fully understand the concerns which shareholders, employees and the public have expressed in recent times about executive remuneration and compensation payments. There have been, in our view, mistakes and misjudgments.

The key recommendations of the report are as follows:

Remuneration committee

- This should consist exclusively of non-executive directors and should determine remuneration policy and the reward packages of individual executive directors.

- A report from the committee should form a self-contained section of, or annex to, the annual report.

- The chairman of the remuneration committee should attend the company's AGM to answer questions about directors' remuneration.

Disclosure of executive remuneration

- The remuneration committee report should include statements on remuneration policy and the methods used to form that policy.

- Listed companies should make full disclosure of named individual directors' remuneration – levels and components of pay, performance criteria and measurements, pension provision, contracts of service and compensation arrangements for early termination.

- Information on share options should conform with the Accounting Standards Board's Urgent Issues Task Force Abstract 10.

Remuneration policy

- Remuneration committees must provide a remuneration package sufficient to attract, retain and motivate directors but should avoid paying more than is necessary. They should be sensitive to wider issues – eg pay and employment conditions elsewhere in the company.

- Performance-related elements should be designed to align the interests of directors and shareholders.

- Any new longer-term incentive arrangement should, preferably, replace existing executive share option plans, or at least form part of an integrated approach which should be approved by shareholders.

- The pension consequences and associated costs to the company of increases in base salary should be considered.

Service contracts

- Notice or service contract periods should be set at, or reduced to, a year or less. However, in some cases periods of up to two years may be acceptable.

- Remuneration committees should take a robust line on the payment of compensation where performance has been unsatisfactory.

- Companies should consider paying compensation wholly or partly in instalments and reducing or stopping payment where a former director takes up a new job.

The Stock Exchange Listing Requirements Relating to Remuneration 1997

The main provisions are:

- A remuneration committee should be in place to advise on the policy governing executive directors' remuneration. They should advise on specific packages for each executive director, including pension rights and compensation arrangements.

- Remuneration committees should provide the packages needed to attract, retain and motivate directors of the quality required but should avoid paying more than is necessary for this purpose.

- Remuneration committees should judge where to position the company relative to other companies. They should be aware of what comparable companies are paying and should take account of relative performance.

- Remuneration committees should be sensitive to the wider scene, including pay and employment conditions elsewhere in the group, especially when determining annual salary increases.

- The performance-related elements of remuneration should be designed to align the interests of directors and shareholders and to give directors the incentive to perform at the highest levels.

- There is a strong case for setting notice or contract periods at, or reducing them to, one year or less.

The Hampel Report January 1998

This report laid the foundations for pulling together the Cadbury and Greenbury recommendations, as well giving its own views on corporate governance. The key principles for directors' remuneration it set out are that:

- Levels of remuneration should be sufficient to attract and retain the directors needed to run the company successfully.

- The component parts of remuneration should link rewards to corporate and individual performance.

- Companies should establish a formal and transparent procedure for developing policy on executive remuneration and for fixing remuneration packages.

- The company's annual report should contain a statement of remuneration policy and details of the remuneration of each director.

Committee on Corporate Governance; The Combined Code 1998

This code, incorporating the findings of earlier reports by the Halpern Committee, contained similar provisions to the Stock Exchange Listing Rules in most respects, with the significant additional point that 'the performance-related elements of remuneration should form a significant proportion of the total remuneration package of executive directors'.

REMUNERATION COMMITTEES

All the recent reports and codes on directors' pay have emphasised the importance of having a committee with the responsibility for making decisions on the remuneration of chief executives and directors, including basic salaries, bonus and incentive schemes and targets, policy on share options, pension arrangements, car entitlement and other benefits.

The purpose of remuneration committees is to provide an independent basis for setting the salary levels and the rules covering incentives, share options, benefit entitlements and contract provisions for executive directors. Such committees are accountable to shareholders for the decisions they take, and the non-executive directors who sit on them should have no personal financial interests at stake. They should be constituted as sub-committees of company boards, and boards should elect both the chairman and the members. Greenbury recommends that remuneration committees in larger companies should consist of at least three members.

The role of the remuneration committee is to

- set broad policy for executive remuneration as a whole, as well as the remuneration packages of executive directors and, sometimes, other senior executives

- focus on encouraging corporate performance contribution, and to ensure that individuals are fairly but responsibly rewarded for their individual contribution

- comply with the appropriate codes (the Stock Exchange and Halpern)

- report and account to shareholders directly for their decisions on behalf of the board

- ensure that the relationship between boardroom remuneration and remuneration for employees below this level remains consistent and sensible

- ensure that proper and professional advice is obtained to assist in its deliberations.

Greenbury recommended that the remuneration committee should be supported by a senior executive of the company who has suitable expertise in remuneration issues, and that it should seek external help from consultants as required. The committee should certainly obtain information on remuneration levels and practices in comparable companies from an internal or external adviser.

DIRECTORS' AND EXECUTIVES' REMUNERATION

The main elements of directors' and executives' remuneration are basic pay, short- and long-term bonus or incentive schemes, share option and share ownership schemes, benefits, and service contracts.

Decisions on the base salary of directors and senior executives are usually founded on views about the market worth of the individuals concerned. At this level the positions may not be evaluated through a formal scheme and are frequently excluded from the pay structure, although most companies take some account formally or informally of internal relativities. They may, for example, lay down that directors and senior managers should be paid respectively 70 per cent and 50 per cent of the chief executive's salary.

Remuneration on joining the company is usually settled by negotiation, often subject to the approval of a remuneration committee. Reviews of base salaries are then undertaken by reference to market movements and success as measured by company performance. Decisions on base salary are important not only in themselves but also because the level agreed is likely to be the platform on which so much else rests. Bonuses are expressed as a percentage of base salary, share options may be allocated as a declared multiple of basic pay, and, commonly, pension is a proportion of final salary.

BONUS SCHEMES

Bonus schemes provide directors and executives with cash sums based on the measures of company and, frequently, individual performance. Recent surveys have shown that about 90 per cent of participating organisations have bonus schemes for main board directors.

Aims

The aims of an executive bonus scheme are to

- increase executive motivation, and therefore business performance

- reward individual contributions

- focus the attention of directors and executives on the company's critical success factors and on the achievement of defined objectives

- ensure that total remuneration levels are competitive

- enable executives to share in the prosperity of the business.

How these aims can be specified is outlined below in sections on the bonus period, the performance measures used, how the bonus is related to performance and the size of the bonus.

Bonus scheme period

Bonus schemes may be short- or long-term. A short-term scheme rewards individual directors and executives on the basis of some measure of company and, often, individual performance. Cash payments are usually made annually, although shorter periodicities such as half-yearly are sometimes adopted in fast-moving businesses.

The objection to short-term bonuses (sometimes called STIs, for short-term incentives) is that they encourage 'short-termism' – that is, paying more attention to immediate profits than to the longer-term growth and prosperity of the business. There has therefore been a marked shift in the direction of long-term incentives (LTIs) related to performance over three years or more. (According to Towers Perrin, 40 per cent of the *Financial Times* 'Top 100' companies had such schemes in 1993.) This move has the overwhelming support of the institutional investors who are the majority shareholders in many organisations. They and, increasingly, remuneration committees favour LTIs because such schemes can motivate directors to concentrate on longer-term strategic objectives and so be less influenced by the short-term negative aspects of investment decisions which should pay off in the longer term. A further perceived virtue of LTIs is that they provide a strong retention incentive (the so-called golden handcuff) because payment is not generally made until the end of the prescribed period. Longer-term incentives may be provided in the form of cash and/or shares.

Performance measures

At executive director level most, if not all, the bonus is usually related to the performance of the business as a whole on the grounds that directors are jointly accountable for that performance. Part of the bonus, however, may be related to the achievement of individual targets. Below board level there may be more emphasis on linking bonuses with the achievement of such targets.

Recent surveys have indicated that by far the most used performance criterion is pre-tax profit. The next most popular measure is earnings per share (profit after interest, taxation and ordinary dividends divided by the number of ordinary shares issued by the company), followed by return on capital employed and then cash flow. Profit and earnings per share are the most common criteria used by analysts and the financial press to assess company performance.

Individual targets would be linked with the key result areas of the role. To concentrate attention on these areas and to avoid complicating the scheme, it is best not to have more than three or four factors.

Relating bonus to performance

Performance-related bonuses are related to the achievement of a target. This may simply be the profit target in the annual budget or the longer-term plan. An alternative method of setting a target is to relate it to a minimum level of improvement compared with the previous year or, if the previous year was a poor one, the highest level reached in the previous two or three years. (This avoids setting the target at too low a figure.)

Three levels of payout may then be determined:

- the threshold or trigger-point – the level at which the bonus first becomes payable

- the target

- the maximum bonus or 'cap' – not all bonus schemes have one, although many organisations believe that there should be a limit.

It is quite common for schemes to exclude payment for 'windfall' profits arising from circumstances which are not affected by the quality of the directors' and executives' performance, such as the sale of company assets or favourable movements in exchange rates.

A bonus formula has then to be determined to establish the relationship between the achievement of the levels defined above and the amount paid out. This is sometimes known as gearing, and it could be a simple arithmetical relationship between percentage achievement of target and the percentage bonus. A threshold might be introduced below which no bonus would be paid. It could be the target figure, or slightly below it. There are, however, many variations on this pattern.

Size of bonus
In a short-term scheme the bonus for achieving the target is typically between 20 per cent and 30 per cent of base pay. But the figure can vary considerably. The 1993 Hay *Boardroom Guide* revealed that the average percentages of threshold, target and maximum bonus for main board directors in the companies covered by the survey were 11 per cent, 25 per cent and 37 per cent respectively.

Criteria for directors' and executives' bonus schemes
The criteria for bonus schemes are that:

• Targets should be tough but achievable.

• The reward should be commensurate with the achievement.

• The targets should be quantified and agreed.

• The measures used should refer to the key factors which affect company performance, and these performance areas should be those that can be directly affected by the efforts of those eligible for bonus payments.

• The formula should be simple and clear.

SHARE OPTIONS

Executive share option schemes provide individual directors and executives with the right to buy a block of shares on some future date at the share price ruling when the option was granted. They are a form of long-term incentive on the assumption that executives will be motivated to perform more effectively if they can anticipate a substantial capital gain when they sell their shares at a price above that prevailing when the option was granted. When share options first became popular in the 1980s, one of the attractions was that money received in this way would be subject only to capital gains tax and not income tax, although a subsequent equalisation of income tax and capital gains tax diminished the advantage. The November 1995 budget provided that options granted in share schemes which on the date of grant have a market value of up to £20,000 will not be subject to income tax either on the date of grant or on the date of exercise, and any subsequent increase in the value of the shares under option will be subject only to capital gains tax. Options above that level granted since 17 July 1995 will, however, be subject to income tax.

The two other arguments advanced in favour of executive share options are that, first, it is right for executives to share in the success of their company, which, it is assumed, they have contributed to; and, second, they encourage executives to align their interests more closely with those of the shareholders as a whole. The first point is valid as long as the reward for exercising share options is commensurate with the contribution of the executive to the improved performance of the business. The second point is dubious. The vast majority of shares acquired in this way are sold almost immediately and the gain is pocketed as extra income.

APPROVED SHARE OPTION SCHEMES

For a scheme to be approved by the Inland Revenue,

- The grant price must be the market price at the time of grant. Options can be issued at a discount of up to 15 per cent off the market value but only if the company operates a share purchase scheme open to all employees. Greenbury, however, recommended that discounting should not be allowed.

- The amount granted to any one individual may not exceed four times his or her emoluments for the current or preceding year.

- The option is not transferable.

Institutional shareholder restrictions

Institutions such as the National Association of Pension Funds and the Association of British Insurers have been concerned about the way in which some share options have operated and have produced guidelines which it would be inadvisable for any company to ignore. Perhaps the most important of these guidelines is that options may be exercised only if appropriate performance criteria are laid down by a remuneration committee which demonstrate 'sustained and significant improvement in underlying financial performance'. This provision recognises the fact that increases in share prices can take place to which directors and executives have made no contribution. Another feature of executive share options which has been fairly universally condemned is that executive share option holders can only gain from their options. Unlike shareholders, they cannot lose.

The future of share options

Share options have been severely criticised recently because of the enormous gains made by some executives in the privatised industries where the initial share price was set at an artificially low level. There is a strong feeling among the institutions and some companies that share options do not achieve community of interest between executives and shareholders and are in effect no more than a form of cash bonus in which the pay-out has little or nothing to do with the executive's performance.

Share option schemes may continue because they are well understood and have become an accepted feature of executive remuneration. But since the tax advantage has been reduced companies may be more interested in developing schemes which are medium- to long-term and are designed to deal with pay for performance, accountability and shareholder alignment. Such schemes may require personal investment in shares.

SHARE OWNERSHIP SCHEMES

Share ownership schemes are relatively uncommon in the UK, but more interest is now being expressed in them as an alternative to share options. Their aim is to align the interests of the executive with the shareholder, which means that they take the same risks – they can lose as well as gain, which is not the case with share options. The main methods available are:

- restricted share schemes – in which shares are held for executives in a trust for a predetermined period (two or three years or more), which means that they cannot be sold during that time. Dividends may or may not be sold during this period. At the end of the restricted period the shares are 'vested' – ie handed over to the executive, but usually only if a performance criterion has been met, such as increase in shareholder value against a group of comparators over the period. For example, in the Reuters scheme, if the performance criterion of total shareholder return is completely met, all rights granted to shares will be vested. If the criterion is not met, the executive will receive no shares. In between these extremes the executive will receive some shares depending on the degree to which the criterion is satisfied.

- bonus-paid-in-shares arrangements – under which executives may elect to take their annual bonus in cash or in restricted shares. If they choose shares, the amount may be increased considerably (often doubled, in which case the shares are offered at half price).

BENEFITS

Employee benefits for executives may amount to over 20 per cent of the total reward package. The most important element is the pension scheme, and directors may be provided with a much higher accrual rate in a final salary scheme. This means that, typically, the maximum two-thirds pension can be achieved after 20 years' service rather than the 40 years it takes in a typical one-sixtieth scheme. Additional pensions through unapproved pension schemes (which do not attract income tax exemptions) may be provided to take the director's pension above the maximum amount permitted in an approved pension scheme (the 'cap').

Directors and executives may receive the same range of benefits as other staff but on a larger scale (a bigger car) or in the form of more generous arrangements for such benefits as medical care.

SERVICE CONTRACTS

Three-year service contracts for directors, which have been fairly typical, attracted much adverse publicity in the middle 1990s because of the high severance payments to departing chief executives and directors, even when it was suspected or actually the case that they had been voted off the board because of inadequate performance. Following the outcry and the Greenbury report, rolling contracts for directors are likely to be restricted to one year in most cases.

THE IMPACT OF PERFORMANCE-RELATED PAY ON EXECUTIVES

Research conducted by Morris and Fenton-O'Creevy (1996) found that 'Equitable base pay does not motivate people to stay; it is the variable element and the pay-performance link which do this.' Their overall conclusion was that 'The variable element of the reward and a clear pay-performance link were strong predictors of the motivation to stay and to perform well.'

SUMMARY

- The Cadbury, Greenbury and Hampel reports and codes on directors' pay have all emphasised the importance of having a committee with the responsibility for making decisions on the remuneration of chief executives and directors, including basic salaries, bonus and incentive schemes and targets, policy on share options, pension arrangements, car entitlement and other benefits.

- The main elements of directors' and executives' remuneration are basic pay, short- and long-term bonus or incentive schemes, share option and share ownership schemes, benefits, and service contracts.

- Bonus schemes provide directors and executives with cash sums based on the measures of company and, frequently, individual performance. Recent surveys have shown that about 90 per cent of participating organisations have bonus schemes for main board directors.

- Executive share option schemes provide individual directors and executives with the right to buy a block of shares on some future date at the share price ruling when the option was granted. They are a form of long-term incentive on the assumption that executives will be motivated to perform more effectively if they can anticipate a substantial capital gain when they sell their shares at a price above that prevailing when the option was granted.

- Share ownership schemes are relatively uncommon in the UK, but more interest is now being expressed in them as an alternative to share options. Their aim is to align the interests of the executive with the shareholder, which means that they take the same risks – they can lose as well as gain, which is not the case with share options.

- Employee benefits for executives may amount to over 20 per cent of the total reward package. The most important element is the pension scheme, and directors may be provided with a much higher accrual rate in a final salary scheme.

FURTHER READING

Because of the constantly changing executive pay scene following the various reports and new income tax regulations, any book (or chapter) on this subject becomes out of date almost immediately. *Just Reward? The Truth about Top Executive Pay* by A. P. Williams (Kogan Page, 1994) is the best and most recent book on the subject although it was published before Greenbury and Halpern. In Armstrong and Murlis,

Reward Management (Kogan Page, 1998) executive incentive and bonus schemes are described in some detail in Chapter 27 and executive share schemes are dealt with in Chapter 37. Examples of incentive schemes are given in Appendix H. To keep up to date, the monthly IDS *Management Pay Review* is essential reading.

33 International pay and expatriates' rewards

Businesses may be involved internationally in any of the following activities:

- manufacturing, with the aim of extending the market for their products or as a result of inducements by overseas governments

- marketing or selling, through agents or direct to customers

- service industries which operate in foreign locations, such as airlines, hotels and telecommunications.

In these circumstances parent companies may transfer staff to work abroad as expatriates for periods of from a few months to a number of years, although there is an increasing tendency to rely on nationals of the overseas country who will be recruited locally. (This may be encouraged or required by the governments concerned.)

Companies may also supply technical expertise to an overseas country. It could be on a 'turnkey' basis, where help is provided in building a factory or a power station which on completion is handed over as a going concern. Alternatively, the business may supply teams of skilled people, such as maintenance engineers to a Middle Eastern country.

The main types of expatriate workers are:

- employees transferred to an overseas operation for two or three years who then return to the parent company: this may be on special assignment or it could be part of a career development programme

- 'long-term mobile' employees who pursue most of their career abroad, changing assignments from time to time or moving up a promotion ladder

- contract employees who are engaged for a predetermined period, often two to three years, to provide specific skills for the company on an overseas project

- third-country nationals (TCNs) whose home country is not that of their employer but who are assigned to a third country – for example, a citizen of the US working in France for a British company.

The employment of expatriates can raise a number of personnel and development policy issues. Among them is the problem of persuading people to work abroad, perhaps in unpleasant locations. Or people may have working partners who do not want their career disrupted. Career planning may also be a problem: an employee's career must not be prejudiced by absence abroad. But the major issue concerns remuneration and other terms and conditions of employment (pay, allowances, benefits) as discussed in this chapter.

At the end of the chapter the reader will understand the basic principles governing expatriates' reward and the alternative methods available.

EXPATRIATE PAY

There are two basic approaches to devising expatriate pay packages: home-based pay and host-based pay, as described below.

Home-based pay

The home-based pay approach aims to ensure that the value of the expatriate's salary is the same as in the home country. The home-base salary may be a notional one for long-term assignments (ie the salary which it is assumed would be paid to expatriates were they employed in a job of equivalent level at the parent company). For shorter-term assignments it may be the actual salary of the individual.

The notional or actual home-base salary is used as the foundation upon which the total remuneration package is built. This is sometimes called the 'build-up' or 'balance sheet' approach.

The policy of most organisations which employ expatriates is to ensure that they are no worse off because they have been posted abroad. In practice, various additional allowances or payments, such as hardship allowances or incentive premia (as described in the next section of this chapter), mean that they are usually better off financially than if they had stayed at home.

The salary 'build-up' starts with the actual or notional home-base salary. To it is added a cost-of-living adjustment which is applied to 'spendable income' – the portion of salary which would be used at home for everyday living. It usually excludes income tax, social security, pensions and insurance, and can exclude discretionary expenditure on major purchases or holidays on the grounds that these do not constitute day-to-day living expenses. The cost of housing in the home country (mortgage payments) is a special case. It is usually treated separately, consideration being given to factors such as the housing arrangements in the host country and any income earned from renting the home property.

Spendable income varies widely, although Employment Conditions Abroad (ECA), the consultancy specialising in expatriate remuneration, says that it averages 65 per cent of salary. The cost-of-living adjustment is usually based on the overseas cost of living indices produced by organisations such as ECA. Thus, if the index for an overseas location were 120 (UK = 100) and the spendable income were 65 per cent of home-base salary, an individual whose notional UK salary was £30,000 would receive a cost of living allowance of £3,900:

The expatriate's salary would then consist of the actual or notional home-base salary plus the cost of living adjustment. In addition, it may be necessary to adjust salaries to take account of the host country's tax regime in order to achieve tax equalisation. Moves of less than a year which might give rise to double taxation require particular attention.

Some or all of the following allowances as described later in the chapter may be added to this salary:

- 'incentive to work abroad' premium

- hardship and location allowance

- housing and utilities allowance

- school fees

- 'rest and recuperation' leave.

The expatriate's total home-based remuneration package would consist of this sum plus, as appropriate, pension, insurance, company car and home leave.

Total earnings expressed in the local currency may be paid entirely to the expatriates in their host country. Generally, however, the salary is split between the home and host countries. Expatriates can then pay for continuing domestic commitments such as mortgage and insurance payments and build up some capital. (The opportunity to acquire capital is often a major inducement for people to work as expatriates.)

Surveys conducted by the CBI (1994) and ECA (1994) established that the great majority of British organisations use the home-based pay method. Home-based pay can at least ensure that expatriates will not be worse off through working abroad and can be developed as an attractive package. It can also be used for third-country nationals using their own country salary as a base. But it can be costly, and an Industrial Data Services (IDS) 1995 survey found that a number of companies wanted to cut back on expatriate packages.

The other problem with home-based pay is that it can create inequities between the remuneration of expatriates and that of their colleagues who are nationals of the host country. If a number of third-country nationals from different parts of the world are employed, home-based pay can create an even more complicated situation. As noted by IDS, some companies are therefore changing or considering changing to a host-based system as described below.

A variation on the home-based approach is the so-called budget system, which assesses the costs incurred by the expatriate in both the home country and the host country. These combined costs are expressed in the currency of the host country and grossed up for tax. But it can be a time-consuming and costly system to administer and is little used.

Host-based pay
The host-based pay approach provides expatriates with salaries and benefits such as company cars and holidays which are in line with those given to nationals of the host country in similar jobs.

The host-based method ensures equity between expatriates and host country nationals. It is adopted by companies using the so-called market-rate system, which ensures that the salaries of expatriates match the market levels of pay in the host country for similar jobs.

Companies using the host-based approach commonly pay traditional allowances such as school fees, accommodation and medical insurance. They may also fund long-term benefits like social security, life assurance and pensions from home.

The host-based method is certainly equitable from the viewpoint of local nationals, and it can be less expensive than home-based pay. But it may be much less attractive as an inducement for employees to work abroad, especially in unpleasant locations, and it can be difficult to collect market-rate data locally to provide a basis for setting pay levels.

TAX CONSIDERATIONS

A key concern when calculating expatriates' pay and benefits package is tax liability. Either a tax equalisation or a tax protection policy can be adopted. A tax equalisation policy means that employees' pay is kept in line with the level of pay they would have received at home. They neither gain nor lose. A tax protection policy means that the company makes up the difference if expatriates pay more tax abroad, but if the tax is less, they keep the difference. Fewer companies use the latter approach.

ALLOWANCES

Housing and utilities
A housing allowance for renting overseas accommodation may be provided (with an upper limit) or free housing may be available. The cost of utilities can be high, and if it is felt not to be covered adequately by the cost of living adjustment, a special allowance to cover extra costs may be paid.

School fees
The cost of boarding schools for the expatriate's children may be paid, with an upper limit or as a percentage (eg 75 per cent) of the cost of fees. Such an allowance is usually reserved for expatriates on long-term assignments or those who are likely to be moved over a number of years to different overseas locations.

Rest and recuperation leave
Expatriates and their families living in hardship areas may be entitled to free trips to more pleasant locations for fairly brief periods (up to a week).

BENEFITS

Expatriates retain home-based benefits such as pension and insurance. They may be entitled to a company car or an appropriate allowance in the host country, but this may be restricted to the level of car other local country employees receive. Home leave flights may be paid for once a year or more frequently from particularly unpleasant locations.

SUMMARY

- There are two basic approaches to devising expatriate pay packages: home-based pay and host-based pay.

- The home-based pay approach aims to ensure that the value of the expatriate's salary is the same as in the home country.

- The host-based pay approach provides expatriates with salaries and benefits such as company cars and holidays which are in line with those given to nationals of the host country in similar jobs.

- A key concern when calculating expatriates' pay and benefits package is tax liability.

FURTHER READING

EIU (1995) *Determining the Expatriate Package.* New York, Economic Intelligence Unit.

ARMSTRONG, M. AND MURLIS, H. (1998) *Reward Management.* Fourth edition, London, Kogan Page, Chapter 38.

34 Rewarding sales staff

Personal selling is the key element in the promotional mix. The other elements – advertising, sales promotion and publicity – are, of course, important, but in most organisations that sell goods or services to customers it is the person-to-person contact that counts. Sales people operate at what they sometimes refer to as the 'sharp end' of the business, where, they claim, they are primarily responsible for generating sales turnover and, therefore, profit. Because of the nature of their work, sales people have traditionally been more results-oriented than other salaried employees. Their efforts can easily be measured in quantified terms such as sales volume, profit, gross margin or contribution to profit and the fixed expenses of the business. (Contribution is defined in accounting terms as sales revenue minus the variable costs of material, labour and other expenses.) Increasingly, the customer service aspect of their work – creating and maintaining customer satisfaction and generating repeat business – is being measured through consumer reaction surveys and more sophisticated methods of quantifying continuing sales to satisfied customers.

These aspects of the role of sales representatives combine to create the belief in many organisations that sales people are unique and should therefore be treated differently from all other employees. Whether this is true or not, reward packages for sales staff are often designed and operated quite separately from the reward system applied to other employees. Sales people, for example, are much more likely to have a significant proportion of their earnings at risk – that is, dependent on their performance. Indeed, they are sometimes entirely dependent on their performance for income when they are on commission-only terms. Sales staff are often excluded from the job evaluation system and their base rates will be more influenced by market rates – job mobility is generally much higher than in other occupations because companies tend to adopt competitive pay policies to attract high performers from other firms.

This perceived difference means that in some businesses it is the sales management team that decides on the payment systems – the personnel function may not be consulted. But the basic principles of reward and motivation described earlier in this book apply to sales people just as much as to other staff. And it can be disruptive if the sales force is treated as a special case without reference to reward strategies and policies elsewhere in the organisation. Personnel and pay specialists should therefore have much to offer in the way of advice on developing reward systems for the sales force which motivate its members effectively. In the rest of this chapter, general approaches to rewarding sales people are considered first, and then the different approaches to paying sales representatives are examined – namely basic salary and performance-related pay, commission schemes and bonus schemes.

At the end of this chapter the reader should be able to offer sound advice on the principles that affect the design and administration of a remuneration package for the sales force. He or she will understand the different approaches available, and the advantages and disadvantages of each of them.

GENERAL CONSIDERATIONS

There are no hard-and-fast rules governing how sales people should be paid. It depends on the type of company, the products or services it offers its customers, and the nature of the sales process – how sales are organised and made. The factors that affect sales force rewards are:

- the types of product, service and customers
- the type of sales staff employed
- how sales are organised – in territories and/or in teams
- the influence sales people have on sales, and the difficulties they meet in achieving their targets
- the sales cycle.

Types of products, services and customers
The products or services offered by the company and the types of customer to whom they are sold will have an important influence on the type of sales staff required and how they will function. Sales representatives who promote ethical pharmaceutical products to doctors will clearly require different qualifications and abilities from those developing new outlets for fast-moving consumer goods and taking orders from existing ones. They will operate differently and their reward package will need to be tailored to what they do and how they do it.

Types of sales staff
Sales people can be divided into three broad categories:

- direct sales people – those who sell directly to customers in a territory, over the telephone or over the counter
- account managers – those who develop and maintain relations with accounts, often on a national or industrial basis
- technical support – those who provide continuing technical support as sales engineers, technical sales representatives, etc.

Different approaches may be required to reward staff in each of these categories. Direct sales staff may receive commissions and/or a bonus. Account managers may be paid a target-related bonus but could be on a basic salary plus performance-related pay. Technical support staff are most likely to be on a basic salary with the possibility of performance-related pay.

The organisation of sales

The extent to which sales representatives are operating internationally, nationally, in a large region or area, or in a well-defined territory will influence how they are rewarded. The reward arrangements for a representative working throughout, for example, the European Union will be very different from those of one operating in a closely-defined territory in south-east London.

The extent to which sales depend on teamwork will affect the use of entirely individual payment systems or approaches which recognise the fact that sales staff are interdependent and sales are achieved only by joint action.

Types of sales activities

Sales activities can be divided broadly into three categories:

- customer identification – following up leads, cold calling and local market analysis

- customer development – direct selling, demonstrating, merchandising, providing a consultancy advice, overseeing customer service delivery, handling queries and complaints

- direct selling – face-to-face or by tele- or written communications.

The mix of these and any other related activities should be analysed when deciding on the most appropriate form of remuneration.

Sales prominence and difficulty

Sales prominence, as defined by Moynahan (1991), is a measure of the sales person's impact on the buying decision. It captures the relative influence of the sales person compared with the influence of pricing, advertising, product quality, the sales force organisation structure and the level of customer service.

The role of the individual sales representative in 'closing' a sale is likely to be much more prominent when there is

- considerable competition on price, quality or service

- a weak company image

- low product acceptance

- a new product or service to be sold

- a new territory to be developed involving much prospecting for customers, cold calling, and opening and nursing new accounts

- little support from advertising or promotion

- low-level support from other parts of the company

- a creative rather than a routine sales message to be delivered

- little or no repeat business.

Competitive salaries and generous commission or bonus schemes may be required to attract and retain staff who can overcome these problems. When some sales territories are easier than others from the point of view of achieving profitable sales it could be hard to reward staff fairly. Pay, commission or bonus may have to be adjusted to take account of the relative ease or difficulty of sales, so that, for example, a representative who opens up a new territory would receive a special bonus for sales generated from new accounts.

The sales cycle

If a considerable period elapses between making the contact and closing the sale, involving prolonged negotiations, it will be difficult to reward individuals simply on the basis of the sales volume they eventually generate. In these circumstances sales are more likely to be achieved by team rather than individual effort, and staff may not receive any immediate form of individual bonus or commission. If it is felt that some form of incentive pay is appropriate, it may be shared between team members and/or staged over the sales cycle, successful accomplishment of a stage in the negotiations resulting in a bonus payment.

THE REWARD MIX FOR THE SALES FORCE

The main elements of the sales reward mix as described in the rest of this chapter are basic salary, commission, bonus, and other motivators such as incentives (rewards in kind in the form of gifts, travel vouchers, etc), competitions and non-financial rewards generally.

Basic salary

Some organisations, such as Albright & Wilson, BP Oil, Digital, Lombard North Central and Pilkington Glass, pay basic salary only. Although salary progression is likely to be performance-related in companies like these, there are no specific commission or bonus schemes related solely to sales volume or the achievement of sales targets. This approach may be adopted when companies want to discourage 'quick sales at all costs' attitudes and actions. Their main concern is to encourage sales staff to build up long-term relationships with their customers, the emphasis being on customer service rather than on high-pressure selling.

Research by Langley (1987) and colleagues established that a company may adopt a salary-only policy when

- there is a high incidence of non-selling activity in the representative's job

- representing the company is a more important part of the job than direct selling

- sales staff have little or no influence on sales volume

- the industry's products are demand-led

- there are 'ethical' reasons for eschewing bonuses or commission.

Basic salary only may also be paid to sales staff who work in

- highly seasonal industries where sales fluctuate considerably

- 'route selling' – milk, bread, drink, etc

- businesses where regular orders for food and other consumer goods give little opportunity for creative selling.

Performance-related pay arrangements for companies which do not pay commission or bonus will be based on agreed objectives and, increasingly, an assessment of competence in such areas as teamwork, customer relations, interpersonal skills and communications.

Companies with a salary-only policy have to adopt competitive pay policies if they want to attract and retain high-quality staff. They have to take account of the regular total earnings of sales staff in markets from which they recruit people or where their own staff move. If they cannot or do not want at least to match average earnings, they may have to offer other inducements to join or stay with the company. These can include opportunities for promotion, learning new skills, more stable pay and greater security.

The advantages of a salary-only or 'straight salary' approach are that it

- encourages customer service
- discourages too high-pressure selling
- helps in team selling situations where it is difficult to apportion the credit for sales between team members
- avoids the problem of over- or under-rewarding staff who are lucky enough to have been allocated a good territory or unlucky enough to have been landed with a poor one
- protects income when sales vary considerably for reasons beyond the sales person's control
- gives sales managers more scope to change the territories or responsibilities of sales representatives.

The disadvantages are that it

- limits the ability of the company to use pay as a means of shaping or modifying behaviour
- may attract unadventurous, under-achieving sales representatives
- results in high achievers' subsidising low achievers
- increases fixed selling costs because pay costs cannot be varied in line with business results.

Sales managers have traditionally believed that the disadvantages of a fixed salary policy considerably outweigh the advantages, especially when sales people can make a direct and significant impact on sales performance. Many still hold to this view, although, increasingly, the emphasis on customer service and the reaction against high-pressure selling are convincing them that a straight salary approach is advantageous, or at least that the proportion of bonus or commission in relation to total earnings should be much lower. Team pay, as at Norwich Union, may also be regarded as more appropriate in situations when the results depend largely on teamwork.

Basic salary plus commission and/or bonus

Although the advantages of basic salary only may be becoming more apparent in some businesses, many companies still believe that the special nature of selling and the type of person they need to attract to their sales force requires some form of additional bonus or commission to be paid. This is intended to act as an incentive and as a reward and a means of recognising achievement. The different types of commission or bonus scheme are considered later in this chapter, but a policy decision has to be made on what percentage of total earnings should be variable or at risk. The proportion of the reward package that is represented by high-risk pay is sometimes called leverage.

Leverage is likely to be high when creative personal selling and highly-developed persuasive skills are required to get customers to buy. But leverage will be lower when sales staff are mainly order-takers, when customer service is an important factor, or when sales people spend a considerable proportion of their selling day in non-selling activities. It may be even lower (or non-existent) in high-technology businesses when the sales force is involved in persuasive communication with highly-trained engineers or buyers and sales representatives must possess the technological know-how to talk to these people on equal terms.

Commission as a percentage of earnings has traditionally been high in the financial services sector, although the adverse publicity given to the high-pressure selling of personal pension plans is changing this situation. A survey conducted in 1990 by Remuneration Economics showed that in all sales functions commission amounted to 32.8 per cent of earnings. In the pensions and investment sector, however, commission was 44.3 per cent, and in financial and business services it was 46.5 per cent (the highest sector of all). Commission is much lower in the food, drink and tobacco sector (5 per cent) and in fast-moving consumer goods (9.6 per cent).

It is suggested by Holmes and Smith (1987) that there is no single right answer to what the split should be between basic salary and commission or bonus. But they do say that 'It is difficult to imagine that an incentive of less than 20 per cent of total compensation would be perceived as an attractive reward by sales people, least of all as one that will motivate them to extraordinary performance.'

Commission plans

Commission plans provide sales representatives with payments based on a percentage of the sales turnover they generate. The simplest form of plan is straight commission, by which the sales person receives only a commission on sales and no basic salary. More commonly, commission is paid in addition to a basic salary.

Straight commission

Commission-only plans may be adopted when

- the performance of sales staff depends primarily on their personal selling ability and can be measured by short-term results – ie immediate sales

- representatives are not required to perform any non-selling activities

- continuing relations with customers are relatively unimportant.

They are most common in the home improvement and direct-selling insurance businesses.

The advantages of commission-only plans are that they

- attract high-performing sales people who are willing to share the risks of the business

- provide a direct financial incentive to maximise sales

- ensure that selling costs vary directly with sales results

- convey a message to poor performers that they might do better elsewhere

- eliminate the need for close supervision.

The disadvantages are that they:

- encourage sales people to take a short-term view, 'milking' mature territories or good customers and neglecting to pursue new sales opportunities

- focus the attention of representatives on sales volume rather than on profitable sales

- can lead to high-pressure selling which does not take into account the real needs of customers

- provide the same pay-outs irrespective of the time taken to secure the sale, thus offering no incentive to quick sales

- lead to lack of identification on the part of representatives with the company or its products.

Commission-only schemes are attractive to companies that want to maximise sales volume in the short term and do not worry too much about long-term customer relations. They are less attractive to businesses where the emphasis is on developing and maintaining continuing profitable business by means of a skilled, loyal and committed sales force.

Salary plus commission
Salary-plus-commission plans provide for a proportion of total earnings to be paid in commission, the rest in the form of a fixed salary. The proportion of commission varies widely. As a general rule it is higher when results depend on the ability and effort of individual representatives and/or when there is less emphasis on non-selling activities.

The commission element of a salary-plus-commission plan may be designed to operate flexibly. Higher rates may be paid for new business.

Differential rates may be attached to different products so that sales people will focus their efforts on more profitable areas.

The commission may be calculated as a fixed percentage of all sales, possibly with a 'cap' or upper limit on commission earnings. Alternatively, an accelerating commission rate formula may be adopted which increases the rate at a series of sales-value thresholds – for example, 5 per cent up to £250,000 of sales per quarter, 7.5 per cent on sales between £250,000 and £300,000, and so on. This is designed to encourage sales staff to strive for even higher sales.

The advantages of salary-plus-commission plans are that they

- enable the company to emphasise the importance of non-sales as well as selling activities

- facilitate the development of a flexible approach to rewarding sales people in accordance with the relative profitability of the products they sell or in situations where they may need to move good staff to new and more difficult territories or to selling new products

- attract sales people who are prepared to spend time on building long-term relationships by providing high levels of customer service rather than 'going for the quick buck'.

But many organisations think that relating pay – even a proportion of pay – directly to sales volume is too crude an approach for any reasonably sophisticated selling operation. And even if more flexible approaches are adopted they can become too complex and thereby detract from their value as motivators. This is why some businesses prefer to use bonus schemes.

Bonus schemes
Bonus schemes provide pay in addition to basic salary which is related to the achievement of defined and, preferably, agreed targets. The latter may refer simply to sales volume or profit, and such bonus arrangements are akin to commission schemes, with one vital difference – they are based on the achievement of targets rather than on an essentially crude percentage of whatever sales have been attained. Such bonus plans, which are often called quota schemes, therefore clarify expectations of what is to be accomplished and have defined levels of achievement which will be rewarded.

More sophisticated bonus schemes are based on rewarding sales people for their achievements in relation to a range of agreed objectives or targets. These may include not only overall sales but also such aspects of the sales representative's role as:

- sales of selected or new products

- sales to new accounts

- reviving moribund accounts

- the incidence of bad debts

- the quality of service to customers

- how well customer complaints are handled

- the volume of repeat or continuing business

- the number of productive calls made

- product knowledge and technical expertise

- the provision of information on competitors

- working effectively as a member of a sales team

- effectiveness in running a sales territory, including the quality and timeliness of reports and the control of expenses.

The bonus may be calculated by awarding points according to performance against each of the agreed objectives and targets. The points are translated at the end of the bonus period (which may be only two or three months) into flat-rate payments of so much a point, or converted to a percentage of salary.

Bonus schemes can also be more discretionary, along the lines of a standard performance-related pay scheme. In such cases an overall decision is made on the level of bonus payable in percentage terms by reference to achievement over the whole range of targets. This is somewhat more subjective than a points scheme.

The total pay package may consist of basic salary plus bonus or basic salary plus bonus and commission. In the latter case the commission is related to sales volume and the bonus is based on achievement in less quantifiable aspects of the sales person's job, such as product knowledge or customer service (although levels of customer service can be quantified by means of customer reaction surveys).

Bonuses are paid as a lump sum to individuals, although they may be divided between team members when sales are based on team efforts. The Remuneration Economics 1990 survey found that the average bonus was 8.2 per cent of earnings, and 43.9 per cent of the survey sample received a bonus.

Bonus plans may pay a bonus of, say, 10 per cent only when the sales target has been achieved. A higher bonus is paid for achievement above target, possibly on a straight-line basis – eg 0.5 per cent for every 1 per cent above target – although some schemes pay an accelerated bonus – eg 0.5 per cent for every 1 per cent of target up to 110 per cent of target, and 1 per cent for every 1 per cent of target between 110 and 120 per cent. The total bonus may be 'capped' at a maximum of, say, 120 per cent of target.

Alternatively, a threshold of, say, 90 per cent of target is set at which a bonus of 5 per cent is payable and the bonus thereafter increases in steps of, say, 5 per cent – 10 per cent for hitting the target, 15 per cent when sales reach 110 per cent of target, and 20 per cent for sales amounting to 120 per cent of target.

There is no standard formula. Every business must determine its own plan in the light of an assessment of its circumstances and needs. This will cover the nature of the sales operation, the type of sales people employed and how they can best be motivated, what the bonus scheme is intended to achieve, and how much money should be spent on bonuses.

Variations to the basic plans described above consist of

- the size of bonus for achieving the target

- the maximum bonus that will be paid out (if it is decided to cap the scheme)

- the formula for relating bonus to sales – this will cover any threshold and the relationship between additional bonus and increased sales (eg straight-line or accelerating)

- the figures to be used for bonus purposes – the most common figure is sales revenue, but some companies use profit or contribution/gross margin (sales revenue minus variable expenses) to demonstrate that they want sales people to concentrate on increasing profit or selling products with higher gross margins rather than just going for volume sales

- the extent to which other factors are included in the bonus plan, such as quality of customer service, sales to new accounts and number of productive calls made – if such items are included, a points system is often used so that sales representatives receive so many points for meeting or exceeding each of their objectives and targets, and the total score is converted into cash.

The advantages and disadvantages of bonus schemes
The advantages of bonus schemes are that they

- provide flexibility in determining the basis of reward

- can be used to define expectations and modify behaviour by highlighting the key result areas of the sales person's job and indicating priorities in terms of what should be sold and non-selling activities

- enable management to change territory structure and sales targets easily while preserving adequate levels of incentive

- can be adapted to reward sales teams as well as individuals.

The disadvantages of bonus schemes which incorporate a range of objectives and targets are that they

- can be complex to administer and hard to understand

- may confuse sales representatives, who could be diverted from their main task of generating profitable sales

- may be perceived by sales people as unfair because they seem to rely on subjective judgements by management on their performance

- do not have the clear-cut relationship between results and rewards which exist in commission plans and bonus schemes that are based entirely on the achievement of sales targets.

CHOICE OF APPROACH

The factors that affect a choice between the main methods of payment are, broadly,

- basic salary only when the aim is to build and maintain long-term relationships with customers through non-selling activities

- salary plus commission where a more flexible approach is required and non-selling activities are important

- salary plus bonus where flexibility in providing rewards for different aspects of the sales task is important and where attention needs to focus on more profitable lines and the various selling and non-selling activities which contribute to effective sales performance

- salary plus commission and bonus where the company wants to get the best of both worlds – a clear link between sales revenue and reward and the scope to modify behaviour by rewarding particular aspects of the sales representative's performance. But this approach can be unduly complex.

DEVELOPING A COMMISSION OR BONUS SCHEME

Commission or bonus schemes should be developed on the basis of an understanding of the particular requirements of the business and a definition of how the scheme should meet them. It is necessary first to decide what behaviours are needed and then to determine how to encourage those behaviours.

Development programme
The development programme should consist of the following stages:

- Analyse requirements. This means assessing all the factors concerning the sales operation listed at the beginning of this chapter.

- Define objectives. What is the scheme intended to achieve?

- Involve the sales force. Obtain the views of field sales management and the sales representatives themselves about what sort of approach they would prefer.

- Decide on the approach. In the light of the initial analysis and the consultation process decide broadly on the type of scheme or combination of schemes.

- Design the scheme in detail, defining the criteria, how performance will be measured and the relation between results and reward. The design should cover not only the formula linking performance and rewards but also when bonuses should be paid. Timely feedback is essential to ensure that a bonus scheme is motivational, and there is more to be said for frequent pay-outs, say every quarter, than waiting until the end of the year. If business is highly seasonal, some companies hold back a proportion of the bonus until the year end so as not to overpay in one period, thus encouraging the workforce to leave in the knowledge that there are leaner times ahead. In general, payments should be made often enough to motivate sales representatives but far enough apart to conform to the company's sale cycle and to ensure that targets can be hit in the time allowed.

- Test the formula. As far as possible test the formula retrospectively, using actual sales figures to calculate what levels of rewards would be obtained and, importantly, how much the scheme will cost in terms of pay-outs (the impact on gross margin).

- Consider the implications. Assess whether the levels of reward that can be achieved by the scheme are likely to ensure that capable and well-motivated staff join and stay with the company.

- Consult the sales force. Check the proposed scheme with field sales management and sales representatives to obtain their views on how it could be improved.

• Modify the scheme as required in the light of the processes of testing, considering the implications and consultation.

• Introduce the scheme, ensuring that everyone understands how it operates and how they will benefit from it.

It is essential to monitor the scheme thoroughly after it has been introduced. The impact of the scheme and reactions to it should be assessed, and the results should be evaluated. If any aspects of the plan need to be modified – and some usually do – it should be done without delay. It is desirable when introducing the scheme to spell out that it will be monitored and evaluated carefully and that it may be subject to change.

OTHER METHODS OF MOTIVATION

There are other and sometimes more effective ways of motivating people besides cash, and for sales representatives they include incentives, competitions, perks and non-financial rewards generally.

Incentives

Gifts, travel vouchers, 'candle-lit dinners for two', etc, can be used as incentives. They provide tangible rewards and a means of recognising achievement which can usefully reinforce or supplement cash payments. The fact that gifts can be shared with the sales representative's family or partner may increase their value as a reward.

Gifts can be linked with achieving specified targets, but care has to be taken not to reward only the high-flyers and demotivate those who are doing a good but not spectacular job. And unrealistic targets will only create a cynical reaction.

Remember that gifts are subject to income tax.

Competitions

On the reasonable assumption that the nature of good sales people is essentially competitive, many businesses organise competitions in which prizes are awarded to the individuals or teams who, for example, create most new business, achieve the highest sales of a particular product or service (which the company wants to promote) or receive the most satisfactory feedback reports from customers. However, competitions can demotivate those who do not win prizes, and they should be designed to ensure that all those who are doing well feel that they have a good chance of winning or at least gaining a prize. (It is advisable to be reasonably generous in the distribution of prizes, even token ones.)

Cars as perks

The stereotype of the sales rep is of someone who proudly burns up the motorway miles in this year's two-litre model and returns home in it to impress the neighbours. Like all stereotypes this may be an exaggeration, but to sales representatives cars are a major tool of the trade and reps can be motivated by the opportunity to get a bigger and better one if they are particularly successful. Some companies do not like doing this because it is easier to give people a car than to take it away from them – the demotivational impact of removing a better car may be much greater than the motivational effect of giving it in the first place. Other companies have attempted to avoid the problem by allocating better cars as prizes which can be retained by the sales representatives for the next six months or a year and, possibly, won again at the end of that period.

Non-financial motivators

Good sales people are natural achievers but they should still be given the scope to use their natural talents, and even people with very high levels of achievement motivation still like their successes to be recognised. Additional training, the opportunity to take on a more challenging and potentially rewarding role and greater responsibility, either in a managerial capacity or for handling larger accounts, can also act as motivating forces.

Recognition is very important. Of course financial rewards, incentives and prizes are highly tangible forms of recognition, but praise for work well done will underpin such rewards, and public recognition – 'applause' – can be even more valuable. The motivational impact of inviting successful sales representatives to attend an overseas conference – an international one if the company conducts its business globally – can be considerable.

SUMMARY

- There are no hard-and-fast rules governing how salespeople should be paid. It depends on the type of company, the products or services it offers its customers and the nature of the sales process – how sales are organised and made.

- The main elements of the sales reward mix are basic salary, commission, bonus and other motivators such as incentives (rewards in kind in the form of gifts, travel vouchers, etc), competitions and non-financial rewards generally.

- Some organisations, such as Albright & Wilson, BP Oil, Digital, Lombard North Central and Pilkington Glass, pay basic salary only. Although salary progression is likely to be performance-related in companies like these, there are no specific commission or bonus schemes related solely to sales volume or the achievement of sales targets. This approach may be adopted when companies want to discourage 'quick sales at all costs' attitudes and actions. Their main concern is to encourage sales staff to build up long-term relationships with their customers, the emphasis being on customer service rather than on high-pressure selling.

- Commission plans provide sales representatives with payments based on a percentage of the sales turnover they generate. The simplest form of plan is straight commission, by which the sales person receives only a commission on sales and no basic salary. More commonly, commission is paid in addition to a basic salary.

- Bonus schemes provide pay in addition to basic salary which is related to the achievement of defined and, preferably, agreed targets.

• There are other and sometimes more effective ways of motivating people besides cash, and for sales representatives they include incentives, competitions, perks and non-financial rewards generally.

FURTHER READING

The best general text is Langley (1987), which is research-based and includes some good examples of incentive schemes. John Moynahan's book (1991) is very comprehensive. Chapters 10 (pp. 150–60) and 14 (pp. 187–200) provide the most useful guidance on the choice and design of reward packages.

Part 9

MANAGING EMPLOYEE REWARD SYSTEMS

35 Managing employee rewards

Reward systems incorporate complex processes which deeply affect everyone in the organisation and generate considerable costs. Payroll budgets have to be formulated and controlled, the implementation of reward policies has to be audited and monitored, procedures have to be set up and managed, line managers and the personnel department have to work together in dealing with pay issues, reward policies are communicated to employees, individuals have to be informed of how they are affected by pay policies and decisions, employees and their representatives are involved in developing reward processes and informed of reward policies, consultation and negotiations take place, and resources have to be mobilised to develop the system, which may mean seeking outside help from management consultants. All these matters are dealt with in this chapter. At the end of the chapter the reader will understand:

- the basis upon which management can be advised on reward policies
- the principles to be followed in implementing the policies
- how to audit, monitor and evaluate the effectiveness of reward policies and practices
- how to prepare reward forecasts and budgets, costing changes and ensuring value for money
- the reward procedures which must be developed and administered to manage the reward system
- the respective responsibilities of line managers and personnel professionals for administering employee rewards
- how to advise managers on pay practices and decisions
- how to communicate to employees individually and collectively on reward policies and proposals

- how to employ management consultants.

Approaches that can be adopted to conducting general and individual pay reviews, including policy formulation and implementation, are considered in the next chapter. The use of the computer in employee reward is dealt with in Chapter 37.

POLICY ADVICE AND IMPLEMENTATION

The content of reward policies and methods of formulating and reviewing them were described in Chapter 8. Policy should always be formulated in consultation with top management, who will need to be convinced that any proposals produced by the personnel function will add value.

Policy advice
Policy advice should spell out

- why the new policy is required or the existing policy has to be changed

- the benefits that will result from the implementation of the policy: these should be quantified as far as possible in terms of improved performance or cost savings

- the resources required to develop and implement the policy, including the use of management consultants as necessary

- the costs of developing and implementing the policy, including:

  - the costs of using management consultants

  - opportunity costs arising from diverting management and personnel resources to the development programme

  - increases in payroll costs arising from a job evaluation exercise or a revision of the pay structure

  - the costs of new or improved employee benefits

- the programme for development and implementation

- how managers and employees will be involved in developing the new policy

- how the policy should be communicated to employees.

Policy implementation
The policies should be implemented by means of a carefully planned and managed project. The normal rules of project management should apply – namely:

- The objectives should be defined in terms of what has to be achieved, and why.

- A project director should be appointed with clear accountability to the board, a steering committee or a senior manager for the success of the project.

- A project plan should be prepared, setting out the timetable, the resources required, the cost budget and the responsibility for each part of the programme.

- Arrangements should be made for monitoring and reporting on progress, which should include designating review points in the form of 'milestones' at crucial stages of the project.

- Procedures should be set up for evaluating the outcome of the project against its objectives.

Policy administration

The effective administration of reward policies depends on setting up appropriate procedures as described in the next section of this chapter, ensuring that line managers and personnel specialists work effectively together in managing them, monitoring policy implementation, and carrying out regular audits to ensure that the policies are working well and giving value for money. A balance has to be struck between, on the one hand, the need for controls to ensure consistency and, on the other, the need for flexibility in administering the policies, giving line managers a reasonable degree of freedom to act within their budgets and in accordance with policy guidelines. The problem of achieving this balance can be alleviated if the policy guidelines are not too rigid. So far as possible, policies should be expressed in ways which allow managers a reasonable degree of freedom to decide how they should be applied in the light of local circumstances.

AUDITING, MONITORING AND EVALUATING THE REWARD SYSTEM

Auditing the system

An audit of the reward system as described in Chapter 9 should consist of:

- an analysis of each component of the reward system to assess its effectiveness, the extent to which it is adding value, and its relevance to the present and future needs of the organisation

- an assessment of opinions about the reward system by its key users and those who are affected by it: this may be conducted by means of interviews or through attitude surveys and/or focus groups

- a diagnosis of strengths and weaknesses, leading to an assessment of what needs to be done, and why.

Monitoring the implementation of pay policies and practices

Monitoring should be carried out continually by the personnel department through such audits and by the use of compa-ratios, as discussed below. In particular it is necessary to analyse data on upgradings, the effectiveness with which performance management processes are functioning, and the amount paid out on pay-for-performance schemes and the impact they are making on results.

Internal relativities should also be monitored by carrying out periodical studies of the differentials that exist vertically within departments or between categories of employees. The study should examine the differentials built into the pay structure and also analyse the differences between the average rates of pay at different levels. If it is revealed that because of changes in roles or the impact of pay reviews differentials no longer properly reflect increases in job values and/or are no longer 'felt fair', further investigations to establish the reasons for the situation can be conducted and, if necessary, corrective action taken.

External relativities should be monitored by tracking movements in market rates by studying published data and conducting pay surveys as described in Chapter 13.

Evaluating the reward system

No reward innovations should take place unless a cost-benefit analysis has forecast that they will add value. The audit and monitoring processes should establish that the extent to which the predicted benefits have been obtained and check the costs against the forecast.

Compa-ratio analysis

A compa-ratio (short for 'comparative ratio') measures the relationship in a graded pay structure between actual and policy rates of pay as a percentage. The policy value used is the midpoint or reference-point in a pay range which represents the target rate for a fully competent individual in any job in the grade. This point is aligned with market rates in accordance with the organisation's market stance.

Compa-ratios are used to define where an individual is placed in a pay range. The analysis of compa-ratios indicates what action may have to be taken to slow down or accelerate increases if compa-ratios are too high or too low compared with the policy level. The process is sometimes called 'midpoint management'.

A compa-ratio of 100 per cent means that actual pay and policy pay are the same. Compa-ratios which are higher or lower than 100 per cent mean that pay is respectively above or below the policy target rate. For example, if the target (policy) rate in a range was £20,000 and the average pay of all the individuals in the grade was £18,000, the compa-ratio would be 90 per cent.

Compa-ratios establish differences between policy and practice. The reasons for such differences need to be established. They may be attributable to one or more of the following factors:

- differences in aggregate performance levels or performance ratings

- differences in average job tenure – average tenure may be short if people leave the job through promotion, transfer or resignation before they have moved far through the range, and that would result in a lower compa-ratio; a higher ratio may result if people tend to remain in the job for some time

- the payment of higher rates within the range to people for market reasons which may require recruits to start some way up the range

- the existence of anomalies after implementing a new pay structure

- the rate of growth of the organisation – a fast-growing organisation may recruit more people towards the bottom of the range or, conversely, may be forced to recruit people at high points in the range because of market forces: in a more stable or stagnant organisation, however, people may generally have progressed further up their range for a lack of promotion opportunities.

Some differences may be entirely justified; others may need action, such as accelerating or decelerating increases or exercising greater control over ratings and pay reviews.

Analysing attrition

Attrition or slippage takes place when employees enter jobs at lower rates of pay than the previous incumbents. If this happens, payroll costs will go down, given an even flow of starters and leavers and a consistent approach to the determination of rates of pay. In theory attrition can help to finance pay increases within a range. It has been claimed that fixed incremental systems can be entirely self-financing because of attrition, but the conditions under which this can happen are so exceptional that it probably never does.

Attrition can be calculated by the formula: *total percentage increase to payroll arising from general or individual pay increases* minus *total percentage increase in average rates of pay*. If it can be proved that attrition is going to take place, the amount involved can be taken into account as a means of at least partly financing individual pay increases. Attrition in a pay system with regular progression through ranges and a fairly even flow of starters and leavers is typically between 2 per cent and 3 per cent, but this should not be regarded as a norm.

REWARD PROCEDURES

Reward management procedures are required to achieve and monitor the implementation of reward management policies. They deal with methods of fixing pay on appointment or promotion and resolving anomalies. They also refer to methods of appealing against grading or pay decisions, usually through the organisation's normal appeals procedure.

Procedures for grading jobs

The procedures for grading new jobs or regrading existing ones in a conventional graded structure may lay down that grading or regrading can take place only after a proper job evaluation study in order to control grade drift. Pressure to upgrade because of market forces or difficulties in recruitment or retention should be resisted. These problems should be addressed by such methods as market premiums or creating special market groups of jobs.

However, in a more flexible broad-banded structure, job evaluation may not be used to check on movements within the band. It may only be undertaken when a new job is created and its position in the band structure has to be determined. In these increasingly typical situations, job evaluation takes on a supporting role and may seldom be used. Market forces may be dealt with by fixing new anchor points in the band as described in Chapter17. Rates of pay may be market-driven and adjusted whenever a case can be made that it is necessary to keep pace with external pay levels.

Fixing rates of pay on appointment

Line managers should have a major say in pay offers and some freedom to negotiate when necessary, but they should be required to take account of relevant pay policy guidelines which set out the circumstances in which pay offers above the minimum of the range or zone can be made. It is customary to allow a reasonable degree of freedom to make offers up to a certain point – eg the 90 per cent level in an 80–120 per cent pay range. Pay policies frequently allow offers to be made up to the midpoint or reference-point in a graded structure or the anchor rate in a broad-banded structure, depending on the extent to which the recruit has the necessary experience, skills and competences. In a conventional structure, offers above the midpoint should be discouraged because they would leave relatively little room for expansion. Such offers are sometimes made because of market pressures, but they need to be very carefully considered because of the inevitability of grade drift unless the individual is promoted fairly soon. If the current rates are too low to attract good candidates, it may be necessary to reconsider the scales or to agree on special market-rate premiums. To keep the latter under control, it is advisable to require that they cannot be awarded unless they are authorised by the HR department or a more senior manager. Many organisations require that all offers be vetted and approved by a member of the HR function and/or a higher authority. In a broad-banded structure there will be more flexibility but it is still essential to ensure that offers above the anchor point are justified.

Promotion increases

In a conventional graded structure promotion increases should be meaningful, say 10 per cent or more. They should not normally take the promoted employee above the midpoint or reference-point in the pay range for his or her new job, so that there remains adequate scope for performance-related increases. One good reason for having reasonably wide differentials is to allow space for promotion. In a broad-banded structure a move to a different role in the same or a higher band is treated as if it were a new appointment and the salary is set within the zone for the role at a point which depends on the individual's assumed level of competence in that role. Lateral movements through the band as roles expand are dealt with in accordance with an assessment of the level of the individual's contribution in the expanded role and by reference to the rate of pay of other people who are carrying out work at a similar level.

Dealing with anomalies

Within any pay structure, however carefully monitored and maintained, anomalies will occur and they need to be addressed during a pay review. Correction of anomalies will require higher increases for those who are underpaid relative to their performance and time in the job, and lower increases for those who are correspondingly overpaid. It is worth noting that overpayment anomalies cannot be corrected in fixed incremental structures, and this is a major disadvantage of such systems. The cost of anomaly correction should not be huge in normal circumstances if at every review managers are encouraged to 'fine-tune' their pay recommendations as suggested earlier. In broad-banded systems it is much easier to monitor rates of pay to prevent the occurrence of anomalies, but if they do arise, there is sufficient flexibility in the arrangements for progressing pay to enable managers to propose adjustments which may completely correct the anomaly or, if the gap is very high, which may be phased to achieve a target rate of pay over a longer period of time.

In a severely anomalous situation, such as may be found at the implementation stage of a new structure or at a major review, a longer-term correction programme may be necessary either to mitigate the demotivating effects of reducing relative rates of pay or to spread costs over a number of years.

As well as individual anomaly correction there may be a need to correct a historical tendency to overpay or underpay whole departments, divisions or functions by applying higher or lower levels of increases over a period of time. This would involve adjustments to pay review budgets and guidelines, and it would obviously have to be handled with great care.

Appeals

There should be an appeals procedure which enables employees to query decisions about their pay.

RESPONSIBILITY FOR REWARD

The trend is to devolve more responsibility for pay decisions to line managers, especially those concerned with individual pay reviews. As Murlis and Wright (1993) point out: 'Devolution of remuneration practice goes with devolution of decision-making and accountability.'

Devolution implies that managers are given the authority to decide on pay increases as long as they keep within their budgets and follow policy guidelines. The latter may be quite broad. But there are obvious dangers. They include inconsistency between managers' decisions, favouritism, prejudice (gender or racial) and illogical distribution of rewards. Research has shown that many managers tend not to differentiate between the performance of individual members of their staff. Ratings can be compressed, so that most people are clustered around the midpoint and very few staff are rated as good or poor performers.

Devolving more authority to line managers may in principle be highly desirable but managers must be briefed thoroughly on their responsibilities, the organisation's pay policies (including methods of progressing pay), the principles to be followed in conducting reviews, and how they should interpret and apply pay review guidelines. The need to achieve equity and a reasonable degree of consistency across the organisation should be emphasised. Managers should be given whatever training, guidance and help they need to ensure that they are capable of exercising their discretionary powers wisely. Such training should cover:

- how information on market rates supplied by the personnel department should be interpreted and used

- how data provided by the personnel department on the levels of pay and pay progression histories of individual members of staff and the distribution of pay by occupation throughout the department should be used as the basis for planning pay

- methods of assessing performance and contribution levels – as Murlis and Wright (1993) indicate: 'The performance management process needs to be put firmly into place as an integral part of the general management process'

- how to interpret any generic competence profiles to assess individual development needs and agree career pathways

- how to assess competence requirements for specific roles (as they exist now or as they may develop), and how to counsel employees on the preparation of personal development plans

- methods of reviewing progress in achieving these plans and in career development, and how to interpret information from the reviews when making pay decisions

- generally, how to distribute rewards within budgets, fairly, equitably and consistently by reference to assessments of contribution, competence, progress or growth

- the guidance available from the personnel function on how to manage pay – it should be emphasised that guidance must always be sought if line managers have any doubts as to how they should exercise their discretion.

However, it is usual for senior managers, personnel or pay specialists to monitor pay proposals to spot inconsistencies or what appear to be illogical recommendations, especially when the scheme is initiated or with newly appointed managers. The use of computerised personnel information systems makes it easier for managers to communicate their proposals and for the personnel department to monitor them. If the personnel department is involved, it should offer support and guidance, not act as a police force. Monitoring can be relaxed as managers prove that they are capable of making good pay decisions.

COMMUNICATING TO EMPLOYEES

Employee reward systems communicate messages to employees about the beliefs of the organisation on what is felt to be important when valuing people in their roles. They convey two messages: this is how we value your contribution; this is what we are paying for. Reward policies and practices likewise affect two of the major concerns of people at work – what and how they are paid now; what pay opportunities will be available in the future. Even if legitimate doubts can be held about relying on financial incentives to motivate people, they will not work at all if those affected are not aware of the behaviours expected of them if they are to receive greater rewards and how rewards will be related to those behaviours. Reward systems will demotivate if they are not 'felt fair', and how can employees know whether they are fair or not if they do not understand how they function or how they are affected by them? Certainly, employee reward will motivate only if people are told that what they have got is worth having – if that is the case – and, even more important, informed of what they can expect to get. This is in line with what is perhaps the key motivational theory relating to reward: expectancy theory.

It is therefore important to communicate to employees collectively about the reward policies and practices of the organisation and individually about how those policies affect them – now and in the future. Transparency is essential.

What to communicate to employees generally
Employees generally should understand:

- the reward policies of the organisation in setting pay levels, providing benefits and progressing pay

- the pay structure – grades and pay ranges and how the structure is managed

- the benefits structure – the range of benefits provided, with details of the pension scheme and other major benefits

- methods of grading and regrading jobs – the job evaluation scheme and how it operates

- pay progression – how pay progresses within the pay structure, and how pay decisions affecting employees collectively and individually are made

- pay-for-performance schemes – how individual, team and organisation-wide schemes work, and how employees can benefit from them

- pay for skill or competence – how any skill-based or competence-based schemes work, the aims of the organisation in using such schemes, and how employees can benefit from them

- performance management – how performance management processes operate, and the parts played by managers and employees

- reward developments and initiatives – details of any changes in the reward system, the reasons for such changes, and how employees will be affected by them: the importance of doing this thoroughly cannot be over-emphasised.

What to communicate to individual employees
Individual employees should know and understand:

- their job grade and how it has been determined

- the basis upon which their present rate of pay has been determined

- the pay opportunities available to them – the scope in their grade for pay progression, the basis upon which their pay will be linked with their performance and the acquisition and effective use of skills and competences as their career develops, and what action and behaviour are expected of them if their pay is to progress

- performance management – how their performance will be reviewed, and the part they play in agreeing objectives and formulating personal development and performance improvement plans

- the value of the employee benefits they receive – the level of total remuneration provided for individuals by the organisation, including the values of such benefits as pension and sick pay schemes

- appeals and grievances – how they can appeal against grading and pay decisions or take up a grievance on any aspect of their remuneration.

How to communicate collectively

The media of collective communication include employee handbooks and special brochures or handbooks explaining reward policies and procedures and the pension scheme and other benefits. The company magazine and notice-boards can also be used. Written media should be reinforced by briefing consultative committees and through team briefings (face-to face meetings between team leaders and the members of their teams).

How to communicate individually

Individuals will be given details of their terms and conditions in letters of appointment supplemented by handbooks. Changes in those terms will be communicated in writing, including confirmation of pay increases. Some companies produce benefit statements which set out in full the value to employees of their total remuneration package. But the emphasis should always be on face-to-face communication. Letters should be handed over personally by managers, who should explain the basis upon which pay decisions have been made and discuss with individuals what pay opportunities are available to them and what they have to do to benefit from them. However, care has to be taken to ensure that the picture painted to employees about the future is realistic – false expectations must not be created. The value of the total remuneration package can be conveyed through benefit statements which set out how much the individual employee is receiving under each benefit heading.

Conveying information on a face-to-face basis to individual employees is the role of line managers and team leaders, not members of the personnel function. But this task has to be carried out skilfully, and guidance or training should be provided on how to perform it.

INVOLVEMENT, PARTICIPATION AND NEGOTIATION

The need to treat employees as stakeholders has been stressed throughout this book. Employees should be given every opportunity to participate and contribute to the decision-making processes concerning the development of reward policies and practices. This is a matter of involvement in working parties, project teams and panels, not just consultation, although the normal consultative channels have to be used.

Trade unions and their representatives should take part in the processes of participation and consultation. If they have negotiating rights, it is wise to involve them in the initial stages, to sound out their opinions and reach as much agreement as possible on the way forward. This is particularly important when plans are being made to develop new pay structures and pay-for-performance schemes or to introduce job evaluation. Trade unions have been known to veto the use of a particular brand of job evaluation, and their views should be sought in advance on what they are prepared to support. It may be advisable to discuss major developments in advance with full-time officials at local and even national level.

If there are trade unions with negotiating rights 'across the board', increases will have to be negotiated with them. Proposed changes in the pay structure or methods of payment may also have to be negotiated. If the proposals affect the members of a number of unions, the possibility of 'single-table bargaining' should be explored, if it does not already exist. The aim should be to avoid confrontation, and this is much less likely to happen if trade union representatives are involved at all stages of a development programme.

USING MANAGEMENT CONSULTANTS

Management consultants may be used to supply expertise and additional resources when introducing job evaluation, developing pay structures and pay-for-performance or competence schemes, carrying out pay and benefit surveys and advising on employee benefits and pension schemes. They can conduct diagnostic reviews and employee attitude surveys, provide disinterested advice on reward policies, and carry out independent audits and evaluations of the employee reward system and its components. They can be expensive, but good consultants can add value because they have the knowledge of best practice and experience in managing development projects which may not be available in the organisation. Consultants can add an extra dimension of credibility to any radical proposals for change.

To make good use of consultants it is necessary to

- specify the objectives of the exercise and the 'deliverables' – ie what the consultants are expected to achieve, and the expenditure that can be incurred: consultants should be engaged only if it is clear that they will add value

- select the consultants with great care, ensuring that they have the expertise and experience required, understand the problem, propose deliverables and methodologies which will meet the specification, and are likely to 'fit' the culture and management style of the organisation

- agree explicit terms of reference and a detailed project plan which covers deliverables, the timetable, the resources required and the costs

- ask for regular progress reports and check them against the project plan

- hold regular 'milestone' meetings at prearranged points in the project programme which coincide with the completion of a project stage and the start of the next stage

- scrutinise any proposals made by the consultants thoroughly to ensure that they are relevant to the project objectives, are realistic, and can be implemented with the agreement of those concerned and within the cost budget

- step in quickly if the programme seems to be drifting or the deliverables have not been produced on time, to ensure that corrective action is taken.

SUMMARY

- The reward system should be monitored and evaluated continually by analysing data on upgradings, the effectiveness with which performance management processes are functioning and the amount paid out on pay-for-performance schemes and the impact they are making on results.

- Reward management procedures are required to achieve and monitor the implementation of reward management policies. They deal with methods of fixing pay on appointment or promotion and resolving anomalies. They also refer to methods of appealing against grading or pay decisions, usually through the organisation's normal appeals procedure.

- Within any pay structure, however carefully monitored and maintained, anomalies will occur and they need to be addressed during a pay review.

- The trend is to devolve more responsibility for pay decisions to line managers, especially those concerned with individual pay reviews.

- Employee reward systems communicate messages to employees about the beliefs of the organisation on what is felt to be important when valuing people in their roles. They convey two messages: this is how we value your contribution; this is what we are paying for.

- Employees generally should understand the reward policies of the organisation, the pay and benefits structure, methods of grading and regrading jobs, how pay progresses within the pay structure (contingent pay schemes) and how performance management processes operate.

- Individual employees should know and understand: their job grade and how it has been determined, the basis upon which their present rate of pay and pay increases have been determined, the pay opportunities available to them, how their performance will be reviewed, the value of the employee benefits they receive – the level of total remuneration provided for individuals by the organisation, including the values of such benefits as pension and sick pay schemes – and how they can appeal against grading and pay decisions or take up a grievance on any aspect of their remuneration.

- Employees should be given every opportunity to participate and contribute to the decision-making processes concerning the development of reward policies and practices.

- Management consultants may be used to supply expertise and additional resources when introducing job evaluation, developing pay structures and pay-for-performance or competence schemes, carrying out pay and benefit surveys, and advising on employee benefits and pension schemes.

FURTHER READING

In *Reward Management* (fourth edition, 1998, Kogan Page) by Michael Armstrong and Helen Murlis the items covered by a benefit statement are set out on pp. 566–567, and Chapter 43 goes into more detail on communicating the benefits.

36 Conducting pay reviews

The most visible aspect of the management of employee reward systems is that of conducting pay reviews – either general, 'across the board' reviews, or those affecting individual awards. If this is mishandled, all the work which has gone into developing a 'best-practice' system can be wasted. When the organisation is trying to achieve fairness, equity, consistency and transparency in its reward processes, the pay review is the occasion on which these ideals should be put into practice.

On completing this chapter the reader will be familiar with the practice of conducting general, structural and individual pay reviews including the preparation and control of pay review budgets.

TYPES OF REVIEWS

The three types of reviews are:

- *general or 'across-the-board' reviews* in response to movements in the cost of living or market rates, or following pay negotiations with trade unions

- *structural reviews* which deal with changes required to the pay structure to cater for the need to reflect market rates or to change differentials: these may affect the whole structure or a job family

- *individual reviews* which provide individuals with pay increases in accordance with their contribution.

AIMS

As Armstrong and Murlis (1998) state:

> Pay reviews are a major means of implementing the organisation's reward policies for improving performance and ensuring the continued motivation and retention of employees. They are also the manifestation to employees of those reward policies.

Increases to the payroll following general and individual reviews have to be affordable, and cost constraints may restrict the amount of money available. In times of low inflation, percentage increases may be restricted. This can make it difficult to differentiate rewards sufficiently to reflect levels of performance, competence, skill or contribution. But within financial constraints, the review should aim to satisfy employees' expectations on how they will be rewarded in accordance with their performance and contribution.

Overall, employees expect that general reviews will maintain the purchasing power of their pay by compensating for increases in the cost of living. They will want their levels of pay to be competitive with what they could earn elsewhere. And they, and certainly their union representatives, if any, will be suspicious of any organisation that uses affordability as a reason for a restricted review when the company is clearly prospering (or paying inflated salaries or bonuses to top managers).

Individuals will want the review to be conducted in ways which achieve

- *fairness* – people are appropriately rewarded in relation to their contribution

- *equity* – people are appropriately rewarded in relation to others in the organisation

- *consistency* – the decisions made about pay should be consistent across the organisation and over time in that they do not deviate without good cause from the organisation's pay policies and review guidelines

- *transparency* – employees know the basis upon which pay decisions are made and the reason for the decisions that affect them personally.

The objectives of pay reviews will also have to take into account the views, actions and reactions of trade unions if they have negotiating rights.

GENERAL REVIEWS

General reviews take place when employees are given an increase in response to general market-rate movements, increases in the cost of living or union negotiations. General reviews are often combined with individual reviews but employees are usually informed of the general and individual components of any increase they receive. Alternatively, the general review may be conducted separately to enable better control to be achieved over costs and to focus employees' attention on the performance-related aspect of their remuneration.

Many organisations, however, prefer not to link pay rises explicitly to the cost of living. Their policy is to respond to movements in market rates in order to maintain their competitive position, bearing in mind that increases in market rates are affected by the cost of living. They do not want to be committed to an 'index-linked' approach, even in times of low inflation.

Some organisations have completely abandoned the use of across-the-board reviews. They argue that the decision on what people should be paid should be an individual matter, taking into account the personal contribution people are making and their 'market worth' – how they as individuals are valued in the marketplace. This enables the organisation to adopt a more flexible approach to allocating pay increases in accordance with the perceived value of individuals to the organisation.

Conducting general reviews in a non-union situation

The steps required to plan and implement a non-negotiated across-the-board review are:

1 Agree budget.

2 Obtain and analyse data on market rates of pay, trends in increases made by comparable organisations, and rates of inflation. The data on market rates can be obtained from published pay surveys issued by Remuneration Economics Ltd, The Reward Group, Monks Partnership, and, if the organisation is eligible, Hay Management Consultants. Information on pay settlements, trends and inflation rates can be obtained from the *Pay and Benefits Bulletin* produced by Industrial Relations Services

3 Calculate the cost.

4 Adjust the pay structure – in a conventional graded structure this may mean increasing the pay brackets of each grade by the percentage general increase. Alternatively, only the midpoint of each grade may be increased by the general percentage and different increases given to the upper or lower limits of the bracket, thus altering the shape of the structure. In a broad-banded structure the increase may be applied to the anchor rates, although when such structures exist, the tendency is to avoid general increases and adjust the anchor rates and zones by reference to market-rate movements.

5 Inform employees of the decision and the reasons for taking it.

Conducting negotiated general pay reviews

The following steps should be taken:

1 Obtain and analyse data on pay settlements, movements in market rates and rates of inflation.

2 Agree a target settlement, taking into account affordability, comparability, the effect, if any, on other units, divisions or employee groups in the company, and the balance of power between management and trade unions.

3 Prepare a negotiating brief.

4 Negotiate to achieve the best settlement in accordance with targets.

5 Reach agreement.

6 Implement.

CONDUCTING STRUCTURAL REVIEWS

Reviews of the pay structure are carried out in response to internal changes in the organisation structure or the type and levels of work carried out. Such changes may affect relativities which have to be adjusted. Pay structure reviews may also be initiated by the need to adjust pay levels because of differential changes in market rates. In the latter case, the review may prompt the establishment of job families or may institute changes to the levels of pay and differentials in existing job families.

CONDUCTING INDIVIDUAL REVIEWS

Individual pay reviews determine performance-related, competence-related, contribution-related or skill-based consolidated increases to base pay. Reviews are usually carried out for all employees at a fixed time or times during the year, and it is this type of review that is discussed below. Such pay reviews do not, of course, preclude special increases to individuals at other times because they are carrying out more highly-valued work.

Individual pay reviews may also be concerned with the award of special achievement or sustained good performance bonuses, as additions or alternatives to base pay rate increases. These may be considered as part of a periodical formal review but can be awarded individually at any time if a particular achievement needs to be recognised financially.

The considerations that affect individual pay reviews as discussed below are the size and distribution of awards, the use of ratings, achieving consistency if ratings are used, alternative approaches if there are no overall 'bottom-line' ratings, the link between the pay review and the performance review, the conduct of reviews if rating is not used, and the procedure for conducting reviews.

The size of awards

The size of awards is a matter of what the organisation can afford but will be much smaller in times of low inflation. The IPD 1998 survey of PRP showed that the majority of respondents (58 per cent) made awards of between 1 and 6 per cent to senior managers, although 29 per cent paid more than 7 per cent. However the 1998 IRS survey showed that the average increase to the paybill for merit awards was only 1.5 per cent. Clearly the motivational impact of a low reward is likely to be poor, even non-existent, and 36 per cent of the respondents to the IPD survey said that this was a serious problem (a further 38 per cent thought it was a minor problem). Low awards may constitute a form of financial recognition, but they are not direct motivators.

Some organisations allow for the average size of the award to vary between departments and functions, depending on relative levels of performance. This can be done fairly easily if relative performance can be measured in financial terms as between different profit centres or sales regions. In effect, this would be a performance-related bonus for distribution to all staff in the unit or area. This may be fair if the basis for financial comparisons is in accordance with the same formula and significant differences do not exist between the profit or revenue-earning capacities of the units concerned. It may be more difficult to provide for a demonstrably fair means of distribution when the performance of entirely different functions is compared – for example, sales and finance. One solution adopted by some companies is not to vary the funds available for base pay increase funds but to create a separate bonus fund from which special awards can be made and which can be flexed to respond to particular achievements.

The distribution of awards

The distribution of rewards in terms of size can also be a problem. Some organisations such as Pfizer International and Book Club

Associates contend that it is only necessary to provide for three levels – average, above average and below average – on the grounds that these levels can easily be distinguished and that any further shading will lead to problems in maintaining consistency. Other organisations, more typically, believe that some shading should be provided for, possibly by having four levels: below average, average, above average and exceptional. These levels refer to the amount of the increase, not the capability of the employee. It is generally believed that it is degrading to categorise someone as average (no one can accept that they are 'average' and it is even worse to be told that you are below average). To avoid this semantic problem some companies prefer to use the terms 'normal' for an increase to someone whose performance meets expectations, and 'above' or 'below the norm' to those who exceed expectations or fail to meet them.

It is usual to assume that the distribution of awards should broadly conform to the shape of the normal curve of distribution, although this may be skewed in the direction of the higher levels. Thus, if there were three levels of reward, the expected distribution might be 70 per cent normal, 20 per cent above the norm and 10 per cent below the norm. If there were four levels, the distribution could be 60 per cent normal, 20 per cent above the norm, 10 per cent considerably above the norm and 10 per cent below the norm. There are no rules on distribution. Organisations decide for themselves on the extent to which they want to differentiate between various levels of performance.

Individual pay reviews based on ratings

Individual pay reviews when there is a contingent pay scheme relating pay to performance, competence or contribution are commonly but not universally based on some form of performance and/or competence rating (approaches to rating were examined in Chapter 28). There is a choice of approaches.

1 There is a direct link between the performance or competence rating and the pay increase. For example:

Rating	% increase
A	7
B	5
C	3
D	1–2
E	0

Managers are provided with guidelines on the relationship between pay increases and performance rating and, often, on the distribution of increases and the maximum and minimum increases that can be awarded. They will be required to work within a pay review budget.

2 There is a direct link between performance and competence ratings on a pay matrix which determines percentage increases as shown in Table 31.

Table 31 A performance/competence pay matrix

	Rating	Competence			
		A %	B %	C %	D %
Performance	a	10	7	5	3
	b	7	5	3	2
	c	5	3	2	0
	d	2	0	0	0

3 The increase depends on both the rating and the position in the pay range by using a pay matrix as illustrated in Table 32.

Table 32 A pay matrix

Rating	Position in pay range (compa-ratio)			
	80–90%	91–100%	101–110%	111–120%
Exceptional	12	10	8	6
Very effective	10	8	6	4
Effective	6	4	3	0
Developing	4	3	0	0
Ineligible	0	0	0	0

4 The use of 'equity shares' in organisations such as government departments and agencies and large insurance companies with formal pay structures and systems which relate pay increases precisely to merit ratings. The size of the increase may be determined by a formula which allocates money according to points or 'equity shares'. Thus, so many points could be awarded for a particular level of performance which indicates, according to the value of the points or shares, how much the increase will be. The value of the points is determined by how much money is allocated for distribution. Equity share systems often use software packages to establish the value of shares by reference to the available money.

Achieving consistency in rating

The problem with rating is that it is difficult to ensure that a consistent approach is adopted by managers. Some people may be more generous than others, while others may be harder on their staff. Managers may be unwilling or unable to discriminate between good and poor performers and give everyone, or almost everyone, the same rating (this is known as the 'central tendency' in rating). And sexual discrimination may take place.

Ratings can, of course, be monitored and challenged if their distribution is significantly out of line, and computer-based systems have been developed for this purpose. But many managers want to do the best for their staff, either because they genuinely believe that they are better or because they are trying to curry favour. It can be difficult in these circumstances to challenge them. There are five possible approaches to achieving consistency.

Forced distribution

This requires managers to conform to a pattern which quite often corresponds with the normal curve of distribution on the questionable assumption that performance levels are distributed normally. This is sometimes called a quota system. A typical distribution is shown in Table 33.

Table 33 **Forced distribution**

Rating	%
A	5
B	15
C	60
D	15
E	5

However, in the many evaluations of performance management and performance-related pay that have been conducted over the last few years, forced distributions and quotas have been heavily criticised. There is no certainty that performance or ability is normally distributed within an organisation.

Ranking systems

As described later, ranking systems place staff in order of merit and then distribute performance ratings through the rank order. A typical forced distribution in a ranking system would be to give the top 10 per cent an A rating, the next 15 per cent a B rating, the next 60 per cent a C rating and the remaining 15 per cent a D rating. Such systems ensure a consistent distribution of ratings but still depend on the relative objectivity and accuracy of the rankings.

Training

Consistency workshops can be run with managers from different departments to define the different levels in the rating-scale by reference to actual examples, discuss how ratings are perceived, explore differences, practise rating in 'case-study' performance reviews and, over time, build up a better common understanding and level of comfort with the rating process. This can be extended to bringing managers together after their performance-ratings have been set and getting them to exchange information and, where necessary, justify their distribution of assessments.

Monitoring

Monitoring provides for the rater's manager and possibly the personnel function to check on both the quality of formal performance reviews and the consistency of performance ratings. This process should be supported by training workshops.

Moderating or peer review

This requires getting raters together with their peers to exchange information about the distribution of ratings and to justify them if challenged by colleagues. (It works best if the members of the moderating group are drawn from a function or department where managers know each other well and have regular contacts with at least the more senior members of each other's teams.) It is necessary for such meetings to be facilitated to help participants reach agreed and positive conclusions.

Guidance

The personnel department can play a useful part in helping to achieve fairly distributed and consistent ratings – not by taking on a 'policing' role and compelling managers to accept a forced distribution, but by providing guidance and encouraging managers to reconsider their ratings if they seem misjudged.

Individual pay reviews where there are no overall ratings

It is often assumed that a performance- or competence-related pay review depends upon ratings. But the 1998 IPD research revealed that 24 per cent of the respondents with performance-related pay did not have ratings.

Even when there are no ratings it is still necessary to reach a decision on the level of a pay increase, but this may take the form of a proposal which takes into account a number of factors besides rated performance. These include relativities, market rates and potential. Account may also be taken of the extent to which the individual's salary has unjustifiably fallen behind or risen above the level appropriate to his or her contribution relative to what other people contributing at the same level in the same job are paid. If this is the case, the individual's rate of pay progression may require to be accelerated or decelerated.

This may be called the 'holistic' approach to pay reviews, in which a number of factors are taken into account before reaching an overall conclusion on how an individual should be valued in financial terms. The decision may be expressed in the form of a statement that an individual is now worth £22,000 rather than £20,000. The increase is 10 per cent, but what counts is the overall view of the value of the person to the organisation, not the percentage increase to that person's pay.

At BP Exploration managers propose where people should be placed in the pay range for their grade, taking into account their contribution relative to others in similar jobs and the relationship of their current pay to market rates. This is carried out separately from the performance review, but individuals are given the opportunity to discuss their manager's proposal and to advance reasons why they should be paid more. And managers are expected to respond and to take account of these submissions.

At Book Club Associates managers were asked to give an indication of the proposed increase – eg above average, average, below average – rather than a rating of the individual's performance. The following guidelines were given.

- An above-average increase of, say, 5 per cent to 8 per cent could be given to people when there was evidence that they were clearly and consistently contributing at a high level compared to their peers, and that they were displaying more than the required level of competence.

- An average increase of, say, 3 per cent could be given to people when evidence was available that they were performing in accordance with expectations and were successfully applying the required level of competence.

- A below-average increase of less than 3 per cent would be given to those for whom the evidence was that they were not meeting the expected standards of performance and competence.

Managers were given an overall pay budget which they had to work within. They were encouraged to identify high and low levels of contribution and to reward or not to reward accordingly. But there was no forced distribution or quota. The other factors managers were asked to take into account were the rate of pay compared with those in similar jobs, any special market-rate pressures, and the need to increase or decrease the rate of pay progression for those whose pay had fallen behind market rate or who, without good reason, were paid above market rate.

As reported by Brown and Armstrong (1999), a modified version of this approach is practised by Scottish and Newcastle Retail. Managers are asked to assess people in respect of current performance, future potential and marketability. But there is no final rating or forced distribution. Instead, there is a fixed pay budget and suggested range between high and low performers. The Woolwich has moved away from a uniform, corporate points-based system with a fixed quota of performance ratings to a similar more flexible approach. Staff are indeed rated in respect of competencies and results, but the emphasis is on agreeing an appropriate rate of pay with the individual, given their performance and data on their market value. Only the total budget constrains the size of individual awards.

At Bristol Myers Squibb, as also reported by Brown and Armstrong, there was a reaction against the 'school-report', 'box-ticking' nature of the appraisal which tended to 'focus on the negative' and on the pay review, ignoring personal growth and development. It was also felt that performance and pay review were inflexible and 'did not address what you do for the rest of the year'. Pay increases were perceived as being determined in advance, making the process 'something of a charade'. The new procedure stipulated an open, joint discussion and an agreed summary description of the level of performance. Third-party input from internal and external customers, agreed in advance by employees and their managers, is provided for in these discussions. On the basis of these performance summaries, managers recommend an appropriate rate of increase for each member of staff, taking account of:

- the level at which individuals contribute – their performance against objectives and the level of competence displayed

- the development and growth of individuals

- the relative performance of other staff.

These recommendations are monitored by the HR department for consistency and finally reviewed by a meeting of all department managers.

Other approaches
The two other approaches to making performance pay decisions without rating are ranking and what in the USA is called 'performance clustering'.

Ranking

Ranking is carried out by managers who place staff in comparable categories in order of merit. This order may be determined through the old-fashioned system of merit-rating which allocates points on a scale according to the assessed level of merit for each characteristic in the assessment schedule. Alternatively, a less analytical but not necessarily more arbitrary method is to place 'the whole person' in the rank order according to an overall assessment of relative contribution or merit. The rank order is divided into groups so that someone in the top 10 per cent of the rank order could get an 8 per cent increase, while someone in the next 20 per cent might receive 6 per cent, and so on. Guidelines can be issued to managers on the distribution of awards within the budget which they have some discretion to apply flexibly. Or they may be forced to conform to a standard distribution. Ranking can be justified on the grounds that comparative judgements of the relative merit of people are easier and therefore more valid than absolute judgements of a person's merit against a scale. But ranking depends on what could be invidious comparisons and works better when it is used in situations where there are a number of people in similar jobs to be ranked.

Clustering

Performance clustering is a variation of the ranking approach. It involves managers' making comparisons of the relative performance of their staff and placing them into 'clusters' or groups of people who are broadly performing at the same level. Thus there may be three clusters: the largest one for the majority of staff, whose performance meets expectations; one for those whose performance far exceeds expectations and one for those where there is room for improvement. Like ranking, clustering is only feasible when there are a number of employees in similar jobs. And like other forms of assessing eligibility for performance, competence or contribution-related pay increases, facilitated peer reviews may take place in which managers compare and discuss each other's groupings.

Guidelines for managers on conducting individual pay reviews

When conducting individual reviews, managers are encouraged to 'fine-tune' their pay recommendations to ensure that individuals are on the right track within their grade according to their level of performance, competence and time in the job. It is important, therefore, that managers should be given the scope to do such fine-tuning by making adjustments to the rate of progression as necessary. To do this, they will need general guidelines on typical rates of progression in relation to performance, skill or competence, and specific guidance on what they can and should do. They will also need information on the relative positions of their staff in the pay structure in relation to the policy guidelines. Data can be generated through a computerised personnel record system which sets out individual compa-ratios and illustrates the distribution of pay within grades by means of scattergrams.

The conduct of pay reviews can have a major impact not only on motivation and commitment but also on the perceptions of employees about the fairness of the whole process of reward management.

Reviews should not, therefore, be carried out mechanically. Policies and data should only provide general guidelines and each decision should be made on the merits of the case. The guidelines should not become straitjackets. Some freedom should be allowed for individual judgements as long as they can be justified.

Individual pay reviews usually take place on a fixed date, typically once a year, although fast-moving organisations may prefer more frequent reviews, say, twice a year. The review date can be varied to suit the circumstances of the organisation. Rolling reviews may be held for employees based on their birthday or starting/promotion date in order to allow more attention to be paid to the individual's reward. But this method is more difficult to budget for and control.

Basic guidelines

The basic guidelines should be on the policy of the organisation on pay progression and the awards that can be made. These could cover:

- the limits of progression in a conventional grade or a zone in a broad-banded structure; in the latter case the guidelines would indicate that progression would normally be within a zone but could go beyond the zone for those who were clearly making a contribution that was significantly above expectations

- the use of cash bonuses as an alternative to a consolidated increase – for example, when people are at the top of their range or zone

- the need to keep within the pay review budget

- methods of conducting the review, including making judgements on the amount of the award with or without performance review ratings

- the information that will be made available to reviewing managers, including existing salaries, records of previous increases, the distribution of salaries for individuals under review, and market-rate data

- the use that should be made of this data – for example, the guidelines may indicate that pay decisions should take account of internal relativities and the market worth of individuals as well as their performance, contribution and level of competence

- the procedures that are to be followed to review proposals, and who will be involved – eg the line manager's manager, peers, the personnel department

- how individuals will be informed of the decision, and the part that managers should play

- the amount of discretion allowed to managers, and the guidelines that will be made available.

Some companies allow line managers complete discretion to award pay increases within their budgets. But most organisations believe that guidelines are necessary. There is a choice of approaches which vary in the degree to which control is exercised. These are described below in order of the amount of discretion allowed to managers.

Discretion with minimum guidance

Line managers can be given discretion to award PRP within their budgets, although they may be told the target rate of pay for a fully competent individual and the circumstances in which cash should be given rather than a pay increase. Devolving pay decisions to line managers can create the problem of ensuring that such decisions are equitable, fair and consistent. The responsibility of line managers for reward matters was discussed in Chapter 35.

Guidance on maximum and minimum increases

Guidelines for managers making pay review decisions can set out the minimum and maximum increases that can be given – for example, 3 per cent and 10 per cent. This, of course, must be within the pay review budget.

Award guidelines with some discretion

A suggested distribution of awards can be issued to managers. This might, for example, recommend that the normal increase should be 3 per cent, while those who merited above-average increases could get up to 6 per cent, and 2 per cent or less could be given to those who were assessed as deserving a less-than-normal increase.

Links to rating

The guidelines could state how ratings should be translated into percentage increases. The distribution of ratings might not be stipulated but, more usually, a typical distribution would be suggested of, say, 70 per cent normal, 20 per cent above the norm and 10 per cent below the norm. However, managers would be informed that they have some discretion to vary this distribution as long as they keep within their budgets and on the understanding that out-of-ordinary distributions – such as everyone's getting the same, or a few very high increases – may be challenged and would have to be justified.

Use of pay matrices and ranking

Pay matrices, as described earlier, indicate precisely the size of the reward according to the rating and position in the pay range.

Forced distribution

As mentioned earlier in this chapter, forced distribution lays down the allocation of ratings at different levels that correspond to the size of the increase. It can be used in conjunction with a pay matrix or ranking. This Procrustean approach guarantees consistency in the arithmetical distribution of increases but not necessarily fairness in the shape of awarding people what they deserve.

Normalising

Normalising or operating a quota system is an even more autocratic technique. The distributions of ratings or merit scores are adjusted by the personnel department to conform with what is believed to be the 'correct' pattern of distribution. A quota of percentage pay increases allowed for each rating or merit-score range is then determined centrally and imposed on line managers. Managers' ratings in some organisations are analysed centrally and the financial implications of the pay increases arising from these ratings assessed. If they result in an overall payroll increase above the budget, the ratings are adjusted to bring increases within the budget and managers are informed of the changes made to their ratings. Neither of these approaches is desirable. The latter is particularly pernicious because it can largely destroy any value that was obtained from the performance review process.

Links between the performance review and the pay review

As explained in Chapter 28, the focus of performance management has moved significantly in recent years from using it to inform pay decisions to using it for developmental purposes. The IPD research clearly indicated that the important developmental aspects of performance management could be seriously damaged by diverting attention to ratings and consequential pay decisions.

Increasingly, therefore, organisations are separating the performance and development review from the pay review. The former is concerned with providing feedback and motivation and with the agreement of personal development and performance improvement plans. Overall ratings may not be made. The latter concentrates on making a pay decision which is related not only to levels of performance, competence and contribution but also to internal and external relativities and position in the range or band. There is, of course, a read-across between the two. The performance and contribution of an individual discussed at the performance review is the same as the performance and contribution of the individual which is taken into account at the pay review. But the processes followed are different. In the performance review the emphasis is on what the individual has achieved and how more can be achieved in the future. It is an opportunity to provide non-financial rewards in the shape of positive feedback, recognition and development opportunities. Although it is recognised that at a later date performance will be taken into account in the pay review, the focus of the review meeting is on development, not the financial implications of performance.

As reported by Towers Perrin at the American Compensation Association's 1999 Boston conference (unpublished), the prime objective of 'de-coupling' the performance review from the pay review is to improve the quality of the discussion between managers and staff and to move away from a discussion focused only on pay issues. Discussions leading to pay decisions tend to 'crowd out' critical performance feedback and a forward-looking dialogue on areas for improvement and development needs.

A typical procedure in the UK is to separate the two reviews by between three and six months, as at Pfizer, Nuffield Hospitals and Bristol Myers Squibb. Research conducted by Saville and Holdsworth as reported by IRS (1998) found that 41 per cent of the organisations they surveyed now separated the two reviews compared to 22 per cent when they last conducted a survey. Another increasingly favoured procedure is to hold the pay review on a fixed date but conduct the performance review on the anniversary of the date the individual joined the organisation, although avoiding too close a proximity to the pay review date. This distinguishes between the two reviews and also spreads the load of performance review meetings for managers. The performance review meeting might be expected to be a thorough affair, lasting an hour or two. But the pay review meeting could be much briefer, requiring the manager simply to inform the individual of the pay decision and why it has been made.

Combined reviews

Some organisations do not conduct separate general and individual reviews. Instead, they hold one combined review, and increases (if any) for individual employees are related to performance, skill or competence and their market worth – that is, what the organisation believes people should be paid to keep pace with increases in market rates and their 'marketability'. A policy may be established to the effect that pay levels should be protected against inflation, but the organisation may decide not to do this for individuals who are performing poorly, thus reducing their real earnings.

Combined reviews allow more scope to flex rewards according to the individual's value to the organisation, but employees often prefer to be informed about the different elements of their pay increase, and it can be argued that the motivational impact of a performance-related increase will be greater if it is distinguished from general market-related or cost-of-living increases.

Procedure for individual pay reviews

The steps required to plan and implement a non-negotiated pay review are:

1 Consider the financial situation (affordability) and special factors such as attraction and retention problems or market-rate pressures which may affect pay review decisions.

2 Agree the budget.

3 Obtain and analyse data – market rates of pay, market pay increase trends, the distribution of existing levels of pay in relation to pay policies, compa-ratios, attrition, performance ratings, etc.

4 Prepare and obtain agreement to review guidelines on the size, range and distribution of awards and on methods of conducting the review (the use of ratings, if any, and the factors to be taken into account).

5 Issue procedural guidelines on timetable, approval and monitoring processes, dealing with anomalies, discussions with individuals and communicating outcomes.

6 Provide advice and support.

7 Iterate to achieve acceptable proposals in relation to budget, pay policies and review guidelines.

8 Summarise and cost proposals.

9 Obtain approval.

10 Update payroll.

11 Inform employees.

12 Deal with any queries or appeals.

In developing procedures for pay reviews the importance of providing advice, guidance *and* training to line managers cannot be overestimated. Some managers will be confident and capable from the start. Others will have a lot to learn. There may be some who have previously sheltered behind decisions made by 'them' and are not ready to face up to their responsibilities. The HR department has an important role not only in producing guidelines and training for managers but also – as a pay and benefits manager once put it – in 'holding their hands'.

Communications are also important. Manager and all employees need to know the basis upon which the review is carried out, how decisions are made, and the steps being taken to be fair and consistent. Without such transparency, pay reviews can lead to lack of trust and can damage rather than improve the employment relationship and the performance of the organisation.

PAY REVIEW BUDGETS

Pay review budgets set out the overall increase in its payroll that the organisation believes it can or should afford. This forms the basis of the pay review budgets issued to departmental reviewing managers. It is the key control mechanism, and managers should be accountable for keeping strictly within their budgets.

Pay review budgets are usually concerned only with performance or competence/skill-related awards. They may not therefore control the payroll costs arising from new appointments, transfers and promotions. Some companies set budgets which control increases arising from promotions and upgradings as well as contingent pay. Others aim to achieve complete control through total payroll budgeting.

SUMMARY

- The three types of reviews are general or 'across-the-board' reviews; structural reviews, which deal with changes required to the pay structure to cater for the need to reflect market rates or to change differentials; and individual reviews which provide individuals with pay increases in accordance with their contribution.

- Pay reviews are a major means of implementing the organisation's reward policies for improving performance and ensuring the continued motivation and retention of employees. They are also the manifestation to employees of those reward policies.

- General reviews take place when employees are given an award in response to general market-rate movements, increases in the cost of living or union negotiations. General reviews are often combined with individual reviews.

- Structural reviews are carried out in response to internal changes in the organisation structure or the type and levels of work carried out. Such changes may affect relativities which have to be adjusted.

- Individual pay reviews determine performance-related, competence-related, contribution-related or consolidated increases to base pay. They may also cover the award of cash bonuses (variable pay).

- The size of awards is a matter of what the organisation can afford but will be much smaller in times of low inflation. The IPD 1998 survey of PRP showed that the majority of respondents (58 per cent) made awards of between 1 and 6 per cent to senior managers.

- Awards may be distributed broadly to conform to the shape of the normal curve of distribution, although this may be skewed in the direction of the higher levels. Thus, if there were three levels of reward, the expected distribution might be 70 per cent normal, 20 per cent above the norm and 10 per cent below the norm.

- Individual pay reviews when there is a contingent pay scheme relating pay to performance, competence or contribution are commonly but not universally based on some form of performance and/or competence rating.

- There are a number of methods of linking ratings and pay increases, including a direct link between the rating and the pay increase, and the use of a pay matrix.

- There are a number of ways of achieving consistency in rating, including forced distribution, ranking, training, monitoring and moderating or peer reviews.

- Ranking as an alternative to rating is carried out by managers who place staff in a rank order according to an overall assessment of relative contribution or merit. The rank order is divided into groups so that someone in the top 10 per cent of the rank order could get an 8 per cent increase, while someone in the next 20 per cent might receive 6 per cent, and so on.

- Another alternative to rating is 'clustering' which involves dividing staff into groups according to their level of performance.

- Guidelines should be provided to managers on the policy of the organisation on pay progression and on the awards that can be made, and the basis upon which they can make pay awards in terms of size, range and distribution.

- Organisations are tending to separate the performance and development review from the pay review.

- The 1998 IPD research revealed that 24 per cent of the respondents with performance-related pay did not have rating.

- Even when there are no ratings it is still necessary to reach a decision on the level of a pay increase, but this may take the form of a proposal which takes into account a number of factors besides rated performance. These include relativities, market rates and potential. Account may also be taken of the extent to which the individual's salary has unjustifiably fallen behind or risen above the level appropriate to his or her contribution relative to what other people contributing at the same level in the same job are paid.

- Some organisations do not conduct separate general and individual reviews. Instead, they hold one combined review, and increases (if any) for individual employees are related to performance, skill or competence and their market worth – that is, what the organisation believes people should be paid to keep pace with increases in market rates and their 'marketability'.

• Pay review budgets set out the overall increase in its payroll that the organisation believes it can or should afford. This forms the basis of the pay review budgets issued to departmental reviewing managers. It is the key control mechanism, and managers should be accountable for keeping strictly within their budgets.

37 Using computers

Employee reward processes can benefit considerably from the use of computers to provide administrative support and to assist in decision-making. The four main uses for computers are in providing an employee reward database, pay review modelling, job evaluation, and pay structure modelling. At the end of this chapter the reader will understand how computers can be used in administering employee rewards, including computer modelling to calculate the cost of alternative reward policies.

THE EMPLOYEE REWARD DATABASE

The employee reward database is the information technology (IT) platform which allows data on employees' pay, earnings and benefits to be held, processed and communicated as information to users. The database consists of systematically organised and interrelated sets of files (collections of records serving as the basic unit of data storage) and allows for combinations of data to be selected as required by different users.

The reward database will be part of a computerised personnel information system (CPIS). Pay information from the payroll or personnel information system can be downloaded on to the reward database section of the system. The information required to administer rewards and to assist in decision-making will be captured on that database. This information may include personal and job details, job grade, basic pay, position in the pay range (compa-ratio), earnings through variable pay, pay history (progression, and general and individual pay increases), performance management ratings and details of employee benefits, including pension contributions. From the database, the personnel function can:

- produce listings of employees by job category, job grade, rate of pay, position in range and size in actual or percentage terms of the last increase, and, if required, previous individual performance pay increases

- generate reports analysing distributions of pay by grade, including compa-ratios for each grade and the organisation as a whole, to assist in managing and auditing the reward system: extracts from these reports can be downloaded to the personal computers of managers responsible for pay decisions to assist them in conducting pay reviews

- initiate and print notifications of pay increases and update the payroll database

- use electronic mail (e-mail) facilities to transmit data.

In using the database and distributing data, the personnel function must, however, ensure that the provisions of the Data Protection Act 1984 are met. This requires *inter alia* that personal data held for any purpose should not be used or disclosed in any manner incompatible with that purpose, and appropriate security measures must be taken against unauthorised access to or disclosure of those data. If data are going to be downloaded, it will be essential to control who gets what. The importance of data protection will also have to be spelt out to managers.

Managing the reward database for pay administration purposes will involve the collection, storage and preparation of data to ensure that they are available and appropriate for the uses to which they may be applied. The uses to which the data will be put will have to be analysed and the data will have to be organised to suit those needs: ensuring that they can be located and extracted quickly, maintaining and updating them as necessary, and providing for security. Database management systems (DBMS) in the shape of a set of programs can be used to create and maintain the database and to provide the means of executing programs for the delivery of the information required.

PAY REVIEW MODELLING

General pay reviews require information on the cost of across-the-board increases in terms of increases in basic payroll costs and the knock-on effects of such increases on other pay and employment costs – performance pay, pensions, etc. Computers can be used to model alternative scenarios to assess the costs of different levels of increase.

Central data
Individual pay reviews require information at the centre on the aggregate costs of the total review to be compared with the budget. Again, 'what if' calculations may be required to estimate the costs of different levels and distributions of awards. Variables may include:

- alternative budgeted costs for the whole organisation, including both basic payroll increases and knock-on effects

- the costs of different distributions of awards in relation to alternative distributions of ratings or the costs of performance-related pay increases in relation to budget

- different configurations of a pay matrix and the compa-ratios of individuals in each grade.

Departmental data
Line managers can be provided with programs which enable them to manipulate the pay data for members of their department and calculate the costs of alternative distributions of awards within their budgets. The data for these 'what if' calculations can be downloaded from the central database. Managers of outlying units – eg regional offices – can manage their own database, which could be linked through a network to a central database for monitoring and costing purposes.

Checking and monitoring review proposals

To assist in conducting and monitoring departmental reviews, scattergrams can be produced showing the distribution by grade of the current rates for employees, highlighting any anomalies which may have to be dealt with. After proposed increases have been loaded into the computer, revised scattergrams can be generated showing what changes have taken place. Alternative distributions of awards can be tried, costed and reproduced graphically. The outcome of departmental proposals can be scheduled in a report and illustrated by the scattergram for review by a more senior manager and/or the personnel department. They can then check that the proposals are within the budget and that the distribution of increases is logical and in accordance with policy guidelines. Line managers would have to justify any unusual distributions and awards. The total outcome of the departmental reviews can then be scheduled and graphed.

The use of spreadsheets

Spreadsheets such as Lotus 1-2-3 and Excel can be used for pay review modelling. They provide the user with a worksheet, divided into cells, into which can be inserted text, numbers or formulae. This allows the user to carry out complex 'what if' analyses and gives the flexibility to make adjustments in accordance with alternative levels and distributions of awards and policy changes on budgets or distributions. Analyses can be saved as a separate file for future recall when the proposals are approved. Spreadsheets can be printed out in report or graphical form.

The problem with spreadsheets is that they can be quite cumbersome to deal with in larger applications and may require a considerable amount of skill on the part of the operator. Also, most spreadsheets function only within the available memory of the computer, which may run out of processing space when dealing with medium to large populations.

Software packages

Micro-based software packages have been developed to carry out the various processes referred to above. Proprietary software is usually designed as a standard software shell within which there are a number of functions that allow users to customise the system to meet their own needs.

COMPUTER-ASSISTED JOB EVALUATION

Computer-assisted job evaluation (CAJE) supports job evaluation in two ways:

• It helps with the administration and maintenance of a job evaluation scheme, keeping evaluation records and auditing the operation of the scheme.

• It helps with the whole process of evaluating jobs rather than simply administering the scheme.

The second of these two applications embraces the first – and when reference is made to computer-assisted job evaluation, that is what most people are talking about.

Aims

The aims of computer-assisted job evaluation are:

- to set up and maintain a database of job analyses and evaluations

- to assist in the process of making judgements about job values by functioning as an expert system which captures the knowledge of experts in the domain of job evaluation and emulates the reasoning processes of those experts

- to help to achieve consistency in evaluation judgements by reference to the database of previous evaluations

- to speed up the process of evaluation

- to reduce the bureaucracy often built into job evaluation systems and, incidentally, save paper.

However, a full computer-assisted job evaluation system does not replace human judgement. It simply provides an efficient means of applying the evaluation criteria and values which have been incorporated by the designers into the system on the basis of their analysis of the reasoning processes and rules used by evaluators.

The administration and maintenance of CAJE systems

A CAJE system designed to help with administration and maintenance is in effect a database which holds records of evaluations. This database maintains details of the scoring, ranking and grading of all benchmark and other jobs. The data can be held for each factor on a level-by-level basis so that information can be obtained on which benchmark jobs have been rated at a particular level in a factor, thus facilitating comparisons.

These data can be used for:

- comparing jobs being evaluated with the overall scores and gradings given to benchmark jobs in similar occupations or functions elsewhere in the organisation (internal benchmarking on a whole-job basis)

- comparing for validation purposes the levels at which benchmark jobs have been evaluated for particular factors (internal benchmarking on a factor-by-factor basis)

- carrying out consistency checks on evaluations by different job evaluation panels or groups of evaluators

- conducting comparative audits of the evaluation scores and grade distributions of jobs on different functions, departments or units.

Evaluating jobs with the help of computers

A full CAJE system will not only maintain a database for the purposes listed above but will also assist in the actual process of evaluating jobs. In the latter application it functions in effect as an expert system – ie one that is based on 'rules' for processing, analysing and drawing conclusions from data which have been developed by 'experts' in this field.

A CAJE 'expert' system simply replicates in computer language the thought-processes followed by evaluators when conducting a 'manual' evaluation. What expert systems do is to:

* ask intelligent questions on the extent to which a particular factor is present in a job

* compare the answers with the factor-level definitions in the factor plan and decide which is the most appropriate level

* continue to do this with each of the factors in the plan

* add the scores for the levels given for each factor to produce the total score for the job

* compare the total score for the job with the points brackets which define the grade in the pay structure and allocate a grade to the job.

The rationale behind any expert CAJE system is that there must be clear and discernible reasons for deciding on the levels to be allocated to a factor in any job. Indeed, if there were no apparent reasons or 'rules', the job evaluation process could not operate consistently. However, the 'rules' may be quite complex.

In a CAJE system the evaluation decision rules are defined quantitatively or qualitatively or both, and built into the system shell. The system then operates as follows:

* Information about the job relating to each factor is entered into the computer in the form of answers to a questionnaire. The answers may first be recorded manually on the questionnaire before being loaded into the computer, or as in the Gauge system marketed by Pilat (UK) Ltd, they may be generated by the software (ie displayed on the computer screen) and the answers input direct to the computer without the need for completing a separate questionnaire.

* The computer applies the rules to these answers and determines the factor scores.

* The total score for the job is calculated by the computer.

* The job is graded.

* The job information in the form of a factor analysis is stored in the computer.

The computer can also be used for consistency checks. It may establish internal consistency between the answers to different questions. If one answer seems inconsistent with another (for example, a high score on number of people managed and a low score on leadership skills), the fact could be highlighted by the computer and the evaluator directed to reconsider those answers. The computer can also carry out consistency checks with other benchmark jobs by displaying the scores for the job in question alongside those of a relevant benchmark job (or any other previously evaluated job) and highlighting the scoring differences.

The system can generate instant information in the form of print-outs. For example, the Gauge system as used at Burnley Healthcare Trust allows the code for each answer option selected during the evaluation of a job to be stated in sequence by the system, which also has a pre-loaded phrase or statement for each answer code. The system can then assemble all the statements associated with the relevant answer codes and present them in narrative form, reflecting the way in which the job has been described through the answers chosen. There is thus a full rationale on a factor-by-factor basis of how the overall score and the job grade were derived.

Developing a CAJE system

A tailor-made CAJE system can be developed for an organisation from its existing point-factor scheme. This avoids the discontinuities which arise when an established system is being replaced, and means that the original investment in the scheme, and the expertise created over the years in its use, are not wasted.

However, it may be decided that the existing factor plan needs to be modified or that an entirely new factor plan, possibly competence-based, has to be devised. The factor and sub-factor definitions and weighting in this revised or new plan would provide the framework for the CAJE system.

The development process for a CAJE system, whether based on an existing plan or on a revised or new plan, consists of the following stages:

1 Identify and analyse benchmark jobs. (Even if the existing plan is being maintained it is still necessary to carry out this analysis and the subsequent steps.)

2 Define and weight the factors and sub-factors.

3 Analyse and define the different levels at which the factors and sub-factors apply in the benchmark jobs.

4 On the basis of this analysis, develop a questionnaire aimed at establishing for individual jobs the levels at which the factors and sub-factors apply.

5 Use the factor plan and questionnaire developed in stages 2 to 4 above to score and rank the benchmark jobs.

6 Assess the validity of the results obtained at stage 5 and the effectiveness of the questionnaire as a means of producing acceptable results. Validity may be assessed by ranking the benchmark jobs by the paired-comparison method and measuring the correlation between that ranking and one achieved by the use of the factor plan at stage 5.

7 Modify the factor plan and questionnaire and re-evaluate as necessary in the light of the assessment at stage 6.

8 Define the evaluation rules for use in the system, which means developing an algorithm (ie a process containing rules which enables certain calculations to be carried out). This relates the dependent variable of the evaluation or ranking produced at stage 5, or modified at stage 7, to questionnaire responses so that the factors and jobs can be scored direct from the questionnaire responses.

9 Test the evaluation rules (the algorithm) to ensure that they deliver satisfactory results for the benchmark jobs – ie results which correspond with those produced by the manual evaluation. If necessary, modify the algorithm and, possibly, the questionnaire until a valid result is obtained. This is often an iterative process.

10 Configure the software to carry out the following functions:

- Score factors and complete jobs.
- Grade jobs.
- Conduct consistency checks.
- Display the results of the evaluations and consistency checks on screens.
- Generate print-outs of the results.
- Create and maintain the database.
- Enable authorised users to access the database.
- Enable authorised persons to modify the system (eg factors, weightings, questions).

11 Test and as necessary amend the program.

12 Prepare a users' manual.

13 Train users.

14 Provide maintenance and support services.

The sequence of actions listed above assumes that a tailor-made system is being developed from scratch. But consultants and software houses can be used to install their own system which may be customised to a greater or lesser degree.

PAY STRUCTURE MODELLING

Software packages can be developed which use the output from a computerised job evaluation exercise as contained in the database to model alternative grade structures by reference to the distribution of points scores. The computer analyses where existing employees would be placed in the proposed grade structures and produces a report which assesses the cost of increasing the pay of those who are undergraded following the evaluation up to the minimum or some other designated point in the new grade. Scattergrams are produced which show graphically the location and number of anomalies. The program enables alternative grade configurations to be tested to establish the extent to which they reduce the number of anomalies and therefore the cost of introducing the new structure. The program will also calculate costs in accordance with parameters of the maximum increase that can be awarded and the stages which should be adopted for bringing pay up to the minimum. In fixed incremental systems, or those in which pay progression is closely controlled, the model can be used to forecast future payroll costs on the basis of parameters for movements through the grade and the amount of increases.

EXAMPLE OF A REWARD SOFTWARE PROGRAM

The Pay Modeller marketed by Link Consultants is a software program designed to assist organisations to model both existing and potential pay structures. For each potential pay scenario it provides instant feedback of the costs and other implications. Graphics illustrate the results of pay structure and review decisions. It is aimed at medium-sized and large organisations where spreadsheet solutions have become unwieldy, difficult to manipulate and potentially simplistic. The key features are:

Data input
Pay information for all employees can be downloaded from the organisation's payroll or personnel system(s) or entered manually.

Pay structure data
A mouse-driven graphic interface allows the user to view the entire population in the form of a scattergram. Grade lines, pay ranges and (optionally) pay points can then be specified and manipulated on the screen. By 'clicking' a point on the scattergram it is possible to display the actual salary or salaries of the individual or individuals represented by that point. A zoom facility allows the user to view parts of the graph in more detail. A cost window instantly feeds back the effect of each change.

The system tracks and identifies 'red circles' (those currently paid above the proposed grade pay maximum) and 'green circles' (those paid below the proposed pay minimum). Market lines can be displayed to assist users who want to align their structures more closely with the market. A range of statistical facilities allow further detailed analysis of a proposed grade structure. Each structure can be saved to a 'structure manager' and retrieved at a later date.

Performance pay
The system enables the user to set up performance pay structures. Performance grids (performance pay matrices) can be constructed. The progression of job-holders through the pay range can be linked directly with the performance pay matrices or tables.

Modelling the entire pay bill
The entire pay bill can be modelled as follows:

- fixed allowances – the user can change the value of each existing allowance, consolidate allowances into basic pay and develop new allowances

- variable allowances – the user can change hourly rates and other payments; the effects of changing the length of the working week can be determined

- pensions – various pension structures can be modelled and allowances made pensionable or non-pensionable

- National Insurance – employer's contribution NI tables can be set up and NI contributions modelled.

A single control centre screen provides the user with an overview of total costs and enables the effect of knock-on costs to be seen.

Filters and reports
The system allows the user to work on sub-populations by means of a filter. For example, an analysis of the distribution of salaries within a

department could be extracted from the overall company analysis for use by a departmental manager. A range of cost reports provide feedback on the effects of any changes at any level from the whole organisation to the individual.

Predicting the future

The modeller can roll forward any pay structure 10 years into the future. Users can enter predictions about

- employee turnover

- establishment requirements

- employee progression through the pay structure

- the effects of inflation

- the treatment of red-circled job-holders.

The user can then obtain information about the results of these predictions by means of reports which can be customised to meet their needs.

SUMMARY

- The four main uses for computers are: providing an employee reward database, pay review modelling, job evaluation, and pay structure modelling.

- The employee reward database is the information technology (IT) platform which allows data on employees' pay, earnings and benefits to be held, processed and communicated as information to users.

- General pay reviews require information on the cost of across-the-board increases in terms of increases in basic payroll costs and the knock-on effects of such increases on other pay and employment costs – performance pay, pensions, etc.

- Computers can be used to model alternative scenarios to assess the costs of different levels of increase.

- Individual pay reviews require information at the centre on the aggregate costs of the total review to be compared with the budget. 'What if' calculations may be required to estimate the costs of different levels and distributions of awards.

- Line managers can be provided with programs which enable them to manipulate the pay data for members of their department and calculate the costs of alternative distributions of awards within their budgets.

- Departmental reviews can be monitored from computerised data to check that they are within budget and follow review guidelines.

- Computer-assisted job evaluation (CAJE) supports job evaluation by helping with the administration and maintenance of a job evaluation scheme (keeping evaluation records and auditing the operation of the scheme) and by assisting with the whole process of evaluating jobs.

- Software packages can be developed which use the output from a computerised job evaluation exercise as contained in the database to model alternative grade structures by reference to the distribution of points scores.

FURTHER READING

Further details of computerised pay applications are given in *Reward Management* by Armstrong and Murlis (fourth edition, Appendix F) and *The Job Evaluation Handbook* by Armstrong and Baron (Chapter 10 and Appendix F).

References

ABOSCH, K. S. (1998) 'Variable pay: do we have the basics in place?' *Compensation and Benefits Review*, May/June, pp. 12–22.

ACAS (1988) *Job Evaluation: An Introduction*. London.

ACAS (1994) *Introduction to Payment Systems*. London.

ADAMS, J. (1965) 'Injustice in social exchange', in L. Berkowitz (ed.) *Advances in Experimental Psychology*. New York, Academic Press.

ADAMS, K. (1998) 'Competencies and the unions: pay and grading'. *Competency*, Autumn, pp. 23–27.

ADAMS, K. (1998) 'Rethinking competency-based pay'. *Competency*, Autumn, pp. 16–19.

ALDERFER, C. (1972) *Existence, Relatedness and Growth*. New York, The Free Press.

ARKIN, A. (1994) 'Team-based pay – an incentive to work together'. *Personnel Management Plus*, November, pp. 22–23.

ARMSTRONG, M. AND BARON, A. (1995) *The Job Evaluation Handbook*. London, Institute of Personnel and Development.

ARMSTRONG, M. AND LONG, P. (1994) *The Reality of Strategic HRM*. London, Institute of Personnel and Development.

ARMSTRONG, M. AND MURLIS, H. (1988) *Reward Management*. First edition, London, Institute of Personnel Management.

ARMSTRONG, M. AND MURLIS, H. (1998) *Reward Management*. Fourth edition, London, Kogan Page.

ARVEY, R. D. (1986) 'Sex bias in job evaluation procedures'. *Personnel Psychology*, Vol. 39, pp. 315–35.

BANDURA, A. (1982) 'Self-efficacy mechanism in human agency'. *American Psychologist*, Vol. 37, pp. 122–47.

BEER, M. (1984) 'Reward systems', in M. Beer, B. Spector, P. R. Lawrence, Quinn D. Mills and R. Walton (eds), *Managing Human Assets*. New York, The Free Press.

BEER, M., SPECTOR, B., LAWRENCE, P. R., QUINN D. MILLS AND WALTON, R. (1984) *Managing Human Assets*. New York, The Free Press.

BERLET, K. R. AND CRAVENS, D. M. (1991) *Performance Pay as a Competitive Weapon*. New York, Wiley.

BINDER, A. S. (1990) *Paying for Productivity*. Washington DC, Brookings Institution.

BOWEY, E. AND THORPE, R. (1982) 'The effects of incentive payment systems'. *Department of Employment Research Paper No 36*. London, DOE.

BRADICK, C. A., JONES, M. B. AND SHAFER. P. M, (1992) 'A look at broadbanding in practice'. *Compensation and Benefits Review*. July/August. pp. 28–32.

BREHM, J. W. (1966) *A Theory of Psychological Reactance*. New York, Academic Press.

BROWN, D. (1998) *A Practical Guide to Competency-Related Pay*. London, Financial Times.

BROWN, D. AND ARMSTRONG, M. (1999) *Paying for Contribution*. London, Kogan Page.

BROWN, W. (1962) *Piecework Abandoned: The effect of wage incentive schemes on managerial authority*. London, Heinemann.

BRUMBACH, G. B. (1988) 'Some ideas, issues and predictions about performance management'. *Public Personnel Management*. Winter, pp 387–402.

CAUDRON, S. (1994) 'Tie individual pay to team success'. Personnel Journal, October, pp. 40–6.

CAULKIN, S. (1999) 'A poisoned apple for teacher'. *The Observer Business Section*, 31 January, p. 9.

CBI (1994) *Remuneration Practices for International Transferees*. London.

CBI/MERCER (1994) *Survey of Pensions*, London, CBI.

CBI/WYATT COMPANY (1993) *Variable Pay*. London, CBI.

CBI/HAY MANAGEMENT CONSULTANTS (1996) *Trends in Pay and Benefits Systems*. London, CBI.

CIRA, D. J. AND BENJAMIN, E. R. (1998) 'Competency-based pay: a concept in evolution', *Compensation and Benefits Review*. September/October, pp. 21–28.

CORKERTON, R. M. AND BEVAN, S. (1998) 'Paying hard to get.' *People Management*, 13 August, pp. 40–42

CYERT, R. M. AND MARCH, J. G. (1963) *A Behavioural Theory of the Firm*. Englewood Cliffs, NJ, Prentice-Hall.

Deming, W. (1986) Out of the Crisis, Cambridge, Mass., Massachusetts Institute of Technology, Centre for Advanced Engineering Studies.

DICKENS, CHARLES (1844) *Martin Chuzzlewit*. London, Chapman & Hall.

ECONOMIC INTELLIGENCE UNIT (1995) *Determining the Expatriate Package*. New York, EIU.

EHRENBERG, R. G. AND SMITH R. S. (1994) *Modern Labor Economics*. New York, HarperCollins.

ELLIOTT, R. F. (1991) *Labor Economics*. Maidenhead, McGraw-Hill.

EMERSON, S. M. (1991) 'Job evaluation: a barrier to excellence'. *Compensation and Benefits Review*, January/February, pp 39–51.

EQUAL OPPORTUNITIES COMMISSION (1985) *Job Evaluation Schemes Free of Sex Bias*. London.

EQUAL OPPORTUNITIES COMMISSION (1997) *Code of Practice on Equal Pay*. Manchester.

EMPLOYMENT CONDITIONS ABROAD (1994) *Survey Report on Changes in Expatriate Remuneration and Organisations*. London.

FLANNERY, T. P., HOFRICHTER, D. A. AND PLATTEN, P. E. (1996) *People, Performance, and Pay*. New York, The Free Press.

FOWLER, A. (1992) 'Choose a job evaluation system'. *Personnel Management Plus*, October, pp. 33–4.

GILBERT, D. AND ABOSCH, K. S. (1996) *Improving Organisational Effectiveness through Broadbanding*. Scottsdale, Ariz., American Compensation Association.

GOMEZ-MEJIA, L. R. AND BALKIN, D. B. (1992) *Compensation, Organisational Strategy, and Firm Performance.* Cincinnati, Southwestern Publishing.

GRAYSON, D. (1987) *Job Evaluation in Transition.* London, Work Research Unit, ACAS.

GREENHAM, R. (1998) 'Reward strategy: a practical experience'. Presentation at the Reward Strategy Forum, London, IPD (unpublished).

GUEST, D. E. (1989) 'Personnel and HRM: can you tell the difference?' *Personnel Management,* January, pp. 48–51.

GUEST, D. E. (1992) 'Motivation after Herzberg'. Unpublished paper delivered at the Compensation Forum. London.

GUEST, D. E. (1994) 'Rewarding talent and keeping staff motivated in the flatter organisation'. Unpublished paper delivered at the Institute of Personnel and Development's annual conference. Harrogate.

GUEST, D. E. AND CONWAY, N. (1997) *Employee Motivation and the Psychological Contract.* London, Institute of Personnel and Development.

GUEST, D. E. AND CONWAY, N. (1998) *Fairness at Work and the Psychological Contract.* London, Institute of Personnel and Development.

GUEST, D. E., CONWAY, N., BRINER, R., AND DICKMAN, M. (1996) *The State of the Psychological Contract in Employment.* London, Institute of Personnel and Development.

GUPTA, N. AND SHAW, J. D. (1998) 'Financial incentives *are* effective!', *Compensation and Benefits Review,* March/April, pp. 26, 28–32.

GUZZO, R. A., JETTE, R. D. AND KATSELL, R. A. (1985) 'The effect of psychological-based intervention programmes on worker productivity: a meta-analysis'. *Personnel Psychology,* Vol. 38, pp. 275–91.

HAGUE, H. (1996) 'The end for merit pay?', *Personnel Today,* 4 June, pp. 28–29.

HANDY, C. (1994) *The Empty Raincoat.* London, Hutchinson.

HASTINGS, S. (1989) *Identifying Discrimination in Job Evaluation Schemes.* Trade Union Research Unit Technical Note No. 108. Oxford.

HASTINGS, S. (1991) *Developing a Less Discriminatory Job Evaluation Scheme.* Trade Union Research Unit Technical Note No. 109. Oxford.

HASTINGS, S. (1992) *Virgin Territory: Job Evaluation in the Health Service and other Recently Privatised Sectors.* Trade Union Research Unit Technical Note No. 110. Oxford.

HERZBERG, F., MAUSNER, B. AND SNYDERMAN, B. (1957) *The Motivation to Work.* New York, Wiley.

HILTROP, J. (1995) 'The changing psychological contract: the human resources challenge', *European Management Journal,* Vol. 33, No. 3, pp. 286–294.

HOFFRICHTER, D. AND SPENCER, S. (1996) 'Competencies: the right foundation for effective management'. *Compensation and Benefits Review,* November/December, pp. 21–7.

HOLBECHE, L. (1998) *Motivating People in Lean Organisations*. Oxford. Butterworth-Heinemann.

HOLMES, S. G. AND SMITH N. (1987) Sales Force Incentives. London, Heinemann.

INCOMES DATA SERVICES (1990) *Putting Pay Philosophies into Practice*. London, IDS.

INCOMES DATA SERVICES (1991) *Shopfloor Incentive Schemes*. IDS Study No. 488. London, IDS.

INCOMES DATA SERVICES (1992) *Skilling Up*. IDS Study No. 500. London, IDS.

INCOMES DATA SERVICES (1993) 'Managers, teams and reward'. August, pp. 20–23.

INCOMES DATA SERVICES (1995) *Executive Benefits*. Management Pay Review, No. 174, August.

INCOMES DATA SERVICES (1995) 'Costing the expatriate package'. *Management Pay Review*, June 1995, pp. 19–22.

INCOMES DATA SERVICES (1995) *Profit Sharing Study No. 583*. London, IDS.

INCOMES DATA SERVICES (1997) 'General awards: fact or fiction', *Management Pay Review*, July.

INCOMES DATA SERVICES (1998) *IDS Study No 650*, June.

INCOMES DATA SERVICES (1998) *IDS StudyPlus*, July.

INDUSTRIAL RELATIONS SERVICES (1992) 'Skill-based pay: the new training initiative'. *Employee Development Bulletin No. 31*, July, pp. 2–6.

INDUSTRIAL RELATIONS SERVICES (1993) 'Job evaluation in the 1990s'. *Pay and Benefits Bulletin*, October, pp. 4–12.

INDUSTRIAL RELATIONS SERVICES (1994) 'Paying for performance: a survey of merit pay', *Pay and Benefits Bulletin No. 361*, October, pp. 4–7.

INDUSTRIAL RELATIONS SERVICES (1995) 'Key issues in team working'. *Employee Development Bulletin No. 69*, September, 5–15.

INDUSTRIAL RELATIONS SERVICES (1996) 'Gainsharing at BP Exploration', *Pay and Benefits Bulletin No. 393*, February, pp. 6–9.

INDUSTRIAL RELATIONS SERVICES (1997) 'Sharing the gains at Rank Xerox', *Pay and Benefits Bulletin No. 431, September*, pp. 4–9.

INDUSTRIAL RELATIONS SERVICES (1998) 'There is merit in merit pay', *Pay and Benefits Bulletin No. 445*, April.

INDUSTRIAL RELATIONS SERVICES (1998) 'Flexible benefits evolve at Cable & Wireless', *Pay and Benefits Bulletin No. 450*, June, pp. 2–4.

INDUSTRIAL RELATIONS SERVICES (1998) 'Pay prospects survey', *Pay and Benefits Bulletin No. 459*, November pp. 10–13.

INSTITUTE OF PERSONNEL AND DEVELOPMENT (1998) *Executive Summary: IPD 1998 Performance Pay Survey*. London, IPD.

INSTITUTE OF PERSONNEL AND DEVELOPMENT (1996) *The IPD Guide to Team Reward*. London, Institute of Personnel and Development.

INSTITUTE OF PERSONNEL MANAGEMENT (1992) *Performance Management in the UK: An Analysis of the Issues*. London, IPM.

INTERNATIONAL LABOUR OFFICE (1984) *Payment by Results*. Geneva, ILO.

JAQUES, E. (1961) *Equitable Payment*. London, Heinemann.

KANTER, R. M. (1987) 'The attack on pay'. *Harvard Business Review*, March–April, pp. 64–78.

KAPLAN, R. S. AND NORTON, D. P. (1992) 'The balanced scorecard – measures that drive performance'. *Harvard Business Review,* January–February, pp. 71–9.

KATZ, D. AND KAHN, R. L. (1964) *The Social Psychology of Organisations.* New York, Wiley.

KATZENBACH, J. AND SMITH, D. (1993) *The Magic of Teams.* Boston, Mass., Harvard Business School Press.

KEAR, S. (1999) 'Bass: brewing a balanced approach to competency and performance pay'. Presentation at the IPD Compensation Forum Conference, 9 February (unpublished).

KELLEY, H. H. (1967) 'Attribution theory in social psychology', in D. Levine (ed.), Nebraska Symposium on Motivation. Lincoln, NB, University of Nebraska Press.

KESSLER, I. AND PURCELL, J. (1992) 'Performance-related pay: objectives and application', *Human Resource Management Journal,* Vol. 2, No. 3, Spring, pp. 16–33.

KESSLER, I. AND PURCELL, J. (1993) *The Templeton Performance-Related Pay Project: Summary of Key Findings.* Oxford, Templeton College.

KINNIE, N. AND LOWE, D. (1990) 'Performance-related pay on the shop floor', *Personnel Management,* November, pp. 45–49.

KOHN, A. (1993) 'Why incentive plans cannot work', *Harvard Business Review,* September–October, pp. 54–63.

KOHN, A. (1998) 'Incentives and competition', *INC Journal,* January, pp. 91–94.

KOHN, A. (1998) 'Challenging behaviorist dogma: myths about money and motivation', *Compensation and Benefits Review,* March/April, pp. 27, 33–37.

LATHAM, G. AND LOCKE, E. A. (1979) 'Goal-setting – a motivational technique that works'. *Organisational Dynamics,* Autumn, pp. 68–80.

LAWLER, E. E. (1969) 'Job design and employee motivation'. *Personnel Psychology,* Vol. 22, pp. 426–35.

LAWLER, E. E. (1971) *Pay and Organisational Effectiveness.* New York, McGraw-Hill.

LAWLER, E. E. (1988) 'Pay for performance: making it work', *Personnel,* October, pp. 68–71.

LAWLER, E. E. (1990) *Strategic Pay.* San Francisco, Jossey-Bass.

LAWLER, E. (1993) 'Who uses skill-based pay, and why'. *Compensation and Benefits Review,* March–April, pp. 22–6.

LAWLER, E. E. (1995) 'The new pay: a strategic approach'. *Compensation and Benefits Review,* July–August, pp. 14–22.

LOCKE, E. A. (1984) 'The effect of self-efficacy, goals and task strategies on task performance'. *Journal of Applied Psychology,* Vol. 69, No. 2, pp. 241–51.

LUTHANS, F. AND KREITNER, R. (1975) *Organizational Behavior Modification.* Glenview, IL, Scott-Foresman.

MADIGAN, R. M. AND HILLS, F. S. (1988) 'Job evaluation and pay equity'. *Personnel Management,* Vol. 17 No. 3, pp. 323–30.

MANT, A. (1996) 'The psychological contract'. Unpublished address to IPD National Conference.

MARSDEN, D. AND FRENCH, S. (1998) *What a Performance: Performance-*

Related Pay in the Public Services. London, London School of Economics, Centre for Economic Performance.

MARSDEN, D. AND RICHARDSON, R. (1994) 'Performing for pay? The effects of "merit pay" in a public service', *British Journal of Industrial Relations,* June, pp. 243–261.

MASLOW, A. (1954) *Motivation and Personality.* New York, Harper & Row.

MCCLELLAND, D. (1975) *Power – the Inner Experience.* New York, Irvington.

MCGREGOR, D. (1960) *The Human Side of Enterprise.* New York, McGraw-Hill.

MCHALE, P. 'Putting competencies to work: competency-based job evaluation'. *Competency,* Summer 1990, pp. 39–40.

MCNALLY, J. AND SHIMMIN, S. (1988) 'Job evaluation: equal work – equal pay?', *Management Decision,* Vol. 26, No. 5, pp. 22–7.

MILES, R. E. AND SNOW, C. C. (1978) *Organizational Strategy, Structure and Process.* New York, McGraw-Hill.

MILLWARD, N., STEVENS, M., SMART, D. AND HAWES, W. R. (1992) *Workplace Industrial Relations in Transition.* Aldershot, Dartmouth Publishing.

MIRVIS, P. AND HALL, D. (1994) 'Psychological success and the boundaryless career', *Journal of Occupational Psychology,* 15, pp. 361–380.

MORRIS, T. M. AND FENTON-O'CREEVY, M. (1996) 'UK top manager's attitudes to their performance pay', *The International Journal of Human Resource Management,* September, pp. 708–720.

MURLIS, H. (ed.) (1996) *Pay at the Crossroads.* London, Institute of Personnel and Development.

MURLIS, H. AND WRIGHT, V. (1993) 'Decentralising pay systems: empowerment or abdication?' *Personnel Management,* March, pp. 28–33.

NALBANTIAN, H. (1987) *Incentives, Cooperation and Risk Sharing.* Totowa, NJ, Rowman & Littlefield.

NATIONAL ASSOCIATION OF PENSION FUNDS (1994) *Survey of Pension Arrangements.* London.

NATIONAL INSTITUTE FOR ECONOMIC AND SOCIAL RESEARCH (1994) *Report on Directors' Remuneration.* London.

NEATHEY, F. (1994) *Job Evaluation in the 1990s.* London, Industrial Relations Services.

OFFICE OF MANPOWER ECONOMICS (1973) *Wage Drift.* London, HMSO.

O'NEAL, S. (1994) 'Work and pay in the 21st century'. *ACA News,* February, p. 16.

PFEFFER, J. (1998) 'Six dangerous myths about pay'. *Harvard Business Review.* May–June.

PICKARD, J. AND FOWLER, A. (1999) 'Grade expectations'. *Personnel Management,* 11 February, pp. 32–8.

PORTER, M. E. (1985) *Competitive Advantage: Creating and Sustaining Superior Performance.* New York, The Free Press

PORTER, L. W. (1961) 'A study of perceived need satisfaction in bottom and middle management jobs'. *Journal of Applied Psychology,* Vol. 45, No. 1, pp. 165–77.

PORTER, L. AND LAWLER, E. E. (1968) *Management Attitudes and Behavior.* Homewood, IL, Irwin-Dorsey.

PRITCHARD, D. AND MURLIS, H. (1992) *Jobs, Roles and People.* London, Nicholas Brealey.

QUAID, M. (1993) *Job Evaluation: The myth of equitable assessment.* Toronto, University of Toronto Press.

RILEY, E. (1992) *Motivating and Rewarding Employees: Some Aspects of Theory and Practice.* London, ACAS.

ROBINSON, S. (1992) 'The trouble with PRP', *Human Resources,* Spring, pp. 66–70.

ROSE, M. (1998) 'Rewarding with recognition', *Human Resource Management Yearbook,* London, AP Information Services.

ROUSSEAU, D. M. AND GRELLER, M. M. (1994) 'Human resource practices: administrative contract makers'. *Human Resource Management,* Vol. 33, No. 3, pp. 385–401.

ROUSSEAU, D. M. AND WADE-BENZONI, K. A. (1994) 'Linking strategy and human resource practices: how employee and customer contracts are created'. *Human Resource Management,* Vol. 33, No. 3, pp. 463–89.

RUBERY, J. (1992) *The Economics of Equal Value.* London, Equal Opportunities Commission.

RUBINSTEIN, M. (1992) as reported in 'Making the visible invisible: rewarding women's work', *Equal Opportunities Review,* September–October, pp. 23–32.

SCHEIN, E. H. (1965) *Organisational Psychology,* Englewood Cliffs, NJ, Prentice-Hall.

SCHUSTER, J. R. AND ZINGHEIM, P. K. (1992) *The New Pay.* New York, Lexington Books.

SELF, R. (1995) 'Changing roles for company pensions'. *People Management,* 5 October, pp. 24–9.

SIMS, R. R. (1994) 'Human resource management's role in clarifying the psychological contract'. *Human Resource Management,* Vol. 33, No. 3, pp. 373–82.

SIMS, R. R. (1994) 'Human resource management's role in clarifying the new psychological contract', *Human Resource Management,* Vol. 33 No. 3, Fall, pp. 373–82.

SKINNER, B. F. (1974) *About Behaviorism.* New York, Knopf.

SLATER, P. (1980) *Wealth Education.* New York, Dutton.

SMITH, ADAM [1776] (1976) *The Wealth of Nations.* Oxford, Clarendon.

SOCIETY OF BRITISH TELECOM ENGINEERS (1993) 'More stressing performance: a survey of British Telecom Executives', *Journal of the Society of British Telecom Engineers,* September, pp. 34–7.

SPARROW, P. (1996) 'Too good to be true'. *People Management,* 5 December, pp. 22–7.

SPINDLER, G.S. (1994) 'Psychological contracts in the workplace: a lawyer's view', *Human Resource Management,* Vol. 33, No. 3, pp. 325–33.

SUPEL, T. M. 'Equivalence and redundance in the point-factor job evaluation system'. *Compensation and Benefits Review,* March/April, pp. 48–55.

TAYLOR, F. W. (1911) *Principles of Scientific Management.* New York, Harper.

THOMPSON, M. (1992) *Pay and performance: The Employee Experience.* IMS Report No 218. Brighton, Institute of Manpower Studies.

TIJOU, F. 'Just rewards: implementing competency related pay', *Human Resources,* Autumn, 1991, pp. 147–50.

TRADE UNION RESEARCH UNIT (1986) *Job Evaluation and Equal Value: Similarities and Differences.* Oxford.

VROOM, V. (1964) *Work and Motivation.* New York, Wiley.

WALLACE, M. J. AND SZILAGYI, A. D. (1982) *Managing Behavior in Organizations.* Glenview, IL., Scott-Foresman.

WOMACK, J. AND JONES, D. (1970) *The Machine That Changed the World.* New York, Rawson.

WOODRUFFE, C. (1991) 'Competent by any other name'. *Personnel Management,* September, pp 30–33.

WYATT COMPANY AND INSTITUTE OF PERSONNEL MANAGEMENT (1989) *Survey of Job Evaluation Policies and Practices.* London, Institute of Personnel Management.

ZISKIN, L. V. (1986) 'Knowledge-based pay: a strategic analysis'. *ILR Report.* Fall, pp. 56–66.

Index